Lecture Notes in Artificial Intelligence 3955

Edited by J. G. Carbonell and J. Siekmann

Subseries of Lecture Notes in Computer Science

Grigoris Antoniou   George Potamias
Costas Spyropoulos   Dimitris Plexousakis (Eds.)

Advances in Artificial Intelligence

4th Helenic Conference on AI, SETN 2006
Heraklion, Crete, Greece, May 18-20, 2006
Proceedings

 Springer

Series Editors

Jaime G. Carbonell, Carnegie Mellon University, Pittsburgh, PA, USA
Jörg Siekmann, University of Saarland, Saarbrücken, Germany

Volume Editors

Grigoris Antoniou
George Potamias
Dimitris Plexousakis
University of Crete
Department of Computer Science F.O.R.T.H.
Institute of Computer Science, 71409, Heraklion, Crete, Greece
E-mail:{antoniou,potamias, dp}@ics.forth.gr

Costas Spyropoulos
NCSR "Demokritos" Institute of Informatics and Telecommunications
15310 A. Paraskevi Attikis, Greece
E-mail: costass@iit.demokritos.gr

Library of Congress Control Number: 2006924682

CR Subject Classification (1998): I.2, H.3, H.4, H.2.8, F.2.2, I.4

LNCS Sublibrary: SL 7 – Artificial Intelligence

ISSN   0302-9743
ISBN-10   3-540-34117-X Springer Berlin Heidelberg New York
ISBN-13   978-3-540-34117-8 Springer Berlin Heidelberg New York

Springer is a part of Springer Science+Business Media

springer.com

© Springer-Verlag Berlin Heidelberg 2006
Printed in Germany

Typesetting: Camera-ready by author, data conversion by Scientific Publishing Services, Chennai, India
Printed on acid-free paper   SPIN: 11752912   06/3142   5 4 3 2 1 0

Preface

Artificial intelligence is a dynamic field that continuously finds new application areas with new research challenges. The ever-increasing volume, complexity and heterogeneity of knowledge, as well as the increasingly rapid change in the technological, economic and social environment, post new needs and raise novel challenges for managing complexity and change. AI provides methods to address these challenges and develop solutions.

This volume contains papers selected for presentation at the 4th Hellenic Conference on Artificial Intelligence (SETN 2006), the official meeting of the Hellenic Society for Artificial Intelligence (EETN). Previous conferences were held at the University of Piraeus (1996), Aristotle University of Thessaloniki (2002) and the University of the Aegean (2004). SETN conferences play an important role in the dissemination of the innovative and high-quality scientific results in artificial intelligence which are being produced mainly by Greek scientists in institutes all over the world. However, the most important effect of SETN conferences is that they provide the context in which AI researchers meet, get to know each other's work, as well as a very good opportunity for students to get closer to the results of innovative artificial intelligence research. In addition, the conference series seeks to raise international participation. This year we had submissons from all over the world: USA, Australia, UK, Germany, Italy, France, Romania, Spain, Denmark, Finland, Mexico, Korea, China.

SETN 2006 was organized by EETN, in collaboration with the Institute of Computer Science of FORTH, and the Department of Computer Science of the University of Crete. The conference took place in Heraklion, on the island of Crete, during May 18–20, 2006.

The conference attracted 125 submissions, which underwent a thorough reviewing process; 43 of these were accepted as full papers. In addition, another 34 submissions were accepted as short papers. This proceedings volume includes the full papers and extended abstracts of the short papers. An indication of the scientific quality of the papers is that the *International Journal of Artificial Intelligence Tools* decided to have a special issue based on the best papers of the conference.

SETN 2006 was honored to have hosted invited talks by two distinguished keynote speakers:

- "Planning with Stochastis Nets and Neural Nets" by Nikolaos Bourbakis, OBR Distinguished Professor of Information Technology and Director of the Information Technology Research Institute at Wright State University, USA
- "Data Mining using Fractals and Power Laws" by Professor Christos Faloutsos of Carnegie Mellon University, USA

Finally, SETN 2006 included in its program an invited session on AI in Power System Operation and Fault Diagnosis, chaired by Nikos Hatziargyriou.

The members of the SETN 2006 Programme Committee and the additional reviewers did an enormous amount of work and deserve the special gratitude of all participants. Our sincere thanks go to our sponsors for their generous financial support and to the Conference Advisory Board for its assistance and support. The conference operations were supported in an excellent way by the Confious conference management system; many thanks to Manos Papagelis for his assistance with running the system. Special thanks go to to Theodosia Bitzou for the design of the conference poster, to Babis Meramveliotakis and Vassilis Minopoulos for the design and maintenance of the conference Web-site, and Maria Moutsaki and Antonis Bikakis for assisting with the preparation of the proceedings. We also wish to thank Round Travel, the conference travel and organization agent, and Alfred Hofmann, Ursula Barth and the Springer team for their continuous help and support.

May 2006

Grigoris Antoniou
George Potamias
Costas Spyropoulos
Dimitris Plexousakis

Organization

Conference Chair

George Potamias, FORTH-ICS, Greece

Conference Co-chairs

Costas Spyropoulos, NCSR "Demokritos," Greece
Dimitris Plexousakis, FORTH-ICS and University of Crete, Greece

Programme Committee Chair

Grigoris Antoniou, FORTH-ICS and University of Crete, Greece

Steering Committee

Ioannis Hatzilygeroudis, University of Patras, Greece
Themistoklis Panayiotopoulos, University of Piraeus, Greece
Ioannis Vlahavas, Aristotle University, Greece
George Vouros, University of the Aegean, Greece

Programme Committee

Ion Androutsopoulos, Athens University of Economics and Business, Greece
Nick Bassiliades, Aristotle University, Greece
Basilis Boutsinas, University of Patras, Greece
George Demetriou, University of Sheffield, UK
Yannis Dimopoulos, University of Cyprus, Cyprus
Christos Douligeris, University of Piraeus, Greece
Giorgos Dounias, University of the Aegean, Greece
Theodoros Evgeniou, INSEAD, France
Nikos Fakotakis, University of Patras, Greece
Eleni Galiotou, University of Athens, Greece
Manolis Gergatsoulis, Ionian University, Greece
Nikos Hatziargyriou, Technical University of Athens, Greece
Katerina Kabassi, University of Piraeus, Greece
Dimitris Kalles, Hellenic Open University and AHEAD, Greece
Nikos Karacapilidis, University of Patras, Greece

Vangelis Karkaletsis, NCSR "Demokritos," Greece
Dimitris Karras, Technological Educational Institute of Halkida, Greece
Petros Kefalas, City Liberal Studies, Greece
Stefanos Kollias, Technical University of Athens, Greece
Yiannis Kompatsiaris, CERTH, Greece
Kostas Kotropoulos, Aristotle University, Greece
Manolis Koubarakis, University of Athens, Greece
Kostas Koutroumbas, National Observatory of Athens, Greece
Aristidis Lykas, University of Ioannina, Greece
Spyridon Lykothanasis, University of Patras, Greece
Ilias Magloyannis, University of the Aegean, Greece
Giorgos Magoulas, Birkbeck College, University of London, UK
Filia Makedon, University of the Aegean, Greece, and Dartmouth College, USA
Basilis Moustakis, Technical University of Crete and FORTH-ICS, Greece
Giorgos Paliouras, NCSR "Demokritos," Greece
Giorgos Papakonstantinou, Technical University of Athens, Greece
Christos Papatheodorou, Ionian University, Greece
Pavlos Peppas, University of Patras, Greece
Stavros Perantonis, NCSR "Demokritos," Greece
Stelios Piperidis, Institute for Language and Speech Processing, Greece
Ioannis Pitas, Aristotle University, Greece
Ioannis Pratikakis, NCSR "Demokritos," Greece
Ioannis Refanidis, University of Macedonia, Greece
Timos Sellis, Technical University of Athens, Greece
Kyriakos Sgarbas, University of Patras, Greece
Panagiotis Stamatopoulos, University of Athens, Greece
Michael Strintzis, CERTH, Greece
George Tsichrintzis, University of Pireaus, Greece
Nikos Vasilas, Technological Educational Institute of Athens, Greece
Maria Virvou, University of Piraeus, Greece

Additional Reviewers

Adam Adamopoulos
Nicholas Ampazis
Grigorios N. Beligiannis
Christina Evangelou
Basilis Gatos
Heng Huang
Antonis Kakas
Sarantos Kapidakis
Isambo Karali
Stasinos Konstantopoulos
Dimitrios Kosmopoulos

Georgios Kouroupetroglou
Pavlos Moraitis
Pantelis Nasikas
Yi Ouyang
Vasileios Papastathis
Ioannis Partalas
C. Pattichis
Sergios Petridis
Dimitrios Pierrakos
Nikolaos Pothitos
Lambros Skarlas

Spiros Skiadopoulos
Stefanos Souldatos
George Stamou
Manolis Terrovitis
Nikolaos Thomaidis
Dimitris Tsakiris
Athanasios Tsakonas
Grigorios Tsoumakas

George Tzanis
Yurong Xu
Song Ye
Nick Z. Zacharis
John Zeleznikow
Kyriakos Zervoudakis
Rong Zhang
Sheng Zhang

Table of Contents

Invited Talks

Full Papers

Short Papers

Planning with Stochastic Petri-Nets and Neural Nets

Nikolaos Bourbakis

Information Technology Research Institute, Wright State University, USA
bourbaki@cs.wright.edu

Abstract. This talk presents a synergistic methodology based on generalized stochastic Petri-nets (SPN) and neural nets for efficiently developing planning strategies. The SPN planning method generates global plans based on the states of the elements of the Universe of Discourse. Each plan includes all the possible conflict free planning paths for achieving the desirable goals under certain constraints occurred at the problem to be solved. The a neural network is used for searching the vectors of markings generated by the SPN reachability graph for the appropriate selection of plans. The SPN model presents high complexity issues, but at the same time offers to the synergic important features, such as stochastic modeling, synchronization, parallelism, concurrency and timing of events, valuable for developing plans under uncertainty. The neural network does contribute to the high complexity, but it offers learning capability to the synergy for future use. An example for coordinating two robotic arms under the constraints of time, space, and placement of the objects will be presented.

G. Antoniou et al. (Eds.): SETN 2006, LNAI 3955, p. 1, 2006.
© Springer-Verlag Berlin Heidelberg 2006

Data Mining Using Fractals and Power Laws

Christos Faloutsos

Department of Computer Science, Carnegie Mellon University, USA
christos@cs.cmu.edu

Abstract. What patterns can we find in a bursty web traffic? On the web or on the internet graph itself? How about the distributions of galaxies in the sky, or the distribution of a company's customers in geographical space? How long should we expect a nearest-neighbour search to take, when there are 100 attributes per patient or customer record? The traditional assumptions (uniformity, independence, Poisson arrivals, Gaussian distributions), often fail miserably. Should we give up trying to find patterns in such settings? Self-similarity, fractals and power laws are extremely successful in describing real datasets (coast-lines, rivers basins, stock-prices, brain-surfaces, communication-line noise, to name a few). We show some old and new successes, involving modeling of graph topologies (internet, web and social networks); modeling galaxy and video data; dimensionality reduction; and more.

G. Antoniou et al. (Eds.): SETN 2006, LNAI 3955, p. 2, 2006.

Voice Activity Detection Using
Generalized Gamma Distribution

George Almpanidis and Constantine Kotropoulos

Department of Informatics, Aristotle University of Thessaloniki,
Box 451 Thessaloniki, GR-54124, Greece
{galba, costas}@aiia.csd.auth.gr
http://www.aiia.csd.auth.gr/index.html

Abstract. In this work, we model speech samples with a two-sided generalized
Gamma distribution and evaluate its efficiency for voice activity detection. Using a computationally inexpensive maximum likelihood approach, we employ
the Bayesian Information Criterion for identifying the phoneme boundaries in
noisy speech.

1 Introduction

A common problem in many areas of speech processing is the identification of the
presence or absence of a voice component in a given signal, especially the determination of the beginning and ending boundaries of voice segments. In many cases voice
activity detection (VAD), endpoint detection, speaker segmentation, and audio classification can be seen as similar problems and they share a common methodology. In
this work, we are interested in off-line VAD algorithms that are suitable for applications such as automatic transcription and speech segmentation in broadcast news. Our
goal is to implement and evaluate a robust VAD and end-point detection algorithm
under noisy conditions, various classes of noise, and short frames. Categorisation of
audio signal at such a small scale has applications to phoneme segmentation and consequently, to speech recognition and speech synthesis. In particular, speech synthesis
requires accurate knowledge of phoneme transitions, in order to obtain a naturally
sounding speech waveform from stored parameters.

The detection principles of conventional VADs are usually based on the signal full-
band energy levels, subband short-energy, Itakura linear prediction coefficient (LPC)
distance measure [1], spectral density, zero crossing rate, Teager energy operator [2],
cepstral coefficients, line spectral frequencies, etc. Energy-based approaches have
been proved to work relatively well in high signal to noise ratios (SNR) and for
known stationary noise [1]. Moreover, these methods have been proved to be computationally efficient to such an extent that they allow real-time signal processing [3].
But in highly noisy environments the performance and robustness of energy-based
voice activity detectors are not optimal. An important disadvantage is that they rely
on simple energy thresholds, so they are not able to identify unvoiced speech segments like fricatives satisfactorily, because the latter can be masked by noise. They
may also incorrectly classify clicking and other non-stationary noise as speech

G. Antoniou et al. (Eds.): SETN 2006, LNAI 3955, pp. 3–12, 2006.

activity. Furthermore, they are not always very efficient in real-world recordings where speakers tend to leave "artifacts" including breathing/sighing, teeth chatters, and echoes. Many efforts have been made to use adaptive schemes for noise estimation but these are usually heuristic-based or limited to stationary noise. A discussion for classical and geometrically adaptive energy threshold methods can be found in [4].

Recently, much research discussion has been done regarding the exploration of the speech and noise signal statistics for VAD and endpoint detection. Statistical model-based methods/approaches typically employ a statistical model with the decision rule being derived from the Likelihood Ratio Test (LRT) applied to a set of hypotheses [5]. These approaches can be further improved by incorporating soft decision rules [6] and High Order Statistics (HOS) [7]. The main disadvantage of statistical model-based methods is that they are more complicated than the energy-based detectors regarding computation time and storage requirements, so they have limited appeal in online applications. Furthermore, model-based segmentation does not generalize to unseen acoustic conditions.

In this paper, we present a statistical model-based method for VAD using the generalised version of the Gamma distribution and evaluate its performance in phoneme boundary identification under noisy environments.

2   Voice Activity Detection Using the BIC Criterion

Bayesian Information Criterion (BIC) is an asymptotically optimal method for estimating the best model using only an in-sample estimate [8], [9]. It is an approximation to minimum description length (MDL) and can be viewed as a penalized maximum likelihood technique [10]. BIC can also be applied as a termination criterion in hierarchical methods for clustering of audio segments: two nodes can be merged only if the merging increases the BIC value. BIC is more frequently applied for speaker-turn detection. However, nothing precludes its application to VAD.

In BIC, adjacent signal segments are modelled using different multivariate Gaussian distributions (GD) while their concatenation are assumed to obey a third multivariate Gaussian pdf, as in Fig.1. The problem is to decide whether the data in the large segment fits better a single multivariate Gaussian pdf or whether a two-segment representation describes more accurately the data. A sliding window moves over the signal making statistical decisions at its middle using BIC. The step-size of the sliding window indicates the resolution of the system.

The problem is formulated as a hypothesis testing problem. For the purpose of VAD, we need to evaluate the following statistical hypotheses:

- H_0: $(x_1, x_2, ..., x_B) \sim N(\mu_Z, \Sigma_Z)$: the sequence data comes from one source Z (i.e., noisy speech)
- H_1: $(x_1, x_2, ..., x_A) \sim N(\mu_X, \Sigma_X)$ and $(x_{A+1}, x_{A+2}, ..., x_B) \sim N(\mu_Y, \Sigma_Y)$: the sequence data comes from two sources X and Y, meaning that there is a transition from speech utterance to silence or vice versa

where x_i are K-dimensional feature vectors in a transformed domain such as Mel Frequency Cepstral Coefficients (MFCCs). In the example of Fig.1 Σ_X, Σ_Y, Σ_Z are respectively the covariance matrices of the complete sequence Z and the two subsets X and Y while A and $B\text{-}A$ are the number of feature vectors for each subset.

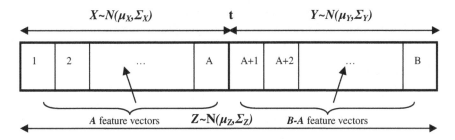

Fig. 1. Models for two adjacent speech segments

The GLR associated with the defined hypothesis test is

$$R=\frac{L(z,\mu_z;\Sigma_z)}{L(x,\mu_x;\Sigma_x)L(y,\mu_y;\Sigma_y)} \tag{1}$$

where, for example, $L(x,\mu_x;\Sigma_x)$ represents the likelihood of the sequence of feature vectors X given the multi-dimensional Gaussian process $N(x,\mu_x;\Sigma_x)$. $L(y,\mu_y;\Sigma_y)$ and $L(z,\mu_z;\Sigma_z)$ are similarly defined. The distance between the two segments in Fig.1 is obtained using the log-value of this ratio,

$$d_R = -\log R \tag{2}$$

The variation of the BIC value between the two models is given by [11]

$$\Delta BIC = -\frac{B}{2}\log|\Sigma_z|-\frac{A}{2}\log|\Sigma_x|-\frac{B-A}{2}\log|\Sigma_Y| + \lambda P \tag{3}$$

$$P = \frac{1}{2}\left(K+\frac{1}{2}K(K+1)\right)\times\log B \tag{4}$$

where P is the penalty for model complexity and λ a tuning parameter for the penalty factor. Negative values of ΔBIC indicate that the multi-dimensional Gaussian mixtures best fit the data, meaning that t is change point from speech to silence or vice versa.

One advantage of BIC is that it does not involve thresholds, but there is still the penalty factor λ which is depended on the type of analysed data and must be estimated heuristically [12]. Also, BIC tends to choose models that are too simple due to heavy penalty on complexity. Nevertheless, BIC is a consistent estimate and various algorithms based on this criterion have extended the basic algorithm combining it with other metrics such as Generalized Likelihood Ratio (GLR), Kullback-Leibler (KL) distance, sphericity tests and other HOS [7].

A variant of BIC that attempts to deal with some of the problems mentioned above is DISTBIC [11]. The algorithm performs two steps. The first step uses a distance computation to choose the possible candidates for a change point. Different criteria such as KL and GLR can be applied to this pre-segmentation step. The second step uses the BIC to validate or discard the candidates determined in the first step.

3 Speech Distributions

One common assumption for most VAD algorithms that operate in the DFT domain, such as DISTBIC, is that both noise and speech spectra can be modelled satisfactorily by GDs. Furthermore, using a transformed feature space, it is possible to assume that these two Gaussian random processes are independent of each other. When both speech and noise are Gaussians the Minimum Mean-Squared Error Estimator (MMSE) estimator is linear and the spectral coefficients of the filter are real. Consequently, the clean speech and noisy coefficients differ only in magnitude. In such cases, maximum a posteriori estimators can be used to determine the signal parameters. Another reason for selecting GD in parametric modelling is the central limit theorem. This justifies the GD for speech signals in the DFT domain. Generally, GDs are simple to use, their properties are theoretically clear and consequently, they have been used extensively for statistical modelling in VAD and generally in speech processing.

Nevertheless, previous work has demonstrated that Laplacian (LD), Gamma (ΓD), and the Generalized Gaussian Distribution (GGD) can yield better performance than GD. Using likelihoods, coefficients of variation (CVs), and Kolmogorov-Smirnov (KS) tests, [13] has concluded that LD is more suitable for approximating active voice segments in most cases and for different frame sizes. More specifically, LD fits well the highly correlated univariate space of the speech amplitudes as well as the uncorrelated multivariate space of the feature values after a Karhunen- Loeve Transformation (KLT) or Discrete Cosine Transformation (DCT) [14].

While some reports attest that LD offers only a marginally better fit than GD, this is not valid when silence segments are absent from the testing [13]. The reason is that while clean speech segments best exhibit Laplacian or Gamma statistical properties the silence segments are Gaussian random processes. [15] and others have also asserted that Laplacian and Gamma distributions fit better the voiced speech signal than normal distributions.

Both LD and GD are members of the family of exponential distributions and can be considered as special cases of ΓD. They are specified by the location and the scale parameters. But the LD compared to GD has a sharper peak and a wider spread so that samples far from the mean are assigned a higher likelihood than in GD. Due to this property of the decreased likelihood, in segments that include periods locally deviating from the model the correct hypothesis is less likely to be rejected. On the other hand, both distributions have insufficient representation powers with respect to the distribution shape [16].

4   DISTBIC Using Generalized Gamma Distribution

Our goal is to accomplish the task of phoneme boundary identification without any previous knowledge of the audio stream while achieving a robust performance under noisy environments. For this purpose, we try to improve the performance of the DISTBIC algorithm in VAD. In order to model the signal in a more theoretically complete manner and to conform to the experimental findings mentioned in Sect. 3, we need to consider generalized versions of distributions that have GD and LD as special cases. A generalized LD (GLD) [16] or the two-sided generalized gamma distribution (GΓD) [17] for an efficient parametric characterization of speech spectra can be used. In this paper, we modify the first step of the DISTBIC algorithm by assuming a GΓD distribution model for our signal in the analysis windows. Let us call the proposed method DISTBIC-Γ from now on.

The GΓD is an extremely flexible distribution that is useful for reliability model-ling. Among its many special cases are the Weibull and exponential distributions. It is defined as

$$f_X(x) = \frac{\gamma \beta^\eta}{2\Gamma(\eta)} |x|^{\eta\gamma - 1} e^{-\beta|x|^\gamma} \tag{5}$$

where $\Gamma(z)$ denotes the gamma function and γ, η, β are real values corresponding to location, scale and shape parameters. GD is a special case for $\gamma=2$ and $\eta=0.5$, for ($\gamma=1$ and $\eta=1$) it represents the LD, while for ($\gamma=1$ and $\eta=0.5$) it represents the common ΓD.

The parameter estimation of this family of distributions with both known and un-known location parameters can be achieved using the maximum likelihood estimation (MLE) method. Unfortunately, estimating the parameters of these distributions with MLE in an analytic way is difficult because the maximised likelihood results in nonlinear equations. Regarding GLD, the location parameter can be numerically de-termined by using the gradient ascend algorithm according to the MLE principle. Using a learning factor we can then reestimate the location value that locally maxi-mizes the logarithmic likelihood function L, until L reaches convergence. Using this value and the data samples we can determine the scale and shape parameters. It must be stated that in MLE it is difficult to apply the same analytical procedure for the shape parameter and moreover the convergence of the gradient method is not always good [16]. The principal parameters of GΓD are estimated similarly according to the MLE principle. A computationally inexpensive on-line algorithm based on the gradi-ent ascent algorithm is introduced in [17]. Here, we use the online ML algorithm proposed by [18]. Given N data $x = \{x_1, x_2, ... x_N\}$ of a sample and assuming the data is mutually independent, we iteratively update the statistics

$$S_1(n) = (1 - \lambda)S_1(n-1) + \lambda |x_n|^{\hat{\gamma}(n)} \tag{6}$$

$$S_2(n) = (1 - \lambda)S_2(n-1) + \lambda \log |x_n|^{\hat{\gamma}(n)} \tag{7}$$

$$S_3(n) = (1 - \lambda)S_3(n-1) + \lambda|x_n|^{\hat{\gamma}(n)} \log|x_n|^{\hat{\gamma}(n)} \tag{8}$$

over the frame N values, updating each time the parameter γ as

$$\hat{\gamma}(n+1) = \hat{\gamma}(n) + \mu\left(\frac{1}{\hat{\eta}(n)} + S_2(n) - \frac{S_3(n)}{S_1(n)}\right) \tag{9}$$

where λ is a forgetting factor and μ is the learning rate of the gradient ascent approach. Using appropriate initial estimates for the parameters (e.g. $\hat{\gamma}(1) = 1$, which corresponds to GD or LD), we are able to recursively estimate the remaining parameters by solving the equations:

$$\psi_0(\hat{\eta}(n)) - \log\hat{\eta}(n) = S_2(n) - \log S_1(n) \tag{10}$$

$$\hat{\beta}(n) = \frac{\hat{\eta}(n)}{S_1(n)} \tag{11}$$

where ψ_0 is the digamma function. The left part of (10) is monotonically increasing function of $\hat{\eta}(n)$, so we are able to uniquely determine the solution by having an inverse table.

The proposed algorithm, DISTBIC-Γ, is implemented in two steps. First, using a sufficiently big sliding window and modelling it and its adjacent sub-segments using GΓD instead of GD, we calculate the distance associated with the GLR. Here, as in [14], we are making the assumption that both noise and speech signals have uncorrelated components in the DCT domain. Depending on the window size, this assumption gives a reasonable approximation for their multivariate PDFs using the marginal PDFs. A potential problem arouses when using MLE for short segments [17]. Nevertheless, we can relax the convergence conditions of the gradient ascend method and still yield improved results. Then, we create a plot of the distances as output with respect to time and filter out insignificant peaks using the same criteria as [11].

In the second step, using the BIC test as a merging criterion we compute the ΔBIC values for each change point candidate in order to validate the results of the first step. Because small frame lengths suggest a GD according to [13] and due to the length limitation of the [18] method for GΓD parameter estimation, we choose to use Gaussians in this step.

5   Experiments

The testing of automatic phoneme boundary detection requires an expansive, annotated speech corpus. In order to evaluate the performance of the proposed method, two sets of preliminary experiments on VAD were conducted on two different corpora. In the first experiment we compare the efficiency of the proposed method using samples from the M2VTS audio-visual database [19]. In our tests we used 15 audio recordings that consist of the utterances of ten digits from zero to nine in French. We measured the mismatch between manual segmentation of audio performed by a human transcriber and the automatic segmentation. Samples were manually segmented or concatenated using sound editing software. The human error and accuracy of visually and acoustically identifying break points were taken into account. In the second set of experiments we used samples from the TIMIT dataset [20] totaling 100 seconds of speech time. For both experiments we used the same set of parameter values and features were used (500ms initial window, 5ms shift of analysis window, first 12 MFCCs for GD, 10 DCTs for GΓD, λ=7). White and babble noise from the NOISEX-92 database [21] was added to the clean speech samples at various SNR levels ranging from 20 to 5 dB.

The errors that can be identified in VADs are distinguished by whether speech is misclassified as noise or vice versa, and by the position in an utterance in which the error occurs (beginning, middle or end). A point incorrectly identified as a change point gives a type-2 error (false alarm) while a point totally missed by the detector is a type-1 error (missed detection). The detection error rate of the system is described by False Alarm Rate (FAR) and Missed Detection Rate (MDR) defined below. ACP stands for the Actual Change Points in the signal as determined by human in our case.

$$FAR = \frac{\text{number of FA}}{\text{number of AST + number of FA}} * 100\% \qquad (12)$$

$$MDR = \frac{\text{number of MD}}{\text{number of AST}} * 100\% \qquad (13)$$

A high value of FAR means that an over-segmentation of the speech signal is obtained while a high value of MDR means that the algorithm does not segment the audio signal properly. The results for the VAD error rates are illustrated in Table 1, 2, 3, and 4.

Table 1. Performance of VAD in M2VTS (voiced phonemes)

Noise	SNR	DISTBIC-Γ		DISTBIC	
		FAR (%)	MDR(%)	FAR (%)	MDR(%)
(clean speech)	-	22.6	16.4	27.5	19.2
White	20	24.8	19.7	29.4	23.4
White	10	25.1	20.3	30.5	24.4
white	5	28.2	23.5	35.4	29.8
babble	20	27.5	21.3	32.7	24.7
babble	10	28.8	24.1	34.9	28.4
babble	5	31.4	26.8	38.5	32.7

Table 2. Performance of VAD in TIMIT (voiced phonemes)

Noise	SNR	DISTBIC-Γ		DISTBIC	
		FAR (%)	MDR(%)	FAR (%)	MDR(%)
(clean speech)	-	25.5	17.1	31.4	19.6
white	20	26.9	18.5	32.2	23.2
white	10	29.4	22.8	33.3	26.9
white	5	32.4	25.0	38.8	31.9
babble	20	30.5	20.6	33.8	25.6
babble	10	31.8	24.4	36.6	29.3
babble	5	34.9	27.7	40.8	35.3

Table 3. Performance of VAD in M2VTS (voiced + unvoiced phonemes)

Noise	SNR	DISTBIC-Γ		DISTBIC	
		FAR (%)	MDR(%)	FAR (%)	MDR(%)
(clean speech)	-	27.5	18.2	29.9	21.5
white	20	28.9	19.4	32.5	23.9
white	10	30.3	22.5	35.4	28.0
white	5	34.1	25.9	39.8	33.1
babble	20	28.8	21.6	33.5	26.2
babble	10	31.6	24.2	37.6	31.4
babble	5	36.1	28.0	42.4	37.5

Table 4. Performance of VAD in TIMIT (voiced + unvoiced phonemes)

Noise	SNR	DISTBIC-Γ		DISTBIC	
		FAR (%)	MDR(%)	FAR (%)	MDR(%)
(clean speech)	-	28.3	18.7	32.1	24.5
white	20	31.2	20.9	34.5	25.7
white	10	33.1	24.4	37.5	30.5
white	5	35.7	28.5	40.4	36.4
babble	20	33.1	22.1	35.0	27.8
babble	10	34.0	25.8	38.6	32.5
babble	5	36.5	29.1	43.5	38.7

Comparing the four tables, we can deduce that there is notable improvement especially at low SNR levels. These results showed that the VAD accuracy of the proposed method DISTBIC-Γ is improved by an average of 16% in FAR and 23.8% in MDR compared to that of the conventional DISTBIC method. We can also indicate the improvement in the recognition of unvoiced speech elements. The improved results denote the higher representation power of the GΓD distribution.

6 Conclusions

The identification of phoneme boundaries in continuous speech is an important problem in areas of speech synthesis and recognition. As we have seen, there are numerous combinations worth exploring for offline 2-step speech activity detection. We have demonstrated that by representing the signal samples with a GΓD we are able to yield improved results than simple normal distributions. We concluded that the Generalised Gamma model is more adequate characterising noisy speech than the Gaussian model. This conforms with the findings of [22]. Also, despite making assumptions on the correlation of distribution components for the computation of the likelihood ratio in GΓD, the proposed algorithm, DISTBIC-Γ, yielded better results than DISTBIC especially in noisy signals. Using the KL distance instead of GLR we could further improve the system performance since the first offers better discriminative ability [23]. Nevertheless, the size of experiments was limited and the computation time was multiple times greater for the method with GΓDs than using the simple DISTBIC algorithms. An open problem worth investigating is the criterion for convergence in the gradient ascend algorithm.

Acknowledgements

G. Almpanidis was granted a basic research fellowship "HERAKLEITOS" by the Greek Ministry of Education.

References

[1] L. R. Rabiner and M. R. Sambur, "An algorithm for determining the endpoints of isolated utterances", *Bell Syst. Tech. Journal,* vol. 54, no. 2, pp. 297-315, 1975.

[2] G. S.Ying, C. D. Mitchell, and L. H. Jamieson, "Endpoint detection of isolated utterances based on a modified Teager energy measurement", In Proc. *IEEE Int. Conf. Acoustics, Speech, and Signal Processing*, pp.732-735, 1992.

[3] A. Ganapathiraju, L. Webster, J. Trimble, K. Bush, and P. Kornman., "Comparison of Energy-Based Endpoint Detectors for Speech Signal Processing", in Proc. *IEEE Southeastcon Bringing Together Education, Science and Technology*, pp. 500-503, Florida, April 1996.

[4] S. Tanyer and H. Ozer "Voice activity detection in nonstationary noise", *IEEE Trans. Speech and Audio Processing,* vol. 8, no. 4, pp.478-482, April 2000.

[5] J. Sohn, N. S. Kim, and W. Sung, "A statistical model based voice activity detection", *IEEE Signal Processing Letters*, vol. 6, no. 1 pp.1-3, January 1999.

[6] J. Chang, J. Shin, and N. S. Kim, "Likelihood ratio test with complex Laplacian model for voice activity detection", in Proc. *European Conf. Speech Communication Technology*, 2003.

[7] E. Nemer, R. Goubran, and S. Mahmould, "Robust voice activity detection using higher-order statistics in the LPC residual domain", *IEEE Trans. Speech and Audio Processing*, vol.9, no. 3, pp. 217-231, March 2001.

[8] G. Schwartz, "Estimating the dimension of a model", *Annals of Statistics*, vol. 6, pp. 461-464, 1978.

[9] S. Chen and P. Gopalakrishnam, "Speaker, environment and channel change detection and clustering via the Bayesian information criterion", in *DARPA Broadcast News Workshop,* 1998.

[10] P. Grunwald, "Minimum description length tutorial", *Advances in Minimum Description Length: Theory and Applications.* pp. 23-80. Cambridge, MA: MIT Press.

[11] P. Delacourt and C. J. Wellekens, "DISTBIC: a speaker-based segmentation for audio data indexing", *Speech Communication*, vol. 32, no. 1-2, pp. 111-126, September 2000.

[12] A. Tritschler and R. Gopinath, "Improved speaker segmentation and segments clustering using the Bayesian information criterion", in Proc. *1999 European Speech Processing*, vol. 2, pp. 679-682, 1999.

[13] S. Gazor and W. Zhang, "Speech probability distribution", *IEEE Signal Processing Letters*, vol. 10, no. 7, pp. 204-207, July 2003.

[14] S. Gazor and W. Zhang "A soft voice activity detector based on a Laplacian-Gaussian model", *IEEE Trans. on Speech and Audio Processing*, vol. 11, no. 5, pp. 498-505, 2003.

[15] R. Martin, "Speech enhancement using short time spectral estimation with Gamma distributed priors", in Proc. *IEEE Int. Conf. Acoustics, Speech, Signal Proc.*, vol. 1, pp. 253-256, 2005.

[16] A. Nakamura, "Acoustic modeling for speech recognition based on a generalized Laplacian mixture distribution", *Electronics and Communications in Japan Part II: Electronics*, vol. 85, no. 11, pp. 32-42, October 2002.

[17] W. -H. Shin, B. –S. Lee, Y. –K. Lee, and J. –S. Lee, "Speech/non-speech classification using multiple features for robust endpoint detection", in Proc. *IEEE Intl Conf. Acoustics, Speech, and Signal Processing*, vol. 3, pp. 1399-1402, 2000.

[18] J.W. Shin and J-H. Chang, "Statistical Modeling of Speech Signals Based on Generalized Gamma Distribution", *IEEE Signal Processing Letters*, vol. 12, no. 3 pp.258-261, March 2005.

[19] S. Pigeon and L. Vandendorpe, "The M2VTS multimodal face database", in *Lecture Notes in Computer Science: Audio- and Video- based Biometric Person Authentication*, (J. Bigun, G. Chollet, and G. Borgefors, Eds.), vol. 1206, pp. 403-409, 1997.

[20] TIMIT Acoustic-Phonetic Continuous Speech Corpus. National Institute of Standards and Technology Speech. Disc 1-1.1, NTIS Order No. PB91-505065, 1990.

[21] A. Varga, H. Steeneken, M. Tomlinson, and D. Jones, "The NOISEX-92 study on the affect of additive noise on automatic speech recognition", Technical Report, DRA Speech Research Unit, Malvern, England, 1992.

[22] J.W. Shi, J-H Chang, H.S. Yun, and N.S. Kim, "Voice Activity Detection based on Generalized Gamma Distribution", in Proc. *IEEE Int. Conf. Acoustics, Speech, and Signal Processing*, vol. 1, pp. 781-784, 2005.

[23] J. Ramirez, C. Segura, C. Benitez, A. Torre, and A. Rubio, "A new Kullback-Leibler VAD for speech recognition in noise", *IEEE Signal Processing Letters*, vol. 11, no. 2, pp. 266-269, February 2004.

A Framework for Uniform Development of Intelligent Virtual Agents

George Anastassakis and Themis Panayiotopoulos

Department of Informatics, University of Piraeus
{anastas, themisp}@unipi.gr

Abstract. As the field of Intelligent Virtual Agents evolves and advances, an ever increasing number of functional and useful applications are presented. Intelligent Virtual Agents have become more realistic, intelligent and sociable, with apparent and substantial benefits to domains such as training, tutoring, simulation and entertainment. However, even though many end-users can enjoy these benefits today, the development of such applications is restricted to specialized research groups and companies. Obvious and difficult-to-overcome factors contribute to this. The inherent complexity of such applications results in increased theoretical and technical requirements to their development. Furthermore, Intelligent Virtual Agent systems today typically offer ad hoc, if any, design and development means that lack completeness and a general-purpose character. Significant efforts have been successfully made towards deriving globally accepted standards; nevertheless these mostly focus on communication between heterogeneous systems and not on design and development. In this paper, we present our current efforts towards a novel architecture for Intelligent Virtual Agents which is based on our previous work in the field and encompasses the full range of characteristics considered today as fundamental to achieving believable Intelligent Virtual Agent behaviour. In the spirit of enabling and easing application design and development, as well as facilitating further research, our architecture is tightly coupled with a behaviour specification language that uniformly covers all aspects and stages of the development process. We also present the key guidelines for a minimal but functional implementation, aimed in validation and experimentation.

1 Introduction

A number of approaches have been attempted until today to deliver believable synthetic character applications using *Intelligent Virtual Agents* (*IVAs*). Some are based in integrating individual components, most usually designed and implemented by separate research groups or companies; others, of a more top-down nature, design and implement their systems from scratch, most often expanding on previous own work. A common conclusion emerging from most, if not all, attempts, is that believability in synthetic characters, whether these be virtual humans, animals or even imaginary beings, demands coexistence and cooperation of a set of features. This set includes at least the following: perception of and action upon a simulated 3D world

G. Antoniou et al. (Eds.): SETN 2006, LNAI 3955, pp. 13–24, 2006.
© Springer-Verlag Berlin Heidelberg 2006

implemented as a *Virtual Environment* (*VE*); a solid AI background for planning, belief representation and reasoning on the world, the character's self and other characters; emotion; agent-human interaction. In addition, in order for frameworks incorporating these characteristics to be actually useful rather than serving a specific predefined application or set of applications, a means to define the world contents, agent behaviour and interactions must be available.

SOAR [1] is a reasoning system preferred by many of those following the component integration approach. SOAR has been used to drive STEVE [2], a virtual human-like agent originally designed to support various forms of training for humans, also incorporated in more complex applications such as the Mission Rehearsal System [3] used in military crisis situations training and, lately, negotiation modelling [4]. Closer to the top-down architectural approach, the FearNot project [5] aims in experimentation with children in bullying situations. The system is based on the concept of *emergent narrative* [6] which requires the plot and dialogue evolution to *emerge*, based on the participants' personalities, beliefs and intentions, rather than be generated by structures of predefined rules. Another synthetic character architecture focusing mostly on virtual humans and their uses in simulation is ACE [7], which offers a degree of flexibility in scenario design through the use of plugins.

The above mentioned projects along with a surplus of others, represent substantial progress in using IVAs for real-world applications with an actual benefit for the participants, as well as notable examples of theory put to working practice. Each, to a certain degree, incorporates some, or all, of the crucial features discussed above. However, they remain research systems with little or unclear potential to employ in mass-production of synthetic character applications, at least at their current stage. Towards this direction, the availability of a design and definition technique becomes essential. Such techniques, ranging from Shoham's *Agent0* agent-oriented programming language [8], formal definition languages such as Z as it has been used for defining agents [9] and graphical environments such as SOAR's ViSoar, to scripting languages such as those offered by Transom JACK and HUMANOID [10], seem to be insufficient and inappropriate for today's synthetic character systems as they do not address the full range of requirements listed above. Also, software toolkits, such as AgentBuilder [11], Jack agents [12] and others, are available for implementation of agent applications but, in each case, they lack important features such as emotion, physical modelling and interaction, belief representation, planning or reasoning.

A diversity of emotional models have been used, from the time their importance in believability has first been emphasized on in projects like Oz [13]. These range from simple models where emotions are modelled as gauges whose value varies over time according to a predefined format, to far more advanced ones, such as the *appraisal theory* [14] and the *OCC model* [15].

As an overall conclusion, today's systems and frameworks, either lack features that are crucial to believability, or lack the means to define applications that will take advantage of such features and address real-world needs.

In this paper, we present our own attempts to address this problem through a novel synthetic character framework, based on our previous work in the field [16] and offering the full range of features crucial to believability, together with a consistent and uniform definition means for IVAs and their VE. This paper intends to present the framework's overall architecture and functionality, rather than provide a detailed and exhaustive analysis of its design, as this would require substantially more space and a technical discussion.

2 Architecture Overview

Virtual agents, whether intelligent or not, inhabit VEs; this relationship is reflected on our framework in a not only conceptual, but also structural manner. At the highest level, the framework can be seen as a set of *agent* components implementing IVAs, interacting with a *world* component implementing a VE. This interaction involves sensory data agents receive from, as well as action data they send to, the world.

Agents and worlds are also subdivided into further components with specific interactions with each other. This high-level view of the framework is illustrated in the following diagram, where a single agent interacts with a world.

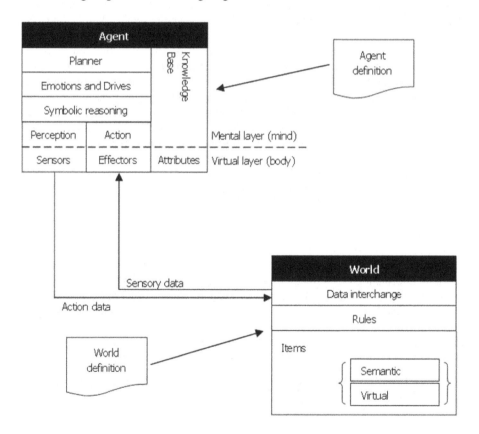

Fig. 1. Architecture overview

As shown in the diagram, in addition to a world and agent(s), the framework also involves definitions for the agents as well as the world. A world definition is an XML file describing the contents and functionality of a VE. An agent definition is the means to achieve a specific IVA behaviour within the context of the framework. Agent definitions are based on a novel version of our VAL language [17] which has been redesigned to comply with the framework's requirements for uniform definition of both mental and physical aspects of an IVA. Definitions can be modified at runtime, offering a high degree of flexibility in application design and experimentation.

3 World

The modelling approach adopted by the world specifies that a VE is modelled as a three-dimensional space of finite dimensions containing *items*.

An item is an abstraction for a real- (or even an imaginary-) world object, a property of the world, an event and others. Items are manifested at mainly two levels. At one level, the item's virtual-reality-related aspects are defined. This enables the item to be rendered on a computer graphics context, generate sound, exhibit simulated physical properties such as volume, mass and structure, as well as move, animate and generally alter its appearance and other properties. It is defined as the item's *virtual representation*. At the other level, the item's semantic content is defined using a Prolog-like symbolic notation. This enables the item to be sensed or acted-upon by an agent. It is defined as the item's *semantic representation*. The two representations are tightly coupled as they essentially describe the same thing from different perspectives, at different levels of abstraction and for different purposes. Specific relationships are provided within a world definition to link semantic with virtual properties, essentially ensuring that the two representations are consistent at all times.

Interaction with items is possible through *access points*. An access point is linked to an element of the virtual and/or semantic representation and specifically defines how these are modified when it is accessed. An access point is virtually represented as a subtotal of the item's virtual representation and can be uni- (a point), two- (a surface) or three-dimensional (a volume).

A semantic representation is needed because the architecture does not specify any mechanism for extracting semantic information from sensory data. Therefore, semantic information needs to be provided to an agent's sensors rather than generated from image or sound data. This approach enables satisfactorily functional sensory processes without the need for complicated and error-prone image and sound analysis techniques. It is a solution suiting a very large application domain without substantial tradeoffs apart from the extra effort required to derive a symbolic representation.

A sample world definition in XML is shown below:

```
<world version="1.0" name="sampleWorld">
  <info contentVersion="1.0.1.1211.b"
    date="12/11/2005"
    author="G. Anastassakis"
    organization=""
    email=""
  />
```

```
<dimension x="1024.0" y="128.0" z="1024.0"/>
<scene name="sampleScene">
  <spawnLocation name="sampleSpawn"
    location="0.0, 0.0"
  />
  <item name="sampleItem"
    class="BaseItem"
    translation="0.0, 0.0, 0.0"
    rotation="0.0, 1.0, 0.0, 0.0"
    scale="1.0, 1.0, 1.0"
  >
    <dimension x="0.0" y="0.0" z="0.0"/>
    <virtualModel>
      <element class="X3D" version=""
        source="sampleWorld.x3d"
      />
    </virtualModel>
    <semanticModel>
      <element name="powerLed" initial="1"
        default="0" domain="[on, off]"
      >
        <binding class="X3D"
          target="led01Mat.emissiveColor"
        >
          <valueBinding semanticValue="on"
            virtualValue="255 64 64"
          />
          <valueBinding semanticValue="off"
            virtualValue="64 64 64"
          />
        </binding>
      </element>
    </semanticModel>
  </item>
</scene>
</world>
```

The above sample, which is simplified to serve the discussion, defines a world with a single item whose virtual model is represented by an X3D (the successor of VRML) scene graph. On the other hand, the item's semantic model defines a single element which is the symbolic equivalent of a node in the scene graph visually representing a power led. The two values defined for the powerLed symbol are bound to two individual values of the power led node's emissive colour property, essentially linking the two instances of the symbol ("powerLed(on)" and "powerLed(off)") to two different visual states.

Ideally, these two representations of an item – virtual and semantic – should be equivalent. The degree to which this is desired is up to a given application's designer to decide and comply with. It is expected, though, that a semantic representation will be less detailed than its virtual counterpart, as the amount of information required for functional item-agent interactions is generally less, as this information is of higher level, than that required for realistic visual and auditory rendering.

Sensory operations as well as interaction with items consist of semantic data only. This data are derived from the symbolic representation of the items involved and are subject to certain rules which essentially drive data generation. For instance, a sensory operation aiming to provide an agent with symbolic data corresponding to which items they can "see" when at a certain location in the VE is subject to range and obstruction rules derived from a line-of-sight vicinity model. Similarly, items that represent sounds have a time-limited lifespan which represents fade-out of sounds in the real-world – although longer so that agents that, in contrast to humans, operate on a discrete time domain, can also "hear" them.

Interaction between agents and human users is possible, but not required for the framework's operation. According to a given application's demands, a human user can "take-over" an agent and gain complete control over its behaviour, immerse into the world and be perceived by other agents as another agent. A different scenario might involve special kinds of items that will enable transfer of information between a human user and an agent inside the world, such as items representing speech, etc. In any case, human-agent interaction follows the same rules that apply to any other kind of interaction in the world.

4 Mental Layer

The mental layer of an agent consists of several components operating concurrently. This component-based nature of the framework's architecture enables extensions on a per-component basis, with no modifications to other components necessary. In addition, concurrent operation ensures that no processing time is wasted while a component waits for another to complete its operation, essentially resulting in optimal utilization of a multi-processing execution context's capabilities. A synchronization mechanism ensures data safety at all times, by scheduling data access requests as issued by components.

It must be noted that the behaviour of each component described below is defined by an agent definition to suit the requirements of a particular application. The general form of an agent definition is shown below in XML syntax:

```
<agent name="smith">
  ...
  <(component)>
    ... (component definition)
  </(component>
  ...
</agent>
```

In the above example, "(component)" is a placeholder for a component name, such "KnowledgeBase", "Reasoning", etc, whereas the enclosed component definition defines the specific component's behaviour as well as its interactions with other components.

Following in this section, each component is described in an order of increasing number of functional dependencies to other components.

4.1 Knowledge Base

The *Knowledge Base* (*KB*) reflects the agent's "knowledge" up to a certain point in time. It contains Prolog-like symbolic data. It is roughly based on the BDI model [18] which enables symbolic representation of beliefs and goal-driven behaviour, yet introduces certain structural and semantic features. For instance, an IVA's abilities, as well as its emotional state – defined later in this text, are reflected by reserved symbols in the KB's beliefs section. This enables the IVA to be aware of its abilities and emotions, a fact that, as discussed later, directly affects action selection and planning. The KB also contains the agent's memory which stores subsets of beliefs representing episodes along with a timestamp. Episodes are retrievable either by context or by temporal conditions.

All components – with a few exceptions – exchange information only with the KB which acts as a synchronized data manager required for concurrent operation.

4.2 Logic-Based Reasoning

This component consists of a meta-interpreter able to produce beliefs according to a set of rules. It enables refinement of beliefs to various abstraction levels. It also provides the necessary facilities for simple reasoning such as arithmetics, spatial and temporal reasoning, resolution of action preconditions, and others.

The meta-interpreter maintains a set of rules, following a Prolog-like syntax, that define *expressions*. When the body of a rule can be unified with beliefs from the KB, the instantiated rule head is either asserted into the KB as a new belief, or used during reasoning, ability precondition resolution, etc. This process ensures availability of beliefs of an arbitrarily higher conceptual level than that of plain sensory data.

4.3 Perception and Action

This lowest level of an agent's mental layer enables production of complex symbolic constructs using *sensory rules* that are applied to sensory data, as well as decomposition of high-level *actions* to *action primitives* that will be sent to the world during action operations. For instance, data involving the absolute locations of a group of items might be processed based on a meta-interpreter rule to produce facts about the items' arrangement and relative positions. Similarly, a location-change action involving a certain destination might trigger a path finding mechanism to generate a path to the destination traversable by primitive movement actions only. Essentially, these primitive actions are the analogue of the abilities of a real-world living creature's physical body, as well as of higher-level actions that are performed automatically, with little or no reasoning – to a certain extent and given certain preconditions – by a real-world intelligent creature. Such actions include walking, grasping, speaking, sitting on a chair, climbing a ladder, or even driving a car.

An action is the result of the application of an *ability*. An ability is a definition for an action the IVA can perform, consisting of a set of *preconditions* and *effects* defined symbolically. Preconditions consist of a set of expressions that must evaluate as true in order for an ability to be applicable. On the other hand, effects specify desired changes to the VE referred to as *world effects*, as well as expressions that will be asserted, retracted, or evaluated against, the KB, representing desired changes to the IVA's mental state and referred to as *agent effects.*

Effects can be action primitives directly executable by effectors, low-level actions processed by the Action component, or actions defined by other abilities. This way, definition of abilities of various levels of complexity is possible. In order for a complex ability to be applicable, its own preconditions as well as preconditions of all abilities referenced by its effects, must evaluate as true. Similarly, a complex ability's low-level action primitive set consists of its own action primitives as well as action primitives produced by the Action layer by processing the effects of all abilities referenced by the complex ability's effects, recursively.

Apart from exchanging information with the KB, the Perception and Action components are also able of immediate information interchange. This feature enables efficient reactive behavioural elements that require little reasoning restricted only to sensory rules.

4.4 Emotions and Drives

Crucial to believability, emotions are modelled as gauges whose value changes over time between two extremes, tending towards an idle value. Emotions can affect each other on a per-change or a per-value basis. Drives can also be defined upon the same mechanism. The selection of emotions and drives to be defined for a particular application is up to the application designer and not specified by the architecture. This enables definition of and experimentation with a variety of affective models appropriate for a range of applications. A (simplified) emotion definition that would appear inside the "Emotion" component's definition is shown below in XML syntax:

```
<emotion name="comfort" min="-100" max="100" idle="30"
  initial="0" change="0.01">
  <emotionEffect target="mood" value="0.2">
</agent>
```

The above sample presents a definition for a "comfort" emotion which might, for instance, represent the degree to which an IVA "feels" comfortable with their surroundings. The value of the defined emotion ranges between -100 and 100, is initially equal to 0 and changes over time towards 30 at a rate of 0.01 per ms. Also, the enclosed "emotionEffect" element defines that each positive unit change to the value of the "comfort" emotion will result in a contribution of 0.2 to the value of another emotion named "mood".

It is important to note that, as mentioned earlier, an IVA's emotional state is reflected by specific beliefs in the KB; therefore, emotional conditions can be seamlessly employed to define ability preconditions. In addition, specific action primitives are reserved to represent changes to emotion values; hence an action can have specifically defined impact to an IVA's emotional state as well. This is shown in the shortened and simplified example below, which presents, in XML syntax, a definition of an ability:

```
<ability name="pickup(Item)">

<preconditions>...,fatigue(X),X<10,...</preconditions>
  <effects>...,-fatigue(X),+fatigue(X+1),...</effects>
</ability>
```

The example shows how, in order for a "pickup" action to be available, the value of "fatigue" emotion must be less than 10, as well as how execution of the "pickup" action positively contributes to the value of the "fatigue" emotion.

4.5 Planning

Planning in our architecture is performed by a STRIPS-based planner operating on the same symbolically defined abilities as those used by the Perception and Action layers. Planning is goal-driven, based on goals contained in the KB's Desires section.

Plan generation is affected by emotions in the same way as actual plan execution. More specifically, the contribution, either negative or positive, of each particular action selected by the planning process is taken under account while planning, simulating the actual emotional impact that this action would have if executed. This feature greatly contributes to an IVA's behavioural believability as, not only its immediate actions, but also its long-term course of action, exhibit an emotion-affected character.

5 Virtual Layer

Being the lowest level of an agent, the virtual layer represents the functionality of an IVA's simulated physical body. This body is not only there for visualization purposes; it plays an important part in the framework's functionality as all interaction between a world and an agent is carried-out through it. For this reason, an agent definition also involves definition of various aspects of a virtual layer.

The two main components of a virtual layer are Sensors and Effectors. Sensors are responsible for gathering symbolic information sent by the world as a result of a sensory operation, forming them into symbolic constructs and delivering them to the Perception component for further processing. Likewise, effectors are responsible for breaking-down symbolically represented action primitives received by the Action component and sending them to the world during an action operation.

As the mental layer's functionality is affected by Emotions and Drives, so is the virtual layer's. A set of *attributes* representing physical properties affect reception of sensory information and the outcome of actions in a way that simulates the corresponding effect on an actual physical body. For instance, a "tiredness" attribute of increased value might cause a sensory operation to receive partial data simulating a living creature missing-out information when sensing its surrounding environment while being tired and, therefore, inattentive. Similarly, a "constitution" attribute of reduced value might cause a targeting action to fail when an IVA tries to access an item's access point. Attributes function similarly to Emotions and Drives, that is, their values can be varying over time, or be constant. Attribute values, behaviour and relationships to sensory and action operations are seamlessly defined by agent definitions, as higher-level components are, essentially enabling uniform and consistent definition of all aspects, both virtual and mental, of an IVA.

6 Implementation

Implementation decisions were taken along a number of key guidelines. First, the framework should constitute a contemporary software product, able to take full advantage of today's technologies for data manipulation, intuitive user interfacing, distributed operation – aiming in effective workload management – and others. Additional requirements include concurrent operation of components, platform independence, maintainability and extendibility. Finally, the framework should be easily accessible and deployable by end users.

For the above reasons, we have chosen Java as the main platform for implementation of our framework. Distributed operation is achieved by enabling component communication through TCP/IP, effectively allowing a given application to be deployed over networks of various extents, ranging from small LANs to the Internet. Concurrency is achieved by implementing each component as a discrete thread – or a group of threads – and providing a synchronization mechanism to achieve thread safety for data accessed by multiple or all threads, such as, for instance, the Knowledge Base.

Additionally, a number of freely available, cross-platform Java-based libraries have been chosen, including SAX for XML parsing, Java3D for VE rendering and Xj3D for VRML and X3D (VRML's successor) files parsing. Apart from the availability of such libraries, the choice of Java guarantees platform-independence, as well as strong support by the community, a crucial factor in maintainability and extendibility of a software product.

Concluding, all forms of symbolic representation and processing, including symbolic reasoning and planning, have been implemented in SICStus Prolog. Interfacing between SICStus Prolog and Java is based on the Jasper library which is part of the SICStus package.

7 Conclusions and Future Work

We have presented our current efforts towards an architecture that encompasses the full range of characteristics that are today considered as crucial to believable IVA behaviour. Our architecture also exhibits a number of additional features, including a by-definition component-based extendible nature, strong focus on intelligence capacities of IVAs, as well as a uniform tool for defining applications, supporting both the VE and IVA aspects at a conceptual, implementation-independent level. We have also presented the guidelines for a minimal but functional implementation which we aim to employ in defining and running evaluation and experimentation scenarios.

The admittedly simplistic approach upon which some components, such as the Emotions and Drives component, are designed, may nonetheless substantially contribute to agent behaviour in terms of believability, if carefully-designed definitions are provided – especially as to the rate of emotion value change over time and interactions between emotions. In any case, the Emotions and Drives component can be re-designed based on more sophisticated approaches without the need for modifications to other components, as explained before. The same also applies to the Planning component and various aspects of Sensors and Effectors, such as pathfinding, etc. In fact, one of the key purposes of this framework is to act, in extended versions, as a testbed for various methodologies and technologies requiring co-operation with other components in order to generate believable IVA behaviours.

Future work includes focus on individual components, so that more sophisticated approaches to various aspects of the framework will collectively enhance its functionality. In particular, we intend to explore potential improvements to emotional modelling, planning and agent-human interaction. Specifically with respect to emotion, we intend to investigate the use of a more advanced theory of emotion such as the appraisal theory or the OCC model. We also mean to explore several areas untouched by the current version of our architecture, such as verbal and non-verbal communication and expression, through speech synthesis and recognition, facial expressions, gaze control and gesture generation. We also plan to design various scenarios and use them to isolate potential real-world uses as well as problems and lacking features. Furthermore, we intend to provide complete and formal syntax and semantics for our behaviour specification language based on VAL. In conclusion, we intend to evolve our framework towards being able to serve as both a basis for contemporary research as well as a means to design and run functional applications.

References

1. Laird, J.E., Newell, A., Rosenbloom, P.S.: SOAR: An Architecture for General Intelligence. Artificial Intelligence, Elsevier Science Publishers B.V., 1987, pp. 1-64.
2. Rickel, J., Johnson, W.: Integrating pedagogical capabilities in a virtual environment agent. In Proceedings of the First International Conference on Autonomous Agents, Johnson, W.L., Hayes-Roth, B. (Eds.), ACM Press, 1997.
3. Swartout, W., Gratch, J., Hill, R., Hovy, E., Marsella, S., Rickel, J., Traum, D.: Toward Virtual Humans. In working notes of the AAAI Fall symposium on Achieving Human-Level Intelligence through Integrated Systems and Research, Crystal City, VA, 2004.
4. Traum, D., Swartout, W., Marsella, S., Gratch, J.: Fight, Flight, or Negotiate: Believable Strategies for Conversing under Crisis. Intelligent Virtual Agents 2005, Panayiotopoulos, T., Gratch, J., Aylett, R., Ballin, D., Olivier, P., Rist, T. (Eds.), LNAI 3661, Springer, 2005, pp. 52-64.
5. Aylett, R., Louchart, S., Dias, J., Paiva, A., Vala, M.: FearNot! - an experiment in emergent narrative. Intelligent Virtual Agents 2005, Panayiotopoulos, T., Gratch, J., Aylett, R., Ballin, D., Olivier, P., Rist, T. (Eds.), LNAI 3661, Springer, 2005, pp. 305-316.
6. Aylett, R.: Narrative in virtual environments – towards emergent narrative. AAAI Symposium on Narrative Intelligence, 1996, pp. 83-86.
7. Kallmann, M., Monzani, J. S., Caicedo, A., Thalmann, D.: ACE: A Platform for the Real Time Simulation of Virtual Human Agents. In Proceedings of EGCAS'2000, 11th Eurographics Workshop on Animation and Simulation, Interlaken, Switzerland, August, 2000.
8. Shoham, Y,: Agent0: A Simple Agent Language and its Interpreter. In Proceedings of the Ninth National Conference on Artificial Intelligence, 1991, pp. 704-709.
9. Luck, M., Griffiths, N., d'Inverno, M.: From Agent Theory to Agent Construction: A Case Study. Intelligent Agents III, Müller, J. P., Wooldridge, M., Jennings, N. R. (Eds.), LNAI 1193, Springer, 1997, pp. 49-64.

10. Boulic, R., Capin, T. K., Huang, Z., Kalra, P., Linterrnann, B., Magnenat-Thalmann, N., Moccozet, L., Molet, T., Pandzic, I. S., Saar, K., Schmitt, A., Shen, J., Thalmann, D.: The HUMANOID Environment for Interactive Animation of Multiple Deformable Human Characters. Computer Graphics Forum, Vol. 14(3), 1995, pp. 337-348.

11. Reticular Systems, Inc.: AgentBuilder: an Integrated Tookit for Constructing Intelligent Software Agents. http://www.agentbuilder.com/, 1999.

12. Busetta, P., Ronnquist, R., Hodgson, A., Lucas, A.: JACK Intelligent Agents – Components for Intelligent Agents in Java. AgentLink Newsletter, 1999.

13. Bates, J.: The Role of Emotion in Believable Agents. Communications of the ACM, Vol. 37, Issue 7, 1994, pp. 122-125.

14. Lazarus, R.: Emotion and Adaptation. Oxford University Press, 1991.

15. Orthony, A., Clore, G., Collins, A.: The Cognitive Structure of Emotions. Cambridge University Press, New York, 1988.

16. Anastassakis, G., Panayiotopoulos, T.: A System for Logic-Based Intelligent Virtual Agents. International Journal of Artificial Intelligence Tools (IJAIT), Vol. 13, N3, World Scientific Publishing, September 2004.

17. Panayiotopoulos, T., Anastassakis, G.: Towards a Virtual Reality Intelligent Agent Language. Advances in Informatics, Fotiadis, D., Nikolopoulos, S.D. (Eds.), World Scientific, 2000, pp. 249-259.

18. Bratman, M. E.: Intentions, Plans and Practical Reason. Harvard University Press, 1987.

A Mixture Model Based Markov Random Field for Discovering Patterns in Sequences

Konstantinos Blekas

Department of Computer Science,
University of Ioannina, 45110 Ioannina, Greece
kblekas@cs.uoi.gr

Abstract. In this paper a new maximum a posteriori (MAP) approach based on mixtures of multinomials is proposed for discovering probabilistic patterns in sequences. The main advantage of the method is the ability to bypass the problem of overlapping patterns in neighboring positions of sequences by using a Markov random field (MRF) prior. This model consists of two components, the first models the pattern and the second the background. The Expectation-Maximization (EM) algorithm is used to estimate the model parameters and provides closed form updates. Special care is also taken to overcome the known dependence of the EM algorithm to initialization. This is done by applying an adaptive clustering scheme based on the k-means algorithm in order to produce good initial values for the pattern multinomial model. Experiments with artificial sets of sequences show that the proposed approach discovers qualitatively better patterns, in comparison with maximum likelihood (ML) and Gibbs sampling (GS) approaches.

Keywords: Pattern discovering, Markov random field, mixture of multinomials model, Expectation-Maximization (EM) algorithm.

1   Introduction

Discovering patterns in sequences is an important problem in many application areas, such as bioinformatics, web mining, etc. Given a set of sequences a pattern (or *motif*) can be represented as a common substring that is repeated in the set. Sequence patterns are focused on highly conserved residues present in active sites of sequences and can be further used for generating rules for classification purposes [1, 2].

Various methods have been introduced for solving this problem that are classified based on the model of the pattern. Under the Bayesian framework, a pattern can be modeled using independent multinomial distributions for its positions. The Gibbs sampling [3, 4], the MEME [5], the SAM [6], the BioProspector [7], the Greedy EM [8] and the LOGOS [9] represent statistical methods for discovering shared patterns in a set of sequences. They all formulate the problem using either mixture models or hidden Markov models, and use the Expectation-Maximization (EM) algorithm [10, 11] or variational EM schemes to estimate the model parameters.

G. Antoniou et al. (Eds.): SETN 2006, LNAI 3955, pp. 25–34, 2006.
© Springer-Verlag Berlin Heidelberg 2006

The application of statistical methods to discovering sequence patterns usually forces the assumption that all the possible starting positions in sequences are independent. Nevertheless, the problem has the particular characteristic that spatial information should be taken into account. That is, apart from the content of a subsequence, its location must be also used in order to determine its posterior probability for matching it as pattern. In other words, it is not desired to identify overlapping patterns. In most of these methods, the common framework used is the maximum likelihood (ML) where the pattern model parameters are estimated by maximizing the likelihood of the observations, while the spatial constraints are indirectly enforced to the model. Therefore, in a sense, there is an inconsistency between the computed pattern distribution and the one defined by the model [9].

In this paper we present a *maximum a posteriori* (MAP) approach that provides a direct method to implement these ideas. The basic scheme is a two-component mixture of multinomials model, where one component models the pattern and the other the remaining non-pattern regions (background). Following this framework, a likelihood term is used to capture the content information of the data, while a bias term is also used to capture the spatial information of the neighborhood locations. This is accomplished by considering the pattern labels of each starting position of sequences through a Markov random field (MRF) model [12, 13]. This constrains the local characteristics of the sequences and thus provides useful information to the pattern estimation process. The EM algorithm is used to estimate the model parameters which provides closed form update equations for all parameters. Since the EM algorithm is very sensitive to the initial parameter values, we also present a clustering scheme based on the well-known k-means algorithm for initializing properly the pattern model. Finally, multiple patterns are discovered by iteratively applying the two-component mixture model after erasing old pattern occurrences. As will be demonstrated in the experimental study, in contrast to the classical unconstrained mixture model and the Gibbs sampling approach, the proposed one overcomes the problem of overlapping subsequences and also estimates qualitatively better pattern models.

Section 2 presents the two-components mixture of multinomials model that is used for discovering a single pattern in two methods: the classical ML and the proposed MAP approach. Experimental results are given in section 3 using artificial sets of sequences, while section 4 presents conclusions and discussion.

2   Mixture Models for Discovering Patterns

Consider a finite set $\Sigma = \{c_1, \ldots, c_\Omega\}$ consisting of Ω individual characters. An arbitrary string over the set Σ is any sequence $S_j = \{s_{jk}\}_{k=1}^{L_j}$ of length L_j, where $s_{jk} \in \Sigma$ denotes the character at the k-th position of the j-th sequence. Now, let $S = \{S_1, \ldots, S_N\}$ be a set of N strings of length $L_1, \ldots, L_N$, respectively. The pattern discovery problem deals with finding a common subsequence of length K that is repeated at different sites among the sequences of set S. In order to deal with this, we collect all the possible substrings of set S having length equal to K. This can be done by sliding a window of size K in every sequence S_j, obtaining a set of $L_j - K + 1$ substrings. Each substring indicates the starting position of a possible pattern occurrence in sequences. Therefore, we construct a set of n substrings $X = \{x_i\}_{i=1}^n$, $n = \sum_{j=1}^N (L_j - K + 1)$, that constitute the observation data. In the next subsections two mixture model based approaches will be presented: the classical maximum likelihood without any constraint, as well as, a new proposed maximum a posteriori approach that uses spatial information.

2.1 The ML Approach

Lets assume that the set X has been generated from a two-component mixture of multinomials, i.e. we assume that each substring x_i belongs to either a pattern class ($y_i = 1$) or a background class ($y_i = 0$) which is indexed by the hidden (binary) variable y_i. The first component models the pattern with a *common* prior probability of $\pi = p(y_i = 1)$, while the second one models the background and represents all the subsequences which do not contribute to the pattern, with a prior probability equal to $1 - \pi = p(y_i = 0)$. The density function $f(x_i|\pi, \Theta)$ of the model for an observation x_i is given by

$$f(x_i|\pi, \Theta) = \pi p(x_i|\theta) + (1 - \pi)p(x_i|b) , \tag{1}$$

where $\Theta = \{\theta, b\}$ is the set of parameters for the two multinomial densities. To parameterize the pattern we use a position weight matrix $\theta = [\theta_{kl}]$ of size $\Omega \times K$, where each element θ_{kl} denotes the probability that character $c_l \in \Sigma$ is at the k-th position of the pattern. For each position k it holds $\sum_l \theta_{kl} = 1$. The background distribution is represented with an Ω-vector of probabilities $b = [b_1, \ldots, b_\Omega]$ common for each substring position ($\sum_l b_l = 1$). Following the multinomial distribution and assuming independence among positions, the probability densities function of the pattern and the background model are

$$p(x_i|y_i = 1, \theta) = \prod_{k=1}^K \prod_{l=1}^\Omega \theta_{kl}^{\delta_{ikl}} \ , \ p(x_i|y_i = 0, b) = \prod_{l=1}^\Omega b_l^{\sum_{k=1}^K \delta_{ikl}} , \tag{2}$$

where δ_{ikl} is the Kronecker delta (1 if character c_l is at the k-th position of substring x_i, 0 otherwise).

Based on the above formulation, the model parameters can be estimated through maximum likelihood (ML). The log-likelihood function is then given by

$$L(X|\pi, \Theta) = \sum_{i=1}^n \log f(x_i|\pi, \Theta) . \tag{3}$$

The EM algorithm [10, 11] is an efficient framework to estimate the model parameters π, $\{\theta_{kl}\}$ and $\{b_l\}$. It requires the computation of conditional expectation z_i of the hidden variables y_i at the E-step, which are given by

$$z_i^{(t)} = p(y_i = 1|x_i, \pi^{(t)}, \Theta^{(t)}) = \frac{\pi^{(t)} p(x_i|y_i = 1, \theta^{(t)})}{\pi^{(t)} p(x_i|y_i = 1, \theta^{(t)}) + (1 - \pi^{(t)}) p(x_i|y_i = 0, b^{(t)})} , \tag{4}$$

while at the M-step the complete log-likelihood is maximized over the model parameters. This gives the following update equations

$$\pi^{(t+1)} = \frac{\sum_{i=1}^{n} z_i^{(t)}}{n} ,$$

$$b_l^{(t+1)} = \frac{\sum_{i=1}^{n}(1 - z_i^{(t)})\sum_{k=1}^{K}\delta_{ikl}}{K\sum_{i=1}^{n}(1 - z_i^{(t)})} , \theta_{kl}^{(t+1)} = \frac{\sum_{i=1}^{n} z_i^{(t)}\delta_{ikl}}{\sum_{i=1}^{n} z_i^{(t)}\sum_{l=1}^{\Omega}\delta_{ikl}} . \tag{5}$$

EM algorithm guarantees the convergence of the likelihood fuction to a local maximum and also satisfies all the constraints of the parameters.

Nevertheless, a significant drawback of the ML approach, arising from the assumption that the observations x_i are i.i.d., is the fact that the spatial information of the subsequences is not taken into account. This results in the estimation of overlapping subsequences as pattern occurrences of the set X, especially in cases where a pattern consists of one or more repeated characters. However, by enforcing spatial constraints one can avoid this problem and estimates better patterns. In [5] for example, a normalization of the posterior value z_i of the adjacent sequences is performed so that guarantees in any window of length K the sum of z_i values remains less than or equal to 1. In this study, we introduce a new approach that deals with this problem in a more systematic way by modeling the spatial arrangements of a pattern.

2.2 The Proposed Spatially-Constrained Mixture Model

In the proposed model, the pattern label priors $\Pi = \{\pi_i = p(y_i = 1)\}_{i=1}^{n}$ are considered as random variables that satisfy the constraint $0 \le \pi_i \le 1$. Since they are spatially dependent, we assume that they form a Markov random field (MRF) being sampled by a Gibbs distribution function [12, 13]

$$p(\Pi|\beta) = \frac{1}{Z}\exp(-U(\Pi|\beta)) . \tag{6}$$

The normalization constant Z is called the partition function, while the β is a regularization parameter. The energy function $U(\Pi|\beta)$ is decomposed into a sum of *clique potentials* $V_{\ i}$

$$U(\Pi|\beta) = \beta \sum_{i=1}^{n} V_{\ i}(\Pi) , \tag{7}$$

that involves neighboring sites $\mathcal{N}_i$ in the proposed sequential field. A similar in principle spatially-constrained model has been also used for the image segmentation problem [14]. In this study, we consider as neighborhood $\mathcal{N}_i$ all the m positions around the position i whose corresponding subsequences x_m overlaps with the subsequence x_i. In the general case, there are $2(K-1)$ such sites which are mutually dependent. When a pattern is found at position i ($\pi_i \approx 1$), it is desired that none substring $x_m \in \mathcal{N}_i$ to be also labeled as pattern ($\pi_m \approx 0$). An appropriated potential function that meets this behavior is the following simple inner product of pattern labels

$$V_i(\Pi) = \sum_m \pi_i \pi_m = \pi_i \pi_i \; . \tag{8}$$

Since Dirichlet densities are conjugate to multinomial densities, it is convenient to use them in order to introduce priors for the pattern parameters θ. Thus, for every pattern position k we consider a Dirichlet prior of the form

$$p(\theta_k|\alpha_k) = \frac{\Gamma(\sum_{l=1}^{\Omega} \alpha_{kl})}{\prod_{l=1}^{\Omega} \Gamma(\alpha_{kl})} \prod_{l=1}^{\Omega} \theta_{kl}^{\alpha_{kl}-1} \; , \tag{9}$$

where the parameter α_k is a Ω-vector with components $\alpha_{kl} > 0$ and $\Gamma(\alpha)$ is the Gamma function. Adding Dirichlet priors in effect introduces pseudo-counts at each pattern position. During the experimental study, the Dirichlet prior parameters were the same for every position and set equal to $1+\epsilon_l$, where ϵ_l was some low percentage (e.g. 10%) of the total predefined frequency of character c_l.

Given the above prior densities (Eqs. (6)-(9)) for the model parameters Π and θ, we can formulate the problem as a *maximum a posteriori* (MAP) problem, i.e. maximize the following posteriori log-density function

$$p(\Pi, \Theta|X) \propto \sum_{i=1}^{n} \log f(x_i|\Pi, \Theta) + \log p(\Pi|\beta) + \sum_{k=1}^{K} \log p(\theta_k|\alpha_k) \; . \tag{10}$$

The use of EM algorithm for MAP estimation requires at each step the computation of the conditional expectation values $z_i^{(t)}$ of the hidden parameters y_i at the E-step, which is the same as ML approach (Eq. 4) by substituting the common prior π with the label parameter π_i. During the M-step the maximization of the following complete-data log-likelihood function is performed

$$Q(\Pi, \Theta \mid \Pi^{(t)}, \Theta^{(t)}) = \sum_{i=1}^{n} z_i^{(t)} \{\log(\pi_i) + \log(p(x_i|\theta))\} + (1 - z_i^{(t)})\{\log(1 - \pi_i) +$$

$$+ \log(p(x_i|b))\} - \beta \sum_{i=1}^{n} \pi_i \pi_i + \sum_{k=1}^{K} \sum_{l=1}^{\Omega} (\alpha_{kl} - 1) \log(\theta_{kl}) \; , \tag{11}$$

independently for each parameter. This gives the following update equation for the pattern multinomial parameters:

$$\theta_{kl}^{(t+1)} = \frac{\sum_{i=1}^{n} z_i^{(t)} \delta_{ikl} + (\alpha_{kl} - 1)}{\sum_{i=1}^{n} z_i^{(t)} \sum_{l=1}^{\Omega} \delta_{ikl} + \sum_{l=1}^{\Omega} (\alpha_{kl} - 1)} \; , \tag{12}$$

while for the background model the update rules are the same as in the case of the ML approach (Eq. 5).

The maximization of the function Q with respect to the label parameters π_i reduces to the next quadratic expression

$$\beta\pi_{,i}(\pi_i^{(t+1)})^2 - (1 + \beta\pi_{,i})(\pi_i^{(t+1)}) + z_i^{(t)} = 0 , \qquad (13)$$

where the summation term $\pi_{,i}$ can include both updated labels $(\pi_m^{(t+1)})$ and not yet updated $(\pi_m^{(t)})$. The above equation has two roots

$$\pi_i^{(t+1)} = \frac{(1 + \beta\pi_{,i}) \pm \sqrt{(1 + \beta\pi_{,i})^2 - 4\beta\pi_{,i}z_i^{(t)}}}{2\beta\pi_{,i}} . \qquad (14)$$

It can be easily shown that only the root with the negative sign is valid, since the other one is discarded due to the constraint $0 \le \pi_i \le 1$. Therefore, the above equation provides a simple update rule for the label parameters π_i which ensures the uniqueness of the solution and satisfies the constraint. Looking carefully at Eq. 14 we can make some useful observations. In the case where a substring x_i has high posterior probability value $(z_i^{(t)} \approx 1)$, one of the following two scenarios will occur in the neighborhood $\mathcal{N}_i$:

- None of sites $m \in \mathcal{N}_i$ is labeled as a pattern, i.e. $\pi_{,i} \lesssim 1$, and thus, following Eq. 14, this site will be labeled as pattern $(\pi_i^{(t+1)} \approx 1)$.
- There is at least one site labeled as pattern in $\mathcal{N}_i$, i.e. $\pi_{,i} \gtrsim 1$. Then, according to Eq. 14, the new label value will be approximately $\pi_i^{(t+1)} \approx \frac{1}{\beta\pi_{\mathcal{N}_i}}$. The larger the value of $\pi_{,i}$, the smaller the update label values of π_i. In this "overlapping" neighborhood only one pattern occurrence will be the most probable to survive, the one having the higher posterior value z_i.

On the other hand, when a substring x_i has small posterior value of being a pattern $(z_i^{(t)} \approx 0)$ it will continue to be labeled as background $(\pi_i^{(t+1)} \approx 0)$, independently of its neighborhood $\mathcal{N}_i$.

From the above analysis it is clear that the regularization parameter β of the Gibbs distribution function plays a significant role. Only large values of this parameter $(\beta \gg 1)$ are acceptable in order to discourage overlapping substrings being labeled as pattern. However, in our experiments, a large range of values of β seems to yield a satisfactory behavior, which implies that the proposed method is not sensitive to this parameter. A typical value that has been used successfully during experiments is $\beta = 100$.

Discovering multiple patterns. This can be accomplished by iteratively apply the two-component mixture of multinomials model, after erasing from the set of sequences S the patterns that have been already found. In particular, after convergence of the EM algorithm all substrings x_i whose label parameters π_i surpass a threshold value T (e.g. $T = 0.9$) are deleted from the S. A new set S is then created, and the initial model is sequentially applied to it to discover another pattern.

2.3   Initializing Pattern Multinomial Models

The major drawback of the EM algorithm is the dependence on the initial values of the model parameters that may cause it to get stuck in local maxima of the likelihood function [11]. In our study, this problem is mainly concentrated on initializing the pattern multinomial θ, since for the background density b we can use the total relative frequencies of characters in sequences. To overcome this weakness we present here a clustering scheme that is based on the classical k-means algorithm and its recent extensions to categorical data [15].

In the general case the k-means algorithm aims at finding a partition of M disjoint clusters to a set of n objects, so as the overall sum of distances between cluster centers μ_j and objects is minimized. Depending on the type of objects, one must determine an appropriate distance function and also a method for estimating cluster centers. Since we are dealing with discrete data, we define the simple Hamming distance $d(x_i, \mu_j) = \sum_{k=1}^{R}(1 - \delta(x_{ik}, \mu_{jk}))$ to measure similarities among the samples and the cluster centers. Moreover, the cluster center μ_j $j = 1, \ldots, M$ is determined as the *median* substring of the cluster members, i.e. $\mu_j = x_{i*}$, where $i = \arg\min_i \sum_{x_k} d(x_i, x_k)$. When finishing, we initialize the pattern model with the relative frequencies of characters from the cluster j that has the minimum average distance (*intracluster* distance) between all cluster members and its center μ_{j*}. It must be also noted that, in order to avoid selection of outliers, we isolate our search over clusters whose size (number of members) is above a threshold value, e.g. $N/2$. The experimental study has shown that this clustering scheme provides excellent initial values of parameter θ in a very fast way.

3   Experimental Results

Several experiments were performed in an attempt to study the effectiveness of the proposed MAP approach. During all experiments the proposed clustering scheme of k-means was first applied to generate an initial pattern multinomial model, and then the EM algorithm was used for MAP estimation of the model parameters. The pattern labels π_i were all initialized to $\pi_i = 0.5$. Comparative results have been also obtained using the ML approach without spatial constraints (initialized identically to the MAP approach), as well as the Gibbs sampling (GS) method [3, 4]. Starting by an initial (random) estimation of the positions of the patterns $(\theta^{(0)})$, the GS method performs iteratively two steps until likelihood convergence: first, it randomly selects a sequence S_i and re-estimates the pattern model $\theta^{(t+1)}$ using the current pattern positions of all sequences but S_i, and then, a new pattern position is selected in S_i by sampling from the posterior distribution over positions. Obviously, this version of the GS assumes that each sequence has a unique occurrence of the pattern. However, this is not true for our model that permits an arbitrary number of pattern copies in each sequence. Thus, in order to provide fair comparisons, we created sets with a single copy of any pattern to every sequence. Moreover, we execute the GS method 10 times and keep the best solution found.

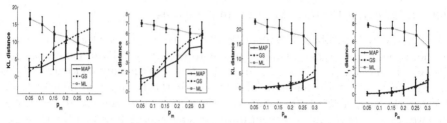

(a) seed pattern: TATATATATATATTTT (b) seed pattern: HIERHIERVIEWVIEW

Fig. 1. Mean values and stds of KL and l_1 as calculated by the three methods in two single-pattern discovery problems (a), (b) using six values of noise parameter p_m.

The artificial sets used in the experiments were generated as follows: Using a number of *seed* patterns (one or two in our cases), every sequence contained a noisy copy of any of these seeds, according to a probability p_m common to every pattern position. The rest (non-pattern) positions were filled arbitrarily with characters following a uniform distribution over the alphabet Σ. Six different values for the noise parameter were used $p_m = [0.05, 0.1, 0.15, 0.2, 0.25, 0.3]$, and for each value we generated 40 different sets of $N = 20$ sequences with a mean length of 100 characters (totally 6×40 sets for each problem). From the above it is clear that we are aware of each true pattern density ϑ (estimated from the relative frequencies of characters of each noisy pattern copies). Following this scheme, four such pattern discovery problems were constructed using the DNA alphabet ($\Omega = 4$) and the protein alphabet ($\Omega = 20$), while the pattern length was always $K = 16$. To evaluate the discovered patterns by each method two information content criteria were used: the Kullback-Libler (KL) distance and the sum of the absolute differences (l_1 distance) between the estimated $\hat{\theta}$ and the true density $\vartheta = [\vartheta_{kl}]$, given by

$$KL(\hat{\theta}||\vartheta) = \sum_{k=1}^{K}\sum_{l=1}^{\Omega} \hat{\theta}_{kl} \log \frac{\hat{\theta}_{kl}}{\vartheta kl} \quad , \quad l_1(\hat{\theta}||\vartheta) = \sum_{k=1}^{K}\sum_{l=1}^{\Omega} |\hat{\theta}_{kl} - \vartheta kl| \ . \quad (15)$$

At first we examined the capability of the proposed MAP approach to clearly identify a single pattern without estimating overlapping copies of it. The results of the three comparative methods are shown in Fig. 1, for two such problems (a), (b). These diagrams illustrate the average values and standard deviations of the two evaluation measurements (KL and l_1) obtained by each method to the created 6×40 different set of sequences. As it is obvious, the proposed MAP approach achieves properly the identification of the patterns in all noisy environments, while the GS method maintains satisfactory performance only to low levels of noise rate. On the other hand, as expected, the weakness of ML approach to distinguish overlapping copies of patterns leads to lower discrimination ability.

We have also tested our method to problems with two sequence patterns. In an attempt to increase the difficulty of their discovery, half of the sites in both seed patterns presented identical characters. The results (mean values and stds of

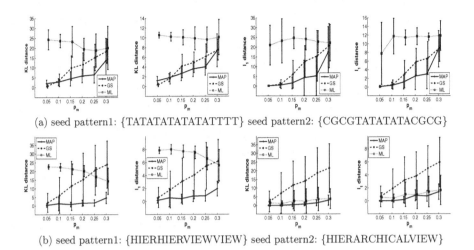

(a) seed pattern1: {TATATATATATATTTT} seed pattern2: {CGCGTATATATACGCG}

(b) seed pattern1: {HIERHIERVIEWVIEW} seed pattern2: {HIERARCHICALVIEW}

Fig. 2. Comparative results taken by applying the three methods in two discovery problems with two seed patterns. Again, calculated mean values and stds of KL and l_1 are illustrated in those diagrams.

KL and l_1) for two such problems (one from each alphabet) are demonstrated in Fig. 2 as obtained by each method. The weakness of the GS method to separate them is apparent, especially in sets with low homology patterns (large values of p_m). On the other hand, the MAP method exhibits almost perfect distinguishing capability by estimating properly the true model of both patterns. Finally, the ML approach presents the tendency to discover only one complex pattern obtained from the synthesis of both, and has shown good performance only in the case of the 2nd pattern of problem (b), where there are not repeated characters.

4   Conclusions

This paper presents a new spatially-constrained approach for discovering probabilistic patterns in sequences. The method uses a mixture of multinomials model with two components for modeling the pattern and the background of sequences. The spatial information is embodied in the model by treating the pattern labels as random variables that form a MRF to modeling their dependencies. The EM algorithm is then used to the reduced MAP problem for estimating the model parameters, after initializing with a clustering scheme that hires properties from the popular k-means algorithm. Experiments, conducted on a variety of categorical time-series, have shown the ability of the MAP method to identify qualitatively better patterns with repeated characters in comparison with the ML approach without constraints and the GS method. Further research can be focused on designing more complex pattern models that can also take into account gaps among sites, as well as on considering patterns of variable length.

References

1. Brāzma A., Jonasses I., Eidhammer I., and Gilbert D. Approaches to the automatic discovery of patterns in biosequences. *Journal of Computational Biology*, 5(2): 277–303, 1998.
2. Bréjova B., DiMarco C., Vinař T., Hidalgo S.R., Holguin G., and Patten C. Finding patterns in biological sequences. Project Report for CS798g, University of Waterloo, 2000.
3. Lawrence C.E., Altschul S.F., Boguski M.S., Liu J.S., Neuwland A.F., and Wootton J.C. Detecting subtle sequence signals: a Gibbs sampling strategy for multiple alignment. *Science*, 226:208–214, 1993.
4. Liu J.S., Neuwald A.F., and Lawrence C.E. Bayesian models for multiple local sequence alignment and Gibbs sampling strategies. *J. Amer. Statistical Assoc*, 90:1156–1169, 1995.
5. Bailey T.L. and C. Elkan C. Unsupervised learning of multiple motifs in Biopolymers using Expectation Maximization. *Machine Learning*, 21:51–83, 1995.
6. Hughey R. and Krogh A. Hidden Markov models for sequence analysis: Extension and analysis of the basic method. *CABIOS*, 12(2):95–107, 1996.
7. Liu X., Brutlag D.L., and Liu J.S. BioProspector: discovering conserved DNA motifs in upstream regulatory regions of co-expressed genes. In *Pac. Symp. Biocomput*, pages 127–138, 2001.
8. Blekas K., Fotiadis D.I., and Likas A. Greedy mixture learning for multiple motif discovering in biological sequences. *Bioinformatics*, 19(5):607–617, 2003.
9. Xing E.P., Wu W., Jordan M.I., and Karp R.M. LOGOS: A modular Bayesian model for *de novo* motif detection. *Journal of Bioinformatics and Computational Biology*, 2(1):127–154, 2004.
10. Dempster A.P., Laird N.M., and Rubin D.B. Maximum likelihood from incomplete data via the EM algorithm. *J. Roy. Statist. Soc. B*, 39:1–38, 1977.
11. McLachlan G.M. and Peel D. *Finite Mixture Models*. New York: John Wiley & Sons, Inc., 2001.
12. Besag J. Spatial interaction and the statistical analysis of lattice systems (with discussion). *J. Roy. Stat. Soc., ser. B*, 36(2):192–326, 1975.
13. Geman S. and Geman D. Stochastic relaxation, Gibbs distributions, and the Bayesian restoration of images. *IEEE Trans. on Pattern Analysis and Machine Intelligence*, 6:721–741, 1984.
14. Blekas K., Likas A., Galatsanos N.P., and Lagaris I.E. A Spatially-Constrained Mixture Model for Image Segmentation. *IEEE Trans. on Neural Networks*, 62(2):494–498, 2005.
15. Huang Z. Extensions to the k-Means algorithm for clustering large data sets with categorical values. *Data Mining and Knowledge Discovery*, 2(3):283–304, 1998.

An Efficient Hardware Implementation for AI Applications

Alexandros Dimopoulos, Christos Pavlatos, Ioannis Panagopoulos,
and George Papakonstantinou

National Technical University of Athens, Dept. of Electrical and Computer Engineering,
Zographou Campus, 157 73 Athens, Greece
{alexdem, pavlatos, ioannis, papakon}@cslab.ece.ntua.gr

Abstract. A hardware architecture is presented, which accelerates the performance of intelligent applications that are based on logic programming. The
logic programs are mapped on hardware and more precisely on FPGAs (Field
Programmable Gate Array). Since logic programs may easily be transformed into
an equivalent Attribute Grammar (AG), the underlying model of implementing an
embedded system for the aforementioned applications can be that of an AG
evaluator. Previous attempts to the same problem were based on the use of two
separate components. An FPGA was used for mapping the inference engine and a
conventional RISC microprocessor for mapping the unification mechanism and
user defined additional semantics. In this paper a new architecture is presented, in
order to drastically reduce the number of the required processing elements by a
factor of n (length of input string). This fact and the fact of using, for the inference
engine, an extension of the most efficient parsing algorithm, allowed us to use
only one component i.e. a single FPGA board, eliminating the need for an
additional external RISC microprocessor, since we have embedded two
"PicoBlaze" Soft Processors into the FPGA. The proposed architecture is suitable
for embedded system applications where low cost, portability and low power
consumption is of crucial importance. Our approach was tested with numerous
examples in order to establish the performance improvement over previous
attempts.

1 Introduction

Although Artificial Intelligence (AI) has already been a challenging research area for
more than 50 years, it still remains one of the most modern and interesting fields.
Knowledge engineering and logic programming approaches have extensively been
used in a considerable number of application domains, which range from medicine to
game theory [1]. It's common for various research areas to resort in AI techniques,
seeking for intelligent tools to enhance their performance. On the other hand,
techniques from other research fields can be embedded into AI applications. Such an
approach is reported in the present paper, in which we show how hardware/software
co design techniques can be exploited, so as to map AI application on a single FPGA
(Field Programmable Gate Array) board. Since most AI applications need to conform
to very strict real-time margins, one of the key requirements for the efficiency of such
systems is that of performance. As a result, designing fast algorithms for logic

G. Antoniou et al. (Eds.): SETN 2006, LNAI 3955, pp. 35–45, 2006.
© Springer-Verlag Berlin Heidelberg 2006

derivations is a key requirement for the efficiency of the implementation of an intelligent embedded system.

It is well known that knowledge representation and processing can be accomplished by two approaches, the declarative and the procedural one. Since Attribute Grammars (AGs) [2] can easily integrate the two approaches in a single tool, this approach appears to be ideal [3], [4], [5], to model AI applications and specifically PROLOG logic programs [6]. Moreover, the field of AGs' processing is fairly mature and many efficient implementations of compilers and interpreters for such evaluation processes can be utilized.

AGs were introduced in 1968 by Knuth [2]. The addition of attributes and semantic rules to Context Free Grammars (CFGs) augmented their expressional capabilities, making them in this way a really useful tool for a considerable number of applications. AGs have extensively been utilized in AI applications [3], [4], [5], [7], [8] structural pattern recognition [9], [10], compiler construction [11], and even text editing [12]. However, the additional complexity imposed by the added characteristics, along with the need for fast CF parsing by special applications, dictates the parallization of the whole procedure (parsing and attribute evaluation) as an attractive alternative to classical solutions.

In this paper we present a new hardware implementation for AI applications, based on AGs. We have improved previous approaches by reducing the number of required processing elements by a factor of n (length of input string). This fact allowed us to use only one component i.e. a single FPGA board, eliminating the need for an external microprocessor, as presented in previous works [7], [8], [13], [14], [15]. Additionally the attribute evaluation algorithm – that implements the unification mechanism and user defined additional semantics – has been improved as well and has been divided into two parts that are executed simultaneously into two processors. Both processors are mapped on the same Xilinx Spartan-II FPGA board, together with the inference engine. Consequently the unification process and the inference mechanism are executed on the same component, an FPGA board. Therefore the proposed architecture is suitable for embedded system applications where low cost, portability and low power consumption is of crucial importance. The downloaded processors, responsible for the attribute evaluation process, are two "PicoBlaze Soft Processor" [16] provided by Xilinx. The PicoBlaze Soft Processor is a very simple 8-bit micro controller designed to be 100% embedded into devices such as the Spartan-II we used. The processors interface with the parser using hardware/software co design methods (see Fig.1), while all data are stored in a shared by all components RAM.

Our approach has been simulated for validation, synthesized and tested on a Xilinx Spartan-II FPGA board, with numerous examples in order to establish the performance improvement over previous attempts. The performance speed up is application depended, i.e. on the length of the produced AG. Our contribution in this work is summarized as follows:

- We improved the parallel parsing architecture by eliminating the required processing elements by a factor of n (input string length) for the subset of AGs produced by PROLOG logic programs.
- We divided the attribute evaluation process into two pieces so as to be executed in parallel on two separate processors, concurrently with the parsing task.

- We mapped the whole implementation (two processors, parser, RAM) into a single component (FPGA).

The rest of the paper is organized as follows. In Section 2, the necessary theoretical background is presented. In Section 3, the implementation details are analyzed, while in Section 4, an illustrative example is demonstrated and performance evaluation is discussed. Finally, Section 5 concludes and presents our future work.

2   Theoretical Background

In this section we give the necessary fundamental definitions and a brief description of how PROLOG logic programs can be transformed into AGs. We will not explain in details theoretical issues, trying to focus on architectural aspects.

An AG is based upon a CFG. A CFG is a quadruple $G = (N, T, R, S)$, where N is the set of non-terminal symbols, T is the set of terminal symbols, R is the set of syntactic rules, written in the form $A \longrightarrow \alpha$, where $A \in N$ and $\alpha \in (N \cup T)^*)$ and S is the start symbol. We use capital letters A, B, C... to denote non terminal symbols, lowercases a, b, c... to denote terminal symbols and Greek lowercases and α, β, γ... for $(N \cup T)^*$ strings. An AG is a quadruple $AG = \{G, A, SR, d\}$ where G is a CFG, $A = \cup A(X)$ where $A(X)$ is a finite set of attributes associated with each symbol $X \in V$. Each attribute represents a specific context-sensitive property of the corresponding symbol. The notation X.a is used to indicate that attribute a is an element of $A(X)$. $A(X)$ is partitioned into two disjoint sets; the set of synthesized attributes $A_s(X)$ and the set of inherited attributes $A_i(X)$. Synthesized attributes X.s are those whose values are defined in terms of attributes at descendant nodes of node X of the corresponding semantic tree. Inherited attributes X.i are those whose values are defined in terms of attributes at the parent and (possibly) the sibling nodes of node X of the corresponding semantic tree. Each of the productions $p \in R$ (p: $X_0 \longrightarrow X_1...X_k$) of the CFG is augmented by a set of semantic rules $SR(p)$ that defines attributes in terms of other attributes of terminals and on terminals appearing in the same production. The way attributes will be evaluated depends both on their dependencies to other attributes in the tree and also on the way the tree is traversed. Finally d is a function that gives for each attribute a its domain $d(a)$.

In [4], [5] an effective method based on Floyd's parser [17] was presented that transforms any initial logic programming problem to its attribute grammar equivalent representation. The basic concepts underlying this approach are the following: every logic rule in the initial logic program can be transformed to an equivalent syntax rule consisting solely of non-terminal symbols. The general idea of using an AG for knowledge representation is to use only one terminal symbol, the NULL symbol. Thus, the grammar recognizes only empty strings of characters. During the recognition of an empty string the semantics can be such that at the time they are evaluated they accomplish the inference required. For example: $R_0(...) \leftarrow R_1(...) \wedge ... \wedge R_m(...)$ is transformed to the syntax rule: $R_0(...) \longrightarrow R_1...R_m|$. ("." represents the end of the rule and "|" represents logic OR). Finally facts of the inference rules are transformed to terminal leaf nodes of the syntax tree referring to the empty string. For example the facts: $R_g(a,b)$, $R_g(c,d)$, $R_g(e,f)$ are transformed to: $R_g \longrightarrow ||||$. For every variable existing in the initial predicates, two attributes are attached to the corresponding node of the syntax tree, one synthesized and one inherited. Those attributes assist in the unification process of the inference engine. The attribute evaluation rules are constructed based on the initial logic program. A detailed methodology for specifying those rules can be found in [5]. Attributes at the leaf nodes of the tree are assigned values from the constants in the facts of the logic program. The inference process is carried out during tree derivations and a function is evaluated at the insertion/visit of each node that computes the attribute rules performing the unification procedure. The way knowledge representation can be accomplished using AGs is illustrated in the example of Sec. 4.

3 The Proposed Implementation

3.1 Overview of Our Approach

In this paper the underlying model of implementing an embedded system for AI applications is that of an AG evaluator. The AG evaluation process is usually divided into two discrete tasks, that of syntactic parsing and that of semantic evaluation. The first corresponds to the inference engine, while the second to the unification mechanism. In the proposed embedded system, the inference engine is implemented using the hardware parsing architecture presented in [13], applying the necessary modifications analyzed in 3.2. The unification mechanism is carried out by the use of two processors embedded in the same FPGA with the parser. The whole process is controlled by the Control Unit, while all data are stored and retrieved by all components in a shared RAM. Our architecture is illustrated in Fig. 1 and analytically presented in the next sections.

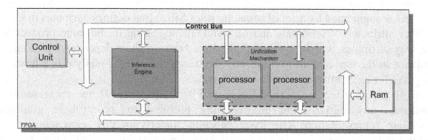

Fig. 1. The proposed architecture

3.2 The Inference Engine (Hardware Parser)

As referred in Sec. 2, every logic rule or fact corresponds to a syntactic rule. The set of these rules produces a CFG, which should be syntactically recognized. Hence, the inference task is carried out by a parser. The underlying algorithm of the parser is based on the most efficient parsing algorithm [18] in a parallel version presented by Chiang & Fu [14].

The basic innovation of the top-down parser that Earley [18], was the introduction of a symbol called dot "•" that does not belong to the grammar. The utility of the dot in a rule (now called dotted rule) is to separate the right part of the rule into two subparts. For the subpart at the left of the dot, it has been verified that it can generate the input string examined so far. However, for the subpart at the right of the dot, it still remains to check whether or not it can generate the rest of the input string. The algorithm scans the input string $a_1a_2a_3...a_n$ from left to right (where n is the input string length). As each symbol a_i is scanned, a set S_i of states is constructed which represents the condition of the recognition process at the point in the scan. A state is a 3-tuple $\{r, l, f\}$ where r is the number of the rule, l is the position of the dot and f is the set that the state was first created.

In 1980 Graham et al [19] proposed the use of an array PT (Parse Table) instead of Earley's set structure. The element of the array pt(i,j) contains all the dotted rules that belong to set S_j and were firstly created in set S_i. Particularly the jth column of the array PT corresponds to set S_j. Only the elements on or above the diagonal are used.

Chiang & Fu proved that the construction of the parsing table can be parallelized with respect to n by computing, in parallel, at every step k the cells pt(i,j) for which $j-i=k\geq1$. The architecture they proposed needs $n^2/2$ processing elements that each one computes the states of a cell of array PT. In every execution step $(te_1, te_2, ... te_n)$ each processor computes one cell and then transmits this cell to others processors as shown in Fig. 2(a). Chiang & Fu also introduced a new operator $\otimes$. Every cell pt(i,j) is a set of dotted rules (states) that can be calculated by the use of this operation $\otimes$, the cells of the same column and the cells of the same row as shown in equation 1.

An enhanced version of Chiang & Fu architecture was presented in [13] that computed the elements of the PT by the use of only n processing elements that each one handled the cells belonging to the same column of the PT, as shown in Fig. 2(b).

The general idea of using an AG for knowledge representation is to use only one terminal symbol, the NULL symbol. Thus, the grammar recognizes only empty strings of symbols. During the recognition of an empty string (actually the empty string) the semantics can be such that at the time they are evaluated they accomplish the inference required. In order to make the grammar compatible with the chosen parser, we introduce the use of a dummy terminal symbol "d". Consequently, the parser recognizes inputs strings of the form "dd...d⊩". The length of the input is problem length depended. Since $a_i=d$ for $1\leq i\leq n$, the cells that are executed during execution step te_1, as shown in equation 1 are equal to pt(i,j) = pt(i,j -1) $\otimes$ d. However, the cells that belong to the main diagonal are the same syntax-wise. Therefore, all the cells that are executed during execution step te_1 i.e. pt(i,j), $1\leq i<n$, $j=i+1$, are the same. Inductively, based on that critical comment and due to the form of equation 1, it can easily be proven that all the cells pt(i,j) that belong to the same diagonal contain the same states.

It must be clarified that although the cells may have the same states, the values of the attributes are clearly different, since the attributes are strictly connected to their position in the parse table and to the values of the attributes of the predecessor and successor symbols.

$$
pt(i,j) = \begin{cases} scanner: & pt(i,j-1)\otimes a_j \quad\quad \cup \\[2mm] & pt(i,i+1)\otimes pt(i+1,j) \quad \cup \\ completer: & pt(i,i+2)\otimes pt(i+2,j) \quad \cup \\ & \quad\quad\quad ... \quad\quad\quad\quad\quad \cup \\ & pt(i,j-1)\otimes pt(j-1,j) \end{cases} \tag{1}
$$

Thus, the parsing task can be accomplished by the use of one processing element, instead of n, that computes only the cells of the first row of the PT, as shown in Fig. 2(c). Once a cell is calculated, it is replicated to the others of the same diagonal so as to fill, the necessary for the attribute evaluation, PT. For example pt(0,1) will be copied to pt(1,2) and pt(2,3). The overhead for this transition is negligible relatively to the overall procedure. The architecture of the one parsing element follows the one presented in [13] achieving a speed-up by a factor of approximately 5, compared to software approaches. Additionally, the fact that we should compute the cells that belong only to the first row, augments drastically the speed-up. As the input string length and therefore the PT size increases, the speed-up increases as well. Experimental results are given in the next section.

The reduction of the required parsing processing elements simplifies the design allowing us to incorporate the processors responsible for the Attribute Evaluation into the same FPGA board, eliminating the need for an external microprocessor.

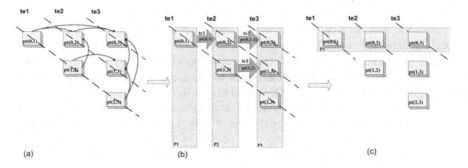

Fig. 2. (a) Chiang & Fu's parallel architecture (n=4) (b) Parsing Architecture for Grammar with Terminal Symbols (c) Parsing Architecture for Grammar without Terminal Symbols

3.3 The Unification Mechanism (Attribute Evaluator)

Once the parser has completed the computation of a PT cell pt(0,j), the attribute evaluation process may begin –evaluating the jth column– concurrently with the parser that computes the next cell pt(0,j+1).

In order to compute the inherited attributes of a state ($state_{current}$) in some cases, data from two other states ($state_1$ and $state_2$) are needed; one from the same row and one from the same column. The state from the same column may be placed either in the same cell or in one bellow.

To face both abovementioned cases, the way the column should be traversed is from bottom to top in relation to the cells and top to bottom in relation to the states inside each cell. Due to the nature of Earley's parsing algorithm (top-down, left to right) synthesized attributes may be evaluated correctly with solely the data that have already been transferred there. This action takes place when the dot symbol "•" reaches the end of the rule.

The attribute evaluation takes place in the PicoBlaze Soft Processors. The PicoBlaze Soft Processor is a very simple 8-bit micro controller designed to be 100% embedded into Spartan-II device. The PicoBlaze Soft Processor features 16 general purpose registers. A simple ALU supporting ADD/SUB, logical, shifts and rotates, conditional jumps and nested subroutine calls.

In the proposed implementation we divided the attribute evaluation process into two parts, so as to be evaluated to two separate processors in an attempt to increase the performance. Since the attribute evaluation of a column in processor1 completes to the point that the evaluation of the next column may start, processor1 sends an interrupt to processor2 to notify it that it may start. Then processor2 handles the evaluation of the next column and so on, as shown in Fig.3. In Fig. 3, it is clearly shown how our approach outperforms the conventional one, mainly due to the three following factors:

- The parsing is carried out in hardware and consequently is completed in shorter time.
- The attribute evaluation is taking place concurrently with the parsing task and not sequentially after the computation of the whole PT.
- The burden of the attribute evaluation is handled by two processors, reducing the time required, due to the pipeline parallelization.

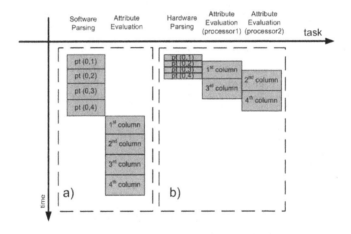

Fig. 3. Comparison of our approach (b) against the software approach (a)

4 An Illustrative Example

The way knowledge representation can be accomplished using AGs is illustrated in the following example. Consider the case where an application needs to find whether a path exists in a directed acyclic graph (Table 1) between two nodes of the graph and if so how many such paths exist. For a graph of k nodes with each node represented by a number i, where $0<i<k$ we define the predicate connected(i,j) which is true whenever there is a directed edge leading from i to j. A simple logic program, for finding paths from an arbitrary node x to another node z in the directed acyclic graph, is provided in Table 1(a). The equivalent attribute grammar syntax rules handling this inference procedure are provided in Table 1 (b) and the attribute evaluation rules for the unification process are shown in Table 1 (c). In the syntax rules the goal is

represented by "G", path by "P" and connected by "C". Let's assume that the goal connection is from 1 to13.

Table 1. (a) Directed acyclic graph and Logic Program for finding a path in a directed acyclic graph (b) Equivalent syntax rules for the attribute grammar to be used as inference engine (c) Semantic Rules

(a) Logic Program	(b) Syntax Rules	(c) Semantic Rules
	0. G → Pl.	$P.ia_1 = 1$; $P.ia_2 = 13$;
	1. P_1 → C P_2l.	$C_1.ia_1 = P_1.ia_1$; $P_2.ia_2 = P_1.ia_2$; $P_2.ia_1 = C_1.sa_2$;
	2. P → Cl.	$C.ia_1 = P.ia_1$; $C.ia_2 = P.ia_2$;
goal(x,y) ← path(1,13) path(x,z) ← path(y,z) ∧ connected(x,y) path(x,z) ← connected(x,z)	3. C → l.	**if** ($(C.ia_1 == 1)$ OR $(C.ia_1 ==$ nil)) **then** $C.sa_1$=1; **else** flag=0; **if** ($(C.ia_2 == 2)$ OR $(C.ia_2 ==$ nil)) **then** $C.sa_2$=2; **else** flag=0;
connected (1,2) connected (1,5) connected (2,3) ... connected (19,20)	4. C → l. 5. C → l. 6. C → l. ... 30. C → l.	...

Provided that the technology used for the hardware implementation is the same for both the FPGA and the microprocessor (if we run the application using a prolog program on a conventional microprocessor) we can safely use the number of the required clock cycles as measure of the efficiency of the two approaches (hardware versus software). Additionally, the computational power of processors used in embedded system, is comparable to that of an FPGA. Hence the performance in all implementations is measured using the number of the required clock cycles, so as to purely compare the architecture, regardless of the technology used. The clock cycles in the software implementations refer to those needed by the processor to execute the algorithm.

In Table 2 measurements are presented for both the software and the hardware approach. Specifically, we have taken individual measurements for i) The software Parser, ii) The Hardware Parser (computation of the first row), iii) The Hardware Parser including the transmission process (filling all the PT), iv) The Attribute Evaluation using only one processor (Pentium II 350 MHz) and v) The Attribute Evaluation using our approach with two PicoBlaze Soft Processors embedded in the Xilinx Spartan-II FPGA. Finally we present the speed-up individually for the parser, the attribute evaluation and the total speed-up (see Fig.4). Furthermore, in Fig. 5 we compare the hardware against the software approach. Unfortunately, due to the difference in magnitude, some measurements cannot appear. Mainly the hardware parser that is under the attribute evaluation (in the FPGA using the two processors).

Table 2. Measurements in clock cycles

Input String Length	4	8	12	16	20
Software Parser	13,560	49,358	115,789	223,153	381,450
Hardware Parser	4,173	9,274	12,997	17,988	25,349
Transmission	96	336	704	1,200	1,824
Hardware Parser + Transmission	4,269	9,610	13,701	19,188	27,173
Attribute Evaluation using one processor	256,342	860,578	1.565,480	2,464,523	3,629,427
Attribute Evaluation using two processors	229,687	622,222	948,842	1,286,956	1,674,223
Parsing Speed-up	3.18	5.14	8.45	11.63	14.04
Attribute Evaluation Speed-up	1.12	1.38	1.65	1.92	2.17
Software approach	269,902	909,936	1,681,269	2,687,676	4,010,877
Our approach	233,956	631,832	962,543	1,306,144	1,701,396
Final Speed-up	1.15	1.44	1.75	2.06	2.36

We can see from Table 2 and Fig. 4, 5 that although we have a very high speed-up for the hardware inference machine (hardware parser), the corresponding speed-up for the unification mechanism (attribute evaluation) is non analogous. These results were expected according to Fig.3. Hence, the overall performance is reduced due to the unification mechanism, i.e. the bottleneck is in the unification.

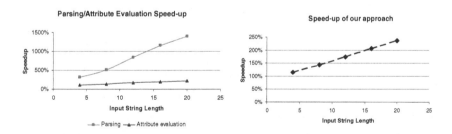

Fig. 4. (a) Parsing/Attribute Evaluation Speed-up (b) Speed-up of our approach compared against software approach

There are four solutions to the above problem. One is to use more processors embedded in the FPGA for the parallel evaluation of the semantics. The second is to use a very fast general purpose external microprocessor for only the evaluation of the semantics. The third is to implement the semantics mapping them directly on the FPGA hardware and not through software on the microprocessor embedded on the FPGA board. The fourth solution is to choose another parallel parsing algorithm which will probably be more suitable for AGs evaluation.

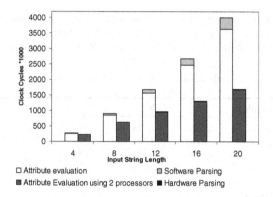

Fig. 5. Comparison of hardware against software approach

The first solution is limited due to the specific size of the FPGA, while the second one violates the requirements of small scale embedded systems which are: low cost, portability, small size, low power consumption e.t.c. The proposed architecture fulfills the above described characteristics, improving also the performance over the software solution, when we use a microprocessor of the same technology. We are currently working for implementing the third solution and we investigate the use of other parallel parsing algorithms more suitable for AGs

5   Conclusion and Future Work

In this paper we present an efficient embedded system for AI applications. The inference engine, as well as the unification mechanism is incorporated in a single FPGA. The proposed architecture is suitable for embedded system applications where low cost, portability and low power consumption is of crucial importance. Interesting enhancements have been applied to both aforementioned tasks, achieving a total speed-up that is depended on the size of the application.

This work is a part of a project[1] for developing a platform (based on AGs) in order to automatically generate special purpose embedded systems. The application area will be that Artificial Intelligence (AI) and of Syntactic Pattern Recognition for Electrocardiogram (ECG) analysis using software hardware co design techniques.

Our future research interest is to automate the whole procedure, so as to automatically map PROLOG logic programs into FPGAs. Furthermore, the speed-up would drastically increase if the attribute evaluation process was described in Hardware Description Language (HDL) and download into the FPGA.

References

1. Russel, S., Norvig P.: Artificial Intelligence, a modern approach. Prentice Hall, (1995)
2. Knuth, D.: Semantics of context free languages. Math. Syst. Theory, Vol.2, No.2, (1971) 127-145

[1] This work is co - funded by the European Social Fund (75%) and National Resources (25%) - the Program PENED 2003.

3. Deransart, P., Maluszynski J.: A grammatical view of logic programming. MIT Press, (1993)
4. Papakonstantinou, G., Kontos J.: Knowledge Representation with Attribute Grammars. The Computer Journal, Vol. 29, No. 3, (1986)
5. Papakonstantinou, G., Moraitis, C., Panayiotopoulos, T.: An attribute grammar interpreter as a knowledge engineering tool. Applied Informatics 9/86, (1986) 382-388
6. Clocksin, WF and. Mellish, C.S.: Programming in PROLOG
7. Panagopoulos, I., Pavlatos, C.and Papakonstantinou,G. :An Embedded System for Artificial Intelligence Applications, International Journal of Computational Intelligence, 2004
8. Panagopoulos, I., Pavlatos, C.and Papakonstantinou, G.: An Embedded Microprocessor for Intelligence Control, Journal of Rob. and Intel. Systems
9. Fu, K.: Syntactic Pattern recognition and Applications, Prentice-Hall 1982
10. Chen, H., Chen, X.: Shape recognition using VLSI Architecture, The International Journal of Pattern Recognition and Artificial Intelligence, 1993
11. Aho, A., Sethi, R., and. Ullman, J.: Compilers – Principles, Techniques and Tools. Reading, MA:Addison-Wesley, 1986, pp. 293-296
12. Demers, A., Reps, T., and Teitelbaum, T.: Incremental evaluation for attribute grammars with application to syntax-directed editors, in Conf. Rec. 8th Annu. ACM symp. Principles Programming Languages, Jan.1981,pp.415-418
13. Pavlatos, C. , Panagopoulos, I. , Papakonstantinou, G,: A programmable Pipelined Coprocessor for Parsing Applications, Workshop on Application Specific Processors (WASP) CODES, Stockholm, Sept. 2004
14. Chiang, Y., Fu, K.: Parallel parsing algorithms and VLSI implementation for syntactic pattern recognition". IEEE Trans. on Pattern Analysis and Machine Intelligence, PAMI-6 (1984)
15. Pavlatos C., Dimopoulos A. and Papakonstantinou G.: An Intelligent Embedded System for Control Applications, Workshop on Modeling and Control of Complex Systems, Cyprus,2005
16. www.xilinx.com/products/design_resources/proc_central/grouping/picoblaze.htm
17. Floyd, R.: The Syntax of Programming Languages-A Survey. IEEE Transactions on Electr. Comp., Vol. EC 13, No 4, (1964)
18. Earley, J.: An efficient context–free parsing algorithm. Communications of the ACM, Vol.13, (1970) 94-102
19. Graham, S.L., Harrison, M.A., Ruzzo, W.L.: An Improved context – free Recognizer. ACM Trans. On Programming Languages and System, 2(3) (1980) 415-462

Handling Knowledge-Based Decision Making Issues in Collaborative Settings: An Integrated Approach

Christina E. Evangelou and Nikos Karacapilidis

Industrial Management and Information Systems Lab, MEAD
University of Patras, 26500 Rio Patras, Greece
{chriseva, nikos}@mech.upatras.gr

Abstract. Decision making is widely considered as a fundamental organizational activity that comprises a series of knowledge representation and processing tasks. Admitting that the quality of a decision depends on the quality of the knowledge used to make it, it is argued that the enhancement of the decision making efficiency and effectiveness is strongly related to the appropriate exploitation of all possible organizational knowledge resources. Taking the above remarks into account, this paper presents a multidisciplinary approach for capturing the organizational knowledge in order to augment teamwork in terms of knowledge elicitation, sharing and construction, thus enhancing decision making quality. Based on a properly defined ontology model, our approach is supported by a web-based tool that serves as a forum of reciprocal knowledge exchange, conveyed through structured argumentative discourses, the ultimate aim being to support the related decision making process. The related knowledge is represented through a Discourse Graph, which is structured and evaluated according to the knowledge domain of the problem under consideration.

1 Introduction

Decision making is widely considered as a fundamental organizational activity that comprises a series of knowledge representation and processing tasks, the final aim being to resolve a problem, attain a goal or seize an opportunity [1, 2]. Empirical evidence shows that collaborative decision making is an interplay between social and knowledge processes [3]. Furthermore, the quality of a decision depends on the quality of the knowledge used to make it. Thus, the enhancement of the decision making efficiency and effectiveness is strongly related to the appropriate exploitation of all possible organizational knowledge resources [4]. The majority of organizational decisions require the collaboration of a group of managers, who are experts in a specific knowledge domain and often represent diverse functions or departments of an organization. Organizational forms created (or emerged) for such purposes are recently known as Communities of Practice (CoPs) [5]. Members of a CoP, especially when working in an asynchronous mode, need support to address their collaboration and communication requirements.

This paper presents an integrated, multidisciplinary approach for supporting knowledge-based collaborative decision making, aiming at "bringing together" decision makers holding complementary knowledge. According to our approach, this knowledge can be

G. Antoniou et al. (Eds.): SETN 2006, LNAI 3955, pp. 46–55, 2006.

unified, revised and improved while it is being used for decision making processes. This is achieved through structured argumentative discourses conducted among stakeholders of the issue under consideration. Our overall work is based on an ontology model that appropriately serves the capturing of the organizational knowledge and augments teamwork in terms of knowledge elicitation, representation, sharing and storage, thus enhancing decision making quality. Moreover, due to the fact that characteristics of information needs and problem solving models differ with respect to the specific decision support environment [6], our approach can easily integrate concepts and models from the particular knowledge domain considered each time.

The remainder of the paper is structured as follows: Section 2 comments on the domain-independent and domain-specific processes that shape our approach. Section 3 presents an implemented web-based tool that fully supports the proposed approach, and demonstrates its features and functionalities through an example case. Section 4 concludes our work by outlining final remarks.

2 Knowledge-Based Decision Making

2.1 Domain-Independent Processes

We view decision making as a collaborative process that comprises a series of argumentative discourses carried out among members of a CoP formed to solve a particular issue. Such discourses are based on the exchange of the involved individuals' knowledge in the form of linguistic statements. These statements express the experience, values, contextual information and experts' insights that enable stakeholders (i.e. decision makers, domain experts, knowledge workers) evaluate and incorporate new experiences and information [7]. As argumentative discourses evolve, the stakeholders' knowledge is usually clustered around specific ideas, solutions and views, while the whole collaboration process can result in knowledge exchange and reconstruction [8]. The final outcome of such discourses is usually a set of decisions, resulted out of appropriate reasoning and evaluation mechanisms, which may then constitute new knowledge. If this new knowledge is made explicit properly (e.g. in the form of a structured argument), it can be reused in a future (context-related) decision making process. What derives from the above rationale is that, in a collaborative setting, there is a clear interrelation between the processes of knowledge management, argumentation and decision making. Consequently, there is a strong interplay between the concepts of knowledge, argument, and decision. It is this very interrelation, as sketched in Figure 1, which characterizes the conceptual modelling of our overall approach and forms the domain-independent part of the ontology model used.

2.2 Domain-Specific Processes

It has been widely argued that visualization of argumentation, conducted by a group of experts working collaboratively towards solving a problem, can facilitate the overall process in many ways, such as in explicating and sharing individual representations of the problem, maintaining focus on the overall process, as well as in maintaining consistency and increasing plausibility and accuracy [9]. Moreover, it leads to the enhancement of the group's collective knowledge. For the above reasons, visualization issues received much attention while shaping the proposed approach.

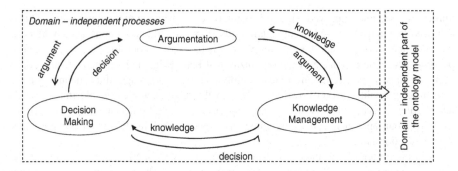

Fig. 1. Domain-independent processes

More specifically, in order to visualize knowledge-driven collaborative decision making processes, our approach takes into account how an argumentative (decision making related) discourse is *structured* and *evaluated*. Our approach comprises a set of *Decision Making Frameworks* (DMFs) in order to provide the necessary procedures for the structuring of complex organizational problems. Actually, DMFs can be considered as models that enable the formalization of the above discourses. Being employed as a "backbone" of a particular discourse, a DMF does not limit participants in the expression of their diverse views, but it provides the guidelines for the evolvement of the underlying argumentation.

At the same time, in order to evaluate the alternative courses of action, our approach employs a set of *Scoring Mechanisms* (SMs), which are actually models based on methods and techniques coming from the Multiple Criteria Decision Aid discipline [10]. These facilitate the selection of the most acceptable alternative solution by measuring the extent to which the alternative solutions meet the objectives set by the stakeholders (and accordingly sort the proposed courses of action). Furthermore, they provide the means for integrating multiple views of a problem and support both quantitative and qualitative criteria.

Both DMFs and SMs are strongly dependent on the knowledge domain of the issue under consideration and delineate the domain-specific part of the ontology model to be used in a particular collaborative decision making setting (see Figure 2).

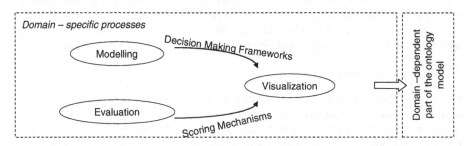

Fig. 2. Domain-specific processes

To give an example, let the knowledge domain of a decision making process being that of strategy development. In such a context, the overall process is carried out by a group of managers (strategists) aiming at matching the organization's resources to the opportunities arising from the competitive environment [11]. This involves the identification of the basic goals of an enterprise, the consideration of alternative courses of action and the allocation of resources necessary for carrying out these goals [12]. The modelling of the underlying argumentative discourses in this context will be performed according to widely used theories stemming from the Strategic Management research field. These theories provide CoPs developed in a business context with the means to develop strategic plans. For strategy development issues, we have adopted the SWOT (Strengths, Weaknesses, Opportunities, and Threats) framework [13], the Resource Based View (RBV) of the firm [14], and the Porter's Five Forces analysis [15]. Each of these three approaches actually shapes a domain-specific DMF to be used for the modelling of the problem under consideration. On the other hand, for the calculation of a discourse's outcome, we have employed a set of alternative SMs, which are based on the Analytic Hierarchy Process [16], the Multi-Attribute Utility Theory [17] and the Outranking Relations Techniques [18].

3   The Supporting Tool

Exploiting features and functionalities from diverse Artificial Intelligence and Operational Research fields (i.e. Decision Support Systems, Knowledge Management Systems, Multicriteria Decision Aid, Argumentation, Semantic Web), we have developed a web-based tool that can be employed as a forum of reciprocal knowledge exchange, conveyed through structured argumentative discourses, the ultimate aim being to support the related decision making process.

3.1   Features and Functionalities

According to our approach, a discourse can be initiated after a registered user's request. The mandatory registration of the users' personal and professional information serves their assignment to certain roles (i.e. discourse moderator, decision maker, domain expert, knowledge manager, external participant). With respect to the role assigned, each user has a specific access level; accordingly, each of them is associated to a specific set of permitted actions (for a particular discourse).

After the definition of the issue under consideration (and the identification of the related knowledge domain), a set of rules is triggered in order to define the structuring of the *Discourse Graph,* which serves the visualization of a discourse. Actually, these rules associate the knowledge domain with the available DMFs and SMs. Although our tool is able to propose the appropriate structure of the Discourse Graph (by exploiting meta-data), the final selection of the DMF and SM to be adopted is up to the discourse moderator. Discourse participants may then contribute their positions through the above graph. In order to assure a high level of expressiveness, the proposed tool enables stakeholders to contribute their individual positions in the form of linguistic statements. The creation of a statement comprises an insertion request and the definition of its *type, content, related criterion* (if applicable), and *placement* on the Discourse Graph. Individual positions inserted in the graph, called hereafter *discourse items*, are considered and treated as knowledge items, and are associated with a specific semantic value according to their placement (in the graph) and their creator.

The supported types of discourse items (i.e. *goal, alternative, argument in favour* or *against, criterion* and *supporting evidence*) comply with semantics explicitly defined in our approach's ontology model, while they are also associated with the set of parameters used in DMFs and SMs. More specifically, a goal corresponds to the discourse item that briefly describes the overall aim of a conducted discourse. This is always defined by the discourse moderator. Alternatives are the items representing the proposed courses of action. In order to state their personal beliefs about the proposed alternatives, discourse participants may attach arguments to them (speaking in favour or against them). Furthermore, discourse participants may relate their arguments to one or more criteria. A list of criteria is always provided to the users whenever a new argument is inserted in the Discourse Graph. In order not to limit participants in expressing their views, new criteria may be also asserted. In this case, such criteria are registered in the tool's Knowledge Base (KB) and added to the above list. Finally, users can upload supporting evidence items (e.g. multimedia documents, URLs), thus providing additional information for their statements. Discourse items of past discourses, containing related bodies of knowledge, can also be retrieved and reused in an ongoing discourse as supporting evidence.

A key functionality of the proposed tool concerns the exploration of the decision makers' statements, as these are expressed during argumentative discourses, in order to elicit knowledge related to the decision making process, the decision makers and the decision *per se*. In order to efficiently and effectively exploit the decision makers' knowledge, the proposed approach maintains a set of user profiles. These provide information about the decision makers' expertise, as well as their behaviour during their participation in the argumentative discourses and knowledge sharing activities. Besides the recording of the users' personal and professional information (discussed above), this is accomplished by extracting a behaviour pattern (mental model), which is built by taking into account the users' involvement in the overall process (e.g. number and type of discourse items inserted, frequency of their appearance, intervention on items inserted by others, etc.). Towards this aim, our approach exploits the decision makers' actions to maintain a set of metadata reflecting their attitude in the specific knowledge domain [19]. Speaking about metadata, we refer to the structured information that describes, explains, locates, or makes it easier to retrieve, use or manage an information resource (e.g., information about how often the "cost" criterion becomes the decisive factor for the resolution of a discourse, and which decision makers are always contributing to this issue).

Another functionality enhancing knowledge elicitation builds around the construction of a *chronicle* that provides a summary of the decision makers' actions during the evolution of a discourse. Pieces of these chronicles can be easily retrieved from the KB through a search engine (in order, for instance, to be reused in future discourses). The information acquired through chronicles can be further analysed through cluster analysis or causal maps in order to enrich the users' profiles and amend their mental models. Furthermore, it can be used for the analysis and validation of the related decision making process.

3.2   An Example Case

In this section, we demonstrate the features and functionalities of the proposed tool through a strategy development case concerning the choice of the location where a new plant should be placed. For this particular case, the RBV Decision Making Framework was employed for the structuring (modelling) of the discourse. This particular DMF involves two basic criteria, i.e. supporting activities and supporting resources, which actually consist the core concepts of the RBV approach. Each of these criteria is associated with a list of sub-criteria (activities with the set {history, cost, dependability, flexibility, speed, quality} and resources with the set {level, cost, dependability, flexibility, speed, quality}). As far as the SM is concerned, a generic algorithm, based on the principles of the Analytic Hierarchy Process, was employed for the evaluation of the overall discourse.

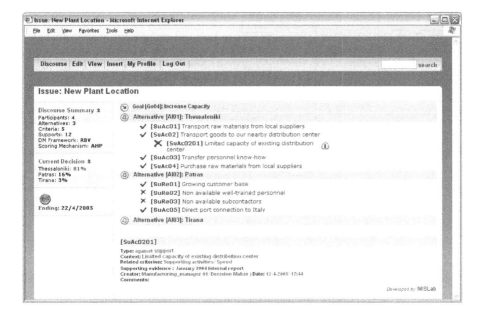

Fig. 3. An instance of the Discourse Graph

Figure 3 illustrates an instance of the Discourse Graph structured for this case. As shown, the overall issue was "New plant location" (appearing on the top of the window), while the goal to be met was "Increase capacity" (top of the Discourse Graph). Discourse participants have proposed (so far) three alternative solutions, namely Thessaloniki, Patras and Tirana. These solutions are supported by in favour and challenged by against arguments. For instance, a decision maker placed the in favour argument "Transport goods to our nearby distribution center" for the alternative "Thessaloniki". This argument was associated to the "supporting activities" criterion and the "speed" sub-criterion, in particular. Discourse items are preceded by an identification label which is associated to their type (e.g. [SuAc02] refers to a supporting activity). Different colours and images are used in order for the users to better visualize the different types of discourse items. Furthermore, by right clicking on them, users may see the list of permitted actions and act accordingly.

Argumentation in our approach can be performed in multiple levels. As shown in Figure 3, another user has attached the item "Limited capacity of existing distribution center", which is an argument against the above in favour argument. In the instance shown, this particular item has been selected (by clicking on it). Details concerning a selected item appear at the bottom right part of the window. This comprises information about the item's type, content, related criteria, supporting evidence, creator, date-time of insertion, as well as related comments.

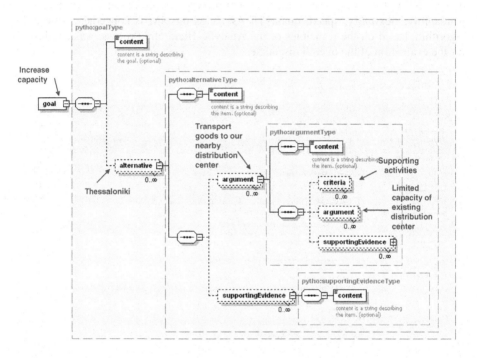

Fig. 4. The XML Schema for the structure of the Discourse Graph

In general, whenever a new discourse item is inserted in the graph, a set of procedures is executed by the tool to update the discourse status and evaluate the alternative solutions. At the same time, the chronicle functionality records the corresponding user's action. These procedures are automatically triggered and are hidden from the discourse participants. The Discourse Graph gets automatically refreshed in order to graphically display the new entry and update the Discourse Summary and Current Decision results (appearing at the left part of the window). The Discourse Summary provides information about the number of participants that have contributed to the overall discourse, the number of alternative solutions that have been proposed, the number of in favour and against arguments inserted in the graph, as well as the number of criteria considered (i.e. the number of criteria associated with the discourse items). Furthermore, users can see the DMF and SM employed for the structure and evaluation, respectively, of the discourse. The Current Decision part of the window provides a sorting of the proposed alternatives, according to the score they get each time (this score is calculated by the SM). At the instance shown in Figure 3, the alternative "Thessaloniki" appears to be winning (its priority is 81%). The date set for the closure of the discourse can be also indicated.

After the closure of a discourse, all statements expressed are stored in the tool's KB, classified according to their type and placement on the Discourse Graph. In general, the storage of the overall discourse to the KB conforms to the XML Schema employed for the structuring of the discourse. For the strategy development issue under consideration, the discourse's structure was delineated by the XML Schema appearing in Figure 4 (the figure also illustrates some instantiations of the Schema's elements according to the discourse instance considered above). This particular Schema has derived after the joint consideration of the RBV DMF and the SM that is based on the principles of the Analytic Hierarchy Process. The overall discourse was stored as an XML document that complies with this Schema.

3.3 Technological Issues

In order to provide users with the necessary means to communicate in a distant and asynchronous mode, the proposed tool is a web-based application. The three-tier architecture of the proposed tool first of all comprises a *Graphical User Interface* (GUI), which is an ASP.NET application (it can be accessed via any common web browser). This is actually the core component of our approach, since it reflects the tool's decision support and knowledge management features and provides users with integrated services.

A *Knowledge Management module* is responsible for the gathering and sharing of knowledge. More specifically, this module handles the extraction and collection of the pieces of knowledge that are embedded in the discourse participants' statements (these are submitted to the tool via the GUI), as well as the uploading of them to the tool's KB. Moreover, it provides users with the necessary functionalities for knowledge extraction and sharing, thus aiding decision making activities. It also facilitates the generation and maintenance of the users' profiles. The conceptual modelling of the KB complies with the KAD ontology model [20]. This ontology model has derived after the thorough consideration of the domain-independent and the domain-specific processes described in Sections 2.1 and 2.2, respectively.

A *Decision Support module* is responsible for the appropriate handling of the argumentative discourses conducted by users, the ultimate aim being to support them in the underlying decision making processes. This module closely collaborates with the tool's *Model Base*, where the DMFs and SMs models are maintained. A set of XML Schemata that comply with the abovementioned ontology's semantics has been used for the representation of the DMFs. The mathematical models of the SMs have been implemented in C#.

Finally, much attention was paid to openness and extensibility issues; we have thoroughly exploited the .NET and XML technologies in order to establish a high level of interoperability, as well as to assure generic, neutral and extensible information modelling.

4 Conclusions

We have argued that a proper integration of Knowledge Management functionalities appears as a very promising solution for contemporary organizations to resolve decision making issues. Towards this aim, we presented a multidisciplinary approach that provides the means for capturing the organizational knowledge in order to augment teamwork in terms of knowledge elicitation, sharing and construction, thus enhancing decision making quality. The proposed web-based tool can serve as a forum of knowledge exchange in natural language. This is through a Discourse Graph, which is structured according to the knowledge domain of the problem under consideration and is based on a properly defined ontology model for providing and accessing knowledge sources. The proposed approach elaborates a set of metadata to make explicit the relations occurring between the decision makers and their statements. In such a way, argumentative discourses carried out in collaborative decision making settings can be exploited for the elicitation of the decision makers' knowledge. At the same time, our approach exploits well-established decision making models and techniques, with respect to the problem domain, in order to evaluate the proposed alternatives and establish an acceptable solution. We envisage it not just as another groupware solution, but as a highly active tool that provides a structured way for modelling and solving complex organizational problems.

References

1. Harrison, E.F., Pelletier, M.A.: The Essence of Management Decision. Management Decision 38 (2000) 462-469.
2. Karacapilidis, N., Adamides, E., Evangelou, C.E.: Leveraging Organizational Knowledge to Formulate Manufacturing Strategy. In Proceedings of the 11th European Conference on Information Systems (ECIS'03), Naples, Italy (2003)16-21.
3. Schwarz, M.: A Multilevel Analysis of the Strategic Decision Process and the Evolution of Shared Beliefs. In Chakravarthy, B., Mueller-Stewens, G., Lorange P., Lechner, C. (Eds.), Strategy Process: Shaping the Contours of the Field, Blackwell Publishing, Oxford (2003) 110-136.
4. Li, E.Y., Lai, H.: Collaborative work and knowledge management in electronic business. Decision Support Systems 39 (2005) 545-547.
5. Wenger, E., McDermott, R., Snyder, W.M.: Cultivating Communities of Practice. Harvard Business School Press, Boston, MA (2002).
6. Gorry, G.A., Scott Morton, M.S.: A Framework for Management Information Systems. Sloan Management Review 13 (1971) 55-70.
7. Davenport, T., Prusak, L.: Working Knowledge: Managing what your Organization Knows. Harvard Business School Press, Boston, MA (1998).
8. Evangelou, C.E., Karacapilidis, N.: Knowledge-Based Strategy Development: An Integrated Approach. In Proceedings of the I-KNOW'05 Conference, Graz, Austria (2005) 4-11.
9. Kirschner, P., Buckingham Shum, S., Carr, C.: Visualizing Argumentation: Software Tools for Collaborative and Educational Sense-Making. Springer-Verlag, London, UK (2003).

10. Zopounidis, C., Doumpos, M.: Multicriteria classification and sorting methods: A literature review. European Journal of Operational Research 138 (2002) 229-246.
11. Andrews, K.R.: The Concept of Corporate Strategy. Richard D. Irwin, Homewood, IL (1971).
12. Chandler, A.D. Jr.: Strategy and structure: Concepts in the History of the Industrial Enterprise. MIT Press, Casender, MA (1962).
13. Porter, M.E.: Competitive Strategy. The Free Press, New York (1980).
14. Wernerfelt, B.: A Resource-Based View of the Firm. Strategic Management Journal 5 (1984) 171-180.
15. Porter, M.E.: How competitive forces shape strategy. Harvard Business Review 57 (1979) 86-93.
16. Saaty, T.L.: The Analytic Hierarchy Process. McGraw-Hill, New York (1980).
17. Edwards, W.: SMARTS and SMARTER: Improved Simple Methods for Multi-attribute Utility Measurement. Organizational Behaviour and Human Decision Processes 60 (1994) 306-325.
18. Roy, B.: The Outranking Approach and the Foundations of ELECTRE Methods. Theory and Decision 31 (1991) 49-73.
19. Widener, P., Eisenhauer, G., Schwan, K.: Open Metadata Formats: Efficient XML-based Communication for High Performance Computing. In Proceedings of the 10th IEEE International Symposium on High Performance Distributed Computing (2001) 371–380.
20. Evangelou, C.E., Karacapilidis, N., Abou Khaled, O.: Interweaving Knowledge Management, Argumentation and Decision Making in a Collaborative Setting: The KAD Ontology Model. International Journal of Knowledge and Learning 1 (2005) 130-145.

Market Clearing Price Forecasting in Deregulated Electricity Markets Using Adaptively Trained Neural Networks

Pavlos S. Georgilakis

Technical University of Crete, University Campus, Kounoupidiana, Chania, Greece
pgeorg@dpem.tuc.gr

Abstract. The market clearing prices in deregulated electricity markets are volatile. Good market clearing price forecasting will help producers and consumers to prepare their corresponding bidding strategies so as to maximize their profits. Market clearing price prediction is a difficult task since bidding strategies used by market participants are complicated and various uncertainties interact in an intricate way. This paper proposes an adaptively trained neural network to forecast the 24 day-ahead market-clearing prices. The adaptive training mechanism includes a feedback process that allows the artificial neural network to learn from its mistakes and correct its output by adjusting its architecture as new data becomes available. The methodology is applied to the California power market and the results prove the efficiency and practicality of the proposed method.

1 Introduction

Deregulation has a great impact on the electric power industry nowadays. In a deregulated environment, electricity is supplied in a competitive market, and the pricing system plays an important role. In a pool-based electric energy market, producers submit to the market operator selling bids consisting of energy blocks and their corresponding minimum selling prices, and consumers submit to the market operator buying bids consisting of energy blocks and their corresponding maximum buying prices. In turn, the market operator runs an unconstrained dispatch algorithm without transmission and other security constraints, assuming the system as a single node interconnected to neighboring systems through single transmission lines. This dispatch defines the market-clearing price (MCP) as the cost of supplying one more megawatt beyond the point where supply and demand matches for each market period, typically one hour.

Producers and consumers rely on price forecast information to prepare their corresponding bidding strategies. A producer with low capability of altering MCPs (price-taker producer) needs day-ahead price forecasts to optimally self-schedule and to derive his bidding strategy in the pool. Retailers and large consumers need day-ahead MCPs for the same reasons as producers. However, MCPs in deregulated power markets are volatile. MCP prediction is a difficult task [1] since bidding strategies used by market participants are complicated and various uncertainties interact in an intricate way.

G. Antoniou et al. (Eds.): SETN 2006, LNAI 3955, pp. 56 – 66, 2006.

Many attempts have been made to forecast day-ahead electricity prices. Reported techniques include ARIMA models [2], dynamic regression models [3], other time series techniques [4,5], wavelet transform models [6,7], heuristics [8], Bayesian techniques [9], and simulations and others [10-12].

Artificial neural network (ANN) method, because of its effectiveness and easy-to-implement, is very promising in fulfilling MCP forecasting task. ANNs have been applied to forecasting prices in the England-Wales pool [13], the Australian market [14], the PJM Interconnection [15] and the New England ISO [16].

This paper proposes an adaptively trained neural network to forecast the 24 day-ahead market-clearing prices. The adaptive training mechanism includes a feedback process that allows the ANN to learn from its mistakes and correct its output by adjusting its architecture as new data becomes available. The methodology is applied to the California power market.

The paper is organized as follows: Section 2 formulates the forecasting problem. Section 3 describes the proposed methodology for MCP forecasting and presents the persistence method with which the proposed method is compared based on the mean average percentage error on the test set. The application of the proposed methodology to the California power market and the obtained results are described in Section 4. Section 5 concludes the paper.

2 Problem Formulation

In a deregulated market environment, the unconstrained market-clearing price of an electricity pool is essentially calculated as follows:

- Generating companies submit bids to the electricity pool to supply a certain amount of electrical energy at a certain price for the period under consideration. These bids are ranked in order of increasing price. From this ranking, a curve showing the bid price as a function of the cumulative bid quantity is built. This curve is the supply curve of the market.
- The demand curve of the market is established based on the consumer offers that consist of quantity and price and ranking these offers in decreasing order of price. Since the demand for electricity is highly inelastic, this step is sometimes omitted and the demand is set at a value determined using a forecast of the load, i.e. in this case the demand curve is assumed to be a vertical line at the value of the load forecast.
- The intersection of the supply and demand curves represents the market-clearing price, i.e. the market equilibrium.

All the bids submitted at a price lower than or equal to the market-clearing price are accepted and generators are instructed to produce the amount of energy corresponding to their accepted bids. Similarly, all the offers submitted at a price greater than or equal to the market-clearing price are accepted and the consumers are informed of the amount of energy that they are allowed to draw from the system.

The market-clearing price represents the price of one additional megawatt-hour of energy. Generators are paid this MCP for every megawatt-hour that they produce, whereas consumers pay the MCP for every megawatt-hour that they consume, irrespective of the bids and offers that they submitted.

Producers and consumers rely on price forecast information to prepare their corresponding bidding strategies. A producer with low capability of altering MCPs (price-taker producer) needs day-ahead price forecasts to optimally self-schedule and to derive his bidding strategy in the pool [17,18].

Retailers and large consumers need day-ahead MCPs for the same reasons as producers. If a consumer is to buy on the spot market, it is essential that he predicts as accurately as possible the evolution of MCPs over the time horizon used to self-schedule [19].

Forecasting MCPs accurately is extremely complex because of the number of influential factors and the lack of information on some of these factors. Since the MCP derives from the market equilibrium, it is influenced by both load and generation factors [10,12]. On the load side, all the temporal, meteorological, economic and special factors that are used in load forecasting should also be taken into account when forecasting prices. The generation side is considerably more troublesome because some events occur at random (e.g., failures leading to withdrawal of capacity and price spikes) and others are not always publicly announced in advance (e.g., planned outages for maintenance). In addition, when the locational marginal price is needed, transmission congestion can have a sudden and hard to predict effect. Finally, when competition is less perfect, some generators have the ability to influence prices to suit their own objectives. From the above, it is concluded that MCPs are volatile and MCP prediction is a difficult task since bidding strategies used by market participants are complicated and various uncertainties interact in an intricate way.

The time framework to forecast the day-ahead MCPs in most markets is as follows. The 24 hourly MCPs for day d are required on day d-1, typically at hour h_b (around 10 am). On the other hand, data concerning results for day d-1 are available on day d-2 at hour h_c (around noon). Therefore, the actual forecasting of market prices for day d can take place between hour h_c of day d-2 and hour h_b of day d-1. Therefore, to forecast the 24 hourly prices for day d, price data up to hour 24 of day d-1 are considered known.

3   Forecasting Methodology

3.1   ANN Method

ANN is a computer information processing system that is capable of sufficiently representing any non-linear functions [20]. The techniques based on ANN are especially effective in the solution of high complexity problems for which a traditional mathematical model is difficult to build, where the nature of the input-output relationship is neither well defined nor easily computable.

The most popular ANN architecture is the three-layer feed-forward system trained with a back-propagation algorithm. The success of this approach dwells in the fact that it can learn the relationship between input and output, by training the network off-line using historical data derived from the system, with a supervised learning technique.

In case of MCP forecasting, there is no simple relationship among the parameters involved in the determination of the MCP. ANNs, due to their highly non-linear capabilities and universal approximation properties, are proposed in this paper for MCP forecasting. At the training stage, the proper ANN architecture (e.g., number and type of neurons and layers) is selected. An adaptive training mechanism allows the ANN to learn from its mistakes and correct its output by adjusting the parameters (weights) of its neurons. The adaptive training process enhances the performance of the proposed method as additional training data get to be available.

As input parameters to the ANN, three factors are considered: 1) historical MCP, 2) historical load and 3) forecasted load. Historical information refers to the previous day information, e.g. historical load information includes the 24 hourly actual (known) loads of the previous day. Similarly, forecasted load information includes the 24 hourly forecasted loads of the day-ahead, i.e., the day for which the MCP is to be forecasted. If all the above three factors are considered as inputs to the ANN, then the input layer has 72 neurons. The proposed training mechanism ensures that the optimum number of hidden neurons is selected. The output layer of the ANN has 24 neurons, each one corresponding to the MCP of one of the 24 hours of the day-ahead.

3.2 Persistence Method

In order to evaluate the performance of the ANN, its forecasts are compared with those of the persistence method. According to the persistence method, the forecasted price, Price(d,h), for the hour h of the day-ahead d is calculated as follows:

$$\text{Price}(d, h) = \frac{\text{Load}(d, h)}{\text{Load}(d-1, h)} \cdot \text{Price}(d-1, h) \tag{1}$$

where Load(d,h) is the forecasted load for the hour h of the day-ahead d, Load(d-1,h) is the actual load for the hour h of the previous day d-1 and Price(d-1,h) is the actual price for the hour h of the previous day d-1.

3.3 Performance Evaluation

To assess the prediction capacity of the ANN model and the persistence model, the mean average percentage error, MAPE, can be used:

$$\text{MAPE} = \frac{1}{N} \cdot \sum_{i=1}^{N} \frac{\left| \text{Actual\_Price}(i) - \text{Forecast\_Price}(i) \right|}{\text{Actual\_Price}(i)} \cdot 100\% \tag{2}$$

where N is the number of hours, Actual_Price(i) is the actual MCP for the hour i and Forecast_Price(i) is the forecasted MCP for the hour i calculated by the model under consideration (persistence or ANN).

However, the MAPE, as defined in (2), is not suitable for price forecasting, since it causes problems for zero MCPs. To overcome this problem, the following calculation for the MAPE is proposed and used throughout this paper:

$$\text{MAPE} = \frac{1}{N} \cdot \sum_{i=1}^{N} \frac{\left| \text{Actual\_Price(i)} - \text{Forecast\_Price(i)} \right|}{\text{Average\_Price}} \cdot 100\% \qquad (3)$$

where Average_Price is calculated as follows:

$$\text{Average\_Price} = \frac{1}{N} \cdot \sum_{i=1}^{N} \text{Actual\_Price(i)} \qquad (4)$$

To assess the prediction capacity of the ANN model and the persistence model, the MAPE is used, as defined in (3). The model with the lower MAPE on the test set is the most suitable for MCP forecasting.

3.4 Overview of the Proposed Methodology

The proposed methodology for MCP forecasting has three steps:

1. In the first step, the day-ahead load is predicted with the ANN method;
2. In the second step, the MCPs are forecasted with the persistence method;
3. In the third step, the MCPs are forecasted with the ANN method.

The first step is to predict the day-ahead load, since this information is needed by the persistence method and also it is expected to be an important input parameter for the ANN model to predict the day-ahead MCPs. This load forecasting is implemented with a multilayer feedforward neural network, which has 48 input neurons and 24 output neurons. The first 24 input neurons correspond to the 24 loads of the previous day (relatively to the day-ahead) and the rest 24 neurons correspond to the 24 loads of the same day (with the day-ahead) of the previous week.

The second step is to forecast MCPs with the persistence method by using (1) and to evaluate the performance of the persistence method by using the MAPE definition of (3).

The third step is to obtain the MCP forecast by using the ANN model. After many experiments, it was found that for the considered case study of Section 4, the best MCP forecasts are obtained by using 72 input neurons, out of which the 24 are for the 24 MCPs of the previous day, the next 24 neurons are for the previous day hourly loads and the rest 24 neurons correspond to the day-ahead hourly loads. The ANN has 24 output neurons, corresponding to day-ahead MCPs.

MATLAB Neural Network Toolbox [21] is used for implementing the above steps 1 and 3 (load and MCP forecasting with ANN).

Since the weights of the ANN are initialized randomly in MATLAB neural network toolbox, different executions of the ANN training and testing algorithm lead to different MAPE results. However, the objective is to train the ANN so as to provide the minimum MAPE for the test set. The proposed training mechanism automatically selects the neural network architecture with the minimum mean absolute percentage error on the test set for both the day-ahead load and MCP forecasting and this is achieved through the following steps:

1. Various ANN architectures are considered;
2. For each ANN architecture, the training and testing algorithm is executed 10 times and the trained ANN with the minimum MAPE on the test set is stored;

3. Among all the ANN architectures, the optimum architecture is the one with the minimum MAPE on the test set.

The structure of the ANN adapts itself as new data becomes available. This adaptation mechanism improves the ANN performance.

Fig. 1 presents the MCP forecasting methodology.

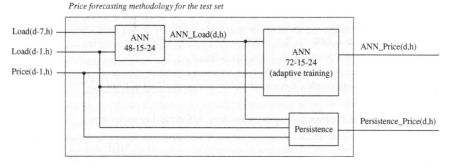

d: forecast day, d-1: previous day, h: hour (h=1,2,...,24)

Fig. 1. MCP forecasting methodology

4   Case Studies

In this Section, the effectiveness of the proposed methodology is checked for the data of the California power market [22] for the year 1999. In the sequel, two case studies are analyzed in detail: in the first case study, the MCP data series are without price spikes, while in the second case study, the MCP data series include price spikes and as a consequence the MCP forecasting problem is more challenging.

4.1   Case 1: Without Price Spikes

In this section, the performance of the ANN model is compared with the performance of the persistence model for a time period without price spikes. The training period is from 1/3/1999 to 28/3/1999 and the testing period is from 29/3/1999 to 4/4/1999. As it can be seen from Fig. 2, the whole training and testing period has no price spikes. More specifically, the maximum MCP during that period is 35 \$/MWh. On the other hand, the minimum MCP is 0 and this value justifies the necessity to define the MAPE from (3) instead of (2).

Table 1 presents the impact of input parameters on the forecasting performance for the test set. It is concluded from Table 1 that the minimum MAPE (optimum performance) for MCP forecasting is obtained when using historical MCP, historical load and forecasted load as inputs to the ANN, in line with the proposed forecasting framework of Fig. 1.

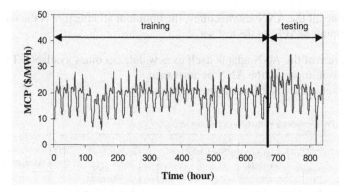

Fig. 2. Actual unconstrained MCP curve of California power market from 1/3/1999 to 4/4/1999

Table 1. Impact of input parameters on forecasting performance

		MCP MAPE (%)	
Case	Inputs	ANN	Persistence
1	Historical MCP	9.78	
2	Historical MCP, historical load	9.09	
3	Historical MCP, historical load, forecasted load	8.44	10.19

Table 2. Impact of quantity of training vectors on forecasting performance

	Training vectors		MCP MAPE (%)	
Case	Period	Quantity	ANN	Persistence
1	15/3-28/3	14	9.20	11.05
2	1/3-28/3	28	8.44	10.19
3	1/2-28/3	56	8.81	10.72
4	4/1-28/3	84	9.13	10.99

Table 2 presents the impact of the quantity of input vectors on the forecasting per-formance. It is concluded from Table 2 that the optimum performance for MCP fore-casting is obtained when using 28 vectors that correspond to the 28 days before the week of the test set. That is why the training period has been selected to be from 1/3/1999 to 28/3/1999 (i.e. 28 days).

Having defined the appropriate input parameters (historical MCP, historical load, forecasted load) and the proper quantity of training vectors (28), in the sequel it is presented the way that the proposed methodology of Section 3.4 is applied in this particular case study.

According to the proposed methodology in Section 3.4, the first step is to predict the day-ahead load. After trial and error, it was found that the optimum forecasting results are obtained with an ANN having the architecture 48-15-24, i.e., 48 input neurons, 15 neurons in the hidden layer and 24 output neurons. For this ANN, the MAPE on the training set and the test set is 1.31% and 1.77%, respectively.

The second step is to forecast MCPs with the persistence method. The results show that the training MAPE is 6.92% and the testing MAPE is 10.19%.

The third step is to forecast MCPs with the ANN method. Table 3 shows the minimum testing MAPE for ANN architectures with different number of neurons in the hidden layer. Following the training mechanism of Section 3.4 and using the results of Table 3, it is concluded that the optimum ANN architecture is 72-15-24, since it provides a minimum testing MAPE of 8.44%, which is 17.17% better than the testing MAPE of the persistence method (10.19%). In Fig. 3, the MCP forecast of the optimum ANN versus the actual MCP is shown for the test set.

Table 3. Evaluation of alternative ANN architectures for MCP forecasting

Hidden neurons	Minimum MAPE (%)	Improvement versus persistence (%)
10	8.93	12.37
15	8.44	17.17
20	9.19	9.81
30	8.92	12.46
40	9.44	7.36

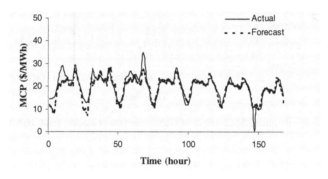

Fig. 3. MCP forecast versus actual MCP for the test set (from 29/3/1999 to 4/4/1999)

4.2 Case 2: With Price Spikes

In this section, the performance of the ANN model is compared with the performance of the persistence model for a time period with price spikes. The training period is from 16/6/1999 to 13/7/1999 and the testing period is from 14/7/1999 to 20/7/1999.

As it can be seen from Fig. 4, there are price spikes (e.g. prices over 80 $/MWh) in the period under consideration. More specifically, price spikes exist in 29/6, 30/6, 1/7, 12/7, 13/7, 14/7 and 15/7/1999. The appearance of price spikes makes the forecasting problem more difficult.

Table 4 presents the impact of the ANN adaptive training on the MCP forecasting performance for the test set using the MCP forecasting framework proposed in Fig. 1. It is concluded from Table 4 that the MCP MAPE obtained with the ANN is improved (reduced) as new data becomes available that is used for retraining the ANN. Moreover, the superiority of the proposed ANN method versus the persistence method is obvious.

Table 4. Impact of ANN adaptive training on ANN forecasting performance

	Training vectors		Testing vectors		MCP MAPE (%)	
Case	Period	Quantity	Period	Quantity	ANN	Persistence
1	14/6-11/7	28	14/7-20/7	7	22.63	35.28
2	15/6-12/7	28	14/7-20/7	7	18.45	30.12
3	16/6-13/7	28	14/7-20/7	7	15.87	27.33

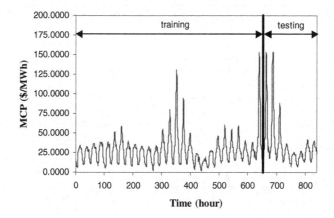

Fig. 4. Actual unconstrained MCP curve of California power market from 16/6 to 20/7/1999

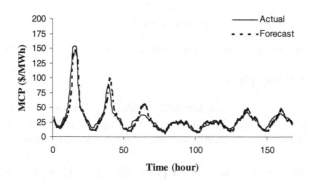

Fig. 5. MCP forecast versus actual MCP for the test set (from 14/7/1999 to 20/7/1999)

In Fig. 5, the MCP forecast of the optimum ANN (case 3 of Table 4) versus the actual MCP is shown for the test set.

5 Conclusions

The objective of this paper is to develop a simple and easy-to-use technique for the prediction of the hourly market clearing price in a deregulated electricity market environment using only the publicly available information. The proposed method uses two ANNs: the first ANN predicts the hourly load and the second ANN estimates the hourly market clearing price. The output of the first ANN together with the previous day load and the previous day market-clearing price are used as input to the second ANN.

An adaptive training mechanism is proposed, which includes a feedback process that allows the artificial neural network to learn from its mistakes and correct its output by adjusting its architecture as new data becomes available. The adaptively trained ANN provides the minimum MAPE for the test set, i.e. the optimum performance. The testing MAPE of the ANN is compared with the testing MAPE of a persistence method.

The methodology is applied to the California power market. Two case studies are analyzed: the first is without price spikes, while in the second case study there are price spikes in the MCP data series. In the first case study, the ANN testing MAPE is 8.44%, which is 17.17% better than the testing MAPE of the persistence method. In the second case study, the ANN testing MAPE is 15.87%, which is 41.93% better than the testing MAPE of the persistence method. These results prove the efficiency and practicality of the proposed method for forecasting the market-clearing price in deregulated electricity markets.

References

1. Schweppe, F., Caramanis, M., Tabors, R., Bohn, R.: Spot pricing of electricity. Kluwer, Norwell, MA (1988)
2. Contreras, J., Espínola, R., Nogales, F.G., Conejo, A.J.: ARIMA models to predict next-day electricity prices. IEEE Trans. Power Systems **18** (2003) 1014-1020
3. Nogales, F.G., Contreras, J., Conejo, A.J., Espínola, R.: Forecasting next-day electricity prices by time series models. IEEE Trans. Power Systems **17** (2002) 342-348
4. Obradovic, Z., Tomsovic, K.: Time series methods for forecasting electricity market pricing. IEEE Power Eng. Soc. Summer Meeting, 1999
5. Crespo, J., Hlouskova J., Kossmeier, S., Obersteiner, M.: Forecasting electricity spot prices using linear univariate time series models. App. Energy **77** (2002) 87-106
6. Yao, S.J., Song, Y.H.: Prediction of system marginal prices by wavelet transform and neural network. Elect. Mach. Power Syst. **28** (2000) 983-993
7. Kim, C.-I., Yu, I.-K., Song, Y.H.: Prediction of system marginal price of electricity using wavelet transform analysis. Energy Convers. Manag. **43** (2002) 1839-1851
8. Jau-Jia, G., Luh, P.B.: Market clearing price prediction using a committee machine with adaptive weighting coefficients. IEEE Power Eng. Soc. Winter Meeting, 2002
9. Ni, E., Luh, P.B.: Forecasting power market clearing price and its discrete PDF using a Bayesian-based classification method. IEEE Power Eng. Soc. Winter Meeting, 2001
10. Bunn, D.W.: Forecasting loads and prices in competitive power markets. Proc. IEEE **88** (2000) 163-169
11. Angelus, A.: Electricity price forecasting in deregulated markets. Elect. J. **14** (2001) 32-41

12. Breipohl, A.M.: Electricity price forecasting models. IEEE Power Eng. Soc. Winter Meeting, 2002
13. Ramsay, B., Wang, A.J.: A neural network based estimator for electricity spot-pricing with particular reference to weekend and public holidays. Neurocomputing **23** (1998) 47-57
14. Szkuta, B.R., Sanabria, L.A., Dillon, T.S.: Electricity price short-term forecasting using artificial neural networks. IEEE Trans. Power Systems **14** (1999) 851-857
15. Hong, Y.-Y., Hsiao, C.-Y.: Locational marginal price forecasting in deregulated electricity markets using artificial intelligence. IEE Proc. Gen. Transm. Distr. **149** (2002) 621-626
16. Zhang, L., Luh, P.B., Kasiviswanathan, K.: Energy clearing price prediction and confidence interval estimation with cascaded neural networks. IEEE Trans. Power Systems **18** (2003) 99-105
17. Arroyo, J.M., Conejo, A.J.: Optimal response of a thermal unit to an electricity spot market. IEEE Trans. Power Systems **15** (2000) 1098-1104
18. Chan, C.J.S.: Development of a profit maximization unit commitment program. MSc Dissertation, UMIST, UK (2000)
19. Kirschen, D.S.: A demand-side view of electricity markets. IEEE Trans. Power Systems **18** (2003) 520-527
20. Haykin, S.: Neural networks: a comprehensive foundation. Prentice-Hall, New Jersey (1999)
21. Demuth, H., Beale, M.: Neural network toobox for use with MATLAB, User's guide, Version 4. MathWorks, MA (2001)
22. http://www.ucei.berkeley.edu/ucei/datamine/datamine.htm, accessed on 18/10/2005. Sponsored by University of California Energy Institute (UCEI)

Adaptive-Partitioning-Based Stochastic Optimization Algorithm and Its Application to Fuzzy Control Design

Chang-Wook Han and Jung-Il Park

School of Electrical Engineering and Computer Science, Yeungnam University,
214-1 Dae-dong, Gyongsan, Gyongbuk, 712-749 South Korea
{cwhan, jipark}@yumail.ac.kr

Abstract. A random signal-based learning merged with simulated annealing (SARSL), which is serial algorithm, has been considered by the authors. But the serial nature of SARSL degrades its performance as the complexity of the search space is increasing. To solve this problem, this paper proposes a population structure of SARSL (PSARSL) which enables multi-point search. Moreover, adaptive partitioning method (APM) is used to reduce the optimization time. The validity of the proposed algorithm is conformed by applying it to a simple test function example and a general version of fuzzy controller design.

1 Introduction

During the past decades, the role of optimization has steadily increased in such diverse areas, such as, electrical engineering, computer science, and communication. In practice, optimization problems become more and more complex. Many large-scale combinatorial optimization problems can only be solved approximately, which is closely related to the fact that many of these problems have been proved NP-hard. Their deterministic polynomial time algorithms are unlikely to exist. The quality of the final solution is in contradiction with computation time. To search an optimum of a function with continuous variables is difficult if there are many peaks and valleys. In these cases, traditional optimization methods are not competent. They will either be trapped to local optima or need much more search time. In recent years, many researchers have been trying to find new ways to solve these difficult problems, and stochastic approaches have attracted much attention [1]-[3].

Random signal-based learning merged with simulated annealing (SARSL) is a powerful optimization algorithm as proved in [3]. But it can not find the global optimum of complex problem very well because of its serial nature. In this paper, a population structure of SARSL (PSARSL) is proposed. The PSARSL is an extended version of SARSL as a population structure. The PSARSL enables the SARSL to explore the search space starting from various random initial states, and then each SARSL in the population exploits the search space with the help of SA. Besides, this paper considers an adaptive partitioning method (APM) to reduce the optimization time and enhance the accuracy. The performance of the proposed method is compared with that of other stochastic optimization algorithms with respect to computational effort and accuracy. For this comparison, the test functions optimization and a fuzzy controller optimization for an inverted pendulum are considered.

G. Antoniou et al. (Eds.): SETN 2006, LNAI 3955, pp. 67–76, 2006.

2 Overview of SARSL

The main idea of the random signal-based learning (RSL) [3] is that the random value randomly agitates the state in the range of learning rate in order to find the optimal state. If the learning rate is quite small, the state can exploit the search space (fine learning), but can not explore (coarse leaning). On the contrary, if the learning rate is large enough, then exploration of the search rather than exploitation is emphasized. This is a trade-off between small and large learning rate. Since the candidate solution moves in a downhill direction very quickly with a small learning rate, RSL is a very effective algorithm for the local search.

The SARSL [3] is a modified RSL with the help of simulated annealing (SA). The SA allows a system to change its state to a higher energy state occasionally such that it has a chance to jump out of local minima and seek the global minimum [4]. The SA possesses a formal proof of convergence to the global optimum [5][6]. This convergence proof relies on a very slow cooling schedule of setting the temperature. While this cooling schedule is impractical, it identifies a useful trade-off where longer cooling schedules tend to lead to better quality solutions. In SA, the downhill moves are always accepted, whereas the uphill moves are accepted with the probability (P) that is a function of temperature. A brief explanation of SARSL is described as follows:

Step 1. Initialize the state at random. Initialize the temperature T.
Step 2. Evaluate the new state using RSL.
Step 3. Q_{old}=performance of the old state, Q_{new}=performance of the new state.
Step 4. If $Q_{new} < Q_{old}$ then the new state is accepted for the next epoch, else compute P and then compare P with the random generated number in [0,1]. If P>random number, then the new state is accepted, else the new state is rejected.
Step 5. Cooling down the temperature as $T=T*$cooling rate.
Step 6. If the stopping criterion is satisfied end algorithm, else go to Step 2.

Example 1. To show the local search ability of RSL, the following nonlinear function, described in Fig. 1, is used [7]

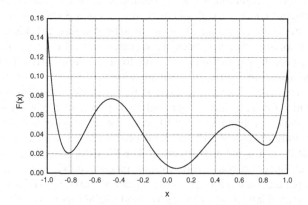

Fig. 1. The shape of nonlinear function $F(x)$ that has a global minimum in x=0.07715

$$F(x)=(x+0.9)(x+0.7)(x+0.2)(x-0.4)(x-0.7)(x-0.9)+0.04. \tag{1}$$

where $-1<x<1$. $F(x)$ has two local minima and one global minimum. The purpose of this example is to find the x that makes the $F(x)$ minimum. Figs. 2 and 3 depict the results of RSL and SARSL for different initial states. Fig. 2 shows that RSL is a good local search algorithm because all the initial states converge into each local minimum exactly. But Fig. 3 shows that the results of SARSL converge into a global minimum for all initial states. This means that SARSL, though it is serial algorithm, is more powerful local search algorithm for the function with many peaks and valleys.

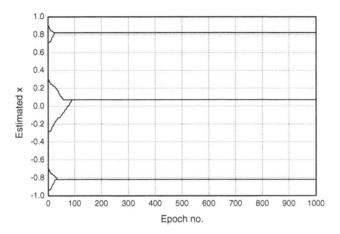

Fig. 2. The result of RSL for different initial states

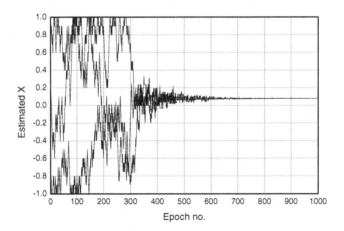

Fig. 3. The result of SARSL for different initial states

3   Description of the Proposed Algorithm

Though, SARSL is a good optimization algorithm for a simple optimization problem, as shown in Example 1, it may not be a good algorithm for a complex one because of

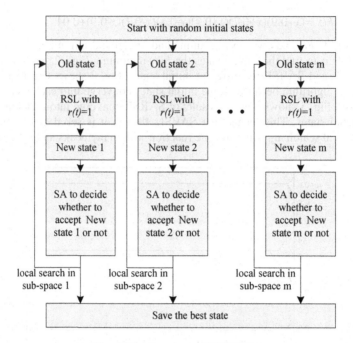

Fig. 4. The flowchart of PSARSL

its serial nature. To overcome this shortcoming, a population structure of SARSL (PSARSL), that is an extension of SARSL as a population structure, is proposed as described in Fig. 4. The PSARSL can get the diversity of solution set by starting with different initial states, and then performs local search for each local area. Therefore, PSARSL can find more accurate solution than SARSL with lower computational effort, because PSARSL searches different local areas with corresponding initial states and SARSL (serial algorithm) is a good local search algorithm as proved in Fig. 3. As shown in Fig. 4, each serial algorithm of PSARSL starts from corresponding initial states generated at random. These *m* serial algorithms search each local area and finally converge on the near global optima.

In case of complex optimization problems, adaptive partitioning method (APM) is very helpful in the reduction of computational effort and enhancement of accuracy [8]. In this paper, the following APM is used to enhance the performance of PSARSL:

Step 1. The original search region is equally partitioned into K rectangles (subregions).

Step 2. Generate R uniformly distributed random states for each subregion, and then evaluate the performance index for all random states.

Step 3. The subregion that contains the best performed state is further equally partitioned into K subregions, and the best performed state is updated.

Step 4. If the partitioning has not been performed in the surrounding subregions (the subregions except the currently partitioning subregion) for S steps, go to next step, else go to Step 2.

Step 5. Use PSARSL in the most promising subregion that has taken from APM to find the global optimum, and additionally, apply simple genetic algorithm (SGA) with small population to the surrounding subregions (consider these subregions as one) because there is a little possibility to exist the global optimum.

Example 2. In this example, the following two-dimensional test function [1] is considered to clarify the APM described above:

$$F(x, y) = 0.5 - (\sin\sqrt{x^2 + y^2} - 0.5)^2 / (1 + 0.001(x^2 + y^2))^2 \qquad -1 \le x, \ y \le -4 . \qquad (2)$$

This function has a global maximum in $(x, y) = (0, 0)$ as 1, and many local maxima, whose values are 0.990283, are around the global maximum. Fig. 5 describes the

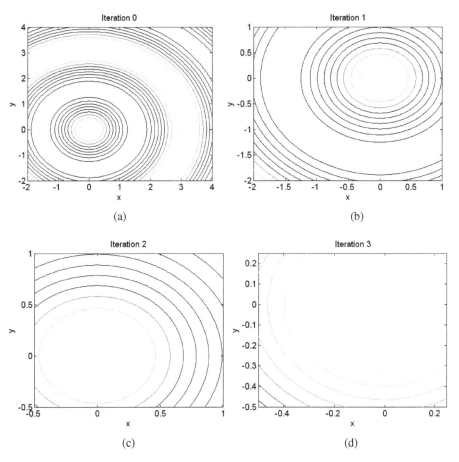

Fig. 5. Contours of the most promising subregions for each APM iterations: (a) Iteration 0=[-2, 4]x[-2, 4] (original region), (b) Iteration 1=[-2, 1]x[-2, 1] (subregion taken from the 1st iteration), (c) Iteration 2=[-0.5, 1]x[-0.5, 1] (subregion taken from the 2nd iteration), (d) Iteration 3=[-0.5, 0.25]x[-0.5, 0.25] (subregion taken from the 3rd iteration)

contours of the most promising subregions for each APM iterations, where K=4, R=20, and S=4. This APM has been performed 30 independent times, and finally, the subregion including global optimum is always survived in the last iteration step of APM as the most promising subregion. Once the most promising subregion has been taken from APM, the PSARSL can find the global optimum in the subregion, as shown in Fig. 5(d), more easily.

From this example we can expect that the complexity of the search space for the most promising subregion obtained by APM is much reduced than that of the original one, and the probability of containing the global optimum inside the obtained subregion is very high. This makes PSARSL to find the optimal state more effectively. Additionally, a SGA is used to explore the surrounding subregions with small population because there is a small possibility that the global optimum can be found in the surrounding subregions.

4 Experimental Results

To verify the effectiveness of the proposed method, we consider several benchmark functions and a fuzzy controller design example. The parameters used in the experiment are set by trial and error, and are defined as follows: learning rate=0.01, cooling rate=0.98, initial temperature=0.1, population size of PSARSL and SGA=20, maximum number of parallel epoch for PSARSL and SGA=200, crossover rate=0.8, mutation rate=0.1, K=4, R=20, and S=4. The proposed method will be compared with PSARSL without APM. Moreover, in this simulation, standard version of genetic algorithm (GA), which is well-known population structure optimization algorithm, is considered as well. For the reasonable comparison the maximum number of parallel epoch for PSARSL and GA without APM=1000, and initial temperature for PSARSL without APM=1.0 (others are the same as above), and each algorithm is run 30 times independently.

4.1 Optimization of the Test Functions

We employ four real-valued benchmark test functions [1], given in Table 1, to demonstrate the mechanics of the proposed method. This table shows high dimensional problem (f1, f4) and low dimensional problem (f5, f6) together.

The results of optimization are summarized in Table 2. This table shows the percentage of global optimum (optimization accuracy) and the average number of function evaluation (optimization speed) to reach 10^{-5} error, respectively. The optimization accuracy of the proposed method and GA is very similar, while the optimization speed is very different, i.e. the proposed method is much faster than GA in these four test functions because of using APM. In the proposed method, the most promising subregion obtained by APM contains a global optimum as 97.5% for all test function optimizations. The performance of PSARSL (without APM) is inferior to that of others as we expected above.

4.2 Applications to Fuzzy Controller Design

To show the effectiveness of the proposed method, optimization of the fuzzy controller for balancing an inverted pendulum system, where a free-falling pole is mounted

Table 1. Test functions and their specifications

Name	Function	Global optimum
f1	$f_1(\mathbf{x}) = \sum_{i=1}^{n} x_i^2$ where n=10, -4.12 < x_i < 5.12	0
f4	$f_4(\mathbf{x}) = \sum_{i=1}^{n} i \cdot x_i^4$ where n=10, -1.0 < x_i < 1.28	0
f5	$f_5(\mathbf{x}) = 1/(0.002 + \sum_{j=1}^{25} \dfrac{1}{j + \sum_{i=1}^{2}(x_i - a_{ij})^6})$ where -64.0 < x_1, x_2 < 65.356	0.998004
f6	$f_6(\mathbf{x}) = 0.5 - \dfrac{Sin^2(\sqrt{x_1^2 + x_2^2}) - 0.5}{(1 + 0.001(x_1^2 + x_2^2))^2}$ where -1.0 < x_1, x_2 < -4.0	1

Table 2. Optimization results of the test functions

Name	Algorithms	% of global optimum	Average number of function evaluation to reach global optimum
f1	Proposed method	96.7	5317.5
f1	PSARSL without APM	76.7	12836.1
f1	GA	93.3	7162.6
f4	Proposed method	93.3	6024.7
f4	PSARSL without APM	73.3	15520.3
f4	GA	90	8317.9
f5	Proposed method	100	3492.3
f5	PSARSL without APM	80	10893.6
f5	GA	100	5351.1
f6	Proposed method	100	3016.8
f6	PSARSL without APM	86.7	7921.3
f6	GA	100	5719.6

on a cart that is controlled by an actuator, is considered here. The control objective is to produce an appropriate actuator force to control the motion of the cart so that the pole can be balanced in a vertical position. Given that no friction exists in the system, and let $x_1 = \theta$ and $x_2 = \dot{\theta}$, then the state equation can be expressed as [3]:

$$\dot{x}_1 = x_2$$
$$\dot{x}_2 = \frac{(M + m)g \sin x_1 - (F + mlx_2^2 \sin x_1)\cos x_1}{\{4/3(M + m) - m(\cos x_1)^2\}l} \quad (3)$$

where M (mass of the cart) is 1.0Kg, m (mass of the pole) is 0.1Kg, l (half length of the pole) is 0.5m, g (gravity acceleration) is 9.8m/s^2, and F is the applied force in

Newton. To simplify the problem, only the control of the pole is considered for the inverted pendulum system, that is, the considered states are the angle, θ, and the angular velocity, $\dot{\theta}$, of the pole with respect to the vertical axis. The fuzzy controller for this system consists of 25 possible rules that have antecedent parts with 5 fixed triangular membership functions (fuzzy sets) for each input variable, and 25 consequent part membership functions [3]. Mamdani-type fuzzy model [9] is used in this example. The proposed algorithm optimizes 25 centers and 25 widths of the consequent part membership functions of the rule. The range of centers and width is [-1, 1]. In this experiment, the following performance index, pursue decreasing, is used:

$$Q = \sum_{i=1}^{q} [e_i^2 + \dot{e}_i^2] \cdot \tag{4}$$

where q is the number of input-output pairs. The performance index is evaluated by controlling the inverted pendulum during 5s (seconds), where the initial angle and angular velocity of the pendulum are ±0.3rad (radian) and zero, respectively. The failure limit of the angle of the pendulum is ±1.0rad and the sampling period is 0.01s.

Table 3 describes the average simulation results (average over 30 independent simulations) for each algorithm. The maximum number of function (performance index) evaluation for each algorithm is 20000. This means that each algorithm has been performed with the same computational effort. In this table, the average best Q (performance index) and the average number of function evaluation to reach 1% of the best Q

Table 3. Average simulation results

Algorithm	The avg. best Q	The avg. number of function evaluation to reach 1% of the best Q
Proposed method	12.01	10346.2
PSARSL without APM	15.12	15274.7
GA	12.27	12154.9

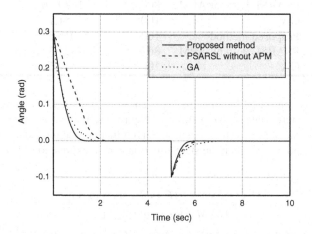

Fig. 6. Average control result of each algorithm

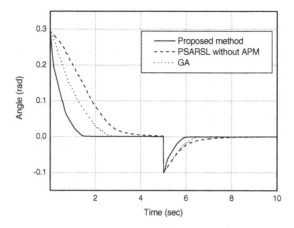

Fig. 7. Averaged control result of each algorithm: l=1.0m

show the accuracy and speed, respectively. As can be seen, the proposed method is superior to other algorithms with respect to optimization accuracy and speed.

Fig. 6 shows the average control result of the inverted pendulum obtained by the 30 optimized fuzzy controllers for each algorithm. From this figure, we can see that the fuzzy controllers optimized by the proposed method control the inverted pendulum much better than other algorithms.

Fig. 7 describes the result when half length of pole, l, is changed as 1.0m long. This result shows the robustness of the optimized fuzzy controllers for the system parameter change. As can bee seen, the fuzzy controllers constructed by the proposed method are more robust than those of other algorithms in terms of parameter change of the system.

5   Conclusions

This paper proposed the adaptive partitioning-based stochastic optimization algorithm to reduce the optimization time and enhance the accuracy. The adaptive partitioning method (APM) finds the most promising subregion containing the global or near global optima to decrease the complexity of the search space. The population structure of SARSL (PSARSL) was applied to this subregion to find the optimum state, while a simple genetic algorithm was used to search the surrounding subregions to find the missing optimum state which may occur very rarely. The validity was confirmed by the optimization of the benchmark test functions and the fuzzy controller for the inverted pendulum. As is shown, the proposed method is superior to PSARSL and GA (without APM) with respect to optimization speed and accuracy. This means that APM is very effective to enhance the performance of PSARSL. For the further research, the more complex general problems should be considered, and the more deep theoretical analysis rather than heuristic approach is needed.

References

1. De Jong, K.: An Analysis of the Behavior of a Class of Genetic Adaptive Systems. Ph.D. dissertation, Dept. Computer Sci., Univ. Michigan, Ann Arbor, MI (1975)
2. Goldberg, D.E.: Genetic Algorithms in Search, Optimization and Machine Learning. Addison-Wesley, Reading, MA (1989)
3. Han, C.W., Park, J.I.: Design of a Fuzzy Controller using Random Signal-based Learning Employing Simulated Annealing. Proc. of the IEEE Conference on Decision and Control, Sydney, Australia (2000) 396-397
4. Kirkpatrick, S., Gelatt Jr., C.D., Vecchi, M.P.: Optimization by Simulated Annealing. Science, Vol. 220, No. 4598 (1983) 671-680
5. Romeo, F., Sangiovanni-Vincentelli, A.: A Theoretical Framework for Simulated Annealing. Algorithmica, Vol. 6 (1991) 302-345
6. Sullivan, K.A., Jacobson, S.H.: A Convergence Analysis of Generalized Hill Climbing Algorithms. IEEE Trans. Automatic Control, Vol. 46, No. 8 (2001) 1288-1293
7. Jeong, I.K., Lee, J.J.: Adaptive Simulated Annealing Genetic Algorithm for Control Applications. International Journal of Systems Science, Vol. 27, No. 2 (1996) 241-253
8. Tang, Z.B.: Partitioned Random Search to Optimization. Proc. of the American Control Conference, San Francisco (1993)
9. Procyk, T.J., Mamdani, E.H.: A Linguistic Self-organizing Process Controller. Automatica, Vol. 15, No. 1 (1979) 15-30

Fuzzy Granulation-Based Cascade Fuzzy Neural Networks Optimized by GA-RSL

Chang-Wook Han and Jung-Il Park

School of Electrical Engineering and Computer Science, Yeungnam University,
214-1 Dae-dong, Gyongsan, Gyongbuk, 712-749 South Korea
{cwhan, jipark}@yumail.ac.kr

Abstract. This paper is concerned with cascade fuzzy neural networks and its optimization. These networks come with sound and transparent logic character-istics by being developed with the aid of AND and OR fuzzy neurons and sub-sequently logic processors (LPs). We discuss main functional properties of the model and relate them to its form of cascade type of systems formed as a stack of LPs. The structure of the network that deals with a selection of a subset of input variables and their distribution across the individual LPs is optimized with the use of genetic algorithms (GA). We discuss random signal-based learning (RSL), a local search technique, aimed at further refinement of the connections of the neurons (GA-RSL). We elaborate on the interpretation aspects of the network and show how this leads to a Boolean or multi-valued logic description of the experimental data. Two kinds of standard data sets are discussed with re-spect to the performance of the constructed networks and their interpretability.

1 Introduction

The essential feature of fuzzy and neurofuzy systems lies in its logic fabric. It can manifest in many different conceptual ways and is realized at different implementa-tion levels. A general framework of fuzzy modeling that is general and yet specific enough to support realization of detailed models can be envisioned as a two-layer ar-chitecture. The interface layer realizes all communication between the external world and the processing core of the model. More specifically, the role of the interface is to accept any input datum no matter what its format is (say, numeric values, fuzzy sets or sets) and translate it into the internal format acceptable for the processing purposes. No matter what the details of such transformation are, in essence it converts physical variables into more abstract and logic-driven format of membership grades of the cor-responding fuzzy sets. There has been an array of approaches to realize such trans-formation, say through possibility, necessity and compatibility measures. Likewise to communicate the results of logic processing back to the physical environment, we end up with a broad range of so-called defuzzification procedures [1]-[4]. As the entire processing done by the model is realized on a more abstract level, it implies that we have to confine ourselves to the logic-oriented nature of the model as well as develop logic-based processing within such model.

The primary objective of this study is to develop a cascade fuzzy neural network [1] with genetic algorithm (GA) [5][6] and random signal-based learning (RSL)

G. Antoniou et al. (Eds.): SETN 2006, LNAI 3955, pp. 77–86, 2006.

[7]-[9], analyze its properties and introduce a comprehensive development environment. These networks implement the logic-based mapping between input and output spaces viewed as multidimensional unit hyper-cubes that is we are concerned about the relationship from $[0,1]^n$ to $[0,1]^m$, and thus come with interpretation transparency augmented by learning capabilities. The cascade nature of the network supports modularity and allows building reduced models on a basis of a subset of the most essential input variables. This feature is particularly appealing when we are concerned with the design of fuzzy models in presence of a high number of variables whose reduction becomes inevitable. GA optimizes the order of the variables and the binary connections of the neurons, and then RSL refines the binary connections, namely GA-RSL optimization. To verify the effectiveness of the GA-RSL optimization, two kinds of numeric data sets are discussed with respect to the performance of the constructed networks and their interpretability.

2 The Logic Processor (LP)

As originally introduced in [1], fuzzy neurons emerge as result of a vivid synergy between fuzzy set constructs and neural networks. In essence, these neurons are functional units that retain logic aspects of processing and learning capabilities characteristic for artificial neurons and neural networks. Two generic types of fuzzy neurons are considered:

AND neuron is a nonlinear logic processing element with n-inputs $\mathbf{x}\ [0,1]^n$ producing an output y governed by the expression

$$y = \text{AND}(\mathbf{x}; \mathbf{w}) = \mathop{T}_{i=1}^{n}(w_i s x_i) \cdot \tag{1}$$

where $\mathbf{w}$ denotes an n-dimensional vector of adjustable connections (weights). The composition of $\mathbf{x}$ and $\mathbf{w}$ is realized by an t-s composition operator based on t- and s-norms, that is, "s" denoting some s-norm and "t" standing for a t-norm. As t- norms (s-norms) carry a transparent logic interpretation, we can look at as a two-phase aggregation process: first individual inputs (coordinates of $\mathbf{x}$) are combined *or*-wise with the corresponding weights and these results produced at the level of the individual aggregation are aggregated *and*-wise with the aid of the t-norm.

By reverting the order of the t- and s-norms in the aggregation of the inputs, we end up with a category of OR neurons,

$$y = \text{OR}(\mathbf{x}; \mathbf{w}) = \mathop{S}_{i=1}^{n}(w_i t x_i) \cdot \tag{2}$$

We note that this neuron carries out some *and*-wise aggregation of the inputs followed by the global *or*-wise combination of these partial results.

Some obvious observations hold:

- For binary inputs and connections, the neurons transform to standard AND and OR gates.
- The higher the values of the connections in the OR neuron, the more essential the corresponding inputs. This observation helps eliminate irrelevant

inputs; the inputs associated with the connections whose values are below a certain threshold are eliminated. An opposite relationship holds for the AND neuron; here the connections close to zero identify the relevant inputs.

- The change in the values of the connections of the neuron is essential to the development of the learning capabilities of a network formed by such neurons; this parametric flexibility is an important feature to be exploited in the design of the networks.

The LP, described in Fig. 1, is a basic two-level construct formed by a collection of "h" AND neurons whose results of computing are then processed by a single OR neuron located in the output layer. Because of the location of the AND neurons, we will be referring to them as a hidden layer of the LP.

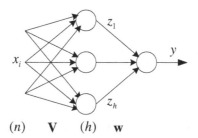

Fig. 1. Architecture of the LP regarded as a generic processing unit

Each LP is uniquely characterized by a number of parameters: a number of inputs (n), number of nodes in the hidden layer (h) and an array of connections of the AND neurons as well as the OR neuron in the output layer. Bearing in mind the topology of the LP, the connections of the AND neurons can be systematically represented in a matrix form **V** while the connections of the OR neuron are collected in a single vector form (**w**). We write the following detailed expressions

$$z_j = \mathrm{AND}(\mathbf{x}, \mathbf{V}_j), j=1,2,\ldots, h \qquad y = \mathrm{OR}\ (\mathbf{z}, \mathbf{w}). \tag{3}$$

where **z** is a vector of outputs of the AND neurons ($\mathbf{z} = [z_1\ z_2\ldots z_h]^{\mathrm{T}}$) while $\mathbf{V}_j$ denotes the j-th column of the connection matrix **V**.

3   A Cascade Fuzzy Neural Network

As LPs are our basic functional modules, there are several viable options to build an overall architecture. Here we discuss them and analyze its functional properties.

LPs are basic functional modules of the network that are combined into a cascaded structure. The essence of this architecture is to stack the LPs one on another. This results in a certain sequence of input variables. To assure that the resulting network is homogeneous, we use LPs with only two inputs, as shown in Fig. 2. In this sense, with "n" input variables, we end up with (n-1) LPs being used in the network. Each LP is fully described by a set of the connections (**V** and **w**). To emphasize the

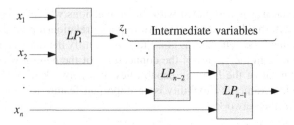

Fig. 2. A cascaded network realized as a nested collection of LPs

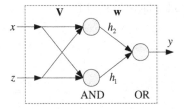

Fig. 3. Logic processor along with its possible logic descriptors; see description in the text

cascade-type of architecture of the network, we index each LP by referring to its connections as $\mathbf{V}$[ii] and $\mathbf{w}$[ii] with "ii' being an index of the LP in the cascade sequence.

To gain a better view at the mapping realized by the network, it is advantageous to
discuss the functional aspects of a single logic processor. We start with the simplest
possible topology. We assume that the number of AND neurons (hidden layer) is
equal to 2 and consider a binary character of the connections, see Fig. 3.

Based on the values of the connection matrices ($\mathbf{w}$ and $\mathbf{V}$) we arrive at the following logic expressions (let us remind that the rows of $\mathbf{V}$ contain the values of the connections originating from a certain input node to the two AND neurons in the hidden
layer; the columns are labeled by the corresponding AND nodes)

$$\mathbf{w} = [1 \ \ 0] \quad \mathbf{V} = \begin{bmatrix} 0 & 0 \\ 1 & 1 \end{bmatrix} \quad h_1 = x \qquad h_2 = x \qquad y = h_1 \ \text{OR} \ 0 = x$$

$$\mathbf{w} = [1 \ \ 0] \quad \mathbf{V} = \begin{bmatrix} 0 & 1 \\ 0 & 1 \end{bmatrix} \quad h_1 = x \ \text{AND} \ z, \quad h_2 = 1, \quad y = h_1 \ \text{OR} \ 0 = x \ \text{AND} \ z$$

In a nutshell, the proposed network realizes a successive realization of the logic
model by incorporating more variables by augmenting its structure by a basic (generic) unit once at a time.

4 Development of the Cascade Type Network

The evolutionary optimization [5][6] is an attractive avenue to exploit in the development of the cascade network. In this learning scenario, we arrange all elements to
be optimized (that is a sequence and a subset of input variables, and the connections

of the logic processors) into a single chromosome and carry out their genetic optimization [1]. The considered form of the chromosome for this optimization is described in Fig. 4. The input sequence of the variables (and thus is involved in the structural optimization of the network) and the connections (parametric optimization) are the phenotype of the chromosome. The sequence gene of input variables to be used in the model (we allow for a high level of flexibility by choosing only a subset of the input variables) consists of "n" real numbers in the unit interval. These entries are assigned integer numbers that correspond to their ranking in the chromosome. The first "p" entries of the chromosome (assuming that we are interested in "p" variables) are then used in the structure of the network. For instance, if the chromosome consists of the following entries: 0.5 0.94 0.1 0.82 0.7 (n = 5) and we are interested in p=3 variables, the ranking leads to the sequence of integers 2 4 5 1 3 and we choose x_2, x_4, and x_5.

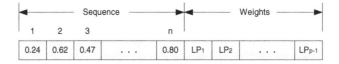

Fig. 4. Structure of a chromosome for the optimization of cascade fuzzy neural networks

The resulting connections of GA are binary. Instead of going ahead with the continuous connections, the intent of GA is to focus on the structure and rough (binary) values of the connections. This is legitimate in light of the general character of genetic optimization: we can explore the search space however there is no guarantee that the detailed solution could be found. The promising Boolean solution can be next refined by allowing for the values of the connections confined to the unit interval. Such refinement is accomplished by the RSL [7-9] that is quite complementary to the GA; while could be easily trapped in a local minimum, it leads to a detailed solution. The complete learning mode is composed then as a sequence of GA followed by the RSL, let us express as GA-RSL (two-step optimization). A brief explanation of the RSL is described as follows:

Step 1. Initialize the states at random.
Step 2. Evaluate the new state using RSL.
Step 3. Q_{old}=performance of the old state, Q_{new}=performance of the new state.
Step 4. If $Q_{new}<Q_{old}$ then the new state is accepted for the next epoch, else the new state is rejected.
Step 5. If the stopping criterion is satisfied end algorithm, else go to Step 2.

To shows the local search ability of the RSL, the following nonlinear function is considered when -1<x<1:

$$F(x)=(x+0.9)(x+0.7)(x+0.2)(x-0.4)(x-0.7)(x-0.9)+0.04 \qquad (4)$$

The optimization goal of this example is to find the x that makes the $F(x)$ minimum. Fig. 5 shows the shape of $F(x)$ which has two local minima and one global minimum. Fig. 6 describes six curves which are the estimated x from six independent executions of the RSL with different initial states. As is shown in this figure, the accurate local optima are always found very quickly by the RSL.

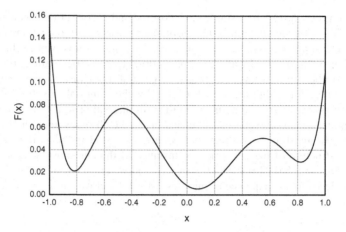

Fig. 5. The shape of the nonlinear function $F(x)$

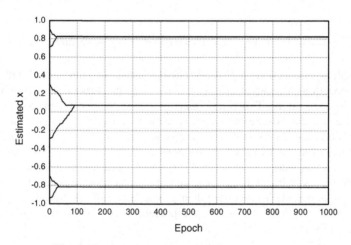

Fig. 6. The estimated x for each different initial state

5   Experimental Studies

The experiments deal with a standard data set, i.e. Auto- MPG data (available on the Machine Learning site at the University of California at Irvine) and Box-Jenkins gas-furnace data [15], those are commonly used in the development of various models.

The genetic optimization is supported by a standard form of GA with real-number encoding as shown in Fig. 4. The parameters of the optimization environment are included in Table 1 and these are fixed for all experiments; it has been found that under these conditions the optimization was carried out efficiently and resulted in meaningful results. In the experiments, we confine ourselves to the two commonly encountered models of triangular norms by implementing t-norm as an algebraic product and realizing s-norm in the form of the probabilistic sum.

Table 1. Experimental setup of the parameters of the optimization environment

Algorithm	Parameter	Value
GA	Population size	50
	Maximum generation	100
	Crossover rate	0.8
	Mutation rate	0.1
RSL	Learning rate	0.05
	λ	5
	Maximum iteration no.	2000

Apparently, the optimization of the fuzzy sets standing in the interfaces could be beneficial to the model and contribute to the enhancement of its quality. Accepting this point of view, for the purpose of this study we assume that fuzzy sets of the input and output interfaces are given in advance and left unchanged. Our focal point is the cascade fuzzy neural network and its optimization. We do not claim that the selection and number of fuzzy sets forming the interfaces are not important in general. For the purpose of this study we keep this part fixed and this allows us to concentrate on the core processing realized in a cascade type of fuzzy neural network [1].

To support interpretation, when it comes to the presentation of the resulting rules, we "binarize" the connections, that is, convert them to 0 or 1 depending where they are originally positioned with respect to the threshold level of 0.5 (the connections whose values are located in the vicinity of 0.5 are less obvious than those positioned close to 0 or 1).

A GA optimizes all parameters (binary connections) and structure. By carrying out RSL refinement we enhance the parametric details of the network and reveal how much these impact its performance. The performance of the network is described by means of RMSE between the desired output and the actual output. To get the reasonable experimental results, each network has been simulated 10 times independently. In this experiment, Auto-MPG and Box-Jenkins gas-furnace data are used to compare the performance of the proposed method with the method in [10] which constructed the fuzzy system based on the significance degree of the input variable.

5.1 Auto-MPG Data

Auto-MPG data comes from the Machine Learning repository and deals with fuel consumption in miles per gallon. Each vehicle is described by the following variables: number of cylinders (CYL), displacement (DIS), horsepower (HP), weight (W), acceleration (ACC), model year (MODEL), and miles per gallon (MPG, treated as the output). For each variable, we set up three Gaussian fuzzy sets with an overlap of 0.5. Because of these fuzzy sets, we end up with 18 input variables (6*3). For all but the model year we accept three labels, those are SMALL, MEDIUM, and LARGE. The age of the vehicle is quantified as OLD, MEDIUM, and NEW. Among 392 data vector, we divide it 2/3 for training and 1/3 for testing.

We again exercised the learning scenarios that GA optimizes the input sequence and binary connections for different number of input and then the RSL refines the connections of the neurons positioned in the unit interval. All logic processors have two AND neurons in their hidden layers. In the experiments, we limit the number of input variables (note that each original variable has its internal manifestation through three fuzzy sets) and consider 3, 5, 7, and 9 number of input. The selection of these variables is also genetically optimized and in this way we can reduce the size of the model as well as reveal a hierarchy of the input fuzzy sets.

Table 2 shows the average performance index (RMSE) over 10 independent simulations for the GA mode of learning with 3, 5, 7, and 9 input variables (fuzzy sets) and RSL refinement of the result obtained by GA (GA-RSL). Shadowed entries indicate the best results of the performance index. The values in the brackets are the result of the testing set. From the results we can see that the binary connections optimized by GA are further refined by RSL. Actually, it is not possible to compare the proposed method with the algorithm introduce in [1] and [10] because the same training and testing data are not used. However, the performance of the proposed method is superior to that of the algorithm in [10] with respect to the accuracy and the reduction ability of the input variables. But we can not see the superiority of the proposed method to the algorithm in [1], i.e., the performance is very similar. Though the performance is very similar, the proposed method is very simple algorithm that does not need very complex mathematics (gradient-based method in [1] needs very complex differential equations).

The interpretation of the networks leads to interesting results. We assume that the inputs are binary to simplify the rules and organize them in Table 3 which reveals one of the ten simulations with 5 input variables (fuzzy sets). The resulting rules are highly intuitive both in terms of how we would sense about fuel efficiency of a vehicle depending on its features.

Table 2. Average performance index (RMSE) over 10 independent simulations for the GA mode of learning with 3, 5, 7, and 9 input variables and RSL refinement for the result obtained by GA (GA-RSL). The values in the brackets are the result of the testing set.

Algorithm	3	5	7	9
GA	2.62	2.59	2.60	2.60
	(2.64)	(2.63)	(2.63)	(2.64)
GA-RSL	2.57	2.48	2.50	2.51
	(2.58)	(2.50)	(2.53)	(2.54)

Table 3. A collection of fuzzy rules produced by the resulting networks

Algorithm	Rules
GA	If [HP is large] OR [W is large] OR [ACC is small] then [MPG is small]
	If [MODEL is new] OR [HP is small] then [MPG is medium]
	If [W is small] AND [HP is small] AND [CYL is medium] then [MPG is large]
GA-RSL	If [HP is large] OR [W is large] then [MPG is small]
	If [MODEL is new] OR [HP is small] then [MPG is medium]
	If [W is small] AND [HP is small] then [MPG is large]

Table 4. Average performance index (RMSE) over 10 independent simulations for the GA mode of learning with 3, 5, 7, and 9 input variables and RSL refinement for the result obtained by GA (GA-RSL). The values in the brackets are the result of the testing set.

Algorithm	3	5	7	9
GA	0.50	0.45	0.46	0.45
	(0.53)	(0.47)	(0.49)	(0.48)
GA-RSL	0.40	0.35	0.37	0.36
	(0.42)	(0.37)	(0.38)	(0.38)

Table 5. A collection of fuzzy rules produced by the resulting networks

Algo-rithm	Rules
GA	If [$y(t-1)$ is small AND $u(t-4)$ is large AND $u(t-3)$ is large] OR [$y(t-2)$ is small] then [$y(t)$ is small]
	If [$y(t-1)$ is medium] and [$u(t-4)$ is medium] then [$y(t)$ is medium]
	If [$y(t-1)$ is large] AND [$u(t-4)$ is medium] AND [$u(t-3)$ is medium] then [$y(t)$ is large]
GA-RSL	If [$y(t-1)$ is small AND $u(t-4)$ is large AND $u(t-3)$ is large] then [$y(t)$ is small]
	If [$y(t-1)$ is medium] and [$u(t-4)$ is medium] then [$y(t)$ is medium]
	If [$y(t-1)$ is large] AND [$u(t-4)$ is medium] AND [$u(t-3)$ is medium] then [$y(t)$ is large]

5.2 Box-Jenkins Gas-Furnace Data

Another example for the comparison is Box-Jenkins gas-furnace data which is a single input-output time series data for a gas furnace process with gas flow rate $u(t)$ as input and the CO_2 concentration $y(t)$ as output. We consider 10 input variables described in [10]. The first half of the date is used as training and remaining data is used as testing. All the experimental conditions are the same as the previous example (Auto-MPG data). The simulation results are described in Table 4 with respect to RMSE. Though, the considered data for training and testing are different, the proposed method performs better than the algorithm in [10] with respect to the testing data prediction RMSE. The comparison result of the GA-RSL with the algorithm in [1] is similar to the case of Auto-MPG data. A collection of resulting fuzzy rules translated from the data are summarized in Table 5.

6 Conclusions

We have introduced and developed cascade fuzzy neural networks with the use of GA-RSL. The network exhibits a transparent logic structure that supports all interpretation faculties. We showed that the genetically optimized network help concentrate on the processing a subset of the most essential variables. The comprehensive development environment consisting of GA-RSL helps complete structural and parametric design of the network. The experimental results help quantify the performance of the network and provide interesting interpretation of the available data.

References

1. Pedrycz, W., Reformat, M., Han, C.W.: Cascade Architectures of Fuzzy Neural Networks. Fuzzy Optimization and Decision Making 3(1) (2004) 5-37
2. Babuska, R.: Fuzzy Modeling for Control. Kluwer Academic Publishers, Norwell, MA (1998)
3. Bargiela, A., Pedrycz, W.: Granular Computing: An Introduction. Kluwer Academic Publishers, Dordrecht (2002)
4. Mitaim, S., Kosko, B.: The Shape of Fuzzy Sets in Adaptive Function Approximation. IEEE Trans. Fuzzy Systems 9(4) (2001) 647-656
5. Goldberg, D.E.: Genetic Algorithms in Search, Optimization and Machine Learning. Addison-Wesley, New York (1989)
6. Michalewicz, Z.: Genetic Algorithm + Data Structures = Evolution Programs. 3rd edn. Springer Verlag, Berlin (1996)
7. Han, C.W., Park, J.I.: Design of a Fuzzy Controller using Random Signal-based Learning Employing Simulated Annealing. Proc. of the 39th IEEE Conference on Decision and Control (2000) 396-397
8. Han, C.W., Park, J.I.: A Study on Hybrid Genetic Algorithms using Random Signal-based Learning Employing Simulated Annealing. Proc. of the 2001 American Control Conference (2001) 198-199
9. Han, C.W., Park, J.I.: A Study on Hybrid Random Signal-based Learning ant Its Applications. International Journal of Systems Science 35(4) (2004) 243-253
10. Kilic, K., Sproule, B.A., Turksen, I.B., Naranjo, C.A.: A Fuzzy System Modeling Algorithm for Data Analysis and Approximate Reasoning. Robotics and Autonomous Systems, Vol. 49 (2004) 173-180

Using Self-similarity Matrices for Structure Mining on News Video

Arne Jacobs

Center for Computing Technologies, University of Bremen
jarne@tzi.de

Abstract. Video broadcast series like news or magazine broadcasts usually expose a strong temporal structure, along with a characteristic audio-visual appearance. This results in frequent patterns occurring in the video signal. We propose an algorithm for the automatic detection of such patterns that exploits the video's self-similarity induced by the patterns. The approach is applied to the problem of anchor shot detection, but can also be used for other related purposes. Tests on real-world video data show that it is possible with our method to detect anchor shots fully automatically with high reliability.

1 Introduction / Related Work

The detection of frequent patterns in video is useful in the case when the given videos expose a strong temporal structure. The results of an anchor shot detection, for example, may be used to help finding story boundaries in news or magazine broadcasts. Other examples are special screens or video sequences used in news videos to announce different topics. Patterns are used in these videos to make it possible for the viewer to easily follow the broadcast and to recognize its structure. They also make it possible to do this so-called "Video Parsing" [1] automatically.

Hauptmann et al. [2] use an SVM on color and face features to identify anchor shots in news videos. In addition to training the SVM, their classifier requires learning of a weighted image grid for the color features to account for changing anchors, clothing, etc. between the different news videos.

In [3], similar features are used, but instead of training, models for each expected presentation type have to be provided manually.

Kobla et al. [4] use the notion of "Video Trails" to identify similar shots in a video without training. However, they directly work on features extracted from the video frames, which makes it difficult to identify clusters because of the vast amount of frames that do not belong to any class and clog the feature space.

In this paper we present an automatic method for identifying frequent patterns, that does not work directly on image features, but on a matrix of similarity between different time points in the video. The method is very general and may be applied to other problems as well, but here we focus on the problem of anchor shot detection.

The next section descibes our algorithm, which is followed by our experimental results. We conclude with Sect. 4.

G. Antoniou et al. (Eds.): SETN 2006, LNAI 3955, pp. 87–94, 2006.

2   Proposed Approach

Our proposed algorithm consists of two steps:

- Computation of a self-similarity matrix
  Based on a similarity measure between two time points in the video, a two-dimensional symmetric matrix is computed, whose height and width is dependent on the length of the video.
- Clustering on rows of the self-similarity matrix
  Here we use a simple K-Means clustering algorithm to find patterns in the matrix, but other clustering methods might also be used.

Both steps can be customized depending on the problem at hand. Here we focus on anchor shot detection. In the next section, the computation of the self-similarity matrix is described in further detail, followed by an overview of the clustering step.

2.1   Self-similarity Matrix

The self-similarity matrix M is a $N \times N$ matrix defined as:

$$M_{ij} = S(t_i, t_j), \tag{1}$$

where $S(t_i, t_j)$ is a similarity measure between two timepoints t_i and t_j in the video. In our case, we choose frame-based timepoints $t_1, \ldots, t_i, \ldots, t_j, \ldots, t_N$ that are multiples of ten, i.e., $N = N'/10$ for a video with N' frames.

The form of the similarity measure $S \in [0, 1]$ (where 1 corresponds to maximal similarity, and 0 corresponds to minimal similarity) depends on the kind of patterns to be detected. Assuming that presentations are always shot in a certain setting and show the same presenter, for our purpose we define S as the product of a color distribution-based and a face-based similarity:

$$S(t_i, t_j) = S_{color}(I(t_i), I(t_j)) \cdot S_{face}(I(t_i), I(t_j)), \tag{2}$$

where $I(t)$ is the video frame at timepoint t. This measure is based on visual information only, i.e., the video frames, but other modes, e.g., audio data, may also be incorporated, if they contain information useful for the solution of the problem.

The color-based similarity is given by:

$$S_{color}(I(t_i), I(t_j)) = s(\|CC(I(t_i)) - CC(I(t_j))\|), \tag{3}$$

where $CC(I(t))$ is the color correlogram according to [5] of frame $I(t)$, and $\|\ldots\|$ denotes the L_2-Norm. Our assumption here is that presentations are always placed in the same or just a limited number of different studio settings. We choose the color correlogram feature as a representation of the visual appearance of the setting.

The face-based similarity is given by:

$$S_{face}(I(t_i), I(t_j)) = \begin{cases} 0 & \text{if } \neg face\_in(I(t_i)) \vee \neg face\_in(I(t_j)) \\ s(\|face(I(t_i)) - face(I(t_j))\|) & \text{otherwise} \end{cases} \quad (4)$$

where $face\_in(I(t)) \in \{true, false\}$ is true iff a face was detected in $I(t)$, and $face(I(t)) \in \mathcal{N}^4$ are the coordinates of the rectangle enclosing the dominant detected face in $I(t)$, if any. For face detection we use the algorithm by Lienhardt et al. [6].

Note that the form of the face-based measure means that a frame is dissimilar to each other frame (including itself) if it contains no face. However, this does not affect the algorithm in general. It just reflects our assumption that the anchor shots we want to find always show a face, and that this face is always shown at the same or a limited number of different positions in the video.

Finally, $s(x)$ as referenced in Equations 3 and 4 is the *GemanMcLure* probability distribution, scaled to $[0, 1]$:

$$s(x_i) = \frac{e^{\frac{-x_i^2}{\sigma^2 + x_i^2}} - e^{-1}}{1 - e^{-1}} \quad (5)$$

where the scale σ is proportional to the median of the distance values:

$$\sigma = \frac{\text{median}(x_1, \ldots, x_i, \ldots, x_{N^2})}{3} \quad (6)$$

We use $s(x)$ to convert distance values (low values correspond to high similarity) to similarity values between 0 and 1 (where high values denote high similarity).

Figure 1 shows an example similarity matrx. Dark areas denote high similarity. The main anchor sequences in the beginning and the financial news presentations at the beginning of the second half can be easily identified by the human eye.

2.2 Clustering

The similarity matrix computed in the previous section reveals temporal patterns of reoccurring frames, which in our case correspond to frames showing a face in a similar size and position, and a similar color distribution. Each row of the matrix contains a frame's similarity to each other considered frame. Frames belonging to a type of presentation will be more similar to other frames of the same type, and those in turn will also be similar to all the other frames of that type. If we see a row in the similarity matrix as a multidimensional feature vector, we find that rows corresponding to a frame of the same type of presentation will form a cluster in this new feature space.

Note that by clustering using the similarity matrix instead of using image features directly, we just need a similarity or distance measure between two frames (or time points in a video, respectively). We thus omit the need for features that lie in a vector space.

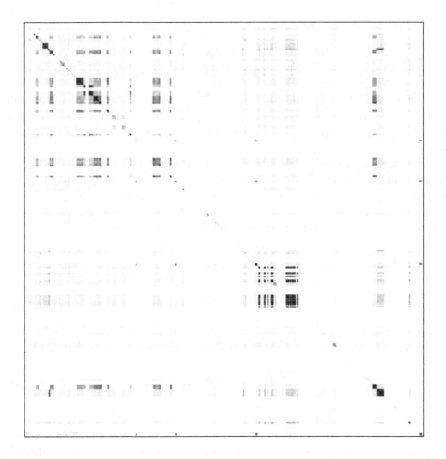

Fig. 1. Example of a similarity matrix computed on a video of "CNN Headline News", using color and face similarity

By applying a clustering algorithm to the matrix rows we can find the different types of presentations and we will also have a mapping from frame to presentation type. We use an adapted simple K-Means clustering algorithm. The number of classes to use as input for the algorithm depends on how many frequently occurring different presentation types we expect in a video. One additional class is added for all frames not belonging to any presentation. Our changes to the original K-Means algorithm ensure that these frames are all put into the same class.

We adapt the K-Means algorithm by weighting rows according to the sum of all entries, and by using a slightly different distance measure and a slightly different mean. The reasons for these changes are given below. The distance $d(i, j)$ between two matrix rows i and j used for clustering is defined as:

$$d(i,j) = \sqrt{\sum_{k=1}^{N} d(i,j,k)^2} \tag{7}$$

$$d(i, j, k) = (M_{ik} - M_{jk}) \cdot w_d(i, j) \tag{8}$$

$$w_d(i, j) = \begin{cases} 0 & \text{if } |i - j| < 50, \\ 1 & \text{otherwise} \end{cases} \tag{9}$$

By using this adapted distance measure we give more weight to similar frames that are not temporally adjacent, supporting frequently occurring patterns. The adapted mean $c(C, k)$ for column k of all rows belonging to the class C is defined by:

$$c(C, k) = \frac{\sum_{i \in C} M_{ik} \cdot w_d(i, k) \cdot w_r(i)}{\sum_{i \in C} w_d(i, k) \cdot w_r(i)} \tag{10}$$

where

$$w_r(i) = \sum_{k=1}^{N} M_{ik} \tag{11}$$

is the weight of row i. The adapted mean makes sure that high values in the diagonal of the similarity matrix do not distort clustering and that all frames not belonging to any frequently occurring pattern are clustered in the same class.

3 Experimental Results

We test our algorithm on several videos from the news broadcast series "CNN Headline News" from 1998 and the german magazine broadcast "ZDF Auslandsjournal" from 2002. In "CNN Headline News" we expect three frequently used types of presentations (see Fig. 2 for examples): Main anchor centered (a), main anchor with image on the right (b), and financial news presenter (c). We therefore cluster using four classes, three for the presentation types, and one for all other frames. For "ZDF Auslandsjournal" we use two classes, one for the main presentation (see Fig. 2 (d) as an example), and one for all other frames.

Figure 3 shows the results of our algorithm compared to the manually annotated ground truth. Table 1 lists the error rate. The second column shows the total amount of false classified frames. The third column shows the amount of false classified frames in relation to the total number of frames that belong to one presentation type. The latter measure is shown because the number of frames not belonging to any presentation type is comparatively large. Note that there is only one presentation (at the end of the third video) that was not detected at all, and just one presentation (in the beginning of the first video) that was mistaken for another presentation type. The other errors are mainly due to single missed frames, probably caused by a wrong face detection result.

Figure 4 shows example frames from the detected presentations, one for each type and video. Note that a model for each presentation type would be difficult to create because of varying setting, clothing, and camera position between the different videos. It would probably at least require some supervision, which means a considerable effort for a human annotator.

Fig. 2. Examples of frequent presentations in "CNN Headline News" (a), (b), (c) and "ZDF Auslandsjournal" (d)

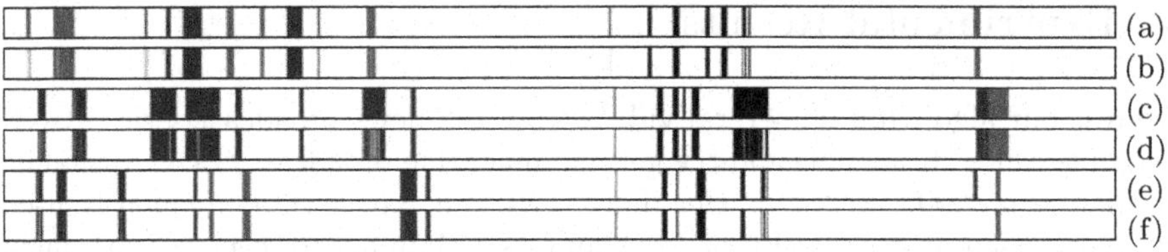

Fig. 3. Ground truth (a, c, e) and results of our algorithm (b, d, f) applied to three instances of the news broadcast series "CNN Headline News". The three identified types of presentations are shown in red (main anchor centered), blue (main anchor with image on the right), and black (financial news presenter), respectively.

Table 1. Error rate for three test videos from "CNN Headline News"

Video	Total error	Error regarding presentations only
1	1.37%	10.85%
2	1.18%	6.22%
3	0.73%	8.20%

The magazine "ZDF Auslandsjournal" just contains one presentation type that occurs often enough to be identified as a class. All three presentations of that type were correctly detected, Fig. 5 shows example frames from these presentations.

Fig. 4. Examples for each presentation type found by the algorithm. Each row corresponds to one video of "CNN Headline News". Each column corresponds to one identified presentation type.

Fig. 5. Examples for each presentation found in the video from "ZDF Auslandsjournal"

4   Conclusions and Outlook

We have presented a method for detection of frequently occurring patterns in videos and successfully applied it to the problem of anchor shot detection. The method works fully automatically and just needs as input the number of expected presentation types. No examples are required.

A suggestion to further reduce the error rate is to incorporate some kind of temporal constraint to account for the single misclassified frames inside a presentation. It may also be possible to find missed presentations by looking for frames that are similar to examples from the automatically identified classes.

Another extension of our method could be to create an inter-video similarity matrix to find sequences occurring in several videos but not frequently enough in one video to be clustered into one class. This includes, e.g., introduction sequences, weather maps, etc.

Acknowledgement

This work was partly supported by the research project AVAnTA [7] which is funded by the German Research Foundation (DFG) within the strategic research initiative No. 1041 "3D2 - Distributed Processing and Delivery of Digital Document".

References

1. Swanberg, D., Shu, C.F., Jain, R.: Knowledge guided parsing in video databases. In: Proceedings of the IS-T/SPIE Conference on Storage and Retrieval for Image and Video Databases. Volume 1908., San Jose, CA, USA (1993) 13–24
2. Hauptmann, A., Baron, R., Chen, M.Y., Christel, M., Duygulu, P., Huang, C., Jin, R., W.-H.Lin, Ng, T., Moraveji, N., Papernick, N., Snoek, C., Tzanetakis, G., Yang, J., Yang, R., Wactlar, H.: Informedia at TRECVID 2003: Analyzing and searching broadcast news video. In: Proceedings of the 12th Text Retrieval Conference (TREC). (2003)
3. Wang, W., Gao, W.: A fast anchor shot detection algorithm on compressed video. In: IEEE Pacific Rim Conference on Multimedia. (2001) 873–878
4. Kobla, V., Doermann, D.S., Faloutsos, C.: Videotrails : Representing and visualizing structure in video sequences. In: ACM Multimedia. (1997) 335–346
5. Huang, J., Zabih, R.: Combining color and spatial information for content-based image retrieval. In: Proceedings of ECDL 1998. (1998)
6. Lienhart, R., Maydt, J.: An extended set of haar-like features for rapid object detection. In: Proceedings of ICIP 2002. Volume 1. (2002) 900–903
7. Miene, A., Herzog, O.: AVAnTA - Automatische Video Analyse und textuelle Annotation. it + ti Informationstechnik und Technische Informatik **42** (2000) 24 – 27

Spam Detection Using Character N-Grams

Ioannis Kanaris[1], Konstantinos Kanaris[2], and Efstathios Stamatatos[1]

[1] Dept. of Information and Communication Systems Eng.,
University of the Aegean,
83200 – Karlovassi, Greece
stamatatos@aegean.gr
[2] Dept. of Mathematics,
University of the Aegean,
83200 – Karlovassi, Greece

Abstract. This paper presents a content-based approach to spam detection based on low-level information. Instead of the traditional 'bag of words' representation, we use a 'bag of character *n*-grams' representation which avoids the sparse data problem that arises in *n*-grams on the word-level. Moreover, it is language-independent and does not require any lemmatizer or 'deep' text preprocessing. Based on experiments on Ling-Spam corpus we evaluate the proposed representation in combination with support vector machines. Both binary and term-frequency representations achieve high precision rates while maintaining recall on equally high level, which is a crucial factor for anti-spam filters, a cost sensitive application.

1 Introduction

Nowadays, e-mail is one of the cheapest and fastest available means of communication. However, a major problem of any internet user is the increasing number of unsolicited commercial e-mail, or *spam*. Spam messages waste both valuable time of the users and important bandwidth of internet connections. Moreover, they are usually associated with annoying material (e.g. pornographic site advertisements) or the distribution of computer viruses. Hence, there is an increasing need for effective *anti-spam filters* that either automate the detection and removal of spam messages or inform the user of potential spam messages.

Early spam filters were based on blacklists of known spammers and handcrafted rules for detecting typical spam phrases (e.g., 'free pics'). The development of such filters is a time-consuming procedure. Moreover, they can easily be fooled by using forged e-mail addresses or variations of known phrases that is still readable for a human (e.g., f*r*e*e.). Hence, new rules have to be incorporated continuously to maintain the effectiveness of the filter.

Recent advances in applying machine learning techniques to text categorization [1] inspired researchers to develop content-based spam filters. In more detail, a collection of both known spam and legitimate (non-spam) messages is used by a supervised learning algorithm (e.g., decision trees, support vector machines, etc.) to develop a model for automatically classifying new, unseen messages to one of these two

G. Antoniou et al. (Eds.): SETN 2006, LNAI 3955, pp. 95–104, 2006.
© Springer-Verlag Berlin Heidelberg 2006

categories. That way, it is easy to develop personalized filters suitable for either a specific user or a mailing list moderator.

Spam detection is not a typical text categorization task since it has some intriguing characteristics. In particular, both spam and legitimate messages can cover a variety of topics and genres. In other words, both classes are not homogeneous. Moreover, the length of e-mail messages varies from a couple of text lines to dozens of text lines. In addition, the message may contain grammatical errors and strange abbreviations (sometimes inspired by spammers in order to fool spam filters). Therefore, the learning model should be robust in such conditions. Furthermore, besides the content of the body of the e-mail messages, useful information can be found in e-mail address, attachments etc. Such additional information can considerably assist the effectiveness of spam filters [2]. Last, but not least, spam detection is a cost sensitive procedure. In the case of a fully-automated spam filter, the cost of characterizing a legitimate message as spam is much higher than letting a few spam messages pass. This fact of crucial importance should be considered in evaluating spam detection approaches.

All supervised learning algorithms require a suitable representation of the messages, usually in the form of an attribute vector. So far, the vast majority of machine learning approaches to spam detection use the *bag of words* representation, that is, each message is considered as a set of words that occur a certain number of times [2, 3, 4, 5]. Putting it another way, the context information for a word is not taken into account. The word-based text representations require a tokenizer (to split the message into tokens) and usually a lemmatizer (to reduce the set of words). A common practice of spammers is to attempt to confuse tokenizers, using structures such as 'f.r.e.e.', 'f-r-e-e', 'f r e e', etc. The use of a lemmatizer is language-dependent procedure. There is no effective lemmatizers available for any natural language, especially for morphologically rich languages. On the other hand, word n-grams, i.e., contiguous sequences of n words, have also been examined [6]. Such approaches attempt to take advantage of phrasal information (e.g., 'buy now'), that distinguish spam from legitimate messages. However, word n-grams considerably increase the dimensionality of the problem and the results so far are not encouraging.

In this paper, we focus on a different but simple text representation. In particular, each message is considered as a *bag of character n-grams*, that is n contiguous characters. For example, the character 4-grams of the beginning of this paragraph would be: 'In t', 'n th', ' thi', 'this', 'his ', 'is p', 's pa', ' pap', 'pape', 'aper', etc. Character n-grams are able to capture information on various levels: lexical ('the ', 'free'), word-class ('ed ', 'ing '), structural ('!!!', 'f.r.'). In addition, they are robust to grammatical errors and strange usage of abbreviations, punctuation marks etc. The bag of character n-grams representation is language-independent and does not require any text preprocessing (tokenizer, lemmatizer, or other 'deep' NLP tools). It has already been used in several tasks including language identification [7], authorship attribution [8], and topic-based text categorization [9] with remarkable results in comparison to word-based representations.

An important characteristic of the n-grams on the character-level is that it avoids (at least to a great extent) the problem of sparse data that arises when using n-grams on the word level. That is, there is much less character combinations than word combinations, therefore, less n-grams will have zero frequency. On the other hand, the proposed representation still produces a considerably larger feature set in comparison with traditional bag of words representations. Therefore, learning algorithms able to deal with high dimensional spaces should be used. Support Vector Machines (SVM) is a supervised learning algorithm based on the *structural risk minimization* principle [10]. One of the most remarkable properties of SVMs is that their learning ability is independent of the feature space dimensionality, because they measure the complexity of the hypotheses based on the margin with which they separate the data, instead of the features. The application of SVMs to text categorization tasks [11] has shown the effectiveness of this approach when dealing with high dimensional data.

In this paper, we propose a content-based spam detection approach based on a bag of character *n*-grams representation and a SVM. No extra information coming from, e-mail address of the sender, attachments etc. is taken into account. Experiments on the publicly available *Ling-Spam* benchmark corpus provide evidence that our approach achieve high spam precision results while maintaining spam recall on equally-high level. Given a cost sensitive evaluation setting, we show that the proposed approach performs better than previous word-based methods.

The rest of this paper is organized as follows: Section 2 includes related work on spam detection. Section 3 describes our approach and Section 4 contains the performed experiments. Finally, section 5 summarizes the conclusions drawn from this study and indicates future work directions.

2 Related Work

Probably the first study employing machine learning methods for spam filtering was published in 1998 [2]. A Bayesian classifier was trained on manually categorized legitimate and spam messages and its performance on unseen cases was remarkable. Since then, several machine learning algorithms have been tested on this task, including boosting decision trees and support vector machines [5], memory-based algorithms [4], and ensembles of classifiers based on stacking [12].

On the other hand, a number of text representations have been proposed dealing mainly with word tokens and inspired from information retrieval. One common method is to use binary attributes corresponding to word occurrence [2, 4]. Alternative methods include word (term) frequencies [6], tf-idf [5], and word-position-based attributes [13]. The dimensionality of the resulting attribute vectors is usually reduced by removing attributes that correspond to words occurring only a few times. Recent work [13] has showed that the removal of the most frequent words (like 'and', 'to' etc.) considerably improves the classification accuracy. Another common practice is to use a lemmatizer [3] for converting each word-type to its lemma ('copies' becomes 'copy'). Naturally, the performance of the lemmatizer affects the accuracy of the filter and makes the method language-dependent. Finally, the dimensionality of the attribute vector can be further reduced by applying a feature selection method [14] that ranks the attributes according to their significance in distinguishing among the two classes. Only a predefined number of top ranked attributes are, then, used in the learning model.

In addition, word *n*-grams have also been proposed [6, 13] but, so far, the results are not encouraging. Although such a representation captures phrasal information,

sometimes particularly crucial, the dimensionality of the problem increases significantly. Moreover, the sparse data problem arises since there are many word combinations with low frequency of occurrence.

A couple of recent studies attempt to utilize a character-level representation of e-
mail messages. In [15] a suffix-tree approach is described which outperforms a traditional Bayesian classifier that is based on a bag of words representation. On the other
hand, a representation based on the combination of character 2-grams and 3-grams is
proposed in [16]. However, preliminary results in an e-mail categorization task
(where many message classes are available) show that approaches based on word-
based representations perform slightly better.

Research in spam detection was considerably assisted by publicly available
benchmark corpora, so that different approaches to be evaluated on the same testing
ground. Nowadays, there are several such benchmark corpora that come from either
mailing list messages, hence avoiding privacy issues of legitimate messages, (e.g.,
Ling-Spam[1]) or the mailboxes of specific users (e.g., SpamAssasin[2]).

3   Our Approach

First, for a given n, we extract the L most frequent character n-grams of the training
corpus. Let $<g_1, g_2, ..., g_L>$ be the ordered list (in decreasing frequency) of the most
frequent n-grams of the training corpus. Then, each message is represented as a vector of length L $<x_1, x_2, ..., x_L>$, where x_i depends on g_i. In more detail, we examine
two representations:

Binary: The value of x_i may be 1 (if g_i is included at least once in the message) or 0
(if g_i is not included in the message).
Term Frequency (TF): The value of x_i corresponds to the frequency of occurrence
(normalized by the message length) of g_i in the message.

The produced vectors can be arbitrarily long. On one hand, if L is chosen too short,
the messages are not represented adequately. On the other hand, if L is chosen too
long the dimensionality of the problem increases significantly. In the experiments
described in the next section, L was set to 4,000. A feature selection method can then
be applied to the resulting vectors, so that only the most significant attributes contribute to the classification model. A feature selection method that proved to be quite
effective for text categorization tasks is *information gain* [14]. The information gain
of a feature x_i is defined as an expected reduction in entropy by taking x_i as given:

$$IG(C, x_i) = H(C) - H(C \mid x_i) \qquad (1)$$

where C denotes the class of the message ($C \in \{spam, legitimate\}$) and $H(C)$ is the
entropy of C. In other words, $IG(C, x_i)$ is the information gained by knowing x_i. Information gain helps us to sort the features according to their significance in distinguishing between spam and legitimate messages. Only the first m most significant
attributes are, then, taken into account.

---

[1] Available at: http://www.aueb.gr/users/ion/data/lingspam_public.tar.gz
[2] Available at: http://spamassasin.org/publiccorpus/

The produced vectors (of length m) of the training set are used to train a SVM classifier. The Weka [18] implementation of SVM was used (default parameters were set in all reported experiments).

4 Experiments

4.1 Benchmark Corpus

The corpus used in this paper is Ling-Spam consisting of 2,893 emails, 481 spam messages and 2,412 legitimate messages taken from postings of a mailing list about linguistics. This corpus has a relatively low spam rate (16%) and the legitimate messages are not as heterogeneous as the messages found in the personal inbox of a specific user. However, it has already been used in previous studies [3, 4, 15] and comparison of our results with previous word-based methods is feasible. Moreover, it provides evidence about the effectiveness of our approach as assistance to mailing list moderators.

The bare version of this corpus was used (no lemmatizing or stop-word removal was performed) so that to be able to extract accurate character n-gram frequencies. Unfortunately, this corpus was already converted to lower case, so it was not possible to explore the significance of upper case characters.

In the experiments described below, a ten-fold cross-validation procedure was followed. That is, the entire corpus was divided into ten equal parts, in each fold a different part is used as test set and the remaining parts as training set. Final results come from averaging the results of each fold.

4.2 Evaluation Measures

Two well known measures from information retrieval community, *recall* and *precision*, can describe in detail the effectiveness of a spam detection approach. In more detail, given that $n_{S \to S}$ is the amount of spam messages correctly recognized, $n_{S \to L}$ is the amount of spam messages incorrectly categorized as legitimate, and $n_{L \to S}$ is the amount of legitimate messages incorrectly classified as spam, then, spam recall and spam precision can be defined as follows:

$$\text{Spam Recall} = \frac{n_{S \to S}}{n_{S \to S} + n_{S \to L}} \tag{2}$$

$$\text{Spam Precision} = \frac{n_{S \to S}}{n_{S \to S} + n_{L \to S}} \tag{3}$$

In intuitive terms, spam recall is an indication of filter effectiveness (the higher the recall, the less spam messages pass) while spam precision is an indication of filter safety (the higher the precision, the less legitimate messages blocked).

However, spam detection is a cost sensitive classification task. So, it is much worse to misclassify a legitimate message as spam than vice versa. Therefore, we need an evaluation measure that incorporates an indication of this cost. A cost factor λ is assigned to each legitimate message, that is, each legitimate message is considered as λ messages [3, 4]. In other words, if a legitimate message is misclassified, λ errors occur. A cost-sensitive evaluation measure, the *Total Cost Ratio* (TCR) can, then, be defined [3, 4] as follows:

$$\text{TCR} = \frac{n_{S \to S} + n_{S \to L}}{\lambda \cdot n_{L \to S} + n_{S \to L}} \tag{4}$$

The higher the TCR, the better the performance of the approach. In addition, if TCR is lower than 1, then the filter should not be used (the cost of blocking legitimate messages is too high). To be in accordance with previous studies, three cost scenarios were examined:

Low cost scenario (λ=1): This corresponds to an anti-spam filter that lets a message classified as spam to reach the mailbox of the receiver along with a warning that the message is probably spam.
Medium cost scenario (λ=9): This corresponds to an anti-spam filter that blocks a message classified as spam and the sender is informed to resend the message.
High cost scenario (λ=999): This corresponds to a fully-automated filter that deletes a message classified as spam without notifying either the receiver or the sender.

4.3 Results

Three sets of experiments were performed based on character 3-gram, 4-gram, and 5-gram representations, respectively. In all three cases, both binary and TF attributes were examined. Moreover, different values of the *m* attributes left after the feature selection procedure were tested (*m* starts from 250 and then varies from 500 to 4000 by 500).

The results of the application of our approach to Ling-Spam are shown in Fig. 1. As can be seen, for binary attributes, 4-grams seems to provide the more reliable representation (for *m*>2000). On the other hand, for TF attributes there is no clear winner. More significantly, binary attributes seem to provide better spam precision results while TF attributes are better in terms of spam recall. In most cases, spam recall was higher than 97% while, at the same time, spam recall was higher than 98%. Moreover, a few thousands of features are required to get these results. This is in contrast to previous word-based approaches that deal with limited amount (a few hundreds) of attributes. This provides another evidence that SVM can effectively cope with high dimensional data.

The results of the cost-sensitive evaluation are shown in Fig. 2. In particular, TCR values for 3-grams, 4-grams, and 5-grams are given for varying number of attributes. Results are given for both binary and TF attributes as well as the three evaluation scenarios (λ=1, 9, and 999, respectively). As can be seen, in all three scenarios, a representation based on character 4-grams with binary attributes provides the best results. This stands for a relatively high number of attributes (*m*>2500). For λ=1, and λ=9 the TCR results are well above 1 indicating the effectiveness of the filter. On the other hand, for λ=999, the TCR results are less than 1 indicating that the filter should not be used at all. However, it is difficult for this scenario to be used in practice.

Table 1 shows a comparison of the proposed approach with previously published results on the same corpus in terms of spam recall, spam precision, and TCR values.

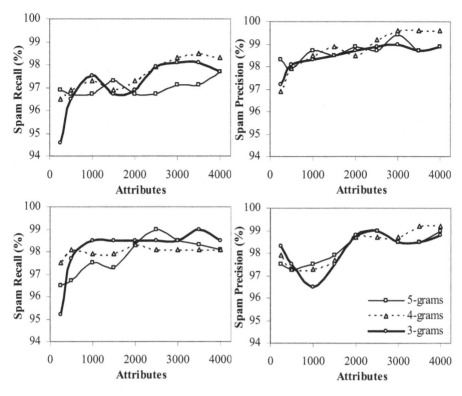

Fig. 1. Spam recall and spam precision of the proposed approach based on character 3-grams, 4-grams, and 5-grams and varying number of attributes. Top: binary attributes. Bottom: TF attributes.

In more detail, best results achieved by three methods are reported: a Naïve Bayes (NB) classifier [3], a Memory-Based Learner (MBL) [4], and a Stacked Generalization approach (SG) [12] using word-based features and a Suffix Tree (ST) [15] approach based on character-level information. The number of attributes that correspond to the best results of each method is also given. It should be noted that the results for the ST approach are referred to a sub-corpus of Ling-Spam with a proportion of spam to legitimate messages approximately equal to the entire Ling-Spam corpus (200 spam and 1,000 legitimate messages). Moreover, no results were reported for the SG approach based on the high cost scenario.

As concerns the TCR, the proposed approach is by far more effective than word-based approaches for the low and medium cost scenarios. This is due to the fact that it manages to achieve high spam recall while maintaining spam precision on equally-high level. ST is also quite competitive. This provides extra evidence that character-based representations are better able to capture the characteristics of spam messages. On the other hand, the proposed approach failed to produce a TCR value greater than 1 for the high cost scenario. That is because the precision failed to be 100%. It must

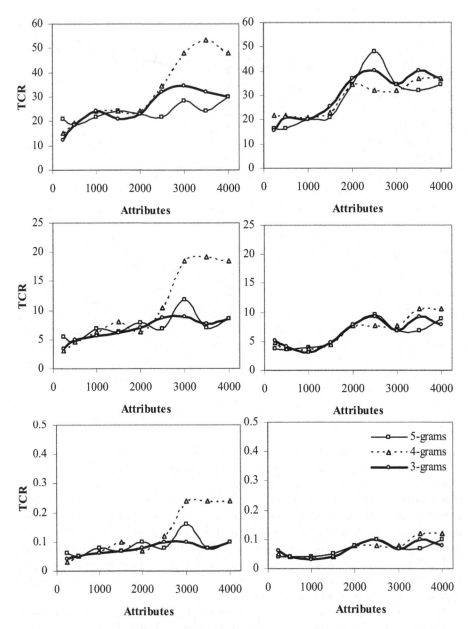

Fig. 2. Results of cost-sensitive evaluation. TCR values for λ=1(top), λ=9 (middle), and λ=999 (bottom) and varying number of attributes and *n*-gram length. Left column: binary attributes. Right column: TF attributes.

be underlined that previous studies [3, 4] show that TCR is not stable for the high cost scenario and it is common for TCR to exceed 1 only for very specific settings. Hence, it is not yet feasible to construct a practical filter based on this scenario.

Table 1. Comparison cost-sensitive evaluation (λ=1, 9, and 999) of the proposed approach with previously published results on Ling-Spam. Best reported results for spam recall, spam precision, and TCR are given. ST results refer to a sub-corpus of Ling-Spam.

Approach	λ	Attributes	Recall	Precision	TCR
NB	1	100	82.35%	99.02%	5.41
MBL	1	600	88.60%	97.39%	7.81
SG	1	300	89.60%	98.70%	8.60
ST	1	-	97.22%	100%	35.97
Proposed	1	3,500	98.50%	99.60%	52.75
NB	9	100	77.57%	99.45%	3.82
MBL	9	700	81.93%	98.79%	3.64
SG	9	100	84.80%	98.80%	4.08
ST	9	-	98.89%	98.89%	9.01
Proposed	9	3,500	98.50%	99.60%	19.76
NB	999	300	63.67%	100%	2.86
MBL	999	600	59.91%	100%	2.49
ST	999	-	97.78%	100%	45.04
Proposed	999	3,500	98.50%	99.60%	0.25

5   Conclusions

In this paper we presented a content-based approach to spam detection. In contrast to the majority of previous studies, character-level information is used to represent the messages. The performed experiments indicate that a character n-gram representation in combination with a support vector classifier is an effective approach for anti-spam filters. The presented results show that the proposed method considerably improves the best reported results on the same corpus for two out of three cost-sensitive scenarios. The amount of attributes required for achieving that performance is considerably higher in comparison to word-based approaches. On the other hand, the proposed method failed to be competitive in the framework of a fully-automated filter (λ=999). However, that scenario does not yet correspond to systems of every-day use.

A publicly available corpus (Ling-Spam) was used for evaluating our approach. Since the legitimate messages of this corpus include mailing list messages about a specific topic (linguistics), they are less heterogeneous than the messages found in the inbox of a particular user. Therefore, the experimental results suggest the application of the proposed method to anti-spam filters assisting mainly mailing list moderators. However, more extensive evaluation on corpora coming from personal user inboxes is needed.

The presented experiments were based on a predefined n-gram length (n=3, 4, or 5) and all messages were converted to lower case. A promising future work direction would be the combination of variable-length n-grams and the distinction between lower case and upper case n-grams.

References

1. Sebastiani, F.: Machine Learning in Automated Text Categorization. ACM Computing Surveys, 34(1) (2002) 1–47
2. Sahami M., Dumais S., Heckerman D., Horvitz E.: A Bayesian Approach to Filtering Junk E-mail. In Proc. of AAAI Workshop on Learning for Text Categorization (1998).
3. Androutsopoulos I., Koutsias J., Chandrinos K.V., Paliouras G., Spyropoulos C.D.: An Evaluation of Naive Bayesian Anti-Spam Filtering. In Potamias, G., Moustakis, V. and van Someren, M. (Eds.), Proc. of the Workshop on Machine Learning in the New Information Age, 11th European Conference on Machine Learning (2000) 9-17
4. Sakkis, G. , Androutsopoulos I., Paliouras G., Karkaletsis V., Spyropoulos C.D., Stamatopoulos P.: A Memory-Based Approach to Anti-Spam Filtering for Mailing Lists. Information Retrieval, 6(1) (2003) 49-73
5. Drucker, H., Wu, D., Vapnik, V.: Support Vector Machines for Spam Categorization. IEEE Trans Neural Network, 10 (1999) 1048-1054
6. Androutsopoulos I., Paliouras G.. Michelakis E.: Learning to Filter Unsolicited Commercial E-Mail. Technical report 2004/2, NCSR "Demokritos" (2004)
7. Cavnar, W., Trenkle, J.: N-gram-based text categorization. In Proc. 3rd Int'l Symposium on Document Analysis and Information Retrieval (1994) 161-169
8. Keselj, V., Peng, F., Cercone, N., Thomas, C.: N-gram-based Author Profiles for Authorship Attribution. In Proc. of the Conference Pacific Assoc. Comp. Linguistics (2003)
9. Lodhi, H., Saunders, C., Shawe-Taylor, J., Cristianini, N., Watkins, C.: Text Classification Using String Kernels The Journal of Machine Learning Research, 2 (2002) 419 – 444
10. Vapnik V.: The Nature of Statistical Learning Theory. Springer, New York (1995).
11. Joachims T.: Text Categorization with Support Vector Machines: Learning with Many Relevant Features. In Proc. of the European Conference on Machine Learning (1998)
12. Sakkis G., Androutsopoulos I., Paliouras G., Karkaletsis V., Spyropoulos C.D., Stamatopoulos P.: Stacking Classifiers for Anti-Spam Filtering of E-Mail. In Proc. of 6th Conf. Empirical Methods in Natural Language Processing (2001) 44-50
13. Hovold J.: Naive Bayes Spam Filtering Using Word-Position-Based Attributes. In Proc. of the Second Conference on Email and Anti-Spam (2005)
14. Yang, Y., Petersen, J.O.: A Comparative Study on Feature Selection in Text Categorization. In Proc. of the 14th Int. Conference on Machine Learning (1997) 412-420
15. Pampapathi, R., Mirkin, B., Levene, M.: A Suffix Tree Approach to Text Categorisation Applied to Spam Filtering. http://arxiv.org/abs/cs.AI/0503030
16. Berger, H., Koehle, M., Merkl, D.: On the Impact of Document Representation on Classifier Performance in e-Mail Categorization. Proc. of the 4th International Conference on Information Systems Technology and its Applications (2005) 19-30
17. Witten I.H., Frank E.: Data Mining: Practical Machine Learning Tools with Java Implementations. Morgan Kaufmann, San Francisco (2000)

Improved Wind Power Forecasting Using a Combined Neuro-fuzzy and Artificial Neural Network Model

Yiannis A. Katsigiannis[1], Antonis G. Tsikalakis[2],
Pavlos S. Georgilakis[1], and Nikos D. Hatziargyriou[2]

[1] Department of Production Engineering and Management, Technical University of Crete,
University Campus, Kounoupidiana, Chania, Greece
{katsigiannis, pgeorg}@dpem.tuc.gr
[2] School of Electrical and Computer Engineering, National Technical University of Athens,
Athens, Greece
{atsikal, nh}@power.ece.ntua.gr

Abstract. The intermittent nature of the wind creates significant uncertainty in the operation of power systems with increased wind power penetration. Considerable efforts have been made for the accurate prediction of the wind power using either statistical or physical models. In this paper, a method based on Artificial Neural Network (ANN) is proposed in order to improve the predictions of an existing neuro-fuzzy wind power forecasting model taking into account the evaluation results from the use of this wind power forecasting tool. Thus, an improved wind power forecasting is achieved and a better estimation of the confidence interval of the proposed model is provided.

Keywords: Artificial neural networks, wind power forecasting, prediction error.

1 Introduction

Wind power is one of the dominant Renewable Energy Sources (RES) since, by the end of 2004, over 47 GW have been installed worldwide, 34 GW of which in Europe [1]. In Greece, the installed wind power capacity is 567 MW, 164.5 MW of which in the autonomous power systems of Greek islands [2]. The intermittent nature of wind power production forces the power systems operators maintaining significant percentage of spinning reserve to compensate for uncertainties in wind power product-ion. Sometimes, especially in autonomous power systems with increased wind power penetration, operators may even consider totally unreliable the wind power production leading the system to operate with excessive spinning reserve and thus increasing its operating cost.

In the past few years, there have been several studies on wind power forecasting. The simplest method of all, more suitable for shorter prediction horizon, is the persistence method, considering that the expected wind power production in the following few hours will be the same as the current hour. The accuracy of the persistence method is reduced as the prediction horizon is increased. Wind power forecasting methods include models based on statistical methods as presented in [3] and methods based on Artificial Neural Networks (ANN), e.g. Radial Basis Functions topology [4]

G. Antoniou et al. (Eds.): SETN 2006, LNAI 3955, pp. 105–115, 2006.
© Springer-Verlag Berlin Heidelberg 2006

or adaptive Fuzzy-Neural networks [5, 6]. Some efforts have been also made with time series and ARMA models, requiring however, transformation and standardization, given the non-Gaussian nature of the hourly wind speed distribution and the non-stationary nature of its daily evolution [7]. A more detailed literature overview of the developed wind power forecasting tools is described in [8]. Some of these methods use meteorological information, mainly wind speed, especially for longer period forecasts, provided by Numerical Weather Prediction (NWP) models like SKIRON and Hirlam.

The impact of improved wind forecasting tool with actual data for the last 4 months of 2001 has shown that improvement of wind forecasting errors has significant economic impact in the operation of the power system due to the reduction of spinning reserve requirements [9]. The reduction in the operating cost is about 1.8%-3.5% if a reliable forecast is used that allows the reduction of spinning reserve in the 50% of wind power production. The reduction in the operating cost is about 2.3%-5.3% if a reliable forecast is used that allows the reduction of spinning reserve in the 20% of wind power production. Therefore, the more reliable the wind power forecasting is, the more confident the operators of the power systems are for the wind power production forecast and thus, the spinning reserve requirements can be further reduced, leading to the reduction of the power system operating cost.

The developers of wind power forecasting models provide their end-users with the Mean Absolute Percentage Error (MAPE) index for their model expressed as a percentage of the installed wind power capacity. This index, however, does not give very much information neither about the performance of the wind power forecasting tool for different forecasting horizon nor about its performance for a variety of forecasted wind power values. Some wind power forecasting tools also provide as output the confidence interval of the wind power forecast based on the estimation of the weather stability and other parameters having to do with the forecasting model itself [10]. Such information helps the operators to estimate the range of the expected wind power production and thus the spinning reserve requirements to cope with the wind power production uncertainty.

In this paper, a method is proposed based on ANN, in order to improve the performance of an existing wind power forecasting tool. This method uses as inputs the outputs of the wind power forecasting model and trains the ANN using the results from the evaluation of the forecasting model. The output of the ANN is a new and improved wind power forecast. Moreover, an 85% confidence interval is provided to the operators for this improved wind power forecast.

The methodology followed to derive the improved wind power forecast is described in detail in Section 2. This methodology is applied to the wind power forecasting model developed within the MORE CARE framework [11, 12] that was executed off-line to produce wind power forecasts for a period with available meteorological data from SKIRON for the power system of Crete. Some information on the power system of Crete is provided in Section 3 concerning mainly the wind power. Section 4 presents results from the application of the proposed methodology to the power system of Crete evaluating the improved forecast obtained using as a criterion the change in the 85% interval and the MAPE. Conclusions are drawn in Section 5.

2   Improved Wind Power Forecasting

In this paper, an existing neuro-fuzzy wind power forecasting tool, considered as a black box, is combined with an ANN, whose general structure is shown in Fig. 1, in order to improve the accuracy of the wind power forecast.

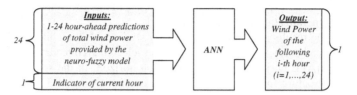

Fig. 1. General structure of the combined ANN and Neural –Fuzzy Network

The improved wind power forecasting methodology consists of the following 4 steps:

1. Creation of two independent Data Sets (DS) by off-line execution of the forecasting model,
2. Split of DS into Learning Set (LS) and Test Set (TS),
3. Creation and Training of the ANNs,
4. Evaluation of the ANN outputs and confidence interval derivation.

2.1   Preparation of the LS and TS

The DS for the ANN model is created as follows: The MORE CARE wind power prediction tool was run off-line for the last 4 months of 2001 providing forecasts for each hour at 24 hour steps. The next 24 hours forecasted values plus an indicator for the current hour are used as inputs for the DS, which consists of 663 time-series in our case study. This DS contains periods of various wind power production levels ranging from very low to very high wind power production.

To ensure more reliable results and to avoid confidence intervals with values below zero or above the wind power capacity, the DS is split into two major classes according to the forecasted values: the first one, with half the data contains values of 0-10 MW (DS1) and the second one with the rest available predictions has prediction values of 10-67.35 MW (DS2).

Each DS is split into a LS and TS. In our case, 2/3 of the data in each DS was used for training and 1/3 was used for the test. The TS data was used for estimating the confidence interval of the existing forecasting tool. Thus, an objective comparison with the same set of data can be performed.

2.2   Creation and Training of the ANNs

For each one of DS1 and DS2 and for each hour, an ANN has been developed, thus a total number of 48 ANNs has been used.

After the training procedure, the neural network is able to learn (generalize) the input-output relationship and thus to predict the wind power to any input vector outside the training set.However, good generalization depends on the network structure. In particular, small size networks are not able to approximate complicated input-output relationships. On the other hand, recent studies on learning versus generalization network capabilities including the VC dimension [13] indicate that an unnecessarily large network size heavily deteriorating generalization. In our approach, we adopt a back-propagation variant [14] in a constructive framework [15], which begins with a small size network and subsequently adds neurons to improve the network perform-ance. A validation data set has been also used during training to control learning with respect to the generalization ability of the network.

In Table 1, the results of different extensively studied ANN architectures for a va-riety of hour-ahead predictions are presented. The selected architecture is the one with the minimum MAPE during the whole prediction horizon. In the specific study, the optimal ANN structure for both classes was the one consisting of 3 hidden layers of 13 neurons each, namely 25-13-13-13-1. In Fig. 2, the performance of the selected ANN architecture for different number of epochs is examined as far as MAPE is con-cerned. According to this figure, the optimal number of epochs was 15.

Table 1. MAPE of TS in the 10-67.35 MW class for different ANN architectures

ANN architecture	MAPE of 10-67.35 MW class		
	1 hour ahead prediction	12 hour ahead prediction	24 hour ahead prediction
25-13-1	10.72%	12.68%	11.27%
25-25-1	10.05%	11.86%	10.74%
25-13-13-1	9.59%	12.06%	10.44%
25-25-25-1	10.01%	11.69%	10.41%
25-13-13-13-1	9.40%	11.66%	10.22%

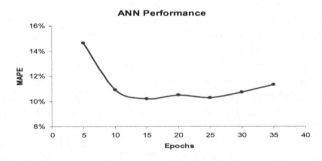

Fig. 2. Performance of the 25-13-13-13-1 ANN architecture for the MAPE estimation of the 24th hour ahead prediction

2.3 Evaluation of the ANN Output and Confidence Interval Derivation

The output of the ANN is the improved wind power prediction for each studied inter-val. In order to evaluate the performance of the ANN, the MAPE is calculated com-paring the outputs of the improved wind power forecast with the actual wind power production from the wind parks of Crete for the period of study; i.e. 4 last months of 2001. The MAPE index for the ANN is calculated as follows:

$$e_r = \left(\frac{P_f - P_a}{P_i} \right) \cdot 100\% \qquad (1)$$

$$MAPE = \frac{1}{N} \sum_{i=1}^{N} |e_r| \qquad (2)$$

where e_r is the wind power prediction error, P_f is the forecasted wind power provided by the ANN, P_a is the actual wind power, P_i is the total installed wind power capacity and N is the number of hours studied (for our application N=24). For the island of Crete, P_i=67.35 MW, for the year 2001. Negative values of e_r mean underestimation of the ANN output, while positive mean overestimation.

Overestimation of wind power, leads to lack of energy unless sufficient spinning reserve has been committed to the power system. Thus, the higher the overestimation of the forecasting model, the higher the spinning reserve that should be maintained, leading to more units to be committed for the same load and thus the higher the operating cost. On the other hand, underestimation of wind power has as an impact that the committed units operate in lower efficiency operating points increasing their operating cost.

After the evaluation of the improved wind power forecast tool is complete, an 85% confidence interval of the forecasting error is derived in order to help the operators to determine their spinning reserve policy as far as wind power forecast uncertainty is concerned.

3 Crete Power System

Crete is the largest isolated power network in Greece with significant wind power penetration around 10% of the annual island demand since 2000. The instantaneous wind power penetration has reached 39% during some valley hours in winter and early spring [9]. The installed wind power capacity on the island is currently 105.15 MW. There are also installed 690 MW of various thermal units, such as diesel, gas turbines, steam turbines and one combined cycle unit in three power plants.

Public Power Corporation (PPC) is the operator of this power system and is obliged to buy at specific price (90% of the retail low voltage price), the energy produced by the wind park installations. Thus, the improved wind power forecasting and the estimation of its confidence interval are significant, especially during low load periods, when slow response units, steam turbines and combined cycle units operate to avoid committing surplus units or not having enough units to compensate for unit loss.

In our study, data from the last 4 months of 2001 was used, when the installed wind power capacity was 67.35 MW.

4 Results

In Table 2, the MAPE for both the existing neuro-fuzzy wind power forecasting model and the proposed methodology are presented for the TS data. In all cases, especially in the 0-10 MW class, the proposed methodology offers much better results.

Table 2. Comparison of TS MAPE for the 0-10 MW class and for the 10-67.35 MW class for the existing wind power forecasting tool (neuro-fuzzy model) and the proposed model (ANN)

Estimation (Hours ahead)	0-10 MW class MAPE on test test		10-67.35 MW class MAPE on test test	
	Neuro-fuzzy model	Improved model (ANN)	Neuro-fuzzy model	Improved model (ANN)
1	19.10%	9.04%	18.10%	9.40%
2	21.70%	11.88%	15.38%	9.54%
3	20.74%	11.53%	16.71%	9.37%
4	21.93%	11.22%	16.70%	11.16%
5	22.27%	12.32%	15.41%	10.03%
6	21.07%	11.29%	15.43%	10.46%
7	23.40%	11.88%	15.63%	10.69%
8	25.58%	14.56%	15.36%	10.43%
9	20.82%	11.37%	16.64%	11.27%
10	21.53%	13.53%	18.53%	11.16%
11	21.46%	12.10%	16.94%	11.02%
12	24.44%	14.37%	17.52%	11.66%
13	23.79%	14.01%	15.30%	11.21%
14	23.14%	12.48%	15.45%	10.82%
15	23.49%	11.53%	16.59%	11.61%
16	24.01%	12.29%	17.12%	11.23%
17	28.10%	14.57%	17.68%	10.00%
18	24.20%	12.18%	17.00%	9.94%
19	22.54%	13.70%	15.48%	11.05%
20	23.67%	11.73%	15.53%	9.51%
21	23.30%	13.45%	17.41%	10.33%
22	23.16%	13.84%	16.46%	9.99%
23	22.40%	13.12%	19.44%	8.96%
24	24.32%	12.79%	17.52%	10.22%

The MAPE differences range from 8.00% (10th hour estimation) to 13.53% (17th hour estimation) for the 0-10 MW class and from 4.09% (13th hour estimation) to 10.48% (23rd hour estimation) for the 10-67.35 MW class.

In Tables 3 and 4, the 85% confidence intervals, expressed as 7.5% and 92.5% percentiles (ptl) on the test set for the two classes of wind power forecasting values are presented, according to both the outputs of the existing model and the proposed method, respectively.

The proposed methodology provides significant reduction to each confidence interval range and much smaller underestimated values, so the power system operator can estimate the wind power production more accurately avoiding committing more units than necessary. More specifically, in the 0-10 MW class, the existing model's lowest underestimating errors are always under -40%, while in the proposed model the corresponding values only once exceed -30%. In the 10-67.35 MW class, the underestimation error differences are smaller, but in almost every case are over 10%.

Table 3. 85% confidence interval (c.i.) for the estimated error of 0-10 MW class and 10-67.35 MW class of the wind power forecasting tool (neuro-fuzzy model)

Estimation (Hours ahead)	0-10 MW class		10-67.35 MW class	
	7.5% ptl	92.5% ptl	7.5% ptl	92.5% ptl
1	-41.80%	2.04%	-42.75%	14.80%
2	-46.52%	0.99%	-40.18%	15.96%
3	-42.52%	3.26%	-35.79%	14.87%
4	-46.38%	1.56%	-43.21%	13.47%
5	-48.88%	2.15%	-31.54%	20.46%
6	-42.88%	0.98%	-33.81%	17.85%
7	-50.01%	0.44%	-31.40%	20.88%
8	-50.09%	0.93%	-32.43%	13.35%
9	-44.91%	7.22%	-35.25%	17.70%
10	-48.35%	8.37%	-35.28%	19.20%
11	-48.08%	8.59%	-36.97%	21.60%
12	-52.55%	7.90%	-42.85%	19.36%
13	-50.71%	8.08%	-33.40%	16.28%
14	-48.77%	2.60%	-30.44%	26.17%
15	-52.14%	5.45%	-33.30%	22.94%
16	-50.47%	7.77%	-35.33%	23.81%
17	-54.43%	0.64%	-34.35%	25.29%
18	-53.52%	2.95%	-31.31%	26.49%
19	-49.90%	6.19%	-28.21%	23.93%
20	-51.27%	7.98%	-29.53%	24.03%
21	-49.34%	2.07%	-33.38%	26.60%
22	-50.36%	8.47%	-27.19%	32.02%
23	-51.51%	3.19%	-31.55%	27.59%
24	-53.64%	1.92%	-30.99%	30.92%

For both classes, smaller differences of the confidence intervals' largest overestimation values are observed, especially in the 0-10 MW class, where for some estimations the initial model gives slightly better results.

Figs. 3 and 4 provide the difference in the forecast and actual operation for specific values of the studied period for the existing neuro-fuzzy model and the proposed ANN model. For each case, the minimum and maximum value of the wind power is also displayed, as it results from the upper and lower boundary of the 85% confidence interval. The reference date is the 28/12/2001 and prediction time 12:00. This prediction time-series offers wide variation of the predicted values from the neuro-fuzzy model, the input data of the ANN model, ranging between 5.18 MW and 45.23 MW. Thus a more representative analysis of models' performance can be done. The selected time-series also provides acceptable number of data for both classes of wind power prediction of the initial model (8 data from the 0-10 MW class and 16 data from 10-67.35 MW class). The comparison of Figs. 3 and 4 proves that the performance of the proposed ANN is much better than the existing model, since the ANN wind power estimation is much more accurate, while its 85% confidence interval is significantly narrower.

Table 4. 85% confidence interval (c.i.) for the estimated error of 0-10 MW class and 10-67.35 MW class of the proposed ANN

Estimation	0-10 MW class		10-67.35 MW class	
(Hours ahead)	7.5% ptl	92.5% ptl	7.5% ptl	92.5% ptl
1	-13.12%	1.36%	-14.94%	6.64%
2	-21.88%	3.18%	-15.56%	10.57%
3	-9.50%	0.70%	-16.73%	6.25%
4	-14.83%	1.31%	-18.17%	4.00%
5	-15.91%	1.81%	-15.72%	8.64%
6	-20.91%	2.83%	-16.32%	6.84%
7	-25.95%	2.07%	-15.90%	6.88%
8	-33.77%	1.88%	-20.45%	9.11%
9	-20.40%	1.87%	-16.48%	10.23%
10	-16.93%	4.43%	-22.03%	6.50%
11	-21.77%	1.90%	-15.97%	9.65%
12	-25.00%	1.54%	-20.39%	7.32%
13	-20.07%	3.54%	-17.29%	9.60%
14	-21.21%	2.46%	-15.86%	12.14%
15	-18.18%	0.80%	-20.65%	13.39%
16	-20.30%	1.95%	-20.03%	9.82%
17	-27.83%	5.50%	-21.10%	8.88%
18	-19.05%	2.62%	-11.62%	8.42%
19	-19.19%	2.81%	-17.35%	10.46%
20	-19.20%	2.88%	-14.00%	8.46%
21	-15.55%	2.32%	-20.10%	8.01%
22	-20.42%	5.06%	-17.02%	8.36%
23	-19.44%	2.92%	-16.32%	6.40%
24	-28.20%	2.69%	-14.99%	12.34%

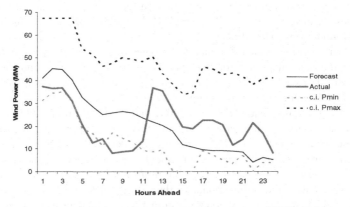

Fig. 3. Forecast versus actual wind power and min/max boundaries of 85% confidence intervals for the existing neuro-fuzzy model for the 28/12/2001 at 12:00

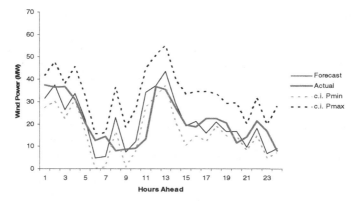

Fig. 4. Forecast versus actual wind power and min/max boundaries of 85% confidence intervals for the proposed ANN model for the 28/12/2001 at 12:00

The economic impact of the improvements of the wind power forecasting, especially for confidence interval, is due to the reduction of spinning reserve requirements to compensate for the wrong estimation of wind. It is considered that the spinning reserve requirements is given by the following equation:

$$Spin\_res = 0.1 \cdot load\_forec + conf\_interval \cdot wind\_power \tag{3}$$

where *conf_interval* is the 92.5% percentile (ptl) values used corresponding to the larger user-defined acceptable wind underestimation level, *load_forec* is the forecasted load and *wind_power* is the installed wind power capacity.

The impact of reduced spinning reserve is shown in Table 5 for two characteristic days corresponding to the two classes of the test sets and for different loading conditions. During Day 1, low loading, the wind power forecast never exceeded 10 MW, while during Day 2, high loading, the wind power forecast was always over 10 MW so the corresponding data should be used from Tables 3 and 4.

It can be seen that there are significant savings in the operating cost during medium to high wind power conditions during high load conditions reaching 1.00%. This is due to the fact that the more expensive gas turbines are committed for less time, or less of these units are required.

Table 5. Characteristic days used for indicating the impact of improved wind power confidence interval

Day	Total daily demand (MWh)	Average Wind Power Production (MW)	Characterization	Percentage Savings
Day 1	5197.4	1.3	Low Load, Low Wind Production	0.05%
Day 2	7396.5	26.6	High Load, Medium Wind Production	1.00%

5 Conclusions

This paper proposes a combined neuro-fuzzy and ANN model for wind power fore-casting. The output of an existing neuro-fuzzy wind power prediction tool is used as input to the proposed ANN structure. It is shown that the proposed ANN model ex-ploits the past performance of the neuro-fuzzy model and provides more accurate wind power forecasting values. More specifically, the proposed method offers signifi-cant improvements in all crucial information for power system operators, concerning wind power prediction and its uncertainty estimation, providing narrower confidence intervals for the predicted wind power. Thus the operator can very quickly and very accurately have improved wind power forecast with narrower confidence intervals based on the initial wind power forecast provided by the Neuro-fuzzy tool or any other wind power forecasting algorithm. Thus, the power systems operators have at their disposal much more accurate information on the expected wind power in the following few hours, that can be used as inputs for the economic scheduling functions of the power systems. Reduction of the uncertainty concerning wind power, especially for autonomous power systems helps in increasing the confidence of the power sys-tems operators on wind power and its further exploitation.

References

1. Web site of European Wind Energy Association (EWEA): On-line www.ewea.org
2. Hatziargyriou, N., Tsikalakis, A.G., Androutsos, A.: Status of Distributed Generation in the Greek Islands. Accepted for presentation at the 2006 Power Engineering Society General Meeting of IEEE, Montreal/Canada
3. Nielsen, T.S., Madsen, H.: Statistical Methods for Predicting Wind Power. Proc. of the European Wind Energy Conference, Dublin Ireland (October 1997) 755-758
4. Wang, X., Sideratos, G., Hatziargyriou, N., Tsoukalas, L.H.: Wind Speed Forecasting for Power System Operational Planning. 8th PMAPS 2004, Iowa (September 12–16 2004)
5. Kariniotakis, G., Stavrakakis, G.S., Nogaret, E.F.: Wind Power Forecasting Using Advanced Neural Network Models. IEEE Transactions on Energy Conversion, Vol. 11, No 4. (December 1996) 762-767
6. Kariniotakis, G.: Forecasting of Wind Parks Production by Dynamic Fuzzy Models with Optimal Generalisation Capacity. Proc. of the 12th ISAP 03, ISAP 03/032, Lemnos (September 2003)
7. Torres, J.L., Garcia, A., De Blas, M., De Francisco, A.: Forecast of Hourly Average Wind Speed with ARMA Models in Navarre (Spain). Solar Energy, Vol. 79. (2005) 65-77
8. Giebel, G., Brownsword, R., Kariniotakis, G.: The State of the Art in Short-Term Prediction of Wind Power: A Literature Overview. Deliverable D1.1 of ANEMOS project, available at: http://anemos.cma.fr
9. Hatziargyriou, N.D., Dimeas, A., Tsikalakis, A., Gigantidou, A., Thalassinakis, E.: Security and Economic Impacts of High Wind Power Penetration in Island Systems. 40th Cigre Session, Paris (August 2004)
10. Pinson, P., Kariniotakis, G.N.: Wind Power Forecasting Using Fuzzy Neural Networks Enhanced with On-line Prediction Risk Assessment. Proc. of 2003 IEEE PowerTech, Bologna, Italy

11. Hatziargyriou, N., et al.: MORE CARE Overview. Proc. of MedPower02, MED02/002, Athens (November 2002)
12. Kariniotakis, G., Mayer, D., Halliday, J.A., Dutton, A.G., Irving, A.D., Brownsword, R.A., Dokopoulos, P.S., Alexiadis, M.C.: Load, Wind and Hydro Power Forecasting Functions of the More-Care EMS System. Proc. of MedPower02
13. Kollias, S.: A Multiresolution Neural Network Approach to Invariant Image Recognition. Neurocomputing, Vol. 12. (1996) 35-57
14. Doulamis, A., Doulamis, N., Kollias, S.: Retrainable Neural Networks for Image Analysis and Classification. Proc.of IEEE Int. Conf. on Systems Man and Cybernetics, Orlando, USA (1997)
15. Kollias, S., Anastassiou, D.: An Adaptive Least Squares Algorithm for the Efficient Training of Artificial Neural Networks. IEEE Trans. on Circuits & Systems, Vol. 36. (1989) 1092-1101

A Long-Term Profit Seeking Strategy for Continuous Double Auctions in a Trading Agent Competition

Dionisis Kehagias[1,2], Panos Toulis[1], and Pericles Mitkas[1,2]

[1] Aristotle University of Thessaloniki,
Department of Electrical and Computer Engineering,
54 124, Thessaloniki, Greece
[2] Centre for Research and Technology Hellas,
Informatics and Telematics Institute,
57 001, Thermi, Greece
diok@iti.gr, ptoulis@olympus.ee.auth.gr, mitkas@eng.auth.gr

Abstract. This paper presents a new bidding strategy for continuous double auctions (CDA) designed for Mertacor, a successful trading agent, which won the first price in the "travel game" of Trading Agent Competition (TAC) for 2005. TAC provides a realistic benchmarking environment in which various travel commodities are offered in simultaneous online auctions. Among these, entertainment tickets are traded in CDA. The latter, represent the most dynamic part of the TAC game, in which agents are both sellers and buyers. In a CDA many uncertainty factors are introduced, because prices are constantly changing during the game and price fluctuations are hard to be predicted. In order to deal with these factors of uncertainty we have designed a strategy based on achieving a pre-defined long-term profit. This preserves the bidding attitude of our agent and shows flexibility in changes of the environment. We finally present and discuss the results of TAC-05, as well as an analysis of agents performance in the entertainment auctions.

1 Introduction

The advent of Internet and accompanying networking infrastructures has significantly contributed to the development of electronic commerce today. As more computational and networking resources become available to the users, electronic transactions move to more sophisticated ways of process automation. Autonomous agents that participate in online trading environments with the goal to increase revenue for humans, represent such an advanced paradigm of process automation. Designing effective bidding strategies for agents that participate in uncertain competitive auction environments, is typically based on the optimization of an objective function of the profit or savings they materialize. As uncertainty increases in the environment, the development of appropriate heuristics becomes a compulsory task for trading agent design. The measurement of agents' performance is commonly provided by a benchmark platform, which encounters the clients' utility accomplished, as well as the expenditure costs. The international Trading Agent Competition (TAC) [10] provides one of the most popular and realistic benchmark environments where a number of autonomous trading agents compete to each other in order to assembly travel packages on

G. Antoniou et al. (Eds.): SETN 2006, LNAI 3955, pp. 116–126, 2006.
© Springer-Verlag Berlin Heidelberg 2006

behalf of a number of clients. Goods are procured in multiple online simultaneous and interrelated auctions of different types. The "travel" (or "classic") game scenario of TAC involves three types of such auctions; a) continuous one-sided that sell flight tickets, b) ascending multi-unit auctions for booking hotel rooms, and c) continuous double auctions (CDA) for entertainment tickets.

In this paper we present *Mertacor*, an agent that ended up first in the finals of TAC for 2005 (TAC-05). In particular, we describe the bidding strategy developed for entertainment auctions, providing at the same time a generic bidding framework for the CDA environment. The latter is the most common variation of double auctions [2] as it is applied in many real life cases, the most typical of which is the stock market. In simple double auctions sellers advertise their offered services or items at prices called asks, while buyers respond, according to their preferences over the available auctioned resources, by posting their desired buying prices called bids. A CDA supports transactions between buyers and sellers that may occur continuously over a specific trading period. In this auction setup, buyers and sellers are allowed to continuously update or even withdraw their bids or asks at any time throughout the trading period [5]. We especially focus on the CDA bidding component of Mertacor, because this is the most generic and non game-specific part of its compound bidding strategy. Thus, this paper's main contribution is the introduction of a new bidding strategy for CDA, realized in the form of entertainment auctions in the context of TAC.

The paper is structured as follows. First, in Section 2 we give an overview of the trading simulation environment on which the developed methodologies are applied. Section 3 reviews related work in trading agent design. Next, Section 4, describes the details of the bidding strategy for CDA deployed by our agent. In Section 5 we present an analysis of the agent performance results taken from TAC-05 environment. Finally, Section 6 concludes the paper.

2   The Trading Agent Competition

The TAC (http://www.sics.se/tac) provides a competitive trading environment in which each participating agent operates with the goal of assembling travel packages on behalf of eight clients. Each package refers to a 5-day period travel and consists of a round-trip flight, a hotel reservation and tickets for three different entertainment events. The clients have separate preferences over the arrival and departure dates, the type of hotel and entertainment events they wish to visit, which are randomly assigned to each client at the beginning of the game. The objective of each agent is to maximize the total satisfaction of its clients. In the TAC simulation environment, all three kinds of commodities (flights, hotels and entertainment tickets) are sold in simultaneous online interrelated auctions of three different types, running over a game, which lasts for 9 minutes. These are described in the following.

Flight auctions: There is only one airline company that sells tickets in single seller continuous one-sided auctions, which close at the end of the game. Each auction sells tickets for a particular day and direction, whereas an unlimited number of seats are available. Prices in flight auctions are updated according to a random walk process.

Hotel auctions: There are two hotels in which clients can stay between the arrival and departure dates. The one is more preferable than the other, thus it is expected to be more expensive. Hotel rooms are traded in standard ascending multi-unit 16th price English auctions, which close at randomly determined times in the last 8 minutes of the game. In each auction 16 rooms are offered for each combination of hotel and night.

Entertainment auctions: Entertainment tickets are traded in continuous double auctions, which are held between the participants during the game. Each agent holds a randomly chosen number of tickets from the beginning of the game and can be either a buyer or a seller. Entertainment ticket auctions clear continuously. On clearing, bids match immediately. A bid that does not completely match remains standing in the auction.

The score that the agent receives at the end of each game is calculated as the utility minus the expenditure costs. The utility function in its general form is:

$$Utility = 1000 - travelPenalty + hotelBonus + FunBonus \qquad (1)$$

Apart from tackling with the utility optimization problem, TAC participants need to also deal with many uncertainty factors introduced by the different nature of each auction types and the interrelations that hold between them. For example, the agents need to acquire flight tickets, hotel rooms and entertainment tickets so that are all consistent with the preferred arrival and departure dates. Moreover, the agents may advance their performance and bidding accuracy when they deploy price prediction mechanisms in their decision-making process. Indeed, price prediction in TAC has been thoroughly used for efficient decision-making various agent-development teams have developed many forecasting methods [10].

Regarding the entertainment ticket auctions, one way to deal with uncertainty is to deduce how much an agent valuates a particular item. This involves an appropriate representation of the profit, which is expected to be obtained from every transaction. Moreover, agents should also take compound decisions, including how much and when to bid and to preserve a consistent bidding behavior in all auctions.

3 Related Work

Since the beginning of the competition in 2000, the TAC problem attracted many participants from different countries and organizations. ATTac-2000 agent [8] made the first key contribution to this challenging area. The intricacies of the game were clarified and attacked in a systematic way. ATTac-2000 was the first agent who won the TAC. The notion of *marginal utility* was then recognized to play an important role in the TAC game framework. In fact it has been proven that bidding marginal values in sequential auctions with deterministic prices is an optimal strategy and a fairly satisfactory one in the TAC environment [3].

Since the first TAC, teams concentrated their efforts mainly on developing effective ways of price prediction. Due to space limitations we only refer here to those approaches that most influenced our work. A novel price prediction method was designed for agent SouthamptonTAC [4], which was a competent in TAC-01 and TAC-02, by the application of fuzzy techniques. Regarding the entertainment auctions, the same agent deploys a strategy, according to which it submits offers (bids or asks) based on the number of items returned by an allocation optimization procedure, driven by Linear Programming (LP) [6]. In order to determine the price to be offered, the agent calculates the bid value using the equation $bid = V - \phi(t)$, where V is the valuation of the item and $\phi(t) > 0$, is a time-dependent descending function. In the case that the agent acts as a seller, the ask price is determined by the equation: $ask = V + \phi(t)$. The $\phi(t)$ function represents the profit that the agent receives as the auction progresses. Being a descending function, $\phi(t)$ leads to a profit, which decreases as the auction reaches its end. SouthamptonTAC team participated in TAC-05 with agent Dolphin. Agent Walverine [1] on the other hand provides an analytical approach relied on the principles of a competitive economy for the hotel and flight auction, while it handles the CDAs as completely unpredictable by the use of heuristics.

Another approach was proposed by agent whitebear [9], which simply, but also interestingly enough, used average prices for the prediction of the hotel auctions closing prices. The main strategy of agent whitbear for CDAs is to buy/sell the entertainment tickets it needs/does not need at a price equal to the current bid/ask plus an increment step. This behavior is modified at the early stages of the game, where the agent intends to buy tickets at low prices, even if it does not really need them. The agent adopts this tactic in order to increase its flexibility in the market. Moreover, when whitebear deduces that its competitor will increase its profit, it retains transactions. This bidding attitude relaxes at the later stages of the auction. Making extensive experimentation on mixing of different 'boundary' strategies and keeping the design as simple as possible, whitebear proved to be the most robust agent in the short TAC classic game history.

LearnAgents [7] also uses an LP model for allocating the acquired items to all the clients the agent serves. LP calculates the optimal allocation of the acquired goods given the buying price of each item. Although this approach works for the flight and hotel auctions, its application in the domain of the entertainment auctions is nontrivial. LearnAgents tries to make predictions about how the transaction prices will evolve during the game. For this reason it preserves a very active bidding behavior.

4   A Strategy for Entertainment Auctions

Entertainment auctions are continuous double sided auctions, where agents receive new price quotes every 30 seconds and bids are processed continuously. Agents involved in CDAs are both buyers and sellers. Although the TAC entertainment auctions adhere to the continuous double auction protocol applied in the stock market, they formulate a more simplified auction environment for two reasons. First, the number of eight participants is significantly lower than the ones met in a typical stock market. Second, the agents remain adherent to their initial plans about acquiring the desired tickets. This is not always the case in a real stock market, where traders may deploy totally unpredicted bidding behaviors. However, the general model of the bidding mechanism presented in this paper applies on any CDA environment with the appropriate parameterization. In particular, the structure of the decision algorithm deployed by Mertacor can be applied as is in the generic CDA case. The only aspect that needs to be taken into account is to change the values of the various variables that determine the decisions to be taken. These are clarified in the description of the Mertacor's bidding algorithm in the remaining section.

As it was previously mentioned, the main problem that a bidding strategy design copes with is the efficient estimation of the unique private valuation that an agent assigns to a particular entertainment ticket at a given moment. Each item in the CDA environment is intended to be acquired by only one client that the agent represents. Each client has a preference over each ticket, expressed by a real number, randomly drawn in the interval [0, 200]. This value represents the bonus that the agent receives by buying one ticket of the desired type for its client. Although assigning a value to each ticket is a TAC-specific manner for evaluating the available items in the auction, it also reflects the client preferences in the real stock market, which is a specific instance of CDA. Indeed, in the stock market a client desires to buy stocks instead of entertainment tickets at a particular price range. The bonus value imposes a constraint to agents according to which, buying a ticket at a price higher than the bonus value is not a preferable action. Although such a statement is intuitively correct, is not a sufficient criterion for the evaluation of a potential transaction. If, for instance, the bonus value for a particular ticket is 120, then buying it at 100 seems undoubtedly a profitable choice, which results in a profit of 120-100=20. However, if the corresponding seller values it for 40, the aforementioned transaction results in a profit of 100-40=60 > 20 for the competitor, hence to a loss for the buyer. Thus, understanding how much the other competitors valuate the auctioned items is a critical strategic element that may significantly improve an agent's performance.

Mertacor's bidding mechanism in entertainment auctions is based on a simple and consistent algorithm that aims to achieve a long-term profit at the end of the auction based on the following hypothesis. Assume that a seller in a CDA wants to sell a resource at a price that will lead to a satisfactory profit M. A successful seller should be flexible, i.e., to accept transactions at different prices. Therefore, there must be some tolerance ranges around the value of M where a transaction is still accepted. Let us also assume that the seller, after finding the best buy offer, accepts a transaction whose profit is R. Then, if R is close to M the buyer decides to sell the ticket, otherwise (if R is far from M) it prefers to send a new sell offer to the potential buyers.

The goal of our seller agent is not the achievement of a profit in every single transaction, because this would result in the completion of very few transactions, but the collection of a positive mean profit from all the transactions it completes.

It is very critical for the agent to posses an effective manner to calculate profit, based on the information available in the CDA environment. When the agent is prepared to complete a transaction it has to firstly evaluate the auctioned item. This involves the calculation of the ticket valuation V, based on the client preferences. E.g., if a client desires to acquire a particular ticket, this will be highly valuated. Otherwise it may have a low or no value to buy. The next step for the agent is to deduce the potential profit that will make from a specific transaction. Apart from the calculated valuation of the item that the agent desires to buy, it also knows the current bid or ask price, if it is a buyer or a seller respectively. An intuition about the notion of profit that stems form the generic CDA environment is that a buyer agent makes a high profit if it buys at a very low price compared to how much it truly evaluates the desired item. Similarly, a seller agent makes a high profit if it sells much higher than it believes the true price of the item is. The question here is "how much it sells?" and the answer depends on the specific CDA environment and the allowed price ranges in this environment. Thus, in general, if a seller asked for a price of P_b for a specific auctioned item, a buyer would make a high profit if its valuation V about the item was $V \gg P_b$, e.g. $V = 2P_b$, and then the profit would be $V - P_b = P_b$. In order to achieve at least such a profit, the agent should assign to its *expected profit* a value of $V - 2P_b$. Thus, the agent submits a buying bid, only if its expected profit is positive.

The notion of profit has been defined in Mertacor in the following manner.

a) If the agent needs to buy a ticket whose value has been estimated equal to V and the current bid price is P_b, then *profit* is defined as: $profit=V-2 \cdot P_b$.

b) If the agent wants to sell the ticket it holds, the value of the ticket is V, and the current ask price is P_a, then *profit* is given by the equation $profit=P_a-2 \cdot V$

Defining profit in this way is a substantial step for the evaluation of both the buying and selling transactions, because it guarantees that profit gained by the competitor it will be relatively close to the one gained by Mertacor. The above definition of profit is valid in the TAC-specific CDA. If we would like to apply our bidding algorithm on the generic CDA case, this definition should be adopted accordingly. Mertacor's selling strategy for the entertainment auctions is implemented by the procedure *MertacorSellStrategy* illustrated in Fig. 1. We describe its functionality in what follows.

The procedure iterates over all tickets that the agents possesses. The *target* variable represents the long-term average profit that the agent aims at achieving. This is set to a pre-specified value for each of the entertainment tickets. Typical values for *target* lie on [5, 10]. The variable *mean* is set equal to the current mean value of profit gained over the previously completed transactions. This is calculated by the function *getMeanValue()* in row 3. Variable M, which is given by the following equation:

$$M=A \cdot target+B \cdot mean \qquad (2)$$

is used to determine the range of the profit sought. After experiments, the weights A and B were chosen to be $A=0.7$ and $B=0.3$. These values show that our agent seeks for a profit highly influenced (70%) by the value of *target*. In order to keep our agent adherent to this goal, we impose (row 5) the variable M to only take values in the range [$a_1 \cdot target$, $a_2 \cdot target$]. Suitable values for the parameters a_2 and a_1 in the TAC environment are $a_1 = 1/2$, $a_2 = 3/2$. For this reason, we use function *relocateM()* (row 6), which returns values in the range [min {*target, mean*}, max {*target, mean*}]. In order to calculate current ticket's valuation V, our agent calls function *calcVal()*, in row 8, which makes use of a LP model. Since we are interested in always selling higher than a determined reserve price V_o, if $V<V_o$ we set $V=V_o$ in row 9. This prevents Mertacor from selling at very low prices. The choice of upper bound V_o for

```
PROCEDURE MertacorSellStrategy
 1:    FOR each entertainment ticket in possession
 2:        Assign a pre-specified value to target;
 3:        mean ← getMeanValue();
 4:        M ← A*target + B*mean;
 5:        IF M ≤ (1/2)*target OR M ≥ (3/2)*target THEN
 6:            M ← relocateM();
 7:        END IF
 8:        V ← calcVal();
 9:        IF V < V₀ THEN V ← V₀; END IF
10:        profit ← Pₐ− 2*V;
11:        Mₜ ← w(t)*M;
12:        Rₐ ← M;
13:        R_b ← 3*M/2;
14:        R_c ← rand(M/2, M);
15:        IF profit ≥ Mₜ-Rₐ THEN sellTicket();
16:        ELSE IF profit ≥ Mₜ-R_b THEN ask (Mₜ-Rₐ+2*V);
17:        ELSE ask (Mₜ- R_c +2*V);
18:        END IF
19:    END FOR
```

Fig. 1. The selling strategy deployed by Metacor in the entertainment auctions

Mertacor was V_o = \$40. In the next step Mertacor calculates the profit it would make in a potential transaction by using the equation

$$profit = P_a - 2V \qquad (3)$$

This preserves our agent's goal, which is to keep $E\{profit\}=target$, where the $E\{.\}$ operator denotes the mean value.

As it was previously stated, M is the profit that Mertacor assumes to be satisfactory. Any CDA market offers different opportunities for a bidder to make profit with respect to different times in the game. Thus, M is actually a time-dependant variable. For this purpose we define in row 11 a new variable $M_t=w(t)M$ that introduces a time-depended low bound for the desired profit. The $w(t)$ function is graphically represented in Fig. 2. From this graph we can quantitatively monitor the time in the game at which Mertacor seeks for the highest profit. The form of the $w(t)$ function is determined based on the specific requirements of the auction environment. For instance, in TAC the duration of all auctions is 9 minutes, while the hotel auctions close every minute on the minute. Thus, in the middle of the game half of the hotel auctions are closed. At this point uncertainty about how feasible is to assemble valid travel packages reaches its maximum value. After the fifth minute, the game approaches its end, since all hotel auctions for at least one particular day will be closed. This is the reason why we have chosen the form of $w(t)$ depicted in Fig. 2. The peak that appears in the middle of the game (4.5 minutes) represents the maximum profit sought at that time. The demand for profit decreases and then remains constant at a relatively low value as the game reaches its end. The specific $w(t)$ is based on the intuition that big uncertainty results in big profit.

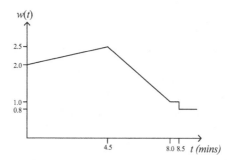

Fig. 2. The $w(t)$ function plotted over time (in minutes)

Next, we define three variables, namely R_a, R_b and R_c, in rows 12, 13 and 14 respectively. The variable R_a determines the case where R is near M. This case indicates that there is an explicit interest from buyers and the transaction is still satisfactory. The variable R_b is used to handle a second case, where R is neither near nor far from the desired profit M. It represents the case where the buyer is interested in the procured resource but the transaction is not yet satisfactory. The variable R_c is defined to cover the case where there is no real interest from the buyers' side to obtain the auctioned resource. In this case our agent sends an offer that results in a bigger profit than in the first case. Function *rand()* in row 14 returns a random number uniformly distributed in the range $[M/2, M]$.

In order to decide when to bid, our agent uses the three decision rules shown in rows 15-17. According to these rules, Mertacor sells the ticket it currently possesses if the profit to be achieved is M_t-R_a or above. This is done by function *sellTicket()*, in row 15. Otherwise, it asks for those prices that will result in a profit equal to or bigger than either M_t-R_a or M_t-R_c. Our agent submits its ask price (derived from Eq. (3)) for both cases, by invoking the *ask()* function in rows 16 and 17, respectively.

Since $R_c \leq R_a$ the expected profit will be at least equal to $(w(t)$-$1)M$. From Fig. 2 we can see that $w(t) \geq 1$ for most of the time. During the last 30 seconds of the game $w(t)$ is fixed to value 0.8 and the profit becomes -0.2M, which is negative. Thus, if M has a big value, a transaction occurred during the last 30 seconds of the game, will lead to a big loss. In addition to this, transactions occurring at times close to the middle of the game are not so likely to happen, because the quantity $(w(t)$-$1)M$ is relatively big. This will lead to a decrease of the overall average profit. In addition, from Eq. (3) it is derived that M will also decrease. On the other hand, if M is small, transactions that lead to a positive profit are more likely to happen, while negative profit transactions will result in a small loss. The aforementioned mechanism is highly adaptive to changes in the market environment, since when a big profit is assumed the number of transactions is reduced and vice versa. The buying bidding strategy of Mertacor is completely symmetrical to the selling strategy.

The decision mechanism described above ensures that each increase/decrease of the M variable results in certain conditions in the environment that strive M to the opposite direction. These conditions become more active as the M variable is monotonic. Preserving such a dynamic equilibrium for M makes Mertacor acting in an autonomous manner, adopting a realistic bidding behavior.

5 Benchmarking Results

In the 6th TAC, the agents were evaluated according to the average score they gained at each round. The TAC servers calculate the score of each agent when a game finishes and this is equal to the utility minus expenditure costs. The utility is given by equation (1). For each round the average score determines the performance metric for all agents. TAC-05 consisted of 4 rounds. In the first (qualifying) round of TAC all eleven agents (for the complete list of participants, please see: http// www.sics.se/tac) participated in 600 games, running for almost two weeks. Our agent ranked fourth, gaining a score of 3918.45, which was 240.33 below the top score achieved by agent whitebear05. In this round Mertacor employed a greedy bidding strategy to deal with the entertainment auctions. Next, in the seeding round 680 games were played using the same server configuration. At the beginning of this round we introduced the bidding algorithm presented in this paper, assigning the relatively high value of 12 to the *target* parameter. In this round Mertacor improved its overall performance. It finished third with the score of 4033.32, managing to reduce its distance from the top score agent whitebear05 to 135.29. In the semi-final round ten participants competed in 56 games. Mertacor only fixed some bugs, compared to its version in the previous round and it finally retained its performance by gaining a score of 4023.88.

Eight out of the ten competitors who participated in the semi-finals were invited to the final round. 40 games in the final round were concurrently played in two TAC servers, namely tac1 and tac2, resulting in 80 games. Compared to the semi-final round, Mertacor improved its entertainment bidding strategy, because it fine-tuned its parameters. In particular, we decided to lower the value of the *target* parameter to 5. This proved to be a critical intervention that significantly increased Mertacor's performance and ranked it as the top-scoring agent of TAC-05. Fig. 3 shows the average scores of the four top-scoring agents in the various rounds of TAC.

Apart from the overall benchmarking results provided by TAC, we have also conducted an additional analysis of the agents' performance regarding only the

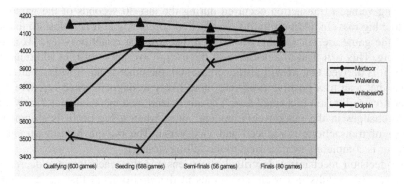

Fig. 3. Performance of the four top scoring agents during the competition rounds. The number of games played in each round is denoted.

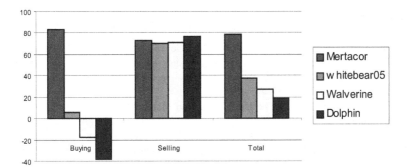

Fig. 4. Average Profit collected by the four top-scoring agents in the final round when they participated in buying, selling and in both types of transactions. The results correspond to data from TAC servers tac1 and tac2.

entertainment auctions. In this respect, we measured the profits that the agents made in their transactions, in all games of the final round. The results of this analysis are shown in Fig. 4. For each agent we measured the average profit collected in buying, selling and both types of transactions. Mertacor's performance with respect to buying transactions is extremely high compared to the other competitors'. This shows that the proposed algorithm is particularly efficient in buying transactions. Mertacor performs almost as well as its competitors in selling transactions. In the latter case the best performing agent is Dolphin. Noticeably, Mertacor is the only agent that manages to receive a positive profit when participating in buying transactions. This aspect of Mertacor's bidding algorithm resulted in an overall better performance of Mertacor in entertainment auctions.

6   Conclusions

This paper presented a bidding strategy for CDA, which was designed for agent Mertacor, the first finalist in the TAC-05. We analyzed our bidding/selling strategy for CDA and provided the details of its internal mechanisms. Our strategy was designed with the goal to achieve a long-term profit specified by a target value. This strategy proved to be robust and easily adaptable to market fluctuations. Our agent, which exploited a combination of strategies, accomplished an outperforming score in the TAC. The element that boosted Mertacor's performance was the CDA bidding component, since a fine-tuning of their parameters resulted in a better performance. The bidding algorithm presented in this paper proved to be valid for the TAC-specific CDA setup. Slight modifications of the proposed strategy allow it to be applied on the generic CDA environment. The strong point of the strategy is that its main decision mechanism is applicable on any CDA setup. In order to build an efficient strategy tailored to the specific needs of any particular CDA we need to define the correct values for the *target*, as well as the R_a, R_b, R_c parameters.

References

1. Cheng, S.-F., Leung, E., Lochner, K.M., O'Malley, K., Reeves D.M., Schvartzman L.J., and Wellman, M.P: Walverine: A walrasian trading agent. In Proceedings of the Second international Joint Conference on Autonomous Agents and Multiagent Systems, ACM Press, New York, NY, (2003) 465-472
2. Friedman, D. and Rust, J.: The Double Auction Market: Institutions, Theories and Evidence, Addison-Wesley (1992).
3. Greenwald, A., and Boyan, J.: Bidding Under Uncertainty: Theory and Experiments. In Proceedings of the 20th Conference on Uncertainty in Artificial Intelligence (2004), 209-216
4. He, M., and Jennings, N.R.: Designing a Successful Trading Agent: A Fuzzy Set Approach. IEEE Transactions on Fuzzy Systems, 12, 3 (2004) 389-410
5. Kagel, J.H. and Vogt, W.: Buyer's bid double auctions; Preliminary Experimental Results, in the Double Auction Market: Institutions, Theories, and Evidence, Friedman D. and Rust J. (ed.) Addison-Wesley, (1991) 285-305.
6. Kolman, B., and Beck, R.: Elementary Linear Programmig with Applications. Academic Press Inc. London, (1995)
7. Sardinha, J.A.R.P., Milidiú, R.L., Paranhos P. M., Cunha P. M., Lucena C.J.P.: An Agent Based Architecture for Highly Competitive Electronic Markets. In Proceedings of the 18th International FLAIRS Conference, Clearwater Beach, Florida, USA, May 16-18 (2005)
8. Stone, P., Schapire, R., Littman, M., Csirik, J. and McAllester, D.: Decision-theoretic bidding based on learned density models in simultaneous, interacting auctions, Journal of Artificial Intelligence Research, 19 (2003) 209-242
9. Vetsikas, I.A. and Selman, B.A.: Principled study of the design tradeoffs for autonomous trading agents. In Proceedings of the Second international Joint Conference on Autonomous Agents and Multiagent Systems. ACM Press, New York, NY (2003) 473-480
10. Wellman, M.P., Wurman, P.R., Oapos M.K., Bangera, R. Lin, S.-D., Reeves, D., Walsh, W.E.: Designing the market game for a trading agent competition. IEEE Internet Computing, 5, 2 (2001) 43-51

A Robust Agent Design for Dynamic SCM Environments

Ioannis Kontogounis[1], Kyriakos C. Chatzidimitriou[2],
Andreas L. Symeonidis[1,3], and Pericles A. Mitkas[1,3]

[1] Electrical and Computer Engineering Dept., Aristotle University of Thessaloniki,
GR541 24, Thessaloniki, Greece
[2] Department of Computer Science, Colorado State University, Fort Collins,
Colorado 80523, USA
[3] Intelligent Systems and Software Engineering Laboratory,
Informatics and Telematics Institute – CERTH, GR570 01, Thessaloniki, Greece
kontogou@auth.gr, kyriakos@cs.colostate.edu, asymeon@iti.gr,
mitkas@eng.auth.gr

Abstract. The leap from decision support to autonomous systems has
often raised a number of issues, namely system safety, soundness and
security. Depending on the field of application, these issues can either
be easily overcome or even hinder progress. In the case of Supply Chain
Management (SCM), where system performance implies loss or profit,
these issues are of high importance. SCM environments are often dynamic markets providing incomplete information, therefore demanding
intelligent solutions which can adhere to environment rules, perceive variations, and act in order to achieve maximum revenue. Advancing on the
way such autonomous solutions deal with the SCM process, we have
built a robust, highly-adaptable and easily-configurable mechanism for
efficiently dealing with all SCM facets, from material procurement and
inventory management to goods production and shipment. Our agent has
been crash-tested in one of the most challenging SCM environments, the
trading agent competition SCM game and has proven capable of providing advanced SCM solutions on behalf of its owner. This paper introduces
`Mertacor` and its main architectural primitives, provides an overview of
the TAC SCM environment, and discusses `Mertacor`'s performance.

1 Introduction

Current trends in Decision Support (DS) Supply Chain Management (SCM)
software tend to integrate Supplier Relationship Management (SRM), Customer
Relationship Management (CRM), and Enterprise Resource Planning (ERP)
primitives, in order to provide competitive business solutions. DS SCM software
efficiently monitors and records all transactions, while supply chain strategies
are applied at various stages of the process, in order to reduce cost and improve
service levels [1].

Nevertheless, in such systems human expertise is imperative, and this usually leads to their deprecation, from advanced DS systems to mere transactional

G. Antoniou et al. (Eds.): SETN 2006, LNAI 3955, pp. 127–136, 2006.
© Springer-Verlag Berlin Heidelberg 2006

databases. In addition, the flourishing of virtual organizations and electronic marketplaces, has led to the shift from traditional markets, relying on long-term trading partner relationships, to more dynamic SCM environments, where goods (raw material, end products) are auctioned between interested parties (suppliers, manufacturers, customers), and advanced bidding strategies are employed in order to achieve optimal results. The structure of these auction environments requires computational strength and accurate timing, therefore implying the need for autonomous SCM solutions, which shall identify rapid market changes and handle them in a cost-effective manner, in order to profit from specific economical regimes. Nevertheless, these SCM solutions should also satisfy all security, safety and soundness issues that may arise in such uncertain environments.

Recent research literature acknowledges intelligent agents as the most appropriate technology for trading and auctioning in electronic markets [2]. Equipped with smart strategies and efficient learning techniques, agents can provide robust solutions to deal with uncertainty and complexity. The more dynamic the SCM environment, the more intelligent the agent has to be.

In this context, we introduce `Mertacor`, an agent that employs a robust SCM mechanism for trading within a dynamic SCM environment. `Mertacor` takes over all company activities, aiming to maximize company revenue. Through extensive analysis, a number of key points within the SCM process have been identified and incorporated into the agent's trading mechanism. By the use of heuristics, SCM business rules, scheduling algorithms, data mining techniques and fail-safe mechanisms, `Mertacor` proves extremely capable of trading with other entities, within a dynamic, multi-variate, uncertain environment. `Mertacor` performance has been extensively tested through its participation in one of the most demanding trading agent competitions, the Trading Agent Competition (TAC) SCM game (http://www.sics.se/tac).

The rest of the paper is organized as follows: Section 2 provides an overview of the TAC SCM environment, in order to specify the framework `Mertacor` was tested on. Section 3 describes the functional characteristics of `Mertacor`, while Section 4 delves deeper into the implementation with respect to TAC SCM. Finally, Section 5 discusses `Mertacor` results at the TAC SCM game, while Section 6 summarizes work conducted and concludes the paper.

2   TAC SCM Overview

Within the TAC SCM game [3], agents act as Personal Computer (PC) manufacturers, competing with others on supplier and customer contracts. Throughout the duration of the game, each agent has to: (a) negotiate supply contracts, (b) bid for customer orders, (c) manage daily assembly activities and, (d) ship completed orders to customers.

A maximum number of six agents can connect to the TAC SCM game server, which simulates the suppliers and customers, and provides banking, production, and warehousing services to the competitors. Each agent is running its own PC assembling unit, which has limited production capacity. Sixteen (16) different types of PCs can be assembled, each requiring a different component compilation. The ten (10) different components available (CPUs, Motherboards, Memory, and Hard disk drives) can be procured through sending RFQs (Request For Quote) and issuing orders to the suppliers. Every day customers send RFQs and agents bid on them, depending on their ability to satisfy delivery dates and prices. The bid price should not exceed the reserve price the customer requires, which is between 75 − 125% of nominal price of PC components. The next day, if an agent's quote is a winning offer, customer sends the order to the agent. To get paid, the agent must either assemble the ordered PCs or supply the customer with PCs already stocked in inventory on time. If an agent fails in delivering customers orders, it is charged with a penalty. Winner is declared the agent with the greater revenue at the end of the game. Game length is 220 days, with each day lasting 15 seconds. Fig. 1 provides a schematic representation of the game. A more detailed description of the game can be found at [4].

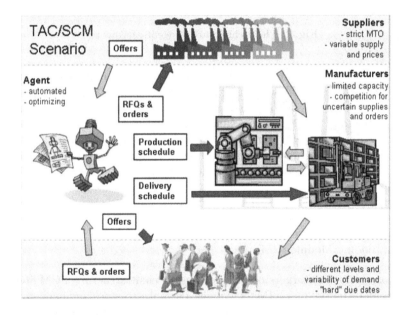

Fig. 1. An overview of the TAC SCM game

3   Agent Mertacor

Taking a closer look at the TAC SCM specifications, one can easily distinguish four (4) primary SCM facets: a. *Component Supplies Procurement*, dealing with negotiations on cheap component contracts, b. *Inventory Management*, managing stock requirements c. *Production and Delivery Scheduling*, and d. *Customer Bidding*, dealing with negotiations on PC sales. In order to better manage and efficiently act on each one, `Mertacor` has employed a modular architecture. Each task is delegated to a specific module, while all modules act in close collaboration.

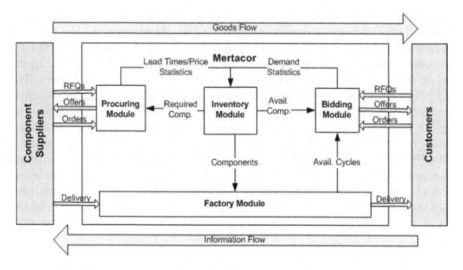

Fig. 2. The architecture of agent Mertacor

`Mertacor`, being a wrapper around the modules, ensures communication with suppliers and customers. Such a modular architecture can be easily applied to other environments also, outside the constraints of the competition. Following other successful paradigms [5, 6], `Mertacor` exploits the integration of techniques from the Operations Research (OR) literature, namely heuristics and adaptive algorithms, as well as statistical modeling. The overall `Mertacor` architecture is illustrated in Fig. 2, where four core modules can be identified:

1. The Inventory Module (IM)
2. The Procuring Module(PM)
3. The Factory Module (FM), and
4. The Bidding Module (BM)

IM constitutes the cornerstone of one's supply chain structure. SCM literature provides many paradigms of IM techniques, i.e. make-to-stock and make-to-order. `Mertacor` realizes an assemble-to-order system (ATO), a hybrid combination of the two aforementioned paradigms, which proves suitable in environments where assembly times are significantly smaller than replenishment times [7]. Additionally, an ATO system eliminates end-product inventory, reduces storage costs, improves forecast accuracy through demand aggregation, and provides quicker response time for order fulfillments through risk pooling.

Both PM and FM are based on heuristics. PM, which is primarily responsible for balancing the need for cheap component procurement to the running needs of the assembly line, attempts prediction of future demands, in order to pre-order affordable components. For FM, which is responsible for producing accurate schedules and for providing the bidder with information on the factory production capacity, a simulation procedure along with some heuristic algorithms was adopted. The simulator creates a projection of what the factory should expect in the near future (usually when conditions are less likely to change) and then diffuses this information to the rest of the modules.

With respect to bidding, a statistical model, capable of predicting the winning price of an order, was developed. Certain customer RFQ properties and the running SCM environment state are used to predict. Training data are derived from logs of previously played games, while some simple but effective fail-safe mechanisms were added, in case the predicted models are invalid. This learning approach proved to be fairly accurate, abiding by the standard rules of a market. Thus, the simulation can be considered realistic and the learning methodology applicable in real life domains.

4   Agent Modules

4.1   Inventory Management

An ATO system works as follows: The main goal of the system is to define certain inventory levels (thresholds) that need to be satisfied and below which replenishment is needed. These thresholds are calculated in real time for each component using the following equation [1, 7]:

$$R = D_{AVG}L_{AVG} + z\sqrt{L_{AVG}D_{STD}^2 + D_{AVG}^2 L_{STD}^2}$$

where D is the demand for specific component, L is the supplier lead time and z is a safety factor denoting the service level.

Demand is given in terms of products from the orders made by the customers. Statistics of product demand may vary making the thresholds more unstable. Nevertheless, by approximating demand in terms of product ranges (high-end, mid-end, low-end), smaller variations can be achieved. Additionally, in ATO no finished product inventory is kept (lower storage costs) and since components are shared along many products: (a) the levels of the thresholds are lowered due to aggregation of demands (b) internal component exchanges are applicable in order to avoid late orders and penalties. Component demand is calculated on the range demand by applying the scheme in Fig. 3, which has been adjusted to the TAC SCM specs. Minimum and maximum levels are also coded as fail-safes. The aforementioned system can handle unique components for the product families and can be extended to become a configure-to-order system (CTO), where there are no pre-specified end-products and the customer can personally select the set of components [7].

4.2   Component Procurement

Mertacor's performance is highly dependent on two factors: (a) having an inventory filled up with cheap components and (b) satisfying the inventory levels, since each delayed order implies a penalty and after five days, order cancellation.

Comp. ID	Low	Medium	High
1	0.4	0.33	0.0
2	0.0	0.17	0.6
3	0.6	0.17	0.0
4	0.0	0.33	0.4
5	0.4	0.5	0.6
6	0.6	0.5	0.4
7	0.8	0.5	0.4
8	0.2	0.5	0.8
9	0.6	0.5	0.4
10	0.4	0.5	0.6

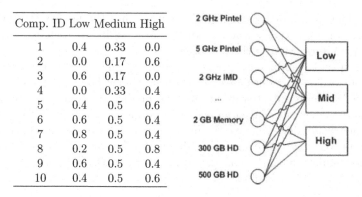

Fig. 3. Mapping range demand to component demand

In order to cope with these requirements, we have developed a simple strategy, which is divided into two distinct phases: initial and standard.

Mertacor initial procurement strategy is followed for the first two days. The RFQs sent to the suppliers on Day-0 and Day-1 aim to build an initial inventory so that Mertacor can start production immediately and therefore start bidding for orders from the first day. The components procured are predictably expensive, nevertheless their usability is increased, since at the beginning of the game, competition is not that strong, leading to higher product prices. On Day-1, another bundle of RFQs is sent, aiming to acquire relatively large quantities of cheap components for the following days.

On Day-2 Mertacor switches to a normal-state procurement strategy, designed to satisfy the aforementioned goals. It uses all five (5) available RFQs per component and per supplier each day, to maximize knowledge of the supplier's selling prices (probing). RFQs sent by our agent can be divided into three categories:

– *Normal procurement RFQs*, aiming to satisfy inventory reorder levels and allow bidding for customer orders in the near future. Quantities for these RFQs are calculated based on the reorder levels of the inventory manager.
– *Critical procurement RFQs*, a special state in which our agent tries to procure components in order to satisfy customer orders.
– *Early procurement RFQs*, in an effort to obtain low-priced components several days before they may be needed. These RFQs indicate quantities that if ordered, they would cause inventory to exceed reorder levels, so that there is no need for normal procurement after some posterior point in the game.

4.3   Production and Delivery Scheduling

The FM is responsible for: (a) generating production and delivery schedules schedules, (b) adjusting inventory levels, and (c) adjusting available factory cycles. This module is also assigned the task of integrating the procuring, inventory and sales parts. FM is the most resource demanding module of the agent. It implements a factory simulator, which simulates the operation of the factory for several days in the future, attempting to produce a draft of what will follow, based on knowledge on future supplier deliveries, customer deliveries, customer orders, future production and delivery schedules. When the schedules are produced, they are communicated to the interested parties. The number of future days Mertacor is simulating is defined as *look-ahead time*. For the current implementation the look-ahead time has been specified to fifteen (15) days.

The algorithm used by the factory simulator to predict forecoming inventory needs is iterative. For each day of the look-ahead period starting from today, the agent has to:

1. Update current inventory with supplier deliveries expected today
2. Update inventory with products assembled from factory (last schedule)
3. Remove components that are needed for tomorrows production
4. Remove products that are to be delivered tomorrow
5. Remaining inventory is the starting inventory for next day

This way the agent is aware of the expected inventory levels and factory cycles for the next 15 days, and alerts the bidder not to exceed these levels.

The daily production schedule includes the orders that fit within the daily factory capacity (2000 cycles). In case there are more orders and the capacity is exhausted, a greedy scheduling procedure is employed:

- Customer orders are sorted based on due date
- Orders with the same due date are sorted based on penalty
- Orders with similar due dates and penalties are sorted based on expected profit, that is unit price x quantity

Another parameter taken into account are the potential orders that should be scheduled. Not all available factory capacity for future days is committed to current RFQs, but a constantly decreasing fraction of the factory's nominal capacity. Thus, it is possible to save cycles for profitable RFQs, expected in the next days. If an RFQ can be successfully scheduled, the bidder is given a signal to go ahead and place a bid for that RFQ.

4.4 Bidding

Our bidding strategy is focused on finding the optimal bidding price for each RFQ received and then deciding on which of these RFQs to bid, sorting on anticipated profit. Mertacor's initial hypothesis is that every bid it places will be successful, and in order to realize it, a bidding mechanism based on machine learning techniques has been implemented. Through this mechanism, the market is modeled off-line based on data from past games. Twenty five (25) attributes were initially selected. Through a cross-validation procedure, using multiple linear regression (MLR) and backward elimination based on the F-statistic, the most parsimonious model within "one-standard-error" from the minimum was picked, leaving seven final predictors [8]. The initial set of attributes, which was formulated by intuition, is the same as in [9], while the data mining algorithm that has eventually been selected to model the market is the M5' [10], since it outperformed other similar

Table 1. The attributes used to predict order prices. These are: the RFQ's due date, its reserve price, the highest and lowest prices for the previous two days, and the current demand of PCs. The value of the intercept was 1515.94.

Feature	Due Date	Res. Price	High-1	High-2	Low-1	Low-2	Demand
β	-8.08	15.69	161.04	66.45	67.97	39.42	9.32

algorithms with respect to root mean square error (RMSE). The optimal, in our case, β coefficients for MLR can be found in Table 1.

This modeling provides us with the parameters that potentially affect the bidding strategies of the marketplace. Since inputs are normalized, the β values are directly comparable and their signs indicate the correlation between the input and the output. Interesting rules that may be derived are: the higher the highest and lowest prices for the past two days, the higher the current price; the later an order is due, the lower its price; the bigger the reserve price, the higher the offer to the customer; the higher the demand from the customer-side, the higher the prices, since there is less competition.

The bidding module also incorporates two on-line modeling mechanisms: a fail-safe mechanism designed to function complementary to the trained models, handling unexpected circumstances of selling prices, and an overbidding mechanism to help with filling the capacity given by the scheduler.

The former, named the follower for its ability to follow prices on-line, evaluates the minimum and maximum prices for PCs ordered the previous day as provided by the daily price reports, and predicts the approximate level of bidding price for each RFQ. The follower deploys linear interpolation based on the assumption that the maximum price paid corresponds to the maximum customer RFQ reserve price, while the minimum price paid corresponds to the minimum RFQ reserve price. Let P_M be the model price and P_F the follower price. Then, the final bid price is calculated as follows:

$$if(|P_F - P_M|/P_M)\% < threshold(10\%), P_M, else, P_F$$

Experimenting has shown that this fail-safe mechanism has significantly helped Mertacor through sudden market changes, especially at the start and end periods of games, when the game unfolded in unpredictable manners. Results showed a 20% improvement in RMSE accuracy compared to other on-line naive mechanisms [11]. Additionally, to support the use of the off-line model versus the on-line, a increase of 13% in RMSE accuracy was measured, favoring the former approach.

As far as overbidding is concerned, a scheme using the k-Nearest Neighbors (k-NN) algorithm [10] was developed to produce a probability of acceptance for each bid placed. Having identified the probability of a RFQ becoming an order, the bidding module signals the scheduler to commit only the fraction of the capacity that corresponds to that probability, letting the remaining capacity for the next RFQ in the row. The probability is calculated as the fraction of the n neighbors that became orders versus the total number of neighbors k (n/k). For the TAC SCM game, a value of $k=10$ was used. The neighbors/exemplars are RFQs sent to the customers the previous day(s) tagged either as accepted or rejected. The set of attributes used are the attributes selected for the off-line model.

5   Competition Results

Mertacor participated in the TAC SCM 2005 competition and performed quite well in all rounds. It came 11th among the 32 teams that participated in the qualifying phase and 10th among the 25 teams in the seeding phase. Going through the results of the qualifying rounds, we came to the conclusion that the reduced Mertacor efficiency was due to the fact that our agent was trained to cope with strong competition, accomplished only when six competitors participated. This, unfortunately, was not certain through the preliminary phase. During the finals, though, where the games played were much more competitive than in the previous rounds, Mertacor was a top scorer in the quarter finals and placed 3rd in the semi finals. At the final round Mertacor competed with the other 5 best scoring agents and finished 3rd, with a positive bank balance (See Table 2).

Even though numerous games must be played in order to evaluate the "true" value of an agent and its game profile with respect to the others, we will restrict our analysis to the results in Table 2 displaying some of the strong points and drawbacks of the developed design. First of all, the ATO system employed, along with the procurement strategy followed, resulted to an agent with the lowest storage costs, high delivery performance rates from agents willing to risk the 100% delivery rate for more profit, and low material costs. One could argue that the last metric also accounts for the inability to compete for orders, but once put into perspective of Mertacor's performance, good inventory management is implied. In addition, the bidding module ensures a high Average Selling Price (ASP) for the agent (2nd with a 0.776 normalized ASP - 0,780 for agent Maxon).

One of the most characteristic drawbacks of the final was the expensive contracts with suppliers, placing Mertacor 6th, with 0,726 average normalized CPU buying price (the most expensive component - 0,694 for agent Southampton-SCM). Another bottleneck was the low factory utilization (equivalent to low revenue) that can be interpreted to low throughput (rate of products out of the

Table 2. Mean skills of the agents in the finals for a total of 16 games. The skills are: final bank balance (Score), revenue, cost of components, storage costs, delivery performance and factory utilization.

Agent	Score ($)	Revenue ($)	Material ($)	Storage ($)	Del. (%)	Util. (%)
TacTex-05	4.741 M	108.586 M	100.614 M	2.013 M	97,75	87,81
SouthamptonSCM	1.604 M	108.246 M	102.375 M	2.843 M	98,06	87,75
Mertacor	546 272	75.582 M	72.639 M	1.730 M	98,88	60,63
Deep Maize	-220 503	107.681 M	103.309 M	2.645 M	97,31	85,13
MinneTAC	-311 844	81.903 M	79.728 M	1.887 M	99,88	65,00
Maxon	-1.985 M	71.105 M	68.588 M	3.520 M	100	56,19

factory versus components in the factory) causing additional reduction to profit. A balance between high selling prices and high throughput is imperative.

6 Conclusions

In this paper, we have introduced `Mertacor`, a SCM agent designed to participate in the TAC SCM game 2005. The agent employs a combination of OR, heuristic and statistical modeling techniques, in order to manage a wide range of activities in an efficient manner. The architecture proposed is generic, and can be applied to other SCM environments also. Focusing on specific points, one can see that the inventory management system, designed for the IBM PC production line, performed very well, in an uncertain and dynamic environment, outside the assumptions made by the authors. The learning models were able to capture the dynamics of the markets at hand, while the heuristics applied to the supplies and the factory modules worked well enough for the agent to be ranked 3rd in the competition. As far as the TAC community is concerned, we have introduced some novel ideas that could help further improve the game. Future research work on `Mertacor` includes the development of more accurate predictors on the behavior of both customers and suppliers. That, along with some improvements in the heuristics, would allow a bigger factory throughput, which is the confining factor for `Mertacor`.

References

1. Levi, S.D., Kaminsky, P., Levi, S.E.: Designing and managing the supply chain. McGraw-Hill, Illinois (2000)
2. He, M., Jennings, N.R., Leung, H.: On agent-mediated electronic commerce. IEEE Transactions on Knowledge and Data Engineering **15**(4) (2003) 985–1003
3. Arunachalam, R., Sadeh, N.: The supply chain trading agent competition. Electronic Commerce Research and Applications **4** (2005) 63–81
4. Collins, J., Arunachalam, R., Sadeh, N., Ericsson, J., Finne, N., Janson, S.: The Supply Chain Management Game for the 2005 Trading Agent Competition. Technical Report CMU-ISRI-04-139, CMU (2004)
5. Pardoe, D., Stone, P.: TacTex-03: A supply chain management agent. SIGecom Exchanges: Special Issue on Trading Agent Design and Analysis **4**(3) (2004) 19–28
6. He, M., Rogers, A., David, E., Jennings, N.R.: Designing and Evaluating an Adaptive Trading Agent for Supply Chain Management Applications. In: IJCAI-05 Workshop on Trading Agent Design and Analysis. (2005)
7. Cheng, F., Ettl, M., Lin, G.: Inventory-Service Optimization in Configure-to-Order Systems. Technical Report RC 21781, IBM (2001)
8. Hastie, T., Tibshirani, R., Friedman, J.: The Elements of Statistical Learning: Data Mining, Inference, and Prediction. Springer (2001)
9. Pardoe, D., Stone, P.: Bidding for customer orders in tac scm: A learning approach. In: Workshop on Trading Agent Design and Analysis. (2004)
10. Witten, I.H., Frank, E.: Data Mining: Practical machine learning tools with Java implementations. Morgan Kaufmann (2000)
11. Dahlgren, E., Wurman, P.R.: Packatac: A conservartive trading agent. SIGecom Exchanges **4**(3) (2004) 33–40

A Novel Updating Scheme for Probabilistic Latent Semantic Indexing

Constantine Kotropoulos and Athanasios Papaioannou

Department of Informatics,
Aristotle University of Thessaloniki,
Thessaloniki 54124 , Greece
{costas, apapaion}@aiia.csd.auth.gr

Abstract. Probabilistic Latent Semantic Indexing (PLSI) is a statistical technique for automatic document indexing. A novel method is proposed for updating PLSI when new documents arrive. The proposed method adds incrementally the words of any new document in the term-document matrix and derives the updating equations for the probability of terms given the class (i.e. latent) variables and the probability of documents given the latent variables. The performance of the proposed method is compared to that of the folding-in algorithm, which is an inexpensive, but potentially inaccurate updating method. It is demonstrated that the proposed updating algorithm outperforms the folding-in method with respect to the mean squared error between the aforementioned probabilities as they are estimated by the two updating methods and the original non-adaptive PLSI algorithm.

1   Introduction

Information Retrieval (IR) is the research topic that examines how people find information and how tools (such as search engines and catalogues) can be constructed to help people to retrieve information. IR has attracted the attention of researchers for more than 40 years. Nowadays, the World Wide Web is one example of information overload and its expansion has generated needs for more efficient access to global and corporate information repositories. Such repositories are usually text-based, but they increasingly include multimedia content. In this paper, we focus on text-based IR.

The paper builds on the *vector space* model [1], where the available textual data of the training corpus along with the query-documents are represented by numerical vectors. Each vector element corresponds to a different *term*, that is, a distinct word in the corpus [2]. It is generally agreed upon that the contextual similarity between documents exists also in their vectorial representation. Therefore, similarity can be assessed by a vector metric. There are two drawbacks in the original vector space model techniques such as word polysemy (i.e., when one word has many meanings e.g saturn) and synonymy (i.e., two or more words have the same meaning e.g. car and automobile). Polysemy tends to reduce precision, while synonymy tends to reduce recall.

Several vector space dimensionality reduction methods have been proposed in order to solve the two aforementioned problems. For example, *latent semantic indexing* (LSI) maps the documents and the terms onto the so-called *latent semantic space* [3]. LSI performs dimensionality reduction by using *singular value decomposition* (SVD).

G. Antoniou et al. (Eds.): SETN 2006, LNAI 3955, pp. 137–147, 2006.

However, although LSI yields good results, many problems arise due to the lack of a statistical foundation. This happens because LSI assumes that words and documents form a joint Gaussian model. However, Gaussian models can generate negative values. Document vectors whose elements are simply the term counts cannot admit negative values. Contrary to the LSI, a method that has a firm statistical foundation is the *probabilistic latent semantic indexing* (PLSI) [4]. PLSI is based on a statistical model, the so called *aspect model* [5, 6]. It allows to deal with polysemous and synonymous words. It has been proved that it outperforms LSI in document and word clustering applications.

In this paper, a novel method is proposed for updating PLSI when new documents arrive. The proposed method adds incrementally the words of any new document in the term-document matrix and derives the updating equations for the probability of terms given the class (i.e. latent) variables and the probability of the documents given the latent variables. Such an updating scheme is very useful when we deal with applications that refresh their term-document matrix very often. A typical example is a web crawler [7]. The performance of the proposed method is compared to that of the folding-in algorithm, which is an inexpensive, but potentially inaccurate updating method. It is demonstrated that the proposed updating algorithm outperforms the folding-in method with respect to the mean squared error between the aforementioned probabilities as they are estimated by the two updating methods and the original non-adaptive PLSI algorithm.

The outline of the paper is as follows. Section 2 describes briefly LSI, while PLSI is presented in Section 3. The proposed updating algorithm is derived in Section 4. Experimental results are demonstrated in Section 5 and conclusions are drawn in Section 6.

2   Latent Semantic Indexing

LSI has demonstrated an improved performance over the traditional vector space techniques and it has been successfully employed in many IR systems [3]. It is an optimal special case of multidimensional scaling [8] that aims at discovering something about the meaning behind the terms and about the topics in the documents, where the topic is an unobservable (i.e., a latent) variable. LSI models the semantics of the domain in order to yield additional relevant keywords and to reveal the "hidden" concepts of a given corpus while eliminating the high order noise. The attractive point of the method is that it captures the higher order "latent" structure of word usage across the documents rather than just the word surface level. This is done by modeling the association between the terms and the documents based on how terms co-occur across documents. The key idea of LSI is to map terms and documents to a vector space with reduced dimensionality, the latent semantic space. Let $\mathbf{X}$ be the $T \times N$ term-document co-occurrence matrix of rank $r <= \min(T, N)$. LSI is based on an application of SVD to $\mathbf{X}$:

$$\mathbf{X} = \mathbf{U} \mathbf{D} \mathbf{V} \tag{1}$$

where $\mathbf{U}$ and $\mathbf{V}$ are both column-orthogonal matrices, $\mathbf{D}$ is an $r \times r$ diagonal matrix that contains the non-zero singular values of $\mathbf{X}$, and $\top$ is the transposition operator. An approximation of $\mathbf{X}$ is computed by preserving only the largest $K < r$ singular values of $\mathbf{D}$ in $\tilde{\mathbf{D}}$ and setting the remaining singular values to zero:

$$\tilde{\mathbf{X}} = \mathbf{U}\tilde{\mathbf{D}}\mathbf{V} . \tag{2}$$

Eq. (2) indicates that the new document-term matrix $\tilde{\mathbf{X}}$ is no more sparse. So we hope to compute a meaningful association between document pairs and that terms with the same meaning will be mapped to the same subspace.

3   Probabilistic Latent Semantic Indexing

Recently, LSI has been criticized, because its probabilistic model does not match the observed data. Thus, a novel alternative is proposed the so called PLSI that is based on a multinomial model. It has been reported to yield better results for document and word clustering than the standard LSI [4]. PLSI is based on the so called aspect model [5]. In the sequel, the variables z, t, and d denote indices to topics, terms, and documents, respectively. The aspect model is a latent variable model for co-occurrence data which associates an unobserved class variable $z = 1, 2, \ldots, K$ with each observation. So, for any text document $d = 1, 2, \ldots, N$ we assume that the occurrence of a term $t = 1, 2, \ldots, T$ in the document is an observed variable and the topic z is an unobserved one. PLSI defines a generative model for term-document co-occurrences. The assumption is that each term t in a given document d is generated from a latent topic z, i.e. a term is conditionally independent from its original document given the latent topic it was generated from. The data generation process can be described as follows[9]:

1. Select a document $d = \delta$ with probability $P(d = \delta)$.
2. Pick a latent topic $z = k$ with probability $P(z = k | d = \delta)$.
3. Generate a term $t = j$ with probability $P(t = j | z = k)$.

Figure 1 depicts the data generation process. The generative process is described by the joint distribution of a term $t = j$, a latent topic $z = k$, and a document $d = \delta$:

$$P(d = \delta, z = k, t = j) = P(d = \delta)P(z = k | d = \delta)P(t = j | z = k) \tag{3}$$

and the joint distribution of the observed data is given by:

$$P(d = \delta, t = j) = \sum_{k=1}^{K} P(d = \delta, z = k, t = j)$$

$$= P(d = \delta) \sum_{k=1}^{K} P(z = k | d = \delta)P(t = j | z = k). \tag{4}$$

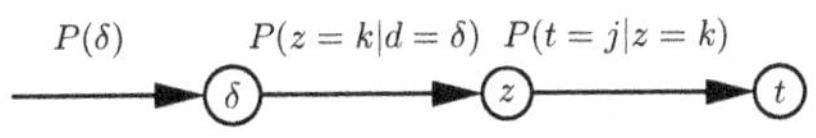

Fig. 1. The data generation process

From (4) one can notice that in contrast to document clustering models, document-specific term distributions $P(t|d)$ are obtained by a convex combination of the aspects or factors $P(t|z)$. Documents are not assigned to clusters. They are characterized by a specific mixture of factors with weights $P(z = k|d = \delta)$. So each word in a document is seen as a sample from a mixture model where mixture components are the multinomial $P(t = j|z = k)$ and the mixing proportions are $P(z = k|d = \delta)$. These mixing weights offer more modeling power and are conceptually very different from posterior probabilities in clustering models and (unsupervised) naive Bayes models.

To further simplify the notation we suppress δ, k, and j hereafter. In order to determine $P(d)$, $P(z|d)$, and $P(t|z)$ we should maximize the log-likelihood function

$$\mathcal{L} = \sum_{d=1}^{N} \sum_{t=1}^{T} n(d,t) \, \log P(d,t) \tag{5}$$

where $n(d,t)$ denotes the term frequency, i.e the number of times t occurred in d. It is worth noting that an equivalent symmetric version of the model can be obtained by inverting the conditional probability $P(z|d)$ with the help of Bayes' rule, which results in

$$P(d,t) = \sum_{z=1}^{K} P(z)P(t|z)P(d|z). \tag{6}$$

Eq. (6) is just a re-parameterized version of the generative models described by (3) and (4).

The PLSI algorithm maximizes the log-likelihood of the model by using the Expectation Maximization (EM) algorithm[10]. EM alternates between two steps:

1. An expectation step (E-step) where posterior probabilities are computed for the latent variables z based on the current estimates of the parameters.
2. A maximization step (M-step), where parameters are updated for given posterior probabilities computed in the previous E-step.

For the aspect model in the symmetric parameterization Bayes' rule yields the E-step

$$P(z|d,t) = \frac{P(z)P(t|z)P(d|z)}{\sum_{z'=1}^{K} P(z')P(t|z')P(d|z')} \tag{7}$$

which is the probability that a term t in a particular document or context d is explained by the factor corresponding to z. By straightforward calculations, one arrives at the following M-step re-estimation equations [4]:

$$P(t|z) = \frac{\sum_{d=1}^{N} n(t,d)P(z|d,t)}{\sum_{d=1}^{N} \sum_{t'=1}^{T} n(t',d)P(z|d,t')} \tag{8}$$

$$P(d|z) = \frac{\sum_{t=1}^{T} n(t,d)P(z|d,t)}{\sum_{d'=1}^{N} \sum_{t=1}^{T} n(t,d')P(z|d',t)} \tag{9}$$

$$P(z) = \frac{1}{R} \sum_{d=1}^{N} \sum_{t=1}^{T} n(t,d)P(z|d,t) \tag{10}$$

where

$$R = \sum_{d=1}^{N} \sum_{t=1}^{T} n(t,d). \tag{11}$$

Alternating (7) with (8)-(10) defines a convergent procedure that approaches a local maxima of the log-likelihood.

In [4], a generalization of the EM algorithm for mixture models is proposed, the so called *tempered EM* (TEM). TEM is based on an entropic regularization and is closely related to the deterministic annealing. In short, a control parameter β (the inverse computational temperature) is introduced and the E-step is modified to

$$P_\beta(z|d,t) = \frac{P(z)[P(d|z)P(t|z)]^\beta}{\sum_{z'=1}^{K} P(z')[P(t|z')P(d|z')]^\beta}. \tag{12}$$

For $\beta = 1$, (12) is the standard E-step, while for $\beta < 1$ the likelihood part in Bayes' formula is discounted. It can be shown that TEM minimizes an objective function known as the free energy [11] and hence it defines a convergent algorithm. In the context of PLSI, the main advantage of TEM is that it avoids overfitting. In order to determine the optimal value of β the use of some held-out data is recommended [4]. The typical number of TEM iterations performed starting from randomized initial conditions is 40-60.

The PLSI model can be used to replace the original term-document representation by a representation in a low-dimensional "latent" space in order to perform term clustering or document retrieval. The components of the document in the low-dimensional space are $P(z = k|d)$, $k = 1, 2, \ldots, K$ and for each unseen document or query the aforementioned components are computed by maximizing the log-likelihood with $P(t|z = k)$ fixed [12]. It is obvious that PLSI is not a well-defined generative model of documents, since there is no direct way to assign a probability to an unseen document. However, a better performance for PLSI than LSI was reported on several corpora in [12]. In particular, PLSI is found to perform well even in the cases where LSI fails completely.

4   Updating Scheme for Probabilistic Latent Semantic Indexing

One open problem for PLSI is its updating scheme. In the literature, the only available solution is the well-known method of *folding-in* of a new document, where we project the new document vector to the latent space [13]. However, this method is suitable for document queries and not when new documents are added in the term-document matrix and PLSI model has to be retrained. This happens because the folding-in method calculates only the mixing proportion $P(z|d)$ while the factors $P(t|z)$ are kept fixed.

A novel method is proposed in this paper for updating all the PLSI model parameters. To distinguish between $P(t|z)$ and $P(d|z)$ we introduce the notation $P_1(t|z) = P(t|z)$ and $P_2(d|z) = P(d|z)$. Let us focus on the computations that take place when we proceed from iteration l to iteration $l + 1$ of the EM algorithm. The E-step for iteration $l + 1$ is given by

$$P(z|d,t)_{l+1} = \frac{P(z)_l P_1(t|z)_l P_2(d|z)_l}{\sum_{z'=1}^{K} P(z)_l P_1(t|z')_l P_2(d|z')_l}. \tag{13}$$

The M-step for updating $P_1(t|z)$ at iteration $l+1$ is rewritten as

$$P_1'(t|z)_{l+1} = \sum_{d=1}^{N} n(t,d)P(z|d,t)_{l+1} \tag{14}$$

$$P_1(t|z)_{l+1} = \frac{P_1'(t|z)_{l+1}}{\sum_{t'=1}^{T} P_1'(t'|z)_{l+1}}. \tag{15}$$

By substituting (13) into (14) we obtain:

$$P_1'(t|z)_{l+1} = P_1(t|z)_l \sum_{d=1}^{N} \left[\frac{n(t,d)\,P_2(d|z)_l}{\sum_{z'=1}^{K} P(z')_l\,P_1(t|z')_l\,P_2(d|z')_l} \right] P(z)_l \tag{16}$$

Similarly, the M-step for updating $P_2(d|z)$ at iteration $l+1$ is rewritten as

$$P_2'(d|z)_{l+1} = P_2(d|z)_l \sum_{t=1}^{T} \left[\frac{n(t,d)\,P_1(t|z)_l}{\sum_{z'=1}^{K} P(z')_l\,P_1(t|z')_l\,P_2(d|z')_l} \right] P(z)_l \tag{17}$$

$$P_2(d|z)_{l+1} = \frac{P_2'(d|z)_{l+1}}{\sum_{d'=1}^{N} P_2'(d'|z)_{l+1}}. \tag{18}$$

Let us assume that a new document indexed by $d = N + 1$ is added at the end of the lth iteration that contains only one word that appears a times. We also assume that the addition of the new document alters neither the number of topics nor the vocabulary of terms. Without any loss of generality, let us assume that the single word is the first word in the vocabulary, i.e. $t = 1$. Therefore, $n(1, N + 1) = a$ and $n(t, N + 1) = 0$, $t = 2, \ldots, T$. Let $\mathbf{P}_2$ be the $N \times T$ matrix with elements $P_2(d|z)$, $d = 1, 2, \ldots, N$ and $t = 1, 2, \ldots, T$. To initialize the recursion for the $(l+1)$th iteration, we simply append a new row to $\mathbf{P}_2$ with elements $P_2(N + 1|z)_l$ that are numbers uniformly distributed in the interval $[0, 1]$ and we normalize so that each column in $\mathbf{P}_2$ has a unit sum. Under the just described conditions, it can be proven that (16) takes the form

$$P_1''(t|z)_{l+1} = P_1'(t|z)_{l+1} + P_1(t|z)_l \frac{n(t, N + 1)\,P_2(N + 1|z)_l}{\sum_{z'=1}^{K} P(z')\,P_1(t|z')_l\,P_2(N + 1|z')_l} P(z)_l \tag{19}$$

where $P_1'(t|z)_{l+1}$ is simply the value predicted by (16) before the addition of the new document. Eq. (19) is further simplified to

$$P_1''(1|z) = \begin{cases} P_1'(1|z)_{l+1} + P_1(1|z)_l \cdot \\ \quad \cdot \frac{a\,P_2(N+1\,z)_l}{\sum_{z'=1}^{K} P(z')_l\,P_1(1\,z')_l\,P_2(N+1\,z')_l} P(z)_l & t = 1 \\ P'(t|z)_{l+1} & \text{if } t \neq 1. \end{cases} \tag{20}$$

Let

$$A_{l+1}' = \sum_{t=1}^{T} P_1'(t|z)_{l+1} \tag{21}$$

$$A_{l+1}'' = \sum_{t=1}^{T} P_1''(t|z)_{l+1} = A_{l+1}' + P_1''(1|z)_{l+1} - P_1'(1|z)_{l+1}. \tag{22}$$

Eq. (15) is simply rewritten as

$$P_1(t|z)_{l+1} = \frac{P_1''(t|z)_{l+1}}{\sum_{t'=1}^{T} P_1''(t'|z)_{l+1}} = \begin{cases} \frac{P_1''(1\ z)_{l+1}}{A_{l+1}'} & \text{if } t = 1 \\ \frac{A_{l+1}'}{A_{l+1}''} P_1(t|z)_{l+1} & \text{otherwise.} \end{cases} \quad (23)$$

Similarly, it can be shown that (17) results in

$$P_2''(d|z) = \begin{cases} P_1''(1|z) - P_1'(1|z) & \text{if } d = N + 1 \\ P_2'(d|z)_{l+1} & \text{otherwise.} \end{cases} \quad (24)$$

Let

$$B_{l+1}' = \sum_{d=1}^{N} P_2'(d|z)_{l+1} \quad (25)$$

$$B_{l+1}'' = \sum_{d=1}^{N+1} P_2''(d|z)_{l+1} = B_{l+1}' + P''(N+1|z)_{l+1}$$

$$= B_{l+1}' + P_1''(1|z)_{l+1} - P_1'(1|z)_{l+1}. \quad (26)$$

Then (18) takes the form

$$P_2(d|z)_{l+1} = \frac{P_2''(t|z)_{l+1}}{\sum_{d'=1}^{N+1} P_2''(d'|z)_{l+1}} = \begin{cases} \frac{P_2''(N+1\ z)_{l+1}}{B_{l+1}''} & \text{if } d = N + 1 \\ \frac{B_{l+1}'}{B_{l+1}''} P_2(d|z)_{l+1} & \text{otherwise.} \end{cases} \quad (27)$$

Finally, we proceed to updating $P(z)_{l+1}$. Let

$$R_l = \sum_{d=1}^{N} \sum_{t=1}^{T} n(t, d) \quad (28)$$

$$P'(z)_{l+1} = \frac{1}{R_l} \sum_{d=1}^{N} \sum_{t=1}^{T} n(t, d) P(z|d, t)_{l+1} \quad (29)$$

be the values admitted by R and $P(z)$, defined by (11) and (10), before appending the $(N + 1)$th document. It is straightforward to show that

$$R_{l+1} = R_l + a \quad (30)$$

$$P(z)_{n+1} = \frac{1}{R_{l+1}} \left[R_l\ P'(z)_{l+1} + P_1''(1|z)_{l+1} - P_1'(1|z)_{l+1} \right]. \quad (31)$$

The method can be generalized for a document with more than one terms, if we assume that every time we deal with an elementary document having just one word and we incrementally append as many incremental documents as the terms found in the document. Additional recursions can be applied in order to process more than one documents. The proposed method will be referred to as *recursive probabilistic latent semantic indexing* (RPLSI).

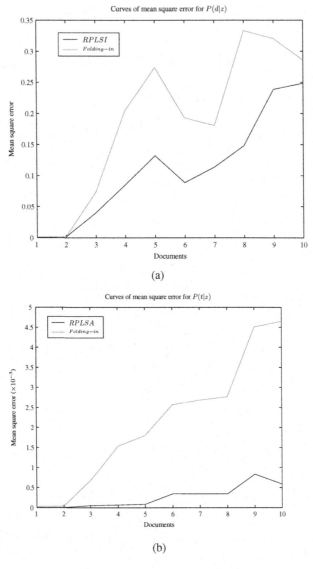

Fig. 2. (a) Mean squared error for $P(d|z)$ for 10 documents. (b) Mean squared error for $P(t|z)$ for 10 documents.

5   Experimental Results

To demonstrate the performance of the proposed updating algorithm for PLSI we have employed a subset of 348 documents from the 20-Newsgroups corpus [14]. The documents used belong to 4 classes. For each document we have kept only 100 terms, those having the highest information gain. After having estimated the parameters of

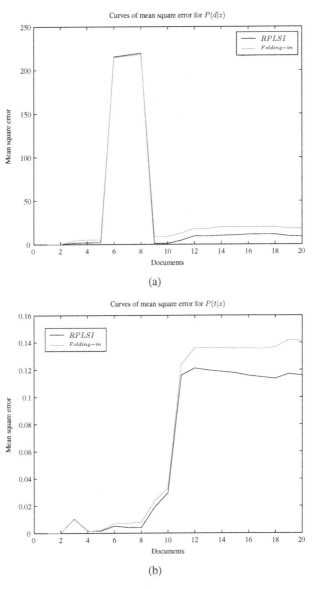

Fig. 3. (a) Mean squared error for $P(d|z)$ for 20 documents.(b) Mean squared error for $P(t|z)$ for 20 documents.

PLSI for the corpus of 348 documents, we start appending a number of documents incrementally. We have compared the accuracy of the proposed updating method with that of the folding-in method. PLSI computes the probabilities $P(t|z)$ and $P(d|z)$, $z = 1, 2, \ldots, K$ for $K = 4$ by resetting the calculation each time a new document is appended. RPLSI and folding-in update the probability values each time a new document is appended. Subsequently, the mean squared error (MSE) has been measured between the exact probability values determined by PLSI and the values estimated by RPLSI by averaging over the latent variable z that refers to classes. The mean squared error between the exact probability values determined by PLSI and the values estimated by folding-in has also been measured. The computations have been performed for 10 and 20 documents. Figures 2 and 3 demonstrate that the proposed method outperforms the folding-in method with respect to the MSE for both $P(t|z)$ and $P(d|z)$. It can be seen that the proposed RPLSI yields almost always a smaller MSE than the folding-in method when a new document is appended. The estimation of $P(t|z)$ is more accurate than $P(d|z)$.

6   Conclusions

A new method for updating the parameters of the PLSI has been proposed that does not require to train the model from the beginning. The proposed method updates not only the probabilities of the new document as folding-in method does, but also all the probabilities of the terms and documents. We have reported first promising experimental results that indicate a better performance than folding-in. In the future, experiments will be conducted with corpora having more documents and more classes. The proposed technique was derived with respect to certain assumptions. Relaxing the constraints is another point of further research. We do not claim that the proposed method yields a new language model. Therefore, it is pointless either to measure perplexity or to compare the model with the latent Dirichlet allocation method.

Acknowledgments

This work has been supported by the FP6 European Union Network of Excellence MUSCLE "Multimedia Understanding through Semantics, Computation and Learning" (FP6-507752). The authors would like to thank the anonymous reviewers for their constructive criticism and their careful proofreading.

References

1. Salton, G., Wong, A., Yang, C.S.: A vector space model for automatic indexing. Commun. ACM **18** (1975) 613–620
2. Yates, R.B., Neto, B.R.: Modern Information Retrieval. ACM Press (1999)
3. Deerwester, S.C., Dumais, S.T., Landauer, T.K., Furnas, G.W., Harshman, R.A.: Indexing by latent semantic analysis. Journal American Society of Information Science **41** (1990) 391–407
4. Hofmann, T.: Probabilistic latent semantic analysis. In: Proc. Uncertainty in Artificial Intelligence, UAI'99, Stockholm (1999)
5. Hofmann, T., Puzicha, J.: Unsupervised learning from dyadic data. Technical Report TR-98-042, International Computer Science Institute, Berkeley, CA (1998)
6. Saul, L., Pereira, F.: Aggregate and mixed-order Markov models for statistical language processing. In Cardie, C., Weischedel, R., eds.: Proc. 2nd Conf. Empirical Methods in Natural Language Processing. Association for Computational Linguistics, Somerset, New Jersey (1997) 81–89

7. Almpanidis, G., Kotropoulos, C.: Combining text and link analysis for focused crawling. In: Proc. Int. Conf. Advances Pattern Recognition. Volume LNCS 3686. (2005) 278–287
8. Bartell, B.T., Cottrell, G.W., Belew, R.K.: Latent semantic indexing is an optimal special case of multidimensional scaling. In: Proc. Research and Development in Information Retrieval. (1992) 161–167
9. Hofmann, T.: Probabilistic latent semantic indexing. In: Proc. Research and Development in Information Retrieval. (1999) 50–57
10. Dempster, A., Laird, N., Rubin, D.: Maximum likelihood from incomplete data via the em algorithm (with discussion). Journal Royal Statistical Society, Series B **39** (1977) 1–38
11. Neal, R., Hinton, G.: A view of the EM algorithm that justifies incremental, sparse, and other variants. Learning in Graphical Models (1999) 355–368
12. Hofmann, T.: Unsupervised learning by probabilistic latent semantic analysis. Machine Learning **42** (2001) 177–196
13. Berry, M.W., Browne, M.: Understanding Search Engines: Mathematical Modeling and Text Retrieval. SIAM (1999)
14. Lang, K.: Newsweeder: Learning to filter netnews. In: Proc. 12th Int. Conf. Machine Learning. (1995) 331–339

Local Additive Regression of Decision Stumps[*]

Sotiris B. Kotsiantis, Dimitris Kanellopoulos, and Panayiotis E. Pintelas

Educational Software Development Laboratory,
Department of Mathematics, University of Patras, Greece
{sotos, pintelas}@math.upatras.gr, dkanellop@teipat.gr

Abstract. Parametric models such as linear regression can provide useful, interpretable descriptions of simple structure in data. However, sometimes such simple structure does not extend across an entire data set and may instead be confined more locally within subsets of the data. Nonparametric regression typically involves local averaging. In this study, local averaging estimator is coupled with a machine learning technique – boosting. In more detail, we propose a technique of local boosting of decision stumps. We performed a comparison with other well known methods and ensembles, on standard benchmark datasets and the performance of the proposed technique was greater in most cases.

1 Introduction

In this paper we consider the following regression setting. Data is generated from an unknown distribution P on some domain X and labeled according to an unknown function g. A learning algorithm receives a sample $S = \{(x_1, g(x_1)), \ldots, (x_m, g(x_m))\}$ and attempts to return a function f close to g on the domain X. Many regression problems involve an investigation of relationships between attributes in databases, where different prediction models can be more appropriate for different regions.

The purpose of ensemble learning is to build a learning model which integrates a number of base learning models, so that the model gives better generalization performance on application to a particular data-set than any of the individual base models [5]. Ensemble generation can be characterized as being homogeneous if each base learning model uses the same learning algorithm or heterogeneous if the base models can be built from a range of learning algorithms.

There has been much research work on ensemble learning for regression in the context of neural networks, however there has been less research carried out in terms of using homogeneous ensemble techniques to improve the performance of simple regression algorithms. Classification problems have dominated research on boosting to date. The application of boosting to regression problems, on the other hand, has received little investigation. In this paper we develop a boosting method for regression problems that works locally.

---

[*] The Project is Co-Funded by the European Social Fund & National Resources - EPEAEK II.

G. Antoniou et al. (Eds.): SETN 2006, LNAI 3955, pp. 148–157, 2006.
© Springer-Verlag Berlin Heidelberg 2006

When all training examples are considered when classifying a new test instance, the algorithm works as a global method, while when the nearest training examples are considered, the algorithm works as a local method, since only data local to the area around the testing case contribute to the classification [1]. Local learning [2] can be understood as a general principle that allows extending learning techniques designed for simple models, to the case of complex data for which the model's assumptions would not necessarily hold globally, but can be thought as valid locally.

When the size of the training set is small compared to the complexity of the classifier, the learning algorithm usually overfits the noise in the training data. Thus effective control of complexity of a method plays an important role in achieving good generalization. Some theoretical and experimental results [20] indicate that a local learning algorithm (that is learning algorithm trained on the training subset) provides a feasible solution to this problem. The authors of [7] proposed a theoretical model of a local learning algorithm and obtained bounds for the local risk minimization estimator for pattern recognition and regression problems using the structural risk minimization principle. The authors of [9] extended the idea of constructing local simple base learners for different regions of input space, searching for ANN architectures that should be locally used and for a criterion to select a proper unit for each region of input space.

In this paper, we propose a technique of local additive regression of decision stumps. We performed a comparison with other well known methods and ensembles, on standard benchmark datasets and the performance of the proposed technique was greater in most cases.

Current ensemble approaches and work are described in section 2. In Section 3 we describe the proposed method and investigate its advantages and limitations. In Section 4, we evaluate the proposed method on several UCI datasets by comparing it with standard bagging and boosting and other lazy methods. Finally, section 5 concludes the paper and suggests further directions in current research.

2   Ensembles of Estimators

Empirical studies showed that ensembles are often much more accurate than the individual base learner that make them up [5], and recently different theoretical explanations have been proposed to justify the effectiveness of some commonly used ensemble methods [16]. Currently, there are two main approaches to model combination. The first is to create a set of learned models by applying an algorithm repeatedly to different training sample data; the second applies various learning algorithms to the same sample data. The predictions of the models are then combined according to an averaging scheme or a stacking algorithm [5]. In this work we propose a combining method that uses one learning algorithm for building an ensemble of regression models. For this reason this section presents the most well-known methods that generate sets of base learners using one base learning algorithm.

The Bagging (Bootstrap Aggregating) algorithm [8] uses sampling on the training set to create many varied but overlapping new sets. The base algorithm is used to create a different base model instance for each sample, and the ensemble output is the average of all base model outputs for a given input.

Another method that uses different subset of training data with a single learning method is the boosting approach [10]. The boosting approach uses the base models in sequential collaboration, where each new model concentrates more on the examples where the previous models had high error. The AdaBoost.R algorithm [13] attacks the regression problem by reducing it to a classification problem. Friedman has also explored regression using the gradient descent approach [14]. In each iteration, the Additive Regression algorithm constructs goal values for each data-point x_i equal to the (negative) gradient of the loss of its current master hypothesis on x_i. The base learner then finds a function in a class minimizing the squared error on this constructed sample.

Recently, theories have been proposed for the effectiveness of bagging and boosting based on bias plus variance decomposition. In this decomposition we can view the expected error of a learning algorithm as having two components:

- A bias term measuring how close the average model produced by the learning algorithm will be to the target function;
- A variance term measuring how much each of the learning algorithm's guesses will vary with respect to each other (how often they disagree)

Regarding the bias – variance tradeoff, bagging method is a primarily variance reduction method, that is, it reduces the likelihood of deploying a poor model by reducing the error variance when evaluating models on out-of-sample data. This does not mean that it cannot reduce model bias, and it does indeed, on average, reduce model bias, but it does not necessarily reduce bias. Methods that operate more directly on the modeling errors themselves, such as boosting are more effective at reducing model bias. One basic theoretical property of boosting is its ability to reduce the training error, or roughly speaking that it boosts a weak learner to be strong. How this works is relatively well understood, subject to the major assumption of a weak base learner that the hypotheses generated by the base learner in boosting are 'weak', or are capable of beating a random guesser [10].

3 Proposed Algorithm

Learning based on the training subset has been an exciting research topic and some important theoretical and experimental results have been obtained. In fact, local learning is not a new concept and it has appeared in the early years of pattern recognition. The obvious example is the k-nearest neighbor method: given a testing pattern, we estimate its value from the closest patterns in the training set.

In local learning, each local model is trained entirely independently of all other local models such that the total number of local models in the learning system does not directly affect how complex a function can be learned - complexity can only be controlled by the level of adaptability of each local model. Local regression estimation was independently introduced in several different fields. An excellent book on the topic is [18]. However, the idea of local regression has never been examined in relation to ensemble techniques.

The proposed algorithm builds a model for each instance to be classified, taking into account only a subset of the training instances. This subset is chosen on the basis of the preferable distance metric between the testing instance and the training instances in the input space. For each testing instance, a boosting ensemble of decision stump models is thus learned using only the training points lying close to the current testing instance.

Decision stumps (DS) are one level decision trees [15]. We can find the best stump just as we would learn a node in a decision tree: we search over all possible features to split on, and for each one, we search over all possible thresholds induced by sorting the observed values. DS (or regression stumps) do regression based on mean-squared error where each node in a decision stump represents a feature in an instance to be predicted, and each branch represents a value that the node can take. At worst a decision stump will reproduce the most common sense baseline, and may do better if the selected feature is particularly informative.

Generally, the proposed ensemble consists of the following four steps (see Fig. 1).

1) Determine a suitable distance metric.
2) Find the k nearest neighbors using the selected distance metric.
3) Apply boosting to the decision stump algorithm using as training instances the k instances
4) The answer of the ensemble is the prediction for the testing instance.

Fig. 1. Local Additive Regression of decision stumps

The proposed ensemble has some free parameters such as the distance metric. In our experiments, we used the most well known -Euclidean similarity function- as distance metric. For two data points, $X = <x_1, x_2, x_3, ..., x_{n-1}>$ and $Y = <y_1, y_2, y_3, ..., y_{n-1}>$, the Euclidean similarity function is defined as $d_2(X,Y) = \sqrt{\sum_{i=1}^{n-1}(x_i - y_i)^2}$.

The performance of additive regression has been shown to exceed or meet that of various other boosting algorithms [10], thus making it a good choice for this research. We used 10 iterations for the boosting process in order to reduce the time needed for the prediction of a new instance.

The proposed algorithm also requires choosing the value of K. There are several ways to do this. A first, simple solution is to fix K a priori before the beginning of the learning process. However, the best K for a specific dataset is obviously not the best one for another dataset. A second, more time-consuming solution is therefore to determine this best K automatically through the minimization of a cost criterion. One way to do that is to evaluate the estimation error on a test set and thus keep as K the value for which the error is the least. In the current implementation we decided to use a fixed value for K (=50): a) in order to keep the training time low and b) about this size of instances is appropriate for a simple algorithm, to build a precise model according to [12].

Our method shares the properties of other instance based learning methods such as no need for training and more computational cost for classification. Besides, our method has some desirable properties, such as better correlation coefficient.

4 Experiments Results

We experimented with 24 datasets from the UCI repository [4]. These datasets cover many different types of problems having discrete, continuous and symbolic variables. The specific datasets are listed in Table 1.

Table 1. Datasets

Datasets	Instances	Categorical features	Numerical features	Missing values
servo	167	4	0	No
autoHorse	205	8	17	Yes
autoMpg	398	3	4	yes
autoPrice	159	0	15	no
baskball	96	0	4	no
bodyfat	252	0	14	no
breastTumor	286	8	1	yes
cholesterol	303	7	6	yes
cleveland	303	7	6	yes
cloud	108	2	4	no
Cpu	209	1	6	no
echoMonths	130	3	6	yes
fishcatch	158	2	5	yes
housing	506	1	12	no
lowbwt	189	7	2	no
Pbc	418	8	10	yes
pwLinear	200	0	10	no
quake	2178	0	3	no
sensory	576	11	0	no
auto93	93	6	16	yes
veteran	137	4	3	no
wisconsin	194	0	32	no
triazines	186	0	60	no
Stock	950	0	9	no

Firstly, we compared the proposed ensemble methodology with other methods that are based on the same learning algorithm - DS:

- Simple DS algorithm
- Local DS using 50 local instances. This method differs from the proposed technique since it has no boosting process.
- Bagging DS and Additive regression DS (using 10 sub-classifiers). Both these methods work globally whereas the proposed method works locally.

The most well known measure for the degree of fit for a regression model to a dataset is the correlation coefficient. If the actual target values are $a_1, a_2, \ldots a_n$ and the predicted target values are: $p_1, p_2, \ldots p_n$ then the correlation coefficient is given by the formula:

$$R = \frac{S_{PA}}{\sqrt{S_P S_A}}, \text{where } S_{PA} = \frac{\sum_i (p_i - \overline{p})(a_i - \overline{a})}{n-1}, \quad S_P = \frac{\sum_i (p_i - \overline{p})^2}{n-1}, \quad S_A = \frac{\sum_i (a_i - \overline{a})^2}{n-1},$$

$\overline{p}$: the average value of p_i and $\overline{a}$: the average value of α_i. In order to calculate the models' correlation coefficient for our experiments, the whole training set was divided into ten mutually exclusive and equal-sized subsets and for each subset the model was trained on the union of all of the other subsets. Then, cross validation was run 10 times for each algorithm and the average value of the 10-cross validations was calculated. It must be mentioned that we used the free available source code for most of the algorithms by [22] for our experiments.

In Table 2, we represent as "v" that the specific algorithm performed statistically better than the proposed ensemble according to t-test with $p<0.05$. Throughout, we speak of two results for a dataset as being "significant different" if the difference is statistical significant at the 5% level according to the corrected resampled t-test [19], with each pair of data points consisting of the estimates obtained in one of the 100 folds for the two learning methods being compared. On the other hand, "*" indicates that the proposed ensemble performed statistically better than the specific algorithm according to t-test with $p<0.05$. In all the other cases, there is no significant statistical difference between the results (Draws). In the last row of the table one can also see the aggregated results in the form (α/b/c). In this notation "α" means that the proposed ensemble is significantly less accurate than the compared algorithm in α out of 24 datasets, "c" means that the proposed algorithm is significantly more accurate than the compared algorithm in c out of 24 datasets, while in the remaining cases (b), there is no significant statistical difference.

In the last raw of the Table 2 one can see the aggregated results. The proposed ensemble (LARDS) is significantly more accurate than simple DS in 17 out of the 24 datasets, whilst it has significantly higher error rate in 5 datasets. In addition, the presented ensemble is significantly more accurate than Local DS in 11 out of the 24 datasets, while it has significantly higher error rate in 6 datasets. What is more, the proposed ensemble is significantly more accurate than Bagging DS in 13 out of the 24 datasets, whilst it has significantly higher error rate in 5 datasets. Furthermore, global additive regression DS have significantly lower error rates in 8 datasets than the proposed ensemble, whereas it is significantly less accurate in 11 datasets.

To sum up, the performance of the presented ensemble is better than the other well-known ensembles that use only the DS algorithm. This indicates that it is possible to obtain a feasible solution to regression problems in the real world by local additive regression because approximating a global target function is hard given that usually not enough training samples are available.

Table 2. Comparing the algorithms

Dataset	Local Additive Regression DS	Local DS		Bagging DS		Additive Regression DS		DS	
servo	0.93	0.89	*	0.79	*	0.85	*	0.79	*
autoHorse	0.92	0.92		0.79	*	0.86	*	0.72	*
autoMpg	0.89	0.89	v	0.77	*	0.87	*	0.74	*
autoPrice	0.92	0.89	*	0.82	*	0.90	*	0.81	*
baskball	0.46	0.44		0.49		0.49		0.48	
bodyfat	0.95	0.94	*	0.84	*	0.95		0.82	*
breastTumor	0.10	0.10		0.23	v	0.28	v	0.22	v
cholesterol	0.10	0.12		0.12		0.15	v	0.04	*
cleveland	0.57	0.63	v	0.59		0.65	v	0.40	*
cloud	0.82	0.69	*	0.76	*	0.87	v	0.39	*
cpu	0.96	0.92	*	0.85	*	0.95	*	0.31	*
echoMonths	0.49	0.62	v	0.69	v	0.63	v	0.70	v
fishcatch	0.96	0.94	*	0.85	*	0.94	*	0.83	*
housing	0.87	0.84	*	0.73	*	0.84	*	0.60	*
lowbwt	0.73	0.78	v	0.78	v	0.78	v	0.78	v
pbc	0.38	0.43	v	0.45	v	0.53	v	0.43	v
pwLinear	0.89	0.84	*	0.68	*	0.83	*	0.68	*
quake	0.10	0.09		0.09		0.10		0.09	
sensory	0.46	0.47		0.29	*	0.38	*	0.29	*
auto93	0.77	0.72	*	0.74		0.77		0.59	*
veteran	0.35	0.28	*	0.32		0.40	v	0.15	*
wisconsin	0.15	0.22	v	0.26	v	0.11		0.27	v
triazines	0.51	0.47	*	0.24	*	0.37	*	0.04	*
stock	0.99	0.99		0.79	*	0.94	*	0.78	*
W-D-L		*6/7/11*		*5/6/13*		*8/5/11*		*5/2/17*	

Several other models have been proposed for modeling and approximating the values of a continuous objective attribute by using the values of conditional attributes, such as local learners, regression trees, and neural networks.

Subsequently, we compared the proposed ensemble methodology with other well known regression algorithms:

- K-nearest neighbors using k=50 because the proposed algorithm uses 50 neighbors. In addition, we tested Kstar: another instance-based learner which uses entropy as distance measure [11].
- The most well known algorithm for training artificial neural networks – Back Propagation (BP) with one hidden layer and five neurons in this layer.
- A well known regression tree algorithm - RepTree [22]
- A well known regression algorithm - Decision Table [17]

In the last raw of Table 3 one can see the aggregated results. The proposed ensemble is significantly more accurate than simple Kstar in 12 out of the 24 datasets, whilst it has significantly higher error rate in 5 datasets. In addition, the presented ensemble is significantly more accurate than 50NN in 15 out of the 24 datasets, while it has significantly higher error rate in 8 datasets. What is more, the proposed ensemble is significantly more accurate than Decision Table in 11 out of the 24 datasets, whilst it has significantly higher error rate in 8 datasets. Furthermore, the BP algorithm has significantly lower error rates in 9 datasets than the proposed ensemble, whereas it is significantly less accurate in 10 datasets. Finally, the RepTree algorithm has significantly lower error rates in 12 datasets than the proposed ensemble, whereas it is significantly less accurate in 7 datasets.

To sum up, the performance of the presented ensemble is more accurate than the other well-known regression methods.

Table 3. Comparing the algorithms

Dataset	LARDS	Kstar		Decision Table		BP		50NN		RepTree	
servo	0.93	0.86	*	0.80	*	0.94		0.65	*	0.86	*
autoHorse	0.92	0.90	*	0.85	*	0.95	v	0.85	*	0.83	*
autoMpg	0.89	0.91	v	0.90	v	0.91	v	0.86	*	0.88	
autoPrice	0.92	0.91		0.81	*	0.90	*	0.89	*	0.88	*
baskball	0.46	0.46		0.53	v	0.54	v	0.56	v	0.39	*
bodyfat	0.95	0.87	*	0.97	v	0.98	v	0.91	*	0.98	v
breastTumor	0.10	0.19	v	0.16	v	0.09		0.23	v	0.15	v
cholesterol	0.10	0.04	*	0.07		0.08		0.17	v	0.07	
cleveland	0.57	0.55		0.52	*	0.44	*	0.71	v	0.54	*
cloud	0.82	0.81		0.84		0.88	v	0.77	*	0.80	*
cpu	0.96	0.97		0.92	*	1.00	v	0.92	*	0.90	*
echoMonths	0.49	0.39	*	0.72	v	0.42	*	0.72	v	0.70	v
fishcatch	0.96	0.99	v	0.94	*	0.99	v	0.78	*	0.95	
housing	0.87	0.90	v	0.81	*	0.90	v	0.77	*	0.85	*
lowbwt	0.73	0.62	*	0.78	v	0.60	*	0.75	v	0.78	v
pbc	0.38	0.30	*	0.40		0.32	*	0.52	v	0.46	v
pwLinear	0.89	0.72	*	0.83	*	0.90		0.85	*	0.89	
quake	0.10	0.08	*	0.09		0.08	*	0.06	*	0.07	*
sensory	0.46	0.39	*	0.57	v	0.29	*	0.36	*	0.45	
auto93	0.77	0.77		0.68	*	0.85	v	0.71	*	0.23	*
veteran	0.35	0.31		0.41	v	0.25	*	0.35		0.23	*
wisconsin	0.15	0.04	*	0.04	*	0.04	*	0.35	v	0.15	
triazines	0.51	0.45	*	0.47		0.44	*	0.25	*	0.27	*
stock	0.99	1.00	v	0.97	*	0.99		0.98	*	0.98	
W-D-L		5/7/12		8/5/11		9/5/10		8/1/15		5/7/12	

The reason for the performance of the proposed technique is the bias-variance trade-off. By increasing the number of observations over which averaging is taking place, one can reduce the variance of a local averaging estimator. On the other hand as progressively less similar observations are introduced in each iteration, the estimator generally becomes more biased and subsequently more appropriate for the boosting.

5 Conclusion

Local regression is a non-parametric statistical methodology that provides smooth modeling by not assuming any particular global form of the unknown regression function. On the contrary these models fit a functional form within the neighborhood of the query points. These models are known to provide highly accurate predictions over a wide range of problems due to the absence of a "pre-defined" functional form.

As it is well known, local techniques are an old idea in time series prediction [3]. Local learning can reduce the complexity of component classifiers and improve the generalization performance although the global complexity of the system can not be guaranteed to be low.

In spite of the attention boosting receives in classification methodology, few results exist that apply the ideas to regression problems. If boosting effectiveness extends beyond classification problems then we might expect that the boosting of simplistic regression models could result in a richer class of regression models.

In this study, local averaging estimator is coupled with boosting technique. In detail, we proposed local additive regression of decision stumps and our experiment for some real datasets shows that the proposed combining method outperforms other well known methods and ensembles.

The benefit of allowing multiple local models is somewhat offset by the cost of storing and querying the training dataset for each test example that means that instance based learners do not scale well for the large amount of data. Local weighted learning algorithms must often decide what instances to store for use during generalization in order to avoid excessive storage and time complexity. By eliminating a set of examples from a database the response time for decisions will decrease, as fewer instances are examined when a query example is presented.

In future work we will focus on the problem of reducing the size of the stored set of examples while trying to maintain or even improve the correlation coefficient by avoiding noise and overfitting. In the articles [6] and [21] numerous instance selection methods can be found that can be combined with a local boosting technique. It must be also mentioned that we will use local additive regression with other weak regression methods such as RepTree [22].

References

1. Aha, D., Lazy Learning. Dordrecht: Kluwer Academic Publishers, (1997).
2. Atkeson, C. G., Moore, A. W. and Schaal, S., Locally weighted learning for control. Artificial Intelligence Review, 11 (1997) 75–113.
3. Atkeson, C. G., Moore, A. W. and Schaal, S., Locally weighted learning. Artificial Intelligence Review, 11 (1997) 11-73.

4. Blake, C. & Merz, C., UCI Repository of machine learning databases. Irvine, CA: University of California, Department of Information and Computer Science. [http:// www. ics. uci.edu/~mlearn/MLRepository.html] (1998)
5. Dietterich, T., Ensemble Methods in Machine Learning, In Proc. 1st International Workshop on Multiple Classifer Systems, LNCS, Vol 1857, (2000) 1-10, Springer-Verlag.
6. Brighton, H., Mellish, C., Advances in Instance Selection for Instance-Based Learning Algorithms, Data Mining and Knowledge Discovery, 6 (2002) 153–172.
7. Bottou, L. and Vapnik, V., Local learning algorithm, Neural Computation, vol. 4, no. 6, (1992) 888-901.
8. Breiman, L., Bagging Predictors. Machine Learning, 24 (1996) 123-140.
9. Cohen S. and Intrator N., Automatic Model Selection in a Hybrid Perceptron/ Radial Network. In Multiple Classifier Systems. 2nd International Workshop, MCS 2001, pages 349–358.
10. Duffy, N. Helmbold, D., Boosting Methods for Regression, Machine Learning, 47, (2002) 153–200.
11. John, C. and Trigg, L., K*: An Instance- based Learner Using an Entropic Distance Measure", Proc. of the 12th International Conference on ML, (1995) 108-114.
12. Frank, E., Hall, M., Pfahringer, B., Locally weighted naive Bayes. Proc. of the 19th Conference on Uncertainty in Artificial Intelligence. Acapulco, Mexico. Morgan Kaufmann, (2003) 249-256.
13. Freund, Y., & Schapire, R. E.. A decision-theoretic generalization of on-line learning and an application to boosting. Journal of Computer and System Sciences, 55:1, (1997) 119–139.
14. Friedman J., "Stochastic Gradient Boosting," Computational Statistics and Data Analysis 38 (2002) 367-378.
15. Iba, W. & Langley, P., Induction of one-level decision trees. Proc. of the Ninth International Machine Learning Conference (1992) 233-240. Aberdeen, Scotland: Morgan Kaufmann.
16. Kleinberg, E.M., A Mathematically Rigorous Foundation for Supervised Learning. In J. Kittler and F. Roli, editors, Multiple Classifier Systems. First International Workshop, MCS 2000, Cagliari, Italy, volume 1857 of Lecture Notes in Computer Science, (2000) 67–76. Springer-Verlag.
17. Kohavi R., The Power of Decision Tables. In Proc European Conference on Machine Learning (1995) 174 - 189.
18. Loader, C., Local Regression and Likelihood. Springer, New York, (1999).
19. Nadeau, C., Bengio, Y., Inference for the Generalization Error. Machine Learning, 52 (2003) 239-281.
20. Vapnik, V.N., Statistical Learning Theory, Wiley, New York, (1998) (chapters:2 & 3).
21. Wilson, D., Martinez, T., Reduction Techniques for Instance-Based Learning Algorithms, Machine Learning, 38 (2000) 257–286.
22. Witten, I., Frank, E., Data Mining: Practical Machine Learning Tools and Techniques with Java Implementations. Morgan Kaufmann, San Mateo, CA, (2000).

Mining Time Series with Mine Time

Lefteris Koumakis[1], Vassilis Moustakis[1,2], Alexandros Kanterakis[1],
and George Potamias[1]

[1] Institute of Computer Science, Foundation for Research and Technology-Hellas (FORTH),
P.O. Box 1385, 71110 Heraklion, Crete, Greece
[2] Department of Production and Management Engineering,
Technical University of Crete, University Campus,
Kounoupidiana, 73100 Chania, Crete, Greece
{koumakis, moustaki, kantale, potamias}@ics.forth.gr

Abstract. We present, *Mine Time*, a tool that supports discovery over time series data. *Mine Time* is realized by the introduction of novel algorithmic processes, which support assessment of coherence and similarity across time-series data. The innovation comes from the inclusion of specific 'control' operations in the elaborated time-series matching metric. The final outcome is the clustering of time-series into similar-groups. Clustering is performed via the appropriate customization of a phylogeny-based clustering algorithm and tool. We demonstrate *Mine Time* via two experiments.

1 Introduction

The article presents *Mine Time*, an apprentice for mining and clustering time series data. Time-Series (TS for short) occur in many aspects of economic, social and scientific activity and TS data modeling has been an active area of research in statistics. A variety of models exist, which manifest interest and provide statistical analysis tools [2]. Expanding interest in data mining and knowledge discovery has contributed to an increase of research awareness in machine-learning and data-mining on TS data – see for instance the work of Morik on time sequences of intensive care unit data [9].

The discovery of relationships in a time sequence is important in many application domains. Yet an important aspect, largely missing from the literature is the discovery of temporal patterns or relationships in sequences of time events.[1, 4, 6, 7, 8], which would eventually support assessment of similarity and clustering across TS.

Mine Time integrates discovery of similar and indicative patterns in TS collections. This is achieved via the clustering of TS into similar-groups. Clustering is performed and visualized by the appropriate customization of phylogeny-based clustering [12].

In the sections that follow, we overview *Mine Time* methodology, present *Mine Time* in action and discuss experimental results. We conclude the article by summarizing our work and point to areas for further research on the subject.

G. Antoniou et al. (Eds.): SETN 2006, LNAI 3955, pp. 158–168, 2006.
© Springer-Verlag Berlin Heidelberg 2006

2 Mine Time Methodology

Geometrical distance does not suffice to assess similarity across TS since sequence data may have outliers, different scaling factors and baseline. As noted in [1] specific functions should be employed to ascertain reliability in similarity matching (see figure 1 for a visual explanation of these functions). In figure 1(part 1) shows two TS sequences. Figure 1(part 2) demonstrates the fist operation via which a time gap between the two TS is removed. Gap removal supports offset alignment in time, which is demonstrated in figure 1(part 3). Finally, amplitude is scaled and the two TS are segmented into two pieces in time, see figure 1(part 4). The two segments are used to support TS matching via the matching of the two sub sequences – see figure 1(5). Mine Time incorporates the heuristics that support gap removal, offset translation, scaling, and similarity matching and clustering of TS. Mine Time methodology is discussed in the subsections that follow. The methodology encompasses two main parts: matching and phylogenetic clustering.

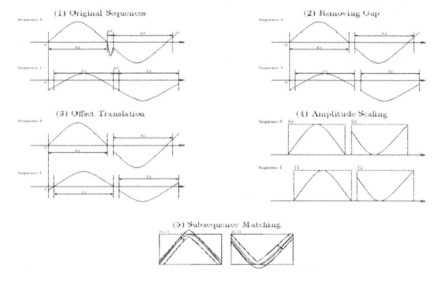

Fig. 1. Critical functions in time-series matching operations. In (1) are the original TS. In (2) non-significant parts are removed. In (3) outliers are removed. In (4) series are smoothed and finally in (5) similarity is assessed (figure from reference [1], p. 2).

2.1 TS Matching and Coherence

Mine Time incorporates five main operations to support matching and modeling of coherence. Operations are denoted by A to E. Notation is described in the text and summarized in the Appendix.

A. *Transformation and Representation.* Piecewise linear segmentation of TS data is used to transform and to decompose into pieces a series of data based on [10]. Breaking a series into component trends is common in TS. Scaling precedes segmentation and scaling proceeds according to time to time differences. Given a TS X_a, evolving over a set of k time-points with respective values y_1, y_2, ... y_k, the percentage change, $c_{a,i}$ is computed by formula (1), which supports scaling, namely:

$$C_{a,i} = \frac{\left| y_{i+1} - y_i \right|}{y_i} \qquad (1)$$

B. *Segmentation.* TS data are decomposed into segments that range over more than one time-to-time changes or fitting windows. A segment's change is computed as the sum over all respective segments' changes. That is, for a segment ranging over I_{seg} time-points.

$$C_{a,seg} = \sum_{i \in seg} C_{a,i} \Big/ (I_{seg} - 1) \qquad (2)$$

With the transformation computed by formula (2), a collection of TS ranging within different vertical (offset) and horizontal (amplitude) widths are calibrated and normalized. Furthermore, TS percentage-changes transformation offers a first approach to the identification of TS trends. Results of the percentage-changes piecewise linear segmentation approach for an artificially generated domain (Synthetic Control Data – SCD, [11]) is shown in figure 2. Even with a fitting window reduced to single sequential time-to-time changes, noticeable smoothing is achieved.

(**a**) TS (raw)   (**b**) %Changes transform

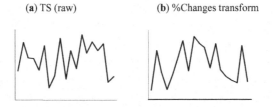

Fig. 2. (a) One unprocessed (raw) time-series for the SCD domain; (b) Processed incorporates percentage transformation changes, which are representative of the same data. The TS in (a) included 600 points and the transformed series in (b) includes 19 time-period associated points.

Segments correspond to TS parts and are determined according to user specified parameter settings. For instance, a time series with 120 data points (such as monthly observations across ten years) may be segmented by taking 12 points at a time. *Mine Time* encompasses two types of segmentation. The first type is called successive and takes a predetermined number of data observations and creates a corresponding number of segments. For instance, in a series of 120 points if the user specifies that 36 points are desired then *Mine Time* will automatically generate 49 segments. The first segment will capture data points one through thirty-six, the second segment will capture points two through thirty-seven and so on. The second segmentation type is region based and optimizes the process by avoiding unnecessary split of data sequences. For instance a series with 120 points may be segmented into 10 parts on 12 points each. The main advantage of the region-based segmentation is that it offers the user the ability to focus his/her exploration activities on specific periods. For example, monthly time-series ranging over 180 months (i.e., 15 years) may be assessed similar because they exhibit a high-similarity figure for the last 12 time-points (i.e., last year). Thus, similarity between TS acquires a more natural interpretation. Moreover, because of the segmentation operations involved, TS may be considered similar because some of their not-overlapping segments (e.g., with 12-months period lag) are similar- regardless of their coherence in other time-periods.

C. *Statistically significant changes.* We compute statistically significant change from Y_i to Y_{i+1} time point for a time series A with l time points by using formula (3). The same formula is also used in step E during TS distance assessment.

$$t_{A,Yi} = \frac{C(X_a, Y_{Y1}) - \overline{C}}{\sqrt{\sigma^2(1 + 1/(l - k - 1))}} \tag{3}$$

D. *Weighting.* Using segments we proceed to the assessment of the 'influence' that each part of a TS has with respect to the overall series in the collection. In other words, we are interested to identify the inter-significance characteristics of the collection. The relative-weight of a TS change is computed by formula (4) and represents the mean of the respective changes over all TS, namely:

$$W_{Ca,i} = \frac{C_{a,i}}{\sum_{\substack{Time-series \\ in\ \{a,b,..\}}} C_{T,i}} \tag{4}$$

E. *Assessment of distance between TS.* We elaborate on a metric that computes pair similarity between TS. This is done because phylogenic clustering is based on the distance between objects. Given two TS, X_a and X_b, distance between the two of them is computed by formula (5), namely:

$$\mathbf{\mathit{dist}}(X_a, X_b) = \sum_{i=1}^{k-1} |(W_{Ca,i} \times C_{a,i}) - (W_{Cb,i} + 1 \times C_{b,i})| \tag{5}$$

- If the respective percentage changes are *statistically significant* (by step C) then their weights are computed by formula (4) above.
- In all other cases, the weight of each non-significant change is fixed to the lowest relative-weight value of the respective time-to-time (or, segment) changes in the time-series collection.

Distance assessment takes into account the relative weight factors, which correspond to changes across segments. In addition, it introduces a control feature in the course of TS matching. At the extremes, non-significant changes of low relative-weight exhibit a weak influence; on the contrast, significant changes of high relative-weight have a strong influence.

2.2 Phylogenetic Clustering

Computed distances between TS form a square distance-matrix, which initiates distance-based clustering. Distance-based clustering methods represents and active area of research and practice. *Mine Time* relies on a distance-based hierarchical clustering approach – *phylogenetic* clustering, and uses the *Neighbor Joining (NJ)* algorithm. *Phylogenetic* clustering is rich in visualization characteristics of the derived hierarchical clustering-tree. Yet construction of a hierarchical clustering-tree for a set of objects based on their pair wise distance is computationally intractable (i.e., NP-complete) according to various optimality criteria [3, 5] and this has led to the development of numerous greedy approaches. Among greedy approaches, *NJ* is widely used in biomedical research due to its efficiency and simplicity. *NJ* was initially proposed by Saitou and Nei [12] and later modified by Studier and Kepler [14]. *NJ* seeks to build a tree which minimizes the sum of all edge lengths in the hierarchical clustering-tree. A number of studies have confirmed efficiency of NJ in clustering and tree construction. [13].

NJ begins with a star tree, then iteratively finds the closest neighboring pair (i.e. the pair that induces a tree of minimum sum of edge lengths) among all possible pairs of nodes (both internal and external). The closest pair is then clustered into a new internal node, and the distances of this node to the rest of the nodes in the tree are computed and used in later iterations. The algorithm terminates when internal nodes have been inserted into the tree (i.e., when the star tree is fully resolved into a binary tree).

3 *Mine Time* in Action

Mine Time encompasses operations at five layers: (1) client side, (2) server side, (3) segmentation, (4) matching and (5) visualization. A query by the user is taken through the TS collection (which resides at a server) and query specifics are interpreted to support segmentation, matching, similarity and clustering. The process is illustrated in figure 3.

Mine Time is built in *Java* with the appropriate customization and integration of a set of Java classes for phylogenetic-based clustering, adopted from the PAL project (Phylogenetic Analysis Library; http://www.cebl.auckland.ac.nz/pal-project/ visited in November 2005).

Using SQL the user forms a query and *Mine Time* conveys the query to the Server. Figure 4 shows the overall system interface. The user has the option to connect to the server, to form a query and to retrieve the relevant time series. To activate this option the user has to select from the Menu *File -> Read TSs from URL*. Furthermore, the user may select a file for input instead of a query by selecting *File -> Read from file*, without the execution of an SQL query to a database or can view an existing scenario by selecting *File -> Read distances* and invoke only the visualization methods.

If the user wants a graphical representation of the output he/she may choose a *'Cycle'* or a *'Dendrogram'* representation from the *"Visualize Results"* option of the menu.

When the user selects to retrieve time-series from a remote server, then a query window appears in which the user has to set the server's URL address and the SQL query. To connect the user must specify JDBC (Java DataBase Connectivity) parameters. The overall interface encompasses parameter selections related to segmentation and visualization of clustering results – see figure 4.

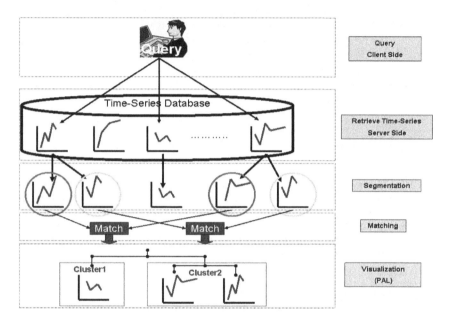

Fig. 3. Five layers of *Mine-Time*. The user specifies a query, which is taken through the TS collection. Based on segmentation matching parameters specification and on clustering preference, *Mine Time* proceeds to clustering and identification of coherence across TS.

Visualization is limited to the segments or series that pass the distance threshold.

The user can set up this threshold from the distance threshold window and view or change value to system parameters, such as number of remaining TS, time points per window, start / end dates, etc.

After the calculation of TS distances, two matrices are generated for both TS segments and for the entire TS. The user may select to display results on an either / or basis.

The final step is the visualization if the user has selected from the initial main window to visualize the results (i.e., one of the two alternatives- cycle; tree, is selected). Then a window appears with the segmented time-series clustered, based on their computed distances (see Figures 5 and 6 for phylogeny and dendogram cluster visualizations).

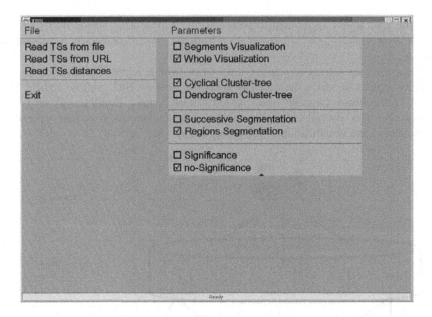

Fig. 4. *Mine Time* system interface. At the **File Menu** the user may select to retrieve time-series directly from: a previously stored file, a remote server or to load a pre-computed time-series distance matrices file. At the **Parameters Menu** the user can select: (a) how to visualize output (entire TS or segments), (b) what type of output she wishes (cyclical or dendrogram), (c) what kind of segmentation she desires (successive or region), and (d) how to handle significance of respective percentage changes during similarity assessment.

4   Experimenting with *Mine Time*

Mine Time experimentation and validation focused in two dimensions:

- To assess reliability of similarity heuristics (and clustering trees) between TS.
- To assess efficiency with respect to the use of computational resources.

In order to perform the evaluation and validation studies we relied on different domains and respective TS datasets. Reliability of Mine Time heuristics was explored with an artificial domain that involved TS data randomly generated from mathematical functions and full scale assessment was based on real-world TS data retrieved from the database of IFO (Institute for Economic Research, Munich, Germany, (www.ifo.de).

4.1   Mathematical Functions Domain

The first experiment concerns a group of simple mathematical functions. Specifically we generated TS with 100 time points using the square, cosine, sine, palm and polynomial functions. Figure 5 shows the results for 20 randomly generated TS. We applied successive segmentation and set minimum similarity equal to 0 (all time series were selected for clustering). *Mine Time* classified correctly 19 of the 20 time series, which corresponds to 19/20 = 95% accuracy. Cluster formation mapped mathematical function definition while it is noticeable that relations between sine, cosine and polynomial functions were also discovered. We repeated the experiment with 30 and 100 time series (randomly generated) and the accuracy, for both experiments, was 100%.

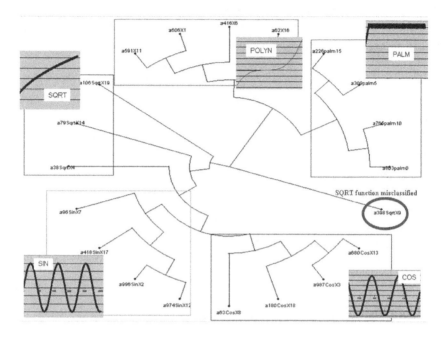

Fig. 5. Phylogeny-clustering (cyclical) tree for the synthetic mathematic functions TS. SQRT is the square function, POLYN relates to polynomial, PALM relates to the palm function, SIN to the sine function and COS relates to the cosine function. All functions were classified correctly except one square function, which was left out during cluster formation (the misclassified TS is circled). Individual TS are listed at the leafs.

4.2 Ifo-Kt Domain

The second experiment draws from a subset of TS from the IRAIA's ifo database, called the *'ifo_Konjunkturtest'*[1]. A subset of about 1000 TS was selected (using the *Mine Time* URL-based direct access, to a remote database). Using the *Mine Time* we narrowed the set of 1000 TS down to 20. Figure 6 shows the results of standard agglomerative clustering dendogram, for the ten most-similar series across the 20 selected TS. The dendogram was generated with a standard algorithmic-statistical procedure without taking in consideration the distances as computed with the aid of the *Mine Time*.

---

[1] Data were collected during the duration of the IRAIA project, IST-1999-10602. See also:
http://www.vdi-nachrichten.com/studien/wirtschaft/ifo-daten2.asp
http://www.cesifo-group.de/link/10DATABASE

Vertical axis reflects similarity measured by the *Mine Time*. Most of the TS, which are part of the denodgram have similarity (according to *Mine Time*) that exceed 90%. Agglomerative clustering results validate Mine Time selection of the 20 TS out of 1000. The experiment took about 10 minutes to run. Time is reasonable and presents a milestone towards real-world utilization and exploitation of the *Mine Time*.

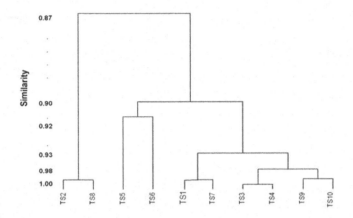

Fig. 6. Agglomerative clustering: The dendogram presents the clustering of the 10 most similar TS for the ifo-kt domain; note that most of the series exhibit similarity levels over 0.9 and across all TS similarity is at least 0.87

5 Conclusions

We have presented tool that supports mining and discovery of coherence across TS data. TS. *Mine Time* supports operations for importing and reading TS data (e.g., from Excel); to compute distances between TS; to cluster TS; and to visualize clustering results. *Mine Time* is built in Java making it portable on various platforms. The Java classes for the clustering algorithm were taken from the public-domain library PAL-Phylogeny Analysis Library, http://www.pal-project.org and were appropriately customized and integrated in our system.

Research and development plans may move towards:

- The elaboration and customization of other time-series matching approaches, e.g., Dynamic Time Warping (DTW); and clustering operations (e.g., agglomerative, k-means etc).
- The elaboration on intelligent time-series indexing techniques, in order to make operations more effective and scalable to huge collections of TS – this will place *Mine Time* in the realm of an 'on-demand' web service to be called at any-time of the navigation and exploration process.
- Porting the whole package at a web server in order to achieve remote operation - access just from a Web browser using jsp (JavaServer Pages).

Acknowledgement

Work reported herein was partially supported via the IRAIA and WS-Talk projects [15], IST-1999-10602, and CRAFT 006026. The partners of both projects were: IFO, DIW, University de Talca, UPS-IRIT, QUB, RHUL, Iteratec, LemonLabs, Soluciones, UDP (Chile), Archimedia, LuckyEye and FORTH-ICS. Opinions and results expressed herein do not correspond to official IRAIA or WS-Talk Consortia position and are the sole responsibility of the authors. We also want to thank the anonymous reviewers who gave us the opportunity to improve in many respects our work and presentation.

References

[1] Agrawal, R., Lin, K., Sawhney, H.S., and Shim, K., Fast Similarity Search in the Presence of Noise, Scaling, and Translation in Time-Series Databases. *Proc. 21st VLDB Conf.* Zurich, Switzerland, 490-501 (1995)

[2] Box, G.E.P., and Jenkins, G.M. *Time Series Analysis, Forecasting and Control.* Prentice Hall (1976).

[3] Day, W., Computational complexity of inferring phylogenies from dissimilarity matrices. *Bull. Math. Biol.,* 49, 4, 461-467 (1987).

[4] Faloutsos, C., Ranganathan, M., and Manolopoulos, Y., Fast Sequence Matching in Time-Series Databases. Proc. *SIGMOD'94* (1994).

[5] Foulds, L. R. and Graham, R. L., The Steiner problem in phylogeny is NP-complete. *Advances Appl. Math.,* 3, 43-49 (1982).

[6] Jagadish, H., Mendelzon, A., and Milo, T., Similarity-Based Queries. *Proc. 14th Symp. on Principles of Database Systems* (*PODS'95*). 36-45 (1995).

[7] Laird, P., *Identifying and using patterns in sequential data.* In: Jantke, K., Kobayashi, S., Tomita, E., and Yokomori, T. (Eds), Algorithmic Learning Theory, 4th International Workshop, Berlin: Springer Verlag, 1-118, (1993).

[8] Mannila, H., Toivonen, H., and Verkamo, A. Discovering frequent episodes in sequences. *Proc. 1st International Conference on Knowledge Discovery and Data Mining* (*KDD'95*), Montreal, Canada, 210-215 (1995).

[9] Morik K., The Representation Race – Pre-processing for Handling Time Phenomena. *Proc. European Conference on Machine Learning (ECML).* Springer Verlag (2000).

[10] Pavlidis, T., and Horowitz, S., Segmentation of plane curves. *IEEE Trans. On Computers*, 23, 8 (1974).

[11] Pham, D.T., and Chan, A.B., Control Chart Pattern Recognition using a New Type of Self Organizing Neural Network. *Instn, Mech, Engrs.* 212, 1,115-127 (1998).

[12] Saitou, N., and Nei, M., The neighbor-joining method: a new method for reconstructing phylogenetic trees. *Mol. Biol. Evo.,* 4, 4, 406-425 (1987).

[13] Saitou, N. and Imanishi, T., Relative efficiencies of the Fitch-Margoliash, maximum-parsimony, maximum-likelihood, minimum-evolution, and neighbor-joining methods of phylogenetic tree construction in obtaining the correct tree. *Mol. Biol. Evol.,* 6, 514-525 (1989).

[14] Studier, J. and Keppler, K., A note on the neighbor-joining algorithm of Saitou and Nei. *Mol. Biol. Evol.,* 5, 729-731 (1988).

[15] http://www.ics.forth.gr/eHealth/projects.jsp

Appendix. Notation

X_a	A Time-Series
k	A set of time-points
y_i	Value of a specific (i) time-point
$c_{a,i}$	the percentage change
I_{seg}	Number of time-points.
$C_{a,seg}$	Statistically significant change of a time series A for a segment ranging over I_{seg} time-points
Y_i	A time-point
l	Total time-points of a Time-series
$t_{A,Yi}$	Statistically significant changes
$W_{Ca,i}$	Weighting of a segment
$dist(X_a,X_b)$	Distance between Time-Series X_a,X_b

Behaviour Flexibility in Dynamic and Unpredictable Environments: The ICAGENT Approach

Vangelis Kourakos-Mavromichalis and George Vouros

Dept. of Information and Communication Systems Engineering,
University of the Aegean, Karlovassi, Samos – Greece
{emav, georgev}@aegean.gr

Abstract. Several agent frameworks have been proposed for developing intelligent software agents and multi-agent systems that are able to perform in dynamic environments. These frameworks and architectures exploit specific reasoning tasks (such as option selection, desire filtering, plan elaboration and means-end reasoning) that support agents to react, deliberate and/or interact/cooperate with other agents. Such reasoning tasks are realized by means of specific modules that agents may trigger according to circumstances, switching their behaviour between predefined discrete behavioural modes. This paper presents the facilities provided by the non-layered BDI-architecture of ICAGENT for supporting performance in dynamic and unpredictable multi-agent environments through efficient balancing between behavioural modes in a continuous space. This space is circumscribed by the purely (individual) reactive, the purely (individual) deliberative and the social deliberative behavioural modes. In a greater extend than existing frameworks; ICAGENT relates agent's flexible behaviour to cognition and sociability, supporting the management of plans constructed by the agent's mental and domain actions in a coordinated manner.

1 Introduction

This paper focuses on agents' autonomous behaviour in dynamic and non-deterministic environments that are populated by multiple agents. Being resource-bounded, an agent that performs in such environments faces inherent limitations with respect to the perception, practical reasoning, performance and cooperation abilities: It cannot be fully aware of the changes that occur in their physical environment, the available time to compute responses is always limited and bounded to the time that it has until its resources exceed, it has to plan and to achieve its goals without exceeding environmental and own resources, and finally, it often needs to collaborate with others to achieve better results (e.g. it can save resources, or increase its expected utility or its fitting advantage).

To overcome the above limitations, a resource bounded agent must be able to deliberate, to plan and act with respect to its own, others', and environment resources, adapting to unforeseen events and to newly detected facts, either individually or in collaboration with others. On the other hand, an agent needs to react to events/facts

G. Antoniou et al. (Eds.): SETN 2006, LNAI 3955, pp. 169 – 180, 2006.

that provide opportunities for achieving its goals or to events/facts that may seriously affect its mission. In either case, an agent may perform individually or in conjunction with other agents.

As already pointed out in [Weiss, 2001], [Kourakos and Vouros 2001], this paper conjectures that for an agent to be flexible (i.e. *to have the ability to adapt and balance between the different behavioural modes*) its behavioural mode cannot be determined by the mere mapping of domain tasks to specific types of behaviour. This is so, because the agent may need to adapt its behavioural mode several times in response to changes in the environment while it pursues a specific goal. Such an adaptation can be considered as a "tuning" process, with respect to the way several mental actions are performed. Therefore, the type of behaviour adopted by an agent at a specific time point must be considered as a property that emerges as the agent performs, according to the perceived state of the environment, the occurring events, and to the agent's mental state.

To adapt their behaviour, agents have to

(a)   Decide about the facts and events whose occurrence in the physical environment they must monitor.
(b)   Decide whether they shall reason about the relative strength of their desires and intentions, or whether they will commit to fulfil a desire without considering conflicts with intentions they already have.
(c)   Decide whether they will assess their options towards fulfilling a desire or, acting purely reactively, whether they will fetch a good solution and start pursuing it.
(d)   Determine whether and how they shall generate and elaborate their plans individually or jointly with other agents.

As it has been proposed by [Pollack and Horty, 1999] the above issues require plan management abilities for performing plan generation, environment monitoring, alternative assessment, commitment management, plan elaboration, meta-level control and cooperation reasoning tasks.

In conjunction to the plan management reasoning tasks, it has been argued [Grosz 1996] that for agents to plan and act effectively, mostly in collaborative settings, they must maintain a mental-state view of plans in terms of beliefs and intentions. Bratman [Bratman 1987] has argued that intentions to do actions constrain the other intentions an agent may adopt, focuses means-ends reasoning and guides re-planning: These are major issues for agent's goal directed flexible behaviour.

Combining these views, this paper describes how the *mental-state view of plan management* of the ICAGENT framework can support agents' flexibility in behaviour (i.e. the ability to adapt and balance between different behavioural modes). This extends previous work on the ICAGENT framework in two major, important directions: (a) The incorporation of facilities for agents' to behave socially [Kourakos and Vouros 2001] either deliberatively or reactively, and (b) The incorporation of generic, advanced collaborative facilities for the collaboration of more than two agents [Kourakos and Vouros 2005].

Specifically, the Intelligent Collaborative Agent (ICAGENT) framework introduces an alternative to the layered approach to balancing between different behavioural modes: While layered architectures implement agent's behavioural modes (such as planning, reaction and cooperation) in different modules, the ICAGENT framework introduces a "tuning" approach to achieving behavioural flexibility: *Plan management reasoning tasks are performed by means of mental actions, which in conjunction to the domain actions are planned and performed according to agents' beliefs and intentions, following a mental state view of plan management. The overall behaviour of the agent results from the combination of the way reasoning tasks are performed.*

Towards this approach, key technologies for realizing the ICAGENT framework are a BDI architecture and the SharedPlans model for collaborative activity. Specifically, the ICAGENT framework supports the development of BDI agents that are able to plan either reactively or deliberatively, and orthogonally, either individually or in a social setting. The BDI model supports practical reasoning and considers that a rational agent must be able to *deliberate* (i.e. decide what state of affairs to achieve) and perform *means-end reasoning* (i.e. decide how to achieve these state of affairs) [Bratman 1987]. ICAGENT exploits these *practical-reasoning* tasks to support the implementation of the SharedPlans [Grosz and Kraus, 1996, 1999] model for agents' *social deliberation*. The *SharedPlans* model provides the mental structures and states that are required for a group of agents to perform jointly (i.e. socially deliberatively). Particularly, it describes the plan refinement process: Starting from a shared goal and a partial shared plan, agents form *intentions to* act and *intentions that* the group of collaborators will succeed towards their shared goal. The latter prohibit agents to commit towards actions that are in conflict with other intended actions of the group, and drive collaborators to exhibit helpful behaviour when one of the collaborating parties needs it. Agents collaborate towards the construction of a full shared-plan by elaborating the partial shared plan jointly.

Summarizing the above, the ICAGENT framework for agent development provides:

- A mental-state view of plans: Agents have plans when they have a particular set of beliefs and intentions.
- Reasoning tasks for agents to manage their plans towards adapting and balancing their behaviour between individual/social reaction and deliberation.
- Mental actions for performing the reasoning tasks: These actions are treated in coordination with the domain actions and their performance can affect "tuning" the reasoning tasks towards one or another behavioural mode according to agents' beliefs and intentions.
- An implementation of collaboration that is based on the SharedPlans [Grosz 1996] model of collaborative activity.

2   The Tileworld

In the paragraphs that follow we present examples of intelligent agents performing in a highly dynamic and unpredictable Tileworld environment.

The Tileworld is a highly parameterized simulated environment proposed by M. Pollack and M. Ringuette [Pollack 1990] for evaluating agent architectures that include rational heuristic policies for managing deliberation. The environment comprises four types of entities: obstacles, tiles, holes and agents. Obstacles are always organized in groups (of three obstacles) that after a while they may form deadlocks for agents. Every a fixed number of milliseconds the state of this physical environment changes: new tiles and obstacles may appear, old ones may disappear, some of them may move by one square randomly and be removed from the chessboard. Holes appear randomly but they may disappear after a given number of seconds (TTL). New agents may be introduced in the environment in random places. Agents may perceive part of the physical environment and may know the expected time to leave (TTL) of holes. We consider that all agents in the Tileworld are capable of perceiving all facts and events that occur in the physical environment in a given range from their current positions, as well as from the positions of other objects of interest (e.g. tiles, holes and other agents). The latter one points on agents' ability to focus on specific "areas" of interest. Each agent has the goal to fill a predefined number of holes. Having achieved this goal, it leaves the environment.

A configuration of the Tileworld is the one shown in Fig. 1

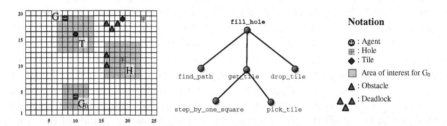

Fig. 1. A configuration of the tile-world chessboard

Intelligent behaviour in the Tileworld environment requires careful balancing between fast reactions and deliberative consideration of long term ramifications, as well as social deliberation when it is necessary. Each agent that performs on the chessboard adapts its behaviour according to the following: (a) the knowledge that it has about the changes that occur in its physical environment (i.e. its beliefs about the physical context), (b) the knowledge that it has about how to elaborate its current (individual or shared) plans in the (possibly shared) context of actions (i.e. knowledge about methods for achieving goals with respect to its intentions) and (c) the "responses" that it receives from the environment when it performs actions.

Let us suppose that we place a new agent, say G_0, on square (10,4). The new agent detects that the hole and the tile that are most close to it are on squares (19,11) and (10,16). The agent recognizes this situation and commits to fill this hole with this tile. Towards achieving this goal it finds a path to the tile, then to the hole, and starts traversing this path in a reactive way until it detects one of the following: (a) a deadlock, (b) other agents that may intent to fill the same hole or to use the same tile, and (c) the potential for collaboration with other agents.

The agent follows the planned route and reacts to changes in the environment. For instance, the agent avoids obstacles reactively by moving them by one square. In such cases the agent does not need to consider other alternatives, reform its commitments or abandon any of them. The agent's behavioural mode towards performing the abstract action "fill the hole" does not change until it detects one of the following facts: A new agent that is close to the intended tile, or an obstacle that compiles a deadlock to the path that it traverses.

In case the agent detects a new agent close to the intended tile, its behaviour changes from reactive to social deliberative. Agents communicate trying to recognize the potential for collaboration, to negotiate about the method that will follow on filling the hole jointly, and to agree on the allocation of tasks between group members. Note that while agents collaborate on filling a hole, they may have different, incomplete and possibly inconsistent views of the world and mental states of the other agents. Thus, to act jointly, communication is required to avoid mis-coordination.

Returning to our example, recognizing the potential for collaboration, the agent G_0 requests from G_1 to work jointly on filling the hole H_0. The agent G_1, being benevolent (this assumption holds for all the agents in the chessboard), accepts the request of G_0 and it commits to perform this activity jointly with G_0. Doing so, G_1 reconciles the recipe proposed by G_0 with its mental state and other intentions it holds in its context of action and recognizes that no conflict occurs (because it believes that the TTL of H_1 will not exceed if it will help G_0 to fill the hole H_0). G_1 informs G_0 that it accepts the proposed recipe, which it becomes a shared one. The recipe comprises three actions: "find a path to the tile and hole", "get the tile" and "drop the tile to the hole".

According to the shared recipe, agents agree to perform as follows: (a) each agent to perform individually the primitive action "find a path to the tile and hole", (b) to perform collaboratively the abstract action "get the tile" and finally, (c) the agent G_0 to perform the abstract action "drop the tile to the hole" individually.

Each agent forms the commitment that each of these actions will be performed successfully. This has as a result both agents to help each other achieving the prescribed goals and to perform actions that are not in conflict with other's goals.

Each agent may collaborate with more than one agent whenever this is needed. For example, during the collaboration session with G_1, if the agent G_0 detects a deadlock in its path to H_0, then, before it gets there, it changes its behaviour from reactive to social or to individual deliberative. In the former case the agent initiates collaboration with the agents that are capable to move the obstacles that constitute the deadlock. In case of social deliberation, and in case agents G_0, G_1, G_2 succeed to form a group of collaborators, they will share the goal to move the detected obstacles. In case of individual deliberation, the agent has not detected any agent that has the capability to help removing the obstacles, or collaboration has failed. In this case, the agent changes its behaviour to individual deliberative: The agent tries to find an alternative plan to fill the hole, it reconciles this plan with its current mental state and other constraints it has, and commits to perform it. Having tackled the problem, the agent may continue towards filling the hole H_0 reactively.

As it seems from the above example, to perform effectively, an agent needs to be able not only to select an appropriate type of behaviour for each domain task, but it must also be able to adapt its behaviour according to the beliefs that it has, other intentions that it holds and the mental state of other agents.

3 Related Work

Although a wide range of architectures have been proposed for building agents, we focus on some representative architectures that balance between deliberative and reactive planning: these are the dMARS [d'Inverno, et. al., 1997], InteRRaP [Müller, 1996] HAC [Atkin et. al., 1999] and AT-Humboldt [Burkhard et. al., 1997].

These architectures do not distinguish in a clear way between reaction, deliberation and social behaviour, or when they distinguish between them, they "restrict" agents' behaviour by "switching" between these three "modes" of planning. Existing systems change their behaviour explicitly between the three types of behavioural modes considering that there is nothing between them [Weiss, 2001]. Every action or goal that they pursue is performed either (socially or individually) reactively or deliberatively, without changing-adapting their behaviour in the light of new changes that occur in the environment. An exception to this case is the previous version of ICAGENT [Kourakos and Vouros, 2001] that although it did deal with the continuum from individual interactive to individual deliberative behaviour, it did not deal with social behaviour.

Close to the objectives of ICAGENT is the Constraint Centered Architectural Framework (CCAF) [Weiss, 2001]. The basic idea underlying CCAF is that flexible behaviour, in contrast to switching between discrete behavioural repertoires, emerges along two continuous axis – cognition ad sociability – as an attempt of agents to handle constraints. CCAF is based on four key conditions identified for achieving continuous flexibility through constraint handling. ICAGENT and CCAF are complementary to the approach towards emergence in agents' behaviour flexibility: ICAGENT emphasizes on the management of plans and on the integration of agents' intentional state with reasoning tasks, while CCAF emphasizes on the use of constraints.

Close to CCAF objectives and basic idea, is the use of preference policies in [Demetriou et al., 2004]. Such policies can be used in any component of the agent to achieve adaptability of behaviour in changing conditions. Preference policies shape decisions of the agent at various levels (which plans to use, which agents to collaborate with, etc) tuning agents' adaptability. However, they have not shown how adaptability is achieved by means of preference policies. Policies are complementary to the techniques used by ICAGENT, as much as constraints are.

This paper aims to show how agents can balance between deliberative, reactive and social behaviour by "tuning" their behaviour between these modes of behaviour. Agents are considered to move in the behavioural modes' space presented in Fig. 2 by performing "more" deliberatively or "more" reactively, either individually or socially.

Fig. 2. An agent in order to be able to adapt efficiently to unforeseen changes in a highly dynamic environment it must be able to adjust its type of behaviour in a space that is circumscribed between the purely reactive, the purely deliberative and the social behaviour modes

An agent is considered to perform in a *purely reactive* way when it builds and/or adjusts/reconsiders its plans only in response to environmental changes, regardless the goals that it already has or that other agents have. In this mode of behaviour the agent does not collaborate with other agents and the only information that it may share concerns the physical environment.

We define that an agent performs in a *purely deliberative* way when it generates and pursues goals pro-actively. As in the reactive behaviour mode, the agent does not collaborate with other agents and the only information that it may share concerns the physical environment.

Finally, we say that the agent behaves in a *social* way when it pursues goals with other agents either in a deliberative or in a reactive way. Information that can be shared in this case may concern goals, recipes for shared actions, mental states, as well as information about the physical environment.

4   The ICAGENT Development Framework

The ICAGENT framework provides a set of features and structures that enable an agent developer to implement software agents capable to act robustly in dynamic and unpredictable environments either individually or collaboratively with other agents.

Following a *mental-state view of plan management* ICAGENT enables agents to adapt their behavioural mode by controlling the plan management reasoning tasks according to their beliefs and intentions: As it will be described in the paragraphs that follow, the architecture realizes five reasoning tasks (environment monitoring, opportunity recognition, reconciliation, plan elaboration and intention realization) for plan management.

As Fig. 3 shows, the ICAGENT overall framework consists of three primary components:

– The Agent's Body.
– The BDI-Control of Practical Reasoning Mechanism.
– The Knowledge Base.

The physical environment is where the agent "lives". Since the mechanisms that drive changes in the physical environment are not part of the ICAGENT framework, the framework supports the representation of the perceived state of the environment, in contrast to simulating the environment itself.

The agent's 'body' comprises (a) *Event-Fact Detectors* for perceiving facts and events that occur in the environment, and (b) *Actuators* for acting.

The knowledge base includes agent's mental state, knowledge concerning (a) the state of the environment, (b) the perception of events and facts in the environment, (b) the context of actions, (c) recipes for actions, and (d) situation recognition rules. The knowledge base is updated by means of sensors that perceive events and facts in the environment, and by the effects of the actions, via the Knowledge Base Update Mechanism.

The recipes in ICAGENT are the methods for performing actions or for achieving goals. Recipes comprise the following constituents: (a) the type of action or goal state that the agent wants to perform or achieve accordingly, (b) a mental condition that specifies the relevance condition, (c) directives that "guide" the agent to reconcile its desire to perform the corresponding action, or to achieve the goal state, with other goals or intentions that it holds, (d) collaboration conditions that determine the situations in which an agent shall consider the potential for collaboration towards the performance of the recipe, (e) a list that enables an agent to allocate the recipe subsidiary actions to potential collaborators, (f) conditions for checking the recipe's applicability in a specific context of action, (g) a list of subsidiary actions that should be performed, (h) a list of facts (effects) that the agent expects to hold, when the recipe has been performed successfully.

As Figure 3 shows, the BDI-Control of Practical Reasoning (BDI-CPR) mechanism comprises six modules that correspond to the reasoning tasks identified above. These run in parallel and communicate via the *KB Consult and Update Mechanism*. They enable an agent to monitor the environment and update its beliefs (*Perception Module*), to take the initiation to act (*Situation Recognition Module*), to reconcile desires in the context of action (*Reconciliation Module*), to elaborate plans and commit to perform actions (*Plan Elaboration Module*) and to perform the intended actions (*Intention Realization Module*).

The following paragraphs show how the performance of these tasks affects the balancing between the behavioural modes of reaction, deliberation and social behaviour.

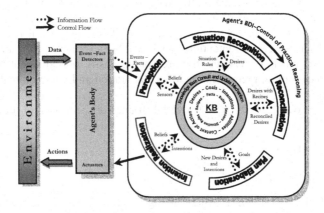

Fig. 3. The Overall ICAGENT Architecture

Environment monitoring: The agent is able to monitor the physical environment and to focus only on specific environmental changes. Perception planning allows an agent to decide when and what type of facts or events it has to monitor.

The Perception Module controls the event-fact detectors and is responsible for the detection of the events/facts that occur in the physical environment. Detectors are controlled by sensor specifications that specify the type of events/facts that must be perceived and the mental condition that must be true in order the agent to assert (or to retract) the specific type of events or facts. Sensor specifications can be asserted or deleted from the agent's knowledge base under specific conditions by means of perception actions. For example, in the Tileworld environment, whenever an agent detects an object of interest (i.e. a tile or a hole) it forms the desire to perform a perception action that results in monitoring an area around the object of interest.

Agents' behaviour mode, as far as perception is concerned, is affected (a) by the way the planning of perception actions is done and (b) by the number of events-facts that the agent decides to monitor at the same time. Reconciling the perception actions results to agents' deliberative behaviour (as far as perception is concerned). On the other hand, in case no perception planning is performed, or in case that no reconciliation of perception actions' is performed and the number of facts/events that are monitored is small, then we consider that the agent behaves in a rather reactive way.

Consult and Update of Beliefs: ICAGENT, through the Knowledge Base Consult and Update Mechanism, can consult and update the knowledge base using the *consult learn* and *forget* mental actions. With these actions the agent is able to keep the KB consistent. This is important not only for an agent to take the right decisions, but also for the BDI-CPR modules to perform in parallel and in coordination. The agent performs the *Belief Update* task whenever it recognizes new events/facts or whenever the agent needs to revise its beliefs. In all these cases, the time that the agent spends may affect its response to unforeseen changes and thus the balance between reaction and deliberation (social or individual).

Opportunity Recognition: The agent constantly tries to recognize situations for which it must take the initiative to act. In the ICAGENT framework this reasoning task is realized by means of the *Situation Recognition Module*. The Situation Recognition Module exploits Situation Rules to recognize configurations and states of the environment that drive subsequent initiatives for action. Such rules may be formed on-the-fly during agent's performance. The recognition of states results to desires towards achieving goals or performing actions, individually or with other agents. The number of states that the agent checks at the same time, as well as the method (e.g. planning from first principles or driven by specific rules) towards forming new situation rules, affects the agent's behaviour towards reactivity and deliberation.

Reconciliation: The agent commits to the performance of actions. In individual and socially deliberative behaviour these commitments may rule out some options. Thus, for each recipe that the agent selects from the knowledge base, it has to decide if it will reconcile this recipe with other intentions it holds or if it will start elaborating it without considering any conflicts that occur. In general, the behaviour of the agent depends on whether it will probe for possible conflicts concerning recipes' constraints, capabilities and context constraints. The agent's adaptability is highly affected by the method(s) that the agent will follow to detect and resolve conflicts.

The ICAGENT framework provides facilities for the detection and resolution of conflicts that occur during the course of activity, taking into account recipes' behaviour directives, recipes' conditions, constraints associated with the context of action, agents' mental states, the perceived state of the environment and agent capabilities. The *Reconciliation Module* controls the *detect conflict* and the *resolve conflict* mental actions. These actions detect and resolve conflicts between recipes and the agent's mental state, as well as between recipes in the context of action, following the behaviour directives of the corresponding recipes.

Once the agent has detected a conflict it has to assess the cost and the benefits of the following options: To resolve the conflict utilizing domain specific knowledge, to find alternative recipes for the current action in the context of action, to reconsider the recipes of parent actions, to override the conflict, to drop the whole plan, to cancel the execution of the action, postpone the execution of the recipe until the conflict is resolved, or to collaborate with other agents in order to resolve the conflict. The decision that the agent will take depends on the current context of action and the corresponding directives for resolving specific (types of) conflicts. Deliberative behaviour requires meta-reasoning capabilities for deciding the proper way for resolving any conflict, while reactivity requires domain specific rules for resolving each (type of) conflict.

Plan Elaboration: In dynamic environments, the plan elaboration task controls the way that partial plans are further elaborated, given the current context of action, the limitations of the physical environment and the constraints posed to agents. This reasoning task is realized by the *Plan Elaboration* module of the ICAGENT framework. This module controls the mental actions that cause changes in the context of action. Specifically, the Plan Elaboration module controls the *select recipe* and the *elaborate recipe* mental actions.

The *select recipe* action enables the agent to select recipes according to their relevance conditions. The Plan Elaboration module, for each action (or state) that the agent has the desire to perform (respectively, to achieve) forms the desire to construct an initial plan. The *select recipe* mental action constructs initial plans either by selecting pre-built recipes or by constructing such recipes, either individually or with other agents. The complexity of this reasoning task affects the agent's balancing between reaction, individual deliberation and social deliberation. A purely reactive behaviour requires that the initial plan will be generated by selecting a pre-specified recipe. On the other hand, the generation of an initial plan by performing long term planning determines a more deliberative behaviour. Also, if the agent needs to communicate with other agents in order to select a recipe, then its behaviour is turned to be either socially reactive (in case agents merely interact so as to select a relevant recipe - which may not be a common one) or socially deliberative (in case agents interact to agree on a common recipe).

The *elaborate recipe* mental action enables an agent to extend individual or shared partial plans to complete ones. Whenever a relevant and applicable recipe has been chosen (either individually or with other agents), the Plan Elaboration module forms the desire to further elaborate it. We distinguish two default methods for elaborating recipes:

The first is relevant when the agent performs the corresponding action individually, while the second one is relevant when the agent commits to perform the corresponding action in conjunction with other agents (i.e. the action is shared).

In the first case, the *elaborate recipe* is considered to be an individual primitive action. Using this action the agent is able to extend a partial individual plan to a full individual one by forming desires for the subsidiary actions specified by the recipe.

In the second case, where the agent has committed to perform an action with others, the recipe elaboration reasoning task extends a partial plan to a full plan. This plan is shared in case agents deliberate socially. In case agents interact, then every agent contributes to a shared goal in a reactive way, being in communication with other agents.

In case the agent commits to act *jointly* with others, the *elaborate recipe* task manipulates mental actions that are responsible for the following: (a) Forming a group of collaborators for planning and performing an action, (b) reaching an agreement for the relevant and applicable recipe to be used, and finally, (c) allocating sub-tasks to collaborators. Each of the above three mental actions results to changes in the intentional context of collaborative parties: The formation of a group of agents results to a shared action for the group. Agreement about the recipe to be followed results to a shared goal, and finally, allocating tasks to agents results to a shared (partial) plan for action.

Notice that for specific types of actions, agents may utilize specific methods for the *elaborate recipe* mental action, other than the default ones. Regardless the method that the agent will choose for elaborating recipes, the list of effects comprises desires for the subsidiary actions of the domain recipe. The agent possesses these desires after the successful execution of the *elaborate recipe* action.

Intention Realization: The Intention Realization Module enables an agent to perform the actions to which it has committed. The agent may interleave actions' execution with planning or not. This decision may be formed depending on the perceived state of the environment, context of action and interaction with other agents.

6   Conclusions – Feature Work

We have presented how the non-layered BDI-architecture of ICAGENT supports performance in dynamic and unpredictable multi-agent environments through efficient balancing between different behavioural modes. The ICAGENT framework introduces a "tuning" approach where each reasoning task controls internal (mental) actions that are "tuned" to the perceived state of the environment, the overall intentional state of the agent and the context of action. The overall behaviour of the agent results from the combination of these reasoning tasks. ICAGENT, in contrast to existing approaches and proposals, places much emphasis on managing plans and to the integrated treatment of agents' mental states with the reasoning tasks realized by its modules. Choosing its behaviour mode in a continuous space that is circumscribed by the purely reactive, purely deliberative and social behaviour, agents can be highly adaptive to the changes of their environment.

Future work concerns studying the incorporation of constraints and preferences to support meta-reasoning and cooperation.

References

1. Atkin, M., Westbrook D., and Cohen P., Capture the Flag: Military Simulation Meets Computer Games. AAAI Spring Symposium on AI and Computer Games (1999).
2. Burkhard, H., Hannebauer, M., Wendler. J. AT Humboldt - Development, Practice and Theory. Proc. First International Workshop on RoboCup, Springer Verlag, LNCS, (1997).
3. Bratman M. E., Israel D. J., Pollack M.E., Plans and Resource-Bounded Practical Reasoning. In: Computational Intelligence, 4(3): 349-355, (1987).
4. Grosz, B.J., Kraus, S.: Collaborative plans for complex group action. In: Artificial Intelligence, 86(2):269-357 (1996).
5. Grosz, B.J., Kraus, S.: The Evolution of SharedPlans. In: Foundations and Theories of Rational Agencies, A. Rao and M. Wooldridge, eds. pp. 227-262 (1999).
6. d'Inverno, M., Kinny, D., Luck, M., Wooldridge, M.: A formal specification of dMARS. Australian Artificial Intelligence Institute, Technical Note 72, (1997).
7. Kourakos-Mavromichalis V., Vouros G.: Building Intelligent Collaborative Interface Agents with the ICAGENT Framework. In: Journal of Autonomous Agents and Multi-Agents Systems, Springer. (Accepted November 2005).

8. Kourakos-Mavromichalis V., Vouros G.: Balancing Between Reactivity and Deliberation in the ICAGENT Framework, In: Balancing Between Reactivity and Social Deliberation in Multi-agent Systems, LNAI Volume 2103, Springer-Verlag, 2001.

9. Müller, J.P.: The Design of Intelligent Agents, Lecture Notes in computer science; Vol. 1177, Springer, (1996).

10. Demetriou N., Kakas A., and Torroni P. Agent Planning, Negotiation, and Control of Operation. In Ramon López de Mántaras and Lorenza Saitta, eds., *Proceedings of the 16th Biennal European Conference on Artificial Intelligence, ECAI 2004,* Valencia, Spain, August (2004).

11. Pollack, M.E., Horty, J.F.: There's More to Life than Making Plans: Plan Management in Dynamic, Multi-agent Environments. In: AAAI Magazine Vol. 20, No.4, (1999).

12. Pollack, M.E., Ringuette, M.: Introducing the Tileworld: Experimentally Evaluating Agent Architectures. In: Proceedings of the Eighth National Conference on Artificial Intelligence, 183-189. Menlo Park, Calif.: American Association for Artificial Intelligence, (1990).

13. Russell, Stuart and Peter Norvig. Artificial Intelligence: A Modern Approach, Prentice-Hall, NJ, (1995).

14. Weiss, Gerhard,: Cognition, Sociability, and Constraints, In: Balancing Between Reactivity and Social Deliberation in Multi-agent Systems, LNAI Volume 2103, Springer-Verlag, (2001).

Investigation of Decision Trees (DTs) Parameters for Power System Voltage Stability Enhancement

Eirini A. Leonidaki and Nikos D. Hatziargyriou

National Technical University of Athens,
Heroon Polytechniou, 157 73 Zografou, Greece
eleonid@central.ntua.gr, nh@power.ece.ntua.gr

Abstract. This paper describes the application of Decision Tress (DTs) in order to specify the most critical location and the rate of series compensation in order to increase power system loading margin. The proposed methodology is applied to a projected model of the Hellenic interconnected system in several system configurations. Investigation of the best system operating point to create the DTs, the effect of attributes number and type on the DTs size and quality are discussed in order to reach the final DTs parameters that lead to the construction of the best DTs for the determination of optimal series compensation location and rate. Finally, the results obtained for several (N-1) contingencies examined are presented.

1 Introduction

A power system is considered voltage secure when a sufficient loading margin from the base case to the point of voltage instability exists, under N and (N-1) conditions. The loading margin is used as a measure of system robustness at a given operating point. In the energy market terminology the loading margin is also known as Available Transfer Capability (ATC) [1].

Flexible AC Transmission Systems (FACTS) such as Thyristor Controlled Series Capacitor (TCSC) and Static Var Compensator (SVC) can increase the system loading margin and alleviate power system congestion. A number of papers have been published proposing methodologies to determine the most critical lines for series compensation or the most effective buses for shunt compensation, based on second order sensitivities [1], Singular Value Decomposition of the load-flow Jacobian [2], cascading line overloading considerations [3] and the larger entries in the right and left eigenvectors associated to the zero eigenvalue at the voltage collapse point [4]. In [5], [6] a technique to evaluate the sensitivity of the power margin to collapse with respect to system parameters has been proposed. In [7] a systematic methodology has been developed for identifying the critical branches for series compensation based on the sensitivity of system loading margin to lines reactance.

DTs methodology and several of its applications in power system operation and planning are proposed in [8]. Steps in order to study the best substation to place an SVC are sketched, but no systematic approach of this application has been presented.

G. Antoniou et al. (Eds.): SETN 2006, LNAI 3955, pp. 181–191, 2006.
© Springer-Verlag Berlin Heidelberg 2006

This paper describes the application procedure of creating suitable DTs in order to specify the most critical location and the rate of series compensation in order to increase power system loading margin. The proposed methodology is applied to a projected model of the Hellenic interconnected system in several system configurations.

Investigation of the best system operating point to create the KB, the effect of attributes number and type on the DTs size and quality as well as on the classification of OPs is discussed in order to reach the final DTs parameters that lead to the construction of the best DTs for optimal series compensation location and rate. Finally, the results obtained for several (N-1) contingencies (i.e. the loss of one main system element like generator unit or transmission line) examined, are presented.

2 Decision Trees Overview

The DTs methodology is a nonparametric learning technique able to produce classifiers about a given problem in order to deduce information for new unobserved cases. A DT has the hierarchical form of a tree, structured upside down. The construction of a DT is based on a knowledge base (KB) consisting of a large number of operating points (OPs) theoretically covering all possible states of the power system under study. A vector of pre-disturbance steady-state variables, called "attributes", characterizes each OP. The KB is divided in a learning set (LS) used for deriving the classifier structures and a test set (TS) used to evaluate the performance of these structures on new, unobserved OPs.

The construction of a DT starts at the root node with the whole LS of pre-classified OPs. These OPs are analyzed in order to select the dichotomic test T that splits them "optimally" into a number of most "purified," mutually exclusive subsets. For a two-class partition (secure or insecure) the test T is defined as

$$T: A_i < t_i \tag{1}$$

where t_i is the optimal threshold value of chosen attribute Ai.

The best attribute and its threshold value are obtained by sequentially testing the attributes and candidate thresholds and comparing their information gain. This way, the selection of the optimal test is based on maximizing the additional information gained through the test. The information gain is based on the entropy of each subset E_n with respect to the class partition of its elements, defined as:

$$H_c(E_n) = -(f_s \log f_s + f_i \log f_i) \tag{2}$$

where f_s and f_i are the relative frequencies of the secure and insecure OPs, respectively, in the subset.

This criterion has proved most successful in similar power systems application. Alternative other criteria are also possible [8].

The selected test is applied to the LS of the node splitting it into two exclusive subsets, corresponding to the two successor nodes. Every subset (node) is characterized by its security index (SI), defined as the ratio of secure OPs to the total number of OPs belonging to this subset. The optimal splitting rule is applied recursively to build the corresponding sub-trees. In order to detect if one node is terminal, i.e., "sufficiently" class pure, the stop splitting rule is used, which checks whether the entropy of the node is lower than a preset minimum value. If it is, the node corresponds to a sufficiently pure subset (states belong to the same class) and is declared a "leaf"; otherwise, a test T is sought to further split the node. If the node cannot be further split in a statistically significant way, it is termed a "deadend", carrying the two class probabilities estimated on the basis of the corresponding OPs subset.

3 The Greek Power System

More than 60% of generating capacity in the Greek power system is provided by coal-fired power plants installed in the North. A significant lignite production exists also in the southern peninsula of Peloponnese, while oil-fired power plants exist near Athens region. In addition, almost 20% of the total generation is provided by hydroplants, situated mainly in the Northern and Western Greece.

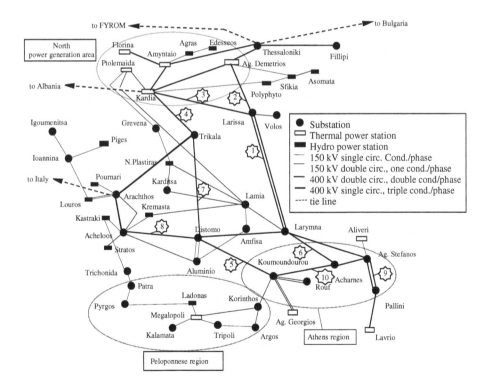

Fig. 1. The Hellenic interconnected power system

Two parallel transmission networks, at 400 kV and 150 kV respectively, operate in the Hellenic interconnected transmission system, as shown in Fig. 1. The 400 kV transmission network has a dominant presence in the northern and central part of the system, playing the primary role in the energy transmission to Athens with three links, while the peninsula of Peloponnese is served exclusively by the 150 kV network. The system is interconnected in the northern part of the country with Albania and F.Y.R.O.M (400kV and 150 kV lines), with Bulgaria (400kV line) and with Italy through an HVDC interconnection of 500 MW.

Several critical operating conditions are associated with the geographical distance between generation in the North and the main consumption center of the metropolitan area of Athens. More specifically, during summer peaks voltage stability problems have been experienced in the southern part of the system (Athens and Peloponnese areas), in case of reduced generation availability in this area.

For this study a model of the Greek system comprising 730 buses, 76 generators, 973 circuits, and 180 transformers, in peak load conditions (total load 10.3 GW), has been developed in EUROSTAG [9]. It represents the Greek generation and transmission system up to 150kV. The external Balkan system is represented by three equivalent generators connected to the three interconnection lines, while the DC inter-connection with Italy is modeled as constant negative load.

4 Decision Trees Development

For each of the examined contingencies a KB is created, with the procedure presented in the flowchart of Fig. 2: at a stressed system condition near the ATC point with total active load equal to 10332 MW, the N candidate transmission lines are series compensated in steps of a % up to the maximum compensation rate $kmax$ %. For each compensation step, all buses load are randomly varied within ±3% for n_{max} times and load flow simulation is performed. This way a KB of $\left(N \cdot \frac{kmax}{a} \cdot n_{max}\right)$ OPs is created for each contingency.

Each of the OPs is classified according to the convergence of the load flow calculation and the technical limits check. More specifically, an OP is characterized as "safe" if the load flow calculation has converged and all technical constraints are met. Otherwise it is labeled as "unsafe".

The "candidate attributes" of each OP comprise the p.u. reactance of the candidate for series compensation transmission lines (twenty 400 kV lines) and other system parameters, such as system total active and reactive load, regional active and reactive loads and voltage profile of critical buses mainly in Athens and Peloponnese area. The 44 "candidate attributes" are named in Table 1. The DT (A) developed for Lavrio Combined Cycle unit outage (470 MW) is presented in Fig. 3. The KB is created around system operating point with peak load 0.30% lower to 10332 MW. Each of the twenty lines is compensated between 5% and 50% (i.e. 10 steps of compensation) and for each compensation step, buses loads are randomly varied 14 times within ±3%. This way, a knowledge base of 2800 OPs is created for each contingency.

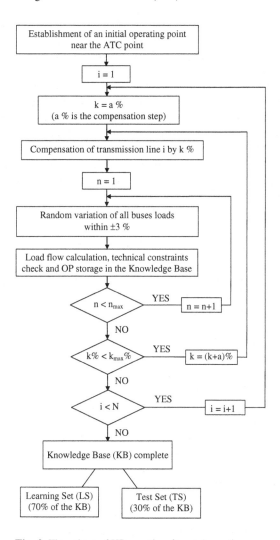

Fig. 2. Flowchart of KB creation for each contingency

Approximately, 70% of the OPs are randomly selected to form the LS (2000 OPs), and the remaining 30% are used as the TS (800 OPs).

In the terminal nodes of this DT, the type of the node is provided and in non-terminal nodes, the splitting test is presented. It is observed that in the DT trunk (nodes 1,3,5,7,11,15,19,21,23 and 25) only splitting tests referring to the candidate lines appear. The splitting test that refers to the reactance of transmission line i has the following form:

$$Xi < k_i \qquad (4)$$

where $k_i = 1$ p.u. when the line i is not compensated and $k_i < 1$ when $(1 - k_i)$ p.u. series capacitor is installed.

Consequently, (4) is equivalent to the following expression:

$$compensation\ rate\ of\ line\ i \geq (1 - k_i) \cdot 100\% \tag{5}$$

If (4) is true ('Y' branch) and a "leaf" with SI greater than 0.95 is reached, then the minimum compensation rate of line i has been found. If (4) is not true ('N' branch), a new splitting test referring to another line is applied. For example, the node 1 in the DT (A) indicate that if line 3 is series compensated by at least 20%, then 70 OPs become secure with SI equal to 0.9750 (exactly 67 safe OPs). Node 25 indicates the amount of system OPs that remain insecure if none of the lines appearing in the DT splitting tests is series compensated at the compensation rate proposed by the DT. In addition, it must be mentioned that, based on DTs optimal splitting criterion, the nearer to the DT root a splitting test appears, the more significant the series compensation of the relevant transmission line is.

In order to investigate the contribution of the candidate attributes that refer to critical buses voltage and regional active and reactive loads, the DTs (B) and (C) in Fig. 4 and 5 respectively have been developed. In DT (B) the critical buses voltage are eliminated, while in DT (C) the regional active and reactive loads are additionally eliminated. By comparing DTs (A) and (B) with DT (C), it is obvious that, while the DT (C) is shorter, it provides the same information about the significant lines and their compensation rate. More specifically, the splitting tests referring to critical voltage buses, nodes 6 and 12 in DT (A), and to regional loads value, node 10 in DT (A) and node 8 in DT (B), clarify the conditions under which the nodes 6 and 8 of DT (C), classified as "deadend", could lead to a "leaf". The same observations occurred in all developed DTs for several contingencies. Consequently, these "candidate attributes" appear only in low significance nodes without influencing the main DT results. For this reason, they have been ignored. Also, it has been observed that only the reactance of the 400 kV transmission lines from North to South appear in all developed DTs. Therefore, the final attributes selected are the reactance of the ten lines numbered in Fig. 1 and correspond to attributes I1-I10 of Table 1.

Additionally, in order to investigate the best system operating point near the ATC point, for the construction of the DTs, the DTs (D) and (E) in Fig. 6 and 7 respectively have been developed. The DT (D) is constructed at system operating point with total active load 0.20% greater to 10332 MW and the DT (E) at total active load equal to 10332 MW. (DT (E) contains 1000 OPs as only the ten candidate lines of Table 2 are included without influencing the results). By comparing DTs (B), (D) and (E), it is concluded that the same lines appear in the nodes near the root and as the total active load increase, the minimum compensation rate of the important lines increases and the DTs become shorter. The critical lines and their minimum compensation rate for the three system loading conditions are presented in Fig. 8. It can be concluded that for best results, the DTs must be developed at an operating point very close to the ATC point.

Using the conclusions derived above for the DTs construction (use of only 10 attributes and KB creation very close to the ATC point), several contingencies

Table 1. Candidate attributes for DTs development

Attribute type	A/A	Symbol in DTs	Described network component
400 kV transmission lines inductive reactance	I 1	X1	Larissa – Larymna (double line)
	I 2	X2	Ag.Demetrios – Larissa
	I 3	X3	Kardia – Larissa
	I 4	X4	Kardia – Trikala
	I 5	X5	Koumoundourou – Distomo
	I 6	X6	Larymna – Acharnes
	I 7	X7	Trikala – Distomo
	I 8	X8	Distomo – Acheloos
	I 9	X9	Ag.Stefanos – Pallini (double line)
	I 10	X10	Koumoudourou - Acharnes
	I 11	X11	Amyntaio – Kardia
	I 12	X12	Larymna – Distomo
	I 13	X13	Pallini-Lavrio
	I 14	X14	Thessaloniki- Ag. Demetrios
	I 15	X15	Acheloos – Arachthos
	I 16	X16	Acharnes – Ag. Stefanos
	I 17	X17	Lagadas - Amyntaio
	I 18	X18	Ag. Demetrios – Kardia
	I 19	X19	Filipopoi – Lagadas
	I 20	X20	Larymna- Ag. Stefanos
Active power	I 21	Psyst	System
	I 22	P1	East Macedonia-Thace
	I 23	P2	West Macedonia
	I 24	P3	Thessalia
	I 25	P4	West Sterea-Evia
	I 26	P5	Attica
	I 27	P6	Peloponnese
	I 28	P7	West Greece
	I 29	P8	Epirus-Seven Islands
Reactive power	I 30	Qsyst	System
	I 31	Q1	East Macedonia-Thace
	I 32	Q2	West Macedonia
	I 33	Q3	Thessalia
	I 34	Q4	West Sterea-Evia
	I 35	Q5	Attica
	I 36	Q6	Peloponnese
	I 37	Q7	West Greece
	I 38	Q8	Epirus-Seven Islands
Voltage at sub-station 150 kV bus	I 39	V1	S/S Kasasandras (Macedonia)
	I 40	V2	S/S Sovel –Tsigeli (Thessalia)
	I 41	V3	S/S Rouf (Attika)
	I 42	V4	S/S Psychiko (Attica)
	I 43	V5	S/S Astros (Peloponnese)
	I 44	V6	S/S Molaoi (south Peloponnese)

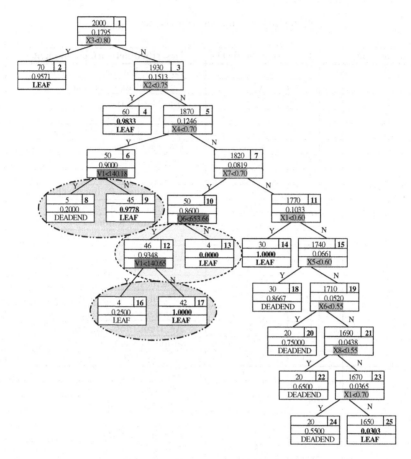

Fig. 3. DT (A) with 44 attributes (p.u. reactance of 20 lines, system and regional active and reactive loads and voltage profile of critical buses). KB creation at (10332 -0.30%) MW.

have been examined. More specifically, four generator unit outages in Athens and Peloponnese area and the Kardia-Trikala line opening are examined. The results from developed DTs are summarized in Table 2, where the critical lines and the minimum compensation rate for each contingency are shown. From this Table it can be concluded that the best locations for series compensation are the transmission lines that have been proposed by DT methodology for all examined contingencies. In addition, the most appropriate rate of the selected lines is the maximum compensation rate that covers all the examined contingencies. This means that, in the Hellenic power system, the 55% series compensation of transmission lines 2 or 3 is the optimal compensation scheme to maximize the loading margin during severe contingent-cies. Comparing these results with the results obtained from the sensitivies analysis presented in [7], it is concluded that the same critical lines have been selected.

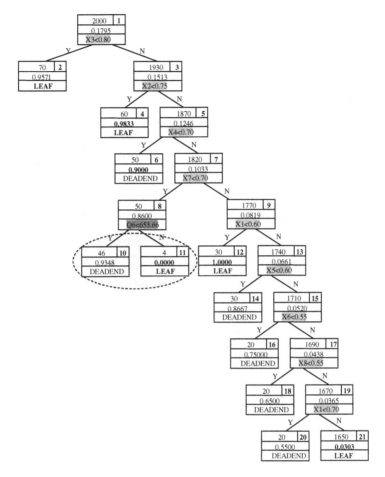

Fig. 4. DT (B) with 38 attributes (p.u. reactance of 20 lines, system and regional active and reactive loads). KB creation at (10332 -0.30%) MW.

Table 2. DTs results for several (N-1) contingencies

	CONTINGENCY	MINIMUM COMPENSATION RATE %							
		Line 1	Line 2	Line 3	Line 4	Line 5	Line 6	Line 7	Lines 8,9,10
1	AG. GEORGIOS 9 OUTAGE	-	35	35	45	-	-	50	-
2	AG. GEORGIOS 8 OUTAGE	45	35	35	45	-	-	45	-
3	LAVRIO 2 OUTAGE	45	30	30	40	-	-	45	-
4	LAVRIO CC OUTAGE	45	35	35	45	-	-	45	-
5	MEGALOPOLI IV OUTAGE	30	20	20	25	30	35	25	-
6	KARDIA-TRIKALA OPENING	-	55	55	-	-	-	-	-

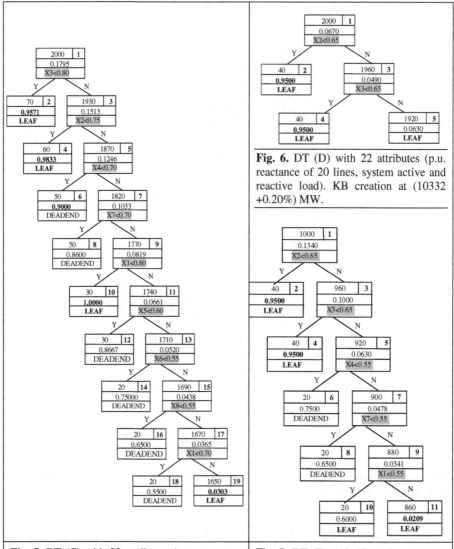

Fig. 6. DT (D) with 22 attributes (p.u. reactance of 20 lines, system active and reactive load). KB creation at (10332 +0.20%) MW.

Fig. 5. DT (C) with 22 attributes (p.u. reactance of 20 lines, system active and reactive load). KB creation at (10332-0.30%) MW.

Fig. 7. DT (E) with 12 attributes (reactance of 10 lines, system active and reactive load). KB creation at (10332 +0.00%) MW.

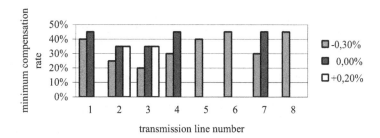

Fig. 8. Critical lines and minimum compensation rate for different system loading conditions

5 Conclusions

In this paper the application of DTs for voltage stability enhancement by means of finding the critical lines for series compensation and their compensation proper rate is proposed. Applicati on of the proposed method to a model of the Hellenic interconnected power system shows that the method succeeds in identifying the most critical lines and the proper rate of series compensation in a very clear way. The basic advantage of the proposed methodology, in comparison with other analytical methods, is that not only the critical lines are selected, but also the minimum compensation rate is specified. In addition, although the method requires a large number of calculations in order to create the necessary knowledge base, it is based on simple load flow calculations and offers a viable alternative to more complicated, techniques.

References

1. C.A. Canizares, A. Berizzi, P. Marannino, "Using FACTS Controllers to Maximize Available Transfer Capability", Proc. Bulk Power Systems Dynamics and Control IV-Restructuring Conference, Santorini, Greece, 1998.
2. A.R. Messina, M.A. Pérez, E. Hernádez, "Co-ordinated application of FACTS devices to enhance steady-state voltage stability", Int. Journal of Electrical Power and Energy Systems 25, 2003.
3. R. Rajaraman, F. Alvarado, A. Maniaci, R. Camfield, S. Jalali, "Determination of Locations and Amount of Series Compensation to Increase Power Transfer Capability", IEEE Trans. on Power Systems, Vol. 13, No. 2, May 1998.
4. C.A. Canizares, Z.T. Faur, "Analysis of SVC and TCSC Controllers in Voltage Collapse", IEEE Trans. on Power Systems, Vol. 14, No. 1, February 1999.
5. S. Greene, I. Dobson, F. Alvarado," Sensitivity of the loading margin to voltage collapse with respect to arbitrary parameters", IEEE Trans. on Power Systems, Vol. 12, No. 1, February 1997.
6. T. Van Cutsem, C. Vournas, "Voltage Stability of Electric Power Systems", Kluwer Academic Press, 1998.
7. E.A. Leonidaki, G.A. Manos, N.D. Hatziargyriou, "An effective method to locate series compensation for voltage stability enhancement", Int. Journal of Electric Power System Research, Volume 74, Issue 1, April 2005, pages 73-81.
8. L. Wehenkel, "Automatic Learning Techniques in Power Systems", Norwell, MA: Kluwer, 1998.
9. Eurostag 3.2 Package user's guide.

An Improved Hybrid Genetic Clustering Algorithm

Yongguo Liu[1,2,3], Jun Peng[4], Kefei Chen[3], and Yi Zhang[1]

[1] College of Computer Science and Engineering, University of Electronic
Science and Technology of China, Chengdu 610054, P.R. China
[2] State Key Laboratory for Novel Software Technology, Nanjing University,
Nanjing 210093, P.R. China
[3] Department of Computer Science and Engineering, Shanghai Jiaotong University,
Shanghai 200030, P.R. China
[4] School of Electronic Information Engineering, Chongqing University of Science and
Technology, Chongqing 400050, P.R. China

Abstract. In this paper, a new genetic clustering algorithm called IHGA-clustering is proposed to deal with the clustering problem under the criterion of minimum sum of squares clustering. In IHGA-clustering, DHB operation is developed to improve the individual and accelerate the convergence speed, and partition-mergence mutation operation is designed to reassign objects among different clusters. Equipped with these two components, IHGA-clustering can stably output the proper result. Its superiority over HGA-clustering, GKA, and KGA-clustering is extensively demonstrated for experimental data sets.

1 Introduction

The clustering problem is a fundamental problem that frequently arises in a great variety of application fields such as machine learning, pattern recognition, and statistics. In this article, we focus on the minimum sum of squares clustering problem stated as follows: Given N objects in R^m, allocate each object to one of K clusters such that the sum of squared Euclidean distances between each object and the center of its belonging cluster for every such allocated object is minimized. This problem can be mathematically described as follows:

$$\min_{W,C} J(W,C) = \sum_{i=1}^{N} \sum_{j=1}^{K} w_{ij} \parallel \mathbf{x}_i - \mathbf{c}_j \parallel^2 \tag{1}$$

Where

$$\begin{cases} \sum_{j=1}^{K} w_{ij} = 1 \\ \mathbf{c}_j = \dfrac{1}{n_j} \sum_{\mathbf{x}_i \in C_j} \mathbf{x}_i \end{cases} \tag{2}$$

In Equation 1, N, K, and m denote the number of objects, clusters, and object attributes, respectively. $\mathbf{x}_i$ denotes object i, $\mathbf{c}_j$ denotes the centroid of cluster C_j,

G. Antoniou et al. (Eds.): SETN 2006, LNAI 3955, pp. 192–202, 2006.

$C = \{C_1, \ldots, C_K\}$ denotes the set of K clusters, and $W = [w_{ij}]$ denotes the $N \times K$ $0 - 1$ matrix. In Equation 2, n_j denotes the number of objects belonging to cluster C_j. This problem is a nonconvex problem which possesses many locally optimal values, resulting that its solution often falls into these traps. It is known that this clustering problem is NP-hard [1]. Many clustering approaches have been reported [2,3]. Among them, K-means algorithm is an important one. But it converges at local minima under certain conditions [4]. Recently, researchers attempt to solve this problem by stochastic optimization methods such as evolutionary computation [5-7], tabu search [8,9], and simulated annealing [10,11]. In [5,12-21], researchers developed different genetic clustering methods. Among them, some researchers integrated K-means algorithm into genetic algorithms so as to deal with the clustering problem [14-21]. After K-means algorithm is combined, the performance of the clustering algorithm is greatly improved. In this paper, we pay our attention to dealing with the clustering problem by genetic algorithms. Due to space limitations, we select three genetic clustering methods and compare them with the proposed algorithm. In [13], a genetic clustering algorithm called HGA-clustering is reported. In HGA-clustering, tabu list is used to prevent fitter individuals from occupying the population so as to keep a high level of population diversification. In addition, aspiration criterion is used to maintain selection pressure. Its superiority over K-means algorithm and GA-clustering [5] is shown by computer simulations. In [15], the clustering algorithm called GKA is proposed. It is proved that GKA can obtain the best result at the expense of less computational cost than ES [6] and EP [7]. In [18], the presented method called KGA-clustering is proved to be better than K-means algorithm and GA-clustering [5]. Both GKA and KGA-clustering employ K-means algorithm as the local improvement operation.

In this article, how to stably achieve the optimal clustering result at the expense of low cost is our motivation. In [13], HGA-clustering filters each individual by tabu operation, keeps the harmony between selection pressure and population diversity, and improves the performance of the clustering algorithm. HGA-clustering is faster than GA-clustering, but it still requires huge computational resource and its number of generations is up to 1000. In [15], the convergence speed of GKA is enhanced, but its improvement is small and not stable in complicated cases. In KGA-clustering, the chromosome encodes the centers of clusters but the assignment of objects is not provided. As a result, when the objective function value is needed, all objects have to be associated with their nearest centers. This increases the computational cost. In addition, the number of generations in KGA-clustering is also 1000. In this paper, we limit the number of generations G to 50 so as to reduce the computational cost. Within small generations, how to stably achieve the optimal result is a huge challenge. Here, we introduce two new operations: DHB operation and partition-mergence mutation operation, and develop a new genetic clustering method called IHGA-clustering. DHB operation is used to improve the individual and accelerate the convergence speed. Without the mutation probability, partition-mergence mutation operation can automatically reassign objects among different clusters. By experimental simulations, its superiority over HGA-clustering, GKA, and KGA-clustering is demonstrated.

The remaining part of this paper is organized as follows: In Section 2, IHGA-clustering and its main components are described in detail. Results of computer simulations are extensively analyzed in Section 3. Finally, some conclusions are drawn in Section 4.

2 IHGA-Clustering Algorithm

The general description of IHGA-clustering is shown as Figure 1. It is seen that its most procedures observe the architecture of genetic algorithms. Here, a new module called DHB operation consisting of one-step DHB algorithm is integrated into the algorithm framework. This operation is used to improve the individual and accelerate the convergence speed of IHGA-clustering. Its function is similar to that of K-means operation in [14-21]. In addition, we design partition-mergence mutation operation to reassign objects among different clusters and do not set the value of the mutation probability in advance.

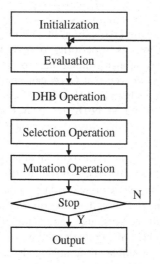

Fig. 1. General description of IHGA-clustering

IHGA-clustering adopts the string-of-group-numbers encoding the same as HGA-clustering and GKA. The individual representation shows the partition of objects, which is suitable for computing the objective function value. Proportional selection and elitist model used in HGA-clustering and KGA-clustering are adopted here. Considering the clustering problem under consideration is a minimum problem, we define the individual fitness as $1/J$. Then the minimum problem is converted into the maximum one suitable for genetic algorithms. In [14-21], mutation operation and crossover operation are mainly performed on the chromosome. In IHGA-clustering, mutation operation is designed for the partition of clusters. Here, we pay main attention to DHB operation and mutation operation.

2.1 DHB Operation

In [22], four local iteration methods (DHB, DHF, ABF, and AFB) are compared with K-means algorithm for experimental data sets. It has been proved that these four methods own stronger convergence states than K-means algorithm. Moreover, they can get much better clustering results sooner than K-means algorithm. Their time complexities are the same as that of K-means algorithm. They own the performance similar to each other. The detail description of these four algorithms can be found in [22]. By experimental simulations, we choose one-step DHB algorithm to fine-tune the individual. We define several variables in order to describe DHB operation. For cluster C_j, its objective function value is defined as follows:

$$J_j = \sum_{\mathbf{x}_i \in C_j} \| \mathbf{x}_i - \mathbf{c}_j \|^2 \tag{3}$$

If object $\mathbf{x}_i$ belonging to cluster C_j is reassigned to cluster C_k, then the cluster centers are moved accordingly, J_j will decrease by ΔJ_{ij}, J_k will increase by ΔJ_{ik}, and the new objective function value $J^{'}$ will be:

$$\begin{cases} J^{'} = J - \Delta J_{ij} + \Delta J_{ik} \\ \Delta J_{ij} = n_j \| \mathbf{x}_i - \mathbf{c}_j \|^2 \big/ (n_j - 1) \\ \Delta J_{ik} = n_k \| \mathbf{x}_i - \mathbf{c}_k \|^2 \big/ (n_k + 1) \end{cases} \tag{4}$$

and the new cluster centers of C_j and C_k will become:

$$\begin{cases} \mathbf{c}_j^{'} = (n_j \mathbf{c}_j - \mathbf{x}_i) \big/ (n_j - 1) \\ \mathbf{c}_k^{'} = (n_k \mathbf{c}_k + \mathbf{x}_i) \big/ (n_k + 1) \end{cases} \tag{5}$$

Based on above equations, DHB operations is described as follows: Object $\mathbf{x}_i$ belonging to cluster C_j is reassigned to cluster C_k, iff

$$\min(\Delta J_{ik}) < \Delta J_{ij} \tag{6}$$

where $i = 1, \ldots, N$, $j, k = 1, \ldots, K$, and $j \neq k$. According to Equations 4 and 5, the corresponding parameters are updated. After all objects are considered, the improved individual is obtained.

2.2 Mutation Operation

In general, researchers determine the value of the mutation probability artificially or by computer simulations. These methods lack adaptability in face of different data sets. In [23], three concepts (under-partitioned state, optimal-partitioned state, and over-partitioned state) are given to describe the variation of two partition functions so as to establish the cluster validity index. Here, we introduce these concepts to design mutation operation. For the cluster, there are only three partition states:

under-partitioned state, optimal-partitioned state, and over-partitioned state. So, partitioning the under-partitioned cluster and merging the over-partitioned cluster are helpful for exploring the correct result. According to this, a new mutation called partition-mergence mutation operation is proposed. It consists of two sub-operations: partition operation and mergence operation. Here, two sub-operations are performed on the individual in random order.

Partition Operation: Suppose cluster C_i is to be partitioned, we introduce proportional selection to choose cluster C_i. The probability of selecting cluster C_i is defined as follows:

$$p_i = \frac{J_i/n_i}{\sum_i (J_i/n_i)} \tag{7}$$

where $i = 1, \ldots, K$ and n_i denotes the number of objects belonging to cluster C_i. That is, the sparser the cluster, the more possibly it is selected to be partitioned, and vice versa. Since local iteration methods such as K-means algorithm and DHB algorithm are simple and free from predefining the cluster centers, we adopt them to divide cluster C_i into two new clusters. By experimental simulations, we choose K-means algorithm to perform this operation. After partition operation, cluster C_i is divided into two clusters and the number of clusters increases by one.

Mergence Operation: Like partition operation, we adopt proportional selection to determine which cluster is to be merged. That is, the closer two clusters to each other, the more possibly one of them is selected as the one to be merged, and vice versa. For cluster C_i, determine the distance between C_i and its nearest neighbor as follows:

$$d_i = \min_{i \neq j} \| \mathbf{c}_i - \mathbf{c}_j \|^2 \tag{8}$$

then the probability of selecting the cluster pair is defined as follows:

$$p_i = \sum_i d_i \Big/ d_i \tag{9}$$

Suppose the cluster pair C_i and C_j is selected, if

$$\frac{J_i}{n_i} > \frac{J_j}{n_j} \tag{10}$$

then C_i is selected; otherwise its nearest neighbor C_j is selected. Suppose cluster C_i is to be merged, object $\mathbf{x}_i$ belonging to cluster C_i is reassigned to cluster C_k, iff

$$\| \mathbf{x}_i - \mathbf{c}_k \|^2 < \| \mathbf{x}_i - \mathbf{c}_j \|^2 \tag{11}$$

where $\mathbf{c}_j \neq \mathbf{c}_k$. After mergence operation, cluster C_i disappears and the number of clusters decreases by one. After mutation operation, objects are automatically reassigned among different clusters and a new individual is created.

3   Experimental Results

Performance comparisons between IHGA-clustering and other three methods are conducted in Matlab on an Intel Pentium III processor running at 800MHz with 128MB real memory.

3.1   Data Sets

Five data sets are chosen to perform computer simulations: German Towns [3], British Towns [24], Data52, Crude Oil [25], and Iris [26]. Here, we consider two cases: one is that the number of clusters is variable, the other is that the number of clusters is fixed. Among them, the number of clusters in German Towns varies in the range [4, 10]. We label them as GT-4C, GT-6C, GT-8C, and GT-10C, respectively. This data set consists of Cartesian coordinates of 59 towns in Germany. The cases of British Towns are the same as those of German Towns which are labeled as BT-4C, BT-6C, BT-8C, and BT-10C, respectively. It is composed of 50 samples each of four variables corresponding to the first four principal components of the original data. Data52 is a two-dimensional data set having 250 overlapping objects where the number of clusters is five. Crude Oil has 56 data points, five features, and three classes. Iris represents different categories of irises having four feature values. The four feature values represent the sepal length, sepal width, petal length, and petal width in centimeters. It has three classes with 50 samples per class.

3.2   Performance Comparison

In [13], the conclusion is drawn that HGA-clustering can obtain better results sooner than GA-clustering [5] and more stably than K-means algorithm. In [15], the conclusion is drawn that GKA can obtain the proper clustering result at the expense of less computational cost than ES [6] and EP [7]. In [18], the conclusion is drawn that KGA-clustering can obtain better results sooner than GA-clustering [5] and more stably than K-means algorithm. In this paper, we compare IHGA-clustering with HGA-clustering, GKA, and KGA-clustering. If IHGA-clustering is better than them, then it is better than K-means algorithm and GA-clustering [5]. The population size P of four methods is the same and equal to 50. Each experiment includes 20 independent trials.

The average (Avg) and standard deviation (SD) values of the clustering results for different data sets are compared as shown in Table 1. Among four methods, HGA-clustering is the worst. It fails to attain the optimal values in most trials, which shows its convergence speed is slow. Equipped with K-means operation, GKA and KGA-clustering can obtain better results sooner than HGA-clustering. For Data52, Iris, and Crude Oil, they can attain the optimal results in most trials. For German Towns and British Towns, they obtain the best results when the number of clusters is small. When this number is close to ten, they fall into local optima in most trials. IHGA-clustering can obtain the optimal outputs in each trial in face of different data sets except BT-10C. For BT-10C, we find its standard deviation value is very small.

Table 1. Comparison of clustering results of four methods

	HGA-clustering Avg(SD)	GKA Avg(SD)	KGA-clustering Avg(SD)	IHGA-clustering Avg(SD)
GT-4C	55975.75(4088.33)	49600.59(0.00)	49600.59(0.00)	49600.59(0.00)
GT-6C	45380.21(4488.04)	30535.39(0.00)	30535.39(0.00)	30535.39(0.00)
GT-8C	36241.56(4555.63)	21661.82(201.87)	21488.56(9.69)	21483.02(0.00)
GT-10C	31943.01(4667.40)	17101.30(346.64)	16436.87(114.10)	16307.96(0.00)
BT-4C	186.52(6.18)	180.91(0.00)	180.91(0.00)	180.91(0.00)
BT-6C	158.82(10.19)	141.97(0.75)	141.64(0.34)	141.46(0.00)
BT-8C	135.81(7.34)	115.37(1.57)	113.94(0.83)	113.50(0.00)
BT-10C	117.43(8.78)	94.89(1.37)	93.33(0.46)	92.70(0.02)
Data52	2301.78(83.98)	488.02(0.01)	488.02(0.00)	488.02(0.00)
Iris	168.87(31.79)	78.94(0.00)	78.94(0.00)	78.94(0.00)
Crude Oil	1770.11(126.04)	1647.19(0.00)	1647.19(0.00)	1647.19(0.00)

Table 2. Comparison of the convergence speed and stability of four methods

	HGA-clustering AvgNG(SDNG)	GKA AvgNG (SDNG)	KGA-clustering AvgNG (SDNG)	IHGA-clustering AvgNG (SDNG)
GT-4C	-	4.70(1.42)	10.10(7.31)	1.95(0.22)
GT-6C	-	6.30(1.31)	19.30(9.83)	2.95(0.50)
GT-8C	-	10.50(2.50)	19.87(10.25)	3.25(0.54)
GT-10C	-	-	32.38(6.24)	9.95(11.64)
BT-4C	47.50(2.50)	5.80(2.01)	8.95(6.27)	2.00(0.00)
BT-6C	-	11.00(6.53)	30.47(9.01)	5.95(2.20)
BT-8C	-	16.17(11.94)	35.58(9.15)	12.10(7.67)
BT-10C	-	24.00(-)	-	25.90(13.25)
Data52	-	8.16(3.56)	22.35(10.93)	3.70(0.95)
Iris	-	6.84(2.94)	4.50(2.97)	2.00(0.00)
Crude Oil	43.00(2.83)	5.05(0.80)	3.95(2.33)	2.35(0.48)

To compare the convergence speed and stability of four methods, we adopt two indicators, the average and standard deviation values of the number of generations (AvgNG and SDNG) where the optimal result is firstly attained. AvgNG and SDNG respectively show the convergence speed and stability of the clustering method. Table 2 shows the results for these two indicators. The symbol "-" denotes the item does not exist. For example, in face of GT-10C, GKA fails to attain the best value within specified generations. Then this item is labeled as "-". In [5], it is proved that HGA-clustering can obtain better results sooner than GA-clustering. When the number of generations decreases to 50, its convergence speed becomes slow. In Table 2, it is seen that this method cannot obtain the proper results within specified generations for most data sets. GKA is faster and more stable than KGA-clustering in many cases. It is seen that IHGA-clustering is faster and more stable than other three methods in face of different data sets.

Table 3. Comparison of the success rates of four methods

	HGA-clustering SR(%)	GKA SR(%)	KGA-clustering SR(%)	IHGA-clustering SR(%)
GT-4C	0	100	100	100
GT-6C	0	100	100	100
GT-8C	0	10	75	100
GT-10C	0	0	40	100
BT-4C	10	100	100	100
BT-6C	0	65	75	100
BT-8C	0	30	60	100
BT-10C	0	5	0	50
Data52	0	95	100	100
Iris	0	95	100	100
Crude Oil	35	100	100	100

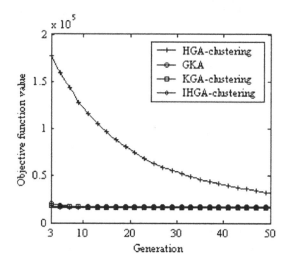

Fig. 2. Comparison of HGA-clustering, GKA, KGA-clustering, and IHGA-clustering

The success rate (SR) of the clustering algorithm is another indicator. It is defined as the number of trials where the best value is obtained divided by the number of total trials, which shows the ability of the clustering approach to achieve the optimal result. The success rates of four methods are compared as show in Table 3. It is found that the success rate of HGA-clustering is the lowest. GKA and KGA-clustering can obtain the ideal success rates for Data52, Iris, and Crude Oil. In face of German Towns and British Towns, they can attain the best results when the number of clusters is small. As the increase of this parameter, their success rates greatly decrease. In all cases, IHGA-clustering can obtain the ideal success rates except BT-10C. In face of BT-10C, IHGA-clustering can attain the optimal result in half trials.

In order to understand the performance of four methods better, we use GT-10C to show the evolution process. In Figure 2, it is seen that HGA-clustering is far inferior to other three methods. It seems that other three algorithms are close to each other. After HGA-clustering is removed, it is seen that IHGA-clustering is superior to GKA and KGA-clustering as shown in Figure 3.

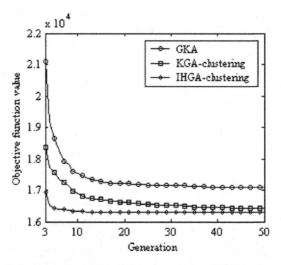

Fig. 3. Comparison of GKA, KGA-clustering, and IHGA-clustering

3.3 Time Complexity Analysis

In this section, we compare the time complexities of four methods. The time complexities of HGA-clustering, GKA, and KGA-clustering are $O(GPN_t mN)$, $O(GPmN^2)$, and $O(GPKmN)$, respectively, where N_t denotes the neighborhood size. Therefore, GKA is the most expensive, HGA-clustering is the second, and KGA-clustering is the third. In the following, we analyze the time complexity of IHGA-clustering. The time complexity of DHB operation is equal to $O(KmN)$. In genetic operations, the computational cost is dominated by mutation operation. The time complexity of mutation operation is discussed as follows: The time complexity of selecting the cluster to be partitioned is $O(K)$. The time complexity of partitioning the cluster is $O(mN)$. The time complexity of selecting the cluster to be merged is $O(K^2 m)$. The time complexity of merging the cluster is $O(KmN)$. Therefore, the total time complexity of IHGA-clustering is $O(GPKmN)$ the same as that of KGA-clustering.

4 Conclusions

In this paper, IHGA-clustering is proposed to deal with the minimum sum of squares clustering problem. In the algorithm framework, DHB operation is used to improve the individual and accelerate the convergence speed of IHGA-clustering, and partition-mergence mutation operation is designed to establish the child population. Here, mutation operation need not the mutation probability and can automatically reassign objects among different clusters. With the same time complexity as KGA-clustering, IHGA-clustering can get much better results faster and more stable than HGA-clustering, GKA, and KGA-clustering, which is demonstrated for experimental data sets.

Acknowledgements

This research was partially supported by National Natural Science Foundation of China (Grants 60573030 and 60471055) and State Key Laboratory for Novel Software Technology at Nanjing University.

References

1. Brucker, P.: On the complexity of clustering problems. Lecture Notes in Economics and Mathematical Systems. 157 (1978) 45-54
2. Jain, A.K., Dubes, R.: Algorithms for clustering data. Prentice-Hall, New Jersey (1988)
3. Spath, H.: Cluster analysis algorithms. Wiley, Chichester (1980)
4. Selim, S.Z., Ismail, M.A.: K-means-type algorithm: generalized convergence theorem and characterization of local optimality. IEEE Trans Pattern Anal Mach Intell. 6 (1984) 81-87
5. Murthy, C.A., Chowdhury, N.: In search of optimal clusters using genetic algorithms. Pattern Recognit Lett. 17 (1996) 825-832
6. Babu, G.P., Murthy, M.N.: Clustering with evolutionary strategies. Pattern Recognit. 27 (1994) 321-329
7. Babu, G.P.: Connectionist and evolutionary approaches for pattern clustering. PhD dissertation. Indian Institute of Science, India (1994)
8. Al-sultan, K.S.: A tabu search approach to the clustering problem. Pattern Recognit. 28 (1995) 1443-1451
9. Sung, C.S., Jin, H.W.: A tabu-search-based heuristic for clustering. Pattern Recognit. 33 (2000) 849-858
10. Selim, S.Z., Al-Sultan, K.S.: A simulated annealing algorithm for the clustering problem. Pattern Recognit. 24 (1991) 1003-1008
11. Bandyopadhyay, S., Maulik, U., Pakhira, M.K.: Clustering using simulated annealing with probabilisitc redistribution. Int J Pattern Recognit Artif Intell. 15 (2001) 269-285
12. Hall, L.O., Ozyurt, B., Bezdek, J.C.: Clustering with a genetically optimized approach. IEEE Trans Evol Comput. 3 (1999) 103-112.
13. Liu, Y.G., Chen, K.F., Li, X.M.: A hybrid genetic based clustering algorithm. In: Proceeding of The Third International Conference on Machine Learning and Cybernetics. Shanghai. (2004) 1677-1682
14. Fränti, P., Kivijärvi, J., Kaukoranta, T., Nevalainen, O.: Genetic algorithm for large-scale clustering problems. Comput J. 40 (1997) 547-554
15. Krishna, K., Murty, M.N.: Genetic K-means algorithm. IEEE Trans Syst Man Cybern Part B-Cybern. 29 (1999) 433-439
16. Maulik, U., Bandyopadhyay, S.: Genetic algorithm-based clustering technique. Pattern Recognit. 33 (2000) 1455-1465

17. Estivill-Castro, V.: Hybrid genetic algorithms are better for spatial clustering. Lecture Notes in Artificial Intelligence. 1886 (2000) 424-434
18. Bandyopadhyay, S., Maulik, U.: An evolutionary technique based on K-means algorithm for optimal clustering in R^N. Inf Sci. 146 (2002) 221-237
19. Kivijärvi, J., Fränti, P., Nevalainen, O.: Self-adaptive genetic algorithm for clustering. J Heuristics. 9 (2003) 113-129
20. Wu, F.X., Zhang, W.J., Kusalik, A.J.: A genetic K-means clustering algorihtm applied to gene expression data. Lecture Notes in Artificial Intelligence. 2671 (2003) 520-526
21. Sheng, W.G., Tucker, A., Liu, X.H.: Clustering with niching genetic K-means algorithm. Lecture Notes in Computer Science. 3103 (2004) 162-173
22. Zhang, Q.W., Boyle, R.D.: A new clustering algorithm with multiple runs of iterative procedures. Pattern Recognit. 24 (1991) 835-848
23. Kim, D.J., Park, Y.W., Park, D.J.: A novel validity index for determination of the optimal number of clusters. IEICE Trans Inf Syst. E84-D (2001) 281-285
24. Chien, Y.T.: Interactive Pattern Recognition. Marcel-Dekker, New York (1978)
25. Johnson, R.A., Wichern, D.W.: Applied multivariate statistical analysis. Prentice-Hall, New Jersey (1982)
26. Fisher, R.A.: The use of multiple measurements in taxonomic problem. Annals of Eugenics. 7 (1936) 179-188

A Greek Named-Entity Recognizer That Uses Support Vector Machines and Active Learning

Georgios Lucarelli and Ion Androutsopoulos

Dept. of Informatics, Athens University of Economics and Business
Patission 76, GR-104 34, Athens, Greece

Abstract. We present a named-entity recognizer for Greek person names and temporal expressions. For temporal expressions, it relies on semi-automatically produced patterns. For person names, it employs two Support Vector Machines, that scan the input text in two passes, and active learning, which reduces the human annotation effort during training.

1 Introduction

Named-entity recognizers (NERs) identify occurrences of entity names in texts, and classify them in predefined categories (e.g., names of persons, organizations, dates). Named-entity recognition is an important sub-process in information extraction, where systems identify relationships and events mentioned in texts, question answering, and many other natural language processing applications.

Earlier NERs that were based on hand-crafted rules [1, 2] have largely been superseded by recognizers that use statistical and machine learning techniques, including Hidden Markov Models (e.g., [3, 4]), Maximum Entropy Models (e.g., [5]), C4.5 (e.g., [6]), Support Vector Machines (SVMs) (e.g., [7, 8]), and Neural Networks (e.g., [9]). Apart from usually performing better, statistical and learning-based recognizers are easier to configure for new text genres and new name categories. However, they still require a tedious annotation phase, during which humans must tag occurrences of entity names in a training corpus. The problem can be alleviated with active learning techniques (e.g., [10, 11]), whereby the system itself selects and presents for human annotation only training instances it expects to improve its performance. Shen et al. [12] recently demonstrated that active learning can reduce significantly the annotation effort in an English SVM-based NER. Similar findings have been reported by Vlachos [13].

Research on NERs is dominated by work on English texts. All previous published work on Greek NERs we are aware of relies on hand-crafted rules or patterns [14, 15, 16] and/or decision tree induction with C4.5 [17, 18]. In this paper, we present a freely available NER for Greek texts, which currently supports person names and temporal expressions (e.g., "end of August", "Easter of 2002"). To recognize temporal expressions, our NER relies on semi-automatically constructed patterns. To recognize person names it uses two SVMs, used in two passes of the input text, respectively.[1] The 2nd-pass takes into account the decisions of the

---

[1] We use LIBSVM with an RBF kernel, including LIBSVM's grid-search parameter-tuning utility; see `http://www.csie.ntu.edu.tw/~cjlin/libsvm/`

G. Antoniou et al. (Eds.): SETN 2006, LNAI 3955, pp. 203–213, 2006.

first-pass, which allows it to learn how to correct mistakes of the first-pass, and whether or not a token was classified with high confidence as a person name elsewhere in the same text during the first-pass, which helps it identify person names in less obvious contexts. An additional initial pass uses simplistic rules to remove from the consideration of the SVMs tokens that are almost certainly not person names. We borrowed the multiple-pass approach from Edinburgh's MUC-7 NER [19]. In that system, however, the multiple passes were implemented in a radically different way, using gradually more permissive hand-crafted transduction rules and consulting a Maximum Entropy-based name-matching component before moving on to a more permissive set of transduction rules.

2   System Description

2.1   Preprocessing and Classification Task

Both during training and at run-time (when using the trained NER on new texts), the system first applies a simplistic tokenizer, which treats any non-alphanumeric character as a separate token (e.g, ['Η', 'κ', '.', 'Τ', '.', 'Α', '.', 'Νικολάου', '-', 'Παπαδάκη', 'δήλωσε', 'ότις', '13', '/', '12', '/', '98', ...]). Words containing both Greek and Latin characters are also split (e.g., "Euroγνώση" becomes ['Euro', 'γνώση']). Any HTML tags are also removed, after marking as sentence delimiters tokens that immediately precede end-of-paragraph tags. An SVM-based sentence splitter is also applied; see [20] for details. Following Bikel et al. [3], named-entity recognition is then viewed as the task of assigning each token to one of the name categories (in our case, person name or temporal expression) or the not-a-name category. Unlike other NERs (e.g., [4]), we have no special categories for the first tokens of names. This simplifies the classification task, but has the disadvantage that we cannot distinguish between adjacent names of the same category (e.g., "the sister of John Smith Mary Rose said"). Such cases, however, are very rare.

2.2   Temporal Expression Recognition

Temporal expressions are recognized using patterns produced semi-automatically. First, all the manually tagged temporal expressions are retrieved from the training corpus, and they are generalized by replacing numbers by regular expressions and other tokens by pre-defined token types (e.g., month, sep(arator), special, article). For instance, "12 December 2005" becomes "[0-9]{2} month [0-9]{4}", "12.1.67" becomes "[0-9]{2} sep [0-9]{1} sep [0-9]{2}", and "Easter of 1995" becomes "special article [0-9]{4}". (Greek uses an article instead of "of". We translate examples in English, when possible.) We use 13 token types, and for each type there is a list with the corresponding tokens. The token types and lists are created manually and may have to be modified when moving to texts of a different genre, but otherwise pattern generation is automatic.

Generalized expressions that differ only in numeric sub-expressions are then combined by creating disjunctions; "[0-9]{2} sep [0-9]{1} sep [0-9]{2}" and "[0-9]{1} sep [0-9]{2} sep [0-9]{4}", deriving from "12.1.67" and "1.11.2005",

become "([0-9]{2}|[0-9]{1}) sep ([0-9]{1}|[0-9]{2}) sep ([0-9]{2}|[0-9]{4})".
The resulting patterns are sorted by length. At run-time, if multiple temporal patterns apply we use the longest (most specific) one.

2.3   Person Name Recognition

Person name recognition assumes that all the tokens of temporal expressions have
been identified correctly, an assumption our experiments confirm is reasonable.
Hence, it is concerned with classifying as person names or non-person-names the
tokens that have not been classified as temporal expressions.

Sure-Fire Rules. The binary classification problem of person name recognition is grossly imbalanced: person name tokens are much fewer than non-person-
name ones. This imbalance is problematic, because learning algorithms will tend
to classify all tokens in the majority class (non-person-names). To reduce the
imbalance, we employ simplistic 'sure-fire' rules. Tokens that satisfy them are
classified as non-person-names without consulting the SVMs; and the SVMs are
trained only on instances corresponding to tokens that do not satisfy the sure-
fire rules (and have not been tagged as temporal expressions). Preliminary experiments indicated that the ratio of person name to other tokens is initially
approximately 1:42; after removing temporal-expressions and tokens satisfying
the sure-fire rules, it becomes 1:3.5, and only 0.2% of the removed tokens are
person names. By "removed tokens" we mean that the SVMs are not invoked to
decide their categories, and that tokens of this type do not give rise to training
instances of the SVMs; however, the SVMs may well examine features of those
tokens when classifying other neighboring tokens.

The sure-fire rules classify as non-person-names all numbers, punctuation
and other non-alphabetic symbols, as well as stop-words and tokens not starting
with a capital letter. They also classify as non-person-names tokens ending in
suffixes like "–ώνω" that are highly indicative of Greek verb forms. The rules
are not applied to tokens directly preceded by other tokens known to be person
names (during training, other tokens that have been tagged as person names;
at run-time, preceding tokens the SVMs have classified as person names). This is
needed in cases like "Λουδοβίκος των Ανωγείων", where "των" is part of the name.

First Pass. Both at run-time and during training, each token to be classified
is represented as a vector containing features of that token and its context.
Henceforth, t_0 denotes the token to be classified, and t_i the $|i|$-th token to the
right (positive i) or left (negative i) of t_0. The 1st-pass SVM uses 65 features, listed
in Table 1.[2] For example, 6 Boolean features indicate whether or not t_{-1}, t_0, and
t_1 are commas or full stops. All features were selected from a larger, manually
created pool of candidate features, using information gain [21] computed on
training data. For instance, there was initially also a feature that checked if t_2
was a full stop, but it was discarded based on its low information gain.

---

[2] Numeric features are normalized in $[-1, 1]$.

Table 1. Features of the 1st-pass SVM

no.	feature descriptions	t_{-2}	t_{-1}	t_0	t_1	t_2	type
1–6	comma? full stop?			•	•	•	Boolean
7–9	number?			•	•	•	Boolean
10–17	Greek characters or not? Latin characters or not?		•	•	•	•	Boolean
18–27	first character capital or not? all characters capital?	•	•	•	•	•	Boolean
28–32	length in characters	•	•	•	•	•	numeric
33–38	common Greek surname prefix/suffix?			•	•	•	Boolean
39	common Greek first name?			•			numeric
40–44	common Greek last character?	•	•	•	•	•	Boolean
45–46	ends in "–ς"? common singular adjective ending?			•			Boolean
47	common plural noun/adjective ending?			•			Boolean
48–52	last token of sentence? (useful for full stops)	•	•	•	•	•	Boolean
53	part of article's title? (different writing conventions)			•			Boolean
54–57	distance from start of person name $\leq$ 1, 2, 3, 6?			•			Boolean
58	directly preceded by "χ." (Mr./Mrs.)?			•			Boolean
59	"χ.χ." (plural of Mr./Mrs.) in previous 10 tokens?			•			Boolean
60–62	directly preceded by tokens accompanying person names			•			numeric
63–65	preceded by tokens accompanying person names			•			numeric

Feature 39 shows the degree (number of initial characters) to which t_0 matches the closest entry of a mini-gazetteer of 350 common Greek first names. This partial matching captures inflectional variations of Greek names. Features 40–44 show if $t_{-2}, \ldots, t_2$ end in "–ς", "–ν", or a vowel, as most Greek words do, or not; if not, this is an indication that the corresponding token may be an abbreviation (as in "Ανδρ. Παπανδρέου"). There is also a feature (45) that checks t_0 for the "–ς" ending in particular, which is very common in masculine Greek first names. We had no Greek POS-tagger; hence, we experimented with features corresponding to common endings of nouns, adjectives, etc. Of those, the information gain selection retained only feature 46, which checks for some common singular adjective endings, and feature 47, which checks for common plural noun or adjective endings.

Features 54–57 check the distance of t_0 from the first token of a continuous sequence of person-name tokens t_0 is part of. For example, in "ο Γεώργιος – Αλέξανδρος Μαγκάκης" the distance of the last token from the first person-name token is 3. These features allow the SVMs to estimate how likely it is for a token to continue a preceding person name, based on the length of the preceding name. We also use 6 numeric features (60–65) that check the degree to which t_0 is preceded (directly or in a window of 7 tokens) by tokens (of 1–2, 3–4, or more characters) that occur frequently before person-name tokens in the training corpus. See [20] for motivation and details.

Active Learning. In a binary classification problem, an SVM in general uses non-linear functions to map the feature vectors to a new vector space of higher dimensionality. It then employs optimization techniques to locate a hyperplane in the new space that separates the training vectors of the two categories with the maximum margin (distance between the closest training vectors of the two categories) and the smallest error (training vectors that end up on the wrong side of the hyperplane or inside the marginal area) [22]. The equation of the resulting optimal hyperplane depends only on training vectors that the hyperplane misclassifies or that fall within the marginal area, jointly called *support vectors*.

Active learning aims to select and present for human annotation only instances of the training dataset that improve the performance of the classifier. In the case of SVMs, adding training instances that are not support vectors does not affect the optimal hyperplane, as the new vectors are ignored. Hence, one should concentrate on adding training instances that fall inside the marginal area (thus, close to the hyperplane) or on the wrong side of the hyperplane. In the latter case, if the SVM has already encountered a large number of training instances, new training instances that fall on the wrong side will most likely also tend to be close to the separating hyperplane (i.e., the SVM will be close to classifying them correctly). Hence, in both cases one should concentrate on adding training instances that fall close to the separating hyperplane the SVM has learnt so far.[3]

Learning-based NERs are typically constructed by picking randomly some texts from a larger pool, annotating them exhaustively, and then training the NERs on the annotated texts. In our 1st-pass, this means annotating all the tokens of the selected texts that do not satisfy the temporal expression patterns nor the sure-fire rules, hereafter called *hard tokens*, and training the SVM on vectors representing the annotated hard tokens. We call this approach *passive learning*. In contrast, when using active learning our NER evaluates repeatedly the hard tokens of the entire pool that have not been annotated, it asks the human annotator to classify a batch of 100 of those tokens it considers most useful (closest to the current hyper-plane), and then retrains the 1st-pass SVM on the extended training set. Selecting the most useful non-annotated hard tokens, however, requires computing the distances from the current hyperplane to all of the non-annotated hard tokens of the pool; the distances are, roughly speaking, the confidence scores the SVM returns for each instance it classifies. For large pools, this becomes impractical. As a compromise, we divide the pool in ten parts, and whenever we need additional training instances, we select cyclically another part of the pool and limit the selection process to the non-annotated hard tokens of that part. This allows active learning to consider eventually all the hard tokens of the pool, while limiting the distance computations.

Second Pass. A person name may occur several times in a text, and context may make some of its occurrences (e.g., "Mr. M. Liapis") easier to identify than others ("According to Liapis..."). Hence, the 1st-pass SVM may have classified some occurrences of a token as person names, and others as non-person-names. However, if the 1st-pass SVM has classified an occurrence of a token as person name with high confidence, any other occurrences of the same token in the same text are probably also person names. Furthermore, if a token (e.g., "Michalis") is

---

[3] See [23] for a more formal account of why selecting training instances close to the hyperplane and other selection criteria are reasonable.

accompanied by another token (e.g., "Liapis" in "Michalis Liapis") that the 1st-pass SVM has classified anywhere in the text as person name with high confidence, then this is an indication that the first token may also be a person name.

Following these observations, at run-time once the first pass is complete we create a set P of all the tokens that the 1st-pass SVM classified as person names anywhere in the text with confidence greater than 0.9. We then re-scan the text, using the 2nd-pass SVM to re-classify all the hard tokens. The 2nd-pass SVM uses the same features as the 1st-pass one, with the addition of six more numeric features. The first three indicate the degree to which t_{-1}, t_0, and t_1 match the closest token in P, as in feature 39. The other three features are the confidence scores of the 1st-pass SVM for t_{-1}, t_0, t_1. They allow the 2nd-pass SVM to learn when and to what degree to trust the decisions of the first pass. Active learning is performed in the 2nd-pass SVM in the same manner as in the 1st-pass SVM.

3   Experimental Results

3.1   Corpora

We evaluated our NER using three collections of newspaper articles. The first one, called *corpus 0*, contains all the articles (ranging from politics and finance to sports) of the Greek newspapers "To Vima" and "Ta Nea" that were published from July 2000 to October 2001 (12,687 articles) and from March 2001 to July 2002 (9,250 articles), respectively. The second collection, *corpus 1*, consists of 400 randomly selected articles of corpus 0, a total of 331,000 tokens, 4,815 person names (possibly multi-token) and 1,563 temporal expressions (possibly multi-token). The third collection, *corpus 2* consists of 715 financial articles from Greek newspapers, and, hence, is more focussed in terms of topics.[4] It contains 205,000 tokens, 1,046 person names, and 1,244 temporal expressions (possibly multi-token). All the tokens of corpora 1 and 2 were manually annotated as temporal expressions or person names.

3.2   Evaluating Temporal Expression Recognition

Temporal expression recognition was evaluated separately on corpora 1 and 2, using 10-fold cross-validation. The results are shown in Table 2. Precision is defined as $\frac{TP}{TP+FP}$, recall as $\frac{TP}{TP+FN}$, and F_β as $\frac{(1+\beta^2)\ precision\ recall}{\beta^2\ precision+recall}$, where TP (true positives) and FP (false positives) are the numbers of tokens that are correctly or wrongly, respectively, classified as temporal expressions, and FN (false negatives) the number of tokens wrongly classified as non-temporal-expressions. Precision shows how certain we can be that a token classified as temporal expression belongs indeed in that category, whereas recall shows how many temporal-expression tokens the system identifies correctly. F_β is a combination of precision and recall; we use $\beta = 1$, which gives equal importance to precision and recall. Performance was very good on both corpora, with slightly worse results, especially in recall, in the first, more varied corpus. See [20] for an error analysis.

---

[4] Corpus 2 was created during MITOS; see http://iit.demokritos.gr/skel/mitos/

Table 2. Cross-validation results of temporal expression recognition

corpus	precision (%)	recall (%)	$F_{\beta=1}$ (%)
corpus 1 (general)	96.62	92.95	94.75
corpus 2 (financial)	97.59	95.35	96.46

3.3   Evaluating Person Name Recognition

Active vs. Passive Learning in the 1st Pass. In this experiment, the 400 articles of corpus 1 were randomly divided in two parts (approx. 200 articles each), hereafter *part 1* and *part 2*. First, part 1 was used to induce temporal expression patterns, as in Section 2.2. Then, in passive learning the 1st-pass SVM was trained on an increasingly larger set of training vectors, corresponding to the first n hard tokens of part 1, with n ranging up to 13,000. (Part 1 contained 17,100 hard tokens. The remaining 4,100 were reserved for the training of the 2nd-pass SVM.) In contrast, in active learning the 1st-pass SVM was trained on the first 4,100 of the 13,000 training vectors of passive learning, and increasingly more additional training vectors corresponding to hard tokens selected from a pool and subsequently annotated by a human (as in Section 2.3), up to a total of 14,000 training vectors. The pool consisted of 5,000 randomly selected articles of corpus 0 (2,500 from each newspaper), excluding the articles of corpus 1, an estimated 425,000 non-annotated hard tokens. The classifiers that active and passive learning produced were both evaluated on part 2.

Precision, recall, and $F_{\beta=1}$ are now defined as in Section 3.2, except that we now count person-name tokens. The $F_{\beta=1}$ results are shown in the left diagram of Figure 1 ("one SVM" curves); error bars correspond to 0.99 confidence intervals. With approximately only 5,500 training vectors, active learning performs as well as passive learning with 12,000 training vectors. Furthermore, active learning clearly leads to superior results, when both methods use the same number of training instances, which is probably due to the wider variety of training instances active learning has access to. The right diagram of Figure 1 shows that overall active learning is better than passive learning in both precision and recall, although with large training sets the difference in precision almost disappears and the precision of active learning deteriorates. In contrast, the recall of active learning is consistently better than that of passive learning, which again suggests that the size of its pool allows active learning to identify a larger variety of person names.

2nd-Pass SVM. In this experiment, we used the 1st-pass SVM that the previous experiment produced with active learning and 9,100 training vectors (approximately the number of training vectors beyond which precision no longer improved). The 2nd-pass SVM was initially also trained on 9,100 vectors: the 5,000 training instances that the 1st-pass SVM had selected with active learning, and the remaining 4,100 tokens of part 1 that had not been used. The latter replaced the initial 4,100 training instances of the 1st-pass SVM that had been obtained with passive learning; motivation follows. In all the training vectors of

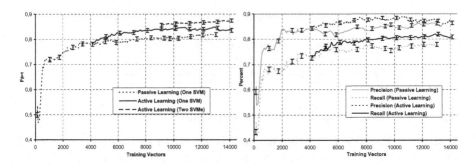

Fig. 1. Left: F-measure of person name recognition with 0.99 confidence intervals. Right: The effect of active learning on the precision and recall of the 1st-pass SVM.

the 2nd-pass SVM, we inserted the additional six features using the decisions of the 1st-pass SVM. We then gradually expanded the training set of the 2nd-pass SVM by selecting with active learning fresh training instances from the pool, manually annotating them, and adding the new six features by invoking the 1st-pass SVM, up to a total of 14,000 training vectors. The fresh instances were now selected by their distance from the hyperplane of the 2nd-pass SVM.

Using as the initial training set of the 2nd-pass SVM exactly the same 9,100 instances that were used to train the 1st-pass SVM might had led the 2nd-pass SVM to over-value the decisions of the 1st-pass SVM (as recorded in the additional features), because the 1st-pass SVM would have encountered all 9,100 instances during its training. As a partial remedy, we replaced only the 4,100 initial training instances, which reduced the annotation effort of the experiment.

Figure 2 shows the effect of the second pass on precision and recall; we include the active learning curves of the right diagram of Figure 1, which were obtained using the 1st-pass SVM only. There is a notable improvement in recall, because the 2nd-pass SVM is now aware of whether or not t_0 or its surrounding tokens have been classified elsewhere in the text as person names with high confidence, which allows it to classify as person names tokens in less obvious contexts. The second pass also has a positive impact on precision, which is probably due to the fact that the second SVM can learn to correct mistakes of the first one. The effect of the second pass on the F-measure is shown in the left diagram of Figure 1. See [20] for an error analysis.

Financial Articles. The last experiment was a 10-fold cross-validation on corpus 2 (financial articles). As we did not have a larger pool of non-annotated texts for this type of articles, we only experimented with passive learning. In each iteration of the cross-validation, the temporal expression patterns were induced from the training articles (90% of the total articles). The iteration's training articles were then divided in two equal parts. The first one was used to train the 1st-pass SVM, which was then applied to the second part to add the additional six features of the 2nd-pass. The 2nd-pass SVM was then trained on the second part. The system, using only one or both of the SVMs, was then tested on the

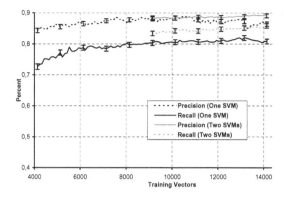

Fig. 2. The effect of the 2nd-pass on the precision and recall of person-name tokens

Table 3. Person name recognition results with 0.99 confidence intervals

corpus	methods (training inst.)	precision (%)	recall (%)	$F_{\beta=1}$ (%)
general articles	1 SVM, passive (13k)	86.29±0.69	77.91±0.83	81.89±0.77
(corpus 1, with	1 SVM, active (9.1k)	88.39±0.64	80.33±0.79	84.17±0.73
corpus 0 as pool)	2 SVMs, active (9.1, 14k)	89.06±0.62	85.83±0.69	87.42±0.66
financial articles	1 SVM, passive (8.8k)	94.96±1.28	88.95±1.83	91.86±1.60
(cross-validation)	2 SVMs, passive (8.8, 8.8k)	95.76±1.18	91.05±1.67	93.34±1.46

iteration's testing articles (10% of the total articles). The results can be seen in the bottom rows of Table 3; the top rows show results from the experiments on general articles. The system performed better than on general articles, even though this time we used only passive training with smaller training sets (on average, in each iteration the SVMs were trained on 8,800 training instances each). We attribute this to the fact that corpus 2 is more focussed in terms of topics, which limits the variety of contexts where person names may appear.

The results compare favorably to previously published results of person name recognition in Greek financial news: Boutsis et al. [14] reported 71% precision and 71% recall, whereas Farmakiotou et al. [15] reported 88% precision and 77% recall ($F_{\beta=1} = 82\%$). No comparison can be made to the other Greek NERs of Section 1, because their results were obtained using very different corpora [17], they do not target person names [16], or no comparable results are available [18].

4   Conclusions

We presented a freely available NER for Greek person names and temporal expressions.[5] For temporal expressions, the system uses manually constructed token lists and automatically generalized regular expression patterns. For person

---

[5] Our NER is available from http://www.aueb.gr/users/ion/publications.html

names, it uses a pair of SVMs that scan the input text in two passes. The 1st-pass SVM uses both hand-crafted features and features corresponding to automatically collected tokens that accompany frequently person names in the training data. The 2nd-pass SVM uses the same features, but it also takes into consideration the decisions of the 1st-pass SVM, which allows it to learn how to correct mistakes of the first pass; it also considers whether or not the same token was tagged elsewhere in the same text as a person name with high confidence by the 1st-pass SVM, which allows it to identify person name occurrences in less obvious contexts. A set of simplistic sure-fire rules is also employed, to reduce the class imbalance of the decision problem the two SVMs face. Both SVMs use active learning, which requires a smaller training set to reach the same performance as passive learning, and allows the system to perform better than with passive learning when using a training set of the same size. The system performed better on a more focussed collection of financial articles than on general newspaper articles.

References

1. Appelt, D., Hobbs, J., Bear, J., Israel, D., Kameyama, M., Kehler, A., Martin, D., Myers, K., Tyson, M.: SRI International FASTUS system MUC-6 test results and analysis. In: 6th Message Understanding Conference, Columbia, MD (1995)
2. Mitchell, B., Huyck, C., Cunningham, H., Humphreys, K., Gaizauskas, R., Azzam, S., Wilks, Y.: University of Sheffield: Description of the laSIE-II system as used for MUC-7. In: 7th Message Understanding Conference, Fairfax, VA (1998)
3. Bikel, D.M., Schwartz, R.L., Weischedel, R.M.: An algorithm that learns what's in a name. Machine Learning **34**(1–3) (1999) 211–231
4. Zhou, G., Su, J.: Machine learning-based named entity recognition via effective integration of various evidences. Natural Language Engineering **11** (2005) 189–206
5. Chieu, H.L., Ng, H.T.: Named entity recognition with a maximum entropy approach. In: 7th Conference on Computational Natural Language Learning, Edmonton, Canada (2003) 160–163
6. Paliouras, G., Karkaletsis, V., Petasis, G., Spyropoulos, C.: Learning decision trees for named-entity recognition and classification. In: 14th European Conference on Artificial Intelligence, Berlin, Germany (2000)
7. Kazama, J., Makino, T., Ohta, Y., Tsujii, J.: Tuning Support Vector Machines for biomedical named entity recognition. In: ACL Workshop on Natural Language Processing in the Biomedical Domain, Philadelphia, PA (2002) 1–8
8. Lee, K., Hwang, Y., Rim, H.: Two-phase biomedical NE recognition based on SVMs. In: ACL Workshop on Natural Language Processing in the Biomedical Domain, Philadelphia, PA (2002)
9. Petasis, G., Petridis, S., Paliouras, G., Karkaletsis, V., Perantonis, S., Spyropoulos, C.: Symbolic and neural learning for named-entity recognition. In: Symposium on Computational Intelligence and Learning, Chios, Greece (2000) 58–66
10. Schohn, G., Cohn, D.: Less is more: Active learning with Support Vector Machines. In: 17th Int. Conference on Machine Learning, Stanford, CA (2000) 839–846
11. Brinker, K.: Incorporating diversity in active learning with Support Vector Machines. In: 20th International Conference on Machine Learning, Washington, D.C. (2003) 59–66

12. Shen, D., Zhang, J., Su, J., Zhou, G., Tan, C.L.: Multi-criteria-based active learning for named entity recognition. In: 42nd Annual Meeting of the Association for Computational Linguistics, Barcelona, Spain (2004) 589–596
13. Vlachos, A.: Active learning with Support Vector Machines. Master's thesis, School of Informatics, University of Edinburgh (2004)
14. Boutsis, S., Demiros, I., Giouli, V., Liakata, M., Papageorgiou, H., Piperidis, S.: A system for recognition of named entities in Greek. In: 2nd International Conference on Natural Language Processing, Patra, Greece (2000) 424–435
15. Farmakiotou, D., Karkaletsis, V., Koutsias, J., Sigletos, G., Spyropoulos, C., Stamatopoulos, P.: Rule-based named entity recognition for Greek financial texts. In: Workshop on Computational Lexicography and Multimedia Dictionaries, Patra, Greece (2000) 75–78
16. Farmakiotou, D., Karkaletsis, V., Samaritakis, G., Petasis, G., Spyropoulos, C.: Named entity recognition in Greek Web pages. In: 2nd Hellenic Conference on Artificial Intelligence, companion volume, Thessaloniki, Greece (2002) 91–102
17. Karkaletsis, V., Paliouras, G., Petasis, G., Manousopoulou, N., Spyropoulos, C.: Named-entity recognition from Greek and English texts. Intelligent and Robotic Systems **26** (1999) 123–135
18. Petasis, G., Vichot, F., Wolinski, F., Paliouras, G., Karkaletsis, V., Spyropoulos, C.: Using machine learning to maintain rule-based named-entity recognition and classification systems. In: 39th ACL/10th EACL, Toulouse, France (2001) 426–433
19. Mikheev, A., Grover, C., Moens, M.: Description of the LTG system used for MUC-7. In: 7th Message Understanding Conference, Fairfax, VA (1998)
20. Lucarelli, G.: Named entity recognition and categorization in Greek texts. Master's thesis, Department of Informatics, Athens University of Economics and Business (2005) `http://www.aueb.gr/users/ion/docs/lucarelli_msc_final_report.pdf`.
21. Manning, C., Schutze, H.: Foundations of Statistical Natural Language Processing. MIT Press (1999)
22. Cristianini, N., Shawe-Taylor, J.: An Introduction to Support Vector Machines. Cambridge University Press (2000)
23. Tong, S., Koller, D.: Support Vector Machine active learning with applications to text classification. Machine Learning Research **2** (2002) 45–66

Intelligent Segmentation and Classification of Pigmented Skin Lesions in Dermatological Images

Ilias Maglogiannis, Elias Zafiropoulos[1], and Christos Kyranoudis[2]

[1] Department of Information and Communication Systems Engineering,
University of the Aegean,
GR 83200 Karlovasi, Samos, Greece
[2] School of Chemical Engineering, National Technical University of Athens,
Zografou Campus, Athens, GR-15780, Greece

Abstract. During the last years, computer vision-based diagnostic systems have been used in several hospitals and dermatology clinics, aiming mostly at the early detection of malignant melanoma tumor, which is among the most frequent types of skin cancer, versus other types of non-malignant cutaneous diseases. In this paper we discuss intelligent techniques for the segmentation and classification of pigmented skin lesions in such dermatological images. A local thresholding algorithm is proposed for skin lesion separation and border, texture and color based features, are then extracted from the digital images. Extracted features are used to construct a classification module based on Support Vector Machines (SVM) for the recognition of malignant melanoma versus dysplastic nevus.

1 Introduction

A significant amount of studies have proven that the quantification of tissue lesion features may be of essential importance in clinical practice, because several tissue lesions can be identified based on measurable features extracted from an image [1][2] [3], [4], [5], [6], [7], [8], [9], [10]. During the last years, computer vision-based diagnostic systems have been used in several hospitals and dermatology clinics, aiming mostly at the early detection of malignant melanoma tumor, which is among the most frequent types of skin cancer, versus other types of non-malignant cutaneous diseases. The significant interest in melanoma is due to the fact that its incidence has increased faster than that of almost all other cancers and the annual incidence rates have increased on the order of 3–7% in fair-skinned populations in recent decades [11].

The advanced cutaneous melanoma is still incurable, but when diagnosed at early stages it can be cured without complications. However, the differentiation of early melanoma from other non-malignant pigmented skin lesions is not trivial even for experienced dermatologists. In several cases primary care physicians underestimate melanoma in its early stage [12]. In this paper, the problems of skin image segmentation using a local thresholding approach for the separation of pigmented skin lesions from healthy skin and the feature extraction from the separated regions are examined. The extracted features are intended for the recognition of malignant melanoma versus dysplastic nevus. An automated procedure based on the Support Vector Machine

G. Antoniou et al. (Eds.): SETN 2006, LNAI 3955, pp. 214–223, 2006.
© Springer-Verlag Berlin Heidelberg 2006

(SVM) algorithm and proper feature selection and kernel function employment is proposed for this purpose, which exhibited excellent results of accuracy, sensitivity and specificity indices. The paper is organized as follows: In section 1 a brief outline of the presented research work is given. In section 2 the materials and methods employed in the paper are described, providing details concerning the description of the image data set, image pre-processing and segmentation and feature extraction. In section 3, the basic features of the SVM classifier implementation on the data set are described, followed by the corresponding results and discussion. Finally in section 4, the paper concludes.

2   Materials and Methods

2.1   Description of Image Data Set

The image data set used in this study is an extraction of the skin database that exists at the Vienna Hospital, kindly provided by Prof. Ganster. The whole data set consists of 1041 images, 972 of them are displaying nevus and the rest images are containing malignant melanoma cases. The size of the melanomas image set is not so small considering the fact that malignant melanoma cases in primordial state are very rare. It is very common that many patients arrive at specialized hospitals (e.g. the Vienna Hospital) with partially removed lesions; lesion removal is a simple operation that may be performed in small health centres.

The total number of images is captured using the Molemax II imaging device. The MoleMax II is an integrated system for digital epiluminescence microscopy and macro imaging in the world, utilizing patented polarized light technology to effectively view beneath the skin's surface, without the need of immersion oil. More details about the MoleMax II system may be found at http://www.dermausa.net/ Pages/ molemaxii.htm. A standard protocol was used for the acquisition of the skin lesion images ensuring the reliability and reproducibility of the collected images. Reproducibility is considered quite essential for the image characterization and recognition attempted in this study, since only standardized images may produce comparable results.

2.2   Image Pre-processing and Segmentation Using Local Thresholding

The segmentation of an image containing a cutaneous disease involves the separation of the skin lesion from the healthy skin. For the special problem of skin lesion segmentation, mainly region-based segmentation methods are applied [13], [14], [15]. A simple approach is Thresholding, which is based on the fact that the values of pixels that belong to a skin lesion differ from the values of the background. By choosing an upper and a lower value it is possible to isolate those pixels that have values within this range. The information for the upper and the lower limits can be extracted from the image histogram, where the different objects are represented as peaks. The bounds of the peeks are good estimates of these limits. It should be noted though that, simple thresholding as it is described here can not be used in all cases because image histograms of skin lesions are not always multi-modal.

Several attempts have been made in literature concerning image segmentation [16]. In this study, a more sophisticated approach of a local thresholding technique was adopted, where the window size, the threshold value and degree of overlap between successive moving windows were the procedure parameters. These parameters were tuned so that skin lesions separation was performed satisfactory. Image thresholding is performed using only the intensity value, therefore the image is firstly converted into grey scale. Furthermore, image pixels are smoothed using a standard Gaussian filter whose moving window size value is appropriately tuned, for reducing noise. According to the proposed method, the characteristic color feature for each pixel in the image (in this case color intensity) is directly compared to the average value of this specific feature computed for all pixels that reside within a wide rectangular area (window) around this pixel. If the pixel feature value is less that the average window value minus a characteristic threshold value the pixel is assumed to be part of the skin lesions region (the pixel is interpreted as "dark" pixel). If the window is wide enough to contain the entire image for all pixels within it, the technique is called global thresholding. Typically, to avoid individual image intensity differences, the feature values are normalized by the average feature value for all pixels in the image. Thus threshold is provided as a per-cent fraction of this value. Local (or global) threshold-ing partitions the image into objects that can be interpreted as "islands" of "dark" pixels within the frame. These objects contain image pixels extracted by the thresh-olding process ("dark" pixels) and are characterized by a certain proximity property in the sense that each pixel in the object has or has not at least one "dark" pixel in the neighborhood, that is to say it is close to the former by a distance of one pixel in any direction. A recursive algorithm was implemented to extract each "island" object. According to this algorithm, the image pixels are scanned one by one. If an un-scanned "dark" pixel is met, the pixel is added to a new "island" object and recur-sively an adjacent "dark" pixel is sought within its neighbor (adjacent pixels in all

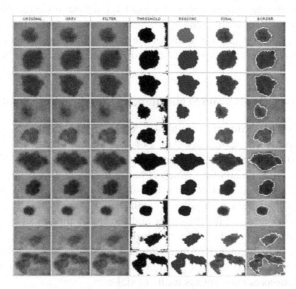

Fig. 1. Local Thresholding Segmentation of digital images containing melanoma lesions

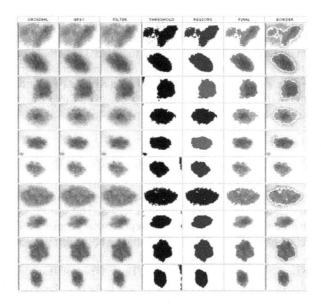

Fig. 2. Local Thresholding Segmentation of digital images containing dysplastic nevus lesions

directions). In this way all coherent "dark" pixels of the object are located and characterized as scanned. The algorithm complexity is polynomial and specifically linear in terms of image dimensions (number of pixels). In this way all "islands" are located. The image features can then be evaluated for all "dark" pixels of the image or for each "island" object separately. The results of the proposed segmentation procedure are depicted in Figures 1 and 2.

In order to determine the validity of the computer-calculated border using the proposed local thresholding method relative to the true border and in compare to more simple methods (i.e. global thresholding and region growing) we asked an expert dermatologist to draw manually the border on the digital image. The metric used for the performance of the segmentation algorithm was the percentage of common pixels between the two areas defined by the two borders, calculated as the ratio of the intersection divided by their union. We have also calculated the percentage of pixels that

Table 1. A measure of performance of the proposed segmentation algorithm

Algorithm	Common Pixels between the two the two segmentations (%)	Pixels that belong to the computer-based segmentation and not to the manually determined (%)	Pixels that belong to the manually determined segmentation and not to the computer-based (%)
Global Thresholding	60.29	19.16	20.59
Region Growing	69.12	22.86	8.02
Window Thresholding	76.31	12.45	11.24

belong to the computer-based lesion and not to the manually determined lesion and vice-versa. Segmentation algorithm tests included 100 digital images acquired by the molemax system and the results are displayed in Table 1. It should be noted though, that manual outlining suffers from low inter- and intra-operator agreement and the results could be different if another physician was selected. At the same time it is very difficult to get the outlines from many operators; however Table 1 gives an indication of local thresholding algorithm's performance.

2.3 Utilized Features

In automated diagnosis of skin lesions, feature design is based on the so-called ABCD-rule of dermatology. ABCD rule, which constitutes the basis for a diagnosis by a dermatologist [17] represents the *Asymmetry*, *Border* structure, variegated *Colour*, and the *Differential Structures* of the skin lesion. The feature extraction is performed by measurements on the pixels that represent a segmented object allowing non-visible features to be computed. Several studies have also proven the efficiency of border shape descriptors for the detection of malignant melanoma on both clinical and computer based evaluation methods [18]. Three types of features are utilized in this study: Border Features which cover the A and B parts of the ABCD-rule of dermatology, Colour Features which correspond to the C rules and Textural Features, which are based on D rules. More specifically the extracted features are as follows:

Border Features

1. Thinness Ratio measures the circularity of the skin lesion defined as TR = 4πArea/(Perimeter)^2
2. Border Asymmetry is computed as the percent of non-overlapping area after a hypothetical folding of the border around the greatest diameter or the maximum symmetry diameters
3. The variance of the distance of the border lesion points from the centroid location
4. Minimum, maximum, average and variance responses of the gradient operator, applied on the intesity image along the lesion border.

Colour Features

1. Plain RGB colour plane average and variance responses for pixels within the lesion
2. Intensity, Hue, Saturation Colour Space average and variance responses for pixels within the lesion

$$I = \frac{R+G+B}{3} \qquad S = 1 - \frac{3}{R+G+B}[\min(R,G,B)] \qquad W = \arccos\{\frac{R - \frac{1}{2}(G+B)}{[(R-G)^2 + (R-B)(G-B)]^{1/2}}\}$$

where
$$H = W(if\ G>B)\ or\ H = 2\pi\text{-}W\ (if\ G<B\ )\ or\ H = 0\ (if\ G=B)$$

3. Spherical coordinates LAB average and variance responses for pixels within the lesion

$$L = \sqrt{R^2 + G^2 + B^2} \qquad AngleA = \cos^{-1}[\frac{B}{L}] \qquad AngleB = \cos^{-1}[\frac{R}{L\sin(AngleA)}]$$

Texture Features

1. Dissimilarity, d, which is a measure related to contrast using linear increase of weights as one moves away from the GLCM diagonal.

$$d = \sum_{i,j=0}^{N-1} P_{i,j} |i - j|, \quad P_{i,j} = \frac{V_{i,j}}{\sum_{i,j=0}^{N-1} V_{i,j}}$$

where i is the row number, j is the column number, N is the total number of rows and columns of the GLCM matrix, and $P_{i,j}$ is the normalisation equation in which $V_{i,j}$ is the DN value of the cell i, j in the image window.

2. Angular Second Moment, *ASM*, which is a measure related to orderliness, where $P_{i,j}$ is used as a weight to itself :

$$ASM = \sum_{i,j=0}^{N-1} P_{i,j}^2$$

3. GLCM Mean, μ_i, which differs from the familiar mean equation in the sense that it denotes the frequency of the occurrence of one pixel value in combination with a certain neighbour pixel value and is given by

$$\mu_i = \sum_{i,j=0}^{N-1} i(P_{i,j})$$

For the symmetrical GLCM, $\mu_i = \mu_j$.

4. GLCM Standard Deviation, σ_i, which gives a measure of the dispersion of the values around the mean

$$\sigma_i = \sqrt{\sum_{i,j=0}^{N-1} P_{i,j} (i - \mu_i)^2}$$

3 Development and Implementation of an Automated Image Classification Method for Skin Lesions

3.1 Reported Results

The development of a robust classification system for skin lesions, enabling the distinction of malignant melanoma from dysplastic nevus, has been an issue of significant research in the recent years. Artificial intelligent techniques provide automated procedures for objective judgments by making use of quantitative measures and machine learning; in most cases these algorithms were proved to be highly efficient. In respective previous research efforts Kjoelen A et al. in [19] report an average success rate of 70% in diagnosing melanoma via features extracted by digital images, while Ercal et al. using a neural network for the detection of malignant melanoma from colour images report a percentage of 86% correct classification [7], [20]. In a similar study the same research team has reported significant results [21]; however fewer image features have been taken into account. Moreover Dreiseitl et al. in [22] have utilized five techniques, namely the k-nearest neighbours clustering, logistic regression, artificial neural networks (ANNs), decision tress, and support vector machines (SVMs) on the task of classifying pigmented skin lesions as common nevi, dysplastic nevi, or melanoma. The success rates they report fluctuate from 79% to 97%. The present research work presents an efficient automated classification algorithm based on SVMs which classifies pigmented skin lesions as melanoma or dysplastic nevus through proper feature selection and SVM kernel function employment.

3.2 Implementation of the Methodology and Results

The Support Vector Machine algorithm has been implemented for the classification of pigmented skin lesion images [23], [24], [25]. In order to reduce the dimensionality of the problem, several features concerning standard deviations and minimum or maximum values of features were ignored and the selected features that construct the input datasets for the automated procedure are depicted in Table 2. A training set of 500 cases was randomly selected from the dataset of the total cases. The accuracy of the classification algorithm was examined using a test set consisted of the full set of 1041 cases, so as a significant number of test instances was not included in the training set. Apart from the accuracy indices, the performance of a binary classifier is further evaluated using the sensitivity and specificity indices.

Table 2. Selected features for the construction of the training and test set, where MM and MD the mean values for the melanoma and the nevus cases respectively

SELECTED FEATURES					
Feature	MM (std)	MD (std)	Feature	MM (std)	MD (std)
mean-R	116.65 (33.65)	157.29(28.09)	Complexity	10.89 (16.87)	8.07 (12.37)
I-mean	75.72 (22.04)	101.66 (22.32)	ASM	8949.96 (7505.5)	7247.92 (6716.8)
L-mean	141.86 (40.50)	190.46 (38.45)	Dissimilarity	3430017(2571071)	2781110(2571071)
mean-G	62.46 (19.60)	83.79(21.74)	Perimeter	2640.49 (1874.6)	2252.06(1592.4)
mean-B	48.03 (16.68)	63.90 (20.31)	Area	68924.59 (25955)	64009.45(23396)
GMSM-mean	140.25 (36.11)	134.51 (32.18)	Eccentricity	1.68 (0.42)	1.77(0.48)
S-mean	93.48 (22.91)	100.56 (18.74)	Asymmetry	30.53 (18.63)	29.68 (16.99)
H-mean	27.66 (22.06)	25.96 (28.56)	Grad-mean	1.26 (0.52)	1.23 (0.45)
B-mean	40.41 (5.48)	38.88 (4.44)	A-mean	98.8 (5.35)	100.52 (4.31)

The SVM algorithm was implemented using numerous kernel functions and the corresponding detailed results as well as the algorithm's performance indices accuracy, specificity and sensitivity are depicted in Table 3. The best performance was achieved using the exponential radial basis function with sigma=7 (accuracy=91.84%, specificity=91.87%, sensitivity=91.30%), while other values of sigma (i.e. sigma=8, 6, 9, 10) exhibit high values of these performance indices as well. Furthermore, the values of accuracy, specificity and sensitivity are presented in the bar chart of figure 3 in comparison for the top four kernel functions exhibiting the best performance.

Table 3. Performance of the SVM algorithm using the exponential radial basis function with various values of sigma

SIGMA	ERRORS	TP	TN	FP	FN	ACCURACY	SPECIFICITY	SENSITIVITY
7	85	63	893	79	6	91.84%	91.87%	91.30%
8	87	62	892	80	7	91.64%	91.77%	89.86%
6	88	62	891	81	7	91.55%	91.67%	89.86%
9	90	62	889	83	7	91.35%	91.46%	89.86%
10	91	62	888	84	7	91.26%	91.36%	89.86%
12	97	62	882	90	7	90.68%	90.74%	89.86%
5	99	61	881	91	8	90.49%	90.64%	88.41%

TP: True Positive (melanoma instances actually classified as melanoma by the SVM algorithm)
TN: True Negative (dysplastic nevus instances actually classified as nevus by the SVM algorithm)
FP: False Positive (melanoma instances classified as nevus by the SVM algorithm)
FN: False Negative (dysplastic nevus instances classified as melanoma by the SVM algorithm)

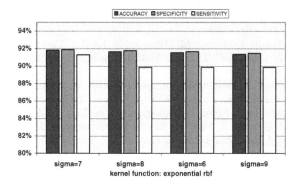

Fig. 3. Accuracy, sensitivity and specificity indices for the kernel functions with the best performance of SVM classifiers

4 Conclusions

The technical achievements of recent years in the areas of image acquisition and processing allow the improvement and lower cost of image analysis systems. Such tools may serve as diagnostic adjuncts for medical professionals for the confirmation of a diagnosis, as well as for the training of new dermatologists. In addition the latest developments in decision support systems give the opportunity of implementing more accurate, faster and reliable classification systems. The introduction of diagnostic tools based on intelligent decision support systems is also capable of enhancing the quality of medical care, particularly in areas where a specialized dermatologist is not available. The inability of general physicians to provide high quality dermatological services leads them to wrong diagnoses, particularly in evaluating fatal skin diseases such as melanoma [12]. In such cases, an expert system may detect the possibility of a serious skin lesion and warn of the need for early treatment.

A new system for analyzing digital images of skin lesions has been presented in the paper. In the present study, a novel segmentation method is presented followed by a classification algorithm which incorporates a great number of image features. The results of the present study are significant and quite promising for the future.

Acknowledgement

Authors wish to thank Prof Harald Ganster of the Graz University Technology for the provision of the skin image data set captured at Hospital of Wien.

References

[1]   Hansen, G., Sparrow, E., Kokate, J. et al., 1997, Wound status evaluation using color image processing, IEEE Transactions on Medical Imaging, 16, 1, pp. 78-86.
[2]   A. Green, N. Martin, G. McKenzie, J. Pfitzner, F. Quintarelli, B. W. Thomas, M. O'Rourke, N. Knight, "Computer image analysis of pigmented skin lesions", Melanoma Res., vol.1, pp.231 -236, 1991.
[3]   A. Green, N. Martin, J. Pfitzner, M. O'Rourke, N. Knight, "Computer image analysis in the diagnosis of melanoma", J. Amer. Acad. Dermatol., vol.31, no.6, pp.958-964, Dec. 1994.
[4]   R. Pompl, W. Bunk, A. Horsch, W. Abmayr, G. Morfill, W. Brauer, W. Stolz, "Computer vision of melanocytic lesions using MELDOQ", Proc. 6th Congress Int. Soc. Skin Imaging, London; Skin Research and Technology, vol. 5, no.2, pp.150-1999.
[5]   H. Ganster, M. Gelautz, A. Pinz, M. Binder, H. Pehamberger, M. Bammer, J. Krocza, "Initial results of automated melanoma recognition", Theory and Applications of Image Analysis II, Selected papers of the 9th SCIA, Scandinavian Conference on Image Analysis, World Scientific, Singapore, pp.343- 354, 1995.
[6]   P. N. Hall, E. Claridge, J. D. M. Smith, "Computer screening for early detection of melanoma — is there a future?", Br. J. Dermatol., vol.132, pp.325-338, 1995.
[7]   F. Ercal, A. Chawla, W. V. Stoecker, H. C. Lee, R. H. Moss, "Neural network diagnosis of malignant melanoma from color images", IEEE Trans. Biomed. Eng., vol.41, pp.837-845, Sept. 1994.
[8]   Kjoelen, M. Thompson, S. Umbaugh, R. Moss, W. Stoecker:, 1995, Performance of Artificial Intelligence Methods In Automated Detection of Melanoma, IEEE Engineering Medicine and Biology, 14, 4 pp. 411-416.
[9]   M. Nishik, C. Foster, 1997, Analysis of Skin Erythema Using True Color Images, IEEE Transactions on Medical Imaging, 16, 6 711-716.
[10] Ganster, H., Pinz, P., Rohrer, R., Wildling, E., Binder, M., Kittler, H. "Automated melanoma recognition", IEEE Transactions on Medical Imaging, 20 (3), Mar 2001 233 -239
[11] Marks R. Epidemiology of melanoma. Clin Exp Dermatol 2000;25:459–63.
[12] Pariser R.J. and Pariser D.M., 1987, Primary care physicians errors in handling cutaneous disorders, J Am Acad Dermatol, 17, pp. 239-245
[13] Zhang, Z., Stoecker, W.V., Moss, R.H.Medical, "Border detection on digitized skin tumor images" IEEE Transactions on Medical Imaging, 19 (11), Nov 2000 1128 -1143
[14] Do Hyun Chung, Sapiro G, "Segmenting skin lesions with partial-differential-equations-based image processing algorithms" IEEE Transactions on Medical Imaging, 19 (7), Jul 2000 763 -767

[15] L. Xu, M. Jackowski, A. Goshtasby, D. Roseman, S. Bines, C. Yu, A. Dhawan, A. Hunt-ley, "Segmentation of skin cancer images", Image and Vision Computing, vol.17, pp.65-74, 1999.

[16] Maglogiannis I.: "Automated Segmentation and Registration of Dermatological Images" Journal of Mathematical Modeling and Algorithms, vol. 2 pp. 277-294 Springer Science Business Media, Formerly Kluwer Academic Publishers (2003).

[17] F. Nachbar, W. Stolz, T. Merkle, A. B. Cognetta, T. Vogt, M. Landthaler, P. Bilek, O. Braun-Falco, and G. Plewig, "The ABCD rule of dermatoscopy: High prospective value in the diagnosis of doubtful melanocytic skin lesions," J. Amer. Acad. Dermatol., vol. 30, no. 4, pp. 551–559, Apr. 1994.

[18] W. V. Stoecker, W. W. Li, R. H. Moss, "Automatic detection of asymmetry in skin tumors", Computerized Med. Imag. Graph., vol.16, no.3, pp. 191-197, May, June 1992.

[19] Kjoelen A et al. "Performance of AI methods in detecting melanoma", IEEE Eng in Medicine and Biology, Vol.14, 4, 1995 pp. 411-416

[20] F. Ercal, H. C. Lee, W. V. Stoecker, R. H. Moss, "Skin cancer classification using hierar-chical neural networks and fuzzy systems", Int. J. Smart Eng. Syst. Design, vol.1, pp.273-289, 1999.

[21] Maglogiannis I., Zafiropoulos E.: "Utilizing Support Vector Machines for the Characteri-zation of Digital Medical Images" BMC Medical Informatics and Decision Making 2004, 4:4.

[22] S. Dreiseitl, L. Ohno-Machado, H. Kittler, S. Vinterbo, H. Billharrt, M. Binder, 2001, "A comparison of Machine Learning Methods for the Diagnosis of Pigmented Skin Lesions", Journal of Biomedical Informatics, 34, 28-36

[23] Burges C.: A tutorial on support vector machines for pattern recognition [http://www.kernel-machines.org/].

[24] Schölkopf B.: Statistical learning and kernel methods [http://research.Microsoft.com/~bsc].

[25] Campbell C.: Kernel methods: a survey of current techniques, [http://www.kernel-machines.org/].

Modelling Robotic Cognitive Mechanisms by Hierarchical Cooperative CoEvolution

Michail Maniadakis[1] and Panos Trahanias[2]

[1]Inst. of Computer Science, Foundation for Research and Technology-Hellas,
71110 Heraklion, Crete, Greece,
[2]Department of Computer Science, University of Crete,
71409 Heraklion, Crete, Greece
{mmaniada, trahania}@ics.forth.gr

Abstract. The current work addresses the development of cognitive abilities in artificial organisms. In the proposed approach, neural network-based agent structures are employed to represent distinct brain areas. We introduce a Hierarchical Cooperative CoEvolutionary (HCCE) approach to design autonomous, yet collaborating agents. Thus, partial brain models consisting of many substructures can be designed. Replication of lesion studies is used as a means to increase reliability of brain model, highlighting the distinct roles of agents. The proposed approach effectively designs cooperating agents by considering the desired pre- and post- lesion performance of the model. In order to verify and assess the implemented model, the latter is embedded in a robotic platform to facilitate its behavioral capabilities.

1 Introduction

The long-term vision of developing artificial organisms with mammal-like cognitive abilities can be facilitated by computational models of the mammalian Central Nervous System (CNS). We have recently introduced a systematic method to design brain-inspired computational models of partial CNS substructures [1, 2]. The models consist of a collection of neural network agents, each one representing a CNS area. Similarly to the epigenetic life-time learning process, the performance of agents is specified by means of environmental interaction. The dynamics of epigenetic learning are designed by an evolutionary process which simulates phylogenesis, similar to [3]. Instead of using a unimodal evolutionary process we employ a cooperative coevolutionary approach which is able to highlight the specialties of brain areas and the integrated performance of substructures in the composite model [4].

In the present work, we propose a hierarchical extension of this approach, introducing a Hierarchical Cooperative CoEvolutionary (HCCE) scheme which supports the coevolution of a large number of populations. Specifically, evolutionary processes at lower levels are driven by their own dynamics to meet the special objectives of each brain area. The evolutionary process at the higher levels, tunes lower level coevolutionary processes integrating the performance of

G. Antoniou et al. (Eds.): SETN 2006, LNAI 3955, pp. 224–234, 2006.

partial components. The architecture of multiple coevolutionary processes tuned by a higher level evolution can be repeated for as many levels as necessary, forming a tree hierarchy.

Furthermore, following recent trends aiming at the study of computational models in lesion conditions [5, 6], we adapt our method to accomplish systematic modelling of biological lesion experiments. Appropriate fitness functions indicate the performance of the model when all substructures are present, and they also indicate the performance when some partial structures are eliminated. Thus, the model is able to replicate brain lesion findings.

The rest of the paper is organized as follows. In the next section, we present the structure of neural agents employed for the representation of CNS areas. In section 3 we introduce the hierarchical cooperative coevolutionary scheme which supports the design of agents. Section 4 presents the application of the proposed approach in the design of a brain-inspired computational structure. Finally, conclusions and suggestions for future work are drawn in the last section.

2   Computational Model

We implement two different neural agents, to provide a general computational framework which facilitates the modelling process: (i) a cortical agent to represent brain areas, and (ii) a link agent to support information flow.

Link Agent. The structure of the link agent is appropriately designed to support connectivity among cortical agents. Using the link agent any two cortical modules can be connected, simulating the connectivity of brain areas.

Each link agent is specified by the projecting axons between two cortical agents (Fig 1(a)). Its formation is based on the representation of cortical modules by planes with excitatory and inhibitory neurons (see below). Only excitatory neurons are used as outputs of the efferent cortical agent. The axons of projecting neurons are defined by their (x, y) coordinates on the receiving plane. Cortical planes have a predefined dimension and thus projecting axons are deactivated if they exceed the borders of the plane. This is illustrated graphically in Fig 1(a), where only the active projections are represented with an × on their termination.

Cortical Agent. Each cortical agent is represented by a rectangular plane. A cortical agent consists of a predefined population of excitatory and inhibitory neurons, which all follow the Wilson-Cowan model described in [1]. Both sets of neurons, are uniformly distributed, defining an excitatory and an inhibitory grid on the cortical plane. On the same plane there are also located the axon terminals from the efferent projected cortical agents.

All neurons receive input information either from i) projecting axons, or ii) excitatory neighbouring neurons, or iii) inhibitory neighbouring neurons. The connectivity of neurons follows the general rule of locality. Synapse formation is based on circular neighbourhood measures. A separate radius for each of the three synapse types, defines the connectivity of neurons. This is illustrated graphically in Fig 1(b), which further explains the example of Fig 1(a).

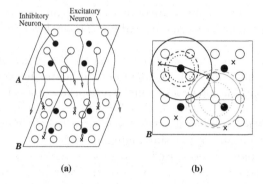

Fig. 1. Schematic representation of the computational model. Part (a) illustrates a link agent which supports information flow from cortical agent A to B. Part (b) illustrates synapse definition in cortical agent B. Neighbourhood radius for i) afferent axons is illustrated by a solid line, for ii) neighbouring excitatory neurons by a dashed line, and for iii) neighbouring inhibitory neurons by a dotted line. Sample neighbourhoods for excitatory neurons are illustrated with grey, while neighbourhoods for inhibitory neurons are illustrated with black.

The performance of cortical agents is adjusted by the experiences of the artificial organism obtained through environmental interaction, similar to epigenetic[1] learning [7]. To enforce experience-based subjective learning, each set of synapses is assigned a Hebbian-like learning rule defining the self-organization dynamics of the agent [8]. This is in contrast to the most common alternative of genetically-encoded synaptic strengths which prevents experience based learning. We have implemented a pool of 10 Hebbian-like rules that can be appropriately combined to produce a wide range of functionalities [1].

3   Hierarchical Cooperative CoEvolution (HCCE)

Similar to a phylogenetic process, the structure of agents can be specified by means of an evolutionary method [3]. However, using a unimodal evolutionary approach, it is not possible to explore effectively partial components, which represent brain substructures. To alleviate that, coevolutionary algorithms have been recently proposed that facilitate exploration, in problems consisting of many decomposable components [4]. Coevolutionary approaches involve separate interactive populations to design each component of the solution. These populations are evolved simultaneously, but in isolation to one another. Partial populations are usually referred as *species* in the coevolutionary literature, and thus this term will be employed henceforth.

The design of brain-inspired models fits very well to coevolutionary approaches, because separate coevolved species can be used to perform design decisions for each component representing a brain area. As a result, coevolution

---

[1] Epigenesis here, includes all learning processes during lifetime.

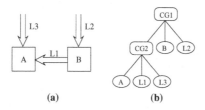

(a)   (b)

Fig. 2. Part (a) represents a hypothetical connectivity of agents. Part (b) represents the hierarchical coevolutionary scheme utilized to evolve partial structures.

is able to highlight the special features of each brain area, and additionally the cooperation within computational modules.

We have presented a new scheme to improve the performance of cooperative coevolutionary algorithms [1, 2]. The present work extends this scheme to a hierarchical multi-level architecture, as it is described below. We employ two different kinds of species to support the coevolutionary process encoding the configurations of either a Primitive agent Structure (PS) or a Coevolved agent Group (CG). PS species specify partial elements of the model, encoding the exact structure of either cortical or link agents. A CG consists of groups of PSs with common objectives. Thus, CGs specify configurations of partial solutions by encoding assemblies of cortical and link agents. The evolution of CG modulates partly the evolutionary process of its lower level PS species to enforce their cooperative performance. A CG can also be a member of another CG. Consequently, several CGs can be organized hierarchically, with the higher levels enforcing the cooperation of the lower ones. The HCCE-based design method for brain modelling is demonstrated by means of an example (Fig 2). We assume the existence of two cortical agents connected by three link agents representing their afferent and efferent projections (Fig 2(a)). One hypothetical HCCE process employed to specify agent structure is illustrated in (Fig 2(b)).

All individuals in all species are assigned an identification number which is preserved during the coevolutionary process. The identification number is employed to form individual assemblies within different species. Each variable in the genome of a CG is joined with one lower level CG or PS species. The value of that variable can be any identification number of the individuals from the species it is joined with. PSs encode the structure of either cortical or link agents. The details of the encoding have been presented in [1, 2], and thus they are omitted here due to space limitations. A snapshot of the exemplar HCCE process described above is illustrated in (Fig 3). CGs enforce cooperation of PS structures by selecting the appropriate cooperable individuals among species.

In order to test the performance of a complete problem solution, populations are sequentially accessed starting by the higher level. The values of CG individuals at various levels are used as guides to select cooperators among PS species. Then, PS individuals are decoded to specify the structure of cortical and link agents, and the performance of the proposed overall solution is tested.

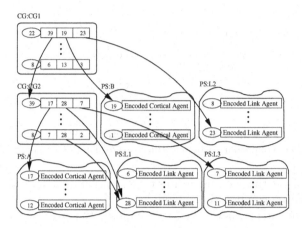

Fig. 3. A snapshot of the hierarchical coevolutionary scheme of Fig 2. Identification numbers are represented with an oval.

The proposed hierarchical scheme is able to support the simulation of lesion conditions which is a typical case for biological experiments. Specifically, by deactivating a CG together with the PS structures corresponding to its lower level species, we can easily simulate lesion of the respective brain areas. Thus, all necessary lesion conditions can be considered during the evolutionary process, and the role of each partial structure in the composite model can be highlighted.

Furthermore, our method employs separate fitness measures for different species. This matches adequately to the agent-based modelling of brain areas, because different objectives can be defined for each partial structure to preserve its autonomy. This feature of HCCE, facilitates additionally the modelling of biological lesion findings, because properly formulated fitness functions can be utilized to specify the desired pre- and post- lesion performance of the model.

For each species s, a fitness function f_s is designed to drive its evolution. All PS species strictly under a CG share a common f_s. Partial fitness functions are also utilized to evaluate the performance of the model in diverse operating conditions. Specifically, $f_{s,t}$ evaluates the ability of an individual to serve task t. The overall fitness function is estimated by:

$$f_s = \prod_t f_{s,t} \tag{1}$$

Furthermore, the cooperator selection process at the higher levels of hierarchical coevolution will probably select an individual to participate in many assemblies (e.g. the case of individual 28 of PS species L1, of Fig 3). Let us assume that an individual participates in K assemblies which means that it will get K fitness values $f_{s,t}$. Then, the ability of the individual to support the accomplishment of the t-th task is estimated by:

$$f_{s,t} = max_k\{f_{s,t}^k\} \tag{2}$$

where $f_{s,t}^k$ is the fitness value of the k-th ($k = 1...K$) solution formed with the membership of the individual under discussion.

A common problem for the coevolutionary approaches evolving assemblies of cooperators, is related to the multiple participation of some individuals in many different collaborator assemblies, while at the same time others are offered no cooperation at all. A large number of multiple cooperations is generally a drawback for the coevolutionary process, because different cooperator assemblies could demand evolution of the same individual in different directions. Non-cooperating individuals can be utilized to decrease the multiplicity of cooperations for those individuals which are heavily reused.

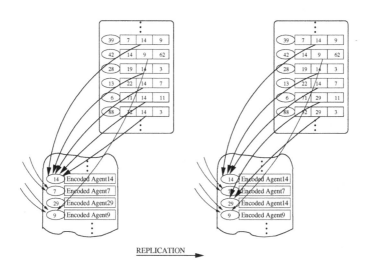

REPLICATION

Fig. 4. Schematic representation of the replication operator ($max_c = 3$)

We have introduced a new genetic operator termed Replication (it does not aim to be a computational representative of the DNA replication), addressing the issue of multiple cooperations [1]. In short, for each unused individual x of a species, replication identifies the fittest individual y with more than max_c cooperations. The genome of y is then copied to x, and x is assigned $max_c - 1$ cooperations of y, by updating properly the CG population at the higher level. After replication, individuals x and y are allowed to evolve separately following independent evolutionary directions. This is illustrated graphically in Fig 4.

Evolutionary steps are performed separately for each species of the HCCE scheme. First, individuals are sorted according to their fitness values. Then, Replication is applied to reduce multiple cooperations. Next, a predefined percentage of individuals are probabilistically crossed over. An individual selects its mate from the whole population, based on their accumulative probabilities. Finally, mutation is performed in a small percentage of the resulted population. This process is repeated for a predefined number of evolutionary epochs.

4   Results

The effectiveness of the proposed approach is illustrated on the design of a partial
brain computational model, which simulates posterior parietal cortex (PPC) -
prefrontal cortex (PFC) - primary motor cortex (M1) - spinal cord (SC) interactions, emphasizing on working memory (WM) usage (Fig 5(a)). The organization
of these areas in the mammalian brain has been extensively studied by means of
delayed response (DR) tasks. M1 encodes primitive motor commands which are
expressed to actions by means of SC. PPC-PFC reciprocal interaction operates in
a higher level encoding WM [9], to develop plans regarding future actions. PFC
activation is then passed to M1 which modulates its performance accordingly. As
a result, all the above mentioned structures cooperate for the accomplishment
of a DR task by the organism. However, PFC lesion affects planning ability of
the organism, resulting in purposeless motion [10].

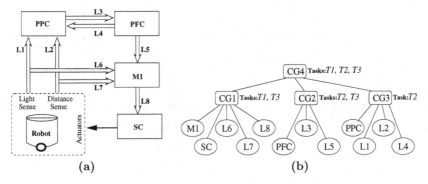

(a)   (b)

Fig. 5. (a) A schematic overview of the model. (b) A graphical illustration of the
coevolutionary process.

The present work employs the hierarchical cooperative coevolutionary approach to design a model of the areas under discussion. Similar to [5,6], the
experimental process aims at reproducing a lesion scenario which is in agreement to the biological findings presented above. The composite computational
model aims at the accomplishment of a DR task, developing a behavior similar
to the one described in pre-lesion performance of animals [11]. This is further
supported by two partial behaviors. The first accounts for the development of
WM-like activation in PPC-PFC which are the brain structures most closely
linked to WM [9]. The second accounts for purposeless motion by M1 when
lesion occurs on the higher level structures [10]. Both partial and composite
models are embedded on the robotic platform to furnish it with cognitive abilities and prove the validity of results. Specifically, we employ a two wheeled
simulated robotic platform equipped with 8 uniformly distributed distance and
light sensors.

Three tasks are designed to demonstrate the effectiveness of the computational procedure and also highlight the role of each agent in the model. The first

task $T1$, accounts for primitive motion abilities without purposeful planning. For mobile robots, a task with the above characteristics is wall avoidance navigation. Thus, for the needs of the present study, M1-SC structures aim at wall avoidance navigation. The successful accomplishment of the task is evaluated by the function:

$$E_1 = \left(\sum_M (sl + sr - 1) * (1.0 - p^2)\right)\left(1 - \frac{2}{M}\left|\sum_M \frac{sl - sr}{sl * sr}\right|\right)^3 \left(1 - 2\sqrt{\frac{B}{M}}\right)^3 \quad (3)$$

where we assume that the robot is tested for M steps, sl, sr are the instant speeds of the left and right wheel, p is the maximum instant activation of distance sensors, and B is the total number of robot bumps. The first term seeks for forward movement far from the walls, the second supports straight movement without unreasonable spinning, and the last term minimizes the number of robot bumps on the walls.

The development of WM-like performance specifies the second task $T2$. Working memory (WM) is the ability to hold and manipulate goal-related information to guide forthcoming actions. In the present experiment, a light cue is presented in the left or right side of the robot. WM performance aims at persistent PFC activity, related each time to the respective side of light cue presentation.

Two different states l, r are defined associated to the left or right side of light source appearance. For each state, separate activation-averages over the time of M simulation steps, a_j, are computed, with j identifying excitatory neurons of PFC agent. The formation of WM related to the side of light cues is evaluated aiming at persistently different activation patterns in PFC:

$$E_2 = \frac{1}{2}\left(\frac{v_l}{m_l} + \frac{v_r}{m_r}\right) \cdot \min\left\{\sum_{j, a_j^l > a_j^r}(a_j^l - a_j^r), \sum_{j, a_j^r > a_j^l}(a_j^r - a_j^l)\right\} \quad (4)$$

where m_l, v_l, m_r, v_r are the mean and variance of average activation at the respective states. The first term seeks for consistent PFC activation, and the second develops distinct sets of active neurons for each state.

Finally, a delayed response (DR) task $T3$, aims to combine the above behaviors formulating a complex model. Specifically, a light cue is presented on the left or right side of the robot. The robot has to move at the end of a corridor memorizing the side of sample cue appearance, and then make a choice related to 90° turn left or right, depending on the side of light cue presence. A target location is defined on each side of the corridor depending on the position of the initial light cue. The robot has to approximate the target location without crashing on the walls. The successful approximation to the target location is estimated by:

$$G = \left(1 + 3.0 * \left(1 - \frac{d}{D}\right)\right)^3 \cdot \left(1 - 2\sqrt{\frac{B}{M}}\right)^2 \quad (5)$$

where d is the minimum Euclidian distance between the target and the robot, D is the Euclidian distance between the target and the starting location of the robot, and B is the total number of robot bumps. The accomplishment of $T3$ is evaluated by means of two subtasks testing separately the right or left turn of the robot for the respective positions of the light cue, employing each time the appropriate target location:

$$E_3 = G^l \cdot G^r \tag{6}$$

We turn now to the HCCE-based design of the model. According to the lesion experiment, each agent needs to serve more than one task, as it is illustrated in Fig 5(b). Specifically, the structures under $CG1$ are related to M1-SC interactions, and they need to serve both the wall avoidance and the delayed response task. The structures under $CG2$ are related to PFC and its afferent and efferent projections, which need to serve working memory persistent activation, and the delayed response task. The structures under $CG3$ are related to PPC and its afferent projections which have to support working memory activation only. Finally, a top level CG is employed to enforce cooperation within partial configurations aiming to support the accomplishment of all the three tasks.

The testing phase for the individuals of the coevolutionary scheme proceeds as follows. The top-level species is sequentially accessed. Each individual of $CG4$, guides cooperator selection among its lower level CG and PS species. Individuals of PS species are decoded to detailed agent structures. The composite model is tested on the accomplishment of DR task $T3$. Next, PPC-PFC interaction is isolated by deactivating the agents under $CG1$. The remaining structures are tested on working memory task $T2$. Finally, $CG1$ agents are activated back, and now $CG2$ structures are deactivated to simulate PFC lesion. The remaining agents are tested on the accomplishment of wall avoidance navigation.

The fitness functions which guide the evolution of species are designed accordingly to support the accomplishment of the respective tasks. The agent structures grouped under $CG1$ serve the success on tasks $T1$, $T3$. Following the formulation introduced in eqs. (1), (2) the fitness function employed for the evolution of $CG1$ is:

$$f_{CG1} = f_{CG1,T1} \cdot f_{CG1,T3} \quad \text{with,} \ f^k_{CG1,T1} = E_1, \quad f^k_{CG1,T3} = \sqrt{E_3} \tag{7}$$

where k represents each membership of an individual in a proposed solution. Similarly, $CG2$ design aims to support both the accomplishment of $T2$ and $T3$ tasks. Thus, the fitness function which guides the evolutionary process is:

$$f_{CG2} = f_{CG2,T2} \cdot f_{CG2,T3} \quad \text{with,} \ f^k_{CG2,T2} = E_2{}^2, \quad f^k_{CG2,T3} = \sqrt{E_3} \tag{8}$$

where k is as above. The third group $CG3$, consists of PPC and all link agents projecting on it. These structures need to serve only the development of working memory activation in PFC. Thus, the fitness function employed for the evolution of $CG3$ is defined by:

$$f_{CG3} = f_{CG3,T2} \quad \text{with,} \ f^k_{CG3,T2} = E_2 \tag{9}$$

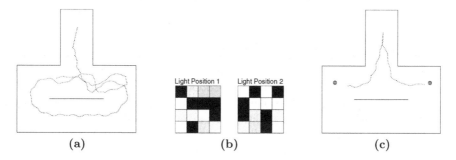

Fig. 6. (a) A sample result of robot performance, driven by M1-SC. The robot moves in a purposeless mode without bumping on the walls. (b) The average activation of excitatory neurons at PFC, for each light position. Evidently, each side of light cue presence is encoded by a different activation pattern. (c) A sample result of robot performance in the delayed match-to-sample task. Goal positions are illustrated with double circles.

where k is as above. Additionally, the top level evolutionary process $CG4$, enforce the integration of partial configurations in a composite model, aiming at the successful accomplishment of all the three tasks. Thus, the fitness function employed for the evolution of $CG4$ supports the concurrent success on wall avoidance task $T1$, working memory task $T2$, and DR task $T3$. It is defined accordingly, following the formulation introduced in eqs. (1), (2), by:

$$f_{CG4} = f_{CG4,T1} \cdot f_{CG4,T2} \cdot f_{CG4,T3} \quad \text{with,}$$
$$f^k_{CG4,T1} = \sqrt{E_1}, \quad f^k_{CG4,T2} = E_2{}^2, \quad f^k_{CG4,T3} = E_3 \tag{10}$$

where k is as above. Following this approach, different species with separate objectives need to cooperate in order to accomplish the composite lesion scenario.

The coevolutionary process described above employed populations of 200 individuals for all PS species, 300 individuals for $CG1$, $CG2$, $CG3$, and 400 individuals for $CG4$ species. After 200 evolutionary epochs the process converged successfully. Sample results of robot performance on each task are illustrated in Fig 6. As indicated by the lesion scenario, M1-SC are able to drive the robot in a purposeless manner, following a wall avoidance policy (Fig 6(a)). At the same time, PPC-PFC interactions are able to encode the side of light cue appearance and memorize it for a brief future period (Fig 6(b)). Moreover, the composite model combines successfully the performance of partial structures to accomplish the DR task (Fig 6(c)). Consequently, the results observed by biological lesion experiments related to delayed response tasks, are successfully replicated by the model highlighting the distinct roles of substructures. It is noted that we have also approached the problem described above following an ordinary unimodal evolutionary approach, without successful outcome.

5   Conclusions

The work described in this paper, addresses the development of cognitive abilities in artificial organisms, by means of brain-inspired computational models. The proposed computational framework employs neural agent modules to represent brain areas. Additionally, a Hierarchical Cooperative CoEvolutionary (HCCE) scheme is utilized to support design specification of agent structures. This approach offers increased search abilities of partial components, and is able to emphasize both the specialty of brain areas and their cooperative performance.

The proposed HCCE scheme can also be utilized to integrate partial brain models, by introducing an appropriate number of additional higher level evolutionary processes [2]. Thus, the incremental integration of gradually more partial brain models on top of existing ones constitutes the main direction of our future work. We believe that by exploiting the proposed approach, a powerful method to design large scale reliable brain models can emerge.

Finally, it is noted that the proposed coevolutionary approach can also be utilized in contexts different from brain modelling, such as the design of cooperating robot teams, or the research on economic and social behaviors. Thus, it can be potentially employed as a general purpose method for the design of distributed complex systems.

References

1. Maniadakis, M., Trahanias, P.: Modelling brain emergent behaviors through co-evolution of neural agents. Neural Networks journal, in print. (2006)
2. Maniadakis, M., Trahanias, P.: Coevolutionary incremental modelling of robotic cognitive mechanisms. In: Proc. VIIIth European Conference on Artificial Life, (ECAL-2005). (2005) 200–209
3. Rolls, E., Stringer, S.: On the design of neural networks in the brain by genetic evolution. Progress in Neurobiology **61** (2000) 557–579
4. Potter, M., De Jong, K.: Cooperative coevolution: An architecture for evolving coadapted subcomponents. Evol. Computation **8** (2000) 1–29
5. Sklavos, S., Moschovakis, A.: Neural network simulations of the primate occulo-motor system iv. a distributed bilateral stochastic model of the neural integrator of the vertical saccadic system. Biological Cybernetics **86** (2002) 97–109
6. Aharonov, R., Segev, L., Meilijson, I., Ruppin, E.: Localization of function via lesion analysis. Neural Computation **15**(4) (2003) 885–913
7. Cotterill, R.: Cooperation of the basal ganglia, cerebellum, sensory cerebrum and hippocampus: possible implications for cognition, consciousness, intelligence and creativity. Progress in Neurobiology **64**(1) (2001) 1 – 33
8. Floreano, D., Urzelai, J.: Evolutionary robots with on-line self-organization and behavioral fitness. Neural Networks **13** (2000) 431–443
9. Compte, A., Brunel, N., Goldman-Rakic, P., Wang, X.J.: Synaptic mechanisms and network dynamics underlying spatial working memory in a cortical network model. Cerebral Cortex **10**(1) (2000) 910–923
10. Ragozzino, M., Kesner, R.: The role of rat dorsomedial prefrontal cortex in working memory for egocentric responces. Neuroscience Letters **308** (2001) 145–148
11. Fuster, J.: Executive frontal functions. Exper. Brain Research **133** (2000) 66–70

Bayesian Feature Construction

Manolis Maragoudakis and Nikos Fakotakis

Artificial Intelligence Group, University of Patras,
26500 Rion, Patras, Greece
{mmarag, fakotaki}@wcl.ee.upatras.gr

Abstract. The present paper discusses the issue of enhancing classification performance by means other than improving the ability of certain Machine Learning algorithms to construct a precise classification model. On the contrary, we approach this significant problem from the scope of an extended coding of training data. More specifically, our method attempts to generate more features in order to reveal the hidden aspects of the domain, modeled by the available training examples. We propose a novel feature construction algorithm, based on the ability of Bayesian networks to represent the conditional independence assumptions of a set of features, thus projecting relational attributes which are not always obvious to a classifier when presented in their original format. The augmented set of features results in a significant increase in terms of classification performance, a fact that is depicted to a plethora of machine learning domains (i.e. data sets from the UCI ML repository and the Artificial Intelligence group) using a variety of classifiers, based on different theoretical backgrounds.

1 Introduction

Research as well as practical, experimental evaluations have proved that the performance of basic classification algorithms, such as C 4.5 [12] and IBL [1] decreases as the training data contain features that are not directly interrelated to the problem class, which should be learned by the algorithm [4]. Two different issues can be identified: features that are not related to the class and features that do not have an interaction among them.

As regards to the former case, researchers have focused on the so-called "feature selection" approach ([4], [6], [13]). The latter case is dealt with techniques that produce a new set of features, based on the initial one. The process is also called "feature construction". The newly-generated features contribute to the construction of better and more precise classifiers. Furthermore, the discovery of reasonable domain knowledge representations leads to better understanding of the extracted classification model, thus to a better and more comprehensive learning model.

The majority of feature construction algorithms have been planned under a specific scope, i.e. the creation under a strictly predefined representation, which the new features should follow in an exact manner. Among the most popular representation

G. Antoniou et al. (Eds.): SETN 2006, LNAI 3955, pp. 235–245, 2006.

formalisms are simple Boolean expressions, M-of-N expressions, hyperplanes, logic rules and bits. Most of them utilize a series of domain dependent heuristics. For example, it has been shown that the M-of-N algorithm performs particularly well in classification problem from the medical domain, where experts make great use of prior knowledge, which is inserted into the classification system in the form of criteria tables, a key concept of the M-of-N algorithm [9].

In the recent years, some grammar based methodologies have been proposed. The grammar can be edited by a domain expert along with the specifications that new features should follow. Nevertheless, there are some issues that point out the fact that using either grammars or representation schemes poses two significant problems:

Both approaches are based on the domain expert specifications. Prior knowledge is not always obtainable, particularly in cases where the selection of features that actually influence the class is being determined by empirical data.

The strictly close nature of the above formalism does not allow the adjustment or tuning of the parameters of the specification, when the latter are needed to change. For example, increasing the number of training data can bring about changes to the classification model.

For the present work, we propose a feature construction algorithm, allowing for insertion of coded prior knowledge, which is manly based on the interrelation of the initial feature set, as this is expressed through training data. More specifically, we propose a novel, stochastic framework, based on Bayesian networks [11], for generating features. Bayesian networks are well known in Machine Learning for being a strong mechanism of knowledge representation. This knowledge can be inserted to the new features, aiming the process of a classifier to better distinguish the concept that determines the prediction of the class. In addition, the Bayesian nature of the algorithm makes insertion of prior knowledge a straightforward approach. The complexity of the approach has been deliberately kept in low levels, allowing at most N new features from an initial set of N primal features.

2   A Bayesian Framework for Feature Construction

In an attempt to enrich the available feature set, the following approach is proposed. A set of basic features along with the set of instances are fed to a supervised classifier in order to "learn" the class variable. The proposed algorithm uses any available prior domain knowledge and generates a new set of features with their corresponding values. The newly created data augment the original feature and instance set. Figure 1 explains the architecture in a graphical manner. The framework extends the ordinary classifier description by introducing new fundamental elements which we named λ-parameters. These parameters are Bayesian in the sense that they encode the degree of interrelation of the basic features. The λ-parameters are actually probabilities and they form the core of the Bayesian feature construction algorithm.

The main idea of the algorithm is the augmentation of a given data set (either training or test) with additional data that will contribute to better classification performance. The algorithm aims to overcome second-order statistics such as covariance allowing distance based methods to exploit the mutual relation or independence between features.

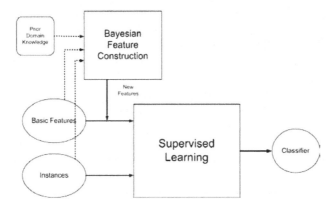

Fig. 1. The feature construction framework

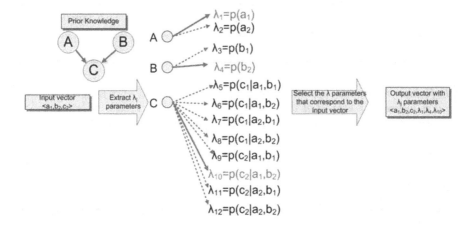

Fig. 2. An example of the proposed methodology for feature generation for a given input instance. Solid arrows denote an acceptance of a λ parameter while dashed denote a rejection.

Every data set contains different values for each feature. If one simply considers each value separately, no particular knowledge of the interrelation with the other can be obtained (if such a relation exists). When a Bayesian network is trained using this dataset, a form of knowledge about the distribution of the features and the relation amongst them is embedded. The goal is to channel such knowledge to the output, expressed in probabilities, which symbolize the belief of the data set itself on the value of each separate value.

The following example will assist in understanding the operation of the algorithm; consider a data set consisting of three variables i.e. A, B and C. We denote feature names in uppercase letters and their values in lowercase letters. Suppose also that each feature is binary, with values a_1, a_2, b_1, b_2 and c_1, c_2 respectively. Figure 2 portrays the aforementioned representation. For the given data set, a Bayesian network has been structured. The construction of the network structure has been made either manually, by a domain expert or automatically, using some learning algorithm such as K2 [2] or MDL [7]. Furthermore, the construction of the conditional probabilities table could be automatically provided by known algorithms such as Junction Trees [3].

When the algorithm encounters an input instance (e.g. $<a_1,b_2,c_2>$), it produces the λ parameters for every possible value a feature may have. These parameters are probabilities, describing the belief of each possible value, given the values of the parent nodes of the feature that contains this value. From the set of the extracted λ parameters, only those who describe the values of the given input instance are taken into account (in the above example these are: $<\lambda_1,\lambda_4,\lambda_{10}>$). Note that the dimension of the λ parameters vector is always equal to the dimension of the initial input instance. As a last step, these new values are inserted to the initial instance, in order for the new one to be used in the classification stage.

Generalizing, if $X_1,...X_N$ is a set of features with values $x_{1i},...x_{Nj}$, the feature construction algorithm binds N new slots for potential new features and provides as values of the new features the λ parameters that correspond to each initialization of the feature values, as they appear in the data set.

Definition 1: *Suppose a data set of m instances, consisted of N features $X_1,...X_N$. Each instance is expressed as a vector of the form $<x_{11},...x_{N1}>$ to $<x_{1m},...x_{Nm}>$. Given a Bayesian network which symbolizes the probability distribution of the data set, a λ parameter is the probability of a value x_{ij} of a feature X_i ($1\leq i\leq N$ and $1\leq j\leq m$) given the values of the features that are parents of Xi in the network. From the space of λ parameters, only N of them are selected, i.e. those who represent the probability of value x_{ij} of the k-th instance, given the values of the features that are parents of X_i and exist in the k-th instance.*

Note that the estimation of all possible λ values is necessary. On the contrary, a reverse approach is followed, significantly decreasing the feature generation time. Knowing the value of each primal feature, the Bayesian network is instructed to output only the λ parameter that refers to the values of the given input instance, rather than all the possible values of λ.

An additional remark is the unbiased behavior of the algorithm both in the training and in the test phase. Contrary to other algorithms that attempt to inherit domain knowledge from the train set to the test, the proposed methodology simply enriches each set independently with information on the degree of interrelation of features. Of course, prior knowledge can be inserted in both sets, but the important is that this is not done spontaneously, but only if the domain expert declares it in the Bayesian network construction phase. The pseudo-code of the Bayesian Feature Construction (BFC) algorithm is shown below:

Input: A dataset D, consisting of N features $X_1, ...X_N$ with m instances of the form $<x_{1i}, ..., x_{Nj}>$, where x_{ir} is the r-th value of the i-th feature.

1. If prior knowledge is known then:
   a. Construct the structure Bayesian network B using it.
   b. Create the conditional probability table (CPT) using either the knowledge or the available data.
2. else:
   a. Learn a Bayesian network from data using the K2 algorithm (for the structure) and Junction Trees (for the CPT)
   b. For each instance of the data set:
      i. For each value of the instance
         1. Estimate the λ parameter so that it depicts the probability of the value in the current instance, given the values of the features that are parent nodes of the current feature, as they appear in the instance.
         2. Insert all extracted parameters in to the initial current instance

Output: A new set of instances, consisting of the primal features plus the new ones, with values taken from the corresponding λ parameters.

2.1 Computational Complexity of BFC

The BFC algorithm constructs a network from a dataset D, of N initial features in computational time less than $O(2^N)$, which is the learning time of general, unrestricted Bayesian networks from data. This is due to the fact that the most probable network is examined using a modified search strategy; initially, the most probable forest-structured network is constructed (i.e. a network in which every node has at most one parent). A greedy search is performed by adding, deleting or reversing the arcs randomly. In case that a change results in a more probable network it is accepted, otherwise cancelled. Throughout this process, a repository of networks with high probability is maintained. When the search reaches a local maximum, a network is randomly selected from the repository and the search process is activated again. It should be noted that in order to avoid the convergence to the previous local maximum the network is slightly modified, meaning that some arcs are deleted. Since the training data set is large we also sub-sample the data to speed the network evaluation process up. During the search, the size of the sub-samples is increased. A restriction on the network complexity is also applied during the search, so that a limited number of arcs is allowed in the beginning and, as the process progresses, more and more arcs are approved. These two annealing schemes (sub-sampling and complexity restrictions) have proven to have the effect of avoiding many bad local maxima.

The following equation expresses the complexity of the BFC algorithm:

$$O_{BFC} = O_{BN} + 2N\log(2^N)m \approx O(2^N) + 2N\log(2N)m$$

One could note that the complexity is heavily influenced by the Bayesian network learning stage. In cases that the structure is known, the algorithm converges smoothly, to levels comparable with that of other feature construction algorithms such as FICUS [8]. In practice, we ascertained that the search strategy reduces learning time by a factor of 3 or 4. Furthermore, a further reduction is being accomplished when the features of the dataset are binary, or they do not have more than 4 distinct values.

3 Experimental Evaluation

The following section discusses the issue of whether the theoretical claims about the improvement of the initial representation space are also reflected in practice. For that purpose, the BFC algorithm was applied to a number of different domains, mostly from the Language Technology discipline. More specifically, seven applications were considered, three of which belong to the Machine Learning domain and can be available through the UCI Machine Learning repository [10]. The rest of them involved Language Technology problems that were faced by the Artificial Intelligence Group, where the authors belong.

3.1 Language Technology Datasets

The following datasets were considered:
- Name Entity Recognition (NER) [14].
- Optical Character Segmentation (OCS) [5].
- Automatic Speaker Verification (ASV) (The 2001 NIST SRE dataset was used).
- Prosodic Word Identification (PWI) from Greek corpora [15].

Table 1 tabulates the characteristics of the data set of each application, as regards to the number of instances, features and values of the class variable.

Table 1. Characteristics of the Language Technology applications

Domain	# instances	# primal features	#BFC features	#class values	Training time (sec)
NER	47,000	8	8	4	160
OCS	4,587	10	10	2	450
ASV	80,000	34	34	2	1580
PWI	3,946	16	16	4	400

3.2 UCI Repositiry Datasets

The following table presents the complexity of the three UCI databases that were considered in the experiments.

Table 2. Characteristics of the UCI ML repository data sets

Domain	# instances	# primal features	#BFC features	#class values	Training time (sec)
Tic-Tac-Toe	958	10	10	2	15
Dermatology	366	35	35	6	66
Votes	435	17	17	2	100

3.3 Performance of BFC

In order to have a clearer view of the BFC performace, several Machine Learning algorithm were utilized as classifiers. Analytically, we used the C4.5, IB1, KNN (K=3), Naive Bayes, SVM and RBF algorithms. Regarding metrics of performance, precision, recall and F-measure were used. The 10-fold cross validation approach was considered. The exact process was as follows: for each training and test set, the BFC algorithm produced additional features and the new, augmented set was fed to the classifiers for evaluation. As can be seen from the tables below, the augmented set clearly outperfoms the initial using all kinds of classification methodologies for all applications. This behaviour is demonstrating that the BFC algorithm produces new datasets where the separation of class is clearer. The percentage of improvement ranges from 3% to 25%, a fact that supports the theoretical claims on the robustness of the proposed methodology.

Table 3. The performance of the BFC algorithm in the AI group datasets

NER				OCS			
C4.5	Primal	BFC	%gain	**C4.5**	Primal	BFC	%gain
precision	0,75	**0,92**	23,5%	precision	0,82	**0,97**	17,8%
recall	0,67	**0,85**	26,7%	recall	0,82	**0,96**	16,5%
F-measure	0,70	**0,88**	25,5%	F-measure	0,82	**0,96**	17,1%
IB1				**IB1**			
precision	0,71	**0,82**	16,3%	precision	0,78	**0,94**	20,7%
recall	0,69	**0,80**	15,6%	recall	0,78	**0,93**	19,9%
F-measure	0,70	**0,81**	15,8%	F-measure	0,78	**0,93**	20,3%
KNN3				**KNN3**			
precision	0,80	**0,86**	8,4%	precision	0,81	**0,91**	12,1%

Table 3. (*continued*)

recall	0,61	**0,74**	21,2%	recall	0,81	**0,90**	10,7%
F-measure	0,66	**0,74**	11,1%	F-measure	0,81	**0,91**	11,4%
Naïve				**Naïve**			
precision	0,57	**0,68**	18,0%	precision	0,78	**0,81**	2,9%
recall	0,56	**0,69**	23,6%	recall	0,79	**0,82**	3,4%
F-measure	0,50	**0,68**	36,5%	F-measure	0,79	**0,81**	3,1%
RBF				**RBF**			
precision	0,33	**0,34**	2,9%	precision	0,64	**0,68**	7,2%
recall	0,25	0,25	0,0%	recall	0,53	**0,54**	2,2%
F-measure	0,24	0,24	0,0%	F-measure	0,47	**0,49**	3,9%
SVM				**SVM**			
precision	0,76	**0,78**	3,0%	precision	0,81	**0,98**	19,8%
recall	0,65	**0,71**	9,9%	recall	0,82	**0,97**	18,2%
F-measure	0,68	**0,73**	6,5%	F-measure	0,81	**0,97**	19,6%
ASV				**Prosodic Words**			
C4.5	Primal	BFC	%gain	**C4.5**	Primal	BFC	%gain
precision	0,84	**1,00**	18,4%	precision	0,80	**0,96**	18,8%
recall	0,76	**0,97**	26,7%	recall	0,76	**0,95**	24,5%
F-measure	0,80	**1,00**	25,5%	F-measure	0,76	**0,95**	24,8%
IB1				**IB1**			
precision	0,80	**0,93**	16,3%	precision	0,70	**0,76**	7,6%
recall	0,79	**0,91**	15,6%	recall	0,71	**0,76**	7,0%
F-measure	0,79	**0,92**	15,8%	F-measure	0,71	**0,76**	7,2%
KNN3				**KNN3**			
precision	0,90	**0,98**	8,4%	precision	0,77	**0,79**	3,2%
recall	0,69	**0,84**	21,2%	recall	0,73	**0,76**	3,0%
F-measure	0,75	**0,84**	11,1%	F-measure	0,74	**0,77**	2,9%
Naïve				**Naïve**			
precision	0,62	**0,73**	18,0%	precision	0,77	**0,79**	2,9%
recall	0,61	**0,75**	23,6%	recall	0,78	**0,81**	2,9%
F-measure	0,54	**0,73**	36,5%	F-measure	0,77	**0,80**	2,7%
RBF				**RBF**			
precision	0,57	**0,58**	2,9%	precision	0,41	**0,48**	18,5%
recall	0,43	0,43	0,0%	recall	0,39	**0,45**	14,1%
F-measure	0,42	0,42	0,0%	F-measure	0,38	**0,42**	9,8%
SVM				**SVM**			
precision	0,82	**0,84**	3,0%	precision	0,78	**0,97**	25,1%
recall	0,70	**0,77**	9,9%	recall	0,76	**0,97**	27,0%
F-measure	0,74	**0,79**	6,5%	F-measure	0,77	**0,97**	26,1%

Table 4. The performance of the BFC algorithm in the UCI ML repository datasets

Dermatology				Tic-tac-toe			
C4.5	Primal	BFC	%gain	**C4.5**	Primal	BFC	%gain
precision	0,95	**0,96**	0,6%	precision	0,84	**0,90**	7,9%
recall	0,96	**0,97**	1,1%	recall	0,83	**0,88**	6,5%
F-measure	0,95	**0,96**	0,8%	F-measure	0,83	**0,89**	7,1%
IB1				**IB1**			
precision	0,95	**0,97**	2,5%	precision	0,80	**0,84**	5,3%
recall	0,95	**0,98**	2,4%	recall	0,79	**0,82**	3,2%
F-measure	0,95	**0,98**	2,8%	F-measure	0,80	**0,83**	4,0%
KNN3				**KNN3**			
precision	0,97	0,97	0,6%	precision	0,88	**0,99**	12,4%
recall	0,97	0,97	0,7%	recall	0,83	**0,98**	17,6%
F-measure	0,97	**0,98**	0,8%	F-measure	0,85	**0,99**	16,5%
Naïve				**Naïve**			
precision	0,96	**0,97**	1,1%	precision	0,66	**0,68**	2,7%
recall	0,96	**0,98**	1,7%	recall	0,63	**0,65**	2,9%
F-measure	0,96	**0,97**	1,9%	F-measure	0,64	**0,66**	3,1%
RBF				**RBF**			
precision	0,29	**0,35**	20,6%	precision	0,55	**0,58**	4,5%
recall	0,36	**0,38**	6,0%	recall	0,50	**0,51**	0,4%
F-measure	0,29	**0,36**	22,2%	F-measure	0,42	**0,42**	0,2%
SVM				**SVM**			
precision	0,97	**1,00**	2,8%	precision	0,99	**0,99**	0,0%
recall	0,97	**0,98**	1,3%	recall	0,98	**0,98**	0,3%
F-measure	0,97	**0,98**	1,6%	F-measure	0,98	**0,98**	0,0%

Votes			
C4.5	Primal	BFC	%gain
precision	0,95	**0,96**	0,3%
recall	0,96	0,96	-0,1%
F-measure	0,96	0,96	-0,2%
IB1			
precision	0,92	**0,93**	1,4%
recall	0,93	**0,94**	1,0%
F-measure	0,92	**0,93**	1,3%
KNN3			
precision	0,92	**0,93**	1,4%

Table 4. (*Continued*)

recall	0,93	**0,94**	1,0%
F-measure	0,92	**0,94**	1,3%
Naïve			
precision	0,88	**0,89**	1,0%
recall	0,89	**0,90**	1,5%
F-measure	0,89	**0,90**	1,1%
RBF			
precision	0,88	**0,89**	1,8%
recall	0,76	**0,84**	9,6%
F-measure	0,78	**0,85**	10,0%
SVM			
precision	0,95	**0,96**	0,4%
recall	0,96	0,96	0,1%
F-measure	0,96	0,96	0,3%

4 Conclusion

The proposed work described a novel algorithm for feature generation, using a methodology based on Bayesian networks. We exploited their functionality of encoding knowledge in a probabilistic form, so that new dataset contain such knowledge within. The algorithm was based on the ability Bayesian networks have to represent conditional independence assumptions about the primal feature set, thus projecting attributed that were not previously obvious, when they were fed to a classification algorithm in their initial form. The algorithm, named BFC, aims to overcome common statistical methods such as covariance and to allow ML algorithms that are based on the distance of instances to make use of the mutual relation between features. Each data set contains different values for each feature. If one simply considers each value independently, no particular knowledge on its relationship with the others is taken into account. When a Bayesian network is trained using this set, some form of knowledge about the distribution of feature and their semantic relation is encoded. This knowledge is piped to the input as probabilities, which reflect the belief of the dataset on the importance of each separate value. The augmented dataset was shown to be more robust as regards to classification, as it was evaluated using various datasets and different classifiers.

References

1. Aha, D., Kibler, D. and Albert, M.K.: Instance based learning algorithms. Machine Learning, 6(1) (1991), 37-66.
2. Cooper, G. and Herskovits, E.: A Bayesian method for the induction of probabilistic networks from data. Machine Learning, 9 (1992), 309-347.
3. Jensen, R.: An Introduction to Bayesian Networks. UCL Press, London (1996).

4. John, G., and Langley, P.: Estimating continuous distributions in Bayesian classifiers. Proceedings of the Eleventh Conference on Uncertainty in Artificial Intelligence (1995), 338-345.

5. Kavallieratou, E.: Σύστημα Αυτόματης Επεξεργασίας Εγγράφου και Αναγνώρισης Χειρόγραφων Χαρακτήρων Συνεχόμενης Γραφής, Ανεξάρτητο Συγγραφέα, PhD Thesis, (2000).

6. Kohavi, R., & Dan, S.: Feature subset selection using the wrapper model: Overfitting and dynamic search space topology. In U. M. Fayyad and R. Uthurusamy (Eds.), First International Conference on Knowledge, Discovery and Data Mining (1995).

7. Lam, W. and Bacchus, R.: Learning Bayesian belief networks: An approach based on the MDL principle. Computational Intelligence, 10(4) (1994), 269-293.

8. Markovich, S and Rosenstein, D.: Feature Generation Using General Constructor Functions, Machine Learning, 49(1) (2002), 59-98.

9. Murphy, P.M. and Aha, D.W.: UCI repository of machine learning databases. [Machine-readable data repository]. University of California, Department of Information and Computer Science, Irvine, CA (1993).

10. Murphy, P.M. and Pazzani, M.J.: Exploring the decision forest: An empirical investigation of Occam's razor in decision tree induction. Journal of Artificial Intelligence Research, 1 (1994), 257-275.

11. Pearl, J.: Probabilistic Reasoning in Intelligent Systems: Networks of Plausible Inference. San Mateo, CA: Morgan Kaufmann (1988).

12. Quinlan, J.: C4.5: Programs for Machine Learning. Morgan Kaufmann. Reiter, R. (1980). A logic for default reasoning. Artificial Intelligence, 13(1-2) (1993), 81-132.

13. Salzberg, S.: Improving classification methods via feature selection. Machine Learning, 1993, 99.

14. Tasikas, A.: Αναγνώριση Ονομάτων Οντοτήτων σε Κείμενα Νέας λληνικής Γλώσσας αποκλειστικά με Μηχανική Μάθηση, Diploma Thesis, University of Patras (2002).

15. Zervas, P., Maragoudakis, M., Fakotakis, N. and Kokkinakis, G.: Learning to predict Pitch Accents using Bayesian Belief Networks for Greek Language, LREC 2004, 4th International Conference on Language Resources and Evaluation, Lisbon, Portugal (2004), 2139-2142.

Musical Instrument Recognition and Classification Using Time Encoded Signal Processing and Fast Artificial Neural Networks

Giorgos Mazarakis[1], Panagiotis Tzevelekos[2], and Georgios Kouroupetroglou[2]

[1] National Technical University of Athens,
Department of Electrical and Computer Engineering
gemazar@mail.ntua.gr
[2] National and Kapodistrian University of Athens,
Department of Informatics and Telecommunications
{taktzev, koupe}@di.uoa.gr

Abstract. Traditionally, musical instrument recognition is mainly based on frequency domain analysis (sinusoidal analysis, cepstral coefficients) and shape analysis to extract a set of various features. Instruments are usually classified using k-NN classifiers, HMM, Kohonen SOM and Neural Networks. In this work, we describe a system for the recognition of musical instruments from isolated notes. We are introducing the use of a Time Encoded Signal Processing method to produce simple matrices from complex sound waveforms, for instrument note encoding and recognition. These matrices are presented to a Fast Artificial Neural Network (FANN) to perform instrument recognition with promising results in organ classification and reduced computational cost. The evaluation material consists of 470 tones from 19 musical instruments synthesized with 5 wide used synthesizers (Microsoft Synth, Creative SB Live! Synth, Yamaha VL-70m Tone Generator, Edirol Soft-Synth, Kontakt Player) and 84 isolated notes from 20 western orchestral instruments (Iowa University Database).

1 Introduction

Automatic music instrument recognition is an essential subtask in many applications regarding music information indexing and retrieval. Computational auditory scene analysis (CASA), automatic music transcription frameworks and content-based search systems, all find such a capability to be extremely helpful. However, musical instrument recognition has not received as much research interest as, for instance, speech and speaker recognition, even though both the amateur music lover and the professional musician would benefit from such systems.

Many attempts in music instrument recognition have taken place in the last thirty years. Most of them have focused on single, isolated notes (either synthesized or natural) and tones taken from professional sound data-bases [1]. Recent works have operated on real-world recordings, polyphonic or monophonic, multi-instrumental or solo [2]. However, the issue is yet far from being solved. The work on recognition from separate notes still remains crucial, since it can lead to further optimization of the methods used and to insights on the recognition of multi-instrumental, commercial recordings.

G. Antoniou et al. (Eds.): SETN 2006, LNAI 3955, pp. 246–255, 2006.

The majority of the recognition systems used so far concentrate on the timbral-spectral characteristics of the notes. Discrimination is based on features such as pitch, spectral centroid, energy ratios, spectral envelopes and mel frequency cepstral coefficients [3,4]. Temporal features, other than attack, duration and tremolo, are seldom taken into account. Classification is done using k-NN classifiers, HMM, Kohonen SOM and Neural Networks [5,6]. A limitation of such methods is that in real instruments the spectral features of the sound are never constant. Even when the same note is being played, the spectral components change. One has to take into consideration many timbral components and the way they can vary, which is often rather random, in order to develop a robust recognition system.

In this paper, we present a different instrument recognition approach, based on Time Encoded Signal Processing and Recognition, a time-domain specific feature extraction process. The method encodes signals in a simple and computational lightweight manner, while producing fixed size and dimension structures regardless of the duration or complexity of the signal. Classification is performed using Fast Artificial Neural Networks. For validation, we use isolated, constant-pitch notes. 470 notes produced with 5 velocity scales from 19 instruments, using 5 synthesizers. 28 notes were taken from a public real-instrument database of 20 instruments.

The paper is organized as follows: in Section 2, we describe the recognition and classification methodology used. Section 3 contains the validation procedure and the recognition results. Section 4 concludes this work.

2 Recognition and Classification Method

2.1 Time Encoded Signal Processing

Time Encoded Signal Processing and Recognition, or TESPAR Coding, is a method proposed by King [7, 8] to digitally code speech waveforms. The method is based on infinite clipping (Fig. 1 shows an example), a coding method proposed by Licklidder and Pollack [9]. According to their work, they managed to achieve mean random-word intelligibility scores of 97.9% by differentiating a speech waveform and then removing all amplitude information by performing infinite clipping i.e. preserving only zero-crossing information.

The infinite clipping coding is a direct representation of the duration between the zero crossings of the waveform, i.e. the real zeros of the waveform, thus it is only dependent on the waveform itself and not at the sampling frequency, as long as sampling is performed according to Shannon's theorem.

The above observations on the importance of zeros to the intelligibility of a coded waveform led scientists to further investigate zero-based methods of signal approximation [10, 11]. Author in [11] showed that the introduction of the concept of complex zeros could help overcoming some deficiencies of infinite clipping.

Let a signal waveform of bandwidth W and duration T. The signal contains 2TW zeros, where typically 2TW exceeds several thousand. While the real zeros are easy to determine, complex zeros extraction is a difficult problem involving the factorization of a $2TW^{th}$ - order polynomial. Such an approach of zeros identification requires significant computational resources and is practically infeasible.

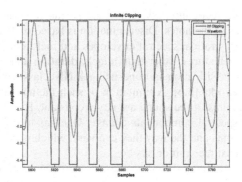

Fig. 1. Infinite Clipping of an oboe waveform

Instead of determining the exact position of complex zeros, which is a complicated task, an approximation of their location could be given. Thus, the waveform is segmented between successive real zeros - the epochs - which comprise the bounds for the complex zeros positions. Complex zeros become visible in the shape of the waveform as minima, maxima or points of inflection and occur in conjugate pairs inside the epoch.

Hence, a band limited waveform may be simply approximated by segmenting it into successive epochs with two features:

- *Duration (D)* which is the number of samples between two successive real zeros
- *Shape (S)* which is the number of local minima (for a positive epoch) or the number of local maxima (for a negative epoch)

Coding Method. The recorded music waveform is presented to the software implemented TESPAR coder (in Matlab), which segments it into successive epochs. Each epoch is described with a set of numbers representing the Duration and Shape (D/S) of it. This pair is then coded according to a predefined alphabet, representing each epoch by a single "letter". In order to reduce the complexity of this mapping procedure, only the more important D/S pairs are encoded according to an alphabet. The alphabet used depends on the complexity, bandwidth and sampling frequency of the input signal. Most frequency components of a speech signals are in the band of 300Hz to 3 kHz. Authors in [8] use a standard 29 symbol alphabet to encode speech signals sampled at 8 kHz. However, musical waveforms are richer in harmonics so the bandwidth of the signal had to be extended to 100Hz to 5.5 kHz. In order to approximate the music waveform more adequately, the alphabet used was extended to 48 symbols by allowing maximum epoch duration (D) to be 54 samples instead of 37 used in [8]. The aforementioned coding procedure results to a symbol stream, as shown in Figure 2, which can be converted into a fixed-dimension matrix. The N-dimension matrix (where N is the number of the symbols in the alphabet) which contains the number of appearances of each character in the symbol stream is called S-Matrix (Figure 3). Histogram-like, S-Matrices are very descriptive of the waveform from which they were created and can be used for classification purposes. Their fixed dimensions make the

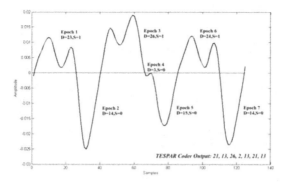

Fig. 2. TESPAR Coding Procedure

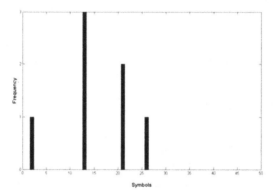

Fig. 3. S-Matrix of figure 2 waveform

classification task using Artificial Neural Networks (ANN) a very enticing solution and the combination of TESPAR with FANNs (Fast Artificial NNs) a very powerful tool for instrument recognition and identification.

2.2   Fast Artificial Neural Networks

FANN is a library which implements a multilayer feedforward ANN, that is, an ANN with neurons ordered in layers, starting with an input layer, continuing with one or more hidden layers and ending with an output layer. The most common networks are fully connected, with connection going only forward, from one layer to the next. The main advantage of this implementation is faster training and testing, compared to similar libraries on systems without a floating point processor, while retaining a comparable performance to other libraries on systems with a floating point processor.

In order to use these networks for classification purposes, two phases must be completed. The first phase is the training phase, where the FANN learns from the imposed input and the requested output. The second phase is the execution phase, where the FANN is presented with unknown input and provides an output. The training process is actually an optimization problem, where the mean square error (MSE) of the entire set of training data must be minimized. The algorithm used to solve this optimization problem is the Backpropagation algorithm. After propagating an input through the network, the error is calculated and then propagated back through the network. In the same time the weights are adjusted in order to make the error smaller. The object of training is to minimize the MSE for all the training data. Training the network on data sequentially one input at a time, instead of training using the whole dataset at once has been proved more efficient. While this means that the order of the data is of importance, this method is a way of avoiding getting stuck in a local minima and stop the training process. A detailed description of FANN library can be found in [12] and a free implementation on different programming languages and platforms is available and maintained under the GNU Lesser General Public License (LGPL) [13].

3   Experimental Dataset and Validation

In order to evaluate the introduced method, several experiments have been conducted with two main objectives: the performance of the system in recognizing synthesized instrument sounds and recognizing instruments from real recordings. All recordings were monophonic, 16-bit wav files downsampled to 11 kHz.

3.1   Synthesized Instruments

Dataset. For this purpose we chose instrument tones, produced with 5 different synthesizers, namely the simple Microsoft Synth, the embedded synthesizer on a Sound Blaster Live! Sound Card, a Yamaha VL-70m Tone Generator, Kontakt player and Edirol Soft-Synth. From each synthesizer 19 instruments (18 instruments for Kontakt player, soprano sax was missing) were selected, each playing C4 note, except the flutes that were all playing C5. Each note was recorded 5 times with 5 different values for velocity (40 for pp-p, 60 for p-mp, 80 for mf-f, 100 for f-ff and 120 for ff-fff) and was named as sample1 - sample5. A total amount of 470 notes was tested.

Validation. For each synthesizer, all notes (19x5=95) were coded with the TESPAR method and the S-Matrices for each note were created. From these matrices, two pairs of datasets were created, each pair used in two experiments accordingly (exp1 and exp2). In exp1, the training data for the FANN was the mean S-Matrix of each instrument (from the 5 note samples) and the test data were all the S-Matrices from the recordings of this synthesizer (95 notes). In exp2, the training data for the FANN were S-Matrices from samples 1,3,5 of each note, while the test data were S-Matrices from samples 2,4. In this experiment training and testing data are completely independent, which is usually the scenario in real-world recognition applications.

3.2   Real Instruments Dataset

Dataset. The evaluation material for testing the system under real conditions is obtained from the original recordings from Iowa University [14]. Recordings from 20 instruments playing C4 and C5 notes (flutes) were used, in vibrato and non vibrato variations and from different strings (for the string family instruments). All instruments were playing in pp, mf and ff, resulting in 3 samples from each note (pp - sample1, mf - sample2 and ff - sample3). A total amount of 84 notes were tested.

Validation. The evaluation method used was almost the same with the one used for the synthesized instruments. S-Matrices were created for each note. In exp1, the training data for the FANN was the mean S-Matrix of each instrument (from the 3 note samples) and the test data were the S-Matrices from the 84 notes. In exp2, the training data were the S-Matrices from pp and ff note samples (sample1,3) and the test data was the S- Matrix from mf note sample (sample2).

3.3 FANN Training

Training a NN is a random procedure that depends on a variety of parameters involving training algorithm, error function, hidden and output layer activation method, learning rate and more. Due to these random results, classification was not based on the results from a single FANN but from 10 parallel FANNs. Five of them were trained using the sigmoid-stepwise function and five using the stepwise function. The averaged result was used for classification purposes. Every one of the 10 parallel FANNs converged after an average of 80 epochs reaching a set Mean Square Error of MSE $\leq$ 0.01.

Each FANN has 48 neurons for the input layer plus one bias neuron, one hidden layer with 30 neurons plus one bias neuron and 19 neurons for output (20 for Iowa Music Database [14]). Each output neuron represents one instrument and can take values from 0 to 1. Its value should be 1 in a correct classification of the according instrument, while all others should be 0. This ideal situation results in a MSE of 0.

3.4 Results

Kontakt Player. Tables 1, 2 show the recognition rates for the exp 1, 2 respectively. In both experiments, the higher recognition rates for all the instruments (in bold numbers) correspond to the correct ones. Recognition is successful for all instruments, with all rates rising above 87%, apart from the violin (50% and 58%). The total MSE is 12% in the first experiment and 6% in the second, values that demonstrate the high success of the process for the specific synthesizer. Detailed recognition matrices will not be shown for all tested synthesizers but the brief description that follows is indicative of the effectiveness of the method in all of them.

Microsoft Synth. Highest errors occurred for the violin, the clarinet and the tuba. The total MSE was 53%. In experiment 2, viola was recognized as violin and tuba as trombone. However, in both cases, the correct instruments did get the second higher rate, while the higher rates did remain in the same instrument family group. The total MSE was 50%.

Sound Blaster Live! Synth. In experiment 1, all instruments were recognized successfully, with very high recognition rates (mostly above 90%) and a very low total MSE of 5%. Equivalent results were taken in experiment 2. In both experiments, the french horn delivered the higher MSE, which was still relatively low (65% and 53%).

Yamaha VL70-m Tone Generator. This tone generator uses physical modelling methods to synthesize sound. Thus, the notes produced share the versatility and complexity of natural instrument notes. In both experiments, the higher recognition rates correspond to the correct instruments, while the total MSE is relatively low (36% and 24% respectively). In the second experiment, 8 instruments gather rates above 90%.

Edirol Soft-Synth. In the first experiment all instruments were successfully recognized, while in the second experiment only the piano was mismatched. In both experiments, some instruments gathered high recognition rates while other gathered low. However, in the second experiment, we find very high rates for the violin, the viola, the piccolo, the soprano saxophone, the tenor sax and the trumpet. The MSEs for the two experiments are respectively 45% and 48%.

Iowa Instrument Database. Tables 3, 4 correspond to exp 1, 2 for real-instrument notes obtained from the Iowa Instrument Database. In the first experiment, 26 out of 28 attempts were correctly recognized, while in the second experiment, 22 out of 28. A flute recording was recognized as violin in both experiments. Eb clarinet and bass clarinet were recognized as Bb clarinet in the second experiment. Total MSE is 43% in the first experiment and 58% percent in the second.

Table 1. Kontakt Player Experiment 1

Stimulus \ Recognized	Violin	Viola	Cello	Contrabass	Piccolo	Flute	Oboe	English Horn	Clarinet	Bassoon	Soprano Sax	Alto Sax	Tenor Sax	Baritone Sax	Trumpet	French Horn	Trombone	Tuba	Piano	MSE
Violin	58	0	5	0	17	0	0	0	1	3	0	9	5	0	1	0	2	0	3	61
Viola	0	94	2	2	0	1	1	0	0	0	0	0	12	0	3	2	0	0	2	14
Cello	0	0	88	1	3	0	0	0	0	0	0	2	4	3	0	0	2	0	0	11
Contrabass	0	0	10	74	1	1	0	0	0	0	0	3	1	3	0	0	0	2	0	30
Piccolo	5	0	1	0	93	0	0	0	0	2	0	1	1	0	0	0	0	1	3	3
Flute	0	0	0	1	0	98	0	0	0	3	0	3	0	0	0	0	0	0	0	1
Oboe	0	0	0	0	0	0	87	0	0	0	0	0	0	0	1	0	1	0	0	2
English Horn	1	1	0	6	0	1	9	87	0	0	0	0	0	0	5	0	0	2	0	19
Clarinet	2	0	0	1	0	0	5	0	93	0	0	0	1	0	1	0	0	0	1	3
Bassoon	1	0	0	0	1	0	0	0	0	96	0	0	0	0	0	0	1	0	2	1
Soprano Sax	-										-									-
Alto Sax	3	0	1	0	1	2	0	0	0	0	0	88	2	1	0	0	0	0	0	8
Tenor Sax	2	8	1	0	1	0	1	1	2	0	0	1	86	0	1	0	1	0	1	11
Baritone Sax	0	0	11	0	0	0	0	0	0	0	0	0	0	81	0	0	0	2	0	23
Trumpet	1	0	0	0	2	0	4	1	0	0	0	1	3	1	93	0	0	0	0	5
French Horn	1	0	0	0	0	0	2	0	0	0	0	0	0	0	0	95	2	0	0	2
Trombone	2	0	0	0	2	0	4	0	0	0	0	0	0	0	0	0	96	0	0	1
Tuba	1	0	0	1	0	0	1	0	0	0	0	0	0	0	0	0	0	99	0	0
Piano	6	0	0	0	8	0	0	0	0	4	0	0	0	0	0	0	0	0	87	13

Total MSE   *12*

Table 2. Kontakt Player Experiment 2

Stimulus \ Recognized	Violin	Viola	Cello	Contrabass	Piccolo	Flute	Oboe	English Horn	Clarinet	Bassoon	Soprano Sax	Alto Sax	Tenor Sax	Baritone Sax	Trumpet	French Horn	Trombone	Tuba	Piano	MSE
Violin	50	0	2	0	2	5	0	0	0	0	0	4	4	0	0	0	1	0	2	55
Viola	0	98	0	1	0	0	1	0	0	0	0	0	1	0	0	0	0	0	0	0
Cello	0	0	87	1	0	0	0	0	0	0	0	2	0	1	0	0	0	0	0	5
Contrabass	0	0	0	92	0	1	0	0	0	0	0	0	0	5	0	0	0	0	0	5
Piccolo	1	0	3	0	99	0	0	0	0	0	0	0	0	0	0	0	0	0	1	0
Flute	1	0	0	1	0	95	0	0	0	1	0	15	0	0	0	0	0	0	0	6
Oboe	0	0	0	0	0	0	97	0	1	0	0	0	0	0	0	0	0	0	0	0
English Horn	1	0	0	3	0	0	0	99	0	0	0	0	0	0	0	0	0	2	0	1
Clarinet	0	0	0	1	0	0	1	0	99	0	0	0	0	0	0	0	0	0	0	0
Bassoon	1	0	0	1	0	0	0	0	0	98	0	0	0	0	0	0	0	0	0	0
Soprano Sax	-	-	-	-	-	-	-	-	-	-	-	-	-	-	-	-	-	-	-	-
Alto Sax	2	0	1	1	0	1	0	0	0	0	0	97	2	1	0	0	0	0	0	1
Tenor Sax	1	4	5	1	0	0	0	0	0	0	0	1	95	0	0	1	0	0	0	3
Baritone Sax	0	0	0	8	0	0	0	0	0	0	0	1	0	87	0	0	0	0	0	12
Trumpet	0	0	0	0	0	0	2	0	0	0	0	0	0	0	98	0	0	0	0	0
French Horn	0	10	0	0	0	0	1	0	0	0	0	0	3	0	0	99	0	0	0	7
Trombone	2	0	0	0	0	0	1	0	0	0	0	0	1	0	0	0	93	0	0	6
Tuba	0	0	0	2	0	0	0	5	0	0	0	0	0	0	0	0	0	99	0	5
Piano	10	0	0	0	1	0	0	0	0	2	0	0	0	0	0	0	0	0	95	4
																			Total MSE	**6**

Table 3. Iowa Instrument Database Experiment 1

Stimulus \ Recognized	Violin	Viola	Cello	Bass	Flute	AltoFlute	BassFlute	Oboe	Bassoon	EbClar	BbClar	BassClar	SopSax	AltoSax	Trumpet	Horn	TenorTromb	BassTromb	Tuba	Piano	MSE
Violin.arco.sulG	84	5	0	0	3	5	5	0	1	1	0	6	0	1	1	0	0	0	1	0	22
Viola.arco.sulC	4	75	0	0	0	0	0	0	0	1	0	0	0	19	0	0	0	2	0		26
Viola.arco.sulG	17	92	0	0	0	0	0	0	0	1	0	0	0	16	0	0	0	1	0		26
Cello.arco.sulA	0	0	68	0	4	2	0	6	0	0	0	0	0	0	1	0	4	0	0	0	29
Cello.arco.sulD	0	0	92	0	2	2	0	3	0	8	0	0	0	0	0	2	0	0	0		13
Cello.arco.sulG	1	0	78	1	0	2	13	2	0	0	0	0	1	0	0	0	1	0	0		32
Bass.arco.sulD	0	2	3	85	0	0	0	1	0	0	0	7	1	0	0	0	0	0	0	4	18
Bass.arco.sulD	0	14	0	97	0	0	0	1	0	1	0	2	1	0	0	0	0	0	0	4	12
flute.vib	0	0	0	0	65	3	56	0	17	0	0	0	1	0	0	0	1	1	0	0	89
flute.novib	32	0	17	0	29	6	6	1	21	0	0	0	0	0	1	0	11	0	0	0	124
AltoFlute	6	0	13	1	16	62	26	2	9	0	0	0	2	0	5	3	10	1	0	0	91
BassFlute	4	1	0	0	27	3	78	0	11	0	0	1	3	0	1	0	1	1	0	4	47
oboe	0	0	2	0	0	0	0	79	0	0	0	0	0	0	1	0	2	0	0	0	11
Bassoon	0	0	0	0	0	0	0	0	91	0	0	0	0	0	0	1	0	1	8	0	7
EbClar	0	2	0	1	0	0	0	1	0	6	64	2	0	5	0	1	0	1	0	0	150
BbClar	0	4	0	0	0	0	0	0	2	3	69	4	0	4	5	0	0	0	13	0	37
BassClarinet	0	8	1	9	0	0	0	0	0	13	10	40	0	3	0	0	0	0	0	2	67
SopSax.NoVib	0	0	0	0	0	0	0	0	0	0	0	2	58	0	0	0	1	1	0	8	42
SopSax.Vib	0	0	0	3	0	0	0	7	0	0	0	5	69	0	0	0	2	7	0	6	45
AltoSax.NoVib	0	2	0	0	0	0	0	0	0	1	33	0	0	77	0	1	0	2	8	8	52
AltoSax.Vib	1	2	0	0	0	0	0	0	0	1	21	1	0	79	0	1	0	0	6	14	42
Trumpet.novib	0	9	0	0	0	0	0	14	0	4	0	0	0	0	95	0	0	0	0	0	11
Trumpet.vib	0	10	0	0	0	0	0	16	0	0	3	0	0	0	95	0	0	0	0	0	13
Horn	0	0	5	0	0	0	0	1	11	0	1	0	0	0	0	57	0	5	11	7	59
TenorTrombone	0	0	0	0	2	5	0	6	2	0	0	0	0	0	0	0	95	8	0	0	8
BassTromb	0	0	0	0	0	0	3	0	18	0	0	0	0	0	0	0	22	3	72	2	49
Tuba	0	4	0	0	0	0	0	0	16	0	1	0	0	0	4	1	1	0	75	1	31
Piano	0	0	0	0	0	0	11	0	0	3	0	3	1	10	0	0	0	0	4	72	39
																				Total MSE	**43**

Table 4. Iowa Instrument Database Experiment 2

Stimulus \ Recognized	Violin	Viola	Cello	Bass	Flute	AltoFlute	BassFlute	Oboe	Bassoon	EbClar	BbClar	BassClar	SopSax	AltoSax	Trumpet	Horn	TenorTromt	BassTromb	Tuba	Piano	MSE
Violin.arco.sulG	89	0	0	0	4	3	3	0	0	1	0	1	8	0	6	0	10	0	2	0	31
Viola.arco.sulC	0	45	0	0	0	0	0	0	0	0	0	0	0	0	6	0	0	0	5	0	49
Viola.arco.sulG	6	84	0	0	0	0	0	0	0	1	0	0	0	0	1	0	0	0	1	0	11
Cello.arco.sulA	0	1	49	0	0	0	0	1	0	0	0	0	0	0	0	0	0	0	0	0	38
Cello.arco.sulD	0	0	88	0	0	4	1	0	0	0	0	1	0	0	0	0	0	0	0	0	9
Cello.arco.sulG	0	2	77	0	0	0	0	1	0	0	0	0	2	0	0	0	0	0	0	0	21
Bass.arco.sulD	3	13	0	70	0	0	0	0	0	1	0	28	8	0	0	0	0	1	0	0	62
Bass.arco.sulD	4	2	0	97	0	0	0	0	0	1	0	14	0	0	0	0	0	0	0	0	10
flute.vib	0	0	0	0	77	13	42	4	0	0	0	0	5	0	0	10	0	2	0	0	63
flute.novib	35	0	5	0	31	8	1	8	0	0	0	0	0	0	0	0	1	0	0	0	99
AltoFlute	18	0	16	1	37	51	12	1	0	10	0	0	5	0	10	0	11	2	0	0	105
BassFlute	0	0	1	1	23	9	50	0	0	0	0	0	10	0	0	0	0	1	0	0	61
oboe	0	0	0	0	0	0	0	96	0	0	0	0	0	0	6	0	0	0	0	0	2
Bassoon	0	0	0	0	5	0	0	0	90	0	0	0	0	0	0	1	0	1	0	0	5
EbClar	0	0	0	0	0	0	0	0	0	2	77	0	0	20	0	0	0	1	2	0	181
BbClar	0	0	0	0	0	0	0	0	2	0	43	0	0	14	0	0	0	0	5	0	61
BassClarinet	0	0	0	2	0	0	0	4	1	9	32	9	0	0	0	0	0	10	0	0	135
SopSax.NoVib	0	0	3	0	0	1	1	0	0	0	0	0	1	0	0	0	0	0	0	6	100
SopSax.Vib	0	0	0	0	4	5	8	0	0	0	0	0	7	1	0	0	4	7	0	9	113
AltoSax.NoVib	0	1	0	0	0	0	0	0	0	0	3	0	0	71	0	0	0	1	39	2	53
AltoSax.Vib	0	12	15	0	0	0	0	0	0	0	7	2	0	67	0	0	0	0	34	0	67
Trumpet.novib	0	4	0	0	1	0	0	9	0	0	0	0	0	0	85	0	0	0	0	0	10
Trumpet.vib	0	0	0	0	1	0	26	0	0	0	0	0	0	0	96	0	0	0	0	0	16
Horn	0	0	0	0	0	0	0	0	19	0	0	0	0	1	0	15	0	15	2	9	110
TenorTrombone	0	0	0	0	9	3	1	0	8	0	0	0	0	1	0	8	95	10	0	0	24
BassTrombone	0	0	0	0	0	2	1	0	17	0	0	0	0	1	0	10	3	35	20	6	89
Tuba	0	0	0	0	0	0	0	0	7	0	0	0	0	4	1	0	0	2	66	0	27
Piano	0	0	8	0	0	1	1	0	0	0	0	3	1	1	0	0	0	0	2	18	85

Total MSE   58

5   Conclusions

In this paper, we presented a promising method for music instrument recognition and classification, using Time Encoded Signal Processing and Fast Artificial Neural Networks. The method proved to provide high recognition rates with notes produced from synthesizers, as well as with notes from real-instrument recordings.

Future works include evaluation with notes having wider pitch range, from a wider range of synthesizers and natural-instrument recordings. Depending on the results of these tasks, one can continue with instrument identification in multi-instrumental, commercial recordings.

References

1. K.D. Martin: Sound-Source Recognition: A Theory and Computational Model, Ph.D. thesis, MIT, 1999
2. A. Livshin, X. Rodet: Musical Instrument Identification in Continuous Recordings, Proc. of the 7th Int. Conference on Digital Audio Effects (DAFX-04), Naples, Italy, October 5-8, 2004
3. A. Eronen, A. Klapuri: Musical Instrument Recognition Using Cepstral Coefficients and Temporal Features, Proc. of the IEEE International Conference on Acoustics, Speech and Signal Processing, ICASSP 2000, pp. 753-756

4. T. Kitahara, M. Goto, H. Okuno: Musical Instrument Identification Based on F0-Dependent Multivariate Normal Distribution, Proc. of the 2003 IEEE Int'l Conf. on Acoustic, Speech and Signal Processing (ICASSP '03), Vol.V, pp.421-424, Apr. 2003
5. A. Eronen: Musical instrument recognition using ICA-based transform of features and discriminatively trained HMMs, Proc. of the Seventh International Symposium on Signal Processing and its Applications, ISSPA 2003, Paris, France, 1-4 July 2003, pp. 133-136
6. G. De Poli, P. Prandoni: Sonological Models for Timbre Characterization, Journal of New Music Research, Vol 26 (1997), pp. 170-197, 1997
7. J. Holbeche, R. D. Hughes, R. A. King: Time Encoded Speech (TES) Descriptors As A Symbol Feature Set For Voice Recognition Systems. IEE International Conference On Speech Input/Output; Techniques And Applications, pp. 310-315, London, March 1986
8. R. A. King, T. C. Phipps: Shannon, TESPAR and Approximation Strategies. ICSPAT 98, Vol. 2, pp. 1204-1212. Toronto, Canada, September 1998
9. J. C. R. Licklidder, I. Pollack: Effects of Differentiation, Integration, and Infinite Peak Clipping Upon the Intelligibility of Speech. Journal of the Acoustical Society of America, vol. 20, no. 1, pp. 42-51, Jan. 1948
10. F. E. Bond, C. R. Cahn: A Relationship between Zero Crossings and Fourier Coefficients for Bandwidth-Limited Functions. IRE Trans. Information Theory, vol. IT-4, pp. 110-113, Sept.1958
11. E. C. Titchmarsh: The Zeros of Certain Integral Functions. Proc. progres. Math. Soc., vol. 25, pp. 283-302, May 1926
12. S. Nissen: Implementation of a Fast Artificial Neural Network Library (FANN). Report, Department of Computer Science University of Copenhagen (DIKU), 31 October 2003
13. Fast Artificial Neural Network Library (fann): http://leenissen.dk/fann/
14. Univ. of Iowa Electr. Music Studios: http://theremin.music.uiowa.edu/index.html

O-DEVICE: An Object-Oriented Knowledge Base System for OWL Ontologies

Georgios Meditskos and Nick Bassiliades

Department of Informatics, Aristotle University of Thessaloniki, Greece
{gmeditsk, nbassili}@csd.auth.gr

Abstract. This paper reports on the implementation of a rule system, called O-DEVICE, for reasoning about OWL instances using deductive rules. O-DEVICE exploits the rule language of the CLIPS production rule system and transforms OWL ontologies into an object-oriented schema of COOL. During the transformation procedure, OWL classes are mapped to COOL classes, OWL properties to class slots and OWL instances to COOL objects. The purpose of this transformation is twofold: a) to exploit the advantages of the object-oriented representation and access all the properties of instances in one step, since properties are encapsulated inside resource objects; b) to be able to use a deductive object-oriented rule language for querying and creating maintainable views of OWL instances, which operates over the object-oriented schema of CLIPS, and c) to answer queries faster, since the implied relationships due to the rich OWL semantics have been pre-computed. The deductive rules are compiled into CLIPS production rules. The rich open-world semantics of OWL are partly handled by the incremental transformation procedure and partly by the rule compilation procedure.

1 Introduction

The vision of the Semantic Web is to provide the necessary standards and infrastructure for transforming the Web into a more automatic environment where agents would have the ability to search for requested information automatically. This is feasible by describing appropriately the already available data on the Web in a way that could be machine-understandable. Ontologies can be considered as a primary key towards this goal since they provide a controlled vocabulary of concepts, each with an explicitly defined and machine processable semantics.

The development of Semantic Web proceeds in layers where each layer is built on top of the others [6]. Currently, the *ontology* layer has reached a sufficient level of maturity, having OWL [19] as the basic form for ontology definition. The next step is to move on the higher levels of *logic* and *proof*, which are built on top of *ontology* layer, where rules now are considered as the primary key, since (a) they can serve as extensions of, or alternatives to, description logic based ontology languages; and (b) they can be used to develop declarative systems on top of (using) ontologies.

A lot of effort is undertaken to define a rule language for the Semantic Web on top of ontologies in order to combine already existing information and deduce new knowledge. Currently, RuleML [8] is the main standardization effort for rules on the

G. Antoniou et al. (Eds.): SETN 2006, LNAI 3955, pp. 256–266, 2006.

Web to specify queries and inferences in Web ontologies, mappings between ontologies, and dynamic Web behaviors of workflows, services, and agents. Furthermore, very recently the Rule Interchange Format Working Group [18] has been formed to produce a core rule language plus extensions which together allow rules to be translated between rule languages and thus transferred between rule systems.

One approach to implement a rule system on top of the Semantic Web ontology layer is to start from scratch and build inference engines that draw conclusions directly on the OWL data model. However, such an approach tends to throw away decades of research and development on efficient and robust rule engines. In this paper we follow a different approach: we re-use an existing rule system (CLIPS [10]) for reasoning on top of OWL data. However, before an existing rule system is used, careful design must be made on how OWL data and semantics are going to be treated in the host system. The design should be sufficient enough to (a) draw the right conclusions stemming from the semantics of the language and (b) complete the inferencing procedure in a reasonable amount of time.

The O-DEVICE system inferences over (on top of) OWL documents. O-DEVICE exploits the advantages of the object-oriented programming model by transforming OWL ontologies into classes, properties and objects of the OO programming language provided within CLIPS, called COOL. The system also features a powerful deductive rule language which supports inferencing over the transformed OWL descriptions. Users can either use this deductive language to express queries or a RuleML-like syntax. The deductive rule language is implemented by translating deductive rules into CLIPS production rules. The semantics of OWL constructors are appropriately handled by O-DEVICE, either by the OWL transformation procedure, using corresponding COOL constructs, or by the deductive rule compilation procedure, rewriting parts of the rule condition.

Our main motivation for doing such a transformation from OWL to objects is to be able to exploit our existing deductive object-oriented rule language ([3], [4], [2]) for querying and creating maintainable views of OWL instances, taking into consideration the complex, implied relationships between classes and instances, due to the rich OWL semantics. Notice that our purpose is not to build another OWL reasoner, i.e. we do not aim to classifying instances under classes, but rather to infer and materialize in advance as much properties for OWL instances as possible under the semantics of OWL constructors. In this way we are able to answer deductive queries at run-time much faster, since all the implied relationships have been pre-computed. Finally, although the host system is restricted by the closed-world assumption, our current mapping scheme is able (in most situations) to cope with the open-world semantics of OWL, due to our incremental transformation algorithms.

This paper extends the work first presented in [16] by adding more OWL constructs to the mapping scheme. However, the work described in this paper is still work in progress. The rest of the paper is organized as follows: Section 2 presents the functionality of the system. Section 3 describes the transformation procedure of OWL constructors into COOL. Section 4 briefly describes the rule language of O-DEVICE. Section 5 presents related work on rule systems on top of ontologies. Finally, Section 6 concludes with a summary and potential future work.

2 O-DEVICE Functionality

In this section we describe in details of the O-DEVICE system architecture and functionality (Fig. 1) and the way of each component participates in the data flow.

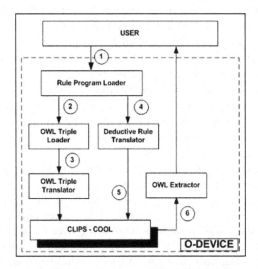

Fig. 1. Architecture of O-DEVICE

System components: The system consists of five basic modules.

i) Rule Program Loader: Accepts from the user the URL of a RuleML file and saves it locally. The rule file also contains information about the location of the OWL files, the names of the derived classes to be exported as results and the name of the output OWL file. The *Rule Program Loader* scans the rule file and collects the appropriate information for later use. The RuleML program is translated into the native O-DEVICE rule notation using an XSLT stylesheet.

ii) OWL Triple Loader: Accepts from the *Rule Program Loader* the URLs of the OWL files that has found from the RuleML document and saves them locally. Furthermore, it uses the ARP Parser [15] to translate the OWL document in the N-Triple format and saves them locally too. The triple loader has been implemented as an extension of the R-DEVICE system [2], which imports RDF Schema ontologies and RDF data into CLIPS.

iii) Deductive Rule Translator: Accepts from the *Rule Program Loader* the set of O-DEVICE rules and translates them into a set of CLIPS production rules. CLIPS runs the production rules and generates the objects that constitute the result of the rule program.

iv) OWL Triple Translator: Accepts from the *OWL Triple Loader* the produced triples from the ARP parser and transforms them into classes, properties and objects of COOL according to the mapping scheme which is described later.

v) OWL Extractor: Accepts objects generated (derived) by the production rules and exports them to the user as an OWL document.

Data flow: The data flow of the system can be considered as a 6-step procedure (Fig. 1): the user inputs (*step 1*) the URL of the RuleML rule file to the *Rule Program Loader*, which downloads it. The *Rule Program Loader* scans the rule file to target the relevant OWL documents and passes theirs URLs to the *OWL Triple Loader* (*step 2*). It uses the ARP Parser to translate the OWL document in the N-Triple format and passes the produced triples to the *OWL Triple Translator* (*step 3*) which transforms them into classes, properties and objects of COOL. The O-DEVICE rule program (from the translation of the RuleML file) is then forwarded to the *Deductive Rule Translator (step 4)* which translates them into a set of CLIPS production rules. After the translation of deductive rules or the loading of the compiled rules, CLIPS runs the production rules (*step 5*) and generates the objects that constitute the result of the rule program. The result-objects are exported to the user (*step 6*) as an OWL document through the *OWL Extractor*.

3 OWL Constructor Transformation

The transformation procedure of OWL constructors is a critical task which affects both the quality of results and the performance of the system. Careful design must be made in order (a) to preserve the open-world OWL semantics by exploiting the available constructs of COOL, whenever possible, (b) to define incremental, rule-based algorithms to emulate some of the semantics that could not be directly mapped to COOL and (c) to make the system efficient enough to complete the tasks in a reasonable amount of time.

3.1 Basic Transformation Principles

The mapping scheme of OWL ontologies and data to objects tries to exploit as many built-in features of COOL as possible, in order to query and reason about OWL objects faster. The main features of the mapping scheme are the following:

Built-in OWL classes: These classes are represented both as classes and as objects, instances of the `rdfs:Class` class. This binary representation is due to the fact that COOL does not support meta-classes, so the role of meta-class is played by the instances of `rdfs:Class` class.

meta-classes: Meta-classes are needed in order to store certain information about a class. So, for example, the OWL class *Male* (in section 3.2.1) is represented in O-DEVICE both by a `defclass Male` construct and a `[Male]` object that is an instance of the `owl:Class` class.

User-defined classes: They follow the same scheme except for the fact that the "meta-class" objects are instances of the class `owl:Class`. Inheritance issues of class hierarchies are treated by the class-inheritance mechanism of COOL, for inheriting properties from superclasses to subclasses, for including the extensions of subclasses to the extensions of the superclasses and for the transitivity of the `rdfs:subClassOf` property.

OWL data: All OWL data (resources) are represented as COOL objects, direct or indirect instances of the `owl:Thing` class.

Properties: Properties are instances of the class `owl:DatatypeProperty` or `owl:ObjectProperty`. This also includes subclasses of the above classes, such as `owl:TransitiveProperty`. Furthermore, properties are defined as slots (attributes) of their domain class(es). The values of properties are stored inside resource objects as slot values. OWL properties are multislots, i.e. they store lists of values, because a resource can have multiple times the same property attached to it.

3.2 Preserving OWL Semantics

O-DEVICE currently handles ontologies in OWL DL, which supports rich expressiveness and gives computational guarantees. In the subsections below, we describe how the system handles some of the OWL constructors, in order to preserve their semantics, giving for each case a short example. A complete list of all transformations can be found in [17].

3.2.1 Property Restrictions
Value constraints are declared with the properties `owl:allValuesFrom`, `owl:someValuesFrom`, `owl:hasValue` and the cardinality constrains with the properties `owl:cardinality`, `owl:minCardinality`, `owl:maxCardinality`.

Restriction owl:hasValue
The `owl:hasValue` constraint is partly implemented using the built-in mechanism of COOL for handling default values. We can declare a *default* value for a slot, making all the instances of the class to have by default this value, if a value is not provided when creating the instance. The following example describes the class of `Male`:

```
<owl:Class rdf:ID="Male">
   <rdfs:subClassOf rdf:resource="#Human"/>
   <rdfs:subClassOf>
      <owl:Restriction>
         <owl:onProperty rdf:resource="#hasGender" />
         <owl:hasValue rdf:resource="#male" />
      </owl:Restriction>
   </rdfs:subClassOf>
</owl:Class>
```

Assuming that there is a class named `Human` with a property `hasGender`, the above example is represented in COOL as follows:

```
(defclass example:Male (is-a example:Human gen1)
   (multislot example:hasGender (type INSTANCE-NAME)
              (default [example:male])))
```

For all instances of class `Male` that do not have any value for slot example:`hasGender`, the value of property `hasGender` will be `[example:male]`. If an instance is created that does have a value for that slot, then a check is performed to see whether the default value is a member of the multislot, otherwise it is added. Such a behaviour is an extension of the simple semantics of the CLIPS default mechanism.

Restriction owl:cardinality
Cardinality restrictions are handled directly via the *cardinality* mechanism of COOL. Consider the following example of `owl:cardinality` property stating that a `Human` has only one biological mother (`hasBiologicalMother` property):

```
<owl:Class rdf:ID="Human">
  <rdfs:subClassOf>
    <owl:Restriction>
      <owl:onProperty rdf:resource="#hasBiologicalMother" />
      <owl:cardinality rdf:datatype="&xsd;nonNegativeInteger">1
      </owl:cardinality>
    </owl:Restriction>
  </rdfs:subClassOf>
</owl:Class>
```

The representation of class Human in COOL is as follows:

```
(defclass example:Human (is-a gen1)
    (multislot example:hasBiologicalMother
        (type INSTANCE-NAME)(cardinality 1 1)))
```

By this definition, the property hasBiologicalMother can take only one value. If more than one values are to be placed in the slot, the system will ignore the others, keeping only the first. For owl:maxCardinality and owl:minCardinality we follow the same implementation using (cardinality ?VARIABLE <value>) and (cardinality <value> ?VARIABLE) respectively.

3.2.2 Boolean Combination of Classes

In OWL it is possible to create new classes by combining existing classes through Boolean operators. For example, the owl:unionOf property links a class to a list of class descriptions and defines the new class extension as those individuals that occur in at least one of the class extensions of the class descriptions in the list. We describe the use of this property using the following simple example.

```
<owl:Class rdf:ID="Fruit">
  <owl:unionOf rdf:parseType="Collection">
    <owl:Class rdf:about="#SweetFruit" />
    <owl:Class rdf:about="#NonSweetFruit" />
  </owl:unionOf>
</owl:Class>
```

Union of classes is implemented as a common superclass. O-DEVICE handles the above example as follows:

```
(defclass example:Fruit (is-a owl:Thing))
(defclass example:NonSweetFruit (is-a example:Fruit))
(defclass example:SweetFruit (is-a example:Fruit))
```

Notice that if the classes NonSweetFruit and SweetFruit have already been defined, then the OO schema should be re-defined at run-time. This includes backing-up all instances and definitions of the re-defined class(es), deleting all instances of the re-defined class(es), including their subclasses, un-defining the re-defined classes (and subclasses) and, finally, re-defining the class(es) and restoring their instances.

3.2.3 Special Properties

In OWL several special characteristics of properties can be defined such as transitivity, symmetry, etc. For example, when a property P is symmetric then if the pair (x,y) is an instance of P, then the pair (y,x) is also an instance of P. Consider the example:

```
<owl:Class rdf:ID="Human" />
<owl:SymmetricProperty rdf:ID="friendOf">
  <rdfs:domain rdf:resource="#Human"/>
  <rdfs:range  rdf:resource="#Human"/>
</owl:SymmetricProperty>
<Human rdf:ID="george"><friendOf rdf:resource="#nick"/></Human>
<Human rdf:ID="nick" />
```

The above example states that george is friendOf nick but because friendOf is symmetric, the system infers that nick is also friendOf george. The corresponding instances in O-DEVICE are:

```
[example:nick] of example:Human        [example:george] of example:Human
(uri example:nick)                     (uri example:george)
.....                                  .....
(example:friendOf [example:george])    (example:friendOf [example:nick])
```

Notice that the materialization of special property characteristics is incremental, i.e. their algorithms will be applied to all future individuals. In this way, our mapping scheme is compatible to the open-world semantics of OWL. Notice, however, that currently our mapping scheme does not handle the existential OWL construct.

4 The Deductive Rule Language of O-DEVICE

The deductive rule language of O-DEVICE supports inferencing over OWL instances represented as objects and defines materialized views over them, possibly incrementally maintained. The conclusions of deductive rules represent derived classes, i.e. classes whose objects are generated by evaluating these rules over the current set of objects. Furthermore, the language supports recursion, stratified negation, path expressions over the objects, generalized path expressions (i.e. path expressions with an unknown number of intermediate steps), derived and aggregate attributes ([2], [3], [4]). Each deductive rule in O-DEVICE is implemented as a CLIPS production rule that inserts a derived object when the condition of the deductive rule is satisfied.

The following rule retrieves the names of all Woman instances that have a value less than 22 in the age property by deriving instances of class young-woman with the value ?fname in the fname property:

```
(deductiverule young-women
  (test:Woman (test:age ?x&:(< ?x 22)) (test:fname ?fname))
  =>
  (young-woman (fname ?fname)))
```

The above deductive rule refers to the following OWL document:

```
<owl:Class rdf:ID="Human" />
<owl:Class rdf:ID="Man">
  <rdfs:subClassOf rdf:resource="#Human" />
</owl:Class>
<owl:Class rdf:ID="Woman" >
  <owl:complementOf rdf:resource="#Man" />
  <rdfs:subClassOf rdf:resource="#Human" />
</owl:Class>
```

Assuming that there are two datatype properties in class Human, namely fname (string) and age (integer), we can see that the class Woman is complementOf the class Man and both classes are subClassOf the class Human.

The above deductive rule is translated into the following CLIPS production rule:

```
(defrule gen1-gen3
  (object (name ?gen2) (is-a test:Human & ~test:Man)
          (test:age ?x&:(< ?x 22)) (test:fname ?fname))
  =>
  (bind ?oid (symbol-to-instance-name (sym-cat young-woman ?fname)))
  (make-instance ?oid of young-woman (fname ?fname)))
```

Notice that the class Woman of the deductive rule is replaced by the "not" connective constraint ~Man in the is-a constraint of the production rule condition, meaning that objects of all but the Man class are retrieved. In this way, we are able to implement the strong negation of OWL into a production rule environment where the closed world assumption holds and only negation-as-failure exists. Of course, the answers to the above rule depend on the time the query runs. If further OWL instances are added and the query is re-run, a different answer will be obtained. This means that the answer involves only the currently existing instances, i.e. it follows the closed-world assumption. However, the non-monotonic semantics of our rule language (incremental materialization) compensates for future changes in the knowledge base, thus we are able to cope with the open-world semantics of OWL. Furthermore, notice that the superclass Human of Woman class is also added in the is-a constraint to avoid searching for all completely irrelevant to this taxonomy objects.

The action-part of the above production rule simply creates the derived object, after generating an OID based on the class name and the derived object's property values. Maintainable deductive rules have a more complex translation.

The semantics of CLIPS production rules are the usual production rule semantics: rules whose condition is successfully matched against the current data are triggered and placed in the conflict set. The conflict resolution mechanism selects a single rule for firing its action, which may alter the data. In subsequent cycles, new rules may be triggered or un-triggered based on the data modifications. The criteria for selecting rules for the conflict set may be priority-based or heuristically based. Rule condition matching is performed incrementally, through the RETE algorithm.

5 Related Work

A lot of effort has been made to develop rule engines for reasoning on top of OWL ontologies. SweetJess [12] is an implementation of a defeasible reasoning system (situated courteous logic programs) based on Jess that integrates well with RuleML. However, SweetJess rules can only express reasoning over ontologies expressed in DAMLRuleML (a DAML-OIL like syntax of RuleML) and not on arbitrary OWL data. Furthermore, SweetJess is restricted to simple terms (variables and atoms).

SweetProlog [14] is a system for translating rules into Prolog. This is achieved via a translation of OWL ontologies and rules expressed in OWLRuleML into a set of facts and rules in Prolog. It makes use of three languages: Prolog as a rule engine, OWL as an ontology and OWLRuleML as a rule language. It enables reasoning (through backward chaining) over OWL ontologies by rules via a translation of OWL subsets into simple Prolog predicates which a JIProlog engine can handle. There are five principle functions that characterize SweetProlog: a) translation of OWL and OWLRuleML ontologies into RDF triples, b) translation of OWL assertions into

Prolog, c) translation of OWLRuleML rules into CLP, d) transformation of CLP rules into Prolog and e) interrogation of the output logic programs.

DR-Prolog [7] is a Prolog-based system for defeasible reasoning on the Web. The system is a) syntactically compatible with RuleML, b) features strict and defeasible rules, priorities and two kinds of negation, c) is based on a translation to logic programming with declarative semantics, and d) can reason with rules, RDF, RDF Schema and part of OWL ontologies. It supports monotonic and non-monotonic rules, open and closed world assumption and reasoning with inconsistencies.

SWRL [13] is a rule language based on a combination of OWL with the Unary/Binary Datalog sublanguages of RuleML. SWRL enables Horn-like rules to be combined with an OWL knowledge base. Negation is not explicitly supported by the SWRL language, but only indirectly through OWL DL (e.g. class complements). Its main purpose is to provide a formal meaning of OWL ontologies and extend OWL DL. There is a concrete implementation of SWRL, called Hoolet. Hoolet translates the ontology to a collection of axioms (based on the OWL semantics) which is then given to a first order prover for consistency checking. Hoolet has been extended to handle rules through the addition of a parser for an RDF rule syntax and an extension of the translator to handle rules, based on the semantics of SWRL rules.

SWSL [5] is a logic-based language for specifying formal characterizations of Web services concepts and descriptions of individual services. It includes two sublanguages: SWSL-FOL and SWSL-Rules. The latter is a rule-based sublanguage, which can be used both as a specification and an implementation language. It is designed to provide support for a variety of tasks that range from service profile specification to service discovery, contracting and policy specification. It is a layered language and its core consists of the pure Horn subset of SWSL-Rules.

WRL [1] is a rule-based ontology language for the Semantic Web. It is derived from the ontology component of the Web Service Modeling Language WSML. The language is located in the Semantic Web stack next to the Description Logic based Ontology language OWL. WRL consists of three variants, namely Core, Flight and Full. WRL-Core marks the common core between OWL and WRL and is thus the basic interoperability layer with OWL. WRL-Flight is based on the Datalog subset of F-Logic, with negation-as-failure under the Perfect Model Semantics. WRL-Full is based on full Horn with negation-as-failure under the Well-Founded Semantics.

ROWL [11] system enables users to frame rules in RDF/XML syntax using ontology in OWL. Using XSLT stylesheets, the rules in RDF/XML are transformed into forward-chaining rules in JESS. Further stylesheets transform ontology and instance files into Jess unordered facts that represent triplets. The file with facts and rules are then fed to JESS which enables inferencing and rule invocation.

F-OWL [9] is an ontology inference engine for OWL, which is implemented using Flora-2, an object-oriented knowledge base language and application development platform that translates a unified language of F-logic, HiLog, and Transaction Logic into the XSB deductive engine. Key features of F-OWL include the ability to reason with the OWL ontology model, the ability to support knowledge consistency checking using axiomatic rules defined in Flora-2, and an open application programming interface (API) for Java application integrations.

6   Conclusions and Future Work

In this paper we have presented O-DEVICE, a deductive object-oriented knowledge base system for reasoning over OWL documents. O-DEVICE imports OWL documents into the CLIPS production rule system by transforming OWL ontologies into an object-oriented schema and OWL instances into objects. In this way, when accessing multiple properties of a single OWL instance, few joins are required. The system also features a powerful deductive rule language which supports inferencing over the transformed OWL descriptions. The transformation scheme of OWL to COOL objects is partly based on the underlying COOL object model and partly on the compilation scheme of the deductive rule language. One of the purposes of the transformation is to infer and materialize in advance as much properties for OWL instances as possible under the rich semantics of OWL constructors. In this way we are able to answer deductive queries at run-time much faster, since all the implied relationships have been pre-computed.

Certain features of the descriptive semantics of OWL are still under development. For example, inverse functional properties are currently not handled at all, whereas they should be handled similarly to key properties, as in databases. Furthermore, when two objects have the same value for an inverse functional property it should be concluded that they stand for the same object. Finally, the existential restriction has not also been implemented.

All these interpretations of OWL constructs are currently being implemented by appropriately extending the *OWL Triple Translator* (Fig. 1) with production rules that assert extra triples, which are further treated by the translator. Notice that asserting new properties to an already imported ontology might call for object and/or class re-definitions, which are efficiently handled by the core triple translator of R-DEVICE [2]. Therefore, the triple translator is non-monotonic, and so is the rule language, since it supports stratified negation as failure and incrementally maintained materialized views. The non-monotonic nature of our transformation algorithms is a key to overcome the closed-world nature of the host system and allows us to emulate OWL's open-world semantics.

In the future we plan to deploy the reasoning system as a Web Service and to implement a Semantic Web Service composition system using OWL-S service descriptions and user-defined service composition rules.

Acknowledgments

This work was partially supported by a PENED program (EPAN M.8.3.1, No. 03EΔ73).

References

1. Angele J, Boley H., J. de Bruijn, Fensel D., Hitzler P., Kifer M., Krummenacher R., Lausen H., Polleres A., Studer R., "Web Rule Language (WRL)", Technical Report, http://www.wsmo.org/wsml/wrl/wrl.html
2. Bassiliades N., Vlahavas I., "R-DEVICE: An Object-Oriented Knowledge Base System for RDF Metadata", *International Journal on Semantic Web and Information Systems*, 2(2) (to appear), 2006.

3. Bassiliades N., Vlahavas I., and Elmagarmid A.K., "E DEVICE: An extensible active knowledge base system with multiple rule type support", *IEEE TKDE*, 12(5), pp. 824-844, 2000.

4. Bassiliades N., Vlahavas I., and Sampson D., "Using Logic for Querying XML Data", in *Web-Powered Databases*, Ch. 1, pp. 1-35, Idea-Group Publishing, 2003

5. Battle S., Bernstein A., Boley H., Grosof B., Gruninger M., Hull R., Kifer M., Martin D., McIlraith S., McGuinness D., Su J., Tabet S., "SWSL-rules: A rule language for the semantic web", *W3C rules workshop*, Washington DC, USA, April 2005

6. Berners-Lee T., Hendler J., and Lassila O., "The Semantic Web", *Scientific American*, 284(5), 2001, pp. 34-43.

7. Bikakis A., Antoniou G., DR-Prolog: A System for Reasoning with Rules and Ontologies on the Semantic Web 2005, *Proc. 25th American National Conference on Artificial Intelligence* (AAAI-2005).

8. Boley, H., Tabet, S., and Wagner, G., "Design Rationale of RuleML: A Markup Language for Semantic Web Rules", *Proc. Int. Semantic Web Working Symp.*, pp. 381-402, 2001.

9. Chen H., Zou Y., Kagal L., Finin T., "F-OWL: An OWL Inference Engine in Flora-2", http://fowl.sourceforge.net/

10. CLIPS 6.23 Basic Programming Guide, http://www.ghg.net/clips

11. Gandon F. L., Sheshagiri M., Sadeh N. M., "ROWL: Rule Language in OWL and Translation Engine for JESS", http://mycampus.sadehlab.cs.cmu.edu/public_pages/ROWL/ROWL.html

12. Grosof B.N., Gandhe M.D., Finin T.W., "SweetJess: Translating DAMLRuleML to JESS", *Proc. RuleML Workshop*, 2002.

13. Horrocks I., Patel-Schneider P.F., Boley H., Tabet S., Grosof B., Dean M., "SWRL: A semantic web rule language combining OWL and RuleML", Member submission, May 2004, W3C. http://www.w3.org/Submission/SWRL/

14. Laera L., Tamma V., Bench-Capon T. and Semeraro G., "SweetProlog: A System to Integrate Ontologies and Rules", *3rd Int. Workshop on Rules and Rule Markup Languages for the Semantic Web (RuleML 2004)*, Springer-Verlag, LNCS 3323, pp. 188-193.

15. McBride B., "Jena: Implementing the RDF Model and Syntax Specification", *Proc. 2nd Int. Workshop on the Semantic Web*, 2001

16. Meditskos G., Bassiliades N., "Towards an Object-Oriented Reasoning System for OWL", *Int. Workshop on OWL Experiences and Directions,* 11-12 Nov. 2005, Galway, Ireland, 2005.

17. O-DEVICE web page, http://iskp.csd.auth.gr/systems/o-device/o-device.html

18. Rule Interchange Format Working Group, W3C, http://www.w3.org/2005/rules/wg

19. Web Ontology Language (OWL), http://www.w3.org/2004/OWL/

Abduction for Extending Incomplete Information Sources

Carlo Meghini[1], Yannis Tzitzikas[2], and Nicolas Spyratos[3]

[1] Consiglio Nazionale delle Ricerche, Istituto della Scienza e delle Tecnologie della Informazione, Pisa, Italy
`meghini@isti.cnr.it`
[2] Department of Computer Science, University of Crete, Heraklion, Crete, Greece
`tzitzik@csi.forth.gr`
[3] Université Paris-Sud, Laboratoire de Recherche en Informatique, Orsay Cedex, France
`spyratos@lri.fr`

Abstract. The extraction of information from a source containing term-classified objects is plagued with uncertainty, due, among other things, to the possible incompleteness of the source index. To overcome this incompleteness, the study proposes to expand the index of the source, in a way that is as reasonable as possible with respect to the original classification of objects. By equating reasonableness with logical implication, the sought expansion turns out to be an explanation of the index, captured by abduction. We study the general problem of query evaluation on the extended information source, providing a polynomial time algorithm which tackles the general case, in which no hypothesis is made on the structure of the taxonomy. We then specialize the algorithm for two well-know structures: DAGs and trees, showing that each specialization results in a more efficient query evaluation.

1   Introduction

The extraction of information from an information source (hereafter, IS) containing term-classified objects is plagued with uncertainty. From the one hand, the indexing of objects, that is the assignment of a set of terms to each object, presents many difficulties, whether it is performed manually by some expert or automatically by a computer programme. In the former case, subjectivity may play a negative role (e.g. see [4]); in the latter case, automatic classification methods may at best produce approximations. On the other hand, the query formulation process, being linguistic in nature, would require perfect attuning of the system and the user language, an assumption that simply does not hold in open settings such as the Web.

A collection of textual documents accessed by users via natural language queries is clearly a kind of IS, where documents play the role of objects and words play the role of terms. In this context, the above mentioned uncertainty is typically dealt with in a quantitative way, i.e. by means of numerical methods:

G. Antoniou et al. (Eds.): SETN 2006, LNAI 3955, pp. 267–278, 2006.

in a document index, each term is assigned a *weight,* expressing the extent to which the document is deemed to be about the term. The same treatment is applied to each user query, producing an index of the query which is a formal representation of the user information need of the same kind as that of each document. Document and query term indexes are then matched against each other in order to estimate the relevance of the document to a query (e.g. see [1]).

In the present study, we take a different approach, and deal with uncertainty in a *qualitative* way. We view an IS as an agent, operating according to an open world philosophy. The agent knows some facts, but it does not interpret these facts as the only ones that hold; the agent is somewhat aware that there could be other facts, compatible with the known ones, that might hold as well, although they are not captured for lack of knowledge. These facts are, indeed, *possibilities.* One way of defining precisely in logical terms the notion of possibility, is to equate it with the notion of *explanation.* That is, the set of terms associated to an object is viewed as a *manifestation* of a phenomenon, the indexing process, for which we wish to find an explanation, justifying why the index itself has come to be the way it is. In logic, the reasoning required to infer explanations from given theory and observations, is known as *abduction.* We will therefore resort to abduction in order to define precisely the possibilities that we want our system to be able to handle. In particular, we will define an operation that extends an IS by adding to it a set (term, object) pairs capturing the sought possibilities, and then study the property of this operation from a mathematical point of view. The introduced operation can be used also for ordering query answers using a *possibility*-based measure of relevance.

2   Information Sources

Definition 1. An *information source* (IS) S is a pair $S = (O, U)$ where (a) O, the *taxonomy,* is a pair $O = (T, K)$ where T is a finite set of symbols, called the *terms* of the taxonomy, and K is a finite set of conditionals on T, *i.e.* formulas of the form $p \rightarrow q$ where p and q are different terms of the taxonomy; (b) U is a *structure on* O, that is a pair $U = (Obj, I)$ where Obj is a countable set of objects, called the *domain* of the structure, and I is a finite relation from T to Obj, that is $I \subseteq T \times Obj$. K is called the *knowledge base* of the taxonomy, while I is called the *interpretation* of the structure.

As customary, we will sometimes write $I(t)$ to denote the set $I(t) = \{o \in Obj \mid (t, o) \in I\}$, which we call the *extension* of term t. Dually, given an object $o \in Obj$, the *index of* o *in* S, $ind_S(o)$, is given by the set of terms which have o in their extension: $ind_S(o) = \{t \in T \mid (t, o) \in I\}$. Finally, the *context of* o *in* S, $C_S(o)$, is defined as: $C_S(o) = ind_S(o) \cup K$. For any object o, $C_S(o)$ consists of terms and simple conditionals that collectively form all the knowledge about o that S has.

Example 1.   Throughout the paper, we will use as an example the IS $S = ((T, K), (Obj, I))$ given in the righthand side of Figure 1. The lefthand side of the Figure graphically illustrates the taxonomy of S.

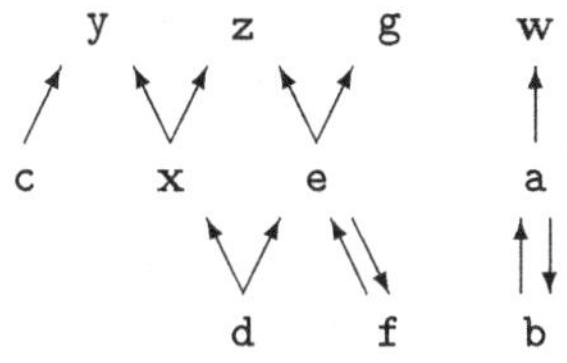

y   z   g   w

c   x   e   a $T = \{a, b, c, d, e, f, g, w, x, y, z\}$

$K = \{c \to y,\ x \to y,\ x \to z,\ d \to x,\ d \to e,\ e \to z,$

$\qquad e \to g,\ e \to f,\ f \to e,\ a \to w,\ a \to b,\ b \to a\}$

d   f   b $Obj = \{1\}$

$I = \{(x, 1),\ (w, 1)\}$

Fig. 1. An information source

We focus on ISs which satisfy an intuitive minimality criterion, to introduce which a few basic notions from propositional logic are now recalled [3]. Given a set of propositional variables P, a *truth assignment for P* is a function mapping P to the true and false truth values, respectively denoted by **T** and **F**. A truth assignment V *satisfies* a sentence σ of the propositional calculus (PC), $V \models \sigma$, if σ is true in V, according to the classical truth valuation rules of PC. A set of sentences Σ *logically implies* the sentence α, $\Sigma \models \alpha$, iff every truth assignment which satisfies every sentence in Σ also satisfies α.

The *instance set* of an object o in an IS S, denoted as $N_S(o)$, is the set of terms that are logically implied by the context of o in S : $N_S(o) = \{t \in T \mid C_S(o) \models t\}$. For each term t in $N_S(o)$, we will say that o is an *instance* of t. Clearly, $ind_S(o) \subseteq N_S(o)$, therefore o is an instance of each term in $ind_S(o)$.

Definition 2. The index of object o in IS S, $ind_S(o)$, is *non-redundant* iff

$$A \subset ind_S(o) \text{ implies } \{v \in T \mid A \cup K \models v\} \subset N_S(o).$$

An IS is *non-redundant* if all its indices are non-redundant.

In practice, the index of an object is non-redundant if no term in it can be removed without loss of information. It can be easily verified that the IS introduced in the previous example is non-redundant. From now on, we will consider "IS" as a synonym of "non-redundant IS".

Definition 3. Given a taxonomy $O = (T, K)$, the *query language for O, $\mathcal{L}_O$,* is defined by the following grammar, where t is a term in T:

$$q ::= t \mid q \wedge q' \mid q \vee q' \mid \neg q \mid (q)$$

Any expression in $\mathcal{L}_O$ is termed a *query*. Given an IS $S = (O, U)$, for every object $o \in Obj$, the *truth model of o in S, $V_{o,S}$,* is the truth assignment for T defined as follows, for each term $t \in T$:

$$V_{o,S}(t) = \begin{cases} \mathbf{T} \text{ if } C_S(o) \models t \\ \mathbf{F} \text{ otherwise} \end{cases}$$

Given a query φ in $\mathcal{L}_O$, the *answer of φ in S* is the set of objects whose truth model satisfies the query:

$$ans(\varphi, S) = \{o \in Obj \mid V_{o,S} \models \varphi\}.$$

In the Boolean model of information retrieval, a document is returned in response to a query if the index of the document satisfies the query. Thus, the above definition extends Boolean retrieval by considering also the knowledge base in the retrieval process.

Query evaluation requires the computation of the truth model of each object o, which in turn requires deciding whether each query term is logically implied by the object context $C_S(o)$. Computing propositional logical implication is in general a difficult task. However, the specific form of the propositional theories considered in this study, makes this computation much simpler, as the remainder of this Section shows. In order to devise an efficient query evaluation procedure, we will resort to graph theoretic concepts.

The *term graph* of a taxonomy O is the directed graph $G_O = (T, E)$, such that $(t, t') \in E$ iff $t \to t'$ is in K. Figure 1 shows indeed the term graph of the example IS. For simplicity, we will use "term" also to refer to a vertex of the term graph. The *tail of a term* t in G_O, *tail(t)*, is the set of terms that can be reached from t by walking the graph edges backward, that is:

$$tail(t) = \{u \in T \mid \text{ there exists a path from } u \text{ to } t \text{ in } G_O\}$$

Proposition 1. For all ISs S and queries $\varphi \in \mathcal{L}_O$, $ans(\varphi, S) = \alpha_S(\varphi)$, where α_S is the *solver* of the IS S, defined as follows:

$$\alpha_S(t) = \bigcup \{I(u) \mid u \in tail(t)\}$$
$$\alpha_S(q \wedge q') = \alpha_S(q) \cap \alpha_S(q')$$
$$\alpha_S(q \vee q') = \alpha_S(q) \cup \alpha_S(q')$$
$$\alpha_S(\neg q) = Obj \setminus \alpha_S(q)$$

The proof of the Proposition relies on structural induction on the query language and on the following Lemma: Given an IS S, a set of terms $A \subseteq T$ and a term $t \in T$, $A \cup K \models t$ iff there is a path in G_O from a letter in A to t.

Example 2. In the IS previously introduced, the term z can be reached in the term graph by each of the following terms: z, x, d, e, f. Hence, $tail(z) = \{z, x, d, e, f\}$. According to the last Proposition, then: $ans(z, S) = \alpha_S(z) = I(z) \cup I(x) \cup I(d) \cup I(e) \cup I(f) = \{1\}$.

As a consequence of the last Proposition, we have that $\alpha_S(t)$ can be computed in $O(|T| \cdot |Obj| \cdot log\,|Obj|)$ time. Indeed, computing $\alpha_S(t)$ requires the following steps: (a) to derive *tail(t)* by searching the term graph in order to identify every vertex that is backward reachable from t; (b) to access the extension of each term in *tail(t)*; and (c) to compute the union of the involved extensions. The time complexity of step (a) is $|T|^2$, corresponding to the case in which every term is backward reachable from t in the term graph. We assume that step (b) can be performed in constant time, which is negligible with respect to the other values at stake. Let us now consider step (c). By adopting a merge-sort strategy, the union between two extensions can be performed in $n\,log\,n$ time in the size of the input. Since in the worst case the union of $|T|$ extensions must be computed, and each extension is the whole set Obj, we have a $O(|T| \cdot |Obj| \cdot log\,|Obj|)$ time complexity for step (c). Overall, the upper bound for evaluating single-term queries is therefore $O(|T|^2 + |T| \cdot |Obj| \cdot log\,|Obj|)$. Since the size of the domain is expected to be significantly larger than the size of the terminology, the sought upper bound for singles-term queries evaluation is $O(|T| \cdot |Obj| \cdot log\,|Obj|)$.

3 Extended Information Sources

Let us suppose that a user has issued a query against an IS and is not satisfied with the answer, as the answer does not contain objects that are relevant to the user information need. Further, let us assume that the user is not willing to replace the current query with another one, for instance because of lack of knowledge on the available language or taxonomy. In this type of situation, database systems offer practically no support, as they are based on the assumption that users can always articulate their information need in the form of a query. In an information retrieval setting a user in the above described situation could use relevance feedback to pinpoint interesting (relevant) or uninteresting objects among those returned by the system, and ask the system to re-evaluate the query taking into account this information; but what if all the displayed objects are not relevant? In all these, and probably other, cases, the index of the IS suffers from *incompleteness*: it contains correct information, but at least in some cases not *all* the correct information. In other words, there are other facts, compatible with the known ones, which hold as well, although they are not captured for *lack of knowledge.*

To overcome this lack of knowledge, the idea is to relax the index, by expanding it, in a way that is as *reasonable* as possible with respect to the original classification of objects. But what could be a reasonable expansion? By reasonable expansion we mean a *logically grounded* expansion, that is an expansion that *logically implies* the index as it has been created in the first place. Then, the expansion we are talking about is in fact a logical *explanation* of the index. The most general form of explanation in logic is *abduction,* seen as the generation of causes to explain the observed effects of known laws. In our case, the known laws are the sentences of the IS knowledge base, the observed effects are contents of the index, while the cause is the sought index expansion. We will therefore resort to abduction in order to define precisely the expansion that would address the incompleteness of the index.

3.1 Propositional Abduction Problems

The model of abduction that we adopt is the one presented in [2]. Let $\mathcal{L}_V$ be the language of propositional logic over a finite alphabet V of propositional variables. A *propositional abduction problem* is a tuple $\mathcal{A} = \langle V, H, M, Th \rangle$, where $H \subseteq V$ is the set of hypotheses, $M \subseteq V$ is the manifestation, and $Th \subseteq \mathcal{L}_V$ is a consistent theory. $S \subseteq H$ is a solution (or explanation) for $\mathcal{A}$ iff $Th \cup S$ is consistent and $Th \cup S \models M$. $Sol(\mathcal{A})$ denotes the set of the solutions to $\mathcal{A}$. In the context of an IS S, we will consider each object separately. Thus,

– the terms in T play both the role of the propositional variables V and of the hypotheses H, as there is no reason to exclude *apriori* any term from an explanation;
– the knowledge base K plays the role of the theory Th;
– the role of manifestation is played by the index of the object.

Definition 4. Given an IS $S = (O, U)$ and object $o \in Obj$, the *propositional abduction problem for o in S*, $\mathcal{A}_S(o)$, is the propositional abduction problem $\mathcal{A}_S(o) = \langle T, T, ind_S(o), K \rangle$.

The solutions to $\mathcal{A}_S(o)$ are given by:

$$Sol(\mathcal{A}_S(o)) = \{A \subseteq T \mid K \cup A \models ind_S(o)\}$$

where the consistency requirement on $K \cup A$ has been omitted since for no knowledge base K and set of terms A, $K \cup A$ can be inconsistent. Usually, certain explanations are preferable to others, a fact that is formalized in [2] by defining a preference relation $\preceq$ over $Sol(\mathcal{A})$. Letting $a \prec b$ stand for $a \preceq b$ and $b \not\preceq a$, the set of preferred solutions is given by:

$$Sol_{\prec}(\mathcal{A}) = \{S \in Sol(\mathcal{A}) \mid \nexists S' \in Sol(\mathcal{A}) : S' \prec S\}.$$

Also in the present context a preference relation is desirable, satisfying criteria that reflect the goals of our framework. Here are these criteria, in order of decreasing importance:

1. explanations including only terms in the manifestation are less preferable, as they do not provide any additional information;
2. explanations altering the behavior of the IS to a minimal extent are preferable; this requirement acts in the opposite direction of the previous one, by making preferable solutions that, if incorporated in the IS, minimize the differences in behavior between the so extended IS and the original one;
3. between two explanations that alter the behavior of the IS equally, the simpler one is to be preferred. As explanations are sets, it is natural to equate simplicity with smallness in size.

All the above criteria can be expressed in terms of the effects produced by the extension of an IS, which we term "perturbation".

Definition 5. Given an IS $S = (O, U)$, an object $o \in Obj$ and a set of terms $A \subseteq T$, the *perturbation of A on S with respect to o*, $pert_o(A)$ is given by:

$$pert_o(A) = \{t \in T \mid (C_S(o) \cup A) \models t \text{ and } C_S(o) \not\models t\}$$

that is the set of additional terms in the instance set of o once the index of o is extended with the terms in A.

We can now define the preference relation over solutions of the above stated abduction problem.

Definition 6. Given an IS $S = (O, U)$, an object $o \in Obj$ and two solutions A and A' to the problem $\mathcal{A}_S(o)$, $A \preceq A'$ if either of the following holds:

1. $pert_o(A') = \emptyset$
2. $0 < |pert_o(A)| < |pert_o(A')|$
3. $0 < |pert_o(A)| = |pert_o(A')|$ and $A \subseteq A'$.

The strict correspondence between the clauses in the last Definition and the criteria previously set for the preference relation should be evident. Solutions having an empty perturbation are obviously subsets of the instance set of the object, therefore the first condition of the last Definition captures the first of the three criteria. The second condition establishes preference for solutions that minimize the number of terms that change their truth value from **F** to **T** in the truth model of the object, and thus alter the behavior of the IS *with respect to query answering* to a minimal extent. Between two solutions producing the same alteration, the third condition makes preferable the smaller in size, and so simplicity, criterion number three, is implemented.

We now introduce the notion of *extension* of an IS. The idea is that an extended IS (EIS for short) includes, for each object, the terms of the original index plus those added through the abduction process illustrated above. However, in so doing, non-redundancy may be compromised, since no constraint is posed on the solutions of the abduction problem in order to avoid it. There can be two sources of redundancy when extending a non-redundant index with the solutions to an abduction problem: (1) a solution to an abduction problem may contain taxonomical cycles, and including a whole cycle in the index of an object clearly violates non-redundancy (all terms in the cycle but one can be removed without losing information); and (2) a term in a solution may be a direct descendant of a term in the index. The coexistence of these two terms in the new index violates redundancy, thus the latter can be added only if the former is removed. In order to cope with the former problem, we introduce the operator ρ, which takes as input a set of terms and replaces each cycle occurring in it by any term in the cycle. In order to cope with the latter problem, we introduce a special union operator $\sqcup$ which takes as input two interpretations and adds each pair (t, o) of the second interpretation to the first interpretation after removing any pair (u, o) in the first interpretation such that $t \rightarrow u \in K$. Formally,

$$I_1 \sqcup I_2 = I_2 \cup \{(t, o) \in I_1 \mid \text{for no pair } (v, o) \in I_2, \ v \rightarrow t \in K\}.$$

Definition 7. Given an IS $S = (O, U)$ and an object $o \in Obj$, the *abduced index* of o, $abind_S(o)$, is given by:

$$abind_S(o) = \bigcup Sol \ (\mathcal{A}_S(o)) \setminus ind_S(o).$$

The *abduced interpretation of S*, I^+, is given by

$$I^+ = I \sqcup \{\langle t, o \rangle \mid o \in Obj \text{ and } t \in \rho(abind_S(o))\}.$$

Finally, the *extended* IS, S^e, is given by $S^e = (O, U^e)$ where $U^e = (Obj, I^+)$.

3.2   Querying Extended Information Sources

A key role in solving propositional abduction problems is played by single-letter solutions (SLSs). Given an IS S, an object o and a term $t \in T \setminus N_S(o)$, the *single-letter solution of t* is the set $\mu(t)$ given by:

$$\mu(t) = \{t\} \cup (ind_S(o) \setminus \sigma(t))$$

where $\sigma(t) = \{u \in T \mid$ there is a path in G_O from t to $u\}$. It can be proven that, for any IS S, object $o \in Obj$ and term $t \in T$, $\mu(t)$ is a solution to $\mathcal{A}_S(o)$ whose perturbation is given by $pert_o(\mu(t)) = \sigma(t) \setminus N_S(o)$. Moreover, if $t \notin N_S(o)$, $\mu(t)$ has the smallest perturbation among the solutions to $\mathcal{A}_S(o)$ including t.

Example 3. Let us consider again the IS S introduced in Example 1, and the problem $\mathcal{A}_S(1)$. The manifestation is given by $ind_S(1) = \{w, x\}$ while $N_S(1) = \{x, y, z, w\}$. Table 1 gives, for each term in $T \setminus N_S(1)$, the σ value, the single-letter solution and its perturbation.

We can now state the main result on query answering in EIS.

Table 1. The single-letter solutions of $\mathcal{A}_S(1)$ and their perturbations

t	$\sigma(t)$	$\mu(t)$	$pert_o(\mu(t))$
a	$\{w, a, b\}$	$\{a, x\}$	$\{a, b\}$
b	$\{w, a, b\}$	$\{b, x\}$	$\{a, b\}$
c	$\{c, y\}$	$\{c, x, w\}$	$\{c\}$
d	$\{d, x, y, z, e, f, g\}$	$\{d, w\}$	$\{d, e, f, g\}$
e	$\{e, f, z, g\}$	$\{e, x, w\}$	$\{e, f, g\}$
f	$\{f, e, z, g\}$	$\{f, x, w\}$	$\{e, f, g\}$
g	$\{g\}$	$\{g, x, w\}$	$\{g\}$

Proposition 2. For all ISs S and terms $t \in T$, $ans(t, S^e) = \alpha_{S^e}(t) = \alpha_S(t) \cup \beta(t)$, where

$$\beta(t) = \{o \in Obj \mid t \in abind_S(o)\}.$$

By unfolding the relevant definitions, we have that $ans(t, S^e) = \{o \in Obj \mid ind_S(o) \cup K \models t\} \cup \{o \in Obj \mid abind_S(o) \cup K \models t\} = \alpha_S(t) \cup \{o \in Obj \mid abind_S(o) \cup K \models t\}$. As it can be proven, the second term of the last union operation is given by:

$$\alpha_S(t) \cup \{o \in Obj \mid t \in abind_S(o)\},$$

and the Proposition obtains. In turn, the set $abind_S(o)$ is derived, based on the above stated properties of SLSs, as follows:

Proposition 3. Given an IS S and an object $o \in Obj$, let d_o be the least positive perturbation of the solutions to $\mathcal{A}_S(o)$, that is:

$$d_o = min\{|pert_o(A)| \mid A \in Sol(\mathcal{A}_S(o)) \text{ and } pert_o(A) > 0\}.$$

Then, $abind_s(o) = \{t \in T \setminus N_S(o) \mid |\sigma(t) \setminus N_S(o)| = d_o\}$.

Example 4. Let us consider again the problem $\mathcal{A}_S(1)$ of the last Example. From Table 1 and the last Proposition, it follows that $abind_S(1) = \{\mathtt{c}, \mathtt{g}\}$ and that $I^+ = I \cup \{(\mathtt{c}, 1), (\mathtt{g}, 1)\}$.

Proposition 3 suggests the following algorithm for computing $\beta(t)$: for each object $o \in Obj$, select the letters u in $T \setminus N_S(o)$ that minimize the size of $\sigma(u) \setminus N_S(o)$. If t is amongst these letters, $o \in \beta(t)$, otherwise $o \notin \beta(t)$. This allows us to establish that $\alpha_{S^e}(t)$ can be computed in $O(|T| \cdot |Obj|^2 \cdot log\,|Obj|)$ time (the proof is omitted for reasons of space). It follows that query evaluation on EISs worsens complexity by a factor equals to the size of the domain, and is consistent with the complexity results derived from propositional abduction problems [2].

4   Special Information Sources

We conclude this study by applying the ideas developed so far to two special classes of ISs, corresponding to two special structures of the taxonomy. The first class consists of the ISs whose term graphs are directed acyclic graphs (DAGs) with a maximal element $\top$. We call these ISs "hierarchical". Indeed, hierarchical taxonomies are common in object-oriented models, where subsumption is a partial ordering relation amongst classes and maximal elements are introduced in order to tie classes up, thus making each class reachable from the top. The second class includes a special case of the first, that is term graphs that are rooted trees. This kind of taxonomies are common in catalogs, directories and information retrieval systems on the Web.

Proposition 4. Let a *hierarchical* information source (HIS) be an IS whose term graph is a DAG with a greatest element $\top$. Then, for all HISs S and terms $t \in T$, $t \neq \top$, $ans(t, S^e) = \cap \{\alpha_S(u) \mid t \to u \in K\}$.

Accordingly, an object o is in the result of query t against the EIS S^e just in case it is an instance of all the immediate generalizations of t in S. Indeed, if o were an instance of t, it would, as a consequence, be an instance of all t's generalizations, thus the explanation of the current index offered by the system is the most reasonable one can conceive. As a result, the behavior of the query mechanism turns out to be compliant with intuition. Notice that asking the query $\top$ on the extended IS, a case not dealt with by the last Proposition, does not make much sense, since already $ans(\top, S) = Obj$.

Example 5. Let us consider the HIS S having as taxonomy the one shown in Figure 2, where the index of the only object 1 consists of the terms $\mathtt{Miniatures}$ and $\mathtt{MovingPictureCams}$. The problem $\mathcal{A}_S(1)$ has two minimal solutions, given by $\mu(\mathtt{Reflex})$ and $\mu(\mathtt{UnderwaterDevices})$. Thus, object 1 should be returned in response to the query $\mathtt{Reflex}$ on S^e, and in fact $ans(\mathtt{Reflex}, S^e)$ is given by:

$$\cap \{\alpha_S(u) \mid \mathtt{Reflex} \to u \in K\} = \alpha_S(\mathtt{StillCams})$$
$$= I(\mathtt{StillCams}) \cup I(\mathtt{Miniatures}) \cup I(\mathtt{Reflex}) = \{1\}$$

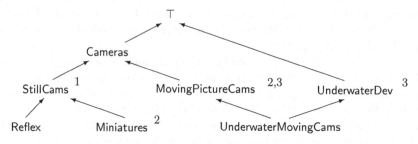

Fig. 2. A hierarchical information source

Letting P stand for S^e and considering $\mathcal{A}_P(1)$, 1 should be included in the answer to the query UnderwaterMovingCams on P^e. Indeed,

$$ans(\text{UnderwaterMovingCams}, P^e) = \cap \{\alpha_P(u) \mid \text{UnderwaterMovingCams} \to u \in K\}$$
$$= \alpha_P(\text{MovingPictureCams}) \cap \alpha_P(\text{UnderwaterDevices}) = \{1\}$$

since 1 is an instance of MovingPictureCams in S and has become an instance of UnderwaterDevices in P.

From a complexity point of view, the Proposition permits to compute an upper bound on the evaluation of queries on an extended HIS. Specifically, it can be proved that $\alpha_{S^e}(t)$, where S is a HIS, can be computed in $O(|T|^2 \cdot |Obj| \cdot log |Obj|)$ time. Table 2 summarizes the complexity results obtained for query evaluation on the classes of IS examined in this study. The last result indicates that the evaluation of queries on extended HISs is worse than that on ISs by a factor proportional to the size of the terminology. This is a significant improvement over the general case, where the factor is proportional to the size of the domain (Proposition 0). This difference reflects the fact that in the general case, $\alpha_{S^e}(t)$ must be computed in an object-based (or class-based) fashion, *i.e.* by considering one object (class) at a time, while the evaluation of $\alpha_{S^e}(t)$ on a HIS proceeds in a term-based fashion, *i.e.* by considering the terms that are immediate successors of t in the term graph. This also simplifies the implementation, as it avoids to compute and keep track of classes.

Table 2. Summary of complexity results for query evaluation

IS type	Complexity
Simple	$O(|T| \cdot |Obj| \cdot log |Obj|)$
Extended	$O(|T| \cdot |Obj|^2 \cdot log |Obj|)$
Extended Hierarchical	$O(|T|^2 \cdot |Obj| \cdot log |Obj|)$
Extended Tree	$O(|T| \cdot |Obj| \cdot log |Obj|)$

Proposition 5. Let a *tree* information source (TIS) be an IS whose term graph is a rooted tree with root $\top$. Then, for all TISs S and terms $t \in T$, $t \neq \top$,

$$ans(t, S^e) = \{\alpha_S(u) \mid t \to u \in K\}.$$

Proof: A TIS is a HIS in which every term different from $\top$ has exactly one immediate successor in the term graph.

The complexity of query evaluation on extended TISs is clearly the same as that on ISs.

5 Ranked Answers

The abduction framework described can be also exploited for obtaining ordered answers. In order to illustrate how, let us use a superscript to indicate the iteration at which an IS is generated, that is, $S = S^0$, $S^e = S^1$, $(S^e)^e = S^2$ and so on. Moreover, let N be the iteration at which the fixed point is reached, *i.e.* $S^{N-1} \subset S^N = S^{N+1} = S^{N+2} = \ldots$. The set of objects that the user will get in response to a query φ on the extensions of the IS S, is given by:

$$answer_S(\varphi) = \bigcup_{i=0}^{N} \alpha_{S^i}(\varphi)$$

We can give all of these objects to the user as a response to the query φ on S, ordered according to the iteration at which each object would start appearing in the answer. In particular, we can define the *rank* of an object $o \in answer_S(\varphi)$, denoted by $rank_S(o, \varphi)$, as follows:

$$rank_S(o, \varphi) = min\{\ k \mid o \in \alpha_{S^k}(\varphi)\}$$

The answer that will be returned by φ on S, the *ranked answer*, is an ordering of sets, i.e. the ordering:

$$rans(\varphi, S) = \langle\{o \mid rank_S(o, \varphi) = 1\}, \ldots, \{o \mid rank_S(o, \varphi) = N\}\rangle$$

For example, consider the hierarchical IS presented in Figure 2, where the extension of each term is shown on the right of the term (*i.e.*, $I(\texttt{MovingPictureCams})$ = $\{2,3\}$). Let suppose that φ = UMC. In this case we have: $\alpha_{S^0}(\texttt{UMC})$ = $\emptyset$, $\alpha_{S^1}(\texttt{UMC})$ = $\{3\}$, $\alpha_{S^2}(\texttt{UMC})\{1,2,3\}$. So the ranked answer to UMC is $rans(\texttt{UMC}, S) = \langle\{3\}, \{1,2\}\rangle$.

6 Conclusions

Indexing accuracy and consistency are difficult to maintain. To alleviate this problem we have proposed a mechanism which allows liberating the index of a source in a gradual manner. This mechanism is governed by the notion of explanation, logically captured by abduction.

The proposed method can be implemented as an answer enlargement[1] process where the user is not required to give additional input, but from expressing his/her desire for more objects. The introduced framework can be also applied for ranking the objects of an answer according to an explanation-based measure of relevance.

---

[1] If the query contains negation then the answer can be reduced.

References

1. R. Baeza-Yates and B. Ribeiro-Neto. *"Modern Information Retrieval"*. ACM Press, Addison-Wesley, 1999.
2. T. Eiter and G. Gottlob. The complexity of logic-based abduction. *Journal of the ACM*, 42(1):3–42, January 1995.
3. H. Enderton. *A mathematical introduction to logic.* Academic Press, N. Y., 1972.
4. P. Zunde and M. Dexter. "Indexing Consistency and Quality". *American Documentation*, 20(3):259–267, July 1969.

Post Supervised Based Learning of Feature Weight Values

Vassilis S. Moustakis

Institute of Computer Science, Foundation for Research and Technology-Hellas (FORTH),
P.O. Box 1385, 71110 Heraklion, Crete, Greece
moustaki@cs.forth.gr
Department of Production and Management Engineering, Technical University of Crete,
University Campus, Kounoupidiana, 73100 Chania, Crete, Greece
moustaki@dpem.tuc.gr

Abstract. The article presents in detail a model for the assessment of feature weight values in context of inductive machine learning. Weight assessment is done based on learned knowledge and can not be used to assess feature values prior to learning. The model is based on Ackoff's theory of behavioral communication. The model is also used to assess rule value importance. We present model heuristics and present a simple application based on the "play" vs. "not play" golf application. Implications about decision making modeling are discussed.

1 Introduction

Often the user of an inductive machine learning (IML) output may wonder about the value importance that learning output implies. Importance may of course be the output itself (such as rules) or in the features IML relied on to generate knowledge. In credit risk assessment the system learns rules [1] yet a user may be interested about the significance of each feature that the system used to generate rules. Such inquiring may also arise in other applications.

The article presents a methodology leading to the assessment of value of features, which are used to represent concepts during IML. IML is supervised learning and is based on a set of training examples, or instances, each of which is known to represent a concept class.

An overview of the instance space on which learning is based is shown in Table 1. There are L training instances, each of which is represented by a set of features $f_1, \ldots, f_M$, Each instance is known to belong to a class C_n where $n = 1, \ldots, N$. Each feature f_i takes values from a domain of values, which may be numeric, symbolic, or binary.

A simple illustration of the learning model presented in Table 1 is provided in Table 2 – illustration is taken from [2]. The simple learning example includes 14 training instances, which are divided in two classes P (for play golf) and N (for not play golf). There are 4 features: (1) *outlook*, with values sunny, overcast, and rain, (2) *temperature*, with values cool, mild and hot, (3) *humidity* with values high and normal, and (4) *windy* with values true and false. The example is used to facilitate presentation of the subject matter and it is used throughout the article.

G. Antoniou et al. (Eds.): SETN 2006, LNAI 3955, pp. 279–289, 2006.
© Springer-Verlag Berlin Heidelberg 2006

Table 1. Representation of training instances in IBL. The last column lists the class to which every training example belongs to. Of course training examples must belong to at least two different classes.

	f_1	f_2		f_M	Class
E_1	$[f_1 = value]$	$[f_2 = value]$	...	$[f_M = value]$	C_n
⋮	⋮	⋮	⋮	⋮	⋮
E_L	$[f_1 = value]$	$[f_2 = value]$	...	$[f_M = value]$	C_n

Table 2. A small IML from instances example. There exist 14 training instances; however, 10 instances are ommited to save space. The full dataset may be found in [2].

Instance	Features				Class
	Outlook (f_1)	Temperature (f_2)	Humidity (f_3)	Windy (f_4)	
E_1	sunny	hot	high	false	N
E_2	sunny	hot	high	true	N
E_3	overcast	hot	high	false	P
...	...	...	...	...	...
E_{14}	rain	mild	high	true	N

Learning is based on instances E_l, $(l = 1...L)$ and leads to the generation of knowledge space Λ which may be seen as the union of identifiable knowledge pieces λ_k ($k = 1, ..., K$) namely: $\Lambda = \bigcup_k \lambda_k$. Knowledge pieces may take the form of IF ... THEN rules. Even if knowledge pieces are not expressed in rules they can be readily transformed to rule format representation, for instance during decision tree based learning [2] the conjunction of feature value sets along branch transversal leading to class identification may be readily formulated in rule format. However, none of the supervised learning systems or methods provides explicit support in feature importance value assessment. Feature importance is implicitly deduced based on the learned λ_k.

In this article we present a formal methodology that addresses feature value importance assessment based on knowledge learned through learning and irrespective of specifics of the method or system used for learning. The proposed methodology estimates the weight value W_i of each feature f_i $(i = 1,2,...,M)$ after learning has been completed. Weight values should satisfy the condition: $\sum_{i=1}^{M} w_i = 1$. Feature weight value assessment is based on the level of involvement of the respective feature in λ_k formation. This means that each w_i is calculated by summing up over λ_k, namely: $w_i = \sum_{k=1}^{K} w_{ik}$, where w_{ik} measures the contribution of f_i in λ_k formation. A schematic overview of w_{ik} and w_i assessment is provided in Table 3. For example, a rule learning system such as SEE5 (see http://www.rulequest.com/see5-info.html) applied on the simple instance data set presented in Table 2 would yield the rules, which are summarized in Figure 1. Each rule represents a piece of knowledge λ_k. A summary of all rules is included in Figure 1. Correspondingly, weight value assessment for the five rules shown in Figure 1 would be based on the specific instantiation of Table 3, which is presented in Table 4.

Table 3. Framework for feature weight value assessment. Feature weight value is assessed by taking into account the weight each feature receives via its participation in individual rule formation.

	λ_1	λ_2	...	λ_K	Overall feature weight value
f_1	w_{11}	w_{12}	...	w_{1K}	
f_2	w_{21}	w_{22}	...	w_{2K}	
f_3	w_{31}	w_{32}	...	w_{3K}	$w_i = \sum_{k=1}^{K} w_{ik}$
$\vdots$	$\vdots$	$\vdots$		$\vdots$	
f_M	w_{M1}	w_{M2}	...	w_{MK}	

```
λ₁: If Outlook = sunny AND Humidity = high Then N
λ₂: If Outlook = sunny AND Humidity = normal Then P
λ₃: If Outlook = overcast THEN P
λ₄: If Outlook = rain AND windy = true THEN N
λ₅: If Outlook = rain AND windy = false THEN P
```

Fig. 1. Simple learning output based on the application of SEE on the dataset summarized in Table 2

We base w_{ik} assessment on a modified heuristic from Ackoff's behavioral theory of communication [3]. In doing so we view learning as a knowledge broadcasting system, which is in a purposeful state. Purposefulness means that choice is available and the system is capable of choice and choice relates to selection of f_i in λ_k formation. Modified of Ackoff's heuristic is based on adjustment according to prize award modeling that captures feature involvement in rules formation.

The significance of features in a post-learning context is invaluable in some domains. For instance, a manager may inquiry into the relative weight of criteria. A medical doctor may have a similar inquiry, and so on.

We organize our presentation in the sections that follow. First, we overview Ackoff's behavioral theory of communication and the relevance of the theory in supervised learning. Then we present and model feature weight assessment heuristics,

Table 4. Feature weight values assessment for the simple learning example. (Zero w_{ik} values are omitted).

Features	Rules					Feature weight value
	λ_1	λ_2	λ_3	λ_4	λ_5	
Outlook	w_{11}	w_{12}	w_{13}	w_{14}	w_{15}	$w_{11} + w_{12} + w_{13} + w_{15}$
Temperature						
Humidity	w_{31}	w_{32}				$w_{31} + w_{32}$
Windy				w_{44}	w_{45}	$w_{44} + w_{45}$

present the model for w_{ik} and w_i assessment and discuss the impact of weight computation in rule importance assessment. We conclude the article by discussing the implications of the methodology presented and discussed herein and proposing areas for further research in the future.

2   Ackoff's Behavioral Theory of Communication and IML

This section introduces briefly Ackoff's behavioral theory of communication [3] in context of IML. The central concepts on which the theory is based are purposefulness and knowledge gain. Purposefulness implies that choice is available and the entity involved is capable of choice. Knowledge gain relates to the added value as result of choice, or, of learning as result of choice.

Consider the learning diagram in Figure 2. Starting from data we proceed to the training instances upon which learning will be performed. Training instances depend on the features (f_i) representation scheme. Learning is achieved via the application of training instances on a learning method, application is dependent on the feature representation scheme and leads to the induction of rules λ_k. Before learning the system is in a *purposeful* state since selection across features is possible and the learning system is (or should be) capable of choice. Let us denote by p_i the probability that feature f_i is selected during learning. Because we are not aware of the feature selection heuristic of the learning system we give all features an equal chance. This means that:

$$p_i = \frac{1}{M}, \forall i = 1...M \tag{1}$$

Knowledge gain is defined as a linear function Γ, which is related to feature selection probability, namely:

$$\Gamma = \sum_{i=1}^{M} \left| p_i - \frac{1}{M} \right| \tag{2}$$

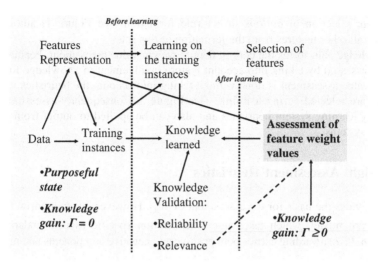

Fig. 2. Learning and feature weight value assessment. The dotted line indicates that feature weight values may also support the assessment of relevance of the learned knowledge – this issue is further elaborated in concluding remarks.

In equation (2) subscript i is omitted from Γ to simplify presentation. Before learning any feature has an equal chance to be selected and according to (1) knowledge gain is equal to zero. During learning some features are selected and included in knowledge learned. Let I be the set of the selected features. If I contains a single feature, say f_i then $p_i = 1$ and $p_j = 0$ for any $j \neq i$. Then:

$$\Gamma(I) = (1 - \frac{1}{M}) + \sum_{i=1}^{M-1} \left| p_i - \frac{1}{M} \right| = 2 - \frac{2}{M} \qquad (3)$$

Alternatively, if cardinality of I, $|I|$, is greater than 1, then (3) is adjusted to:

$$\Gamma(I) = 2 - \frac{2}{M - |I| + 1} \qquad (4)$$

Knowledge gain $\Gamma(I)$ associates with rule λ_k, which incorporates the features that correspond with I selection. By learning one rule knowledge is gained and $\Gamma(I)$ represents a measure of this gain. Gain is a decreasing function with respect to the number of features involved in learned knowledge ($\frac{\partial \Gamma(I)}{\partial |I|} \leq 0$). In the extreme event where $I = M$ knowledge gain $\Gamma(I) = 0$, which means that if all features are used there is no gain.

Feature selection is a mutually exclusive process. Selection of a feature (or features) to form a rule automatically excludes all other features from the specific rule formation; selection of *outlook* in λ_3 rule formation (see Figure 1) automatically excludes all other features from the formation of this rule.

Knowledge gain forms the core in feature weight value assessment. Feature weight value is assessed by taking into account feature involvement in knowledge formation. Weight value assessment is done without taking into account the heuristics via which features are selected during learning – see Figure 2. Consequently assessment is not biased by learning system heuristics and also can be applied to output from different learning systems.

3 Weight Assessment Heuristics

$\Gamma(I)$ provides the basis for the assessment of w_{ik}. However, we transform $\Gamma(I)$ to a *prize* award model, which takes into consideration specific aspects underlying λ_k formation. Prize awarding carries both positive and negative components and relates to:

Rule Coverage of Training Examples. Every rule covers some of the training instances and points to one or more classes. Training instances covered by the rule correspond to the class, or classes, to which the rule is pointing at. The more the training instances covered by the rule the better. We denote the coverage heuristic by α and we suggest a simple formula for its computation, namely:

$$\alpha = \frac{\sum_{n=1}^{N} \sum_{l} e^{*}}{\sum_{N} \sum_{L} e}, 0 \prec \alpha \le 1 \tag{5}$$

Where e^{*} relates to the number of training instances covered by the rule and the summation at the denominator relates to the total number of training instances in the learning set that belong to the class or classes identified by the rule. For instance the α heuristic for rule λ_1 (see Figure 1) is equal to 3/5 because the rule covers 3 training instances from a total of 5 class N training instances included in the training set (see Table 2). Heuristic α is always greater than zero (it would not make much sense to consider a rule, which does not cover at least one training example) and of course is bounded by one since the rule can not cover more than the available training examples.

Rule Modified Consistency. Modified consistency is assessed via a π heuristic that captures: (a) change in probability estimation as result of learning and (b) rule consistency. The π heuristic includes two components: the first component relates to the majority class that the rule points to and the second component captures all other classes pointed incorrectly by the rule. Consider a rule, which correctly identifies class C_1 and also covers training instances that belong to class C_2. Let $P(C_o)$ be the probability that corresponds to the training set of instances for class o $(o = 1,2)$ and $P^{*}(C_o)$ be the probability with which each class is identified by the specific rule. $P^{*}(C_o)$ probabilities are assessed using the examples that the rule covers. As an example, assume that $P(C_1) = 0.2$ and $P(C_2) = 0.3$, and that the rule covers 20 instances of class C_1 and 2 instances of class C_2. Then $P^*(C_1)$ would be equal to 20/22 and $P^*(C_2)$ be equal to 2/22. Credit is provided for class C_1 and would be equal to:

$$-\log P(C_1) + \log P^*(C_1) \tag{6}$$

Penalty for class C_2 would be equal to:

$$-\{-\log(1 - P(C_2)) + \log(1 - P^*(C_2))\} \tag{7}$$

Then calculation of π would be as follows:

$$\pi = \{-\log(P(C_1) + \log P^*(C_1)\} + \{-\{-\log(1 - P(C_2)) + \log(1 - P^*(C_2)\}\} \tag{8}$$

The base of the logarithms does not affect the semantics of the π heuristic. The formula may be readily generalized to incorporate more than one minority classes or classes incorrectly covered by the rule. The formulation of (6), (7) and (8) draws from the work by Kononenko and Bratko [4] on classifier performance assessment using an information theoretic approach. For example, using the probabilities discussed earlier the value of the π heuristic would be ≈ 1.81. Also the value of the π heuristic associated with rule λ_1 (see Figure 1) would be ≈ 1.49.

Thus, π heuristic intervention in prize formation is twofold: (a) credits rule formation in favor of classes with lower frequency distribution in the training set and (b) penalizes for including minority classes in the rule.

Generalization Heuristic. If a feature is valued over a nominal domain, which includes values $\{t, u, x, y, z\}$ and in rule formation it uses two of the values (normally in a disjunctive form, e.g., $f_i = (t, x)$ then the credit should be equal to 2/5. This rather simple definition captures the essence of the β generalization heuristic. If a feature takes values in a numerical interval, say [0, 20] and in rule formation the feature enters with the condition of ≤ 8 then the value of the β heuristic would be equal to 8/20. For example, in rule λ_1 the value of the β heuristic in conjunction with *humidity* being part of it, would be equal to 1/2.

Fairness Heuristic. Fairness is guaranteed via the application of heuristic φ, which divides knowledge gain equally among the features that take part in rule formation. For example, in rule λ_1 *humidity* and *outlook* participate (see Figure 1) and each take a credit equal to 0,5.

Integration: Based on the prize award we proceed to w_{ik} model definition – see Tables 3 and 4. Namely, we adjust knowledge gain, $\Gamma(I)$ - see expression (4) by using the prize award heuristics and proceed to the assessment of w_{ik}, namely:

$$w_{ik} = \Gamma(I) \times \alpha \times \pi \times \beta \times \varphi \tag{9}$$

Feature weight value, which corresponds to w_i is computed by summing over all rules in which the feature participates in rule formation, namely: $w_i = \sum_k w_{ik}$. Specific weight values for the toy domain used in the article are summarized in Table 5.

Table 5. Feature weight values calculation for the simple learning example. In the last column of the table weight values are normalized. The process via which modified rule gain values are computed is explained in the text – see section: Modified rule weight value. The last two columns capture rule value assessment with respect to the learning domain. For instance the first rule (λ_1) has a 35% relative importance in terms of the classification task posed.

Features	Rules					Weight values	Normalized values
	λ_1	λ_2	λ_3	λ_4	λ_s		
Outlook	0.198	0.031	0.126	0.132	0.047	0.534	47%
Temperature							
Humidity	0.297	0,047				0.344	30%
Windy				0,198	0.071	0.269	23%
Modified rule gain	0.198	0.031	0.126	0.132	0.079		
Normalized gain across rules	35%	5%	22%	23%	14%		

The linear additive model via which w_i is computed as the sum of individual w_{ik} holds because of the mutual exclusive nature underlying feature selection and involvement in rule formation and the implicit disjunction of knowledge pieces λ_k to form the entire space of learned knowledge.

We continue by exploring weight value assessment model on different conditions. The conditions are equality of feature importance, inequality in feature importance and the implication of the model in rule weight value assessment.

3.1 Equality and Inequality Between w_i Values

Let us assume that two features f_1 and f_2 are known to be equally important. Importance is expressed with respect to the domain of reference. Then should weights be also equal e.g. $w_1 = w_2$? The question that arises is what would the implication of this condition be in terms of the process for estimating feature weight value discussed herein? According to our procedure $w_i = \sum_k w_{ik}$, which means that total weight comes from the summation of component weights w_{ik}. Of course, we may formulate one rule per concept class learned by taking a disjunction across specific rules. For example, disjunction between rules λ_1 and λ_4 provides one rule for the class N – see Figure 1.

However, if we do so the mathematical computation underlying $\Gamma(I)$ would no longer be valid because disjunction violates the mutual exclusiveness condition, which underlies feature selection in the first place.

If we limit our attention to a case in which there is only one rule in which f_1 and f_2 participate (so no summation across rules is necessary) then weight value would be computed through the expression: $w_{ik} = \Gamma(I) \times \alpha \times \pi \times \beta \times \varphi$. If f_1 and f_2 are part of the same rule then equality would indicate that they are achieving the same level of generalization, e.g., their β heuristic values would be equal. If they are not part of the same rule then equality would reflect a balance between the values of the heuristics that are used in w_{ik} calculation.

Either part of the same rule or part of different rules equality between two feature weight values, e.g., $w_1 = w_2$ (using w_{ik} computation model) can not be formally linked with prior perceived equality in importance. Equality $w_1 = w_2$ is based on post learning assessment of learned knowledge. On the other hand, equality in importance between two features prior to learning would be based on expert judgment or theoretical evidence. Thus $w_1 = w_2$ (using w_{ik} computation model) is based on induction while $f_1 = f_2$ (taken to indicate prior equality in importance) is based on axiomatic definition. Therefore, relation between the two can only be assessed statistically. However, in domains which lack axiomatic definition of f_i importance w_i values may provide useful hints as per the significance of the underlying features.

3.2 Modified Rule Weight Value

The bottom lines of Table 5 express rule weight assessment. We may consider these values as a secondary product of the w_{ik} process. Computation is similar with w_{ik} assessment and fairness heuristic, φ, is excluded and feature value generalization heuristics are multiplied across the features that participate in rule formation. For example, the weight value for rule λ_1 is computed as follows:

$$\left[2 - \frac{2}{4-2+1}\right] \times \left[\frac{3}{5}\right] \times \left[-\log(\frac{5}{14}) + \log(1)\right] \times \left[\frac{1}{3} \times \frac{1}{2}\right] \cong 0,198$$

because two features take part in rule formation, rule points to class N, which has prior probability equal to 5/14, rule covers 3 out of 5 N class examples and the two features that take part in rule formation generalize over one value each.

The 0,198 (or 35% if normalized) value represents a proxy measure of rule importance. The value measures the semantic contribution of the rule in context of the learning problem. Such values may be derived across all classes or with respect to single class. In Table 5 rules λ_2, λ_3 and λ_5 point to class P. Focusing on the modified rule weight values of these rules we may assert that rule contribution to class P identification are: 13% for λ_2, 53% for λ_3 and 34% for λ_5. The result makes sense because rule λ_3 uses just one feature and covers a significant number from the P training instances. It says that rule λ_3 is as valuable as [almost] rules λ_2 and λ_5 considered together are.

4 Conclusions

We have presented, discussed and demonstrated a methodology supporting feature weight value assessment based on post-learning knowledge results. The methodology is inductive and regression based. Inductive means that w_i values reflect feature representation modeling and quality of training instance data. Thus computation is falsity preserving, which means that quality of result depends on quality of input. For example, if we establish a precedence scheme between features (e.g., use feature f_i before using feature f_j), see also Gaga et al [5] this constraint will carry through w_i computation – all other things being equal w_i would be greater than w_j. Pruning will affect value computation and elimination of "soft threshold values" [2] will also affect w_i values. Regression based means that the methodology is able to generate distributional knowledge given singular information point estimates [6]. Singular estimates are the training instances since they implicitly carry information about w_i. Distributional knowledge corresponds to the w_i values since they aggregate in a systematic way the knowledge contribution of each feature across the rules the feature is involved. Feature weight value assessment contributes also to the assessment of learned knowledge comprehensibility. Feature weights or modified rule gains support understanding about a domain. This holds especially in domains at which prior knowledge is minimal. The exemplar domain we used herein to demonstrate our method demonstrates the notion about comprehensibility further.

Proposed methodology complements other approaches, which are oriented towards the assessment of feature weight values *prior* to learning, such as for instance in [8], which are targeted to select a handful of features from a huge amount of features. In gene expression problems the researcher is faced with a rather small set of training examples (from 50 to 200), which are represented by thousands of features (from 5.000 to about 25.000). Then it is *sine qua non* to reduce the size of the domain to a handful yet meaningful features based on which learning will proceed.

The methodology proposed in this article can not be employed to support feature reduction as is. However, it can be extended to so. Extension may not be based on the same heuristics and formulae, which are better suited for post-learning assessment. But, similar heuristics van be devised and used to assess the *forthcoming* importance during learning. Such heuristics may for instance capture the number of changes in value – class assignment with respect to each feature.

Furthermore, weight assessment as proposed herein differs from weight assessment during neural network training [9] where weights are assessed to facilitate learning and fit of training examples to the selected tree or network structure.

Going back to Figure 2 we notice that it may be decomposed into three parts: the left (prior to learning), the center (learning) and the right (post learning). Our methodology relates to the right part. Approaches such as the ones discussed in [8] or [9] relate weight assessment to the left or center parts.

Proposed methodology holds implications for decision making modeling. Numerous models deal with criterion (e.g. feature) weight value assessment. All models proceed to assessment via the incorporation of decision maker's preferences to a model such as linear programming [7]. This procedure assumes that the preference structure of the decision maker is linear. Other approaches exist according to which preference takes alternative functional structures [10]. The proposed approach overcomes this unnecessary assumption. Use of (9) does not necessitate a prior assumption about preference. In addition, it offers the decision maker the option to assess weights with respect to the class of interest alone.

A limitation of the proposed method is that it lacks testing on a real world domain. This can be a subject for further research. A group of decision makers may be asked to express preference about a criteria and then about a set of alternatives. We could then compare initial preference about criteria with values learned via (9).

Acknowledgement

I am indebted to the anonymous reviewers of this article who provided useful insight and guidance on how to improve presentation of the methodology to the reader.

References

[1] Carter C. and Catlett J. Assessing Credit Card Applications Using Machine Learning, *IEEE Expert*, Fall:71—79, (1987).
[2] Quinlan J.R. Induction of decision trees, *Machine Learning*, 1:81--106. (1986),
[3] Ackoff RL., Towards a behavioral model of communication, Management Science, 4:218--234. (1958).
[4] Kononenko I. and Bratko I. Information based evaluation criterion for classifiers' performance, *Machine Learning*,6(1):67--80. (1991).
[5] Gaga, E., Moustakis, V., Vlachakis, Y., and Charissis, G. ID+: Enhancing Medical Knowledge Acquisition Using Inductive Machine Learning. *Applied Artificial Intelligence: An International Journal.* 10(2) 79-94. (1996).
[6] Kahneman D. and Tversky A. Intutive prediction: biases and corrective procedures, TIMS *Studies in the Management Sciences*, 12:313--327. (1979).
[7] Starr M. K. and Zeleny M. MCDM: State and future of the arts. In Starr MK. and Zeleny M., editors, TIMS Studies in Management Sciences 6: Multiple Criteria Decision Making, pages 5--29, North Holland. (1977).
[8] Fujarewicz, K. and Weinch, M. Selecting differentially expressed genes for colon tumor classification, *Int. J. Appl. Math. Comput. Sci.* 13 (3), 327–335 (2003).
[9] Maclin, R., and J. W. Shavlik. Using knowledge based neural networks to improve algorithms: refining the Chou-Fasman algorithm for protein folding. *Machine Learning* 11(2-3): 195-215, (1993).
[10] Doumpos, M. and Zopounidis, C. *Multicriteria Decision Aid Classification Methods*, Kluwer Academic Publishers, Dordrecht. (2002).

Recognition of Greek Phonemes Using Support Vector Machines

Iosif Mporas, Todor Ganchev, Panagiotis Zervas, and Nikos Fakotakis

Wire Communications Laboratory, Dept. of Electrical and Computer Engineering,
University of Patras, 261 10 Rion, Patras, Greece
Tel.: +30 2610 997336; Fax: +30 2610 997336
{imporas, tganchev, pzervas, fakotaki}@wcl.ee.upatras.gr

Abstract. In the present work we study the applicability of Support Vector Machines (SVMs) on the phoneme recognition task. Specifically, the Least Squares version of the algorithm (LS-SVM) is employed in recognition of the Greek phonemes in the framework of telephone-driven voice-enabled information service. The N-best candidate phonemes are identified and consequently feed to the speech and language recognition components. In a comparative evaluation of various classification methods, the SVM-based phoneme recognizer demonstrated a superior performance. Recognition rate of 74.2% was achieved from the N-best list, for N=5, prior to applying the language model.

1 Introduction

The increased interest of the market in multilingual speech-enabled systems, such as telephone-driven information access systems, has raised the necessity of developing computationally efficient and noise-robust speech and language recognition methods. In speech and language recognition, the phonotactic approach became very popular, since it offers a good trade-off between recognition accuracy and amount of data required for training. In brief, in the phonotactic approach the speech signal is decoded to a phoneme sequence, which is further processed by a statistical language model for the language of interest. This technique, proposed by Zissman [1], is known as phoneme recognition followed by language model (PRLM). Due to the success of the phonotactic approach, phoneme recognition became a corner stone in every speech and language recognition component.

At present, various approaches to phoneme recognition have been proposed. In [2], a combination of context-dependent and context-independent ANNs has led a phoneme recognition accuracy of about 46%. Phoneme recognition using independent component analysis (ICA)-based feature extraction [3] yielded accuracy of 51%. Continuous mixture HMM-based phoneme recognizer with a conventional three-state left-to-right architecture [4] achieved recognition performance of 54%. A language-dependent approach to phoneme recognition demonstrated accuracy in the range 45% to 55% [5]. Speaker-independent approach, using multiple codebooks of various LPC parameters and discrete HMMs, achieved 65% accuracy on context-independent test corpus [6]. The Global Phone project provides phoneme recognizers for multiple

G. Antoniou et al. (Eds.): SETN 2006, LNAI 3955, pp. 290–300, 2006.

languages with accuracy varying in the range 55% to 65% [8]. A mixture of language dependent phonemes and language-independent speech units achieved accuracy 38% of phoneme recognition [9]. The language-dependent phone recognition approach, modeling a tree-state context independent HMM, achieved accuracy between 33% and 52% [10]. Broad phoneme recognition approximation, trained with context independent HMMs, yielded accuracy of 50% ÷ 60% [11]. The CMU Sphinx 3 system, which employes a three emitting-state Gaussian mixture HMMs [7] yielded phoneme recognition accuracy of 69%. Finally, an approach [12] similar to ours, which uses SVMs with framewise classification on TIMIT [13], reports 70,6% accuracy of correctly classified frames.

In the present study we employ an SVM-based classifier on the phoneme recognition task. Because of their strong discrimination capabilities, Support Vector Machines (SVMs) became a popular classification tool, which was successfully employed in various real-world applications. Section 3 offers further details about the SVM algorithm, and Section 4 provides comparison with other classification methods.

2 Phoneme Recognition

In a phoneme recognizer built on the PRLM architecture, the sequence of phonemes decoded by the recognizer is matched against a set of phoneme-bigram language models, one for each language of interest. Thus, training of both acoustic models of the phonemes and language model for each language is required. Since the present work aims at selecting the optimal classification approach for phoneme recognition, details about the training of the language model are not discussed.

The typical structure of a generic phoneme recognizer is presented in Fig.1. In brief, firstly the speech signal is sampled and subsequently pre-processed. The pre-processing consists of: (1) band-pass filtering, (2) pre-emphasis, (3) segmentation. The band-pass filtering aims at suppressing the frequency bands with little contribution to the speech contents, eliminating the drift of the signal, reducing the effects caused by saturation by level, and smoothing the clicks. In telephone quality speech, these are frequently observed degradations. The pre-emphasis reduces the spectral tilt for the higher frequencies for enhancing the estimation of the higher formants. Subsequently, segmentation of the speech signal is performed to extract the phoneme borders. As illustrated in Fig.1, during the second step, speech parameterization is performed for each speech segment. Specifically, 13 Mel-frequency cepstral coefficients (MFCC) and the first four formants are estimated. During the post-processing step, the ratios between the second, third and fourth to the first formant F_2/F_1, F_3/F_1, F_4/F_1, respectively, are computed. Next, all speech parameters are grouped together to form the feature vector, and a mean normalization is performed for each parameter. The normalized {$MFCC_0$, ..., $MFCC_{12}$, F_2/F_1, F_3/F_1, F_4/F_1} vectors are fed to the phoneme classifier. The phoneme classifier estimates the degree of proximity between the input and a set of predefined acoustic models of the phonemes. The output of the classifier consists of the N-best list of candidates, which

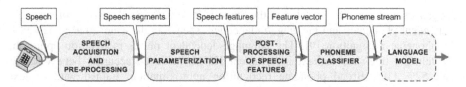

Fig. 1. Structure of a generic phoneme recognizer

is further utilized by a rule-driven language modeling. The output for the language model (specific for each language) is the likelihood of the phoneme sequence in the specific language. Specifically, the N-best list of phonemes is processed by n-gram language models to estimate the likelihood of every hypothesized phoneme sequence. Maximum likelihood selection criterion is utilized to select the most probable phoneme. For a given phoneme sequence $A_i=a_1,a_2,a_3,...a_T$ the likelihood is:

$$L(A_i \mid AM_i) = \frac{1}{T}\log(P(a_i \mid AM_i)) + \sum_{t=2}^{T} \log P(a_t|a_{t-1},...,a_1,AM_i) \qquad (1)$$

where AM_i is the corresponding acoustic model. The sequence with maximum likelihood is detected as:

$$A_i = \arg\max_i L(A_i \mid AM_i) \qquad (2)$$

In the present work we focus on the classification stage. Specifically, seeking out a classifier our choice felt on the SVM method due to its strong discrimination capabilities and the compact models it employs. In the following Section 3 we confine to description of the SVM approach and its least squares version (LS-SVM). Next, in Section 4, the performance of the LS-SVM classifier on the phoneme recognition task is contrasted to the one of other classification algorithms.

3 Fundamentals on Support Vector Machines

Initially, SVMs have been introduced as a two-class classifier for solving pattern recognition problems (Vapnik, 1995;1998). Since many real-world problems, such as phoneme recognition, involve multiple classes, techniques to extend SVMs to multiple classes have been proposed. In the present work we utilize the voting scheme [14] for SVM-based multi-class classification. In this method a binary classification is created for each pair of classes. For K classes the resulting number of binary classifiers is $K(K-1)/2$. The data are mapped into a higher dimensional input space and an optimal separating hyperplane is constructed in this space. Specifically in the present study, we employ the least squares version of SVMs (LS-SVM) [15] for identification of the Greek phonemes. For completeness of exposition, in Section 3.1 we firstly introduce the original SVM theory. Subsequently, in Section 3.2 the specifics of the LS-SVM version are discussed.

3.1 SVMs for Classification

For a training set of N data points , where is the k-th input pattern and $\{y_k, x_k\}_{k=1}^{N}$ is the k-th output pattern, the SVM algorithm constructs a classifier of the form:

$$y(x) = sign\left[\sum_{k=1}^{N} a_k y_k \psi(x, x_k) + b\right] \tag{3}$$

where a_k are positive real coefficients and b is a bias term. Assuming that

$$\begin{cases} w^T \phi(x_k) + b \geq +1, y_k = +1 \\ w^T \phi(x_k) + b \leq -1, y_k = -1 \end{cases} \tag{4}$$

which is equivalent to

$$y_k \left[w^T \phi(x_k) + b \right] \geq 1, k = 1, ..., N , \tag{5}$$

where $\varphi(.)$ is a nonlinear function which maps the input space into a higher dimensional space. To be able to violate (5), in case a separating hyperplane in this higher dimensional space does not exist, variables ξ_k are introduced such that

$$\begin{cases} y_k \left[w^T \phi(x_k) + b \right] \geq 1 - \xi_k, k = 1, ..., N \\ \xi_k \geq 0, k = 1, ..., N \end{cases} \tag{6}$$

According to the structural risk minimization principle, the risk bound is minimized by formulating the optimization problem:

$$\min_{w, \xi_k} J_1(w, \xi_k) = \frac{1}{2} w^T w + c \sum_{k=1}^{N} \xi_k \tag{7}$$

subject to (6), so a Lagrangian is constructed

$$L_1(w, b, \xi_k, a_k, v_k) = J_1(w, \xi_k) - \sum_{k=1}^{N} a_k \{ y_k [w^T \phi(x_k) + b] - 1 + \xi_k \} - \sum_{k=1}^{N} v_k \xi_k \tag{8}$$

by introducing Lagrange multipliers $a_k \geq 0$, $v_k \geq 0$ ($k=1,...,N$). The solution is given by Lagrange's saddle point by computing

$$\max_{w, \xi_k} \min_{w, \xi_k} L1(w, b, \xi_k; a_k, v_k) \tag{9}$$

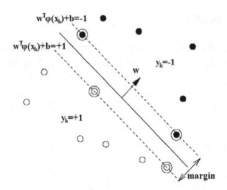

Fig. 2. Linear separating hyperplanes. The support vectors are circled.

This leads to

$$\begin{cases} \dfrac{\partial L_1}{\partial w} = 0 \rightarrow w = \sum_{k=1}^{N} a_k y_k \phi(x_k) \\[2mm] \dfrac{\partial L_1}{\partial b} = 0 \rightarrow \sum_{k=1}^{N} a_k y_k = 0 \\[2mm] \dfrac{\partial L_1}{\partial \xi_k} = 0 \rightarrow 0 \le a_k \le c, k = 1, ..., N \end{cases} \tag{10}$$

which gives the solution of the quadratic programming problem

$$\max_{a_k} Q_1(a_k; \phi(x_k)) = -\frac{1}{2} \sum_{k,l=1}^{N} y_k y_l \phi(x_k)^T \phi(x_l) a_k a_l + \sum_{k=1}^{N} a_k \tag{11}$$

such that

$$\begin{cases} \sum_{k=1}^{N} a_k y_k = 0 \\[2mm] 0 \le a_k \le c, k = 1, ... N \end{cases} \tag{12}$$

The function $\varphi(x_k)$ in (11) is related to $\psi(x, x_k)$ by imposing

$$\phi(x)^T \phi(x_k) = \psi(x, x_k) \tag{13}$$

which is motivated by Mercer's Theorem. The classifier (3) is designed by solving

$$\max_{a_k} Q_1(a_k; \psi(x_k, x_l)) = -\frac{1}{2} \sum_{k,l=1}^{N} y_k y_l \psi(x_k, x_l) a_k a_l + \sum_{k=1}^{N} a_k \tag{14}$$

subject to constraints in (11).

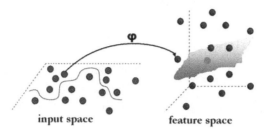

Fig. 3. Mapping (φ) the input space into a higher dimensional space

Neither w nor $\varphi(x_k)$ have to be calculated in order to determine the decision surface. The matrix associated with this quadratic programming problem is not indefinite, so the solution to (14) will be global. Hyperplanes (5) satisfying the constraint $||w||_2 \leq a$ have a Vapnik-Chervonenkis (VC) dimension h which is bounded by

$$h \leq \min([r^2 a^2], n) + 1 \tag{15}$$

where [.] is the integer part and r is the radius of the smallest ball containing the points $\varphi(x_1),\ldots,\varphi(x_N)$. This ball is computed by defining the Lagrangian

$$L_2(r, q, \lambda_k) = r^2 - \sum_{k=1}^{N} \lambda_k (r^2 - \| \phi(x_k) - q \|_2^2) \tag{16}$$

where q is the center of the ball and λ_k are positive Lagrangian multipliers. In a similar way as for (7), the center is equal to $q = \Sigma_k \lambda_k \varphi(x_k)$, where the Lagrangian multipliers follow from

$$\max_{\lambda_k} Q_2(\lambda_k; \phi(x_k)) = - \sum_{k,l=1}^{N} y_k y_l \phi(x_k)^T \phi(x_l) + \sum_{k=1}^{N} \lambda_k \phi(x_k)^T \phi(x_l) \tag{17}$$

such that

$$\begin{cases} \sum_{k=1}^{N} \lambda_k = 0 \\ \lambda_k \geq 0, k = 1, \ldots N \end{cases} \tag{18}$$

Based on (13), Q_2 can also be expressed in terms of $\psi(x_k, x_l)$. Finally, a support vector machine with minimal VC dimension is selected by solving (14) and computing (15) form (17).

3.2 Least Squares Support Vector Machines

Formulating the classification problem as

$$\min_{w,b,e} J_2(w, b, e) = \frac{1}{2} w^T w + \gamma \frac{1}{2} \sum_{k=1}^{N} e_k^2 \tag{19}$$

subject to equality constrains

$$y_k[w^T\phi(x_k)+b]=1-e_k, k=1,...,N \tag{20}$$

a least squares version to SVM classifier is introduced. The Lagrangian is defined as

$$L_3(w,b,e;a)=J_3(w,b,e)-\sum_{k=1}^{N}a_k\{y_k[w^T\phi(x_k)+b]-1+e_k\} \tag{21}$$

where a_k are the Lagrange multipliers, which can further be either positive or negative (Kuhn-Tucker conditions). The conditions for optimality

$$\begin{cases} \dfrac{\partial L_3}{\partial w}=0 \rightarrow w=\sum_{k=1}^{N}a_k y_k\phi(x_k) \\[2mm] \dfrac{\partial L_3}{\partial b}=0 \rightarrow \sum_{k=1}^{N}a_k y_k=0 \\[2mm] \dfrac{\partial L_3}{\partial e_k}=0 \rightarrow a_k=\gamma e_k, k=1,...,N \\[2mm] \dfrac{\partial L_3}{\partial a_k}=0 \rightarrow y_k[w^T\phi(x_k)+b]e_k=0, k=1,...,N \end{cases} \tag{22}$$

are written immediately as the solution to the following linear equations set

$$\begin{bmatrix} I & 0 & 0 & -Z^T \\ 0 & 0 & 0 & -Y^T \\ 0 & 0 & \gamma I & -I \\ Z & Y & I & 0 \end{bmatrix}\begin{bmatrix} w \\ b \\ e \\ a \end{bmatrix}=\begin{bmatrix} 0 \\ 0 \\ 0 \\ \overline{1} \end{bmatrix} \tag{23}$$

where $Z=[\phi(x_1)^T y_1;...; \phi(x_N)^N y_N]$, $Y=[y_1;...;y_N]$, $\overline{1}=[1;...;1]$, $e=[e_1;...;e_N]$, $a=[a_1;...;a_N]$. The solution can also be given by

$$\begin{bmatrix} 0 & -Y^T \\ Y & ZZ^T+\gamma^{-1}I \end{bmatrix}\begin{bmatrix} b \\ a \end{bmatrix}=\begin{bmatrix} 0 \\ \overline{1} \end{bmatrix} \tag{24}$$

Mercer's condition can be applied to the matrix $\Omega=ZZ^T$ where

$$\begin{aligned} \Omega_{kl} &= y_k y_l\phi(x_k)^T \phi(x_l) \\ &= y_k y_l\psi(x_k,x_l) \end{aligned} \tag{25}$$

The classifier (3) is found by solving the linear set of equations (24) – (25) instead of quadratic programming. The support values a_k are proportional to the errors at the data points.

4 Experiments and Results

Evaluation of the recognition was carried out on the SpeechDat (II)- FDB-5000-Greek corpus. It contains recordings from 5000 native Greek speakers (2.405 males, 2.595 females) recorded over the fixed telephone network of Greece. Speech samples are stored as sequences of 8-bit, 8 kHz, A-law format. A comprehensive description of the SpeechDat (II) FDB-5000-Greek corpus is available in [16], [17].

On a common experimental setup, we have evaluated on the phoneme recognition task the following six classification techniques:

- NB: Naïve Bayes [18], using kernel density estimation,
- MLP: Multi Layer Perceptron, using back-propagation for training,
- M5P: regression decision tree based on M5 algorithm,
- J.48: learning algorithm [19], generating a pruned or not C4.5 decision tree,
- Support Vector Machines,
- Least Squares Support Vector Machines.

These algorithms were used alone or combined with several meta-classification algorithms, such as Bagging and AdaBoost [20]. Bagging takes random samples, with replacement, and builds one classifier on each sample. The ensemble decision is made by the majority vote. AdaBoost designs the ensemble members one at a time, based on the performance of the previous member, in order to give more chances to objects that are difficult to classify, to be picked in the subsequent training sets. The WEKA implementation (WEKA machine learning library [21]) of these classification techniques, with default parameter setup, was used. The performance of the evaluated classifiers is presented in Table 1. Two feature vectors were compared: (1) MFCC presented in the second column and (2) MFCC + normalized formants in the third column of the table.

Table 1. Phoneme recognition accuracy in percentage for various classifiers and two feature vectors

CLASSIFIER	Accuracy [%] $\{MFCC_0, ..., MFCC_{12}\}$	Accuracy [%] $\{MFCC_{0-12}, F_2/F_1, F_3/F_1, F_4/F_1\}$
NB	26.17	28.91
MLP	28.83	30.01
J.48	23.11	24.73
Meta-classification via Regression M5P	26.37	28.79
Meta Bagging J.48	28.15	29.82
Meta AdaBoost M1 J.48	28.97	30.09
SVM	34.88	37.98
LS-SVM	34.84	38.06

As the experimental results suggest, the SVM classifier demonstrated the highest accuracy when compared to other classifiers. The observed superiority of the SVM algorithm was expected, since NB and decision trees require discretized attributes. Except this, SVM perform well in higher dimensional spaces since they do not suffer from the *curse of dimensionality*. Moreover, SVMs have the advantage over other approaches, such as neural networks, etc, that their training always reaches a global minimum [22].

In addition to the results presented in Table 1, in Fig. 4 illustrates the *N*-best list for the most successful classifier, namely the Least Squares version of SVM. The results for the *N*-best list for *N*=1 to *N*=5 shown in Fig. 4, illustrate the potential improvement of the accuracy that could be gained after including the language model. As it is well-known some phonemes, which share a similar manner of articulation and therefore possess kindred acoustic features, are often misclassified. Examples of phonemes with similar manner of articulation are the glides /i/ and /j/, the fricatives /f/, /x/ and /T/, the nasals /m/ and /n/ and the palatals /k/ and /x/. This results to pairs as well as groups of phonemes that could be confused during the recognition process. The correlation among the phonemes can be seen from the confusion matrix presented in Table 2.

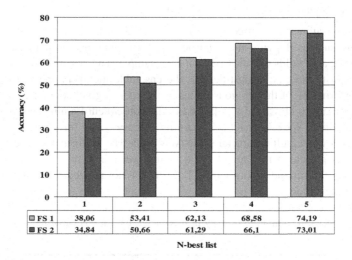

	1	2	3	4	5
FS 1	38,06	53,41	62,13	68,58	74,19
FS 2	34,84	50,66	61,29	66,1	73,01

N-best list

Fig. 4. N-best List accuracy (%) for LS-SVM and two different Feature Sets (FS). FS_1 consists of $\{MFCC_0, ..., MFCC_{12}, F_2/F_1, F_3/F_1, F_4/F_1\}$. FS_2 consists of $\{13\ MFCC\}$.

We deem the lower accuracy we observed in our experiments, when compared to [12], is mainly due to the nature of the recordings in the SpeechDat(II) database. While in [12] the authors experimented with the TIMIT recordings (clean speech sampled at 16 kHz, and recorded with a high-quality microphone) the SpeechDat(II) recordings have been recorded over the fixed telephone network of Greece. Thus, the speech in the SpeechDat(II) database is sampled at 8 kHz, band-limited to telephone quality, and distorted by the nonlinear transfer function of the handset and the transmission channel. Moreover, there is interference from the real-world environment. Finally, the TIMIT recordings consist of read speech, while the SpeechDat(II) contains both prompted and spontaneous speech, which consequences in larger variations in the length of the phonemes, as well as to a stronger co-articulation effects.

Table 2. Confusion matrix of the Greek phonemes (phonemes are transcribed according to SAMPA). The accuracy is presented in percentage.

	a	b	c	d	e	f	g	i	j	k	l	m	n	o	r	s	t	u	v	x	z	N	G	D	dz	T	ts	p	
a	81	6,3	0	0	3,1	0	0	0	0	0	0	0	0	0	0	9,4	0	0	0	0	0	0	0	0	0	0	0	0	a
b	3,1	25	0	0	0	6,3	9,4	3,1	3,1	0	6,3	6,3	0	13	6,3	0	3,1	0	0	0	3,1	6,3	6,3	0	0	0	0	0	b
c	0	0	44	6,3	0	0	3,1	3,1	6,3	0	0	0	0	0	0	3,1	9,4	0	0	0	13	0	3,1	0	6,3	3,1	0	0	c
d	0	6,3	6,3	22	3,1	0	3,1	3,1	13	6,3	3,1	3,1	0	6,3	13	3,1	0	6,3	0	0	0	3,1	0	0	0	0	0	0	d
e	6,3	0	6,3	6,3	66	0	0	0	0	0	0	0	0	3,1	6,3	0	0	3,1	0	0	0	0	3,1	0	0	0	0	0	e
f	0	3,1	0	0	0	44	0	0	0	3,1	0	0	0	0	0	16	0	0	16	0	0	0	0	3,1	13	3,1	0	0	f
g	0	9,4	13	3,1	0	6,3	25	0	0	3,1	0	3,1	0	0	3,1	0	16	3,1	3,1	0	0	0	3,1	9,4	0	0	0	0	g
i	0	0	3,1	0	3,1	0	0	50	19	0	0	3,1	0	0	0	0	0	3,1	0	0	3,1	3,1	9,4	0	3,1	0	0	0	i
j	0	3,1	3,1	0	3,1	0	0	31	31	0	0	9,4	0	0	9,4	0	0	6,3	0	0	0	3,1	0	0	0	0	0	0	j
k	3,1	0	3,1	3,1	0	0	19	0	0	38	0	0	0	0	6,3	3,1	16	0	6,3	3,1	0	0	0	0	0	0	0	0	k
l	0	13	0	3,1	0	0	3,1	0	0	0	25	13	13	6,3	6,3	0	0	9,4	3,1	0	0	3,1	0	3,1	0	0	0	0	l
m	0	6,3	0	0	3,1	0	0	0	6,3	0	6,3	50	13	0	0	0	0	3,1	3,1	0	0	6,3	3,1	0	0	0	0	0	m
n	0	9,4	0	3,1	0	0	3,1	3,1	0	0	6,3	6,3	41	0	0	0	0	6,3	0	0	0	6,3	0	13	0	0	0	0	n
o	3,1	9,4	0	0	3,1	0	0	3,1	3,1	9,4	0	0	0	56	3,1	0	0	3,1	3,1	0	0	3,1	0	0	0	0	0	0	o
r	9,4	6,3	0	6,3	19	0	3,1	6,3	0	3,1	13	0	0	0	22	0	0	3,1	0	0	3,1	0	3,1	0	3,1	0	0	0	r
s	0	0	3,1	0	0	9,4	3,1	0	0	0	0	0	0	0	0	63	0	0	3,1	3,1	0	0	0	0	6,3	6,3	3,1	0	s
t	0	0	13	0	0	0	0	0	0	9,4	3,1	0	0	0	3,1	0	47	0	3,1	0	3,1	0	3,1	0	6,3	9,4	0	0	t
u	0	6,3	0	9,4	0	0	0	0	3,1	0	9,4	0	6,3	13	0	0	0	34	0	0	0	6,3	3,1	0	0	0	0	0	u
v	3,1	13	0	6,3	0	0	3,1	0	0	0	3,1	0	6,3	0	3,1	3,1	3,1	0	25	0	6,3	0	3,1	3,1	0	9,4	3,1	0	v
x	0	0	0	0	0	22	0	0	0	6,3	0	3,1	0	0	0	6,3	0	0	0	50	0	0	0	9,4	0	3,1	0	0	x
z	0	3,1	6,3	0	0	3,1	0	6,3	0	0	0	0	0	3,1	0	3,1	3,1	0	3,1	0	38	3,1	9,4	0	16	0	6,3	0	z
N	0	6,3	0	3,1	0	0	3,1	0	3,1	0	9,4	9,4	0	0	0	0	0	6,3	0	0	0	53	3,1	3,1	0	0	0	0	N
G	0	6,3	3,1	0	3,1	3,1	6,3	9,4	6,3	3,1	9,4	6,3	3,1	13	0	0	0	0	3,1	0	3,1	6,3	63	6,3	0	0	3,1	0	G
D	0	0	3,1	0	0	0	9,4	0	0	6,3	6,3	3,1	6,3	0	3,1	3,1	6,3	0	3,1	0	0	0	9,4	28	3,1	6,3	3,1	0	D
dz	0	0	9,4	0	0	0	0	0	6,3	3,1	0	3,1	0	0	0	0	9,4	0	0	3,1	16	0	0	0	41	0	9,4	0	dz
T	0	3,1	0	6,3	0	22	0	0	0	0	0	3,1	0	0	0	6,3	3,1	0	0	13	3,1	0	3,1	9,4	0	25	3,1	0	T
ts	3,1	3,1	3,1	3,1	0	3,1	0	0	0	3,1	0	3,1	0	0	3,1	16	3,1	0	16	3,1	3,1	0	0	0	9,4	6,3	19	0	ts
p	0	3,1	3,1	0	0	0	6,3	0	0	22	0	0	0	0	9,4	0	0	9,4	3,1	9,4	3,1	0	0	0	9,4	0	3,1	19	p

5 Conclusions

A phoneme recognizer based on Support Vector Machines and specifically on their Least Squares version (LS-SVM) has been presented. It employs a feature vector based on MFCC and formants. A comparative evaluation of the SVM classifier with several other classification methods was performed on the task of Greek phoneme recognition. The SVM method demonstrated the highest accuracy. The N-best list of candidate phonemes produced by the classifier is further feed to language-specific models in order to increase the phoneme recognition performance and facilitate the speech and language recognition components. This phoneme recognizer is intended as a part of telephone-driven voice-enabled information service.

References

1. Zissman M., "Comparison of four Approaches to Automatic Language Identification of Telephone Speech", IEEE Trans. Speech and Audio Proc., vol.4, Jan.96, pp.31-44.
2. Mak M., "Combining ANNs to improve phone recognition", IEEE ICASSP'97, Munich, Germany, 1997,, vol. 4, pp.3253-3256.
3. Kwon O-W, Lee T-W., "Phoneme recognition using ICA-based feature extraction and transformation", Signal Processing, June 2004.
4. Caseiro D., Trancoso I., "Identification of Spoken European Languages", Eusipco, IX European Signal Processing Conference, Greece, Sept. 1998.

5. Yan Y., Barnard E., "Experiments for an approach to Language Identification with conversational telephone speech", ICASSP, Atlanta, USA, May 1996, vol. 1, pp. 789-792.
6. Lee K-F., Hon H-W, "Speaker Independent Phone Recognition using HMM", IEEE Trans. on Acoustics Speech and Audio Processing, vol.37, no.11, Nov.89.
7. Schultz T., Waibel A., "Language Independent and Language Adaptive Acoustic Modeling for Speech Recognition", Speech Communication, vol.35, issue 1-2, pp 31-51, Aug. 01.
8. Dalsgaard P., Andersen O., Hesselager H., Petek B., "Language Identification using Language-dependent phonemes and Language-independent speech units", ICSLP, 1996, p.1808-1811.
9. Corredor-Ardoy C., Gauvain J., Adda_decker M., Lamel L., "Language Identification with Language-independent acoustic models", Proc. of EUROSPEECH 97, September 1997.
10. Martin T., Wong E., Baker B., Mason M., "Pitch and Energy Trajectory Modeling in a Syllable Length Temporal Framework for Language Identification", ODYSSEY 2004, May 31- June 3, 2004, Toledo, Spain.
11. Pusateri E., Thong JM., "N-best List Generation using Word and Phoneme Recognition Fusion", 7th European Conference on Speech Communication and Technology (EuroSpeech), September 2001, Aalborg, Denmark.
12. Salomon J., King S., Osborne M., "Framewise phone classification using support vector machines", In Proceedings International Conference on Spoken Language Processing, Denver, 2002.
13. Garofolo J., "Getting started with the DARPA-TIMIT CD-ROM: An acoustic phonetic continuous speech database", National Institute of Standards and Technology (NIST), Gaithersburgh, MD, USA, 1988.
14. Friedman J., "Another approach to polychotomous classification", Technical report, Stanford University, UA, 1996.
15. Suykens J., Vandewalle J., "Least Squares Support Vector Machine Classifiers", Neural Processing Letters, vol. 9, no. 3, Jun. 1999, pp. 293-300.
16. Hodge H., "SpeechDat multilingual speech databases for teleservices: across the finish line", EUROSPEECH'99, Budapest, Hungary, Sept 5-9 1999, Vol. 6, pp. 2699-2702.
17. Chatzi, I., Fakotakis N. and Kokkinakis G., "Greek speech database for creation of voice driven teleservices", EUROSPEECH'97, Rhodes, Greece, Sept. 22-25 1997, vol. 4, pp.1755-1758.
18. John G., Langley P., "Estimating Continuous Distributions in Bayesian Classifiers", 11th Conference on Uncertainty in Artificial Intelligence, pp. 338-345, Morgan Kaufmann, San Mateo, 1995.
19. Quinlan J. R., "C4.5: Programs for Machine Learning", Morgan Kaufmann Publishers, San Mateo, 1993.
20. Quinlan J. R., "Bagging, Boosting, and C4.5", AAAI/IAAI, Vol. 1, 1996.
21. Witten I., Frank E., "Data Mining: Practical machine learning tools with Java implementations", Morgan Kaufmann, 1999.
22. Burges C., "A tutorial on Support Vector Machines for Pattern Recognition", Data Mining and Knowledge Discovery, Vol. 2, Number 2, p.121-167, Kluwer Academic Publishers, 1998.

Ensemble Pruning Using Reinforcement Learning

Ioannis Partalas, Grigorios Tsoumakas,
Ioannis Katakis, and Ioannis Vlahavas

Department of Informatics,
Aristotle University of Thessaloniki,
54124 Thessaloniki, Greece
{partalas, greg, katak, vlahavas}@csd.auth.gr

Abstract. Multiple Classifier systems have been developed in order to improve classification accuracy using methodologies for effective classifier combination. Classical approaches use heuristics, statistical tests, or a meta-learning level in order to find out the optimal combination function. We study this problem from a Reinforcement Learning perspective. In our modeling, an agent tries to learn the best policy for selecting classifiers by exploring a state space and considering a future cumulative reward from the environment. We evaluate our approach by comparing with state-of-the-art combination methods and obtain very promising results.

1 Introduction

A very active research area during the recent years involves methodologies and systems for the production and combination of multiple predictive models. Within the Machine Learning community this area is commonly referred to as Ensemble Methods [1]. The success of this area is due to the fact that ensembles of predictive models offer higher predictive accuracy than individual models.

The first phase of an Ensemble Method is the production of the different models. An ensemble can be composed of either homogeneous or heterogeneous models. Models that derive from different executions of the same learning algorithm are called Homogeneous. Such models can be produced by injecting randomness into the learning algorithm or through the manipulation of the training instances, the input attributes and the model outputs [2]. Models that derive from running different learning algorithms on the same data set are called Heterogeneous. The second phase of an Ensemble Method is the combination of the models. Common methods here include Selection, Voting, Weighted Voting and Stacking. Recent work [3], [4] has shown that an additional intermediate phase of pruning an ensemble of heterogeneous classifiers (and combining the selected classifiers with Voting) leads to increased predictive performance.

This paper presents a Reinforcement Learning approach to the problem of pruning an ensemble of heterogeneous classifiers. We use the Q-learning algorithm in order to approximate an optimal policy of choosing whether to include

G. Antoniou et al. (Eds.): SETN 2006, LNAI 3955, pp. 301–310, 2006.

or exclude each algorithm from the ensemble. We compare our approach against other pruning methods and state-of-the-art Ensemble methods and obtain very promising results. Additionaly, the proposed approach is an anytime algorithm, meaning that we can obtain a solution at any point.

The rest of this paper is structured as follows: Section 2 presents background information on reinforcement learning and heterogeneous classifier combination, focusing on material that will be later on reffered in the paper. Section 3 reviews related work on pruning ensembles of heterogeneous models, as well as on using reinforcement learning for the combination of different algorithms. Section 4 presents our approach and Section 5 the setup of the experiments for its evaluation. Section 6 discusses the results of the experiments and finally Section 7 concludes this work and points to future research directions.

2   Background

2.1   Reinforcement Learning

Reinforcement Learning (RL) addresses the problem of how an agent can learn a behavior through trial-and-error interactions with a dynamic environment [5]. In an RL task the agent, at each time step, senses the environment's state, $s_t \in S$, where S is the finite set of possible states, and selects an action $a_t \in A(s_t)$ to execute, where $A(s_t)$ is the finite set of possible actions in state s_t. The agent receives a reward, $r_{t+1} \in \Re$, and moves to a new state s_{t+1}. The objective of the agent is to maximize the cumulative reward received over time. More specifically, the agent selects actions that maximize the expected discounted return:

$$R_t = r_{t+1} + \gamma r_{t+2} + \gamma^2 r_{t+3} + \ldots = \sum_{k=0} \gamma^k r_{t+k+1}, \tag{1}$$

where γ, $0 \le \gamma < 1$, is the discount factor and expresses the importance of future rewards.

A *policy* π specifies that in state s the probability of taking action a is $\pi(s, a)$. For any policy π, the value of state s, $V^\pi(s)$, denotes the expected discounted return, if the agent starts from s and follows policy π thereafter. The value $V^\pi(s)$ of s under π is defined as:

$$V^\pi(s) = E_\pi \{R_t \mid s_t = s\} = E_\pi \left\{ \sum_{k=0} \gamma^k r_{t+k+1} \middle| s_t = s \right\}, \tag{2}$$

where s_t and r_{t+1} denote the state at time t and the reward received after acting at time t, respectively.

Similarly, the *action-value function*, $Q^\pi(s, a)$, under a policy π can be defined as the expected discounted return for executing a in state s and thereafter following π:

$$Q^\pi(s, a) = E_\pi \{R_t \mid s_t = a, a_t = a\} = E_\pi \left\{ \sum_{k=0} \gamma^k r_{t+k+1} \middle| s_t = a, a_t = a \right\}. \tag{3}$$

The optimal policy, π , is the one that maximizes the value, $V^\pi(s)$, for all states s, or the action-value, $Q^\pi(s, a)$, for all state-action pairs.

In order to learn the optimal policy, the agent learns the *optimal value function*, V , or the *optimal action-value function*, Q which is defined as the expected return of taking action a in state s and thereafter following the optimal policy π :

$$Q\ (s, a) = E \left\{ r_{t+1} + \gamma \max_{a'} Q\ (s_{t+1}, a') \Big| s_t = s, a_t = a \right\} \tag{4}$$

The optimal policy can now be defined as:

$$\pi\ = \arg \max_a Q\ (s, a) \tag{5}$$

The most widely used algorithm for finding the optimal policy is the Q-learning algorithm [6] which approximates the Q function with the following form:

$$Q(s_t, a_t) = r_{t+1} + \gamma \max_{a'} Q(s_{t+1}, a'). \tag{6}$$

2.2 Combining Heterogeneous Classification Models

A lot of different ideas and methodologies have been proposed in the past for the combination of heterogeneous classification models. The main motivation behind this research is the common observation that there is no independent classifier that performs significantly better in every classification problem. The necessity for high classification performance in some critical domains (e.g. medical, financial, intrusion detection) have urged researchers to explore methods that combine different classification algorithms in order to overcome the limitations of individual learning paradigms.

Unweighted and Weighted Voting are two of the simplest methods for combining not only Heterogeneous but also Homogeneous models. In Voting, each model outputs a class value (or ranking, or probability distribution) and the class with the most votes (or the highest average ranking, or average probability) is the one proposed by the ensemble. In Weighted Voting, the classification models are not treated equally. Each model is associated with a coefficient (weight), usually proportional to its classification accuracy.

Another simple method is Evaluation and Selection. This method evaluates each of the models (typically using 10-fold cross-validation) on the training set and selects the best one for application to the test set.

Stacked Generalization [7], also known as Stacking, is a method that combines multiple classifiers by learning a meta-level (or level-1) model that predicts the correct class based on the decisions of the base-level (or level-0) classifiers. This model is induced on a set of meta-level training data that are typically produced by applying a procedure similar to k-fold cross-validation on the training data:

Let D be the level-0 training data set. D is randomly split into k disjoint parts $D_1 \ldots D_k$ of equal size. For each fold $i = 1 \ldots k$ of the process, the base-level classifiers are trained on the set $D \setminus D_i$ and then applied to the test set D_i.

The output of the classifiers for a test instance along with the true class of that instance form a meta-instance.

A meta-classifier is then trained on the meta-instances and the base-level classifiers are trained on all training data D. When a new instance appears for classification, the output of all base-level classifiers is first calculated and then propagated to the meta-level classifier, which outputs the final result.

3   Related Work

3.1   Pruning Ensembles of Classifiers

Most of the Ensemble Methods in the literature deal either with the production or the combination of multiple classifiers. However, recent work has shown that pruning an ensemble of classifiers (and combining the selected classifiers with Voting) leads to increased predictive performance.

Caruana et al. [4], produce an ensemble of 1000 classification models using different algorithms and different sets of parameters for these algorithms. They subsequently prune the ensemble via forward stepwise selection of the classification models. As a heuristic, they use the accuracy of combining the selected classifiers with the method of voting. This way they manage to achieve very good predictive performance compared to state-of-the-art ensemble methods.

In [3], pruning is performed using statistical procedures that determine whether the differences in predictive performance among the classifiers of the ensemble are significant. Using such procedures only the classifiers with significantly better performance than the rest are retained and subsequently combined with the methods of (weighted) voting. The obtained results are better than those of state-of-the-art ensemble methods.

3.2   Reinforcement Learning for Algorithm Combination

Research work on utilizing Reinforcement Learning (RL) for algorithm combination is limited. We found two past approaches on this subject, one applied to the problem of selecting a single classification algorithm and one of applying the most suitable algorithms on different segments of the dataset. The latest approach applied on two computational problems: order statistic selection and sorting.

In [8], RL is used to adapt a policy for the combination of multiple classifiers. Specifically, an architecture with n experts (classifiers), implemented by multilayer perceptrons (MLPs) and an additional MLP with n-outputs acting as the controlling agent are employed. The state space of the controlling agent consists of the instance space (all the possible different instances) of the particular classification problem and the action is the choice of the expert who will take the classification decision. On top of that, the expert who has been chosen uses the instance to train itself.

In [9], the problem of algorithm selection is formulated as a Markov Decision Process (MDP) and an RL approach is used to solve it. Given a set of algorithms that are equivalent in terms of the problem they solve, and a set of instance features, such as problem size, an RL approach is used to select the right algorithm for each instance based on the set of features. The state of the MDP is represented by the current instantiation of the instance features and the actions are the different algorithms that can be selected. Finally, the immediate cost for choosing some algorithm on some problem is the real time taken for that execution. The learning mechanism is a variation of the Q-learning algorithm.

4   Ensemble Pruning Via Reinforcement Learning

First we must formulate the problem of pruning an ensemble of classifiers as an RL task. To do that, we must define the following components:

1. A set of states, S.
2. A set of actions, A.
3. A reward function, $r(s, a)$.

In our approach, a state represents the set of classifiers that have been selected so far and thus S is the powerset of S_c, $S = P(S_c)$, where $S_c = \{C_1, \ldots, C_n\}$ is the set of classifiers. S has 2^n different states, where n is the number of classifiers available for selection. In each state the agent can select between two actions. It can either include an algorithm into the ensemble or not and thus $A = \{include(C_i)|i = 1 \ldots n\} \cup \{exclude(C_i)|i = 1 \ldots n\}$. Finally, the reward is the accuracy that we obtain if we combine the selected classifiers with the method of voting.

The training phase consists of running a number of episodes, where an *episode* is defined as a sequence of agent-environment interactions. In our approach, each episode starts with an empty set of classifiers and lasts n time steps. At each time step, $t = 1 \ldots n$, of the episode, the agent chooses to include or not a specific classifier into the ensemble, $A(s_{t-1}) = \{include(C_t), exclude(C_t)\}$. Subsequently, the agent receives an immediate reward which equals to the accuracy of the current subset of classifiers combined with voting. The update equation of Q-learning is:

$$Q(s_t, a_t) = Accuracy(s_{t+1}) + \gamma \max_{a'} Q(s_{t+1}, a') \tag{7}$$

The episode ends when the decision to include or exclude the nth algorithm is taken. Figure 1 graphically shows a training episode.

During the training phase the agent must stochastically select actions in order to explore the state space. One way to achieve this aim is to make use of the softmax action selection method, where an action a is selected with probability:

$$P(a) = \frac{\exp^{Q(s,a)/T}}{\sum_{a'} \exp^{Q(s,a')/T}}, \tag{8}$$

where T is a positive parameter, called *temperature*, which starts from a high value and gradually is reduced until it becomes zero. High temperature values

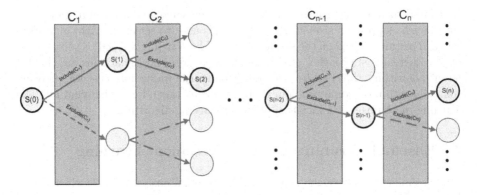

Fig. 1. The procedure of selecting a sequence of classifiers

assign equal probabilities to all actions so the agent explores the state space, while in other case low temperatures cause high probabilities for action with high value estimates and so the agent exploits his knowledge.

At the end of the training phase, the agent executes a final episode choosing the action with the highest Q value at each time step. The resulting subset of classifiers is the output of our approach. This way, the problem of pruning an ensemble of n classifiers has been transformed into the reinforcement learning task of letting an agent learn an optimal policy of taking n actions to maximize the cumulative reward.

5   Experimental Setup

We compare the performance of our approach, Ensemble Pruning via Reinforcement Learning (EPRL), against the following state-of-the-art classifier combination methods: Stacking with Multi-Response Model Trees (SMT), Evaluation and Selection (ES) and Effective Voting (EV).

The methods are applied on top of a heterogeneous ensemble produced using the WEKA [10] implementations of the following 9 different classification algorithms:

- DT: the decision table algorithm of Kohavi [11].
- JRip: the RIPPER rule learning algorithm [12].
- PART: the PART rule learning algorithm [13].
- J48: the decision tree learning algorithm C4.5 [14], using Laplace smoothing for predicted probabilities.
- IBk: the k nearest neighbor algorithm [15].
- K : an instance based learning algorithm with entropic distance measure [16].
- NB: the Naive Bayes algorithm using the kernel density estimator rather than assume normal distributions for numeric attributes [17].
- RBF: WEKA implemenation of an algorithm for training a radial basis function network [18].
- MLP: WEKA implementation of an algorithm for training a multilayer perceptron [18].

We compare the methods on 11 data sets from the UCI Machine Learning repository [19]. Table 1 presents the details of these data sets (Folder in UCI server, number of instances, classes, continuous and discrete attributes, (%) percentage of missing values).

Table 1. Details of the data sets: Folder in UCI server, number of instances, classes, continuous and discrete attributes, percentage of missing values.

UCI Folder	Inst	Cls	Cnt	Dsc	MV
hepatitis	155	2	6	13	5.67
heart-disease (cleveland)	303	5	6	7	0.18
horse-colic	368	2	7	15	23.80
iris	150	3	4	0	0.0
labor	57	2	8	8	35.75
ionosphere	351	2	34	0	0.0
prima-indians-diabetes	768	2	8	0	0.00
soybean	683	19	0	35	9.78
voting-records	435	2	0	16	5.63
wine	178	7	1	16	0.00
zoo	101	7	1	16	0.00

For the evaluation of the methods we perform a 10-fold stratified cross-validation experiment. In each of the 10 repetitions, the same 9 folds are used for training the different methods and 1 fold for evaluating their performance. The accuracy rates are averaged over the 10 folds in order to obtain the average accuracy $acc_m(d_i)$ of each method m in each data set d_i.

Our approach is run using a fixed number of 2000 episodes. For the representation of the value function Q we used a tabular approach, where each value $Q(s, a)$ is stored in a table. The value of T was set to 1000 and decreased by a factor of 2% at each episode. The decisions of the classifiers in the final pruned ensemble are combined using Voting.

6 Results and Discussion

Table 2 presents the accuracy of each classifier combination method on each of the 11 data sets. The last row presents the geometric mean of the accuracy over all data sets. The highest accuracy for each data set is emphasized using bold typeface.

We first notice that our approach has the highest mean accuracy than the rest of the methods. In addition, it has the highest accuracy in 5 data sets, one more than Effective Voting and two more than Stacking with Multi-Response Model Trees that are considered to be state-of-the-art methods for the combination of

Table 2. Folder in UCI server, average accuracy of each combining method on each of the 11 data sets and geometric mean of each combining method over all data sets

UCI Folder	SMT	ES	EV	EPRL
hepatitis	0.8379	0.8383	0.8383	**0.8614**
heart-disease (cleveland)	0.8300	**0.8442**	0.8172	0.8170
horse-colic	0.8290	0.8452	**0.8535**	0.8481
iris	**0.9533**	**0.9533**	0.9467	**0.9533**
labor	0.9100	0.9433	0.9267	**0.9667**
ionosphere	**0.9402**	0.9147	0.9232	0.9203
prima-indians-diabetes	0.7603	0.7720	0.7681	**0.7759**
soybean	0.9254	0.9254	**0.9444**	0.9415
voting-records	**0.9586**	0.9518	0.9563	0.9542
wine	0.9663	0.9722	**0.9889**	0.9722
zoo	0.9509	0.9409	**0.9609**	**0.9609**
geometric mean	0.8940	0.8979	0.8996	**0.9040**

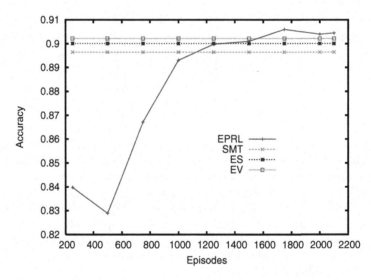

Fig. 2. Average accuracy on all data sets with respect to the episodes

heterogeneous classifiers. Figure 2 shows the average accuracy of our approach over all datasets using a varying number of episodes, starting from 250 up to 2000 with a step of 250 episdoes. It also shows the accuracy of the other classifier combination methods for comparison purposes. As it can be seen, our approach obtains good performance for a small number of episodes and finally outperforms the other methods. In approximately 500 episodes T has acquired a significantly low value and the agent exploits its knowledge. As a result, the accuracy of our approach increases rapidly.

7   Conclusions and Future Work

This paper has presented a method for pruning an ensemble of heterogeneous classifiers based on Reinforcement Learning. The results of combining the subset of classifiers with Voting are very promising as they compare favorably against the results of state-of-the-art methods for heterogeneous classifier combination.

An interesting aspect of the proposed approach is its *anytime* property, which means that it can output a solution at any given time point. As we show from the experimental results, after an initial period of exploration, the approach starts improving by exploiting the knowledge it acquired. Therefore the more the training episodes, the higher the predictive performance of the resulting pruned ensemble, until the approach converges around some good performance.

Another interesting property is that the computational complexity of the method is linear with respect to the ensemble size, as each training episode lasts as many time steps as the number of classifiers in the ensemble. However, the state space that the agent has to explore grows exponentially with the number of classifiers, and so does the complexity of the learning problem.

In the future, we intend to investigate the applicability of the proposed ideas in libraries of thousands of models [4]. In such a case we need to alter the representation of the states, in order to tackle the explosion of the state space. In addition, we plan to explore other methods of action selection, in order to improve not only the exploration of the state space but also the time needed for the algorithm to converge.

Acknowledgements

This work was partially supported by the Greek R&D General Secretariat through a PENED program (EPAN M.8.3.1, No. 03EΔ73).

References

1. Dietterich, T.G.: Machine-learning research: Four current directions. The AI Magazine **18** (1998) 97–136
2. Dietterich, T.G.: Ensemble methods in machine learning. Lecture Notes in Computer Science **1857** (2000) 1–15
3. Tsoumakas, G., Katakis, I., Vlahavas, I.P.: Effective voting of heterogeneous classifiers. In: Proceedings of the 15th European Conference on Machine Learning, ECML 04. (2004) 465–476
4. Caruana, R., Niculescu-Mizil, A., Crew, G., Ksikes, A.: Ensemble selection from libraries of models. In: ICML '04: Proceedings of the twenty-first international conference on Machine learning, New York, NY, USA, ACM Press (2004) 18
5. Sutton, R.S., Barto, A.G.: Reinforcmement Learning, An Introduction. MIT Press (1999)
6. Watkins, C., Dayan, P.: Q-learning. Machine Learning **8** (1992) 279–292
7. Wolpert, D.H.: Stacked generalization. Technical Report LA-UR-90-3460, Los Alamos, NM (1990)

8. Christos Dimitrakakis, S.B.:   Online adaptive policies for ensemble classifiers. Trends in Neurocomputing **64** (2005) 211–221
9. Lagoudakis, M.G., Littman, M.L.: Algorithm selection using reinforcement learning. In: Proc. 17th International Conf. on Machine Learning, Morgan Kaufmann, San Francisco, CA (2000) 511–518
10. Witten, I.H., Frank, E.: Data Mining: Practical machine learning tools and techniques, 2nd Edition. Morgan Kaufmann (2005)
11. Kohavi, R.: The power of decision tables. In Lavrac, N., Wrobel, S., eds.: Proceedings of the European Conference on Machine Learning. Lecture Notes in Artificial Intelligence 914, Berlin, Heidelberg, New York, Springer Verlag (1995) 174–189
12. Cohen, W.W.: Fast effective rule induction. In Prieditis, A., Russell, S., eds.: Proc. of the 12th International Conference on Machine Learning, Tahoe City, CA, Morgan Kaufmann (1995) 115–123
13. Frank, E., Witten, I.H.: Generating accurate rule sets without global optimization. In: Proc. 15th International Conf. on Machine Learning, Morgan Kaufmann, San Francisco, CA (1998) 144–151
14. Quinlan, J.R.: C4.5: programs for machine learning. Morgan Kaufmann Publishers Inc., San Francisco, CA, USA (1993)
15. Aha, D.W., Kibler, D., Albert, M.K.: Instance-based learning algorithms. Mach. Learn. **6** (1991) 37–66
16. Cleary, J.G., Trigg, L.E.: K*: an instance-based learner using an entropic distance measure. In: Proc. 12th International Conference on Machine Learning, Morgan Kaufmann (1995) 108–114
17. John, G.H., Langley, P.: Estimating continuous distributions in Bayesian classifiers. In: Proceedings of the Eleventh Conference on Uncertainty in Artificial Intelligence. (1995) 338–345
18. Bishop, C.M.: Neural networks for pattern recognition. Oxford University Press, Oxford, UK (1996)
19. D.J. Newman, S. Hettich, C.B., Merz, C.: UCI repository of machine learning databases (1998)

Mining Bilingual Lexical Equivalences Out of Parallel Corpora

Stelios Piperidis[1] and Ioannis Harlas[2]

[1] Institute for Language and Speech Processing,
Artemidos 6 & Epidavrou 15125 Marousi, Greece,
and National Technical University of Athens
spip@ilsp.gr
[2] Athens University of Economics & Business
jharlas@cs.aueb.gr

Abstract. The role and importance of methods for lexical knowledge elicitation in the area of multilingual information processing, including machine translation, computer-aided translation and cross-lingual information retrieval is undisputable. The usefulness of such methods becomes even more apparent in cases of language pairs where no appropriate digital language resources exist. This paper presents encouraging experimental results in automatically eliciting bilingual lexica out of Greek-Turkish parallel corpora, consisting of international organizations' documents available in English, Greek and Turkish, in an attempt to aid multilingual document processing involving these languages.

1 Introduction

Of primary importance to the field of machine translation is the deployment of multilingual language resources, usually in the form of a bi-lingual or multi-lingual lexicon establishing translation equivalences between lexical units. The lack of such resources, in a digital form, for language pairs involving less widely used languages in the digital world, such as Greek and Turkish, but also the difficulties of the manual construction of such resources, are the main reasons underlying the necessity and importance of automatic methods for the compilation of such lexicons. Evidence for the applicability of statistical approaches to machine translation is accumulating fast and the performance of statistical techniques coupled with machine learning, proves to be a solution especially when focusing on specific domains. Yet, the main advantage of statistical algorithms is their versatility, as they can be used in many language pairs without minimal methodological changes. The bilingual lexicon extraction method proposed in this paper is based on statistical algorithms over parallel corpora, i.e. corpora consisting of source texts translated to one or more target languages. The language pairs in focus here cover languages with substantial differences in morphology and syntax, Greek (EL) – Turkish (TR) and also Greek (EL) – English (EN). The challenges of tackling the EL-TR pair consist in morphological and syntactical differences between the two languages, stemming from the fact that they belong to different language families. Turkish is an agglutinative

G. Antoniou et al. (Eds.): SETN 2006, LNAI 3955, pp. 311–322, 2006.

language with S-O-V structure, while Greek is non-agglutinative and mostly S-V-O. The value of such methods is highly evaluated especially if we take in consideration a) time costs associated with the manual construction of domain-specific, let alone general language, lexicons, b) the versatility of methods and systems in different kinds of applications and also different language pairs, c) the usability of generated resources in conjunction with translation tools, for learning i.a. new words enriching the original lexicons. In the following chapter we review briefly techniques used up today. In chapter 3 we present the architecture of the proposed method analyzing the phase of single and multi word association. In chapter 4 we present the results from evaluation tests of our method while in chapter 5 we summarize the conclusions of this work.

2 Background

In order to achieve lexicon building automation, usually referred to as word alignment, some basic language processing is involved. Intermediate, well-delineated steps, include: a) Text alignment at sentence level, b) Word conflation to improve statistical relevance, c) Alignment at word level, and d) Spotting and translation of Multi-Word Units (MWUs).

Text alignment at sentence level is the first step for almost any approach [12]. The most commonly used algorithm is the one Gale & Church introduced [4] based on the observation that longer sentences in one language tend to be translated into longer sentences in the other language, and that shorter sentences tend to be translated into shorter sentences. The algorithm manages to align sentences in a ratio of 1:1, 1:0, 0:1, 2:1, 1:2 and 2:2. The sentence length-measure they selected is the number of characters in each sentence. Brown et al. [1] have introduced another algorithm with the main difference of using different metric length of the sentences counting words instead of characters. Their algorithm is also supported by the alignment of "anchor" words. On the word conflation front, word forms that conflate together are reduced to a representative form in order to render the statistical measurements relevant.

The problem of "word conflation" could be solved by grouping all the words based on lemmatization or stemming [13]. Both techniques require the appropriate linguistic processing, usually in terms of a POS tagging and lemmatisation procedure, in order to resolve any ambiguous cases, or in terms of knowledge of morphological classes for stemming purposes. Yet, the existence of usable, possibly with good domain coverage, linguistic processors is not granted for less widely used languages, forcing solutions to be based on "string matching" algorithms. Two of the most popular such solutions are a) Longest Common Sub-sequence Ratio (LCSR), and b) N-Grams [7].

Alignment at word level consists in matching all words of each source sentence with a subset of candidate translations and subsequently selects the most "suitable" association. This phase is usually divided in two sub phases: first eliciting candidate translations and second selecting the most suitable translation. On candidate translations elicitation, for each source word, a set of target words that co-occurred in the aligned target sentences is the original set of candidate translations. However, its size is cut down to a minimal subset of candidate translations for performance reasons and for resolving ambiguous cases. The process of eliminating irrelevant target words has been implemented by Tufiş [16] with the use of a PoS tagger that assosiates only words of the same part of speech category. Another solution proposed by Brown et al. [2] calculates the Mutual Conditional Probability between every source word and its candidate translations and then eliminates those that do not meet a selected threshold. Tufiş [16] and Brown et al. [2] also propose is usage of the relative position of words in the aligned setences they co-occur, eliminating candidates located outside a range of ±2 positions. The problem with these proposals, however, is that they would not work for languages of totally different syntax. A very simple, yet very effective, method has been introduced by Smadja [14] using a modification of the Dice coefficient, substituting the frequency of the target word f(y), with the sum of the co-occurrences of y with the source word. The methods used for selecting the most suitable translation are based on association or estimation techniques [15] or even combining both. The association methods use heuristics, based on the co-occurrences of two words or sometimes on string matching techniques. Widely used association measures include the Dice coefficient and point-wise mutual information. The estimation methods can either be based on probabilistic or graph models. The probabilistic models select a target word y as the translation of the source word x if maximizes the $P(y|x) = P(x|y)* P(y)$. Two of the graph models proposed by Kageura et al. [6] and Gaussier [5] construct graphs whose vertices are the words found in the parallel corpora. Two vertices, derived from words from each language, are connected with an edge only if they are likely to comprise a translation pair. The final word alignment is reached with the use of graph algorithms.

On locating and translating MWUs: MWUs in most cases consist of 2 - 4 (not necessarily contiguous) words with such a concrete meaning that usually translates into a different number of words in another language. The first problem is the identification of the MWU. A common practice used by Kupiec [8] and Van der Eijk [17] locates sequences of nouns supposing that MWUs consist, mainly, of nouns. A more sophisticated system XTRACT has been developed by Smadja et al. [14] locating MWUs using the following criteria: a) up to 4 words can interve between every 2 words of the MWU, b) the MWU has to appear at least 5 times in the text. The only "problem" with XTRACT is that it requires language specific information as part of a PoS tagger and syntax analysis stages. Smadja et al. [14] also introduced "Champollion", a system for translating the MWUs that XTRACT locates. Its iterative structure comes to an end when no more words can be added to the translation of a word or a MWU and still score under a threshold.

3 System Architecture

The proposed method consists of 3 main phases, including a pre-processing phase consisting in aligning the parallel corpus at sentence level. Phase 1 consists in eliciting candidate translations and conflating word forms. Phase 2 consists in aligning at word level, while phase 3 consists in identifying MWUs on both corpus sides and eliciting translation equivalents of MWUs.

The task for the pre-processing phase is to align the sentences of each text in the parallel corpus. Sentence alignment is performed by the "Tr•AID Align" tool [11], based on an improved Gale & Church-like [4] algorithm, running and tested for the first time on EL-TR. The not-unexpected problem encountered involved the inability to locate alignments 3:1, 1:3, 3:2, 2:3, 2:0, 0:2, realized in the corpus.

3.1 Phase 1: Eliciting Candidate Translations and Conflating

For performance reasons, the list of co-occurring target words (candidate translations) gets downsized to a minimum, without loss of correct translations. The methods reviewed in chapter 2 eliminating candidate translations based on their relevant position in a sentence, cannot be used in EL-TR due to the languages' differences. We have therefore introduced another method, appropriate for language pairs of different structure. However the main difference from the evaluation metrics of [2] and [14], is the use of the current frequency of the source and target words, instead of calculating the total occurrences of the two words.

3.1.1 Evaluation Metric

The elimination of irrelevant target words from the list of the source-word's co-occurring words is achieved by use of an evaluation metric introduced in [10], [12] Target words scoring below an empirically defined threshold are ignored from the candidates' list.

$$M(x, y) = \frac{\sqrt{(f(x)-m)^2 + (f(y)-m)^2 + (f(x, y)-m)^2}}{m} \tag{1}$$

$$m = \frac{f(x)+f(y)+f(x, y)}{3}$$

$f(x)$, $f(y)$:   occurrences of source word x and target word y, respectively
$f(x,y)$:   co-occurrences of word x and y in aligned sentences

If y is the only translation of x then they will probably occur the same times in the texts and they furthermore will always occur in aligned sentences thus: $f(x) = f(y) = f(x,y)$ ➔ $M(x,y) = 0$. Actually things are more complicated as it is very common for a word to have more than one translations (y_1, y_2) and therefore $f(x) = f(y_1) + f(y_2)$ ➔ $f(x) > f(y_1)$ ➔ $M(x,y) > 0$. Equation (1) is symmetrical thus: $M(x,y) = M(y,x)$. Generally, the smaller the value of $M(x,y)$ is, the more probable is, that y is the translation of x and vice versa.

3.1.2 Threshold

Tests of the evaluation metric have proven that a sufficient threshold for deciding if y is the translation of x is $M(x,y) < 0.5$. Yet this is a very strict threshold since in the first phase of our algorithm, we do not use the total frequencies but current frequencies. After calculating the first 25 possible combinations (Table 1), excluding symmetrical combinations, for f(x), f(y) and f(x,y) we came up with 3 possible values that could lead to a translation pair. $M(x,y) \in \{0 , 0.816497 , 1.414214 , 1.632993\}$. We have selected as threshold T the greater value: T=1.632993 meaning that any target word y that co-occurred in an aligned sentence with x and $M(x,y) \leq T$ then is added to the list of x's candidate translations.

Table 1. Possible combinations

A/A	$f(x)$	$f(y)$	$f(x,y)$	M(x,y)	Dice(x,y)	Accept.	A/A	$f(x)$	$f(y)$	$f(x,y)$	M(x,y)	Dice(x,y)	Accept.
1	1	1	1	0.000000	1	YES	14	3	2	2	0.816497	0.8	YES
2	1	0	0	0.816497	0	YES	15	3	3	0	2.449490	0	
3	1	1	0	0.816497	0	YES	16	3	3	1	1.632993	0.333333	YES
4	2	0	0	1.632993	0	YES	17	3	3	2	0.816497	0.666667	YES
5	2	1	0	1.414214	0	YES	18	4	1	0	2.943920	0	
6	2	1	1	0.816497	0.666667	YES	19	4	2	0	2.828427	0	
7	2	2	0	1.632993	0	YES	20	4	1	1	2.449490	0.4	
8	2	2	1	0.816497	0.5	YES	21	4	2	1	2.160247	0.333333	
9	3	0	0	2.449490	0		22	4	3	0	2.943920	0	
10	3	1	0	2.160247	0		23	4	3	1	2.160247	0.285714	
11	3	1	1	1.632993	0.5	YES	24	4	3	2	1.414214	0.571429	YES
12	3	2	0	2.160247	0		25	4	3	3	0.816497	0.857143	YES
13	3	2	1	1.414214	0.4	YES							

An additional elimination criterion we have used is the size of the list of candidate translations itself. Assuming that the average size of a sentence is 20-30 words and that the translation of a word should be included in the first 3 aligned sentences, then we can limit the size of candidate translations to a maximum of 100.

3.1.3 M(x,y) vs Dice Coefficient

From a close examination of Table 1, our evalua tion metric appears to be of higher discriminant capacity than the Dice coefficient especially in cases that f(y) and f(x,y) have a very low value (up to 3). In cases {2, 3, 4, 5, 7} and {9, 10, 12, 15, 18, 19, 22} the value of Dice coefficient is always 0, although the first set could be candidate translations and the latter not. On the contrary, the M(x,y) values vary with smaller values for the first set and higher values for the second set, allowing the distinction of the two sets. Moreover, the value of M(x,y) is the same in cases 8 and 11, while Dice coefficient's values are quite different. On the other hand, Dice coefficient scores the same in cases of both sets: {13, 20} and {16, 21}, while on the contrary, the values of M(x,y), correctly vary appropriately. From all the 25 cases examined, Dice coefficient gives better results than M(x,y) in cases 6 and 14.

3.1.4 Word Conflation

For performance reasons the words that conflate together are grouped to sets that are identified by a representative word. The procedures for selecting the representative word and for joining sets are implemented by Union_by_Height and Path_ Compress-ion techniques [3].

Word conflating without linguistic information was based on the observation that in both language (as in most) variations of words are formed by altering their suffix, while their bigger part (from left to right), remains the same. Thus, in order to decide if two words of the same language have a common root, we applied the following: a) from Greek words stresses are deleted, b) depending on the length in characters of word, we ignore up to k and k′ characters from the end of each one respectively (where k, k′ : ∈ {0,1,2,3,4,5}), while the total of ignored characters should never exceed 40% of the total length of the compared word, c) all the strings deriving from each allowed value of k and k′ are being compared to each other and if any two of them are the same, then the two words are considered to have the same root, d) should the two words conflate with each other, the Union_by_Height procedure will set the pointers, of the words, to their representative. In the example of table 5, we test if the words "υποστηρίζεται" and "υποστήριξη" should get conflated.

<table>
<tr><td colspan="3" align="center">**Table 2.** Word conflation</td></tr>
<tr><td>Character length</td><td>Ignored characters</td><td>% of ignored characters</td></tr>
<tr><td>Up to 2</td><td>0</td><td>0 %</td></tr>
<tr><td>3 or 4</td><td>0 or 1</td><td>25% - 33.3%</td></tr>
<tr><td>5 , 6 or 7</td><td>0 , 1 or 2</td><td>28.5% - 40%</td></tr>
<tr><td>8 or 9</td><td>up to 3</td><td>33.3% - 37.5%</td></tr>
<tr><td>10 , 11 or 12</td><td>up to 4</td><td>33.3% - 40%</td></tr>
<tr><td>More than 12</td><td>up to 5</td><td>< 38.46%</td></tr>
</table>

Table 3. Conflation example

Ignored characters	υποστηρίζεται k = 5	υποστήριξη k′ = 4
0	Υποστηριζεται	υποστηριξη
1	Υποστηριζετα	υποστηριξ
2	υποστηριζετ	υποστηρι
3	Υποστηριζε	υποστηρ
4	Υποστηριζ	υποστη
5	υποστηρι	-

This algorithm is not flawless as N-gram's based algorithms. There are several cases that the one algorithm works better than the other (and vice versa). The main advantage of our algorithm is that it works better on word-pairs of different length. The 2-grams score of the word-pair used in our example is 0.6667, quite low for conflating them.

Apart from using purely statistical algorithms we have also tried to embed language specific information in the phase of word conflation. Word conflation using linguistic information was based on the lemmas of the words in the parallel texts. Words with the same lemma are conflated. Lemmatisation for Greek was performed by ILSP's lemmatiser [9], while for Turkish it has been performed by Kemal Oflazer[1].

3.3 Phase 2: Word Alignment

Word alignment takes place in the second phase of the proposed method, by evaluating the possibility of source word x being translated to any of its candidate translations. The evaluation process is augmented by two scoring functions the *Word-Score* and the *Representative-Score*.

3.3.1 Representative-Score (Rep-score)

Again equation 1 is used in order to calculate Rep-score. The difference from W-score is that instead of the single word forms x, y their representatives X, Y respectively, are used for the calculation of $M(X,Y)$ = Rep-score. Thus, for calculating the Rep-score for source word x_1 the following steps are needed: a) The representative of x_1 is retrieved ($X = x_0$), b) All the words $x_1, x_2, \ldots, x_n$ represented by X are retrieved. c) For each of these words there is a corresponding list S_i containing all the sentences the word occurs. We call S_x the union of all these lists. d) The number of members of set S_x is the frequency of x_1's representative = $f(X) \geq f(x_1)$. e) For all the words x_i represented by X, we call WC_X the union of their sets:

[1] Kemal Oflazer , Sabanci University , Faculty of Engineering and Natural Sciences , Orhanli, 81474 Tuzla, Istanbul, Turkey, http://people.sabanciuniv.edu/~oflazer/

WC_{xi} that contain their candidate translations. f) For each target word y_i, contained in WC_X its representative Y is retrieved. g) All the words y_1, y_2 ... y_m represented by Y are retrieved with their corresponding lists T_1, T_2, ..., T_m that contain the sentences in which they occur. h) The number of the members of the union T_Y of all these lists is the frequency of y's representative $= f(Y)$. i) The number of common sentences found in S_X and T_Y is the frequency of common co-occurrences of X and Y : $f(X,Y) = |S_X \cap T_Y|$. j) Finally by replacing $f(x)$, $f(y)$, $f(x,y)$ with $f(X)$, $f(Y)$, $f(X,Y)$ on equation 1 we calculate the $M(X,Y)$ = Rep-score.

3.3.2 Word Translation (Alignment)

The procedure for finding the x's alignment pair is analyzed below: a) All the Rep-scores are calculated between all source words represented by X and each candidate translation. b) All W-scores are calculated between source word x and its candidate translations. c) From the target representatives examined in the first step, the one with the lowest score is selected. d) If more than one words tied in first place, a set of Candidate Representatives (CR) is created. In this case, draws are resolved after calculating the W-score for all the candidate translations of x. e) Finally the target word y, that is represented by the representative selected in step c), is selected as the translation of word x. If more than one representatives have been selected in step d), then the translation of x is the target word, whose representative is included in set CR and has the minimum W-score among all others (whose representatives are also included in set CR). f) In the first step Rep-scores are not calculated only for words co-occurring with x but also for an extended set of target words co-occurring with source words represented by X. As a consequence it is possible that the best scoring representative(s) does not represent any of the candidate translations of x. In these cases, the output of the system will be: all the best scoring representatives (set CR), and any candidate translations with W-score = 0. Even though we try to deal with ties in steps d), e) and f) above, it is still possible that more than one words have a minimum W-score while their representatives also score the minimum Rep-score. In most cases this problem comes up as a result of parallel corpora of insufficient size. In order to deal with these extended ties, the system's output are all the equally scored words, with a certainty percentage equally divided among all the results.

3.4 Phase 3: Translation of MWUs

3.4.1 Spotting the MWUs

The main difference of the proposed system from others such as Smadja's et.al. [14], is that no linguistic information is involved in tracking down MWUs. The method is based on metric $M(x,y)$ with the difference that the two evaluated words are of the same language and in the same sentence. Initially, two-word units are located and in the following recursive steps, n-word units are located by extending, when appropriate, the already found (n-1)-word units.

3.4.1.1 Locating 2-Word Units. The steps of the process are as follows: a) for each source word x all the containing sentences are recalled, b) words contained in the sentences of the previous step will be tested with x for constructing a 2-word unit, excluding words with the same representative with x and words located more than 2 positions away from x. For the selected words, both W-score and Rep-score are calculated ($M(x,y)$ and $M(X,Y)$), c) word pairs with score $M(x,y)$ or $M(X,Y)$ less than an empirically selected threshold $T_2 = 0.3$ and a frequency $f(x,y)$ or $f(X,Y) \geq 3$ are qualified as valid 2-word pairs, d) finally word pairs that do not manage to score both $M(x,y)$ and $M(X,Y) \leq$ than an empirically selected upper limit: $L_{max} = 1.5$, are eliminated.

3.4.1.2   Locating MWUs. Every MWU can be considered as one or more 2-word units + some additional words. Thus, each 2-word or (n-1)-word unit (called x), found in a previous phase, is tested, using $M(x,y)$ and $M(x,Y)$, with any word y (located at most 2 positions further than the first or the last word of x and represented by Y) in order to check if y should be added to the (n-1)-word unit x. The empirically selected thresholds are slightly modified in this phase: $T_n = 0.4$ and $TR_n = 0.3$. If the tested word y passes the following selection criterion:

$$(M(x,y) \leq T_n \textbf{ OR } M(x,Y) \leq TR_n) \textbf{ AND } (M(x,y) \leq L_{max} \textbf{ AND } M(x,Y) \leq L_{max})$$
$$\textbf{AND } (f(x,y) \geq 3 \textbf{ OR } f(x,Y) \geq 3)$$

then it is added to the (n-1)-word unit x which is then updated to a n-word unit.

3.4.2 Translating MWUs
After locating all the MWUs, we seek their translation as follows: a) translating MWU x first of all its container sentences are recalled, b) if the aligned sentences of the target language also contain MWUs: $\{Z_1, Z_2, \ldots Z_k\}$, all $M(x,Z_i)$ are calculated, c) for each target word y (represented by Y) contained in the aligned sentences, $M(x,y)$ and $M(x,Y)$ are calculated, d) the MWU x is then translated either to a single word or to another MWU. After comparing all the calculated scores : $M(x,Z_i)$ $M(x,y)$, $M(x,Y)$ the one with the minimum (=better) score is selected.

4   Evaluation Tests

The lack of sizeable EL-TR parallel corpora made imperative the use of texts of rather limited size. The smaller, text 'A', accounting for 6.011 EL words, 4.227 TR words and 5.234 EN words, is a loosely translated text from NATO texts. The second, bigger text ('B'), accounting for 41.870 EL words, 31.618 TR words and 40.742 EN words, of more accurate translation, is the UN Anan Plan text. For *sentence alignment* purposes, Tr•AID Align did treat 6 cases of 2:1 alignments, 3 cases of 1:2, and 2 cases of 2:2. Most errors were due to strange punctuation use leading to erroneous sentence splitting. The 21 wrong alignments were due to cases of 1:3, 1:0 and 0:2 alignments, due to free translation style. Overall, the performance of Tr•AID Align on EL-TR corpora was quite satisfying: 87% accuracy in text A, 100% in text B.

Word conflation. Table 4 displays the results from applying our word-conflating procedure.

Table 4. Word Conflation Results (EL-TR)

	Word Conflation in Text 'A'	Greek	Turkish
a	Different words	1695	1895
b	Total Conflations	658	723
c	Wrong Conflations	22	22
d	Missing Conflations	28	182
e	Not Conflated	89	85
f	**Precision [b-c/b]**	**95.1368 %**	**96.9571 %**
g	**Recall [b-c/(b-c+d+e)]**	**84.2530 %**	**72.4174 %**

Word alignment results. The system tries to align all the words found in the parallel corpora instead of aligning only the best scoring of them. The main issue in trying to align words between EL-TR is that many Greek words are not aligned with a Turkish word but with a suffix. Results are presented in tables 5, 6 and 7.

Table 5. EL-TR Results

	Word Alignment Text 'B'	Greek	Turkish
a	Different words	5.215	6.663
b	Sample size	919	962
c	Correctly translated	390	410
d	**Precision [c/b]**	**42.4374 %**	**42.6195 %**

Table 6. EL-EN Results

	Word Alignment Text 'A'	Greek	English
a	Different words	1.695	1.299
b	Sample size	1.000	1.000
c	Correctly translated	575	600
d	**Precision [c/b]**	**57.5 %**	**60 %**

Table 7. Word Alignment Examples (EN-EL)

Source word	Translation(s)	
"reduced"	☑ μειωθούν	☑ μειώθηκε
"regular"	☑ τακτικές	☑ τακτικής
"always"	θέσεις	☑ πάντοτε
"appeared"	εξελίξεις	ξέσπασμα
"ability"	☑ ικανότητα	
"accordingly"	☑ συνέπεια	
"achieved"	κοινή	
"act"	☑ δράσης	

"acted"	Ανάπτυξη	
"action"	☑ δράση	
"activities"	☑ δραστηριοτήτων	
"actor"	Αναπτύσσει	
"adapt"	☑ προσαρμόσουν	
"adapting"	☑ προσαρμογή	
"addition"	☑ επιπροσθέτως	
"additional"	☑ επιπρόσθετες	
"address"	☑ αντιμετωπίσει	
"addressing"	☑ αντιμετώπισης	

One of the causes for failing to translate a word is wrong or incomplete word conflation. To illustrate the importance of word conflation, consider the following:

The wordforms "άμυνα"(8), "άμυνας"(7), "αμυντικές"(3), "αμυντικών"(1), "αμυντική"(2), "αμυντικούς"(1), (with frequencies denoted in parentheses) instead of conflating into a single set, they result in two conflation subsets:

A = {*άμυνα, άμυνας*} with representative frequency $f(X_A) = 15$

B = {*αμυντικές, αμυντικών, αμυντικούς, αμυντική*} with $f(X_B) = 7$

The Turkish corresponding word "savunma" and its 6 variations conflate into a single set of representative frequency = 26. However, the system manages to correctly align words of subset A with the appropriate Turkish word. Unfortunately the 4 words of subset B are incorrectly aligned with irrelevant words. The difference in the representative frequencies of $f(X_A+X_B) \neq f(savunma)$ is because of loose translation of the two texts using for example the word «ασφάλεια» (ασφάλεια (EL) = guvenlik (TR) = security (EN)) instead of «άμυνα» (άμυνα (EL) = savunma (TR) = defence (EN)). This example is distinctive of the importance of word conflation where 1 missing conflation link results in 4 wrong word alignments. Another issue denoted by the example above is the problem of translation quality of the parallel corpora, mainly because they are not translations of each other but translations through a pivot language (English).

Table 8. MWU spotting and translation, EL-TR

Multi Word Units Text 'A'	Greek	Turkish
a Total MWUs	30	30
b Spotted	15	13
c Correctly Spotted	14	11
d Correctly Translated	6	5
e **Spotting Recall** [c/a]	**46.67 %**	**36.67 %**
f **Spotting Precision** [c/b]	**93.33 %**	**84.62 %**
g **Translation Precision** [d/c]	**42.86 %**	**45.45 %**

Table 9. MWU spotting and translation, EL-EN

Multi Word Units Text 'A'	Greek	English
a Total MWUs	30	30
b Spotted	15	12
c Correctly Spotted	14	7
d Correctly Translated	7	5
e **Spotting Recall** [c/a]	**46.67 %**	**23.33 %**
f **Spotting Precision** [c/b]	**93,33 %**	**58,33 %**
g **Translation Precision** [d/c]	**50 %**	**71 %**

Table 10. Translating and Spotting Greek MWU in Text A

GREEK (source)			TURKISH (target)		ENGLISH (target)	
Spotted Multi-Word Units	Freq.	correct	Aligned MWU	correct	Aligned MWU	correct
σοβιετικής ένωσης	4	Yes	sovyetler+ birligi'nin	Yes	Soviet	
ίδια στιγμή	4	Yes	Anilan		- NOT SPOTTED -	
βόρεια Αμερική	4	Yes	- NOT SPOTTED -		America	
ευρω-ατλαντικό χώρο	5	Yes	avrupa-atlantik (...)		euro-atlantic+ area	Yes
ηνωμένες πολιτείες	7	Yes	ABD'ye	Yes	united+ states	Yes
ηνωμένων πολιτειών	3	Yes	Tarihinde		united+ states (2nd)	
κράτη μέλη	7	Yes	- NOT SPOTTED -		- NOT SPOTTED -	
κρατών μελών	7	Yes	- NOT SPOTTED -		- NOT SPOTTED -	
ψυχρού πολέμου	8	Yes	soguk (cold)		Cold	
διάσκεψη κορυφής πράγας	4	Yes	prag zirvesinde	Yes	Summit(1st) , prague(2nd)	
αριθμός τοις εκατό	3	Yes	sayisi		cut+ per+ cent	Yes
τρομοκρατικές επιθέσεις Σεπτεμβρίου	4	Yes	ll+ eylül+ terörist	Yes	terrorist+attacks+september	Yes
όπλων μαζικής καταστροφής	9	Yes	kitle+ imha+ silahlari	Yes	weapons+mass+destruction	Yes
όπλα μαζικής καταστροφής	9	Yes	kitle+imha+ silahlarinin	Yes	weapons+mass+destruction	Yes
πρώτη φορά επίκληση άρθρου	3		Maddesini (article)		First , article , invoked	
Total spotted		14	Correctly translated	6	Correctly translated	6
Spotting Precision : 93.3333%			Translation Precision : 45,4545%		Translation Precision : 71%	

MWUs spotting and translation results. The issue in spotting MWUs is the noise coming from words that happen to co-occur more than twice in same sentence. To deal with this, stricter selection criteria were applied leading to reduced recall. Test results are presented in tables 8 9 and 10. Low translation precision is a direct consequence of the also low spotting recall, since it is not possible to correctly translate a MWU if its translation equivalent is not correctly spotted as a MWU.

5 Conclusions

Mining lexical equivalences out of parallel corpora seems to be a promising method for quick and cheap lexicon construction in less widely used language pairs. Analyzing sentence alignment leads to the conclusion that Gale&Church-like approaches can be effectively applied to Greek and Turkish. Word alignment results are promising, too. Though they were better in EL-EN tests, results in EL-TR tests are encouraging. This is obviously due to the simpler morphology of the English language resulting in reduced variations of wordforms in the text. The main cause for failing to translate a word is wrong or incomplete word conflation. By improving the conflation procedure, word alignment will be upgraded. Spotting the MWU was accomplished by using the same metric used for word alignment. The main issue in this task was noise elimination caused by words that casually co-located in the same sentences. Despite the low spotting recall, translation precision is quite good since correctly spotted MWUs in both languages are also correctly translated. Using larger parallel corpora is expected to yield much better results.

References

1. Brown, P., J. Lai, and R. Mercer. "Aligning sentences in parallel corpora." In Proc. 29th Annual Meeting of the ACL, 18-21 June, Berkley, Calif. (1991) 169-176
2. Brown, R, Carbonell, J., Yang, Y. "Automatic Dictionary Extraction for Cross-Language Information Retrieval", (Dec 1998)
3. Cormen, T., Leiserson, C., Rivest, R., Stein, C. "Introduction to Algorithms", ISBN 0-07-013151-1.
4. Gale W.A. and Church K.W., "A Program for Aligning Sentences in Parallel Corpora", Proceedings of the 29th Annual Meeting of the ACL. (1991) 177-184
5. Gaussier, E. "Flow network models for word alignment and terminology extraction from bilingual corpora.", (1998)
6. Kageura, K., Tsuji, K., Aizawa, A. "Automatic Thesaurus Generation through Multiple Filtering.", (2000)
7. Kosinov S. "Evaluation of N-GRAMS Conflation Approach in text-based information retrieval" , (2001)
8. Kupiec, J. "An algorithm for finding noun phrase correspondences in bilingual corpora." Proceedings of the 31st Annual Meeting of the ACL, Columbus, Ohio, (1993).
9. Papageorgiou, H., Prokopidis, P., Giouli, V., Piperidis, S., "A Unified Tagging Architecture and its Application to Greek", Proceedings of Second International Conference on Language Resources and Evaluation-LREC2000, 31 May- 2 June 2000, Athens, Greece, (2000) 1455-1462.
10. Piperidis, S., Boutsis, S., Demiros, I., Automatic Translation Lexicon Generation from Multilingual texts, Workshop on Multilinguality in the Software Industry: the AI Contribution (MULSAIC'97), Fifteenth International Joint Conference on Artificial Intelligence (IJCAI'97), Nagoya, Japan, (25 August 1997), 57-62.

11. Piperidis, S., Malavazos, C., Triantafyllou, Y., A Multi-level Framework for Memory-Based Translation Aid Tools, Aslib, Translating and the Computer 21, London, (November 1999), 10-11.
12. Piperidis S., Papageorgiou H., Boutsis S., From sentences to words and clauses. In Veronis, J. (Ed) Parallel Text Processing, Alignment and use of translation corpora, Kluwer Academic Publishers, Text Speech and Language Technology Series, (2000) 117-138
13. Porter M. "An algorithm for suffix stripping", M.F., (1980) (http:// www.tartarus.org/ ~martin/ index.html)
14. Smadja F., McKeown K.R., Hatzivassiloglou V. "Translating Collocations for Bilingual Lexicons: A Statistical Approach" Computational Linguistics, (1996) 22(1): 1-38
15. Tiedemann, J. "Recycling Translations. Extraction of Lexical Data from Parallel Corpora and their Application in Natural Language Processing". Acta Universitatis Upsaliensis. Studia Linguistica Upsaliensia, Uppsala. ISBN 91-554-5815-7, (2003) 1-130
16. Tufiş, D., Barbu, A-M "Automatic construction of translation lexicons." (2001)
17. Van der Eijk, P. "Automating the Acquisition of Bilingual Terminology." In Proceedings, Sixth Conference of the European Chapter of the Association for Computational Linguistics, Utrecht, The Netherlands, Association for Computational Linguistics, (1993) 113-119

Feed-Forward Neural Networks Using Hermite Polynomial Activation Functions

Gerasimos G. Rigatos[1] and Spyros G. Tzafestas[2]

[1] Industrial Systems Institute,
Unit of Industrial Automation,
26504, Rion Patras, Greece
grigat@isi.gr
http://www.isi.gr
[2] National Technical University of Athens,
Dept. of Electrical and Computer Engineering,
15773, Zografou Campus, Athens, Greece
tzafesta@softlab.ece.ntua.gr
http://www.robotics.ntua.gr

Abstract. In this paper feed-forward neural networks are introduced where hidden units employ orthogonal Hermite polynomials for their activation functions. The proposed neural networks have some interesting properties: (i) the basis functions are invariant under the Fourier transform, subject only to a change of scale, and (ii) the basis functions are the eigenstates of the quantum harmonic oscillator, and stem from the solution of Schrödinger's diffusion equation. The proposed neural networks demonstrate the particle-wave nature of information and can be used in nonparametric estimation. Possible applications of neural networks with Hermite basis functions include system modelling and image processing.

1 Introduction

Feed-forward neural networks (FNN) are the most popular neural architectures due to their structural flexibility, good representational capabilities, and availability of a large number of training algorithms. The hidden units in a FNN usually have the same activation functions and are usually selected as sigmoidal or radial basis functions. This paper presents feed-forward neural networks that use orthogonal Hermite polynomials as the basis functions of the hidden-layer nodes. The proposed neural networks have some interesting properties: (i) the basis functions are invariant under the Fourier transform, subject only to a change of scale, (ii) the basis functions are the eigenstates of the quantum harmonic oscillator and stem from the solution of Schrödinger's diffusion equation. The proposed feed-forward neural networks belong to the general category of nonparametric estimators and are suitable for function approximation and system modelling. Feed-forward neural networks with two dimensional Hermite basis functions can be constructed by taking products of the one-dimensional basis functions. Simulation tests show the approximation capabilities of feed-forward neural networks with Hermite basis functions in case of 1-D and 2-D functions.

G. Antoniou et al. (Eds.): SETN 2006, LNAI 3955, pp. 323–333, 2006.

It worths to be noted that feed-forward neural networks with Hermite basis functions demonstrate the particle-wave nature of information as described by Schrödinger's diffusion equation [1,2]. Attempts to enhance the connectionist neural models with quantum mechanics properties can be found in [3-5]. The proposed FNNs extend previous results on neural structures compatible with quantum mechanics postulates, given in [6,7].

The structure of the paper is as follows: In Section 2, the relation of the eigenstates of the quantum harmonic oscillator to Hermite polynomials is analyzed. Furthermore, the expansion in Gauss-Hermite series is explained and feed-forward neural networks that use Hermite basis functions are introduced. In Section 3 simulation tests show the efficiency of neural networks with Hermite basis functions for function approximation and system modelling applications. The proposed neural networks are compared against conventional feed-forward neural networks. Finally, in Section 4 concluding remarks are stated.

2   Neural Networks Using Hermite Activation Functions

2.1   Function Approximation with Feed-Forward Neural Networks

The idea of function approximation with the use of feed-forward neural networks (FNN) comes from generalized Fourier series. It is known that any function $\psi(x)$ in a L^2 space can be expanded in a generalized Fourier series in a given orthonormal basis, i.e.

$$\psi(x) = \sum_{k=1} c_k \psi_k(x), \ a \leq x \leq b \tag{1}$$

Truncation of the series yields in the sum $S_M(x) = \sum_{k=1}^{M} a_k \psi_k(x)$. If the coefficients a_k are taken to be equal to the generalized Fourier coefficients, i.e. when $a_k = c_k = \int_a^b \psi(x)\psi_k(x)dx$, then $S_M(x)$ is a mean square optimal approximation of $\psi(x)$. Unlike generalized Fourier series, in FNN the basis functions are not necessarily orthogonal. The hidden units in a FNN usually have the same activation functions and are often selected as sigmoidal functions or gaussians.

2.2   The Gauss-Hermite Series Expansion

Feed-forward neural networks with Hermite polynomials as basis functions demonstrate the particle-wave nature of information, as described by Schrödinger's diffusion equation, i.e.

$$i\hbar \frac{\partial \psi(x,t)}{\partial t} = -\frac{\hbar^2}{2m}\nabla^2 \psi(x,t) + V(x)\psi(x,t) \Rightarrow i\hbar \frac{\partial \psi(x,t)}{\partial t} = H\psi(x,t) \tag{2}$$

where H is the Hamiltonian, i.e. the sum of the potential $V(x)$ and of the Laplacian $-\frac{\hbar^2}{2m}\nabla^2 = \frac{\hbar^2}{2m}\frac{\partial^2}{\partial x^2}$. The probability density function $|\psi(x,t)|^2$ gives the probability at time instant t the input x of the NN (quantum particle equivalent) to have a value between x and $x + \Delta x$. The general solution of the quantum harmonic oscillator , i.e. of (2) with $V(x)$ being a parabolic potential, is [1], [2]:

$$\psi_k(x, t) = H_k(x)e^{-x^2/2}e^{-i(2k+1)t} \quad k = 0, 1, 2, \cdots \tag{3}$$

where $\psi_k(x, t)$ are the eigenstates of the quantum harmonic oscillator and $H_k(x)$ are the associated Hermite polynomials. The general relation for the Hermite polynomials is

$$H_k(x) = (-1)^k e^{x^2} \frac{d^{(k)}}{dx^{(k)}} e^{-x^2} \tag{4}$$

According to (4) the first five Hermite polynomials are $H_0(x) = 1$, $H_1(x) = 2x$, $H_2(x) = 4x^2 - 2$, $H_3(x) = 8x^3 - 12x$, and $H_4(x) = 16x^4 - 48x^2 + 12$. Analytic diagrams of the associated basis functions are given in Fig. 1

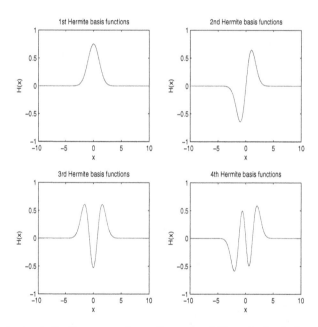

Fig. 1. Analytic diagrams of one-dimensional Hermite basis functions

It is known that Hermite polynomials are orthogonal. The following basis functions can now be defined [8]:

$$\psi_k(x) = [2^k \pi^{\frac{1}{2}} k!]^{-\frac{1}{2}} H_k(x)e^{-\frac{x^2}{2}} \tag{5}$$

where $H_k(x)$ is the associated Hermite polynomial. For the purposes of multi-resolution analysis Hermite basis functions of (5) are multiplied with the scale coefficient α. Thus the following basis functions are derived

$$\beta_k(x,\alpha) = \alpha^{-\frac{1}{2}}\psi_k(\alpha^{-1}x) \tag{6}$$

where α is a characteristic scale. The basis functions of (6) also satisfy orthogonality condition, i.e.

$$\int_{-}^{+} \beta_m(x,\alpha)\beta_k(x,\alpha)dx = \delta_{mk} \tag{7}$$

where δ_{mk} is the Kronecker delta symbol [8]. Any continuous function $f(x)$, $x \in R$ can be written as a weighted sum of the above orthogonal basis functions, i.e.

$$f(x) = \sum_{k=0} c_k \beta_k(x,\alpha) \tag{8}$$

The expansion of $f(x)$ using (8) is a Gauss-Hermite series. It holds that the Fourier transform of the basis function $\psi_k(x)$ of (5) satisfies the relation [8]

$$\Psi_k(s) = i^k \psi_k(s) \tag{9}$$

while for the basis functions $\beta_k(x,\alpha)$ using scale coefficient α it holds that the associated Fourier transform is

$$B_k(s,\alpha) = i^k \beta_k(s,\alpha^{-1}) \tag{10}$$

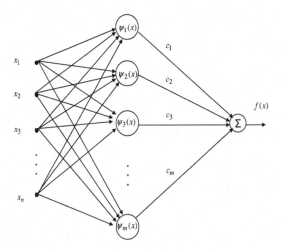

Fig. 2. A feed-forward neural network with Hermite polynomials as basis functions

which means that the Fourier transform acts on the basis functions of (6) with a change of scale $\alpha \to \alpha^{-1}$. Therefore, it holds

$$f(x) = \sum_{k=0} c_k \beta_k(x, \alpha) \xrightarrow{F} F(s) = \sum_{k=0} c_k i^k \beta_k(s, \alpha^{-1}) \tag{11}$$

The structure of a feed-forward neural network with Hermite basis functions is depicted in Fig.2.

2.3 Neural Networks Using the Eigenstates of the 2D Quantum Harmonic Oscillator

Feed-forward neural networks with Hermite basis functions of two variables can be constructed by taking products of the one-variable basis functions $B_k(x, \alpha)$ 8. Thus, setting $x = [x_1, x_2]^T$ one can define the two-variable basis functions

$$B_{k_1,k_2}(x, \alpha) = \frac{1}{\alpha} B_{k_1}(x_1, \alpha) B_{k_2}(x_2, \alpha) \tag{12}$$

These two-variable basis functions are again orthonormal, i.e. it holds

$$\int d^2x B_{n_1,n_2}(x, \alpha) B_{m_1,m_2}(x, \alpha) = \delta_{n_1 m_1} \delta_{n_2 m_2} \tag{13}$$

The basis functions $B_{k_1,k_2}(x)$ are the eigenstates of the two dimensional harmonic oscillator, which is a generalization of (2). These basis functions form a complete basis for integrable functions of two variables. A two dimensional function $f(x)$ can thus be written is the series expansion:

$$f(x) = \sum_{k_1,k_2} c_k B_{k_1,k_2}(x, \alpha) \tag{14}$$

The choice of the maximum order k_1^{max}, k_2^{max} is of practical interest. Appropriate tuning of the scale coefficient α defines the multi-resolution features of FNN with Hermite polynomial activation functions. Thus, an area in the data space can be covered by basis functions with large support or finer resolution so as to pick-up both fine details and courser trends (see Fig. 3).

Indicative basis functions $B_{1,2}(x, \alpha)$ and $B_{3,3}(x, \alpha)$ of a 2D feed-forward quantum neural network are depicted in Fig. 4 and Fig. 5.

It has to be noted that FNN with Hermite basis functions can be also used for function approximation in higher dimensional spaces, if suitable multivariable basis functions are introduced. The tensor product method can be employed to construct appropriate multivariable basis functions.

Remark: The significance of the results of Section 2 is given the sequel:

(i) Orthogonality of the basis functions and invariance under the Fourier transform, (subject only to a change of scale): this means that the energy distribution in the proposed neural network can be estimated without moving to the

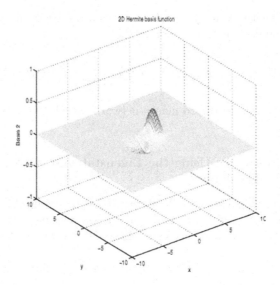

Fig. 3. First five Hermite basis functions in the one-dimensional data space

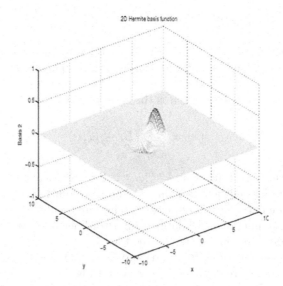

Fig. 4. 2D feed-forward neural network with Hermite polynomial activation functions: basis function $B_{1,2}(x, \alpha)$

frequency domain. The values of the weights of the neural network provide a measure of how energy is distributed in the various modes $\psi_k(x)$ of the signal that is approximated by the neural network.

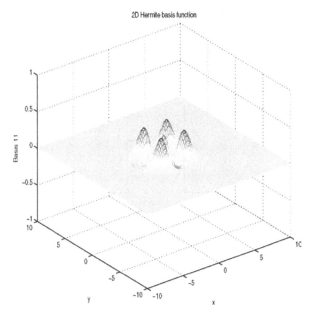

Fig. 5. 2D feed-forward neural network with Hermite polynomial activation functions: basis function $B_{3,3}(x, \alpha)$

(ii) The basis functions of the neural network are the eigenstates of the quantum harmonic oscillator: this means that the proposed neural network can capture the particle-wave nature of information. The input variable x is viewed not only as a crisp value (particle equivalent) but is also distributed to the normal modes of a wave function (wave equivalent).

3   Simulation Results

The performance of neural networks that use the eigenstates of the quantum harmonic oscillator as basis functions is compared to the performance of one hidden layer FNN with sigmoidal basis functions (OHL-FNN). It should be noted that the sigmoidal basis functions $\phi(x) = \frac{1}{1+exp(-x)}$ in OHL-FNN do not satisfy the property of orthogonality. In the case of neural networks with Hermite basis functions, training affects only the output weights, and can be performed with second order gradient algorithms. However, since the speed of convergence is not the primary objective of this study, the LMS (Least Mean Square) algorithm is sufficient for training. In the case of the OHL-FNN with sigmoidal basis functions, training concerns weights of both the hidden and output layer and is carried out using the back-propagation algorithm [9]. Alternatively, second order (Newton) training methods can be used [10].

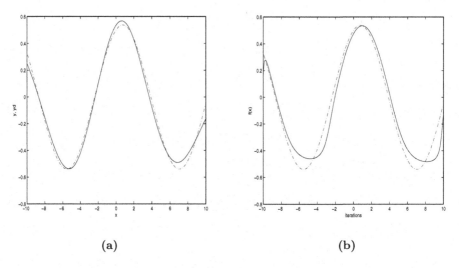

(a)   (b)

Fig. 6. Approximation of function of Eq. (16) using (a) a neural network with Hermite basis functions (b) an one hidden layer feed-forward NN (OHL-FNN)

The following test functions are examined (red dashed lines):

1. Test function 1 given in Eq. (15) over the domain $D = [-10, 10]$:

$$f(x) = 0.5cos(x/2) + 0.3sin(x/2) \tag{15}$$

2. Test function 2 given in Eq. (16) over the domain $D = [-10, 10]$:

$$f(x) = \begin{cases} -2.186x - 12.864 & if \ -10 \leq x < -2 \\ 4.246x & if \ -2 \leq x < 0 \\ 10e^{-(0.05x+0.5)}sin[(0.001x + 0.05)x] & if \ 0 \leq x \leq 10 \end{cases} \tag{16}$$

3. Test function 3 given in Eq. (17) over the domain $D = [-10, 10]$:

$$f(x) = 20.5e^{(-0.3\,x)}sin(0.03x)cos(0.7x) \tag{17}$$

4. Test function 4 given in Eq. (18) over the domain $D = [-10, 10] \times [-10, 10]$:

$$f(x, y) = 1.9e^{(-0.02x^2 - 0.02y^2)}tanh(-0.3y) \tag{18}$$

The approximation results for the 2D function of Eq. (18), obtained by a neural network with Hermite basis functions and by an OHL-FNN, are given in Fig. 8.

5. Test function 5 given in Eq. (19) over the domain $D = [-10, 10] \times [-10, 10]$:

$$f(x, y) = sin(0.3x)sin(0.3y)e^{(-0.1\,y)} \tag{19}$$

Table 1 gives the final root mean square error (RMSE), succeeded by neural networks with Hermite basis functions (quantum harmonic oscillator QHO-FNN) and the OHL-FNN, after 50 epochs. The training data set, in the case of the 1D

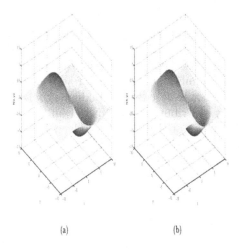

(a)   (b)

Fig. 7. 2D function of Eq. (18)

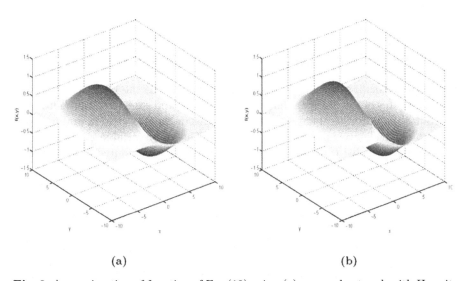

(a)   (b)

Fig. 8. Approximation of function of Eq. (18) using (a) a neural network with Hermite basis functions (b) an one hidden layer feed-forward NN (OHL-FNN)

Table 1. Comparison between NN with Hermite basis functions and OHL-FNN

function	Eq. (15)		Eq. (16)		Eq. (17)		Eq. (18)		Eq. (19)	
NN type	QHO	MLP	QHO	MLP	QHO	MLP	QHO	MLP	QHO	MLP
Num. nodes	6	6	6	6	6	6	16	16	16	16
RMSE	0.613	0.187	0.034	0.059	0.726	0.339	0.047	0.121	0.032	0.117

functions consisted of 200 pairs $[x_k, y_k^d]$ while in the case of the 2D functions it consisted of 3600 triplets $[x_k, y_k, z_k^d]$. Test data consisted of 200 pairs in the case of the 1D functions and 3600 triplets in the case of the 2D functions. To find the optimal number of hidden nodes, the procedure is either constructive, i.e. one starts from a small number of neurons and adds neurons until satisfactory performance is achieved, or is based on shrinking (pruning), i.e. removal of the parameters that do not contribute to the NN output.

As expected, the number of nodes of the hidden layer affects the quality of function approximation. In the case of the 2D functions, the performance of OHL-FNNs is improved when more hidden nodes are added.

To evaluate the quality of the approximation succeeded by the proposed NN, apart from the RMSE two issues should also be taken into account: (i) complexity: FNN with Hermite basis functions are simpler structures than OHL-FNN and contain less tunable parameters, (ii) multi-resolution aspects: suitable scaling of the Hermite basis functions enables multiresolution analysis, i.e. learning of both fine details and courser trends of the approximated functions.

4   Conclusions

In this paper feed-forward neural networks that use orthogonal Hermite polynomials as the basis functions, have been studied. The proposed neural networks have some interesting properties: (i) the basis functions are invariant under the Fourier transform, subject only to a change of scale (ii) the basis functions are the eigenstates of the quantum harmonic oscillator, and stem from the solution of Schrödinger's diffusion equation. These features of the proposed neural network show the particle-wave nature of information. The input variable x is viewed not only as a crisp value (particle equivalent) but is also distributed to the normal modes of a wave function (wave equivalent).

The proposed neural networks belong to the general category of nonparametric estimators and are suitable for function approximation and system modelling. Two dimensional feed-forward quantum neural networks can be constructed by taking products of the one-dimensional basis functions.

In the simulation tests, the approximation capability of feed-forward neural networks with Hermite basis functions was evaluated for 1-D and 2-D functions. The performance of the proposed neural networks was compared to the performance of the OHL-FNN (one hidden layer feed-forward neural networks). It was observed that neural networks with Hermite basis functions can approximate functions at least as effectively as the OHL-FNNs with sigmoidal activation functions. Research on neural structures that can be attributed with quantum information processing capabilities is promising and further work needs to be done in this direction.

References

1. Cohen-Tannoudji,C.,Diu, D. and Laloë, F.:Mécanique Quantique I,(1998) *Hermann*
2. Strauss, W.A.: Partial Differential Equations: An Introduction, (1992) *J. Wiley*

3. Kosko, B.: Neural networks and fuzzy systems : A dynamical systems approach to machine intelligence. (1992) *Prentice Hall*
4. Ventura, D. and Martinez, T.: Quantum Associative Memory, Information Sciences. Elsevier **24** (2000) 273-296
5. Perus, M.: Multi-level Synergetic Computation in Brain. Nonlinear Phenomena in Complex Systems. **4** (2001) 157-193
6. Rigatos, G.G. and Tzafestas, S.G.: Parallelization of a fuzzy control algorithm using quantum computation. IEEE Transactions on Fuzzy Systems **10** (2002) 451-460
7. Rigatos, G.G. and Tzafestas, S.G.: Fuzzy learning compatible with quantum mechanics postulates. *Computational Intelligence and Natural Computation, CINC '03*, (2003) North Carolina
8. Refregier, A.: Shapelets - I. A method for image analysis. Mon. Not. R. Astron. Soc. **338** (2003) 35-47
9. Haykin, S.: Neural Networks: A Comprehensive Foundation (1994) *McMillan.*
10. Ma, L. and K. Khorasani, K.: Constructive Feedforward Neural Networks Using Hermite Polynomial Activation Functions. IEEE Transactions on Neural Networks, **16**, (2005) 821-833

A Distributed Branch-and-Bound Algorithm for Computing Optimal Coalition Structures

Chattrakul Sombattheera and Aditya Ghose

Decision Systems Lab,
School of IT and Computer Science, Faculty of Informatics,
University of Wollongong, NSW 2500, Australia
{cs50, aditya}@uow.edu.au

Abstract. Coalition formation is an important area of research in multi-agent systems. Computing optimal coalition structures for a large number of agents is an important problem in coalition formation but has received little attention in the literature. Previous studies assume that each coalition value is known a priori. This assumption is impractical in real world settings. Furthermore, the problem of finding coalition values become intractable for even a relatively small number of agents. This work proposes a distributed branch-and-bound algorithm for computing optimal coalition structures in linear production domain, where each coalition value is not known a priori. The common goal of the agents is to maximize the system's profit. In our algorithm, agents perform two tasks: i) deliberate profitable coalitions, and ii) cooperatively compute optimal coalition structures. We show that our algorithm outperforms exhaustive search in generating optimal coalition structure in terms of elapses time and number of coalition structures generated.

1 Introduction

Coalition formation is an important area of research in multi-agent systems. It studies the process that leads to cooperation among agents. The process of coalition formation involves i) negotiation in order to exchange information among agents, and ii) deliberation in order to decide with which agents should they cooperate. Coalition formation research has its roots in cooperative game theory [1, 2]. Rather than working on their own individually, agents can jointly create greater value, known as *coalition value*. The coalition value will be distributed among coalition members. This value for each individual agent is known as *payoff*. Mostly, agents in cooperative game theory are self-interested—agents agree to form coalitions if they can obtain greater payoffs. The focus of cooperative game theory is on what coalitions would form and what the payoffs for agents would be. There are two main streams of solution concepts in cooperative game theory, i.e., stability and fairness. Stability concepts, including core, kernel, nucleolus, stable sets, are concerned with the stability of coalitions—once formed, none of the coalition members are likely to deviate. Fairness concept, i.e., Shapley value, is concerned with the fair distribution of coalition value among coalition

G. Antoniou et al. (Eds.): SETN 2006, LNAI 3955, pp. 334–344, 2006.

members. Furthermore, coalition formation in game theory assumes superadditive environment—when a coalition grows larger, it always yields a coalition value not less than it's previous one.

In addition to traditional concepts in cooperative game theory, coalition formation research in multi-agent systems is also concerned with efficiency of the system. In this context, agents are fully cooperative—their common goal is to maximize the system's utility regardless of their own payoffs. Agents in the system need to form coalitions such that the total coalition value is maximal. This problem is known as finding *optimal coalition structures* [3, 4, 5]. It has rich application in real world environments. Examples include internal/external collaboration in third party logistics providers, cooperation among nodes in grid computing systems and cooperation among service providers in composite web services. These real world scenarios usually involve a large number of agents. The problem becomes intractable for a small value of m—the number of coalition structures can be very large (see section 2.2). This makes the problem of finding optimal coalition structures NP-hard [3, 4]. Furthermore, coalition formation in these real world scenarios cannot be assumed to be superadditive because there can be cooperation costs among agents. A larger coalition may yield a smaller coalition value. This kind of environment is known as *non-superadditive* [6].

The problem of finding optimal coalition structures from a large number of agents has received little attention in the literature. A small of number of studies have considered this problem [3, 4, 5]. Although they assume non-superadditive environment, these studies, as in game theory, assume the existence of the *characteristic function* [2], which, given a coalition, returns its coalition value. Designing such a function can be a non-trivial exercise. Sandholm et al. [3, 4] and Dang et al. [5] have proposed anytime algorithms to generate coalition structures within a bound from the optimal value—due to the large search space as mentioned above. The computation is done in centralized fashion. Dang et al. [5] claimed to have a much faster algorithm than Sandholm et al. [4].

We argue that the assumption of the existence of the characteristic function is not pragmatic in real world environments. Given a logistics problem, for example, all the coalition values must be computed on the fly before the process of finding optimal (or generating) coalition structures can commence. For a small number of agents, computing all the coalition values alone can take very long— let alone the time needed for finding optimal (or generating) coalition structures.

The key contribution of this paper are as follows: first, we present an algorithm for computing optimal coalition structures in non-superadditive environment which does not assume the existence of a characteristic function. Second, we offer a distributed approach to computing optimal coalition structures, while the existing work considered only centralized approaches. Finally, our approach is relatively fast, since we do not have to search through the space of all possible coalitions. Our approach in this research is to have agents *i*) compute their profitable coalitions in decentralized fashion, and *ii*) cooperatively compute coalition structures by exchanging profitable coalitions. We modify Owen's linear production game [7] where agents have to agree to pool their resources together in order to produce goods. The original work assumes a superadditive environment, where agents can simply form the grand coalition. Such an assumption is impractical in the real world since the cost of cooperation has to be taken into account as mentioned above.

The outline of this paper is as follows. We introduce our setting. We describe how our algorithm works and discuss both in deliberating and forming coalitions. Then we discuss about the experiment and show empirical results. We discuss related work which followed by conclusion and future work.

2   Coalition Framework

2.1   Linear Production Domain

Linear production games [7] are those in which agents are given resources and try to pool resources to produce goods in order to maximize the system's profit. Owen [7] studied linear production games in superadditive environment. Here, we consider linear production games in non-superadditive environments and the common goal of the agents are to maximize system's profit. We are given a set of agents, $A = \{a_1, a_2, \ldots, a_m\}$, whose goals are to maximize the system's profit. We are also given a set of resources $R = \{r_1, r_2 \ldots, r_n\}$ and a set of goods $G = \{g_1, g_2, \ldots, g_o\}$. Resources themselves are not valuable but they can be used to produce goods, which are valuable to agents. Let $L = [\alpha_{ij}]_{n\ o}$, where $\alpha_{ij} \in \mathbb{Z}^+$, be the matrix that specifies the units of each resource $r_i \in R$ required to produce a unit of the good $g_j \in G$. Such a matrix is called a *linear technology matrix* [7]. The price of each unit of goods produced is specified by the vector $P = [p_j]_{1\ o}$. Each agent $a_k \in A$ is given a resource bundle $b^k = [b_i^k]_{n\ 1}$. In this setting, some agents would have the incentive to cooperate, e.g., if they cannot produce a certain good using only the resources at their disposal. Hence agents have to cooperate, i.e. form coalitions, in order to create value from their resources. Let $S \subseteq A$ be a coalition. It will have a total of

$$b_i^S = \sum_{k \in S} b_i^k$$

of the ith resource. The members of coalition S can use all these resources to produce any vector $x = \langle x_1, x_2, \ldots, x_o \rangle$ of goods that satisfies the following constraints:

$$\alpha_{11}x_1 + \alpha_{12}x_2 + \ldots + \alpha_{1o}x_o \leq b_1^S,$$
$$\alpha_{21}x_1 + \alpha_{22}x_2 + \ldots + \alpha_{2o}x_o \leq b_2^S,$$
$$\vdots \qquad\qquad\qquad \vdots \;\; \vdots,$$
$$\alpha_{n1}x_1 + \alpha_{n2}x_2 + \ldots + \alpha_{no}x_o \leq b_n^S$$

and

$$x_1, x_2, \ldots, x_o \geq 0.$$

We assume that agents have to pool their resources together at a coalition member's location to produce these goods. Thus agents' cooperation incurs some costs, e.g., transportation cost, etc. The cooperation cost among agents is specified by the matrix $C = [c_{kl}]_m \times_m$, which assigns a cooperation cost between each pair (a_k, a_l) of agents such that

$$c_{kl} \in \begin{cases} \mathbb{Z}^+ & \text{if } k \neq l \\ \{0\} & \text{if } k = l \end{cases}$$

We assume that all of the resources of agents are pooled at one location, which can be the location of any agent in the coalition. A singleton coalition yields cooperation cost of 0. For a coalition of size two, $S = \{a_1, a_2\}$, pooling coalition resources at any of the two sites yield the same cost for the coalition (i.e. the cooperation cost matrix is symmetric). The total cost for cooperation incurred by a coalition will be taken to be the sum of the pairwise cooperation costs between the agent at whose location coalition resources are pooled, and the other members of coalition. For a coalition of size three or larger, there is at least one agent, a_k, such that

$$\sum_{k'=1}^{m} c_{kk'} \leq \sum_{l'=1}^{m} c_{ll'}$$

for all $a_l \in S$. We shall call a coalition member a_k who yields the minimal cooperation cost for the coalition a *coalition center*.

Agents in the coalition S have to find a vector x to maximize the revenue accruing to a coalition. Let

$$P_S = \sum_{l=1}^{o} p_l x_l.$$

be the maximal revenue the coalition can generate. Let

$$C_S = \sum_{l \in S} c_{kl}.$$

be the minimal cooperation cost for the coalition (obtained by selecting the optimal coalition center). Obviously, the ultimate objective of agents in the coalition is to maximize profit, i.e., the coalition value v_S, where

$$v_S = P_S - C_S.$$

The linear inequalities referred to above, together with this objective function constitutes a linear programming problem. We shall call the solution, the vector $\langle x_1, x_2, \ldots, x_o \rangle$ that represents the optimal quantities of goods $g_1, g_2, \ldots, g_o$ *optimal product mix*.

2.2   Optimal Coalition Structures

Generating coalition structures can also be considered as a set partitioning problem. The set of all agents will be partitioned into mutually disjoint and proper subsets. Each instance of a partition is known as a *coalition struc-ture*(CS) [5, 4, 2], while each subset is known as a coalition S. The *value* of each coalition structure

$$V(CS) = \sum_{S \in CS} v_S$$

indicates the system' utility yielded by that partitioning. The goal of cooperative agents in coalition formation [4, 5] is to maximize the system's utility.

Computing the optimal coalition structures in a non-sedative environment is non-trivial [4]. Previous studies [4, 5] assumed the existence of a characteristic function and considered algorithms for computing the optimal coalition structures. Such an assumption is impractical in the real world—each coalition value may not be known a priori. Thus agents have to compute all coalition values first. For a set of m agents, there are $2^m - 1$ coalitions and there are $\sum_{i=1}^{m} Z(m, i)$, where $Z(m, i) = iZ(m - 1, i) + Z(m - 1, i - 1)$ and $Z(m, m) = Z(m, 1) = 1$, coalition structures [4]. Hence the complexity of computing all coalition structures is substantially worse.

This work considers a distributed algorithm that allows agents to compute coalition values and approach the optimal coalition structures as they proceed. Each agent has to do to two tasks: i) Deliberating: deliberate over what coalitions it might form by incrementally improving the initial set of coalitions, and ii) Computing optimal coalition structures: exchange information to form coalitions such that those coalitions yield maximal profit to the system. The sets of such coalitions are the optimal coalition structures. The main goal of the algorithm is to reduce search space for finding the optimal coalition structures. This can be achieved by reducing the number of coalitions to be considered. In our setting, the optimal coalition structures must yield a profit, a non-negative utility, to the system. In the worst case, the system's profit is 0—each agent is a singleton coalition and cannot produce anything at all.

3   Distributed Algorithm for Coalition Formation

3.1   Deliberating Process

We extend our algorithm [8] for agents' deliberation in order to improve the performance. We will review the old algorithm by explaining the early stage of the deliberation where each agent ranks other agents based on their suitability to be coalition members. Then we will explain the extended part where new coalitions will be added into the ranking tree and the most profitable coalition of each size will be explored. Firstly, we will explain the old algorithm below.

In the following, we will identify a coalition by the identifier of its coalition center agent. Thus the coalition S^k will have agent a_k as its center. Hence b^S represents the resource vector of S^k. The reasoning described below is conducted by the coalition center agent for each coalition. Given a coalition S^k, let G^k refer to the set of goods whose resource requirements are fully or partially satisfied by b^S, the resources available in S^k (excluding goods whose resource requirement might be trivially satisfied because these are 0). For each good $g_j \in G^k$, the coalition center agent a_k ranks agents not currently in its coalition on a per good basis. For each resource r_i of good g_j, agent a_k ranks non-member agents by computing for each $a_l \notin S^k$, whose $b_i^l > 0$, the value π_i^j—its *proportional contribution* to the profit of the good (using its fraction of the resource requirements for that good provided by the a_l)—minus the (pair-wise) collaboration cost between a_l and a_k, i.e.,

$$\pi_i^j = \frac{b_i^l}{\alpha_{ij}} p_j - c_{kl}.$$

The agent a_k uses this proportional contribution π_i^j to construct a binary tree for each g_j. The only child of the root g_j is the first resource α_{1j}, whose left child is the second resource α_{2j}, and so on. For each α_{ij}, its right child is either *i*) null if $\alpha_j^i = 0$, or *ii*) the agent $a_{1st}^{r_i}$, whose π_i^j value is the greatest. The right child of $a_{1st}^{r_i}$ is the agent $a_{2nd}^{r_i}$, whose π_i^j value is the second greatest, and so on. Every time a_k wants to produce additional units of g_j, it traverses the tree down to the appropriate resource r_i and add more agents into its coalition based on b^S.

The agent a_k uses b^S to determine additional resources needed to produce additional units of a good g_j. For each $g_j \in G^k$ and resource r_i,

$$\beta_i^j = I(\alpha_{ij}) - b_i^S,$$

where $I \in \mathbb{Z}^+$ is the smallest integer such that $\beta_i^j > 0$, represents the amount of r_i that coalition S^k lacks to produce good g_j, provided the amount is non-negative ($\beta = 0$ otherwise). The *indicative vector*, $\beta^j = [\beta_i^j]_{1 \ n}$, represents un-met requirements for each resource r_i of good g_j.

The agent a_k uses the indicative vector β^j to help collecting additional coalition members into its coalition. If the agent a_k wants to produce an additional unit of g_j, it identifies the resource that is needed the most, $\beta_{i*}^j = max_{i=1}^n(b_i^j)$, from the indicative vector. It locates the node β_{i*}^j in T^{g_j} and collects the next available agent a_l^{i*} into the coalition. The total resources of the coalition b^S is updated. Each β_i^j of indicative vector will be subtracted by it corresponding b_i^l. The agent a_k keeps adding more agents into its coalition until there are enough resources to produce an additional unit of g_j, i.e., $\beta_i^j > 0 \ \forall i$.

In the extended part, each agent ranks profitable coalitions in its ranking tree. The root of the tree is the singleton coalition of the agent, S^k. So far, the agent a_k knows that if it wants to produce at least an additional unit of g_j, it needs to acquire additional agents, S', into its S^k. The agent a_k create a trial coalition by merging S' into S. Since each new agent may posses other resources not required for producing g_j, the trial coalitions may find a better solution for producing goods. Hence the profits v of trial coalitions vary. Each S' will be added to the tree as the children of S. The sub-algorithm for selecting profitable members is shown in algorithm 1.

Algorithm 1. Select the most profitable members

Require: A coalition S
Require: ranking trees T^G
  set highest profit $v^* = 0$
  set profitable members $S^+ = null$
  for all $g_j \in G$ **do**
    if S is not capable of producing g_j **then**
      continue
    end if
    get additional agents S'
    set trial coalition $S'_j = S \cup S'_j$
    compute trial coalition's profit $v_{S'_j}$
    set $S^+ = S^+ \cup S'_j$
  end for
  return S^+

In the main algorithm, the agent a_k considers itself a singleton coalition at the beginning of deliberating. It create the ranking tree T^G of all agent for each good. At this point it is only root of the profitable-coalition tree, L^+, and is the base of the growing coalition. It acquires the additional agents S^+ into the coalition. Each $S'_j \in S^+$ will be added as the children of the base coalition. Among all S'_js, the most profitable agents S are those that provide the highest additional profit v and are kept as the base for the further growing coalition. The coalition keeps growing in this fashion until there are no profitable members left in T^G. Then the next profitable sibling of the base S'_j will be the new base. This repetition goes on until it cannot find the new base. This will keep the coalition's marginal profit grows while the size of the coalition is growing. The number of coalitions each agent a_k has to maintain is also much smaller compared to that of the exhaustive search. The main algorithm is shown in algorithm 2.

3.2   Coalition Formation Algorithm

Once each agent finishes its deliberation, it ranks all of its coalitions by profit. Let S^- be a non-profitable coalition, whose value $v_{S-} \leq 0$. and S^+ be a profitable coalition, whose value $v_{S+} > 0$.

Lemma 1. *Any S^- coalition can be replaced by a set of its members' singleton coalitions, whose $v_{a_{k \in S}} \geq 0$, such that the coalition structure's value will not be decreased.*

Therefore, all non-profitable coalitions can be ignored. Each agent will prune all of the non-profitable coalitions, if there is any. The remaining coalitions are profitable. In fact, our algorithm in deliberation process can simply prevent this happening using its tree T^G. It always generate profitable coalitions. Obviously, each singleton coalition is non-negative. Hence, non-profitable coalitions must not exist in the coalition structures. Given that the deliberation algorithm generates all profitable coalitions among agents inclusively, agents can *i*) exchange

---

Algorithm 2. Main

---

set $L^+ = \emptyset$
create a singleton coalition $S = \{a_k\}$
set $A' = A - \{a_k\}$
create ranking trees T^G for all goods
collect profitable members S^+
while $S^+ \neq \emptyset$ **do**
   locate $S^* \in S^+$
   set $A' = A' - S^*$
   set $S = S \cup S^*$
   set $L^+ = L^+ \cup S$
   collect profitable members S^+
   if $S^+ = null$ **then**
      set $S^* =$ the next profitable sibling of S^*
   end if
end while

---

information about coalitions generated and their singleton coalitions, and $ii)$ decide form coalitions that yield the optimal coalition structure value.

Proposition 1. *The optimal coalition structure can be constructed by profitable coalitions generated by agents and their singleton coalitions.*

Next step each agent sends information about coalitions it has generated to each other. For each coalition size, each agent can further reduce the number of coalitions it has by deleting non-centered coalitions and those whose values are non-maximal. Up to this point, the remaining coalitions are likely to be in the coalition structure. Agents exchange information again and compute optimal coalition structures. The algorithm for computing optimal coalition structures is shown below.

1. Each agent a_k deletes non-profitable coalitions from its list
2. Agent a_k sends its list of profitable coalitions to each coalition member
3. For each coalition size, agent a_k deletes all coalitions that their center are not the agent itself and those that do not yield the maximal value
4. Each agent sends the remaining coalitions to each member
5. Each agent compute the optimal coalition structures
6. Optimal coalition structures will be recognized by agents.

4   Experiment

We conduct experiment by simulating agents executing our algorithm against exhaustive search withing the range of $10-50$ agents. We compare the performance of both algorithm in terms of number of partitions generated and elapsed time of generating optimal coalition structures. Since existing exhaustive search algorithms, e.g., [4], does not specify how exactly the partitions are generated, we generate partitions for exhaustive search by i) increasing the number of blocks, e.g., $1, 2, \ldots, n$, and ii) for each block, the coalition size is will be propagated from left to right. For example, given a set of 3 agents, the partitions generated will be {1,2,3}, {1,2}{3}, {1,3}{2}, {2,3}{1} and {1}{2}{3}. In each round, the agents number increases by 5. The number of goods and resources are equal and increase by 1 in every 2 rounds. The technology matrix, agents' resources and co-operation costs among agents are randomly generated with uniform distribution. The number of each resource α_{ij} in the technology matrix is in the range $0 - 10$. The prices of the goods are in the range of $10 - 20$ while the cooperation costs are in the range of 0 and the number of agents in that round, e.g., $10, 15, \ldots$. As our algorithm deals with non-superadditive environments, this setting tends to increase the cooperation cost of a coalition as its size grows. Hence it forces agents to work harder to form profitable coalitions and to achieve optimal coalition structures. Both algorithms uses the Simplex algorithm to find the optimal solution for each coalitions. The revenue generated is subtracted to achieve the coalition's profit.

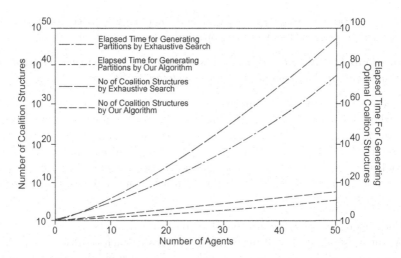

Fig. 1. This graph shows the number of coalition structures generated and elapsed time for generating the optimal coalition structures of our algorithm against those of exhaustive search

The figure 1 compares the performance of our algorithm again that of exhaustive search. The left x-axis is the number of coalition structures generated while the right x-axis is the elapsed time spent for generating optimal coalition structures in milliseconds. The empirical results show that our algorithm performs significantly better than exhaustive search. We experienced that exhaustive algorithm hardly make progress after the number of agents is larger than 40. As shown in the figure, the number of coalition structures generated by exhaustive algorithm is much larger than that of our algorithm. Furthermore, the elapsed time for generating optimal coalition structures of exhaustive search is also much larger than that of our algorithm. Since our computer system could not carry on simulations using exhaustive search for a large number of agents, we limit the comparison only for 50 agents. However, we continued experiment using our algorithm until the number of agents reached 100 but the results are not shown here.)

5   Related Work

Shehory et al. [9] propose an algorithm to allocate tasks to agents in distributed problem solving manner, i.e., agents try to maximize the utility of the system. They consider a domain where a task composed of multiple subtasks, each of which requires specific capacity. These tasks have to be carried out by agents who have specific capacities to carry out tasks. Each agent prepares its list of candidate coalitions and proposes to other agents. Shehory et al. [10] study overlapping coalition formation in distributed problem solving systems in non-superadditive environments. Although agents can belong to multiple coalitions at the same time, agents execute one task at a time. The task allocation process is completed prior to the execution of the tasks. Agents are group-rational, i.e., they form coalition to increase the system's payoff.

Sandholm et al. [11] analyze coalition formation among self-interested agents who are bounded-rational. They consider deliberation cost in terms of monetary cost. The agents' payoffs are directly affected by deliberation cost. In their work, agents agree to form coalition and each of the agents can plan to achieve their goals. Soh et al. [12] propose an integrated learning approach to form coalition in real time, given dynamic and uncertain environments. This work concentrates on finding out potential coalition members by utilizing learning approach in order to quickly form coalitions of acceptable quality (but possibly sub-optimal.) Sandholm et al. [4] study the problem of coalition structure generation. Since the number of coalition structures can be very large for exhaustive search, they argue whether the optimal coalition structure found via a partial search can be guaranteed to be within a bound from optimum. They propose an anytime algorithm that establishes a tight bound withing a minimal amount of search.

6   Conclusion and Future Work

Coalition formation is an important area of research in multi-agent system. The problem of generating optimal coalition structures, the partitioning of a set of agents such that the sum of all coalitions' values within the partitioning is maximal, is an important issue in the area. The small number of existing studies assume each coalition value is known a priori. Such assumption is impractical in real world settings. Furthermore, finding all coalition values becomes intractable for a relatively small number of agents.

We propose a distributed branch-and-bound algorithm for computing optimal coalition structure for linear production domains among fully cooperative agents. In stead of assuming that each coalition value is known a priori, our algorithm tries to reduce the number of coalitions to be involved. We extend our previous algorithm in the deliberation process in order to improve the performance. The non-profitable coalitions are not generated by the deliberation algorithm. Then the information of remaining coalitions will be exchanged among agents. Lastly, each agent uses existing algorithm [4] to compute optimal coalition structures.

The empirical results show that our algorithm help generate the optimal coalition structures much faster than exhaustive search. Our algorithm dramatically reduces the number of coalitions generated hence reducing the number of coalition structures. As a result, the elapsed time of generating the coalition structures is relatively small.

Although this algorithm helps reduce number of coalitions involved in generating optimal coalition structures, there is always rooms to improve. We want to further improve our algorithm for larger number of agents, for example, up to 1000 agents. Lastly, we want to study this problem in related domains, e.g., integer programming, non-linear programming.

References

1. Neumann, J.V., Morgenstern, O.: Theory of Games and Economic Behaviour. Princeton University Press, Princeton, New Jersey (1953 (1963 printing))
2. Kahan, J.P., Rapoport, A.: Theories of Coalition Formation. Lawrence Erlbaum Associates, Hillsdale, New Jersey (1984)
3. Sandholm, T., Larson, K., Andersson, M., Shehory, O., Tohm, F.: Worst-case-optimal anytime coalition structure generation. In: Proceedings of AAAI-98. (1998) 46–53
4. Sandholm, T., Larson, K., Andersson, M., Shehory, O., Tohm, F.: Coalition structure generation with worst case guarantees. Artif. Intell. **111** (1999) 209–238
5. Dang, V.D., Jennings, N.R.: Generating coalition structures with finite bound from the optimal guarantees. In: Third International Joint Conference on Autonomous Agents and Multiagent Systems - Volume 2 (AAMAS'04), pp. 564-571. (2004)
6. Shehory, O., Kraus, S.: Feasible formation of coalitions among autonomous agents in non-super-additive environments. Computational Intelligence **15** (1999) 218–251
7. Owen, G.: On the core of linear production games. Mathematical Programming 9 (1975) 358-370 (1975)
8. Sombattheera, C., Ghose, A.: A distributed algorithm for coalition formation in linear production domain. In: Proceedings of ICEIS 06. (2006)
9. Shehory, O., Kraus, S.: Task allocation via coalition formation among autonomous agents. In: Proc. of IJCAI. (1995) 655–661
10. Shehory, O., Kraus, S.: Formation of overlapping coalitions for precedence-ordered task-execution among autonomous agents. In: ICMAS-96. (1996) 330–337
11. Sandholm, T., Lesser, V.: Coalition Formation among Bounded Rational Agents. 14th International Joint Conference on Artificial Intelligence (1995) 662–669
12. Soh, L.K., Tsatsoulis, C.: Satisficing coalition formation among agents. In: Proceedings of the first international joint conference on Autonomous agents and multiagent systems, ACM Press (2002) 1062–1063

Pattern Matching-Based System for Machine Translation (MT)

George Tambouratzis, Sokratis Sofianopoulos, Vassiliki Spilioti, Marina Vassiliou, Olga Yannoutsou, and Stella Markantonatou

Institute for Language and Speech Processing,
6, Artemidos & Epidavrou Paradissos Amaroussiou 151 25 Athens, Greece
{giorg_t, s_sofian, v_spiliot, mvas, olga, marks}@ilsp.gr

Abstract. The innovative feature of the system presented in this paper is the use of pattern-matching techniques to retrieve translations resulting in a flexible, language-independent approach, which employs a limited amount of explicit a priori linguistic knowledge. Furthermore, while all state-of-the-art corpus-based approaches to Machine Translation (MT) rely on bitexts, this system relies on extensive target language monolingual corpora. The translation process distinguishes three phases: 1) pre-processing with 'light' rule and statistics-based NLP techniques 2) search & retrieval, 3) synthesising. At Phase 1, the source language sentence is mapped onto a lemma-to-lemma translated string. This string then forms the input to the search algorithm, which retrieves similar sentences from the corpus (Phase 2). This retrieval process is performed iteratively at increasing levels of detail, until the best match is detected. The best retrieved sentence is sent to the synthesising algorithm (Phase 3), which handles phenomena such as agreement.

1 Introduction

The work presented in this paper further explores the ideas tested within the METIS[1] system [5], [6], which generated translations from monolingual corpora. In METIS, tagged and lemmatised source language (SL) sentences were translated with a lemma-to-lemma flat bilingual lexicon and the resulting string was matched against a tagged and lemmatised target language (TL) corpus using pattern matching techniques. Results of an adequate quality were retrieved when a similar sentence did exist in the TL corpus, though in general the coverage provided by the corpus is very limited. Efforts, thus, focussed on combining sub-sentential corpus evidence. In METIS-II, the framework of the present work, chunks are exploited to generate translations.

In what follows, we first outline the main features of the system presented. Next, we describe, step by step, our method of using chunks and pattern matching techniques for generating translations. Finally, we evaluate the presented system's

---

[1] METIS was funded by EU under the FET Open Scheme (METIS-I, IST-2001-32775), while METIS-II, the continuation of METIS, is being funded under the FET-STREP scheme of FP6 (METIS-II, IST-FP6-003768). The assessment project METIS ended in February 2003, while the second phase started in October 2004 and has a 36 month duration.

G. Antoniou et al. (Eds.): SETN 2006, LNAI 3955, pp. 345–355, 2006.

performance by contrasting its output with the translations received from established rule-based commercial systems.

2 Main Features

MT systems, whether rule-based, example-based (EBMT) or statistics-based (SMT), often require (very) expensive resources: lexica, grammars/parsers, parallel corpora are among them. EBMT [9] and SMT [3] aimed at using mainly non-manually developed resources. However, it gradually becomes evident that some amount of linguistic knowledge is necessary (see [12] for the case of SMT). On the other hand, all these methods crucially depend on large bitexts [8]. But bitexts are rare [1] and, quite often, of questionable linguistic quality. METIS is innovative, exactly because it relies on monolingual corpora, which are a relatively low-cost, easy-to-construct resource and can be more easily controlled in terms of linguistic quality.

Using sub-sentential corpus evidence has been considered promising for MT [4]. In this context, proposed ways for fragmenting sentences range from the exploitation of highly structured representations of linguistic knowledge [14] to the establishment of string correspondences accompanied by little/trivial linguistic knowledge representation [8]. However, methods combining sub-sentential strings face the problem of boundary friction. 'More linguistic' methods are reported to perform better in this sense than 'less linguistic' ones [14]. METIS is a relatively knowledge-poor approach, as it relies on flat bilingual lexica and on loosely structured syntactic information (which is the normal output of chunkers).

The proposed approach is based on analysing a given SL sentence at clause level. As described in section 3, for each clause, the best-matching clause is retrieved from within an extensive TL corpus, using pattern-matching techniques that take into account the similarity of specific linguistic characteristics at token, chunk and clause level. The best-matching clause is then modified, using pattern recognition techniques and suitable similarity metrics, to provide a better translation.

In a nutshell, the system presented here is modular and language-independent. It uses only 'light' language-specific NLP tools and resources. ILSP has developed the system mainly studying the Greek-English pair. However, three more pairs have been used for testing, namely Dutch, German and Spanish to English.

3 Description of the Proposed System

3.1 Pre-processing Phase

In order for the system to search for the best translation, both the TL corpus and the SL string must be suitably processed. This phase mainly comprises basic NLP tasks (i.e. tagging, lemmatising, chunking etc.) and distinguishes three different procedures:

i. processing of the target monolingual corpus
ii. processing of the source language string
iii. application of an n-gram algorithm for disambiguation purposes

Processing of the target monolingual corpus: This procedure, which is performed off-line, involves the lemmatisation[2] of the TL corpus, the British National Corpus (BNC)[3] in our case, which is already tagged with the CLAWS5[4] tagset. Next, each corpus sentence is split into its constituent finite clauses. This output is subsequently annotated for phrasal chunks (verb groups [VG], noun phrases [NP], prepositional phrases [PP], adjective phrases [ADJ]) [13]. In order to facilitate the search for the best match, the TL corpus is stored into a relational database, containing (a) clauses indexed on the basis of their main verb and the number of their chunks and (b) NP and PP chunks classified according to their label and head.

Processing of the source language string: The annotation of the SL string, being performed on-line, involves its tagging-lemmatising by the respective PAROLE-compatible ILSP tool [7] and annotation for its constituent chunks with the ILSP chunker [2], which yield a sequence of tokens accompanied by grammatical information and organised into labelled chunks.

The output of these tools is subsequently fed to two bilingual lexica, the Expression Lexicon, which provides translations for multi-word units, and the Word Lexicon, which handles single-word units. After the lexicon look-up the SL string is enriched with information about all possible translations of the contained terms. So, for instance, the SL string "Δυστυχώς, διαρκούν για ώρες οι εβδομαδιαίες συναντήσεις των πιο βαρετών ανθρώπων" is represented as in Example 1:

1. Unfortunately last/hold for/about hour/time the weekly meeting the most boring person/people

At this point, it is possible to apply a limited set of mapping rules, which capture the structural and/or lexical differences between the source and the target language and transform the lemma-to-lemma string accordingly. In the above sentence, the "of-insertion" mapping rule applies in order to accommodate the genitive NP "των πιο βαρετών ανθρώπων" (see Example 2). More specifically, a Greek genitive NP is transformed into an English PP headed by "of".

2. Unfortunately [$_{vg}$ last/hold] [$_{PP}$ for/about [$_{np\_ac}$ hour/time]] [$_{np\_nm}$ the weekly meeting] [$_{pp}$ **of** [$_{np\_gen}$ the most boring people/person]]

An n-gram algorithm for disambiguation: In order to narrow down the possible translations provided by the lexicon, the output of the SL processing is then handled by an algorithm based on n-gram (mostly 2-gram) statistics, extracted from the BNC corpus. The main idea is to find the most likely translations of the chunk heads, so that only the best combination of heads in terms of frequency-of-co-occurrence is retained, before proceeding to the search algorithm. More specifically, the following measures are counted:

- The number of co-occurrences of the NP-heads in relation to the VG-head.
- The number of co-occurrences of the VG-head in relation to the PP-heads.
- The number of co-occurrences of the PP-heads in relation to the heads of the embedded NPs.

---

[2] http://iai.iai.uni-sb.de/~carl/metis/lemmatiser
[3] http://www.natcorp.ox.ac.uk/index.html
[4] http://www.comp.lancs.ac.uk/ucrel/claws5tags.html

Hence, for the following sentence (heads are marked with bold),

3. Unfortunately [$_{vg}$ **last/hold**] [$_{pp}$ **for/about** [$_{np\_ac}$ **hour/time**]] [$_{np\_nm}$ the weekly **meeting**] [$_{pp}$ **of** [$_{np\_gen}$ the most boring **people/person**]]

the number of co-occurrences of the following token pairs are measured:

{meeting, last}, {meeting, hold}, {hold, for}, {last, for}, {hold, about}, {last, about}, {of, people}, {of, person}, {for, hour}, {about, hour}, {for, time}, {about, time}.

For obtaining only one translation for every chunk head, the product of every combination is calculated. The possible translations are ranked according to their score and finally the translation with the highest score is chosen. Four possible translations for example 3 are shown below, including (in bold) the highest-scoring one:

Score 1 = {of, people} x {meeting, last} x {last, for} x {for, hour}
Score 2 = {of, people} x {meeting, last} x {last, about} x {about, hour}
Score 3 = {of, person} x {meeting, last} x {last, about} x {about, hour}
Score 4 = {of, person} x {meeting, hold} x {hold, for} x {for, hour}

3.2 Search and Retrieval Phase: Matching Step by Step

Step 1: The first step of the approach is to retrieve clauses from the BNC database that have a similar structure with the lemma-to-lemma translation of the source language (SL). The retrieved BNC clauses must include the translation equivalents of the source verb and contain a number of chunks ranging within [m, $m+2$], where m the number of SL chunks. The SL clause (Example 4) used to search the BNC clauses database is the output of the n-gram statistical algorithm of the pre-processing phase.

4. Unfortunately [$_{vg}$ last] [$_{pp}$ for [$_{np\_ac}$ hour]] [$_{np\_nm}$ the weekly meeting] [$_{pp}$ of [$_{np\_gen}$ the most boring people]]

So, in this example we try to retrieve from the BNC clauses having "*last*" as their main verb and a total number of chunks ranging between 3 and 5.

Step 2: For each candidate translation of the SL clause, which has scored high, a comparison is performed between the SL and the BNC clauses. The search originates within the class of clauses retrieved during the first step.

The result of each comparison is a score for the SL clause-BNC clause pair, based on general chunk information, such as the number of chunks in the clause, chunk labels and chunk heads, using a pattern recognition-based method. The formula for calculating the **ClauseScore** is given in Equation (1), where **m** is the number of chunks in the SL clause, **ChunkScore** is the score of each chunk comparison pair and *ocf* (overall cost factor) is the cost factor for each comparison. The *ocf*, whose value is based on the source chunk, is different per chunk label, since some chunk types are more important than others and should contribute more towards the clause score.

$$ClauseScore = \sum_{n=1}^{m} \left\{ ocf_n \times \frac{ChunkScore_n}{\sum_{j=1}^{m} ocf_j} \right\}, where\ m > 1 \qquad (1)$$

The weighted sum of the chunk label comparison score (***LabelComp***), the chunk head tag comparison score (***TagComp***) and the chunk head lemma comparison score (***LemmaComp***) is the final ***ChunkScore***. Each discrete chunk label is pre-assigned a set of cost factors to determine the comparison scores. These factors are the chunk label cost factor (***bcf***), the chunk head tag cost factor (***tcf***) and the chunk head lemma cost factor (***lcf***). Equation (2) illustrates the score calculation, when comparing two chunks.

$$ChunkScore_n = bcf_n \times LabelComp_n +$$
$$+ tcf_n \times TagComp_n + lcf_n \times LemmaComp_n$$
$$, where \quad bcf_n + tcf_n + lcf_n = 1$$

$$(2)$$

The SL clause and BNC clause comparison pairs are subsequently sorted according to their clause scores. Then, the 30 first clause pairs serve as the input to the next step of the process for further processing, with the constraint that a BNC clause cannot participate in more than one comparison pair.

The employment of sets of weights makes it possible to establish the right constituent order and the appropriate matching of SL and TL chunks, without resorting to the definition of additional explicit mapping rules. For instance, a Greek nominative NP may be mapped with a higher weight onto an English NP, which precedes the main verb than to other NPs. So, the post-verbal NP 'the weekly meeting' will preferably match a BNC clause NP, if it is found before the main verb.

Step 3: In the third step of the algorithm, the SL chunks are checked against the respective chunks in the BNC clause, again using a pattern recognition-based method, but the comparison is more detailed and involves comparing the tokens contained within each chunk. At the end of this step a second score is calculated for each clause pair (and each chunk of the clause) in a similar way to the second step.

The final score for each clause pair is the product of the clause scores obtained at steps 2 and 3. Final scores are calculated for each chunk as well. The BNC clause of the comparison pair with the highest final score is considered to be the best-matching sentence and forms the archetype of the translation.

For the SL clause in Example 4 the retrieval algorithm returns the BNC clause in Example 5 with a final score of 54.8%:

5. [np_nm one charge] [pp of [np_gen the battery]] [vg last] [pp for [np_ac hour]] even [pp at [np_ac top speed]]

The individual chunk scores and mapping are the following:

- [np_nm the weekly meeting] – [np_nm one charge]: 46.7%
- [pp of [np_gen the most boring people]] – [pp of [np_gen the battery]]: 44.6%
- [vg last] – [vg last]: 100.0%
- [pp for [np_ac hour]] – [pp for [np_ac hour]]: 100.0%

Step 4: At this point, the chunk sequence is already settled and we only need to process the chunks. The chunk comparison pairs of the clause are then classified on the basis of their final score using two threshold values ***A*** and ***B***. Chunks scoring higher than ***A*** will be used in the final translation without any changes. Chunks scoring between *A* and *B* (where *A>B*) will be used in the final translation after modifications are made. Finally, chunks with a score lower than *B* are not considered eligible candidate translations. To translate these SL chunks, we need to retrieve new chunks from the BNC based on chunk label and head token information. Values *A* and *B* may function as system parameters, so that the translator can tune the precision of the final translation.

If, for example, *A=90%* and *B=65%* then chunks 3 and 4 of Example 5 will be used without any modifications, while chunks 1 and 2 will be rejected and the BNC will be searched again for a better matching chunk.

3.3 Synthesising Phase

The output of step 4, i.e. the final translation, consists of a sequence of lemmas. In the synthesising phase the following three actions take place:

- Tokens are generated from lemmata. Information for correct morphological generation is taken from the SL extended tags that are assigned in the pre-processing phase.
- Agreement features are checked.
- Word order is checked within chunks as well as for tokens that are not enclosed in chunks, such as adverbs.

4   System Testing – Other Language Pairs

The system is designed to have no limitations as regards the input text; however, as this is the first system prototype, complex sentences were not tested at this phase.

The main aim was to test the language-independent components of the MT system presented and see how the system behaved with other language pairs. In order to achieve that, three more source languages and their respective specific modules were employed: Spanish, Dutch and German, while the target corpus, BNC, remained the same. In total the test corpus consisted of 60 sentences, 15 for each language pair. The majority of sentences were simple as we wanted the results to be as controllable as possible, for example, to check whether the search engine could find the right chunks and put them in the correct order or to check whether the correct translation equivalent would be selected when more than one existed. In addition, it was considered necessary to set equal testing terms for all language pairs, therefore, all sentences met the following specifications:

- Sentences were between 7 and 15 words long and were selected by native speakers.
- Since this was still an early stage in the development of METIS-II, the sentences were not excessively complex, i.e. the majority contained only one clause and only one finite verb.
- All sentences except for the 15 Dutch ones were taken from the BNC either as a whole or as a combination of chunks and were then translated into the respective language by translators that were native speakers.
- The Dutch sentences were taken from Dutch newspapers.
- The verbal subject was specified.

- The number of combinations was limited as no more than three possible translations were given for each source word.
- No expressions were used.

Comparison of the results was on a lemma basis as the synthesising module was not ready at the time.

Complex sentences are planned to be tested at a later stage. The main idea is to break them into clauses, which will then be treated separately. Anticipated problems are clause and chunk boundaries as well as other common problems in machine translation such as anaphora, gapping, etc.

SYSTRAN: Systran[5] was selected among other MT systems for this internal evaluation as it met the following criteria:

a) It is a system with a different architecture i.e. it is mainly a rule-based system with mixed features from both the direct and transfer approach.
b) It is a well-established system used widely both in the private sector as well as in the European Union.

5 System Evaluation

In the present section, the experimental results obtained for the proposed system will be summarised. At an early stage of the development of the system, it was decided to employ established benchmarks that evaluate the accuracy of the generated translation. This, of course needs to be coupled with the detailed analysis of results using specialist human translators. However, in order to generate objective results for a relatively large set of sentences, it is necessary to adopt a metric that compares experimentally-derived translations to a set of reference translations. To that end, the most widely-used benchmarks for tasks involving translation towards the English language has been chosen, these being the BLEU benchmark, which was originally developed at IBM [11] to evaluate the effectiveness of translation for statistical machine-translation systems based on n-grams of words, and the NIST [10] benchmark, which is based on BLEU.

The results obtained are summarized in Tables 1 and 2, where the respective results for the BLEU and NIST metrics are reported. In each table, the average of the 15 scores obtained for each of the sentences within a language pair is indicated, together with the median, the standard deviation and the maximum and minimum sentence scores. As can be seen from Table 1, the proposed system has a consistent average accuracy, giving BLEU scores of 0.44 to 0.47 for the three language pairs (the only language pair with a lower accuracy being the Dutch-to-English pair with a score of 0.30). Similar conclusions are obtained by studying the median of all 15 BLEU scores for each sub-corpus. In comparison to the BLEU scores for the SYSTRAN system, the proposed system always results in a higher average as well as a higher median accuracy. The difference between the two systems is lower in the case of the Spanish-to-English language pair, probably due to the fact that within SYSTRAN this

---

[5] The particular version used for the internal testing is the one on the server of the European Union at the time of writing.

Table 1. Comparative Analysis of the isolated sentence results for the proposed system and SYSTRAN, over each language pair sub-corpus using the **BLEU** metric

	Greek sub-corpus		Spanish sub-corpus		German sub-corpus		Dutch sub-corpus	
	METIS	SYSTRAN	METIS	SYSTRAN	METIS	SYSTRAN	METIS	SYSTRAN
Average accuracy	0.463	0.401	0.470	0.447	0.437	0.250	0.304	0.195
Median accuracy	0.431	0.424	0.483	0.411	0.409	0.290	0.312	0.000
Standard Deviation	0.415	0.295	0.417	0.365	0.281	0.199	0.343	0.267
Maximum accuracy	1.000	0.863	1.000	1.000	1.000	0.580	1.000	0.7369
Minimum accuracy	0.000	0.000	0.000	0.000	0.000	0.000	0.000	0.0000

Table 2. Comparative Analysis of the isolated sentence results for the proposed system and SYSTRAN, over each language pair sub-corpus using the **NIST** metric

	Greek sub-corpus		Spanish sub-corpus		German sub-corpus		Dutch sub-corpus	
	METIS	SYSTRAN	METIS	SYSTRAN	METIS	SYSTRAN	METIS	SYSTRAN
Average accuracy	6.6945	5.6755	6.5263	6.4130	5.6626	4.3264	5.7028	4.2681
Median accuracy	6.3973	5.3800	6.4823	6.3477	5.9267	4.7469	6.1522	3.8937
Standard Deviation	1.4322	1.4002	1.5112	1.2951	1.7617	1.4886	1.5193	1.6322
Maximum accuracy	9.1268	7.9560	9.5637	9.4262	8.5692	6.3856	7.3020	6.9317
Minimum accuracy	4.4601	2.9972	4.0222	4.6576	0.8359	1.4713	2.4596	1.4451

particular language pair has been developed more extensively. Similar observations apply to the median of the isolated sentence scores and the maximum and minimum scores obtained, where the proposed system for all four language pairs has a translation accuracy consistently higher than that of SYSTRAN.

Similar conclusions are obtained when one applies the NIST benchmark (Table 2). The proposed system consistently generates more accurate translations than SYSTRAN, for all four language pairs (as indicated by the average and median translation accuracies). The translation accuracy of the two systems is more similar in the case of the Spanish-to-English sub-experiment, while for the three other cases the proposed system gives a substantially improved performance in comparison to SYSTRAN.

As an example, the actual translation accuracies obtained for the sentences of the Greek-to-English and German-to-English translation sub-experiments are depicted in Figures 1 and 2, respectively. In the case of German-to-English translation, for all sentences, the proposed system generates a more accurate translation than SYSTRAN. For 4 out of the 15 sentences, SYSTRAN generates a wholly inappropriate translation (with a score of 0.00), while in the case of the proposed system this occurs for only a single sentence. Hence, the proposed system is shown to be more robust than SYSTRAN, as a whole.

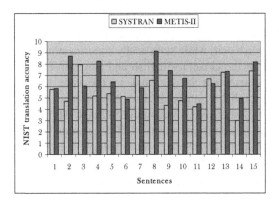

Fig. 1. NIST-derived translation accuracies for each of the 15 sentences within the Greek-to-English experiments, for **SYSTRAN** and the proposed system

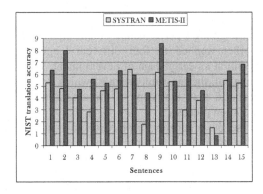

Fig. 2. NIST-derived translation accuracies for each of the 15 sentences within the German-to-English experiments, for **SYSTRAN** and the proposed system

To investigate whether the improved translation accuracy of METIS in comparison to SYSTRAN is statistically significant, a set of t-tests were performed for each combination of metric (BLEU or NIST) and source language (Greek, Spanish, German and Dutch), giving a total of eight combinations. For each of these combinations, a paired t-test was performed to determine whether the means of the translation scores for SYSTRAN and METIS differed significantly. When using the BLEU metric, it was found that for most source languages the two translation systems gave statistically equivalent results. Only for the German-to-English language pair did the METIS system generate significantly better translations, at a significance level of 0.95. On the contrary, in the case of the NIST metric, the higher translation accuracy of METIS was statistically significant for three language pairs (Greek-to-English at a significance level of 0.95; Dutch-to-English, at a significance level of 0.99 and German-to-English at a significance level of 0.995).

This statistical analysis indicates that (i) NIST is a more sensitive measure of the translation accuracy than BLEU, which is expected, since NIST has been based on

BLEU, and (ii) for several language pairs, METIS generates a translation of a higher accuracy than SYSTRAN. More specifically, the main improvement is recorded for the German-to-English pair, while statistically significant improvements (using NIST) are also recorded for the Greek-to-English and Dutch-to-English pairs. The fact that no significant improvement is achieved in the case of the Spanish-to-English translation pair is probably attributable to the fact that this pair has been studied comparatively more extensively within SYSTRAN. However, the fact should be stressed that, for all four language pairs, METIS generated more accurate translations than SYSTRAN in terms of absolute values using the established benchmark metric (NIST), while for three out of four pairs, this improvement in accuracy is statistically significant.

6 Future Work

The results reported in the previous section confirm that the system presented in this article has a considerable potential for machine translation tasks, the existing experimental prototype giving a performance which surpasses that of a commercially-available system, when applied to four different language pairs. However, the proposed system is still at an early stage of development. Thus a number of potential improvements are evident, the most important of which being, at the current stage of development, the expansion of the scope of the algorithm, in order to improve the accuracy of the translation process.

In order to analyse the algorithm, a prerequisite is to considerably expand the experiments, by defining a much larger number of sentences, with more elaborate structures. Also, the system parameters reported in Equations (1) and (2) need to be fine-tuned in a systematic manner. To achieve that, work has already been done to automate the evaluation of system performance, though more work remains to be done.

References

1. Al-Onaizan, Y., Germann, U., Hermjakob, U., Knight, K., Koehn, P., Marcu, D., Yamada, K.: Translating with Scarce Resources. American Association for Artificial Intelligence conference (AAAI '00), Austin, Texas, (2000) 672-678 (Available at http://www.isi.edu/natural-language/projects/rewrite)
2. Boutsis, S., Prokopidis, P., Giouli, V., Piperidis S.: A Robust Parser for Unrestricted Greek Text. In Proceedings of the Second International Conference on Language Resources and Evaluation, Athens, Greece, Vol. 1, (2000) 467-482
3. Brown, P., J. Cocke, S. Della Pietra, V. Della Pietra, F. Jelinek, J. Lafferty, R. Mercer, Roosin P. S.: A Statistical Approach to Machine Translation. Computational Linguistics, Vol. 16, No. 2, (1990) 79-85
4. Cranias, L., H. Papageorgiou, Piperidis, S.: Example Retrieval from a Translation Memory. Natural Language Engineering 3, (1997) 255-277
5. Dologlou, I., Markantonatou, S., Tambouratzis, G., Yannoutsou, O., Fourla, A., Ioannou, N.: Using Monolingual Corpora for Statistical Machine Translation. In Proceedings of EAMT/CLAW 2003, Dublin, Ireland, (2003) 61-68

6. Ioannou, N.: METIS: Statistical Machine Translation Using Monolingual Corpora. Proceedings of the Workshop on Text Processing for Modern Greek: From Symbolic to Statistical Approaches (held in conjunction with the 6th International Conference of Greek Linguistics), Rethymno, Greece, (2003) 11-21

7. Labropoulou, P., Mantzari, E., Gavrilidou, M.: Lexicon-Morphosyntactic Specifications: Language Specific Instantiation (Greek), PP-PAROLE, MLAP report (1996) 63-386

8. McTait, K.: Translation Patterns, Linguistic Knowledge and Complexity in EBMT. In Recent Advances in Example-Based Machine Translation, Michael Carl and Andy Way (eds.), Kluwer Academic Publishers (2003) 307-338

9. Nagao, M.: A Framework of a Mechanical Translation between Japanese and English by Analogy Principle. In Artificial and Human Intelligence, A. Elithorn and R. Banerji (eds.), North-Holland (1984)

10. Nist: Automatic Evaluation of Machine Translation Quality Using n-gram Co-occurrences Statistics (2002) (Available at http://www.nist.gov/speech/tests/mt/)

11. Papineni, K., Roukos, S., Ward, T., Zhu, W.-J.: BLEU: A Method for Automatic Evaluation of Machine Translation. Proceedings of the 40th Annual Meeting of the Association for Computational Linguistics, Philadelphia, U.S.A. (2002) 311-318

12. Popovic, M., Ney, H.: Exploiting Phrasal Lexica and Additional Morpho-Syntactic Language Resources for Statistical Machine Translation with Scarce Training Data. EAMT 10th Annual Conference, Budapest, Hungary (2005)

13. Vandeghinste V.: Manual for ShaRPa 2.0. Internal Report, Centre for Computational Linguistics, K.U.Leuven (2005)

14. Way, A.: Translating with Examples: The LFG-DOT Models of Translation, In Recent Advances in Example-Based Machine Translation, Michael Carl and Andy Way (eds.), Kluwer Academic Publishers (2003) 443-472

Bayesian Metanetwork for Context-Sensitive Feature Relevance

Vagan Terziyan

Industrial Ontologies Group, Agora Center, University of Jyvaskyla,
P.O. Box 35 (Agora), FIN-40014 Jyvaskyla, Finland
vagan@it.jyu.fi

Abstract. Bayesian Networks are proven to be a comprehensive model to describe causal relationships among domain attributes with probabilistic measure of appropriate conditional dependency. However, depending on task and context, many attributes of the model might not be relevant. If a network has been learned across multiple contexts then all uncovered conditional dependencies are averaged over all contexts and cannot guarantee high predictive accuracy when applied to a concrete case. We are considering a context as a set of contextual attributes, which are not directly effect probability distribution of the target attributes, but they effect on a "relevance" of the predictive attributes towards target attributes. In this paper we use the Bayesian Metanetwork vision to model such context-sensitive feature relevance. Such model assumes that the relevance of predictive attributes in a Bayesian network might be a random attribute itself and it provides a tool to reason based not only on probabilities of predictive attributes but also on their relevancies. According to this model, the evidence observed about contextual attributes is used to extract a relevant substructure from a Bayesian network model and then the predictive attributes evidence is used to reason about probability distribution of the target attribute in the extracted sub-network. We provide the basic architecture for such Bayesian Metanetwork, basic reasoning formalism and some examples.

1 Introduction

A *Bayesian network* is a valuable tool for reasoning about probabilistic (causal) relationships [1]. A Bayesian network for a set of attributes $X = \{X1, ..., Xn\}$ is a directed acyclic graph with a network structure S that encodes a set of conditional independence assertions about attributes in X, and a set P of local probability distributions associated with each attribute [2].

An important task in learning Bayesian networks from data is model selection [3]. The models-candidates are evaluated according to measured degree to which a network structure fits the prior knowledge and data. Than the best structure is selected or several good structures are processed in model averaging. Each attribute in ordinary Bayesian network has the same status, so they are just combined in possible models-candidates to encode possible conditional dependencies however many modifications of Bayesian networks require distinguishing between attributes, e.g. as follows:

G. Antoniou et al. (Eds.): SETN 2006, LNAI 3955, pp. 356–366, 2006.
© Springer-Verlag Berlin Heidelberg 2006

- *Target attribute*, which probability is being estimated based on set of evidence.
- *Predictive attribute*, which values being observed and which influences the probability distribution of the target attribute(s).
- *Contextual attribute*, which has not direct visible effect to target attributes but influences relevance of attributes in the predictive model. A contextual attribute can be conditionally dependent on some other contextual attribute.

Causal independence in a Bayesian network refers to the situation where multiple causes provided by predictive attributes contribute independently to a common effect on a target attribute. Context specific independence refers to such dependencies that depend on particular values of contextual attributes. In [4], Butz exploited contextual independencies based on assumption that while a conditional independence must hold over all contexts, a contextual independence need only hold for one particular context. He shows how contextual independencies can be modeled using multiple Bayesian networks. Boutilier et al. [5] presents two algorithms to exploit context specific independence in a Bayesian network. The first one is network transformation and clustering. The other one is a form of cutset conditioning using reasoning by cases, where each case is a possible assignment to the variables in the cutset. Zhang [6] presents a rule-based contextual variable elimination algorithm. Contextual variable elimination represents conditional probabilities in terms of generalized rules, which capture context specific independence in variables. Geiger and Heckerman [7] present method to exploit context specific independence. With the notion of similarity networks, context specific independencies are made explicit in the graphical structure of a Bayesian network. Bayesian Multi-nets were first introduced in ([8]) and then studied in ([9]) as a type of classifiers composed of the prior probability distribution of the class node and a *set* of local networks, each corresponding to a value that the class node can take. A recursive Bayesian multinet was introduced by Pena et al [10] as a decision tree with component Bayesian networks at the leaves. The idea was to decompose the learning problem into learning component networks from incomplete data.

In our previous work [11, 12], is the multilevel probabilistic meta-model (Bayesian Metanetwork), has been presented, which is an extension of traditional BN and modification of recursive multinets. It assumes that interoperability among component- networks can be modeled by another BN. Bayesian Metanetwork is a set of BN, which are put on each other in such a way that conditional or unconditional probability distributions associated with nodes of every previous probabilistic network depend on probability distributions associated with nodes of the next network. We assume parameters (probability distributions) of a BN as random variables and allow conditional dependencies between these probabilities. Algorithms for learning Bayesian Metanetworks were discussed in [13].

As our main goal in this paper, we are presenting another view to the Bayesian Metanetwork by presenting the concept of attribute "relevance" as additional (to an attribute value probability) computational parameter of a Bayesian Network. Based on computed relevance only a specific sub-network from the whole Bayesian Network will be extracted and used for reasoning. The rest of paper organized as follows. In Section 2 we first provide basic architecture of the Bayesian Metanetwork for managing Attribute Relevance. In Section 3 we provide the reasoning formalism and few examples. A general concept of a Relevance Metanetwork is given in Section 4. We conclude in Section 5.

2 Bayesian Metanetwork for Managing Attributes' Relevance

Relevance is a property of an attribute as a whole, not a property of certain values of an attribute (see Fig. 1). This makes a difference between relevance and probability, because the last one has as many values as an attribute itself. Another words, when we say probability, we mean probability of the value of the attribute, when we say relevance, we mean relevance (*probability to be included to the model*) of the attribute as whole.

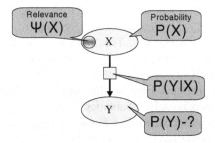

Fig. 1. The relevance of an attribute in a Bayesian Network

Bayesian Network in Fig. 1 actually includes two following subnetworks (see Fig. 2), which illustrate the definition of a "relevance".

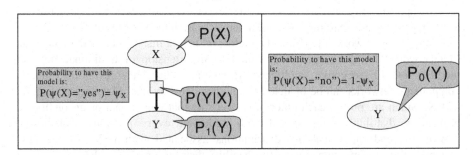

Fig. 2. Two valid subnetworks based on the relevance of the attribute X

In the network from Fig. 1 and Fig. 2 we have: (a) attributes: predictive attribute X with values $\{x_1, x_2, ..., x_{nx}\}$, target attribute Y with values $\{y_1, y_2, ..., y_{ny}\}$; (b) probability distributions of the attributes: $P(X)$, $P(Y|X)$; (c) posteriori probability distributions of the target attribute: $P_1(Y)$ and $P_0(Y)$ for the two cases (X – relevant or X irrelevant) of the valid subnetwork respectively. Relevance predicate:

$\psi(X)$ = "yes", if parameter X is relevant; $\psi(X)$ = "no", if parameter X is not relevant.

Relevance value: $\psi_X = P(\psi(X) = \text{"yes"})$.

Let's estimate $P(Y)$ based on Bayesian reasoning:

$$P(Y) = \psi_X \cdot P_1(Y) + (1 - \psi_X) \cdot P_0(Y), \quad \text{where} \tag{1}$$

$$P_1(Y) = \sum_{i=1}^{nx} P(Y \mid X = x_i) \cdot P(X = x_i). \tag{2}$$

$P_0(Y)$ can be calculated based on $P(Y|X)$ knowing that in that case Y is not depending on X, because X is considered as not relevant:

$$P_0(Y) = \frac{1}{nx} \sum_{i=1}^{nx} P(Y \mid X = x_i). \tag{3}$$

Substituting (2) and (3) to (1) we obtain:

$$P(Y) = \psi_X \cdot \sum_{i=1}^{nx} [P(Y \mid X = x_i) \cdot P(X = x_i)] + (1 - \psi_X) \cdot \frac{1}{nx} \cdot \sum_{i=1}^{nx} P(Y \mid X = x_i) =$$

$$= \sum_{i=1}^{nx} P(Y \mid X = x_i) \cdot [\psi_X \cdot P(X = x_i) + \frac{(1 - \psi_X)}{nx}],$$

which is in compact form is: $P(Y) = \frac{1}{nx} \cdot \sum_X P(Y \mid X) \cdot [nx \cdot \psi_X \cdot P(X) + (1 - \psi_X)]. \tag{4}$

Consider example, where the attribute X will be "state of whether" and attribute Y, which is influenced by X, will be "state of mood". Let the values of the attributes and appropriate prior probabilities will be as follows:

X ("state of weather") ={"sunny", "overcast", "rain"}; Y ("state of mood") ={"good", "bad"};
$P(X=\text{"sunny"}) = 0.4$; $P(X=\text{"overcast"}) = 0.5$; $P(X=\text{"rain"}) = 0.1$;
$P(Y=\text{"good"}|X=\text{"sunny"})=0.7$; $P(Y=\text{"good"}|X=\text{"overcast"})=0.5$; $P(Y=\text{"good"}|X=\text{"rain"})=0.2$;

Let conditional probability, which links X and Y will be as follows:

$P(Y=\text{"bad"}|X=\text{"sunny"})=0.3$; $P(Y=\text{"bad"}|X=\text{"overcast"})=0.5$; $P(Y=\text{"bad"}|X=\text{"rain"})=0.8$;

Assume the value of relevance for the attribute X is known and equal: $\psi_X=0.6$. Now, according to (4) we have:

$$P(Y=\text{" good"}) = \frac{1}{3} \cdot \{P(Y=\text{" good"} | X=\text{" sunny"}) \cdot [1.8 \cdot P(X=\text{" sunny"}) + 0.4] +$$

$$+ P(Y=\text{" good"} | X=\text{" overcast"}) \cdot [1.8 \cdot P(X=\text{" overcast"}) + 0.4] +$$

$$+ P(Y=\text{" good"} | X=\text{" rain"}) \cdot [1.8 \cdot P(X=\text{" rain"}) + 0.4]\} = 0.517;$$

Similarly: $P(Y=\text{"bad"}) = 0.483$.

One can also notice that these values belong to the intervals created by the two extreme cases, when parameter X is not relevant at all or it is fully relevant:

$$0.467 \approx P_0(Y = "good")|_{\psi_x=0} < P(Y = "good")|_{\psi_x=0.6} < P_1(Y = "good")|_{\psi_x=1} = 0.55 ;$$
$$0.45 = P_1(Y = "bad")|_{\psi_x=1} < P(Y = "bad")|_{\psi_x=0.6} < P_0(Y = "bad")|_{\psi_x=0} \approx 0.533 .$$

3   General Formalism and Samples

More complicated case is the management of relevance in the following situation (Fig. 3):

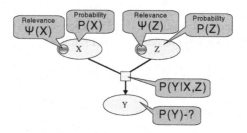

Fig. 3. Relevance management with two predictive attributes

Here we have 4 following subnetworks depending on the relevance (see Fig. 4).

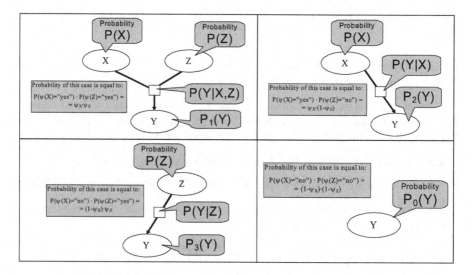

Fig. 4. Subnetworks for the case with two predictive attributes

Here we have: (a) predictive attributes: X with values $\{x_1, x_2, ..., x_{nx}\}$; Z with values $\{z_1, z_2, ..., z_{nz}\}$; (b) target attribute Y with values $\{y_1, y_2, ..., y_{ny}\}$; (c) probabilities: P(X), P(Z), P(Y|X,Z); (d) relevance predicate: $\psi(X)$ = "yes", if X is relevant; $\psi(X)$ = "no", if X is not relevant; (e) relevancies: $\psi_X = P(\psi(X) = "yes")$; $\psi_Z = P(\psi(Z) = "yes")$.

Let's estimate $P(Y)$:

$$P(Y) = \psi_X \cdot \psi_Z \cdot P_1(Y) + \psi_X \cdot (1 - \psi_Z) \cdot P_2(Y) + \\ + (1 - \psi_X) \cdot \psi_Z \cdot P_3(Y) + (1 - \psi_X) \cdot (1 - \psi_Z) \cdot P_0(Y)$$

(5)

$$P_1(Y) = \sum_{i=1}^{nx} \sum_{k=1}^{nz} P(Y \mid X = x_i, Z = z_k) \cdot P(X = x_i) \cdot P(Z = z_k).$$

(6)

$$P_2(Y) = \sum_{i=1}^{nx} P(Y \mid X = x_i) \cdot P(X = x_i).$$

(7)

$$P_3(Y) = \sum_{k=1}^{nz} P(Y \mid Z = z_k) \cdot P(Z = z_k).$$

(8)

Now we should extract $P(Y|X)$, $P(Y|Z)$, $P_0(Y)$ from $P(Y|X,Z)$ and $P(Y|Z)$ from $P(Y|X,Z)$, which is:

$$P(Y \mid X) = \frac{1}{nz} \cdot \sum_{k=1}^{nz} P(Y \mid X, Z = z_k),$$

(9)

$$P(Y \mid Z) = \frac{1}{nx} \cdot \sum_{i=1}^{nx} P(Y \mid X = x_i, Z),$$

(10)

$$P_0(Y) = \frac{1}{nx \cdot nz} \cdot \sum_{i=1}^{nx} \sum_{k=1}^{nz} P(Y \mid X = x_i, Z = z_k),$$

(11)

We can rewrite (7) using (9) as follows:

$$P_2(Y) = \frac{1}{nz} \cdot \sum_{i=1}^{nx} \sum_{k=1}^{nz} P(Y \mid X = x_i, Z = z_k) \cdot P(X = x_i).$$

(12)

From (8) and (10): $P_3(Y) = \dfrac{1}{nx} \cdot \sum_{i=1}^{nx} \sum_{k=1}^{nz} P(Y \mid X = x_i, Z = z_k) \cdot P(Z = z_k).$ (13)

Finally we can substitute (6), (11), (12), (13) to (5):

$$P(Y) = \psi_X \cdot \psi_Z \cdot \sum_{i=1}^{nx} \sum_{k=i}^{nz} P(Y \mid X = x_i, Z = z_k) \cdot P(X = x_i) \cdot P(Z = z_k) + \psi_X \cdot (1 - \psi_Z) \cdot \frac{1}{nz} \cdot \\ \cdot \sum_{i=1}^{nx} \sum_{k=i}^{nz} P(Y \mid X = x_i, Z = z_k) \cdot P(X = x_i) + (1 - \psi_X) \cdot \psi_Z \cdot \frac{1}{nx} \cdot \sum_{i=1}^{nx} \sum_{k=i}^{nz} P(Y \mid X = x_i, Z = z_k) \cdot P(Z = z_k) + \\ + (1 - \psi_X) \cdot (1 - \psi_Z) \cdot \frac{1}{nx \cdot nz} \cdot \sum_{i=1}^{nx} \sum_{k=i}^{nz} P(Y \mid X = x_i, Z = z_k),$$

which is in a more compact form:

$$P(Y) = \frac{1}{nx \cdot nz} \cdot \sum_X \sum_Z P(Y \mid X, Z) \cdot [nx \cdot nz \cdot \psi_X \cdot \psi_Z \cdot P(X) \cdot P(Z) + \\ + nx \cdot \psi_X \cdot (1 - \psi_Z) \cdot P(X) + nz \cdot (1 - \psi_X) \cdot \psi_Z \cdot P(Z) + (1 - \psi_X) \cdot (1 - \psi_Z)].$$

(14)

Consider example. Let we have the following set of data:

X	Z	Y
Sunny	Alone	Good
Overcast	With girlfriend	Bad
Overcast	With dog	Bad
Sunny	With dog	Good
Sunny	Alone	Good
Overcast	Alone	Bad
Rain	With girlfriend	Bad
Sunny	With dog	Good
Overcast	With dog	Bad
Sunny	With girlfriend	Bad
Overcast	With girlfriend	Good
Overcast	Alone	Bad
Overcast	With dog	Bad
Sunny	With girlfriend	Good
Overcast	With dog	Bad
Overcast	Alone	Bad
Sunny	Alone	Bad
Sunny	With dog	Bad
Rain	With girlfriend	Good
Overcast	With dog	Good

X ("state of weather") ={"sunny", "overcast", "rain"}
Z ("companion")   ={"alone", "girlfriend", "dog"}
Y ("state of mood")   ={"good", "bad"};

$P(X="sunny") = 0.4$; $P(X="overcast") = 0.5$; $P(X="rain") = 0.1$;
$P(Z="alone") = 0.3$; $P(Z="girlfriend") = 0.3$; $P(Z="dog") = 0.4$;

P(Y="good"| X, Z)	Z = "alone"	Z="girlfriend"	Z="dog"
X = "sunny"	0.667	0.5	0.667
X = "overcast"	0	0.5	0.25
X = "rain"	0	0.5	0
P(Y="bad"| X, Z)	Z = "alone"	Z="girlfriend"	Z="dog"
X = "sunny"	0.333	0.5	0.333
X = "overcast"	1	0.5	0.75
X = "rain"	1	0.5	1

According to (9):

P(Y | X)	X = "sunny"	X = "overcast"	X = "rain"
Y = "good"	0.611	0.25	0.167
Y = "bad"	0.389	0.75	0.833

According to (10):

P(Y | Z)	Z = "alone"	Z = "girlfriend"	Z = "dog"
Y = "good"	0.222	0.5	0.306
Y = "bad"	0.778	0.5	0.694

According to (11): $P_0(Y="good") = 0.3426$; $P_0(Y="bad") = 0.6574$.

Assuming that relevancies of our parameters are as follows: $\psi_X = 0.8$, $\psi_Z = 0.5$, we can estimate $P(Y)$ based on (14): $P(Y ="good") \approx 0.3773$; $P(Y ="bad") \approx 0.6227$.

One can also notice that these values belong to the interval created by the two extreme cases, when parameters are not relevant at all or they are fully relevant:

$$0.3426 \approx P_0(Y ="good")|_{\psi_x=0,\psi_z=0} < P(Y ="good")|_{\psi_x=0.8,\psi_z=0.5} < P_1(Y ="good")|_{\psi_x=1,\psi_z=1} \approx 0.3867 ;$$

$$0.6133 \approx P_1(Y ="bad")|_{\psi_x=1,\psi_z=1} < P(Y ="bad")|_{\psi_x=0.8,\psi_z=0.5} < P_0(Y ="bad")|_{\psi_x=0,\psi_z=0} \approx 0.6574.$$

Consider the general case of managing relevance (Fig. 5):

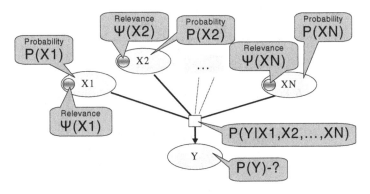

Fig. 5. General case of relevance management

In this case we have the following: (a) predictive attributes: X1 with values $\{x1_1, x1_2, ..., x1_{nx1}\}$; X2 with values $\{x2_1, x2_2, ..., x2_{nx2}\}$; ... XN with values $\{xn_1, xn_2, ..., xn_{nxn}\}$; (b) target attribute: Y with values $\{y_1, y_2, ..., y_{ny}\}$; (c) probabilities: $P(X1)$, $P(X2)$,..., $P(XN)$; $P(Y|X1, X2, ..., XN)$; (d) relevancies: $\psi_{X1} = P(\psi(X1) =$ "yes"); $\psi_{X2} = P(\psi(X2) =$ "yes"); ... $\psi_{XN} = P(\psi(XN) =$ "yes"). Task is to estimate $P(Y)$.

Generalizing (4) and (14) to the case of N predictive variables we finally obtain:

$$P(Y) = \frac{1}{\prod_{s=1}^{N} nxs} \cdot \sum_{X1}\sum_{X2}...\sum_{XN}[P(Y \mid X1, X2,...XN) \cdot \prod_{\forall r(\psi(Xr)="yes")} nxr \cdot \psi_{Xr} \cdot P(Xr) \cdot \prod_{\forall q(\psi(Xq)="no")}(1-\psi_{Xq})]$$

4   A Relevance Metanetwork

Relevance Bayesian Metanetwork can be defined on a given predictive probabilistic network (Fig. 6). It encodes the conditional dependencies over the relevancies. Relevance metanetwork contains prior relevancies and conditional relevancies.

Considering such definition of relevance metanetwork over the predictive network it is clear that the strict correspondence between nodes of both network exists but the arcs do not need to be strictly corresponding (as shown in Fig. 6). It means that relevancies of two variables can be dependent, although their values are conditionally independent and vice versa (Fig. 7). So, the topologies of the networks are different in general case.

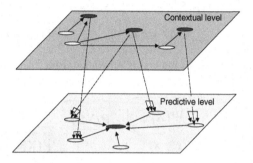

Fig. 6. Relevance network defined over the predictive network

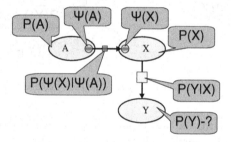

Fig. 7. Architecture of a simple relevance metanetwork

In a relevance network the relevancies are considered as random variables between which the conditional dependencies can be learned. For example in Fig. 7, the probability of target attribute Y can be computed as follows:

$$P(Y) = \frac{1}{nx} \cdot \sum_X \{P(Y \mid X) \cdot [nx \cdot P(X) \cdot \sum_{\psi_A} P(\psi_X \mid \psi_A) \cdot P(\psi_A) + (1 - \psi_X)]\}.$$

More complicated example of a Bayesian metanetwork completed from predictive and relevance networks is shown in Fig. 8. The graph of the Metanetwork in the figure consists of two subgraphs (a) predictive network layer and (b) relevance network layer. The challenge here is that the relevance network subgraph models the relevance conditional dependency and in the same time the posteriori relevance values calculated with this graph effect the calculations at the basic predictive subgraph.

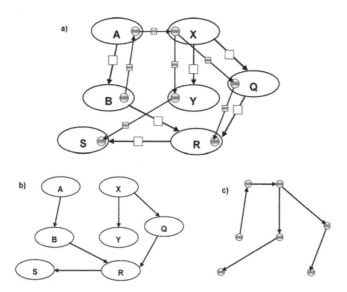

Fig. 8. Example of Bayesian metanetwork (a), consisting of the predictive subnetwork (b) and relevance subnetwork (c) both of which have corresponding nodes, but different topologies

5 Conclusions

Bayesian Networks are proven to be a comprehensive model to describe causal relationships among domain attributes with probabilistic measure of appropriate conditional dependency. However, depending on task and context, many attributes of the model might not be relevant. If a Bayesian Network has been learned across multiple contexts then all uncovered conditional dependencies are averaged over all contexts and cannot guarantee high predictive accuracy when applied to a concrete case. We are considering a context as a set of contextual attributes, which are not directly effect probability distribution of the target attributes, but they effect on a "relevance" of the predictive attributes towards target attributes. In this paper we use the Bayesian Metanetwork vision to model such context-sensitive feature relevance. Such model assumes that the relevance of predictive attributes in a Bayesian network might be a random attribute itself and it provides a tool to reason based not only on probabilities of predictive attributes but also on their relevancies. According to this model, the evidence observed about contextual attributes is used to extract a relevant substructure from a Bayesian network model and then the predictive attributes evidence is used to reason about probability distribution of the target attribute in the extracted sub-network. Such models are useful when the relevance of the attributes essentially depends on the context.

Acknowledgment

This research has been performed as a part of the SmartResource ("Proactive Self-Maintained Resources in Semantic Web") project of Agora Center (University of Jyväskylä, Finland) and funded by TEKES and industrial consortium of following companies: Metso Automation, TeliaSonera, TietoEnator and Science Park.

References

1. J. Pearl, *Probabilistic Reasoning in Intelligent Systems: Networks of Plausible Inference*, (Morgan Kaufmann, 1988).
2. M. Henrion, Some Practical Issues in Constructing Belief Networks, In: *Proceedings of the 3-rd Annual Conference on Uncertainty in Artificial Intelligence*, (Elsevier, 1989), pp. 161-174.
3. D. Heckerman, A Tutorial on Learning with Bayesian Networks, *Technical Report MSR-TR-95-06*, (Microsoft Research, March 1995).
4. C. J. Butz, Exploiting Contextual Independencies in Web Search and User Profiling, In: *Proc. of the World Congress on Computational Intelligence,* (Hawaii, USA, 2002), pp. 1051-1056.
5. C. Boutiler, N. Friedman, M. Goldszmidt and D. Koller, Context-Specific Independence in Bayesian Networks, In: *Proceedings of the 12-th Conference on Uncertainty in Artificial Intelligence*, (Portland, USA, 1996), pp. 115-123.
6. N.L. Zhang, Inference in Bayesian networks: The Role of Context-Specific Independence, *International Journal of Information Technology and Decision Making*, **1**(1) 2002, 91-119.
7. D. Geiger and D. Heckerman, Knowledge Representation and Inference in Similarity Networks and Bayesian Multinets, *Artificial Intelligence*, Vol. 82, (Elsevier, 1996), pp. 45-74.
8. N. Friedman, D. Geiger, and M. Goldszmidt, Bayesian Network Classifiers, *Machine Learning*, **29**(2-3), (Kluwer, 1997), pp. 131-161.
9. J. Cheng and R. Greiner, Learning Bayesian Belief Network Classifiers: Algorithms and System, In: *Proceedings of the 14-th Canadian Conference on Artificial Intelligence*, Lecture Notes in Computer Science, Vol. 2056, (Springer-Verlag Heidelberg, 2001), pp. 141-151.
10. J. Pena, J. A. Lozano, and P. Larranaga, Learning Bayesian Networks for Clustering by Means of Constructive Induction, *Machine Learning*, **47**(1), (Kluwer, 2002), pp. 63-90.
11. V. Terziyan, A Bayesian Metanetwork, *International Journal on Artificial Intelligence Tools*, **14**(3), (World Scientific, 2005), pp. 371-384.
12. V. Terziyan and O. Vitko, Bayesian Metanetwork for Modelling User Preferences in Mobile Environment, In: *Proceedings of KI 2003: Advances in Artificial Intelligence*, Lecture Notes in Artificial Intelligence, Vol. 2821, ed. A. Gunter, R. Kruse and B. Neumann, (Springer-Verlag, 2003), pp.370-384.
13. Terziyan and O. Vitko, Learning Bayesian Metanetworks from Data with Multilevel Uncertainty, In: M. Bramer and V. Devedzic (eds.), *Proc. of the First IFIP International Conf. on Artificial Intelligence and Innovations*, Toulouse, France, (Kluwer, 2004), pp. 187-196.

Prediction of Translation Initiation Sites
Using Classifier Selection

George Tzanis and Ioannis Vlahavas

Department of Informatics, Aristotle University of Thessaloniki,
Thessaloniki 54124, Greece
{gtzanis, vlahavas}@csd.auth.gr
http://mlkd.csd.auth.gr

Abstract. The prediction of the translation initiation site (TIS) in a genomic sequence is an important issue in biological research. Several methods have been proposed to deal with it. However, it is still an open problem. In this paper we follow an approach consisting of a number of steps in order to increase TIS prediction accuracy. First, all the sequences are scanned and the candidate TISs are detected. These sites are grouped according to the length of the sequence upstream and downstream them and a number of features is generated for each one. The features are evaluated among the instances of every group and a number of the top ranked ones are selected for building a classifier. A new instance is assigned to a group and is classified by the corresponding classifier. We experiment with various feature sets and classification algorithms, compare with alternative methods and draw important conclusions.

1 Introduction

The rapid technological advances of the last years have assisted the conduct of large scale experiments and research projects in biology. The completion of these efforts has lead to a giant collection of biological data. The development and use of methods for the management and analysis of these data is necessary. As a consequence to this need, a new research area called bioinformatics has emerged. Bioinformatics is an interdisciplinary area positioned at the intersection of biology, computer science, and information technology.

A large portion of biological data is represented by sequences. These sequences characterize a large molecule that is a succession of a number of smaller molecules. The study of the structure and function of such large molecules (macromolecules) is the mission of molecular biology. The scientists intend to discover useful biological knowledge by analyzing the various genomic sequences. The utilization of exploratory techniques in order to describe the vast amount of data is required. However, the use of traditional analysis techniques is not adequate and novel, high performance tools have to be developed. The field of data mining aims to provide efficient computational tools to overcome the obstacles and constraints posed by the traditional statistical methods.

G. Antoniou et al. (Eds.): SETN 2006, LNAI 3955, pp. 367–377, 2006.

Translation is one of the basic biological operations that attract biologist's attention. Translation along with replication and transcription make possible the transmission and expression of an organism's genetic information. The initiation of translation plays an important role in understanding which part of a sequence is translated and consequently what is the final product of the process. When the way that each of these operations takes place is explained, biologists will be one step closer to the unraveling of the mystery of life, which is the final objective of biology.

A sequence contains a number of sites where the translation might initiate. However, only one of them is the true *translation initiation site* (*TIS*). The recognition of the true TIS among the candidate TISs is not a trivial task and requires the use of data mining tools. Classification methods have been extensively used in order to deal with this problem. The idea of multiple classifier systems is an attempt to construct more accurate classification models by combining a number of classifiers. Classifier combination includes two main paradigms: classifier selection and classifier fusion. In the first case a new instance is classified by selecting the appropriate classifier, while in the second case a new instance is classified according to the decisions of all the classifiers.

In this paper we have followed an approach for classifier selection to tackle the problem of the prediction of TISs in DNA sequences. The traditional data mining methods are not directly applicable to sequence data. Thus, we had to transform the initial set of raw sequences to a new dataset consisting of a number of feature vectors that describe the initial data. In particular, all the sequences are scanned and the candidate TISs are detected. The candidate TISs are grouped according to the length of the sequence compartment upstream and downstream them and a number of features is generated for each one. The features are evaluated among the instances of every group according to their impact in the accuracy of classification. Then, a number of the top ranked features are selected for building a classifier. A new instance is assigned to one of the groups and is classified by the corresponding classifier. We experiment with various feature sets and classification algorithms, we compare with alternative methods and draw important conclusions.

This paper is outlined as follows: In the next section we briefly present the relative work in the area of TIS prediction. In section three we provide the necessary background knowledge. In section four our approach is presented in more detail. Section five contains the description of the dataset, the algorithms and the evaluation method we have used as well as the results of our experiments. Finally, in section six we present our conclusions and some directions for future research.

2 Related Work

The prediction of TISs has been extensively studied using biological approaches, data mining techniques and statistical models. In 1978 Kozak and Shatkin [8] proposed the ribosome scanning model, which was later updated by Kozak [7]. According to this model, translation initiates at the first candidate TIS that has an appropriate context. Later, in 1987 Kozak developed the first weight matrix for the identification of TISs in cDNA sequences [6]. The following consensus pattern was derived from this matrix: GCC[**AG**]CCatg**G**. Bold letters denote the highly conserved positions. Meanwhile, Stormo et al. [16] had used the perceptron algorithm to distinguish the TISs.

Pedersen and Nielsen [13] used artificial neural networks (ANNs) to predict which AUG codons are TISs achieving an overall accuracy of 88% in Arabidopsis thaliana dataset and 85% in vertebrate dataset. Zien et al. [20] studied the same vertebrate dataset, employing support vector machines. Hatzigeorgiou [3] proposed "DIANA-TIS", an ANN system consisting of two modules: the consensus ANN, sensitive to the conserved motif and the coding ANN, sensitive to the coding or non-coding context around the initiation codon. The method was applied in human cDNA data and 94% of the TIS were correctly predicted. ATGpr, developed by Salamov et al. [15], is a program that uses a linear discriminant approach for the recognition of TISs. Nishikawa et al. [12] presented an improvement of ATGpr, named ATGpr_sim, which employs a new prediction algorithm based on both statistical and similarity information and achieves better performance in terms of sensitivity and specificity. Li et al. in [9] utilized Gaussian Mixture Models for the prediction of TISs.

In [11] and [19] the researchers have utilized feature generation and feature selection methods with various machine learning algorithms. In their studies, they used a large number of features concerning the frequency of nucleotide patterns. Using a ribosome scanning model along with the best selected features they achieved an overall accuracy of 94% on the vertebrate dataset of Pedersen and Nielsen. Later, in [10] the same approach was used, but instead of nucleotide patterns, amino acid patterns were generated.

3 Background Knowledge

The main structural and functional molecules of an organism's cell are *proteins*. The information concerning the synthesis of each protein is encoded by the genetic material of the organism. The genetic material of almost every living organism is *deoxyribonucleic acid (DNA)*. There are exceptions of some viruses that have *ribonucleic acid (RNA)* as genetic material. Moreover, RNA has many other functions and plays an important role in protein synthesis. DNA and RNA belong to a family of molecules called nucleic acids. Both proteins and nucleic acids are sequences of smaller molecules, *amino acids* and *nucleotides* respectively. A sequence can be represented as a string of different symbols. There are twenty amino acids and five nucleotides. Every nucleotide is characterized by the nitrogenous base it contains: adenine (A), cytosine (C), guanine (G), thymine (T), or uracil (U). DNA may contain a combination of A, C, G, and T. In RNA U appears instead of T. DNA and RNA sequences have two ends called the 5′ and the 3′ end and are directed from the 5′ to the 3′ end (5′ → 3′).

Proteins are synthesized by the following process. DNA is transcribed into a messenger RNA (mRNA) molecule (transcription). Then mRNA is used as template for the synthesis of a protein molecule (translation). In our setup, we focus on the process of translation, which is further explained below.

Translation takes place by an organelle called ribosome. The mRNA sequence is scanned by the ribosome, which reads triplets, or *codons*, of nucleotides and "translates" them into amino acids. Thus, a protein consisting of n amino acids is encoded by a sequence of $3n$ nucleotides. Since there are 64 different triplets formed from an alphabet of four nucleotides and the total number of amino acids is 20, it is obvious that some amino acids are encoded by more than one codon. Moreover, the triplet AUG, that encodes amino acid methionine is also used as a translation initiation codon. Finally, there are three stop codons for the termination of translation (UAG, UAA and UGA).

An mRNA sequence can be read in three different ways in a given direction. Each of these ways of reading is referred to as *reading frame*. The reading frame that is translated into a protein is named *Open Reading Frame (ORF)*.

Translation, usually, initiates at the AUG codon nearest to the $5'$ end of the mRNA sequence. However this is not always the case, since there are some escape mechanisms that allow the initiation of translation at following, but still near the $5'$ end AUG codons. Due to these mechanisms the recognition of the TIS on a given sequence becomes more difficult.

After the initiation of translation, the ribosome moves along the mRNA molecule, towards the $3'$ end (the direction of translation is $5' \rightarrow 3'$) and reads the next codon. This process is repeated until the ribosome reaches a stop codon. For each codon read the proper amino acid is brought to the protein synthesis site by a transfer RNA (tRNA) molecule. The amino acid is joined to the protein chain, which by this way is elongated.

A codon that is contained in the same reading frame with respect to another codon is referred to as *in-frame codon*. We name *upstream* the region of a nucleotide sequence from a reference point towards the $5'$ end. Respectively, the region of a nucleotide sequence from a reference point towards the $3'$ end is referred to as *downstream*. In TIS prediction problems the reference point is an AUG codon. The above are illustrated in Fig. 1.

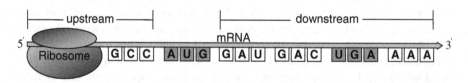

Fig. 1. Translation initiation – The ribosome scans the mRNA sequence from the $5'$ end to the $3'$ end until it reads an AUG codon. If the AUG codon has appropriate context, the translation initiates at that site and terminates when a stop codon (i.e. UGA) is read. An in-frame codon (in relation with AUG) is represented by three consecutive nucleotides that are grouped together.

4   Our Approach

In this section we describe the approach we have followed in order to construct a multiple classifier system for the prediction of TISs in genomic sequences. Our approach consists of a number of steps. Each of these steps is described in detail in the following lines.

- **Step 1:** All sequences are scanned and every candidate TIS is detected as shown in Fig. 2 (In the rest of the paper we use the DNA alphabet, since the original dataset we have used contains DNA sequences. See section 5.1).
- **Step 2:** The candidate TISs found in step 1 are grouped according to the length of the sequence compartment upstream and downstream them. By this way the initial dataset of candidate TISs is divided into a number of smaller datasets (Fig. 3). In our setup we have divided the initial dataset in 4 smaller datasets. Table 1 lists the portion of the whole dataset that each of the four data subsets constitutes. We name D_{m-n} a dataset that contains candidate TISs, that their feature values are calculated by considering m upstream and n downstream nucleotides.
- **Step 3:** For each of the candidate TISs the value of a number of features is calculated. More details about these features are listed in Table 2. Some of them (up-down_x, up_pos_k_x, down_pos_k_x) have been proposed in our previous work [17] and have been found to present good performance in terms of classification accuracy.
- **Step 4:** The features are evaluated among the instances of every group according to their impact in the accuracy of classification. In our setup we have used the information gain measure.
- **Step 5:** A number of the top ranked features is selected and a classifier is built for each of the data subsets.

5' AGCC**ATG**GCATTCCGT**ATG**TTCTG**ATG**TTAA 3'

↓

1, upstream length: 4, downstream length: 24
2, upstream length: 16, downstream length: 12
3, upstream length: 24, downstream length: 4

Fig. 2. A sequence is scanned and every candidate TIS (ATG codon) is detected. Then, its upstream and downstream length is calculated in order to decide in which group belongs.

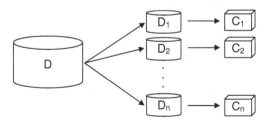

Fig. 3. The initial dataset D is divided into a number of smaller datasets D_i and finally a classifier C_i is built separately for each D_i

Table 1. The four data subsets used in our setup

Dataset	Portion of Initial Dataset
$D_{99\text{-}99}$	12.3 %
$D_{99\text{-}120}$	28.3 %
$D_{120\text{-}99}$	52.5 %
$D_{120\text{-}120}$	6.9 %

Table 2. The features used in our approach

Feature	Description
up_x	Counts the number of occurrences of amino acid x in the upstream region
down_x	Counts the number of occurrences of amino acid x in the downstream region
up-down_x	Counts the difference between the number of occurrences of amino acid x in the upstream region and the number of occurrences of amino acid x in the downstream region
up_pos_k_x	Counts the number of occurrences of nucleotide x in the kth position of the upstream in-frame codons ($k \in \{1, 2, 3\}$)
down_pos_k_x	Counts the number of occurrences of nucleotide x in the kth position of the downstream in-frame codons ($k \in \{1, 2, 3\}$)
up_-3_[AG]	A Boolean feature that is true if there is an A or a G nucleotide three positions before the ATG codon, according to Kozak's pattern (GCC[**AG**]CCatg**G**)
down_+1_G	A Boolean feature that is true if there is a G nucleotide in the first position after the ATG codon, according to Kozak's pattern (GCC[**AG**]CCatg**G**)
up_ATG	A Boolean feature that is true if there is an in-frame upstream ATG codon
down_stop	A Boolean feature that is true if there is an in-frame downstream stop codon (TAA, TAG, TGA)

Finally, a new instance, namely a new candidate ATG, is assigned to one of the groups according to the length of its upstream and downstream regions' length and is classified by the corresponding classifier.

5 Experiments

In this section we describe the dataset, the algorithms and the evaluation method we have used along with the results of our experiments.

5.1 Dataset

The original dataset we have used consists of 3312 genomic sequences collected from various vertebrate organisms. These sequences were extracted from GenBank, the US NIH genetic sequence database [2]. Only the sequences that contain an annotated TIS are included. The dataset is publicly available in [5]. The DNA sequences have been processed and the interlacing non-coding regions (introns) have been removed. Since they are DNA sequences, they contain only the letters A, C, G and T. Thus, a candidate TIS is referred to as ATG codon instead of AUG codon. Almost 25% of the ATGs in these sequences are true TISs.

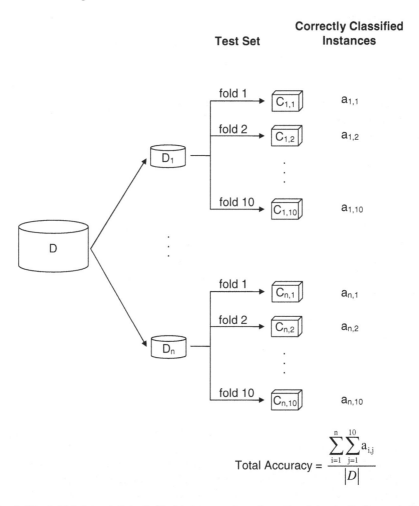

Fig. 4. The initial dataset D is divided into a number of smaller datasets D_i. For each D_i 10 classifiers are built and evaluated according to the 10-fold CV procedure. At the end, each instance of the initial dataset D will have been tested exactly once (in our setup $n = 4$).

In order to compare our approach we have used two datasets -derived from the original- each of them containing the entire set of candidate TISs. The candidate TISs in the first dataset are described by feature values calculated for 99 positions upstream and 99 downstream (D_{99-99}), while in the second dataset are described by feature values calculated for 120 positions upstream and 120 downstream ($D_{120-120}$). Note that D_{m-n} here refers to a dataset containing the complete set of candidate TISs, that their feature values are calculated by considering m upstream and n downstream nucleotides and is different from the corresponding D_{m-n} dataset of our approach, that contains only a portion of candidate TISs (see step 2 in section 4).

5.2 Algorithms

For the conduction of our experiments we have utilized the Weka library of machine learning algorithms [18]. We have used the following three classification algorithms:

- C4.5, that is a decision tree construction algorithm [14].
- Naïve Bayes classifier [4].
- PART, a rule learner [1].

5.3 Evaluation

In order to evaluate the results of our experiments we have used stratified 10-fold cross-validation (CV). In particular, the performance of a classifier on a given dataset using 10-fold CV is evaluated as following. The dataset is divided into 10 non-overlapping almost equal size parts (folds). In stratified CV each class is represented in each fold at the same percentage as in the entire dataset. After the dataset has been divided, a model is built using 9 of the folds as a training set and the remaining fold as a test set. This procedure is repeated 10 times with a different test set. The evaluation procedure of our approach is depicted in Fig. 4.

In order to increase the reliability of the evaluation, we have repeated each experiment 10 times and we finally took into account the average of the results.

5.4 Results

We have built classifiers by using various numbers of the top ranked, according to information gain measure, features. The results concerning the classification accuracy of each classifier are listed in Table 3. As shown in the table our approach performs better in almost every case. In particular, when C4.5 was used the difference between the best accuracy of our method and the best accuracy of anyone of the other approaches was 1.25%. When the Naïve Bayes classifier was used, this difference increased to 2.35% and when PART was used the difference was 1.11%.

We have also conducted experiments for datasets D_{99-99} and $D_{120-120}$, using the features proposed in [10] (up_ATG, down_stop, up_-3_[AG], down_A, down_V, up_A, down_L, down_D, down_E, up_G). The results are presented in Table 4.

Table 3. Classification accuracy of our multiple classifier system (*MCS*) and the classifiers built on datasets D_{99-99} and $D_{120-120}$

Algorithm	Top Features	MCS	D_{99-99}	$D_{120-120}$
C4.5	50	90.30 %	89.82 %	84.15 %
	30	90.70 %	90.10 %	89.77 %
	20	91.43 %	92.82 %	90.21 %
	15	91.97 %	92.95 %	90.43 %
	12	92.26 %	93.01 %	92.79 %
	9	92.98 %	92.63 %	92.65 %
	7	93.27 %	92.21 %	92.36 %
	5	94.26 %	91.44 %	91.98 %
	3	93.59 %	91.12 %	91.92 %
Naïve Bayes	50	91.69 %	88.93 %	83.13 %
	30	92.89 %	88.37 %	89.37 %
	20	92.35 %	90.54 %	89.27 %
	15	91.73 %	90.08 %	88.56 %
	12	88.55 %	89.04 %	88.22 %
	9	88.49 %	88.00 %	86.94 %
	7	87.91 %	87.44 %	85.92 %
	5	86.98 %	85.24 %	84.30 %
	3	85.88 %	82.37 %	81.37 %
PART	50	90.56 %	89.60 %	83.60 %
	30	91.29 %	89.87 %	88.89 %
	20	92.31 %	92.86 %	89.14 %
	15	92.71 %	92.84 %	90.21 %
	12	92.56 %	93.08 %	92.86 %
	9	92.98 %	93.02 %	92.53 %
	7	93.32 %	92.22 %	92.06 %
	5	94.19 %	91.45 %	91.67 %
	3	93.84 %	91.18 %	91.46 %

Using the same reasoning as in the comparisons above we can say that the differences of the best cases for each algorithm range from 3.51% to 3.67%, concluding that our approach performs better.

Table 4. Classification accuracy of classifiers built on datasets D_{99-99} and $D_{120-120}$ using the features proposed in [10]

Algorithm	D_{99-99}	$D_{120-120}$
C4.5	90.29 %	90.59 %
Naïve Bayes	88.24 %	89.00 %
PART	90.34 %	90.68 %

6 Conclusions and Future Work

Translation is one of the basic biological processes and the accurate prediction of the translation initiation site in a genomic sequence is crucial for biologists. However, this is not a trivial task. First of all, the knowledge about the process of translation is limited. It is known that translation initiates at the first AUG codon of mRNA in more than 90% of eukaryotic organisms, but some escape mechanisms prevent this. The exact way that each of these mechanisms works, has not been explained up till now. Moreover, the available sequences are not always complete and contain errors.

In this paper, we considered the utilization of a large number of features. We constructed a multiple classifier system and used classifier selection in order to classify a new instance. For this purpose we developed a method for separating the candidate TISs according to the length of the sequence compartment upstream and downstream them. Then, a classifier is built for each data subset. We applied our approach on a real-world dataset that contains processed DNA sequences from vertebrates. We used various classification algorithms and after extensive experimentation we discovered that the use of our method improves the accuracy of classification.

The study of different ways of separation of the candidate TISs is involved in our future plans. Additionally, we aim to use more datasets and possibly from different kind of organisms. Finally, the experimentation with novel features is always under consideration.

Acknowledgements

This work was partially supported by the Greek R&D General Secretariat through a PABET-NE program (EPAN M.4.3.2, No. 04BEN51).

References

1. Frank, E., and Witten, I.H.: Generating Accurate Rule Sets Without Global Optimization. In Proceedings of the 15th International Conference on Machine Learning, Madison, Wisconson, USA, (1998) 144-151
2. GenBank Overview. http://www.ncbi.nlm.nih.gov/Genbank/index.html
3. Hatzigeorgiou, A.: Translation Initiation Start Prediction in Human cDNAs with High Accuracy. Bioinformatics (2002) 18(2) 343-350

4. John, G.H., Langley, P.: Estimating Continuous Distributions in Bayesian Classifiers. In Proceedings of the 11th Conference on Uncertainty in Artificial Intelligence. Morgan Kaufmann, San Mateo, California, USA (1995) 338-345

5. Kent Ridge Biomedical Data Set Repository. http://sdmc.i2r.a-star.edu.sg/rp/

6. Kozak, M.: An Analysis of 5'-Noncoding Sequences from 699 Vertebrate Messenger RNAs. Nucleic Acids Research (1987) 15(20) 8125-8148

7. Kozak, M.: The Scanning Model for Translation: An Update. The Journal of Cell Biology (1989) 108(2) 229-241

8. Kozak, M., Shatkin. A.J.: Migration of 40 S Ribosomal Subunits on Messenger RNA in the Presence of Edeine. Journal of Biological Chemistry (1978) 253(18) 6568-6577

9. Li, G., Leong, T-Y, Zhang, L: Translation Initiation Sites Prediction with Mixture Gaussian Models in Human cDNA Sequences. IEEE Transactions on Knowledge and Data Engineering (2005) 8(17) 1152-1160.

10. Liu, H., Han, H., Li, J., Wong, L.: Using Amino Acid Patterns to Accurately Predict Translation Initiation Sites. In Silico Biology (2004) 4(3) 255-269

11. Liu, H., Wong, L.: Data Mining Tools for Biological Sequences. Journal of Bioinformatics and Computational Biology, (2003) 1(1) 139-168

12. Nishikawa, T., Ota, T., Isogai, T.: Prediction whether a Human cDNA Sequence Contains Initiation Codon by Combining Statistical Information and Similarity with Protein Sequences. Bioinformatics (2000) 16(11) 960-967

13. Pedersen, A.G., Nielsen, H.: Neural Network Prediction of Translation Initiation Sites in Eukaryotes: Perspectives for EST and Genome analysis. In Proceedings of the 5th International Conference on Intelligent Systems for Molecular Biology, AAAI Press, Menlo Park, California, USA (1997) 226-233

14. Quinlan, J.R.: C4.5: Programs for Machine Learning, Morgan Kaufmann, San Mateo, California, USA (1993).

15. Salamov, A.A., Nishikawa, T., Swindells, M.B.: Assessing Protein Coding Region Integrity in cDNA Sequencing Projects. Bioinformatics (1998) 14(5) 384-390

16. Stormo, G.D., Schneider, T.D., Gold, L., Ehrenfeucht, A.: Use of the 'Perceptron' Algorithm to Distinguish Translational Initiation Sites in E. coli. Nucleic Acids Research (1982) 10 (9) 2997-3011

17. Tzanis, G., Berberidis, C., Alexandridou, A., Vlahavas, I.: Improving the Accuracy of Classifiers for the Prediction of Translation Initiation Sites in Genomic Sequences. In Proceedings of the 10th Panhellenic Conference on Informatics (PCI'2005), Volos, Greece, (2005) 426 – 436

18. Witten, I.H., Frank, E.: Data Mining: Practical Machine Learning Tools with Java Implementations. Morgan Kaufmann, San Francisco (2000)

19. Zeng F., Yap H., Wong, L.: Using Feature Generation and Feature Selection for Accurate Prediction of Translation Initiation Sites. In Proceedings of the 13th International Conference on Genome Informatics, Tokyo, Japan (2002) 192-200

20. Zien, A., Rätsch, G., Mika, S., Schölkopf, B., Lengauer, T., Müller, K.R.: Engineering Support Vector Machine Kernels that Recognize Translation Initiation Sites. Bioinformatics (2000) 16(9) 799-807

Improving Neural Network Based Option Price Forecasting

Vasilios S. Tzastoudis, Nikos S. Thomaidis[*], and George D. Dounias

Decision and Management Engineering Laboratory,
Dept. of Financial Engineering & Management, University of the Aegean, 31 Fostini Str.,
GR-821 00, Chios, Greece
Tel.: +30-2271-0-35454 (35483); Fax: +30-2271-0-35499
{23100072, nthomaid, g.dounias}@fme.aegean.gr
http://decision.fme.aegean.gr

Abstract. As is widely known, the popular Black & Scholes model for option pricing suffers from systematic biases, as it relies on several highly questionable assumptions. In this paper we study the ability of neural networks (MLPs) in pricing call options on the S&P 500 index; in particular we investigate the effect of the hidden neurons in the in- and out-of-sample pricing. We modify the Black & Scholes model given the price of an option based on the no-arbitrage value of a forward contract, written on the same underlying asset, and we derive a modified formula that can be used for our purpose. Instead of using the standard backpropagation training algorithm we replace it with the Levenberg-Marquardt approach. By modifying the objective function of the neural network, we focus the learning process on more interesting areas of the implied volatility surface. The results from this transformation are encouraging.

1 Introduction

An option is a financial contract that gives the *right* to its owner to buy or sell certain quantities of an asset at some future date, at a price that is agreed in advance. In this way, they allow investors to bet on future events and also reduce financial risk.

Every since options trading started in organized markets, there came the problem of what is a reasonable premium to pay for the privilege of not having to exercise the right. The first successful attempt to option pricing was the popular Black & Scholes (BS) model, which gives the fair value of an option in terms of a number of other financial quantities [2]. Although pioneering in its conception, the model has been empirically shown to suffer from significant systematic biases when compared to market prices [1], [6]. Most of the biases steam from the fact that the development of the BS formula was based on a set of assumptions that fail to hold true in practice. In an attempt to relax the BS assumptions, researchers have come up with a variety of other parametric option pricing models, such as the Jump-Diffusion [14], Constant Elasticity of Variance [7], and Hull & White

---

[*] This research is funded by the Public Benefit Foundation "Alexander S. Onassis" and by a grant from "Empeirikion" Foundation.

G. Antoniou et al. (Eds.): SETN 2006, LNAI 3955, pp. 378–388, 2006.
© Springer-Verlag Berlin Heidelberg 2006

Stochastic Volatility [9]. Despite the analytical tractability, the majority of these models are often too complex to be implemented in practice, have poor out-of-sample pricing performance and sometimes inconsistent implied parameters [1]. In addition, they are based on restrictive assumptions concerning the market infrastructure and/or investors' attitudes, which are often questionable from a theoretical or empirical point of view.

On the other hand, computational intelligent nonparametric models, like neural networks or genetic programming, seem to offer a promising alternative to option pricing. This is mainly due to their ability to approximate highly non-linear relationships without relying on the restrictive assumptions and hypotheses implicit in parametric approaches (e.g. assumptions concerning the price process of the underlying asset, the efficiency of the market, the rationality of agents, etc). Option pricing with neural networks, in particular, has attracted the interest of many practitioners and researchers, worldwide. Most studies employ a feedforward network to deduce an empirical pricing formula from option market data that minimizes a certain loss function (e.g. the sum of squared errors)[1].

It is important to note that option pricing in not a typical function approximation task for several reasons. In most option markets, more than one contracts trade simultaneously on the same underlying, which renders option pricing a problem of forecasting a *matrix* of values, the so-called *implied volatility (IV) surface* (see also section 4.1), rather than a single quote. However, not all options are equally spread out the volatility matrix, and most important, not all them share the same liquidity. The absence of an active market usually gives rise to unpleasant phenomena, such as bid\ask spreads and longer average times between consecutive transactions. This means that reliable training data are available for certain areas of the IV surface, which poses a problem to the application of a NN, and in fact to any nonparametric technique. As the out-of-sample performance of nonparametric methods is very much determined by the quality of the training data, a NN would be inefficient for non-liquid areas of the options matrix.

In this paper, we improve the forecasting ability of neural networks by using a *hybrid* intelligent scheme that combines a nonparametric NN model with theoretical option-pricing formulae. In this way, we increase the efficiency of the learning process, by using theoretical arguments for "problematic" data and direct NN learning in actively traded areas of the IV surface. Our main objective is to develop an intelligent model exploiting whatever solid knowledge is available from the problem combining it with a non-parametric computational intelligent model in order to achieve maximum forecasting ability.

The organization of this paper is as follows: in Section 2 we provide the necessary financial background and terminology for the afore-mentioned types of contracts and we also give an overview of the Black & Scholes option pricing model. In Section 3 we detail our approach to option pricing by means of the hybrid intelligent model. Section 4 presents an empirical application to S &P 500 Stock Index options and Section 5 concludes the paper with suggestions for further research.

---

[1] See section 3 for a discussion of approaches.

2 Options Background and the Black & Scholes Pricing Model [2]

An option contract gives the holder the right (not the obligation) to buy or sell a specific commodity, known as the *underlying asset,* at some future date (*maturity/expiry date*) at an agreed price (*exercise/strike price*)[3]. *Call* options give the right to buy while *put* options give the right to sell the underlying. One is said to take a *long (short) position* on a call option when he/she agrees to buy (sell) the underlying at expiry. In standard options terminology, a call option is said to be *in-the-money* if the currently quoted underlying price is greater than the strike price, *out-of-the-money* if the underlying price is lower than the strike price and *at-the-money* if the above two are close to each other. Deep-in-the-money calls are highly priced, especially those that are near to expiration, as the holder can buy the underlying from the counterparty and make profit by selling it at the market at a higher price. For the same reason, out-of-the money calls are worthless as the holder has no benefit from exercising the contract.

The Black & Scholes model [2] is considered to be the first successful attempt to obtain a "fair value" for the price of a call option, which is based on the fundamental idea of replicating options by dynamic hedging strategies. The original Black & Scholes mathematical formula for European-style call options, which was later modified by Merton [15] for dividend-paying underlying asset, is as follows:

$$C = Se^{-\delta T} N(d_1) - Ke^{-rT} N(d_2) \tag{1.a}$$

$$d_1 = \frac{ln(S/K) + [(r-\delta) + 1/2\sigma^2]T}{\sigma\sqrt{T}} \tag{1.b}$$

$$d_2 = d_1 - \sigma\sqrt{T} \tag{1.c}$$

where C is the fair value of a call option at some time T before expiration, S is the current price of the underlying; K is the strike price of the option, r is the risk-free interest rate, δ is the dividend yield, σ is the volatility of the underlying and $N(.)$ denotes the standard normal probability density function.

The BS model links in fact the price of a call option with several factors that affect its value. Intuitively, a rise in the underlying price S or in the volatility σ has a positive impact on the value of the call, as it increases the probability that the option expires in the in-the-money area (i.e. above K). Dividends decrease the price of the underlying (e.g. stock) and hence the value of the call option. The effect of time to maturity and risk-free interest rate is less clear.

Note that at least one parameter of the BS option pricing model, the volatility of the underlying asset, is not directly observable from the market and hence it has to be replaced with sample estimates. Basically, there are two main approaches to computing volatility: the *historical* and the *implied* one. The historical volatility is expressed as the annualized standard deviation of daily returns on the underlying. A modified formula takes the *weighted* average of returns, with more weight put on recent returns.

---

[2] See [10] for more details on options market and pricing models.
[3] When contract settlement takes place only at expiry, the option is said to be *European-style.*

This is a way to incorporate short-term changes in volatility levels. The implied volatility is the value of σ that equals the BS with the market price of the option. Implied volatilities are believed to be a more realistic proxy for the volatility than the historical estimate, as they represent the expectations of agents about future uncertainty.

3 Proposed Methodology

Most previous studies on option pricing with NNs are focused on creating a nonparametric analog to the BS model Eq. (1), $C_{NN} = f_{NN}(S, K, \delta, r, \sigma, T)$, where f_{NN} denotes a neural network model. In an attempt to reduce the number of inputs to the network, some researchers take advantage of the so-called "homogeneity property" of the BS option pricing formula and feed-in the ratio S/K instead of the corresponding absolute terms (see [8], [11],[13]). In some studies [11], [16] the impact of volatility is omitted, as it is assumed that it can be built into the neural nets inductively through the training process. In our case, we follow up a different approach that takes advantage of the no-arbitrage value linking the price F of a forward contract, written on the same index, with the interest rate and the dividend yield, i.e. $F = Se^{(r-\delta)T}$. This transformation proves to be more convenient than the original BS framework, as the forward price is a *well-defined* tradable quantity that incorporates all information about the prevailing interest rate and dividends. In this way, instead of setting-up a neural network mapping the input variables ($S, K, r, \delta, T, \sigma$) to the target value ($C_{NN}$), we can determine the value of the call in terms of (F, K, DF, σ), where $DF = e^{-rT}$ is the discounting term, representing the amount of money that has to be invested in the risk-free interest rate r in order to obtain 1\$ after time T. Another point that differentiates our approach from the current trend is that it builds upon a *hybrid* model rather than a single neural net. This hybrid scheme uses theoretical arguments for "problematic" data of the options matrix and directs NN learning in actively traded areas.

In the experiments presented in following sections, we employ a single-hidden-layer feedforward neural net with hyperbolic tangent activation functions in the hidden layers and a linear function in the output layer. We examined NNs with 1-5 neurons in the hidden layer. We replace the standard steepest-descend backpropagation training algorithm, which is commonly used in previous works, with the Levenberg-Marquardt approach which seems more efficient in terms of convergence and accuracy. According to Charalambous [5], the backpropagation learning algorithm is unable to rapidly converge to an optimal solution. Input data are normalized in the range [-1,1] in order to avoid permanent firing of hidden neurons at the saturation area. Our networks were trained in a batch mode of 1000 epochs. After the final network is estimated, the output is scaled back to its normal range.

3.1 A Hybrid Intelligent Option Pricing Model

Our starting point is that a single neural network need not capture all the geometric characteristics of the volatility surface. Based on financial arguments, we can derive the value of the call at certain problematic areas of the surface (e.g.$|K$-100$|$>50 and T<1) for which not many data are available. For example, one can easily guess the price of an option which is near expiration and deep-in-the-money ($K<<100$). Intuitively, if $S>>K$ the holder of the option can benefit from paying K \$ to buy the underlying from the counter-party and then sell it at the market. This results in an immediate profit of $S-K$ \$. But, $S = Fe^{(\delta-r)T}$ and for options with short time to maturity left $(T << 1)$ $e^{(\delta-r)T} \approx 1$. Hence, the value of a deep-in-the-money option is approximately equal to $F - K$. By using a similar argument, we can show that the value of a deep-out-of-the-money option is close to 0. If $S<<K$ it is not worth exercising the option, as the underlying is sold in the market at a much lower price. Hence, none will be interested in buying a deep-out-of-the-money option, rendering its value close to zero. For options that are around-the-money ($S \approx K$), their value cannot be easily determined as it depends on the short-term volatility of the asset. If S is currently below K and the underlying is highly volatile, then it is likely that S crosses the K-threshold and the option become valuable.

From the above discussion, we see that it makes more sense to direct a NN model to short-maturity at-the-money options and gradually increase the range of strikes as maturity gets longer. In this way, we can define a hybrid model for the call price as:

$$
C = \begin{cases} F - K & S >> K, T \in [T_1, T_2] \\ f_{NN}(F, K, DF, \sigma) & S \approx K, T \in [T_1, T_2] \\ 0 & S << K, T \in [T_1, T_2] \end{cases} \tag{2}
$$

4 Empirical Application

4.1 Sample Data

For the application and testing of the proposed methodology, we used equity option contracts on the American S&P 500 Stock Index, considered to be among the most liquid index options worldwide. S&P 500 options are European-style. We obtained two "snapshots" of the implied volatility surface quoted on 08/05/2002 and 19/07/2002, respectively, which are depicted in figures 1 & 2. Strike and option prices are given as a percentage of the underlying and maturities range from 0.083 to 10 years and 0.083 to 5 years respectively. Note that the value of the call is a U-shaped function of the strike price K and a monotonically increasing function of the time-to-maturity T. These puzzling features of most IV surfaces are known in the literature as "*smile*" and "*skew*", respectively [10],[12].

4.2 Fitting a Neural Network Model to the Whole Option Matrix

In the first experiment, we used 378 market option prices, backed-up from the implied volatility surface on 08/05/2002, to train the networks and the same amount of data corresponding to the implied volatility surface on 19/07/2002 for out-of-sample

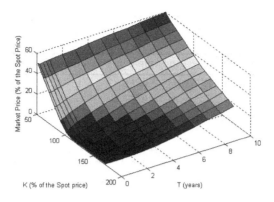

Fig. 1. The S&P 500 call-options matrix quoted on 08/05/2002

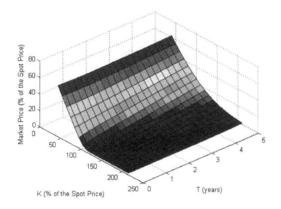

Fig. 2. The S&P 500 call-options matrix quoted on 19/07/2002

evaluation. We employ a historical[4] proxy for the volatility, computed over a period of 45 trading days before the aforementioned dates. As performance measure, we use the *mean absolute error* (MAE) between the network output and target values. Table 1 shows the in- and out-of-sample performance of the neural network models with 1-5 hidden neurons. Note that the in-sample error consistently decreases as more neurons are put in the hidden layer, while the out-of-sample error seems to fluctuate around a constant level. This behaviour is typical of overfitting. In choosing the optimal network topology, we apply a simple criterion which is to pick the number of neurons that corresponds to the first "elbow-point" of the out-of-sample error function (optimal records are denoted with bold letters). Of course, more advanced methods such as Cross Validation, Bayesian Regularization or Bootstrap Aggregating could be applied for that purpose, although the choice of the optimal number of neurons is not the main concern in our work.

---

[4] Experiments were also conducted with the weighted volatility measure without showing any significant improvement in the out-of-sample fitting.

Table 1. The mean absolute error in the in- and out-of-sample period using a historical volatility measure

Hidden Neurons	in-sample error	out-of-sample error
1	3,0296	8,3759
2	**0,9053**	**7,3279**
3	0,4055	7,3782
4	0,2736	7,4370
5	0,2262	7,3111

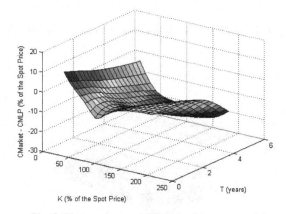

Fig. 3. The goodness-of-fit for the 2-neuron model

Figure 3 shows the error surface of the 2-neuron model estimated with the historical volatility measure. Note that the model tends to under-estimate deep-in and out of-the-money options (as the NN call price is below the market price) and overestimate long-maturity options. Overall, the fitting gets worse as time-to-maturity increases.

4.3   Restriction Areas

In order to guide the fitting in the most liquid areas of the options matrix, we employ a modified weighted objective function for the NN expressed by:

$$MAE = \sum_K \sum_T W_{KT} \mid C_{Market}^{(K,T)} - C_{NN}^{(K,T)} \mid \tag{3}$$

where W_{KT} corresponds to the weight assigned to the (K,T) strike-maturity pair. In this paper, we experimented with three weight schemes, W_1, W_2, and W_3, that cover a range of 60-140% of strike levels and specific ranges of maturities aiming at short, middle and long-horizon fitting.

The three variants are presented in Table 2. Generally, one expects that options falling into the non-zero-weight "cone" area trade with much greater liquidity than those

Table 2. The three weighting schemes W_1, W_2 & W_3 corresponding to a short-, middle- and long- maturity fitting (R_1, R_2 & R_3). The weights of pairs not reported above are all zero.

60	0	0	0	0	0,7	0,7
70	0	0	0,5	0,7	1,0	1,0
80	1,0	1,0	1,2	1,2	1,2	1,2
90	1,5	1,5	1,5	1,5	1,5	1,5
100	2,0	2,0	2,0	2,0	2,0	2,0
110	1,5	1,5	1,5	1,5	1,5	2,0
120	1,0	1,0	1,2	1,2	1,2	1,5
130	0	0,5	0,5	0,7	1,0	1,0
140	0	0	0	0	0,7	0,7
R_1	0,25	0,50	0,75	1,00	2,00	3,00
R_2	2,00	3,00	4,00	5,00	6,00	7,00
R_3	5,00	6,00	7,00	8,00	9,00	10,0

Table 3. The mean absolute error of the hybrid and the BS model in the in- and out-of-sample period for the three maturity ranges

HN	R_1		R_2		R_3	
	in-sample	out-of-sample	in-sample	out-of-sample	in-sample	out-of-sample
1	6,3724	6,8063	**8,2829**	**6,6342**	**10,316**	**8,1509**
2	**0,8090**	**3,9628**	1,4352	10,590	2,0784	13,469
3	0,7152	9,0667	1,2464	10,104	2,0736	13,329
4	0,6567	4,2859	1,0573	10,450	1,7872	13,310
5	0,7435	4,3075	0,9083	10,819	1,6100	13,206
BS	12,001	11,887	15,362	12,223	21,692	13,120

falling outside, hence the graduation of weights. Table 3 presents the in- and out-of-sample error of the hybrid NN models as a function of the number of hidden neurons for the three weights variants[5]. For comparison purposes, we also report the performance of the classical BS model, with the same historical volatility estimate fed in the neural network. Bold letters denote the optimal network topology in each range of maturities. Comparing the results of Table 3 with those of Table 1, we observe that in terms of mean absolute error the hybrid model results in a better output-of-sample fit for the maturity ranges R_1, R_2. In all cases, the hybrid model outperforms the BS one. In figures 4-6, we depict the error surfaces for the three optimal hybrid NN models. Generally, hybrid models provide more reasonable approximations to deep-in and out-of-the money market option prices, which is mainly the result of incorporating the two branches in Eq. (2). Nevertheless, they severely over-estimate around-the-money options, in a negative "ripple" in the error surface.

---

[5] Models assume a historical volatility measure for σ.

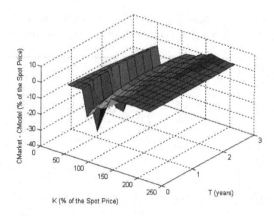

Fig. 4. The goodness-of-fit of the 2-neuron hybrid model corresponding to the short-term range (R_1)

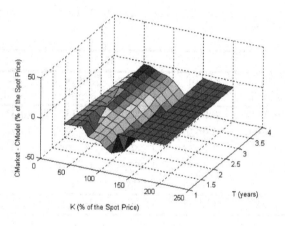

Fig. 5. The goodness-of-fit of the 1- neuron hybrid model corresponding to the medium-term range (R_2)

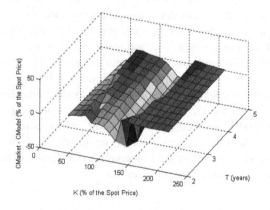

Fig. 6. The goodness-of-fit of the 1- neuron hybrid model corresponding to the long-term range (R_3)

5 Discussion and Conclusions

In this paper we propose a new nonparametric framework for pricing options that comprises a neural network model equipped with theoretical option pricing formulae. In this way, we attempt to make modeling more efficient by directing NN learning into more interesting areas of the options matrix that contain plenty of reliable data. For the pricing of illiquid options we use theoretical no-arbitrage arguments. First experimental results show that theoretical "hints" result in a better pricing performance especially for in- and out-of-the-money areas. The afore-suggested framework can be extended into many directions. We believe that the accuracy of the model would be highly increased with a better estimate for the market volatility. Nowadays, popular models of volatility are based on the time series of the underlying (see e.g. the GARCH family of models [4]). Currently, we are experimenting with various methods for finding the optimal architecture of the neural network model (cross-validation, early-stopping, regularization schemes) as well as an automatic procedure for adjusting the weights of the objective function in order to find the most "hard" areas of the implied volatility matrix to direct the NN learning.

References

1. Bakshi, G., Cao, C. and Chen, Z.: Empirical Performance of Alternative Options Pricing Models, Journal of Finance 52 (1997), 2003-2049.
2. Black and Scholes, M.: The Pricing of Options and Corporate Liabilities, Journal of Political Economy 81 (1973), 659-683.
3. Black, F. and Scholes, M.: Fact and Fantasy in the Use of Options, Journal of Financial Analysts Journal 31 (1975), 36-41 & 61-71.
4. Bollerslev, T., Engle, R.F. and Nelson, D.B.: ARCH models. In: R.F. Engle and D. McFadden (eds): The Handbook of Econometrics, Vol. 4. North-Holland (1994), 2959-3038.
5. Charalambous, C.: A Conjugate Gradient Algorithm for Efficient Training of Artificial Neural Networks, IEEE Proceedings-G 139 (1992), 301-310.
6. Cont, R. and Fonseca, J.: Dynamics of Implied Volatility Surfaces, Quantative Finance, Vol 2, 45-60.
7. Cox, J.C., Ross, S.A. and Stephen, A.: The Valuation of Options for Alternative Stochastic Processes, Journal of Financial Economics 3, (1976), 145-66.
8. Garcia, R. and Gencay, R.: Pricing and Hedging Derivative Securities with Neural Networks and a Homogeneity Hint, Journal of Econometrics 94 (2000), 93-115.
9. Hull, J.C. and White, A.: The Pricing of Options on Assets with Stochastic Volatilities, Journal of Finance 42 (1987), 281-300.
10. Hull, J.C.: Options, Futures and other Derivatives, 5th edition, Prentice Hall, New Jersey, 2002
11. Hutchinson, J.M., Lo, A.W. and Poggio, T.: A Nonparametric Approach to Pricing and Hedging Derivative Securities via Learning Networks, Journal of Finance 3 (1994), 851-889.
12. Jackwerth, C. and Rubinstein, M.: Recovering Probabilities from Option Prices, Journal of Finance 51 (1996), 1611-1631.

13. Lajbcygier, P., Boek, C., Palaniswami, M. and Flitman, A.: Neural Network Pricing of all Ordinaries SPI Options on Futures In: Refenes A - PN, Abu - Mostafa Y, J. Moody and A. Weigend, Neural Networks in Financial Engineering, Proceedings of 3 [rd] International Conference on Neural Networks in the Capital Markets, London, 1995, World Scientific, 1996, 64-77.
14. Merton, R.C.: Option Pricing when Underlying Stock Returns are Discontinuous, Journal of Financial Economics (1976), 125-44.
15. Merton, R.C.: Theory of Rational Option pricing, Bell Journal of Economics and Management Science 4 (1973), 141-83.
16. Yao, J., Li, Y. and Tan, Ch. T.: Option Price Forecasting using Neural Networks, International Journal of Management Science (omega) 28, (2000), 455-466.

Large Scale Multikernel RVM for Object Detection

Dimitris Tzikas, Aristidis Likas, and Nikolas Galatsanos

Department of Computer Science, University of Ioannina, 45110 Ioannina, Greece

Abstract. The Relevance Vector Machine(RVM) is a widely accepted Bayesian model commonly used for regression and classification tasks. In this paper we propose a multikernel version of the RVM and present an alternative inference algorithm based on Fourier domain computation to solve this model for large scale problems, e.g. images. We then apply the proposed method to the object detection problem with promising results.

1 Introduction

The Relevance Vector Machine (RVM) introduced in [1] is a Bayesian treatment of the linear model given by:

$$y(\boldsymbol{x}) = \sum_{i=1}^{M} w_i \phi_i(\boldsymbol{x}), \tag{1}$$

where $\{\phi_m(\boldsymbol{x})\}_{m=1}^{M}$ is a set of basis functions. Learning on such a model, is the process of estimating the weights $\{w_m\}_{m=1}^{M}$ given a training set $\{(x_n, t_n)\}_{n=1}^{N}$. The weights are typically assigned those values that maximize the likelihood of the training set, however the training examples must be significantly more than the parameters in order to achieve good generalization performance. The RVM overcomes this limitation by following Bayesian principles and assuming prior knowledge for the model. Specifically, a suitable hierarchical prior distribution is assumed for the weights of the model, which has most probability mass concentrated in sparse solutions, meaning that it forces most of the weights to be assigned to zero values [1]. This results in pruning basis functions that are not sufficiently supported by the training data, and allows good generalization performance even when using complex models with large number of basis functions and parameters. In a typical RVM there is one basis function centered at each training example, resulting in the following model:

$$y(\boldsymbol{x}) = \sum_{i=1}^{N} w_i \phi(\boldsymbol{x} - x_i), \tag{2}$$

As in most Bayesian models, inference on the RVM is analytically intractable. The most well–known approximations are based on the expectation maximization

G. Antoniou et al. (Eds.): SETN 2006, LNAI 3955, pp. 389–399, 2006.

(EM) algorithm [1] and the variational approximation [3]. Both these approaches, appear to have similar results but the first is generally preferred because it is more computationally efficient. However, time complexity is of order $O(N^3)$ and memory complexity of order $O(N^2)$, making inference on large training sets extremely difficult. The method based on the EM algorithm can be accelerated by considering incrementally adding basis function to an initially empty model [4], improving time complexity to order $O(M^3)$, where M is the number of the basis functions that are included in the model, which, since the model is sparse, should only be a small fraction of the total number of basis functions N.

In this paper we use the RVM for modelling images. Unfortunately, the standard RVM training algorithms are too computationally demanding even for small images. We notice that if the training points x_i lie on a uniform grid, equation (2) can be rewritten as the convolution of the weight vector $\boldsymbol{w} = (w_1, w_2, \ldots, w_N)$ with a vector $\boldsymbol{\phi} = (\phi(x_1), \ldots, \phi(x_N))$, which consists of the basis function $\phi(\boldsymbol{x})$ evaluated at the training points x_i. The RVM can then be written as:

$$\boldsymbol{y} = \boldsymbol{\phi} * \boldsymbol{w}, \tag{3}$$

where $\boldsymbol{y} = (y(x_1), y(x_2), \ldots, y(x_N))$ is the output of the model evaluated at the training points. We propose an alternative implementation of the EM based algorithm [1] that computes convolution in the DFT domain and improves both time and memory requirements. In addition we propose a multikernel RVM model, where more than one types of basis functions is allowed to be used.

2 Large Scale Multikernel RVM

2.1 RVM for Image Analysis

The linear model in (1) is very efficient provided that suitable basis functions ϕ_i are selected and that there are adequate training examples. Thus, finding a basis function set that describes the data well is an important problem, that unfortunately is very difficult to solve. Methods such as cross-validation can be used to estimate the generalization performance of several models and then choose the best one. However, this is very computationally expensive and usually only a small number of candidate basis function sets may be considered. Recently, sparse linear models such as the Support Vector Machine (SVM) [2] and the RVM [1] gain much popularity. These models during the training process select only a small subset of the available basis functions, which is then used for predictions. Thus, a large number of basis functions can be initially used and the most suitable of these will be selected. Usually, the initial set of basis functions consists of shifts of a specific base function centered at each training point. Again, cross-validation can be used to select an appropriate initial basis function set. Alternatively, another linear model can be used for the basis functions [5], estimating the optimal base function shape during the training process.

In this paper, we use several different basis functions centered at each training point, resulting in the following model:

$$y(\boldsymbol{x}) = \sum_{m=1}^{M} \sum_{i=1}^{N} w_{mi} \phi_m(\boldsymbol{x} - x_i), \tag{4}$$

where M is the number of different basis function types. If there is not sufficient prior knowledge to choose the type or scale of the basis functions cross-validation can be used to test the performance of several models and choose the best one. However, this task is very computationally demanding.

The observed image $\boldsymbol{t} = (t_1, \ldots, t_n)$ is assumed to have been generated from the model $y(x)$ evaluated at the training points $\boldsymbol{x} = (x_1, \ldots, x_n)$, after addition of independent white noise:

$$t_i = y(x_i) + \epsilon_i, \tag{5}$$
$$\epsilon_i \sim N(0, \beta^{-1}), \tag{6}$$

where β is the inverse variance of the noise.

Defining $t = (t_1, \ldots, t_N)^T$ to be the vector of observations, (5) can be rewritten as:

$$\boldsymbol{t} = \boldsymbol{\Phi}^T \boldsymbol{w} + \boldsymbol{\epsilon} = \sum_{m=1}^{M} \boldsymbol{\Phi}_m \boldsymbol{w}_m + \boldsymbol{\epsilon}, \tag{7}$$

where $\boldsymbol{\Phi}$ is the $N \times (MN)$ design matrix, each column of which is a vector with the values of a basis function at all the training points. The design matrix can be partitioned as $\boldsymbol{\Phi} = (\boldsymbol{\Phi}_1, \ldots, \boldsymbol{\Phi}_M)$, with $\boldsymbol{\Phi}_m = (\phi_{m1}, \ldots, \phi_{mN})$ being the part of the design matrix corresponding to basis functions of type $\phi_m(x)$ and $\phi_{mi} = (\phi_m(x_1 - x_i), \ldots, \phi_m(x_N - x_i))^T$ being a vector consisting of the basis function $\phi_m(x - x_i)$ evaluated at all the training points. The weight vector $\boldsymbol{w}$ can be similarly partitioned as $\boldsymbol{w} = (\boldsymbol{w}_1, \ldots, \boldsymbol{w}_M)^T$, with each $\boldsymbol{w}_m = (w_{m1}, \ldots, w_{mN})$ consisting of the weights corresponding to basis function $\phi_m(x)$.

The likelihood of the data set can then be written as:

$$p(\boldsymbol{t}|\boldsymbol{w}, \beta) = (2\pi)^{-N/2} \beta \exp \left\{ -\frac{1}{2} \beta \|t - \boldsymbol{\Phi} \boldsymbol{w}\|^2 \right\} \tag{8}$$

Given that the described model has M times more parameters than the training examples are, it is essential to seek a sparse solution. Under the Bayesian framework sparseness is obtained by assigning suitable prior distributions on the parameters. Specifically, independent Gaussian priors with unknown variances are assigned on the weights $\boldsymbol{w}$:

$$p(\boldsymbol{w}) = \prod_{m=1}^{M} \prod_{i=1}^{N} N(0, \alpha_{mi}^{-1}), \tag{9}$$

where α_{mi} is a hyperparameter controlling the inverse variance of the corresponding weight w_{mi}. These hyperparameters are assumed unknown and Gamma hyperpriors are assigned to them. The inverse noise variance β may also be assumed unknown and similarly, a Gamma prior distribution is assigned to it:

$$p(\boldsymbol{\alpha}) = \prod_{m=1}^{M} \prod_{i=1}^{N} \Gamma(a, b), \tag{10}$$

$$p(\beta) = \Gamma(c, d), \tag{11}$$

where $\boldsymbol{\alpha} = (\alpha_{11}, \ldots, \alpha_{1N}, \ldots, \alpha_{MN})$.

Unfortunately, computation of the posterior distribution of the parameters is analytically intractable and an approximation has to be used. An effective approximation, demonstrated in [1], is to consider the posterior distribution of the weights treating the hyperparameters as known parameters and then optimize the hyperparameters. The posterior weight distribution is:

$$p(\boldsymbol{w}|\boldsymbol{t}, \boldsymbol{\alpha}, \beta) = N(\boldsymbol{w}|\mu, \Sigma), \tag{12}$$

with

$$\Sigma = (\beta \boldsymbol{\Phi}^T \boldsymbol{\Phi} + \boldsymbol{A})^{-1} \tag{13}$$

$$\mu = \beta \Sigma \boldsymbol{\Phi}^T \boldsymbol{t} \tag{14}$$

Then the hyperparameters are set to those values that maximize their posterior distribution given by:

$$p(\boldsymbol{\alpha}, \beta|\boldsymbol{t}) \propto p(\boldsymbol{t}|\boldsymbol{\alpha}, \beta) p(\boldsymbol{\alpha}) p(\beta). \tag{15}$$

The quantity $p(\boldsymbol{t}|\boldsymbol{\alpha}, \beta)$ is known as the marginal likelihood and is given by:

$$p(\boldsymbol{t}|\boldsymbol{\alpha}, \beta) = (2\pi)^{-MN/2} |\Sigma|^{-1/2} \exp\left\{ -\frac{1}{2} (\boldsymbol{w} - \mu)^T \Sigma^{-1} (\boldsymbol{w} - \mu) \right\} \tag{16}$$

Differentiation of (16) leads to the following updates for the hyperparameters:

$$\alpha_{mi} = \frac{1 - \alpha_{mi} \Sigma_{ii}}{\mu_{mi}^2}, \tag{17}$$

$$\beta = \frac{N - \sum_{i=1}^{N} (1 - \alpha_i \Sigma_{ii})}{\|t - \boldsymbol{\Phi}\mu\|^2}. \tag{18}$$

Equivalent updates can also be derived from an EM formulation, treating the weights as hidden variables.

The learning algorithm proceeds by iteratively computing the posterior statistics of the weights μ, Σ given by (13) and (14) and then updating the hyperparameters using (17) and (18). Computation of Σ involves inverting a N–by–N matrix which is an $O(N^3)$ procedure, where N is the initial number of basis functions. During the training process, many of the hyperparameters are set to infinite values and the corresponding basis functions can be pruned, allowing computation of the posterior statistics in $O(M^3)$ time, where M is the number of functions that remain in the model. This results in significant speed-up of the later iterations of the algorithm, however in the first iteration all the basis functions have to be considered and the overall complexity is still $O(N^3)$.

An alternative algorithm [4] starts by assuming an empty model and incrementally adds basis functions in each iteration. Computing the posterior statistics require $O(M^3)$ time, since the full model never has to be considered. However, only one base function may be considered at each iteration and if this is chosen at random, then the algorithm requires significantly too many more iterations to reach convergence. Alternatively, the most significant basis function may be selected at each iteration, but this is computationally expensive. Overall, this algorithm is an important improvement but it still cannot be used for large scale problems, such as modelling images. In the next section we propose an RVM implementation based on DFT computations that successfully resolves the problem of computational complexity.

2.2   Multikernel RVM Implementation in the DFT Domain

It can be observed that if the training points are the pixels of an image, or generally uniform samples of a signal, then the RVM given by (4) can be written using a convolution as:

$$y = \sum_{m=1}^{M} \phi_m * w_m. \tag{19}$$

Equation (7) still holds, with the additional property that matrices Φ_m are circulant. This is an important property, implying that the product $\Phi_m w_m$ is a convolution which can be efficiently computed in the DFT domain by multiplying the DFT of the base function $\mathcal{F}$ and the weight vector $\mathcal{W}$.

$$\mathcal{T}_i = \sum_{m=1}^{M} \mathcal{F}_{mi} \mathcal{W}_{mi}, \tag{20}$$

where $\mathcal{T}$ is the DFT of the observations vector t. This observation allows computation of the output of the model without using the complete design matrix but only one basis vector, improving memory complexity from $O(N^2)$ to $O(N)$ and time complexity from $O(N^2)$ to $O(N \log N)$.

The posterior statistics of the weights μ and Σ can also be computed in the DFT domain, benefitting from the same advantages. Beginning with (14), the posterior mean of the weights can be found by solving the equation:

$$\Sigma^{-1}\mu = \beta\Phi^T t \tag{21}$$

$$(\beta\Phi^T\Phi + A)\mu = \beta\Phi^T t \tag{22}$$

Instead of analyticaly inverting the matrix $\beta\Phi^T\Phi + A$, which is computationally expensive and requires the large design matrix Φ, we solve equation (22) by using the conjugate gradient method to minimize the norm:

$$\mu = argmin_{\mu}(\|\beta\Phi^T\Phi\mu + A\mu - \beta\Phi^T t\|). \tag{23}$$

The quantities $\beta\boldsymbol{\Phi}^T\boldsymbol{\Phi}\boldsymbol{\mu}$ and $\beta\boldsymbol{\Phi}^T\boldsymbol{t}$ can be easily computed in the DFT domain since $\boldsymbol{\Phi}$ is circulant, while computation of $\boldsymbol{A}\boldsymbol{\mu}$ is straightforward since A is diagonal. Given an infinite precision machine, the conjugate gradient method is guaranteed to find the exact minimum after N iterations. In practice, a very good estimate can be obtained in only a few iterations.

Unfortunately, in order to compute the posterior weight covariance we have to invert the matrix $\beta\boldsymbol{\Phi}^T\boldsymbol{\Phi}+\boldsymbol{A}$ which is a computational burden. Instead, we notice that we only need to compute the diagonal of $\boldsymbol{\Sigma}$, which can be approximated by $\beta\boldsymbol{\Phi}^T\boldsymbol{\Phi}+\boldsymbol{A}$ with a diagonal matrix, as:

$$\Sigma_{ii} = (\beta\|\phi\|^2 + \alpha_i\mu_i)^{-1} \tag{24}$$

Although this approximation is not generally valid, it has been proved very effective in the experiments, because the matrix A has generally very large values and is the dominant term in $\beta\boldsymbol{\Phi}^T\boldsymbol{\Phi}+\boldsymbol{A}$.

2.3   Evaluation of the Proposed Modification

In order to verify the validity and evaluate the performance of the proposed DFT-based implementation we sampled uniformly the function:

$$t(x,y) = \frac{\sin(\|x+y\|)}{\|x+y\|}, \tag{25}$$

to generate a 30x30 image shown in fig. 1. We then added white Gaussian noise of variance 0.1 and applied both the initial and the DFT-based algorithm to estimate the parameters of an RVM model, which was evaluated at each pixel location to produce an estimate of the original image t. Figure 1 shows the estimates obtained using the initial and the DFT-based algorithms respectively. Averages over 10 noise realizations of the mean squared error (MSE) of each estimate and the number of relevance vectors are shown in Table 1. When computing the posterior weight means $\boldsymbol{\mu}$, stopping the conjugate gradient algorithm after 20 iterations resulted in improving the convergence speed and limiting the execution time.

Table 1. Number of relevance vectors and mean square error of the two algorithms

Algorithm	RVs	MSE
RVM	84	0.039
DFT-RVM	100	0.036

Unfortunately, we can't compare the algorithms for larger images because we can't apply the typical RVM algorithm on larger datasets. However, we demonstrate the effectiveness of the proposed algorithm on large scale regression problems, by training an RVM model with two types of kernels on a large

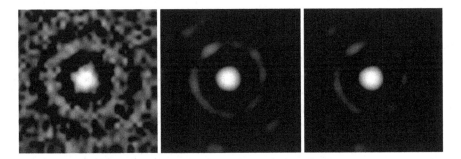

Fig. 1. LEFT: An artificial sine image with added noise. CENTER: Estimate of the RVM algorithm. RIGHT: Estimate of the DFT-RVM algorithm.

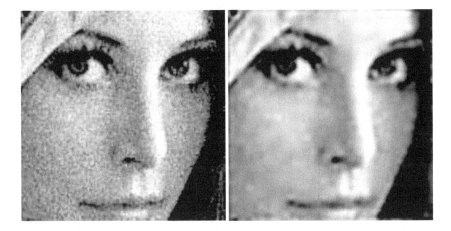

Fig. 2. LEFT: An 128 × 128 image with added gaussian noise. RIGHT: Estimate of the DFT-RVM algorithm using gaussian kernels with variance 2, 4 and 8.

256 × 256 image. The estimated image, shown in fig. 2, is improved with respect to the initial noisy image, having $ISNR = 2.2$. The $ISNR$ is defined as $ISNR = 10 \log \left(\|f - g\|^2 / \|f - \hat{f}\|^2 \right)$ and is a measure of the improvement in quality of the estimated image with respect to the initial noisy image.

3   Object Detection Using the RVM Model

The object detection problem is the problem of finding the location of an unknown number of occurrences of a given 'target' image in another given 'observed' image, under the presence of noise. The 'target' may appear significantly different in the observed image, as a result of being scaled, rotated, occluded by other objects, different illumination conditions and other effects.

The most common approaches to solve the object detection problem are variants of the matched filter, such as the phase-only [9] and the symmetric phase-only [8] matched filters. These are based on computing the correlation image between the 'observed' and 'target' images and then threshold it to determine the locations where the 'target' object is present. Alternatively, the problem can be formulated as an image restoration problem, where the image to restore is considered as an impulse function at the location of the 'target' object. This technique allows many interesting background models to be considered, such as autoregressive models [7].

In the rest of this paper, we present an alternative method for object detection, which is based on training a multikernel RVM model on the 'observation' image. The RVM model consists of two sets of basis functions: basis functions that are used to model the 'target' image and basis functions that are used to model the background. After training the model each 'target' basis function that remains in the model can be considered as a detected 'target' object. However, if the background basis functions are not flexible enough, 'target' functions may also be used to model areas of the background. Thus, we should consider only 'target' basis functions whose corresponding weight is larger than a specified threshold.

We denote by $t = (t_1, \ldots, t_N)$ a vector consisting of the intensity values of the pixels of the 'observed' image. We model this image using the following RVM model:

$$t = \sum_{i=1}^{N} w_{ti}\phi_t(x - x_i) + \sum_{i=1}^{N} w_{bi}\phi_b(x - x_i) + \epsilon, \qquad (26)$$

where ϕ_t is the 'target' basis function which is a vector consisting of the intensity values of the pixels of the 'target' image, and ϕ_b is the background basis function which we choose to be a Gaussian function. After training the RVM model we obtain the vectors μ_t and μ_b which are the posterior weight mean for the kernel and background weights respectively. Ideally, 'target' kernel functions would only be used to model occurrences of the 'target' object. However, because the background basis functions are often not flexible enough to model the background accurately, some 'target' basis functions have been used to model the background as well. In order to decide which 'target' basis functions actually correspond to 'target' occurrences, the posterior 'target' weight means are thresholded, and only those that exceed a specified threshold are considered significant:

$$\text{Target exists at location } i \Leftrightarrow |\mu_{ti}| > T. \qquad (27)$$

Choosing a low threshold may generate false alarms, indicating that the object is present in locations where it actually doesn't exist. On the other hand, choosing a high threshold may result in failing to detect an existing object. There is no unique optimal value for the threshold, but instead it should be chosen depending on the characteristics of the application.

4   Numerical Experiments

In this section we present experiments that demonstrate the improved performance of the DFT-RVM algorithm compared to autoregressive impulse restoration (ARIR), which is a state-of-the-art method, found to be superior than most existing object detection methods [7]. We first demonstrate an example in which the 'observed' image is constructed by adding the 'target' object to a background image and then adding white Gaussian noise. An image consisting of the values of the kernel weights computed with the DFT-RVM algorithm is shown in Fig. 3 along with the output of the model. Notice that because of the RVM sparsness property, only few weights have non-zero values. The 'target' object is the tank located at pixel (100,50), where the bright white spot on the kernel weight image exists.

When evaluating a detection algorithm it is important to consider the detection probability P_D, which is the probability that an existing 'target' is detected and the probability of false alarm P_{FA}, which is the probability that a 'target' is incorrectly detected. Any of these probabilities can be set to an arbitrary value by selecting an appropriate value for the threshold T. The receiver operating characteristics (ROC) curve is a plot of the probability of detection P_D versus the probability of false alarm P_{FA} that provides a comprehensive way to demonstrate the performance of a detection algorithm. However, the ROC curve is not suitable for evaluating object detection algorithms because it only considers if an algorithm has detected an object or not; it does not consider if the object was detected in the correct location. Instead, we can use the localised ROC (LROC) curve which is a plot of the probability of detection and correct localization P_{DL} versus the probability of false alarm and considers also the location where a 'target' has been detected.

In order to evaluate the performance of the algorithm, we created 50 'observed' images by adding a 'target' image to a random location of the background image, and another 50 'observed' images without the 'target' object. White Gaussian

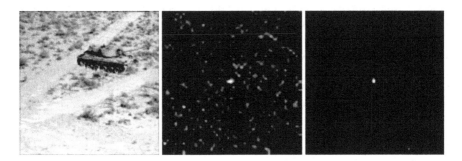

Fig. 3. Object detection example. The 'target' image is a tank located at pixel (100,50). LEFT: The noisy 'observed' image. CENTER: Area around target of the result of the ARIR algorithm. RIGHT: Area around target of the result of the DFT-RVM algorithm.

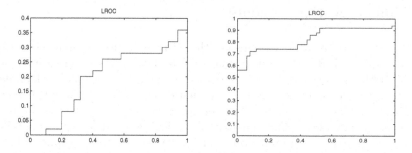

Fig. 4. LROC curve for the ARIR (left) and DFT-RVM (right) algorithms

noise was then added to each 'observed' image. The DFT-RVM algorithm was then used to estimate the parameters of an RVM model with a 'target' kernel and a Gaussian background kernel for each 'observed' image, generating 100 kernel weight images. These kernel weight images were then thresholded for many different threshold values and estimates of the probabilities P_{DL} and P_{FA} were computed for each threshold value. Similar experiments were performed for the ARIR algorithm also. An LROC curve was then plotted for each algorithm, see Fig. 4. The area under the LROC curve, which is a common measure of the performance of a detection algorithm, is significantly larger for the DFT-RVM algorithm. It is important that the LROC curve is high for small values of P_{FA}, since usually the threshold is chosen so that only a small fraction of false detections are allowed.

5   Conclusions

We have proposed an approximate but accelerated inference method for training the RVM model on large scale images, based on fast computation of the posterior statistics in the Fourier domain. Experiments on images demonstrate that the proposed approximation allows inference on large scale images, where the initial RVM argorithm is too computationally demanding to run. We then applied the method to the object detection problem. Experimental results show that the proposed method is more robust than existing methods. Furthermore, the proposed technique can be extended to solve the rotation and scaling invariant object detection problem, by optimizing the model with respect to rotation and scaling of the basis functions.

Acknowledgments

This research was co-funded by the European Union in the framework of the program Pythagoras II of the Operational Program for Education and Initial Vocational Training of the 3rd Community Support Framework of the Hellenic Ministry of Education.

References

1. M. E. Tipping, "Sparse Bayesian Learning and the Relevance Vector Machine", Journal of Machine Learning Research, 1:211-244, 2001.
2. C. Cortes, V.Vapnik, "Support Vector Networks", Machine Learning, 20, 1995.
3. A. C. Faul, M. E. Tipping, "A Variational Approach to Robust Regression", ICANN 2001: 95-102.
4. M. E. Tipping, A. C. Faul, "Fast marginal likelihood maximisation for sparse Bayesian models", In Proceedings of Artificial Intelligence and Statistics '03.
5. M. Girolami, S. Rogers, "Hierarchical Bayesian Models for Kernel Learning", ICML 2005.
6. J. R. Shewchuk, "An Introduction to the Conjugate Gradient Method Without the Agonizing Pain", http://www.cs.cmu.edu/ quake-papers/painless-conjugate-gradient.ps
7. A. Abu-Naser, N. P. Galatsanos, M. N. Wernick and D. Shonfeld, Object Recognition Based on Impulse Restoration Using the Expectation-Maximization Algorithm, Journal of the Optical Society of America, Vol. 15, No. 9, 2327-2340, September 1998.
8. Q. Chen, M. Defrise and F. Decorninck, "Symmetric phase-only matched filtering of Fourier-Mellin transforms for image registration and recognition", Pattern Recognition and Machine Intelligence, 12(12), 1156-1198, 1994.
9. J. L. Horner and P.D. Gianino, "Phase-only matched filtering", Applied Optics, 23(6), 812-816, 1984.

Extraction of Salient Contours in Color Images*

Vassilios Vonikakis[1], Ioannis Andreadis[1], and Antonios Gasteratos[2]

[1] Laboratory of Electronics, Section of Electronics and Information Systems Technology,
Department of Electrical and Computer Engineering,
Democritus University of Thrace, GR-671 00 Xanthi, Greece
{bbonik, iandread}@ee.duth.gr
[2] Laboratory of Robotics and Automation, Section of Production Systems,
Department of Production and Management Engineering,
Democritus University of Thrace, GR-671 00 Xanthi, Greece
agaster@pme.duth.gr

Abstract. In this paper we present an artificial cortical network, inspired by the Human Visual System (HVS), which extracts the salient contours in color images. Similarly to the primary visual cortex, the network consists of orientation hypercolumns. Lateral connections between the hypercolumns are modeled by a new connection pattern based on co-exponentiality. The initial color edges of the image are extracted in a way inspired by the double-opponent cells of the HVS. These edges are inputs to the network, which outputs the salient contours based on the local interactions between the hypercolumns. The proposed network was tested on real color images and displayed promising performance, with execution times small enough even for a conventional personal computer.

1 Introduction

One of the important problems in shape classification is the recognition of shapes in cluttered backgrounds. In such cases, conventional edge detectors extract numerous edges, the majority of which does not belong to any significant object. Thus, shape classification algorithms often deal with irrelevant data. On the other hand, when we look at images, certain salient contours can regularly be perceived regardless of a cluttered background. They draw human attention without the need to scan the entire image in a systematic manner, and without prior expectations regarding their shape.

Research in the automatic detection of salient contours, has been focused on two different directions: conventional and biologically inspired. In one of the early conventional works [1], a network of locally connected processing elements, that iteratively extract salient structures in an image, is presented. Recent techniques assorted into this category are oriented towards graph-theoretic approaches [2, 3]. These methods typically construct a graph where the vertices represent pixels. The weighted edges represent affinity between these pixels. In this context, finding a boundary is reduced to the problem of partitioning the graph in a way that optimizes a

---

* This research was funded by the project PENED 2003 – KE 1354.

G. Antoniou et al. (Eds.): SETN 2006, LNAI 3955, pp. 400–410, 2006.

cost function. A comparison of methods for salient contour detection can be found in [4]. The best algorithms of this category, have reported a polynomial-time execution performance. However, all the aforementioned algorithms refer to grayscale images and no work on the extraction of salient contours in color images has been presented yet.

Biologically inspired methods are based in neuroscientific studies, mainly from the HVS. They attempt to model the way the HVS extracts saliency. The results of these studies suggest that neurons in primary visual cortex integrate information in a way that promotes the integration of salient contours [5]. This means that if a V1 neuron is stimulated by an oriented stimulus within its receptive field, a second collinear stimulus can increase the response of this neuron. Additionally, the same oriented stimulus presented orthogonally to the main axis will produce inhibition [6]. The connection pattern of V1 cells, states that if two edges are locally part of the same contour, there is a high possibility to be co-circular. Two contour elements are co-circular if they are both tangent to the same circle, and smooth if the radius of the circle is large. Many artificial models based on the above studies have been proposed in the recent years [7-11]. They all incorporate a degree of cortical architecture and iteratively process the synchronization of oriented cells. The oriented cortical cells are usually modeled by steerable or Gabor filters. Co-axial connections are similar to the "co-circular" connection scheme [12]. Results are generally good for synthetic images, but performance is relatively poor for real ones. Similarly to the conventional methods, the biologically inspired ones refer only to the extraction of salient contours in grayscale images.

In this paper we present an improvement of a previously proposed system [13] for salient contour extraction, which is loosely inspired by the HVS. It aims at the extraction of the salient contours of a color image, whilst significantly reducing the other edges. The main objective of the method is to acquire optimum results in high-resolution color images, with a high execution performance. One of the drawbacks of the former system [13] was the modest results in the extraction of the initial achromatic edges, which affected the final output of the algorithm. An improved technique is now employed for the extraction of the initial edges, which provides better results. Furthermore, it is extended to the extraction of color edges. This new approach is inspired by the double opponent cells of the HVS. This means that the processing is not done independently in the RGB color planes, but in a similar way to the human color opponency [17]. The proposed method performs well for real color images of high resolution. The execution time does not depend on the complexity of the image and is linear to its size, when the method is executed in parallel. When the algorithm is executed in a serial processor e.g. a conventional PC (P4, 3GHz), color images of up to 700×700 pixels are processed in approximately 2.2 seconds. The rest of the paper is organized as follows: In section 2 we present the network's architecture and the wiring of the connections according to the new connection scheme. In section 3 we describe in detail the system and the new affinity function, as well as the equations of the network. In section 4 we illustrate the experimental results. Finally, concluding remarks are made in section 5.

2 Network Architecture

The hypercolumns of the proposed method are modeled as proposed in [13, 14]. According to this approach, a set of 60 binary kernels, encoding 12 different orientations, are grouped in hypercolumns, which are retinotopically organized, similarly to the ice-cube model of the visual cortex [15]. The image is divided to 10×10-pixel regions. Each region has its own hypercolumn. This is an independent processing unit for the orientation of the edges. Each kernel of a hypercolumn is also an independent processing unit of a particular orientation and a distinct position. In our method, lateral interactions extend to a 5×5 hypercolumn neighborhood. This means that each kernel of the hypercolumn (i, j) is affected by any other kernel, in the hypercolumns found within the square area formed by hypercolumns (i-2, j-2) to (i+2, j+2). Consequently, each kernel of the hypercolumn (i, j), is connected to 1440 other kernels (24 hypercolumns × 60 kernels). The interconnectivity of the network follows the rule that 'everyone is connected to anyone', within the 5×5 hypercolumn neighborhood. These connections are encoded by a set of 1440 fixed weights. A kernel 'k' of the hypercolumn (i, j), has its own 1440 weights. The weights in the proposed scheme are employed in a similar way to the Multi Layer Perceptrons, apart from the fact that they are fixed throughout the whole image. No further training is required after their calculation in the initial design of the network. In the proposed method we introduce a new connection scheme for the calculation of weights. Previous methods [7-11] usually adopt variations of the classical co-circular approach [12] according to which two orientation elements are part of the same curve only if they are tangent to the same circle. Our connection scheme is based on co-exponentiality, meaning that two orientation elements are part of the same curve only if they are tangent to the same exponential curve. Fig. 1 shows a comparison of the co-exponential and co-circular scheme, for the horizontal (0°) orientation.

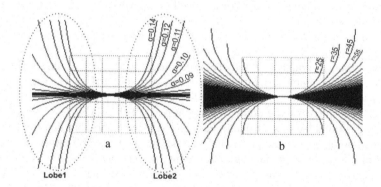

Fig. 1. a. The proposed co-exponential scheme. b. The co-circular scheme. Both refer to the horizontal (0°) orientation. Not all possible curves are depicted for visualization purposes.

The weights of the 60 kernels, should contribute to the formation of a co-exponential connection scheme. In order to calculate the weights of kernel k, it is placed in the central position of a 5×5 neighborhood. The exponential connection scheme is rotated and shifted to the same orientation with the k kernel. Fig. 2a depicts the connection scheme for a kernel of 105° orientation. All the exponential curves of the connection scheme are then separately approximated by combinations of the orientation segments of the kernels. Fig. 2b illustrates the approximation of the right part of the α=0.13 curve. Each kernel used in the approximation, defines an excitatory (positive) weight, which establishes a facilitatory connection with the central kernel at that particular position. Fig. 2c depicts a facilitatory connection of the previous kernel with a kernel of 45° in position (i-2, j+1). This means that any such kernel of an (i, j) hypercolumn facilitates the particular 45° kernel of (i-2, j+1) hypercolumn and inhibits it, in all the other hypercolumns of the 5×5 neighborhood. These are 24 of the 1440 total connection weights only for the particular 105° kernel. The same procedure is followed for all the weights of any other kernel in the set.

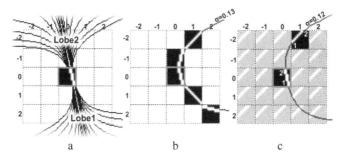

Fig. 2. a. The connection scheme for a 105°-kernel. b. The approximation of the right part of the α=0.13 curve. c. One of the facilitatory connections of the kernel with a 45°-kernel.

The weight values are numbers ranging in the interval [-1, 1]. Positive weights are all set to 1. Negative weights, have a fixed negative value for all the kernels. The selection of this negative value was done after extensive trial and error testing. In the current network configuration, the value of negative weights, in which the network maximizes its performance, was found to be -0.06. This apparent imbalance between the amplitude of the positive and negative weights is reasonable, considering the fact that inhibitory connections significantly outclass the facilitatory ones.

3   Description of the Method

3.1   Extraction of the Color Edges

Most of the conventional methods for salient contour detection initially extract the edges using the Canny edge detector. In the proposed system, we improve the center-surround operator that we previously reported in [13, 14], and was of 3×3 size. Extensive experiments were made in order to define the spatial scale which is more common in every-day images and detects the significant edges, while minimizing the computational burden of the convolution. This would define the optimum size of a center-surround operator for the proposed method. The tests were made with sizes ranging from 3×3 to 21×21. These different operators were tested in the set of real images used in [13]. Center-surround operators of 3×3 size are sensitive to high spatial scales. As a result, they tend to extract many zero-crossings that are not part of significant edges e.g. textures and noise. Sizes exceeding 15×15 tend to extract thick edges of 7-pixel width that are not compatible with the kernel set that the method uses. Additionally, when convolved with an image, they increase the computational burden to undesirable levels. The dimensions that achieve a gainful trade-off between edge extraction and computational burden were found to be the 9×9 operator. This scale is usually sensitive to all the significant edges of an image, not sensitive to high scales, such as textures and noise, and at the same time is small enough to contain the computational burden of the convolution to desirable levels. This is clearly depicted in Fig. 3, where a comparison of the three scales can be seen. The center-surround operator that was adopted for the proposed method can be seen in Fig. 4.

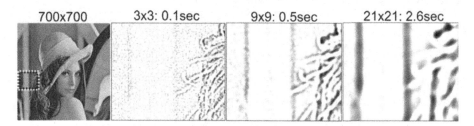

Fig. 3. Extracted edges on a small part of the 'Lena' image by three different center-surround operators

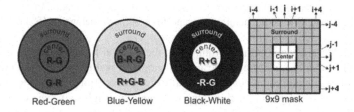

Fig. 4. The three types of double opponent cells carrying the red-green, blue-yellow and achromatic opponency respectively, as well as the 9×9-mask employed for their approximation

Many techniques have been proposed in the past decades for edge detection in color images [16]. However, they are not compatible with the way that the HVS processes color information and usually are computationally intensive. Our aim was to adopt a method for color image edge extraction that would be as simple as the gradient of the R, G and B planes, and at the same time compatible with the HVS. For this reason we have employed a new approach, inspired by the double opponent cells of the HVS [17]. This means that the processing is not done independently in the three color planes, but in a compatible way to the human color opponency. For any pixel in the color image, equations (1), (2) and (3) are employed for the extraction of the color edges. All three equations have two distinct factors. The first refers to the center of the mask $(i-1 \leq y \leq i+1) \cap (j-1 \leq x \leq j+1)$ and the second refers to the surround $(i-1 > y > i+1) \cap (j-1 > x > j+1)$. The center and surround receive always opposite chromatic signals. Normalization is necessary for the center and surround factor, in order to eliminate any DC component and make the equations respond only to color transitions and not to uniform-color regions. Thus, the center factor is divided by 9 which is the number of pixels located in the center of the mask. Similarly, the surround factor is divided by 72 which is the number of pixels found in the surround. It is also known that the strengths of the center and surround are equal [15, 17]. Consequently both factors are divided by 2. The above normalizations ensure that all the equations produce an output ranging from 0 to 1 (or from 0 to 255 depending on the image format) with high values for the color edges and with zero value for the other regions.

$$RG_{i,j} = \frac{1}{2 \cdot 9}\left[\sum_{y=i-4}^{i+4}\sum_{x=j-4}^{j+4}(R_{y,x} - G_{y,x})\right]_{\substack{i-1 \le y \le i+1 \\ j-1 \le x \le j+1}} + \frac{1}{2 \cdot 72}\left[\sum_{y=i-4}^{i+4}\sum_{x=j-4}^{j+4}(G_{y,x} - R_{y,x})\right]_{\substack{i-1 > y > i+1 \\ j-1 > x > j+1}} \quad (1)$$

$$BY_{i,j} = \frac{1}{2 \cdot 9}\left[\sum_{y=i-4}^{i+4}\sum_{x=j-4}^{j+4}\left(B_{y,x} - \frac{(R_{y,x} + G_{y,x})}{2}\right)\right]_{\substack{i-1 \le y \le i+1 \\ j-1 \le x \le j+1}} + \frac{1}{2 \cdot 72}\left[\sum_{y=i-4}^{i+4}\sum_{x=j-4}^{j+4}\left(\frac{(R_{y,x} + G_{y,x})}{2} - B_{y,x}\right)\right]_{\substack{i-1 > y > i+1 \\ j-1 > x > j+1}} \quad (2)$$

$$BW_{i,j} = \frac{1}{2 \cdot 9}\left[\sum_{y=i-4}^{i+4}\sum_{x=j-4}^{j+4}\left(\frac{R_{y,x} + G_{y,x}}{2}\right)\right]_{\substack{i-1 \le y \le i+1 \\ j-1 \le x \le j+1}} - \frac{1}{2 \cdot 72}\left[\sum_{y=i-4}^{i+4}\sum_{x=j-4}^{j+4}\left(\frac{R_{y,x} + G_{y,x}}{2}\right)\right]_{\substack{i-1 > y > i+1 \\ j-1 > x > j+1}} \quad (3)$$

Equation (1) describes the opponency between red and green. It generates a high output only in the transitions between redness and greenness. Similarly, equation (2) describes the opponency between blue and yellow, generating high outputs only in the transitions between blueness and yellowness. Finally, equation (3) describes the achromatic opponency, generating high outputs only in the transitions between blackness and whiteness. For the final extraction of the color edges, we select the maximum value, between the three opponent planes (RG, BY BW), for any (i, j) position.

3.2 Excitation Rules

The extracted color edges are inputs to the network of hypercolumns. The initial local excitation of the hypercolumns is the result of the convolution of the 60 kernels of every hypercolumn with edge image. An extensive description of this can be found in [13, 14]. Having an initial excitation, the hypercolumns interact with each other through the co-exponential connectivity pattern and extract locally the salient contours as described in the following equations:

$$inh_{k(i,j)}(t) = \begin{cases} \sum_{l=1}^{60}\sum_{y=i-2}^{i+2}\sum_{x=j-2}^{j+2} out_{l(y,x)}(t-1) \times weight_{l(y,x) \to k(i,j)} & if\ out_{k(i,j)}(t-1) > 0 \\ 0 & else \end{cases} \quad (4)$$

$$weight_{l(y,x) \to k(i,j)} < 0\ \&\ y \ne i,\ x \ne j$$

$$Lobe\ N_{k(i,j)}(t) = \begin{cases} \sum_{l=1}^{60}\sum_{y=i-2}^{i+2}\sum_{x=j-2}^{j+2} out_{l(y,x)}(t-1) \times weight_{l(y,x) \to k(i,j),N} & if\ out_{k(i,j)}(t-1) > 0 \\ 0 & else \end{cases} \quad (5)$$

$$weight_{l(y,x) \to k(i,j),N} > 0\ ,\ y \ne i,\ x \ne j,\ N = \{1,2\}$$

$$ex_{k(i,j)}(t) = \begin{cases} \dfrac{Lobe1_{k(i,j)}(t) + Lobe2_{k(i,j)}(t)}{2\left(1 + \left| Lobe1_{k(i,j)}(t) - Lobe2_{k(i,j)}(t)\right|\right)} & if\ Lobe1_{k(i,j)}(t), Lobe2_{k(i,j)}(t) > 0 \\ 0 & else \end{cases} \quad (6)$$

$$out_{k(i,j)}(t) = \begin{cases} log\left(out_{k(i,j)}(t-1) + ex_{k(i,j)}(t) + inh_{k(i,j)}(t)\right) & if\ q > 0 \\ 0\ else \end{cases} \quad (7)$$

The total inhibition that a kernel k in hypercolumn (i, j) receives from its 5×5 neighborhood is given by equation (4), where l is the kernel inhibiting kernel k, (y, x) are the coordinates of kernel l in the 5×5 neighborhood and $\text{weight}_{l(y,x) \to k(i,j)}$ is the weight from "kernel l in position (y,x) to kernel k in position (i,j)".

The total facilitation that a kernel receives from the 1440 kernels within its 5×5 neighborhood is pooled in two distinct sets: Lobe1, corresponds to the one side of the oriented segment and Lobe2, corresponds to the other. The concept of lobes was first introduced in [11] with the form of "bipole" cells. Fig. 1a shows the two lobes of the co-exponential connection scheme. Fig 2c also depicts the lobes of two kernels. The facilitation that lobe N of the kernel k in the (i, j) hypercolumn receives from the 1440 kernels of the 5×5 neighborhood is given by equation (5), in which l is the kernel that facilitates kernel k, (y, x) are the coordinates of kernel l in the 5×5 neighborhood and $\text{weight}_{l(y,x) \to k(i,j),N}$ is the weight from "kernel l in position (y, x) to the Nth lobe of kernel k in position (i, j)". Equations (4) and (5) ensure that kernels with high outputs possess a more influential role to the target kernel than those with lower outputs. The nature of this influence (excitatory – inhibitory) is encoded by the weight of the connection between the source and the target kernel.

A kernel receives excitation only if both lobes receive facilitation. This ensures that only the cells which are part of a chain are activated. Additionally, a new affinity function is introduced which defines the excitation of the kernels and favors good continuation. The proposed affinity function is described in equation (6). The novelty that is introduced with equation (6) is the factor of similarity of the two lobes. A kernel that belongs to a smooth contour, will receive in its lobes, approximately equal amounts of facilitation from the other kernels of the chain. Equation (6) ensures that, only the kernels with similar facilitation in the two lobes, receive high excitation.

The total output of kernel k located in the hypercolumn (i, j) at time t, is given by equation (7). The sum q increases exponentially in each iteration, reaching increased values even for a small number of iterations. For this reason a logarithm is introduced, which achieves a linear increase for sum q, averting high values. The initial output of kernel k in the (i, j) hypercolumn, at t = 0, is its local excitation.

According to reported methods [8, 11], every orientation inhibits all the other orientations in the same hypercolumn with a factor proportional to the degree of their dissimilarity. Maximum inhibition accounts for perpendicular orientations. We introduce a different approach based on the "winner takes all" principle, which reduces radically the computational complexity. By the end of each iteration, only the kernel with the maximum output in a hypercolumn survives. This will be called the "winner kernel". The rest of the kernels nullify their outputs. This approach ensures that the active number of kernels is kept to a minimum. For this reason it reduces significantly the required computations in a serial execution of the method. The final output of the method is the drawing of the oriented segment of the winner kernel in each hypercolumn. The intensity of this kernel is proportional to the output of the hypercolumn. Normalization is applied to the output of each hypercolumn in order to achieve a more plausible result. An important feature of equations (4)-(7) is that there are no dependencies in their execution for different kernels and hypercolumns. Hypercolumns and kernels are independent processing modules and, consequently, the method can be fully executed in parallel.

4 Experimental Results

The proposed system was implemented in C code and executed on an Intel Pentium 4 processor running at 3.0 MHz, with 512MB of memory, under Windows XP. One of our primary objectives was to create a method that achieves acceptable results with high resolution images at execution times, ranging into few seconds. Table 1 depicts a comparison between the proposed method for the extraction of color edges and the RGB gradient approach. The image of the third column is obtained by applying a max operator on each pixel of the gradient in the R, G and B planes. It is clear that the proposed technique delivers higher contrast edges, especially in isoluminant regions. Isoluminant regions are regions that have approximately the same luminance and therefore differ only in color. In these cases, the RGB gradient method does not extract high contrast edges contrary to the proposed technique. The luminance component of the images depicted in Table 1 can be seen in Fig. 5. Regions such as the back of the bear or the outline of the parrot are isoluminant and thus, the contrast in these regions is low. Nevertheless, the proposed technique extracts high contrast edges, contrary to the RGB gradient method.

Table 1. Comparison of the proposed technique for the extraction of color edges, to the classical RGB gradient technique

Original	Double-opponent edges	RGB gradient edges

Fig. 5. The luminance component of the images presented in Table 1

Table 2 depicts a comparison between the proposed method and the method presented in [13]. For the comparison we used grayscale images, since the previous method was only for grayscale images. Consequently, the results depict the improvement introduced only by the new center-surround operator. As it is clear the proposed method outperforms the former, creating smoother contours. Additionally, new edges have been extracted, which previously were not detected by the finer scale of the 3×3 operator. At the same time, none of the former detected edges was missed by the 9×9 operator. This is more apparent in the "Lena" image, where the edges of the background, which are not sharp, have been detected by the proposed method. This proves that the new center-surround operator has a scale which detects a broader number of edge sizes, without affecting the finer scales.

Table 2. Comparison of the proposed and the former [13] method

Original	Proposed	Former

Table 3 depicts some of the results of the proposed method, obtained from real color images. All the test images represent objects with smooth contours in cluttered backgrounds. The first column illustrates the original image. The second column presents the results of the extracted color edges with the proposed double-opponent technique. This image is the input to the proposed network. The third column exhibits the results of the network, after 10 iterations, as well as the execution time. As it is demonstrated by the results, the network can extract some of the most salient contours and ignore other high contrast edges. These edges initially excite highly the hypercolumns. However, by the end of the 10th iteration, their contrast has been reduced significantly. It is important to mention that contrary to parallel execution, image complexity affects the execution time when the method is executed serially. Thus, images containing more salient contours than others may require higher execution time.

Table 3. Results of the proposed method in real color images

Original	Color Edges	Salient Contours
1. 700×576		2.2 sec
2. 672×496		1.8 sec
3. 692×519		2.0 sec
4. 700×576		2.5 sec
5. 576×700		2.2 sec

5 Conclusions

A parallel network inspired by the HVS, which extracts the salient contours in color images was presented in this paper. The network consists of independent processing elements, which are organized into hypercolumns and process in parallel the orientation of all the color edges in the image. Saliency enhancement results as a consequence of the local interactions between the kernels. The most important feature of the proposed method is its execution time in accordance to the quality of its results. This allows to process high resolution color images in a few seconds, using a conventional personal computer, even though the high parallelism of the algorithm has not been exploited. Additionally, a new technique for the extraction of color edges was introduced, based on the double-opponent cells of the HVS, which delivers better results in the isoluminant regions of a color image.

The proposed method is intended to be used as a part of a larger cognitive vision system for recognition and categorization. Target applications of such a system include among others robotics systems, image retrieval systems, vision based automation etc.

References

1. Alter, D., Basri, R.: Extracting Salient Curves from Images: An Analysis of the Salience Network. International Journal of Computer Vision 27 (1998) 51–69
2. Mahamud, S., Williamns, R., Thornber, K., Xu, K.: Segmentation of Multiple Salient Closed Contours from Real Images. IEEE Transactions on Pattern Analysis and Machine Intelligence 25 (2003) 433-444
3. Wang, S., Kubota, T., Siskind, M., Wang, J.: Salient Closed Boundary Extraction with Ratio Contour. IEEE Transactions on Pattern Analysis and Machine Intelligence 27 (2005) 546-560
4. Lance, W., Karvel, T.: A Comparison of Measures for Detecting Natural Shapes in Cluttered Backgrounds. International Journal of Computer Vision 34 (2000) 81-96
5. Field, J., Hayes, A.: Contour Integration and the Lateral Connections of V1 Neurons. The Visual Neurosciences, MIT Press (2004)
6. Kapadia, K., Westheimer, G., Gilbert, D.: Spatial Distribution of Contextual Interactions in Primary Visual Cortex and in Visual Perception. F. Neurophysiology 84 (2000) 2048-2062
7. Yen, C., Finkel, L.: Extraction of Perceptually Salient Contours by Striate Cortical Networks. Vision Research 38 (1998) 719-741
8. Li, Z.: A Neural Model of Contour Integration in the Primary Visual Cortex. Neural Computation 10 (1998) 903-940
9. Choe, Y., Miikkulainen, R.: Contour Integration and Segmentation with Self-Organized Lateral Connections. Biological Cybernetics 90 (2004) 75-88
10. Mundhenk, N., Itti, L.: Computational Modeling and Exploration of Contour Integration for Visual Saliency. Biological Cybernetics 93 (2005) 188-212
11. Grossberg, S.: Visual Boundaries and Surfaces. The Visual Neurosciences, MIT Press, (2004)
12. Parent, P., Zucker, W.: Trace Inference, Curvature Consistency, and Curve Detection. IEEE Transactions on Pattern Analysis and Machine Intelligence 11 (1989) 823-839
13. Vonikakis, V., Andreadis, I., Gasteratos, A.: Simple-Shape Classification Based on the Human Visual System. IASTED Int. Conf. on Visualization, Imaging and Image Processing (2005) 162-167
14. Vonikakis, V., Gasteratos, A., Andreadis, I.: Enhancement of Perceptually Salient Contours using a Parallel Artificial Cortical Network. Accepted for publication in Biological Cybernetics
15. Hubel, D., Wiesel, T.: Receptive Fields and Functional Architecture in Nonstriate Areas (188 and 19) of the Cat. Journal of Neurophysiology 28 (1965) 229-289
16. Plataniotis, K., Venetsanopoulos, A.: Color Image Processing and Applications. Springer-Verlag, Berlin Heidelberg (2000)
17. Lennie, P.: Color coding in the cortex. Color Vision – From Genes to Perception. Cambridge University Press (1999)

Dynamic Security Assessment and Load Shedding Schemes Using Self Organized Maps and Decision Trees

Emmanouil M. Voumvoulakis and Nikolaos D. Hatziargyriou

Department of Electrical and Computer Engineering,
National Technical University of Athens,
Zografou 15773, Athens Greece

Abstract. Modern Power Systems often operate close to their stability limits in order to meet the continuously growing demand, due to the difficulties in expanding the generation and transmission system. An effective way to face power system contingencies that can lead to instability is load shedding. In this paper we propose a method to assess the dynamic performance of the Greek mainland Power System and to propose a load shedding scheme in order to maintain voltage stability under various loading conditions and operating states in the presence of critical contingencies including outages of one or more generating units in the south part of the system. A Self Organizing Map is utilized in order to classify the Load profiles of the Power System. With a decision tree the dynamic performance of each class is assessed. The classification of Load Profiles by the SOM, provide the load shedding scheme.

Keywords: Dynamic Security,Load shedding, Self Organizing Maps, Decision Trees.

1 Introduction

As the increase in electric power demand outpaces the installation of new transmission and generation facilities, power systems are forced to operate with narrower margins of security. Security is defined as the capability of guaranteeing the continuous operation of a power system under normal operation even following some significant perturbations ([6]). As security is a major, if not ultimate, goal of power system operation and control, a fast and reliable security assessment is necessary. Dynamic Security Assessment (DSA), can deal with transient stability problems and/or voltage stability problems that respectively require transient stability assessment and voltage stability assessment. This paper focuses on voltage stability assessment.

Voltage stability is concerned with the ability of a power system to maintain steady acceptable voltages at all buses in the system both under normal operating conditions and after being subjected to a disturbance. Instability may occur in case of a progressive fall or rise of voltage of some buses. The main factor causing voltage instability is the inability of the power system to maintain a proper balance of reactive power throughout the system ([7]). One of the objectives in

G. Antoniou et al. (Eds.): SETN 2006, LNAI 3955, pp. 411–420, 2006.

power system security analysis, which is emphasized in this paper, is to indicate corrective actions that would keep the system in operation after a contingency has occurred. Load shedding is one common and effective corrective action to which we resort when the security of a power network is jeopardized.

The Greek system is prone to voltage instability, especially during summer. The phenomenon is related to the power transfer from the generating areas in the North and West of Greece to the main load centre in the Athens metropolitan area reaching its maximum. The problem is due to the long electrical distance between generation and load consisting of generator step-up transformers, 400 kV and 150 kV transmission lines, 400/150 kV autotransformers and bulk power delivery transformers.

In this paper the development of an automatic learning framework both for power system security assessment and load shedding scheme is discussed. With a Kohonen Self Organizing Map (S.O.M.), the power system's state is classified according to the load of the 10 basic areas of Greece. This mapping creates clusters with a large majority of safe or unsafe operational states, and others for which no conclusion regarding system's safety can be deduced. For the latter clusters the method of Decision Trees is applied in order to create simple rules to classify system's states into safe and unsafe. Thus, the dynamic security state of each Operational Point (O.P.), by mapping it onto the SOM and applying the rules derived by the Decision Tree, which belongs to that position of the map. If the state of the O.P. is considered unsafe then we move to the closest safe position of the map. This transposition can be materialized in practice by means of load shedding.

2   Decision Trees

The Decision Tree (D.T.) is a tree, structured upside down, built on the basis of a Learning Set (L.S.) of preclassified states ([2], [4], [5], [8]). The construction of a D.T. starts at the root node with the whole L.S. of preclassified O.Ps. At each step, a tip-node of the growing tree is considered and the algorithm decides whether it will be a terminal node or should be further developed. To develop a node, an appropriate attribute is first identified, together with a dichotomy test on its values. The test T is defined as:

$$T : A_{i_j} = t \tag{1}$$

The subset of its learning examples corresponding to the node is then split according to this dichotomy into two subsets corresponding to the successors of the current node. A more detailed technical description of the approach followed is described in ([5], [8]).

Figure 1 shows a hypothetical decision tree (DT) : to infer the output information corresponding to given input attribute values, one traverses the tree, starting at the top-node, and applying sequentially the dichotomous tests encountered to select the appropriate successor. When a terminal node is reached, the output information stored is retrieved.

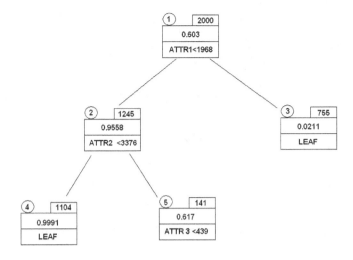

Fig. 1. An example of a Decision Tree

The nodes of the D.T. have the following scheme: There are 4 attributes. In the upper right side is the number of O.Ps, which belong to the node. In the upper left side is the label of the node. In the middle is the safety index which is the safe O.Ps of the node divided to the total O.Ps of the node. Finally in the bottom is the dichotomy test of the node or the characterization of the node as deadend or leaf. In case there is a separation criterion, if it is true we go on the left node, otherwise we go on the right.

D.Ts are evaluated using the Testing Set (T.S.). The most important evaluator of the D.T. reliability and performance is the rate of successful classifications, defined as the ratio of successfully classified O.Ps to the number of O.Ps tested.

$$Success\ Rate = \frac{OPs\ successfully\ classified\ by\ the\ DT}{Total\ number\ of\ OPs\ in\ the\ TS}$$

For a two class partition (Safe-Unsafe) there can be distinguished two types of error, depending on the actual class of the misclassified O.P.:

$$False\ Alarm\ Rate = \frac{Safe\ OPs\ misclassified\ as\ Unsafe\ by\ the\ DT}{Total\ number\ of\ Safe\ OPs\ in\ the\ TS}$$

$$Missed\ Alarm\ Rate = \frac{Unsafe\ OPs\ misclassified\ as\ Safe\ by\ the\ DT}{Total\ number\ of\ Unsafe\ OPs\ in\ the\ TS}$$

3 Self Organized Maps

Unsupervised learning methods are used to guarantee a fast DSA and a good representation of the state space. These methods find characteristic groups and structures in the input data space. Measurement values, which are available in energy management systems, represent the input space. One of the most successful implementation of unsupervised learning is the Kohonen Self Organizing Map ([3], [1])

A S.O.M. maps a high dimensional input space to a low dimensional output space. The mapping of the S.O.M. is done by feature vectors w_j in a way that

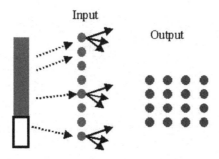

Fig. 2. Kohonen Self-Organizing Map

their main distances to the training vectors are minimized. The feature vectors are structured in a neighbourhood grid. If the grid is two-dimensional, the S.O.M. offers the possibility for the visualization of its mapping. Figure 2 shows a Kohonen network.

During the learning phase the input vectors are presented randomly. At each presentation of an input vector, i.e. at each step of the learning process, every neuron of the network calculates a scalar activation function which depends on the input vector and on its own weight vector w_j. This function is chosen to represent distance $\|...\|$ between the input vector and the weight vector of the neuron under consideration. Possible choices are Euclidean distance or the scalar product. The winning unit is considered to be the one with the largest activation. For Kohonen S.O.Ms, however, one updates not only the winning units weights but also all of the weights in a neighborhood around the winning units. The neighborhoods size generally decreases slowly with each iteration. A sequential description of how to train a Kohonen S.O.M. is as follows:

1. Initialise all weights randomly.
2. Choose input vector randomly in the training set.
3. Select the winning output unit as the one with the largest similarity measure between all weight vectors w_i and the input vector x. If the Euclidean distance is chosen as the dissimilarity measure, then the winning unit c satisfies the following equation:

$$\|x - w_c\| = min \|x - w_i\| \tag{2}$$

4. Define the neighbourhood of the winner, e.g. by using a neighbourhood function $\Omega(i)$ around a winning unit c. For instance the Gaussian function can be used as the neighbourhood function:

$$\Omega_c(i) = exp\left(-\frac{\|p_i - p_c\|^2}{2\sigma^2}\right) \tag{3}$$

where p_i and p_c are the positions of the output units i and c respectively, and σ reflects the scope of the neighbourhood.

After having defined the neighbourhood function we update the weight vector w_c of the selected neuron c and the weight vectors w_i of its neighbours according to the following formula:

$$\Delta w_i = \eta \Omega_c \left(i \right) \left(x - w_i \right) \tag{4}$$

Where η is the learning rate.

5. If neighbourhood function $\geq \epsilon$ goto 2 else stop.

4   Study Case System

The study case system is the model of the Greek mainland system projected to 2005. It comprises steam turbines, which produce the base load and almost 70% of the annual energy, hydro turbines which are used for peak load and frequency regulation and combined cycle units. The above units are represented to the model by 78 generators. The system is interconnected with the rest Balkan system with two 400 kV synchronous interconnections, one with Bulgaria and one with FYROM. The slack bus is considered to be the bus of the interconnection with FYROM (Voltage 408kV, angle 0 deg). There is also a new DC interconnection with Italy which connects the system directly to the European one. The peak load is about 10000 MW (estimate for summer 2005). The model includes the generation and transmission system up to 20 kV buses. The total number of buses is 876, there are 846 lines and 206 transformers.

5   Creation of the Knowledge Base

The application of Automatic Learning techniques is based on previous knowledge about the behaviour of the system, obtained from a large number of off-line dynamic simulations that define a data set. This data set is split into a Learning set (LS), used to derive security evaluation structures, and a Test Set used for testing the developed structures. The data set consists of a large number of operating points, covering the behaviour of the Power System in a region close to its peak loading, as the Hellenic Transmission System Operator (HTSO) estimates it for 2005. More specifically the region covered is between 91% and 110% of the maximum Load. The distribution of the total load of the system is the summation of 20 Gauss distributions with centres 91%,92%,...,110% of the maximum total load respectively. The production of each unit equals to the production of the unit when the system operates at maximum load, multiplied with the coefficient 91% to 110% respectively (as long as it is between its technical minimum and maximum). Each operation point is characterized by a vector of pre-disturbance steady-state variables, called attributes, that can be either directly measured (power, voltages, etc.) or indirectly calculated quantities (wind penetration, spinning reserve, etc.). The quality of the selected attributes and the representativity of the learning set are very important for the successful implementation of the classification.

For the creation of the data set a number of 4000 initial operating points are obtained by varying randomly the load for each bus in the area and the production of the generating units. The simulated disturbance is the loss of a combined cycle unit at Lavrio with 460 MW nominal active power. This disturbance can lead to dangerously low voltage levels, especially in the region of Athens. At the end of the simulation the voltage level in the buses of the area is recorded. It is desired that all voltages are above a security threshold which has be taken 0.9 of nominal voltage, otherwise the system operation is considered unsatisfactory.

Training is performed by random selection of the learning set, while the test set is the rest of the data set. In this way, the learning rate is checked and the capability of the method to classify correctly unforeseen states can be evaluated on a more objective basis.

6   Application of the Method

A 5×5 S.O.M. is utilized in order to classify the load profile of the Greek Power System. The load level of the 10 areas of the Greek Power System is used as the input vector for the construction of the S.O.M. Figure 3 shows the results of the mapping of the testing set onto the S.O.M. At each position of the map we can see the number of Operating Points that belong to that position, the number of Safe O.Ps and the number of Unsafe O.Ps.

We can distinguish three main areas of the map. The first area includes the positions of the map where the large majority of O.Ps are safe (positions 1, 2, 3,

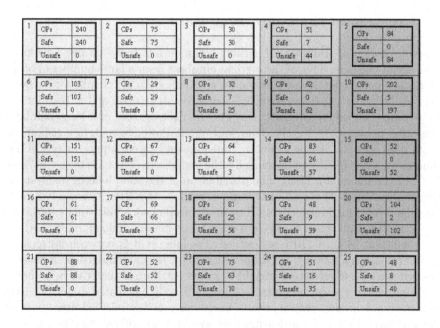

Fig. 3. Mapping of the Testing Set onto the S.O.M

6, 7, 11, 12, 13, 16, 17, 21, 22). When the load profile of the system is mapped onto one of these positions, then the state is assumed safe and there is no need for any corrective action. The second area comprises the positions of the map, where the large majority of O.Ps are unsafe (positions 5, 9, 10, 15, 20). When the load profile is mapped onto one of these positions, then the state is assumed to be unsafe and a corrective action (load shedding) must be followed in case of a contingency. The third area includes the positions of the map where there is no large majority neither of safe nor of unsafe OPs (positions 4, 8, 14, 18, 19, 23, 24, 25). When the load profile of the system is mapped onto one of these positions then no conclusion regarding the safety status of the system can be deduced. With the help of the D.T. method we can construct simple rules in order to determine if the system's state is safe or unsafe. The inputs of the D.T. are the voltage level of its buses.

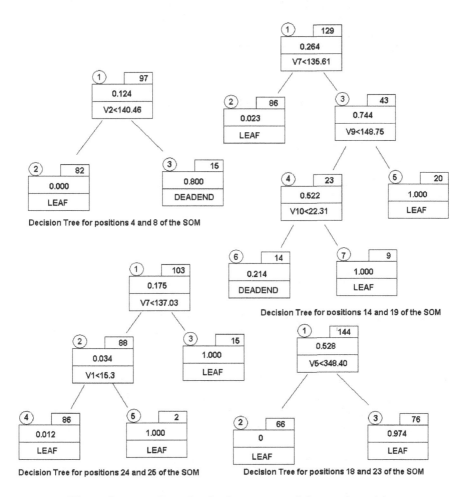

Fig. 4. Decision Trees for the four groups of the map's positions

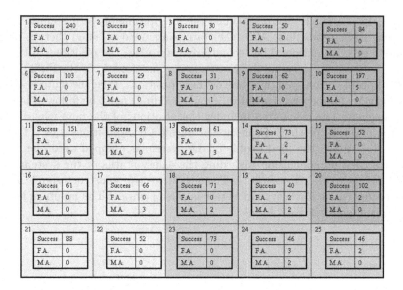

Fig. 5. Performance of the method for each position of the S.O.M.

Table 1. Evaluation of Two-Class Classification Performance

Classification of Test Set		
For TS=2000	Assessed as Safe	Assessed as Unsafe
Safe (1191)	1175	16
Unsafe (809)	18	791
DSA Performance Evaluation		
Success Rate	98.30% (1966/2000)	
False Alarms	1.34% (16/1191)	
Missed Alarms	2.22% (18/809)	

In figure 4 we can see the structure of the decision trees for each of the positions of the map. Instead of constructing a separate D.T. for each position of the map, four groups of adjacent positions (position 4 together with 8, 14 with 19, 18 with 23 and 24 with 25) have been formed, in order to have enough samples to train the D.Ts. After having derived the rules from the D.T., the model is evaluated using the testing set. Figure 5 illustrates the number of the Missed Alarms (M.A.), False Alarms (F.A.) and successfully predicted O.Ps, for each of the positions of the S.O.M. Table 1 illustrates the aggregate results of the D.S.A method.

6.1 Load Shedding Scheme

When the system's state is Unsafe corrective actions must follow a major contingency. In this paper the proposed corrective action is the curtailment of load, in

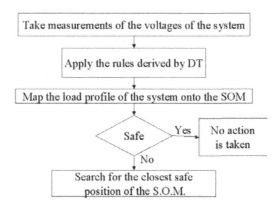

Fig. 6. Load shedding procedure

such a way that both the security of the system is not jeopardized and the economical and social impact is minimized. Figure 6 shows the procedure followed for each O.P.

The concept is rather simple: After having applied the rules derived from D.T., the S.O.M. is divided into two regions, the safe region and the unsafe one. For each O.P. the load profile of the system is mapped onto the S.O.M. If it is mapped onto the safe region, then no action is taken. In case it is mapped onto the unsafe region then a search algorithm finds the closest safe position. The difference between the load profile of the system and the feature weights of the selected position of the map is the load to be curtailed.

7   Conclusions

This paper describes a machine learning based method for the Dynamic Security Assessment of a Power System. The combination of Self Organizing Maps and Decision Trees is capable to evaluate with accuracy the dynamic performance of the Greek Power System. The S.O.M. and D.T. are trained fast, and it is easy to integrate the proposed method to the control centre. The main advantage of this DSA method compared to other machine learning methods (e.g. MLPs) is that it provides also a load shedding scheme, which can be applied when then system's security is in danger.

References

1. Carsten Leder Christian Rehtanz. Stability assessment of electric power systems using growing neural gas and self-organizing maps. *European Symposium on Artificial Neural Networks Bruges (Belgium)*, pages 401–406, 2000.
2. N. Hatziargyriou D. Georgiadis, E. Karapidakis. Application of machine learning technologies on the dynamic security of isolated power systems with large wind power penetration. *SETN Proceedings, Thessaloniki, Companion Volume*, pages 257–268, 2002.

3. Alain J. Germond Dagmar Niebur. Power system static security assessment using the kohonen neural network classifier. *IEEE Transactions on Power Systems*, 7(4):865–871, 1993.
4. P. Georgilakis and N. Hatziargyriou. On the application of artificial intelligence techniques to the quality improvement of industrial processes. *SETN Proceedings, Thessaloniki, LNAI 2308*, pages 473–484, 2002.
5. Pavella M. L.Wehenkel. Decision trees and transient stability of electric power systems. *Automatica*, 27(1):115–134, 1991.
6. Task Force 21 of Advisory Group 02 of Study Committee 38. Power system security assessment. *CIGRE Technical Brochure*, 2004.
7. G.K. Morison P. Kundur. A review of definitions and classification of stability problems in today's power systems. *presented at the panel session on Stability Terms and Definitions, IEEE PES Meeting, New York*, 1997.
8. L. Wehenkel. *Automatic Learning Techniques in Power Systems*. Kluwer Academics, 1998.

Towards Automatic Synthesis of Educational Resources Through Automated Planning

Dimitris Vrakas, Fotis Kokkoras, Nick Bassiliades, and Ioannis Vlahavas

Department of Informatics,
Aristotle University of Thessaloniki
{dvrakas, kokkoras, nbassili, vlahavas}@csd.auth.gr

Abstract. This paper reports on the results of an ongoing project for the development of a platform for e-Learning, which automatically constructs curricula based on available educational resources and the learners needs and abilities. The system under development, called PASER (Planner for the Automatic Synthesis of Educational Resources), uses an automated planner, which given the initial state of the problem (learner's profile, preferences, needs and abilities), the available actions (study an educational resource, take an exam, join an e-learning course, etc.) and the goals (obtain a certificate, learn a subject, acquire a skill, etc.) constructs a complete educational curriculum that achieves the goals. PASER is compliant with the evolving educational metadata standards that describe learning resources (LOM), content packaging (CP), educational objectives (RDCEO) and learner related information (LIP).

1 Introduction

The lack of widely adopted methods for searching the Web by content makes difficult for an instructor or learner to find educational material on the Web that addresses particular learning and pedagogical goals. Aiming at providing automation and personalization in searching and accessing educational material, as well as and interoperability among them, several education related standards have been developed. These standards concern recommended practices and guides for software components, tools, technologies and design methods that facilitate the development, deployment, maintenance and interoperation of computer implementations of educational components and systems.

As more educational e-content is becoming available on-line, the need for systems capable of automatically constructing personalized curricula by combining appropriate autonomous educational units (or learning objects, as they are called) is becoming more intense.

In this paper we report on an ongoing project for the development of such a system. The proposed system, called PASER (Planner for the Automatic Synthesis of Educational Resources) consists of a) a metadata repository storing learning object descriptions, learner profiles and ontological knowledge for the educational domain under consideration, b) a deductive object-oriented knowledge base system for querying and reasoning about RDF/XML metadata, called R-DEVICE and c) a planning system called HAP_{EDU} that automatically constructs course plans.

G. Antoniou et al. (Eds.): SETN 2006, LNAI 3955, pp. 421–431, 2006.

The rest of the paper is organized as follows: Section 2 previous related work on the area of automated course synthesis. Section 3 presents the overall architecture of the proposed system, whereas Sections 4 and 5 present in more detail its major subsystems. Finally, section 6 concludes the paper and poses future directions.

2   Related Work

Automatic course generation has been an active research field for almost two decades. One of the first attempts in creating an automatic system, using planning techniques for the synthesis of educational resources is the work by Peachy and McCalla [9], in which the learning material is structured in concepts and prerequisite knowledge is defined, which states the causal relationships between different concepts. Then they use planning techniques in order to find plans that achieve the learning goals and to monitor the outcomes of the plan.

Karampiperis and Sampson have carried a lot of research in the field of Instructional planning for Adaptive and Dynamic Courseware Generation. In a recent approach [8] they use ontologies and learning object metadata in order to calculate the best path through the learning material.

There are a number of systems that serve as course generators that automatically assemble learning objects retrieved from one or several repositories. These systems usually adopt the HTN planning framework ([4], [5]). In [10] Ulrich uses the JShop2 HTN planner in order to represent the pedagogical objectives as tasks and the ways of achieving the objects as methods in order to obtain a course structure. Similarly, Baldoni et al [1] propose a system for selecting and composing learning resources in the Semantic Web, using the SCORM framework for the representation of learning objects. The learning resources are represented in the knowledge level, in terms of prerequisites and knowledge supplied, in order to enable the use of automated reasoning techniques.

In [2], X-DEVICE, an intelligent XML repository system for educational metadata is presented. X-DEVICE can be used as the intelligent back-end of a WWW portal on which "learning objects" are supplied by educational service providers and accessed by learners according to their individual profiles and educational needs. X-DEVICE transforms the widely adopted XML binding for educational metadata into a flexible, object-oriented representation and uses intelligent second-order logic querying facilities to provide advanced, personalized functionality.

An older approach for a tool that generates individual courses according to the learner's goals and previous knowledge and dynamically adapts the course according to the learner's success in acquiring knowledge is DGC [11]. DGC uses "concept structures" as a road-map to generate the plan of the course.

3   System Architecture

PASER is a synergy of five processing modules (**Fig. 1**), namely a planner, an Ontology & Metadata Server, the R-DEVICE module and two data converters. The system, assumes the availability of three more metadata repositories that feed its modules with certain educational metadata. More specifically, there exists a LOM repository that stores metadata about the available learning objects, a repository of LIP compliant metadata describing the learners that have access to the system and an RDCEO metadata repository. The later provides competency definitions that are referenced by the other two. In addition, it is used by the Ontology & Metadata Server providing in this way a system-wide consistent competency vocabulary. We also assume that all metadata are checked by an expert user before they are entered in to the system. This may introduce additional workload but ensures that a common terminology and semantics are used in the enterprise or organization in which the system is installed.

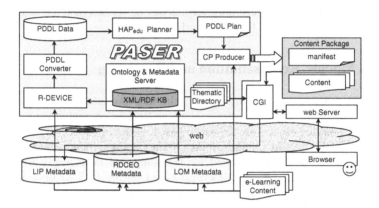

Fig. 1. PASER – System Architecture

We assume that the user is presented (by means of a web page) with a dictionary of themes for which the system may be able to provide educational material. The objective is to provide the user with a plan of activities (interactions with proper learning objects) that will "teach" him about the selected theme. As soon as the user selects a theme, the R-DEVICE module of PASER filters out the available learning objects based on a) the user's preferences and knowledge status, as they described in his LIP record and b) the PASER's understanding of the theme, as it is described in the Ontology & Metadata Server module. R-DEVICE [3] is a deductive object-oriented knowledge base system for querying and reasoning about RDF/XML metadata. It transforms RDF and/or XML documents into objects and uses a deductive rule language for querying and reasoning about them. The properties of RDF resources are treated both as first-class objects and as attributes of resource objects. In this way resource properties are gathered together in one object, resulting in superior query performance than the performance of a triple-based query model.

The output of R-DEVICE is a set of LOM objects (in R-DEVICE terminology) describing learning objects that are directly or indirectly related with the theme selected by the user. Based on these records and keeping only a limited subset of the LOM record elements, the PDDL converter module produces a description of the user's request as a planning problem, encoded in the PDDL language.

HAP$_{EDU}$ is a state – space planning system, based on the HAP planner [12] which is modified in order to implicitly support abstraction hierarchies that are needed in course planning problems.

The PDDL expressed plan produced by the HAP$_{edu}$ planner is forwarded to the CP producer module, which, in turn, creates a content packaging description (compliant to the CP metadata specification) of the learning objects involved in the plan. The produced CP record is finally forwarded to the user. Note that, at the current stage we do not take into account the performance of the user regarding the supplied educational material. In a later stage, assessment results should be taken into account in order to determine the learner's performance and update his LIP record accordingly. At the moment, we provide the user with a simple verification form, related to the material provided, in which he simply verifies that he studied (and learned) the material. This verification updates his LIP record, properly.

4 Data Models, Representation and Reasoning

The PASER system makes extensible use of the various educational metadata specifications developed in the recent years or being under development at the present time. Specifically, learning objects are described based on the IEEE LOM specification, as it is defined in the IMS Learning Resource Meta-Data specification [7]. The characteristics of a learner that are needed for recording and managing learning-related goals, accomplishments, etc. are described based on the IMS Learner Information Package. The XML binding of both specifications is used.

During the data preparation phase performed by the R-DEVICE module of PASER, a phase that will feed the planner with the appropriate data, extensible usage of the *classification* elements of LOM records is done. These elements allow the classification of the host LOM record based on competencies such as educational objectives and prerequisites. This can be formally established using the RDCEO specification. The latter is an emerging specification of an information model for describing, referencing and exchanging definitions of competencies, in the context of e-Learning. The same competency definitions are also used to describe the goals and accomplishments of the learner, in a controlled way. As a result, it is possible to

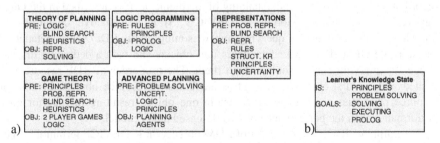

Fig. 2. Prerequisites and educational objectives of some, informally presented, learning objects (left) and initial knowledge state (IS) and learning objectives (GOALS) for a learner (right)

establish links between learning objects and between learning objects and characteristics of the learner. This information together with other constraints imposed over the learning objects due to the learner's preferences, are exploited by the R-DEVICE module, in order to filter out the learning object repository and keep only the "promising" objects. Informally encoded examples of the competency related information located in LOM and LIP metadata, are presented in **Fig. 2** (a) and (b), respectively. Additionally, a partial LOM record encoded in XML, which demonstrates the classification elements and their relation to competency definitions, is presented in Appendix A.

Finally, the same terms defined in the RDCEO metadata, are also organised as depicted in **Fig. 3**. This organisation allows the decomposition of learning objectives into sub-objectives. As a result, the system will be able to relate learning objects with learner objectives in various levels of granularity. Notice that the hierarchy of **Fig. 3** is a part-of hierarchy that is represented in a proprietary ontology of PASER, i.e. it is not represented directly in RDCEO because the latter does not allow the representation of hierarchical relationships.

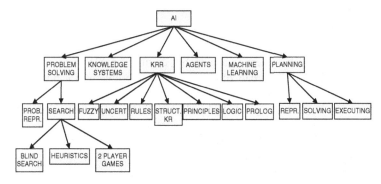

Fig. 3. Sample ontology for the Artificial Intelligence area

The following query filters out the LOM records: *"Find all learning objects that have as educational objective the learner's request or learning objects that have as educational objective the prerequisites of already selected learning objects. At the same time, ensure that all the constraints introduced by the learner's profile are met".*

These queries are formulated in R-DEVICE using deductive rules. An example of such rules follows. We assume that the learner's request is stored in R-DEVICE as objects of the form: (learner-request (competency <string>)). For example, if the user requested educational material for learning Prolog, the stored object will be: (learner-request (competency "Prolog")).

The R-DEVICE rules presented in **Fig. 4** perform the following:

- Rule r_1 keeps the IDs of LOMs that achieve learner requests.
- Rule r_2 recursively searches for prerequisite LOMs, from the already selected ones, and augments the learner requests.

The filtered set of metadata produced by R-DEVICE is transformed into PDDL and is fed to the planning module in order to find a course plan. The details concerning the planning system are presented in the following section. After the planner has constructed the course plan, the CP producer creates a "package" of e-learning content (encoded in XML) and forwards it to the learner.

```
(deductiverule r1
  (learner-request (competency ?comp))
  ?lom <- (lom ((value purpose classification) "Educational Objective")
              ((entry taxon taxonpath classification) ?comp))
  =>
  (result (lomid ?lom))
)
(deductiverule r2
  (result (lomid ?lom))
  ?lom <- (lom ((value purpose classification) "Prerequisite")
              ((entry taxon taxonpath classification) ?comp))
  =>
  (learner-request (competency ?comp))
)
```

Fig. 4. Example of querying the metadata using R-DEVICE deductive rules

5   The Planning System

The core of the PASER system is a planning engine capable of providing curricula that achieve the educational goals of the learner. The problem of synthesizing curricula from a database of educational resources, given the learners objectives and his current knowledge state can be considered as a planning problem and such a view enables the development of fully autonomous systems that generate course plans for each student separately, meeting his needs and capabilities.

A planning problem is usually modeled according to STRIPS (Stanford Research Institute Planning System) notation. A planning problem in STRIPS is a tuple $<I,A,G>$ where I is the Initial state, A a set of available actions and G a set of goals.

States in STRIPS are represented as sets of atomic facts. All the aspects of the initial state of the world, which are of interest to the problem, must be explicitly defined in I. State I contains both static and dynamic information. For example, I may declare that object John is a truck driver and there is a road connecting cities A and B (static information) and also specify that John is initially located in city A (dynamic information). State G on the other hand, is not necessarily complete. G may not specify the final state of all problem objects even because these are implied by the context or because they are of no interest to the specific problem. For example, in the logistics domain the final location of means of transportation is usually omitted, since the only objective is to have the packages transported. Therefore, there are usually many states that contain the goals, so in general, G represents a set of states rather than a simple state.

Set A contains all the actions that can be used to modify states. Each action A_i has three lists of facts containing:

- the preconditions of A_i (noted as $prec(A_i)$)
- the facts that are added to the state (noted as $add(A_i)$) and
- the facts that are deleted from the state (noted as $del(A_i)$).

The following formulae hold for the states in the STRIPS notation:

- An action A_i is applicable to a state S if prec(A_i) $\subseteq S$.
- If A_i is applied to S, the successor state S' is calculated as:
  $S' = S \setminus$ del(A_i)$\cup$add(A_i)
- The solution to such a problem is a sequence of actions, which if applied to I leads to a state S' such as $S' \supseteq G$.

Usually, in the description of domains, action schemas (also called operators) are used instead of actions. Action schemas contain variables that can be instantiated using the available objects and this makes the encoding of the domain easier.

5.1 Problem Representation

There may be a few alternatives in formalizing the problem of automatic synthesis of educational resources, as a planning problem. A straightforward solution that is adopted by PASER is the following:

a) The facts of the problem are the competencies defined in the ontology of the thematic area of interest.

b) A state in the problem is a set of competencies, describing the current knowledge state of the learner.

c) The initial state of the problem is the set of competencies currently mastered by the learner as described in the Learner Information Package.

d) The goals of the problem are defined as a set of competencies that the learner wishes to acquire, as defined in the Learner Information Package.

e) There are three operators in the definition of the problem:

- Consume an educational resource con(L), where L refers to the specific educational resource as described by the IEEE LOM standard. The preconditions of con(L) are the competencies described in the *Classification-prerequisite* field. Similarly, the add effects of con(L) are the competencies described in the *Classification-educational objective* field. The delete list of con(L) is empty.

- Analyze a goal anl(G), which consults the ontology in order to find a set of sub-goals Z that can replace G. This operator is similar to the *methods* in Hierarchical Task Network Planning ([4], [5]) and it is used in order to allow the definition of competencies in various abstraction levels. The precondition list of anl(G) contains only G. The add list contains the sub-goals in which G can be analyzed (Z) and the delete list contains G.

- Synthesize a set of goals sth(S), which consults the ontology in order to find a single goal that can replace a set of sub-goals S. This operator is opposite to anl(G) and is also used in order to allow the definition of competencies in various abstraction levels. The precondition list of anl(S) contains S. The add list contains the goal G which subsumes S and the delete list contains S.

Consider for instance, the example in **Fig. 3**. The specific problem is modeled as described in **Fig. 5**.

```
IS (Initial state) = [principles, problem solving]

G (Goals) = [solving, executing, prolog]

con(Theory of Planning): prec=[logic, blind search,
     heuristics], add=[repr, solving], del=∅

...

anl(ai): prec=[ai], add=[problem solving, knowledge systems,
     krr, agents, machine learning, planning], del=[ai]

...

sth(ai): prec=[problem solving, knowledge systems, krr,
     agents, machine learning, planning], add=[ai],
     del=[problem solving, knowledge systems, krr, agents,
     machine learning, planning]

...
```

Fig. 5. Educational request modeled as a planning problem

5.2 Translation to PDDL

PDDL (Planning Domain Definition Language) [6] is the standard language for encoding planning problems. The basic feature of PDDL is the separation of the domain data from the planning data. The domain describes a family of similar problems and contains all the information that is general and does not depend on the actual instance (problem). Technically, the domain consists of the definitions of the object classes, the relations (predicates) between the classes and the operators (actions with uninstantiated variables) of the domain. The problem on the other hand, contains the information for the specific objects that take part in the problem, the initial state and the goals of the problem.

One difficulty in translating a course planning problem to PDDL is the fact that although according to our representation there are only three operators, each action differs in the number of preconditions and effects, since this depends on the LOM that the action is considered to consume for example. Therefore, the process of creating a general operator for the consume family of actions is not straightforward.

One way to overcome this is to model the specific actions of the problem directly and feed the planner with this information, without modelling the domain in PDDL. However, this process is planner dependent and the PASER system will loose its modularity, as it won't be able to use a different planning module. Moreover, most planners, including HAP$_{EDU}$, have a pre-planning phase in which the domain is analyzed in order to extract information for the guiding mechanisms and this phase must be reorganized if not omitted in order to cope with direct action specifications.

The way to overcome the difficulty that was finally adopted by PASER is to use conditional effects, universal preconditions and explicit declaration of the relations in the definition of the domain. More specifically, the domain contains two classes, named Competency and LOM and the relations

- holds(?Competency): which states that a specific competency is true in a state
- requires(?LOM, ?Competency): which states that the Competency is required in order to consume the LOM
- adds(?LOM, ?Competency): which states that the Competency is learned by the learner after the consumption of the LOM.

- is-part-of(?Competency1,?Competency2): which states that Competency2 is a part of Competency1. This hierarchy information is extracted from the ontology and is used to define competencies in various levels of abstraction.

We suggestively provide the definition of the operator consume in PDDL:

```
(:action con:parameters(?LOM1)
 :precondition(and (LOM ?LOM1)
(forall (requires ?LOM1 ?Competency1) (holds ?Competency1)))
 :effect(and ((forall (?Competency2)
(when (adds ?LOM1 ?Competency2) (holds ?Competency2))))))
```

The definition above says that the operator con (consume) for a specific LOM can be consumed if all the competencies (universal precondition) that are required by the LOM hold in the current state. The operator uses conditional effects in order to state that all the competencies that are added by the LOM will hold in the successor state.

5.3 The HAP$_{EDU}$ Planner

The planning system that was embedded in PASER is called HAP$_{EDU}$, as already stated, is able to handle universal preconditions and conditional effects in a simple way, also adopted by the vast majority of the planning systems. Specifically, it fully instantiates the operators in a preliminary phase and uses the ground actions throughout the rest of the planning process. HAP$_{EDU}$ is a state – space planning system, based on the HAP planner [12] which is modified in order to implicitly support abstraction hierarchies that are needed in course planning problems.

The support for levels of abstraction is realized through actions that analyze competencies in their parts (operator anl) and synthesize higher-level competences from their parts (operator sth). Moreover the planning system must be aware of the existence of different abstraction levels in the encountered facts and deploy the appropriate logical tests in order to see whether for example the competencies required by a LOM are present in the current state. Following the example in **Fig. 3**, note that the LOM "REPRESENTATIONS" can be consumed although the competencies "PROB. REPR." and "BLIND SEARCH" are not included in the initial state, as they are parts of the "PROBLEM SOLVING" competency according to the ontology.

The HAP$_{EDU}$ system works in two phases. In the first phase the systems analyzes the problem structure in order to estimate the distances between all the problem's actions and the goals. The distance between a state S and an action A is merely the number of actions that need to be applied to S in order to reach another state S', in which the preconditions of A hold. The fact that the heuristic function of HAP$_{EDU}$ is based on distances of actions rather than facts enables it to keep better track of the various interactions between the facts, and therefore produce better estimates. In the second phase, the proposed heuristic is used by a regression planner employing a weighted A* search strategy and various other speedup mechanisms.

6 Conclusions

This paper presented PASER, a system aiming at augmenting the educational process in the e-Learning environment. PASER is able to store, manage and synthesize electronic educational material (learning objects) to provide personalized curricula to the learner. We presented the overall architecture of the system, focusing mainly in the core modules, namely the ontology and metadata repository, the knowledge base system that queries and reasons on these metadata and the planning sub-system responsible for synthesizing the curricula.

However, there are still many open design and implementation issues. As stated in the paper, the project is still in its early stages and although initial implementations of some sub-systems have been realized, there is a lot of work to be done. Additionally, there are design aspects that need further investigation in order to improve the system in terms of functionality and efficiency.

Acknowledgment

This work was partially supported by the PYTHAGORAS II program which is jointly funded by the Greek Ministry of Education (EPEAEK) and the European Union.

References

1. Baldoni, M. Baroglio, C., Patti, V., Torasso. L.: Reasoning about learning object metadata for adapting SCORM courseware. In L. Aroyo and C. Tasso, editors, *AH 2004: Workshop Proceedings, Part I, International Workshop on Engineering the Adaptive Web, EAW'04: Methods and Technologies for personalization and Adaptation in the Semantic Web*, Eindhoven, The Netherlands, August (2004): 4-13.
2. Bassiliades, N., Kokkoras, F., Vlahavas, I., Sampson, D.: An Intelligent Educational Metadata Repository. *Intelligent Systems, Techniques and Applications*, C.T. Leondes (ed.), Vol. 4, Ch. 12, 2003, pp. 297-337, CRC Press.
3. Bassiliades, N., Vlahavas, I.: R-DEVICE: A Deductive RDF Rule Language. *Workshop on Rules and Rule Markup Languages for the Semantic Web (RuleML 2004)*, Springer-Verlag, LNCS 3323, pp. 65-80, Hiroshima, Japan, 8 Nov. 2004.
4. Currie, K., Tate, A.: O-Plan: The Open Planning Architecture. *Artificial Intelligence*. Vol. 52(1) (1991) 46-86.
5. Erol, K., Hendler, J., Nau, D.: UMCP: A Sound and Complete Procedure for Hierarchical Task Network Planning. In *Proceedings of the 2nd International Conference on Planning Systems,* Chicago, Illinois (1994) 88-96.
6. Fox, M., Long, D.: PDDL2.1: An extension to PDDL for expressing temporal planning domains. *Journal of Artificial Intelligence Research*, Vol. 20 (2003) 61-124.
7. IMS Global Learning Consortium, Specifications, http://www.imsglobal.org/ specifications.html
8. Karampiperis, P., Sampson, D.: Adaptive instructional planning using ontologies. *Proc. of the 4th IEEE International Conference on Advanced Learning Technologies, ICALT 2004*, (2004) 126–130.
9. Peachy, D. R., Mc-Calla, G. I.: Using planning techniques in intelligent tutoring systems. *International Journal of Man-Machine Studies*, 24 (1986): 77–98.
10. Ullrich, C.: Course generation based on HTN planning. *Proc. 13th Annual Workshop of the SIG Adaptivity and User Modeling in Interactive Systems* (2005): 74-79.
11. Vassileva, J.: Dynamic Course Generation on the WWW. *Proc. 8th World Conf. on AI in Education (AI-ED97), Knowledge and Media in Learning Systems*, Kobe, Japan, 1997.
12. Vrakas, D. Tsoumakas, G., Bassiliades, N., Vlahavas, I.: HAPrc: An Automatically Configurable Planning System, *AI Communications*, 18 (1) (2005) 1-20.

Appendix A

Sample LOM record with reference to competency definitions (*classification* element)

```xml
<?xml version="1.0" encoding="UTF-8"?>
<lom xmlns="http://www...." ....>
  <general>
    <identifier>x-auth-id-v0.ZOE05-107-GR_1272</identifier>
    <title>
      <langstring xml:lang="en-US">Logic Programming</langstring>
    </title>
    <language>en</language>
  </general>
  <technical>
    <format>PDF</format>
    <location>gr_1272.html</location>
  </technical>
  <classification>
    <purpose>
      <source>
        <langstring xml:lang="x-none">LOMv1.0</langstring>
      </source>
      <value>
        <langstring xml:lang="x-none">Educational
Objective</langstring>
      </value>
    </purpose>
    <taxonpath>
      <source>
        <langstring xml:lang="x-
none">"http://www.auth.gr/competencies.xml</langstring>
      </source>
      <taxon>
        <id>definition2</id>
        <entry>
          <langstring xml:lang="en">Prolog</langstring>
        </entry>
      </taxon>
    </taxonpath>
  </classification>
  <classification>
    <purpose>
      <source>
        <langstring xml:lang="x-none">LOMv1.0</langstring>
      </source>
      <value>
        <langstring xml:lang="x-none">Educational
            Objective</langstring>
      </value>
    </purpose>
    <taxonpath>
      <source>
        <langstring xml:lang="x-
none">"http://www.auth.gr/competencies.xml</langstring>
      </source>
      <taxon>
        <id>definition3</id>
        <entry>
          <langstring xml:lang="en">Logic</langstring>
        </entry>
      </taxon>
    </taxonpath>
  </classification>
  <classification>
    <purpose>
      <source>
        <langstring xml:lang="x-none">LOMv1.0</langstring>
      </source>
      <value>
        <langstring xml:lang="x-none">Prerequisite</langstring>
      </value>
    </purpose>
    <taxonpath>
      <source>
        <langstring xml:lang="x-none">"http://www.auth.gr/
competencies.xml</langstring>
      </source>
      <taxon>
        <id>definition5</id>
        <entry>
          <langstring xml:lang="en">Rules</langstring>
        </entry>
      </taxon>
    </taxonpath>
  </classification>
  <classification>
    <purpose>
      <source>
        <langstring xml:lang="x-none">LOMv1.0 </langstring>
      </source>
      <value>
        <langstring xml:lang="x-none">Prerequisite </langstring>
      </value>
    </purpose>
    <taxonpath>
      <source>
        <langstring xml:lang="x-
none">"http://www.auth.gr/competencies.xml</langstring>
      </source>
      <taxon>
        <id>definition5</id>
        <entry>
          <langstring xml:lang="en">Principles</langstring>
        </entry>
      </taxon>
    </taxonpath>
  </classification>
</lom>
```

Towards Capturing and Enhancing Entertainment in Computer Games

Georgios N. Yannakakis and John Hallam

Maersk Institute for production Technology, University of Southern Denmark,
Campusvej 55, Odense M, DK-5230
{georgios, john}@mip.sdu.dk

Abstract. This paper introduces quantitative measurements/metrics of qualitative entertainment features within computer game environments and proposes artificial intelligence (AI) techniques for optimizing entertainment in such interactive systems. A human-verified metric of interest (i.e. player entertainment in real-time) for predator/prey games and a neuro-evolution on-line learning (i.e. during play) approach have already been reported in the literature to serve this purpose. In this paper, an alternative quantitative approach to entertainment modeling based on psychological studies in the field of computer games is introduced and a comparative study of the two approaches is presented. Artificial neural networks (ANNs) and fuzzy ANNs are used to model player satisfaction (interest) in real-time and investigate quantitatively how the qualitative factors of *challenge* and *curiosity* contribute to human entertainment. We demonstrate that appropriate non-extreme levels of challenge and curiosity generate high values of entertainment and we discuss the extensibility of the approach to other genres of digital entertainment and edutainment.

1 Introduction

Cognitive modeling within human-computer interactive systems is a prominent area of research. Computer games, as examples of such systems, provide an ideal environment for research in AI, because they are based on simulations of highly complex and dynamic multi-agent worlds [6, 3, 1], and cognitive modeling since they embed rich forms of interactivity between humans and non-player characters (NPCs). Being able to model the level of user (gamer) engagement or satisfaction in real-time can give insights to the appropriate AI methodology for enhancing the quality of playing experience [15] and furthermore be used to adjust digital entertainment (or edutainment) environments according to individual user preferences.

Motivated by the lack of quantitative cognitive models of entertainment, an endeavor on capturing player satisfaction during gameplay (i.e. entertainment modeling) and providing quantitative measurements of entertainment in real-time is introduced in the work presented here. This is achieved by following the theoretical principles of Malone's intrinsic qualitative factors for engaging gameplay [7], namely *challenge* (i.e. 'provide a goal whose attainment is uncertain'),

G. Antoniou et al. (Eds.): SETN 2006, LNAI 3955, pp. 432–442, 2006.

curiosity (i.e. *'what will happen next in the game?'*) and *fantasy* (i.e. *'show or evoke images of physical objects or social situations not actually present'*) and driven by the basic concepts of the theory of *flow* (*'flow is the mental state in which players are so involved in something that nothing else matters'*) [2]. Quantitative measures for challenge and curiosity are inspired by previous work on entertainment metrics [12] and extracted from the real-time player-opponent interaction. A mapping between the aforementioned factors and human notion of entertainment is derived using prey/predator games as an initial test-bed.

Two types of ANN, namely a feedforward ANN and a fuzzy-neural network (fuzzy-NN), are trained through artificial evolution on gameplay experimental data to approximate the function between the examined entertainment factors and player satisfaction. A comparison between the two methods is presented and the methods are validated against and compared with existing metrics of entertainment in the literature [13]. Results demonstrate that both NNs map a function whose qualitative features are consistent with Malone's corresponding entertainment factors and that the evolved ANN provides a more accurate model of player satisfaction for prey/predator games than previous models designed for this genre of games [12].

The generality of the proposed methodology and its extensibility to other genres of digital entertainment are discussed as well as its applicability as an efficient AI tool for enhancing entertainment in real-time is outlined.

2   Entertainment Modeling

The current state-of-the-art in machine learning in computer games is mainly focused on generating human-like [6] and intelligent [9] characters. Even though complex opponent behaviors emerge through various learning techniques, there is no further analysis of whether these behaviors contribute to the satisfaction of the player. In other words, researchers hypothesize — for instance by observing the vast number of multi-player on-line games played daily on the web — that by generating human-like opponents they enable the player to gain more satisfaction from the game. According to Taatgen et al. [11], believability of computer game opponents, which are generated through cognitive models, is strongly correlated with enjoyable games. These hypotheses might be true up to a point; however, since no notion of interest or enjoyment has been explicitly defined, there is no evidence that a specific opponent behavior generates enjoyable games. This statement is the core of Iida's work on entertainment metrics for variants of chess games [5].

Previous work in the field of entertainment modeling is based on the hypothesis that the player-opponent interaction — rather than the audiovisual features, the context or the genre of the game — is the property that primarily contributes the majority of the quality features of entertainment in a computer game [12]. Based on this fundamental assumption, a metric for measuring the real-time entertainment value of predator/prey games was established as an efficient and reliable entertainment ('interest') metric by validation against human judgement [16]. According to this approach, the three qualitative criteria that collectively define entertainment for any predator/prey game are: the appropriate level of challenge, the opponent behavior diversity and the opponents' spatial diversity. The quantifications of the three criteria provide an estimate — called the I (interest) value, that lies in $[0,1]$ — of real-time entertainment which correlates highly with the human notion of entertainment [16].

As in [12], this paper is primarily focused on the opponents' behavior contributions to the entertainment value of the game since the computer-guided opponent characters contribute to the majority of qualitative features that make a game interesting [7]. However, the work presented here (as an alternative approach to the interest metric introduced in [12]) instead of being based on empirical observations on human entertainment, attempts to introduce quantitative measures for Malone's entertainment factors of challenge and curiosity and extract the mapping between the two aforementioned factors and the human notion of entertainment based on experimental data from a survey with human players (see Section 4).

3   The Test-Bed Game

The test-bed studied is a modified version of the original Pac-Man computer game released by Namco. The player's (*PacMan's*) goal is to eat all the pellets appearing in a maze-shaped stage while avoiding being killed by the four *Ghosts*. The game is over when either all pellets in the stage are eaten by *PacMan*, *Ghosts* manage to kill *PacMan* or a predetermined number of simulation steps is reached without any of the above occurring. In that case, the game restarts from the same initial positions for all five characters. While *PacMan* is controlled by humans, a multi-layered feedforward neural controller is employed to manage the *Ghosts'* motion.

The game is investigated from the opponents' viewpoint and more specifically how the *Ghosts'* adaptive behaviors and the levels of challenge and curiosity they generate can collectively contribute to player satisfaction. The game field (i.e. stage) consists of corridors and walls where both the stage's dimensions and its maze structure are predefined. For the experiments presented in this paper we use a 19×29 grid maze-stage where corridors are 1 grid-cell wide (see [14] for more details on the Pac-Man game design).

We choose predator/prey games as the initial genre of our research in entertainment modeling since, given our aims, they provide us with unique properties. In such games we can deliberately abstract the environment and concentrate on the characters' behavior. Moreover, we are able to easily control a learning process through on-line interaction. Other genres of game (e.g. first person shooters) offer similar properties; however predator/prey games are chosen for their simplicity as far as their development and design are concerned.

4   Experimental Data

The Pac-Man game has been used to acquire data of human judgement on entertainment. To that end, thirty players (43% females, 56% males and 90% Danish, 10% Greek nationality) whose age covered a range between 17 and 51 years participated in a survey [16]. According to this survey, each subject plays a set of 25 games against each of two well-behaved opponents (A and B). In order to minimize any potential of order effects we let each subject play the aforementioned sets in the inverse order too. Each time a pair of sets is finished, the player is asked whether the first set of games was more interesting than the second set of games i.e. whether A or B generated a more interesting game.

An analysis on the subjects' answers shows that the order effect is not statistically significant. Therefore, if the subject's answers in both pairs played in inverse order are not consistent then it is assumed that the two sets of games generate entertainment of non-significant difference. In the opposite situation, it is assumed that the chosen set generates higher entertainment than the non-chosen set. Thus, the total number of comparisons between sets of games equals the number of subjects ($N_s = 30$).

In order to cross-validate the I value against human notion of entertainment, subjects in this survey played against five opponents differing in the I value they generate against a well-behaved computer-programmed player in all combinations of pairs (see [12]). The correlation between human judgement of entertainment and the I value is given by matching the entertainment rankings in which the five opponents are placed by humans and by I value. According to the subjects' answers the I value is correlated highly with human judgement ($r = 0.4444$, p-value $= 1.17 \cdot 10^{-8}$ — see [16]). These five opponents will be used as a baseline for validating both approaches in this paper (see Section 6).

Given the recorded values of human playing times t_k over the 50 (2 times 25) games against a specific opponent, A or B, the average playing time ($E\{t_k\}$) and the standard deviation of playing times ($\sigma\{t_k\}$) for all subjects are computed. We consider the $E\{t_k\}$ and $\sigma\{t_k\}$ values as appropriate measures to represent the level of challenge and the level of curiosity respectively [7] during gameplay. The former provides a notion for a goal whose attainment is uncertain — the lower the $E\{t_k\}$ value, the higher the goal uncertainty and furthermore the higher the challenge — and the latter effectively portrays a notion of unpredictability in the subsequent events of the game — the higher the $\sigma\{t_k\}$ value the higher the opponent unpredictability and therefore the higher the curiosity.

5   Tools

Two alternative neural network structures (a feedforward ANN and a fuzzy-NN) for learning the relation between the challenge and curiosity factors and the entertainment value of a game have been used and are presented here. The pair ($E\{t_k\}$, $\sigma\{t_k\}$) constitutes the input vector and the human judgement of entertainment constitutes the output value for both types of neural network used. Learning is achieved through artificial evolution and is described in Section 5.1.

5.1   Genetic Algorithm

A generational genetic algorithm (GA) [4] is implemented, which uses an "exogenous" evaluation function that promotes the minimization of the difference in matching the human judgement of entertainment. The ANNs and fuzzy-NNs are themselves evolved. In the algorithm presented here, the evolving process is limited to the connection weights of the ANN and the rule weights and membership function parameters of the fuzzy-NN.

The evolutionary procedure used can be described as follows. A population of N networks is initialized randomly. For ANNs, initial real values that lie within [-5, 5] for their connection weights are picked randomly from a uniform distribution, whereas for the fuzzy-NNs, initial rule weight values equal 0.5 and their membership function parameter values lie within [0, 1] (uniformly distributed). Then, at each generation:

Step 1. Each member (neural network) of the population gets two pairs of $(E\{t_k\}, \sigma\{t_k\})$ values one for A and one for B and returns two output values, namely $y_{j,A}$ (output of the game against opponent A) and $y_{j,B}$ (output of the game against opponent B) for each pair j of sets played in the survey ($N_s = 30$). When the $y_{j,A}$, $y_{j,B}$ values are consistent with the judgement of subject j then we state that: 'the values agree with the subject' throughout this paper. In the opposite case, we state that: 'the values disagree with the subject.'

Step 2. Each member i of the population is evaluated via the fitness function f_i:

$$f_i = \sum_{j=1}^{N_s} \begin{cases} 1, \text{ if } y_{j,A}, y_{j,B} \text{ agree with subject } j; \\ \left(\frac{1- y_{j,A}-y_{j,B}}{2}\right)^2, \text{ if } y_{j,A}, y_{j,B} \text{ disagree with subject } j. \end{cases} \tag{1}$$

Step 3. A fitness-proportional scheme is used as the selection method.

Step 4. Selected parents clone an equal number of offspring so that the total population reaches N members or reproduce offspring by crossover. The Montana and Davis [8] and the uniform crossover operator is applied for ANNs and fuzzy-NNs respectively with a probability $p_c = 0.4$.

Step 5. Gaussian mutation occurs in each gene (connection weight) of each offspring's genome with a small probability $p_m = 1/n$, where n is the number of genes.

The algorithm is terminated when either a good solution (i.e. $f_i > 29.0$) is found or a large number of generations g is completed ($g = 10000$).

5.2   Feedforward ANN

A fully-connected multi-layered feedforward ANN has been evolved [17] for the experiments presented here. The sigmoid function is employed at each neuron, the connection weights take values from -5 to 5 and both input values are normalized into [0, 1] before they are entered into the ANN. In an attempt to minimize the controller's size, it was determined that single hidden-layered ANN architectures, containing 20 hidden neurons, are capable of successfully obtaining solutions of high fitness (network topology is not evolved, however).

5.3 Fuzzy-ANN

A fuzzy [18] Sugeno-style [10] inference neural network is trained to develop fuzzy rules by evolving the memberships functions for both the input ($E\{t_k\}$, $\sigma\{t_k\}$) and the output variable y of the network as well as each fuzzy rule's weight. Each of the input and output values is presented by five fuzzy sets corresponding to very low, low, average, high and very high. The membership functions for the input values are triangular and their center α and width β are evolved whereas the output fuzzy sets use singleton membership functions [10] — only the center α of the spike membership function is evolved. The centroid technique is used as a defuzzification method.

6   Results

Results obtained from both ANN and fuzzy-NN evolutionary approaches are presented in this section. In order to diminish the non-deterministic effect of the GA initialization phase, we repeat the learning procedure for each NN type ten times — we believe that this number is adequate to illustrate a clear picture of the behavior of each mechanism — with different random initial conditions.

6.1   Evolving ANN

For space considerations, only the two fittest solutions achieved from the evolving ANN approach are illustrated in Fig. 1. The qualitative features of the surfaces plotted in Fig. 1 appeared in all ten learning attempts. The most important conclusions derived from the ANN mapping between $E\{t_k\}$, $\sigma\{t_k\}$ and entertainment are that:

- Entertainment has a low value when challenge is too high ($E\{t_k\} \approx 0$) and curiosity is low ($\sigma\{t_k\} \approx 0$).
- Even if curiosity is low, if challenge is at an appropriate level ($0.2 < E\{t_k\} < 0.6$), the game's entertainment value is high.
- If challenge is too low ($E\{t_k\} > 0.6$), the game's entertainment value appears to drop, independently of the level of curiosity.
- There is only a single data point present when $\sigma\{t_k\} > 0.8$ and the generalization of the evolved ANNs within this space appears to be poor. Given that only one out of 60 different gameplay data paoints falls in that region of the $E\{t_k\}$-$\sigma\{t_k\}$ two-dimensional space, we can hypothesize that there is low probability for a game to generate curiosity values higher than 0.8. Thus, this region can be safely considered insignificant for these experiments. However, more samples taken from a larger gameplay survey would be required to effectively validate this hypothesis.

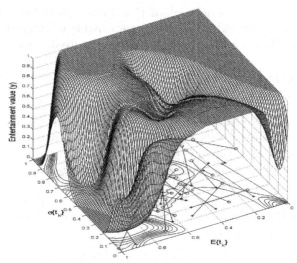

(a) The fittest ANN solution ($f = 29.95$).

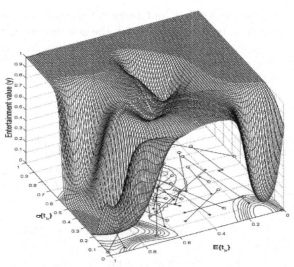

(b) The second fittest ANN solution ($f = 29.67$).

Fig. 1. Circles ('o') and stars ('*') represent $E\{t_k\}$, $\sigma\{t_k\}$ values obtained by playing against opponents A and B respectively. Straight lines are used to connect the sets of games that humans played in pairs.

The fittest evolved ANN is tested against the human-verified I value for cross-validation purposes. The ANN ranks the five different opponents previously mentioned in Section 4 in the order $I_1 = I_2 < I_4 < I_3 < I_5$ (where I_i is the entertainment value the i opponent generates) which yields a correlation of 0.5432 (p-value = $3.89533 \cdot 10^{-12}$) of agreement with human notion of entertainment. Given this ranking of entertainment against these five opponents, the ANN approach appears to model human entertainment better than the interest metric proposed in [12] ($r = 0.4444$, p-value $= 1.17 \cdot 10^{-8}$).

The correlation between entertainment, challenge and curiosity generated through the evolved ANN appears to follow the qualitative principles of Malone's work [7] and the human-verified interest metric developed in our previous work [12] for prey/predator games. According to these, a game should maintain an appropriate level of challenge and curiosity in order to be entertaining. In other words, too difficult and/or too easy and/or too unpredictable and/or too predictable opponents to play against make the game uninteresting.

6.2 Evolving Fuzzy-NN

The evolutionary procedure for the fuzzy-NN approach is also repeated ten times and only the fuzzy-NN that generates the highest fitness ($f = 29.81$) is presented for space considerations. Twenty five fuzzy rules are initially designed based on the conclusions derived from the evolved ANNs. The fittest fuzzy-NN generates 19 fuzzy rules in total — rules with weight values less than 0.1 are not considered significant and therefore are excluded from further consideration — which are presented here with their corresponding weight values w:

- Entertainment is *very low* if (a) challenge is *very high* and curiosity is *low* (Rule 1; $w_1 = 0.4440$) and (b) challenge is *low* and curiosity is *average* (Rule 2; $w_2 = 0.3617$).
- Entertainment is *low* if (a) challenge is *very low* and curiosity is *average* (Rule 3; $w_3 = 0.9897$) or *low* (Rule 4; $w_4 = 0.7068$); (b) challenge is *low* and curiosity is *high* (Rule 5; $w_5 = 0.7107$); (c) challenge is *high* and curiosity is *very low* (Rule 6; $w_6 = 0.5389$) and (d) challenge is *very high* and curiosity is *very low* (Rule 7; $w_7 = 0.9520$) or *high* (Rule 8; $w_8 = 0.9449$).
- Entertainment is *average* if challenge is *very low* and curiosity is *high* (Rule 9; $w_9 = 0.5818$).
- Entertainment is *high* if (a) challenge is *low* and curiosity is *very low* (Rule 10; $w_{10} = 0.8498$) or *very high* (Rule 11; $w_{11} = 0.2058$); (b) challenge is *average* and curiosity is *low* (Rule 12; $w_{12} = 0.5$); (c) challenge is *high* and curiosity is *low* (Rule 13; $w_{13} = 0.2824$) or *average* (Rule 14; $w_{14} = 0.25$) and (d) challenge is *very high* and curiosity is *average* (Rule 15; $w_15 = 0.2103$).
- Entertainment is *very high* if (a) challenge is *very low* and curiosity is *very high* (Rule 16; $w_{16} = 0.7386$); (b) challenge is *average* and curiosity is *very low* (Rule 17; $w_{17} = 0.5571$) or *very high* (Rule 18; $w_18 = 0.8364$) and (c) challenge is *high* and curiosity is *high* (Rule 19; $w_{19} = 0.2500$).

The quantitative means of entertainment achieved through the neuro-fuzzy approach and the majority of the fuzzy rules generated appear to follow Malone's principles on challenge and curiosity, the empirical contributions of the interest metric from the literature [16] as well as the fittest ANN presented in Section 6.1. However, the fittest fuzzy-NN (being less fit than the fittest ANN) generates some few fuzzy rules that are not consistent with the aforementioned principles — e.g. Rule 10: entertainment is *high* if challenge is *low* and curiosity is *very low*. It is not clear whether the poorer performance is intrinsic to the method or a result of unlucky initialization; further tests are needed to distinguish these alternatives.

The fuzzy-NN is tested against the human-verified I value as in the evolved ANN approach. The evolved fuzzy-NN ranks the five opponents in the order $I_2 < I_1 < I_3 < I_4 = I_5$. This ranking demonstrates a correlation of 0.3870 (p-value $= 1.74006 \cdot 10^{-6}$) of agreement with human notion of entertainment which appears to be lower than the correlation achieved through the I value proposed in [12] ($r = 0.4444$, p-value $= 1.17 \cdot 10^{-8}$). However, as in the ANN approach, the generalization of the evolved fuzzy-NNs appears to be poor when $\sigma\{t_k\} > 0.8$ due to the presence of a single data point within this region of the $E\{t_k\}$-$\sigma\{t_k\} > 0.8$ two-dimensional space. Even though we consider this non-frequent region as insignificant as far as this work is concerned, it may be sampled from a more extensive human game experiment in a future study.

7   Conclusions

This paper introduced quantitative metrics for entertainment primarily based on the qualitative principles of Malone's intrinsic factors for engaging gameplay [7]. More specifically, the quantitative impact of the factors of challenge and curiosity on human entertainment were investigated through a prey/predator game.

The two neuro-evolution approaches for modeling entertainment in real-time examined demonstrate qualitative features that share principles with the interest metric (I value) introduced in [12]. Both approaches manage to map successfully between the entertainment factors of challenge and curiosity and the notion of human gameplay satisfaction. Moreover, validation results obtained show that the fittest feedforward ANN gets closer to human notion of entertainment than both the I value [16] and the fittest fuzzy-NN. Therefore, it appears that solely the average and the standard deviation of a human's playing time over a number of games are adequate and more effective than the I value (as reported in [16]) in capturing player entertainment in real-time in prey/predator games.

The current work is limited by the number of participants in the game survey we devised. Therefore, not all regions of the challenge-curiosity search space were sampled by human play which therefore yielded poor NN generalization for these regions. Limited data also restricted the sensible number of inputs to the learning system. Moreover, Malone's entertainment factor of fantasy is omitted in this paper since the focus is on the contribution of the opponent behaviors to the generation of entertainment; however, it needs to be explored in our future game test-bed experiment designs.

The entertainment modeling approach presented here demonstrates generality over the majority of computer game genres since the quantitative means of challenge and curiosity are estimated through a generic feature of gameplay which is the playing time of humans over a number of games. Thus, these or similar measures could be used to adjust player satisfaction in any genre of game. However, each game demonstrates individual entertainment features that might need to be extracted and added on the proposed measures and therefore, more games of the same or other genres need to be tested to cross-validate this hypothesis.

Both approaches can be used for adaptation of the opponents according to the player's individual playing style and as far as the challenge and curiosity factors of entertainment are concerned. The key to this is the observation that the models (ANN or fuzzy-NN) relate game features to entertainment value. It is therefore possible in principle to infer what changes to game features will cause an increase in the interestingness of the game, and to adjust game parameters to make those changes. For the ANN, the partial derivatives of $\vartheta y/\vartheta E\{t_k\}$ and $\vartheta y/\vartheta \sigma\{t_k\}$ indicate the change in entertainment for a small change in an individual game feature. One could use gradient ascent to attempt to improve entertainment with such a model. The fuzzy-NN approach provides qualitative rules relating game features to entertainment, rather than a quantitative function, but an analogous process could be applied to augment game entertainment.

Such a direction constitutes an example of future work within computer, physical and educational games. The level of engagement or motivation of the user/player/gamer of such interactive environments can be increased by the use of the presented approaches. Apart from providing systems of richer interaction and qualitative entertainment [15], such approaches can generate augmented motivation of the user for deep learning in learning environments that use games (i.e. edutainment).

References

1. Champandard, A. J.: AI Game Development. New Riders Publishing (2004)
2. Csikszentmihalyi, M.: Flow: The Psychology of Optimal Experience. New York: Harper & Row (1990)
3. Funge, J. D.: Artificial Intelligence for Computer Games. A. K. Peters Ltd (2004)
4. Holland, J. H.: Adaptation in Natural and Artificial Systems. University of Michigan Press (1975)
5. Iida, H., Takeshita, N., Yoshimura, J.: A Metric for Entertainment of Boardgames: its implication for evolution of chess variants. IWEC2002 Proceedings, Kluwer (2003) 65–72
6. Laird, J. E., van Lent M.: Human-level AI's Killer Application: Interactive Computer Games. Proceedings of the 7th National Conf. on AI, (2000) 1171–1178
7. Malone, T W.: What makes computer games fun? Byte (1981) 6:258–277
8. Montana, D. J., Davis, L. D.: Training feedforward neural networks using genetic algorithms. Proceedings of the 11th IJCAI, Morgan Kauffman (1989) 762–767
9. Nareyek, A.: Intelligent Agents for Computer Games. Computers and Games, Second International Conference, Springer (2002) 414–422
10. Sugeno, M.: Indstrial Applicatios of Fuzzy Control. North-Holland (1985)
11. Taatgen, N. A., van Oploo, M., Braaksma, J., Niemantsverdriet, J.: How to construct a believable opponent using cognitive modeling in the game of set. Proceedings of the fifth international conference on cognitive modeling (2003) 201–206

12. Yannakakis, G. N., Hallam, J.: Evolving Opponents for Interesting Interactive Computer Games. From Animals to Animats 8: Proceedings of the 8th International Conference on Simulation of Adaptive Behavior, The MIT Press (2004) 499–508
13. Yannakakis, G. N., Hallam, J.: A Generic Approach for Obtaining Higher Entertainment in Predator/Prey Computer Games. Journal of Game Development (2005) 3(1):23–50
14. Yannakakis, G. N., Hallam, J.: A Generic Approach for Generating Interesting Interactive Pac-Man Opponents. Proceedings of the IEEE Symposium on Computational Intelligence and Games (2005) 94–101
15. Yannakakis, G. N., Hallam, J.: A Scheme for Creating Digital Entertainment with Substance. Proceedings of the Workshop on Reasoning, Representation, and Learning in Computer Games, 19th IJCAI (2005) 119–124
16. Yannakakis, G. N., Hallam, J.: Towards Optimizing Entertainment in Computer Games. Applied Artificial Intelligence (June 2005) submitted
17. Yao, X.: Evolving Artificial Neural Networks. Proceedings of the IEEE (1999) 87:1423–1447
18. Zadeh, L.: Fuzzy Sets. Information and Control (1965) 8:338–353

Employing Fujisaki's Intonation Model Parameters for Emotion Recognition

Panagiotis Zervas, Iosif Mporas, Nikos Fakotakis, and George Kokkinakis

Wire Communication Laboratory, Electrical and Computer Engineering Dept.,
University of Patras, 26110 Rion, Patras, Greece
{pzervas, imporas, fakotaki, gkokkin}@wcl.ee.upatras.gr

Abstract. In this paper we are introducing the employment of features extracted from Fujisaki's parameterization of pitch contour for the task of emotion recognition from speech. In evaluating the proposed features we have trained a decision tree inducer as well as the instance based learning algorithm. The datasets utilized for training the classification models, were extracted from two emotional speech databases. Fujisaki's parameters benefited all prediction models with an average raise of 9,52% in the total accuracy.

1 Introduction

Extensive research has been conducted lately, regarding speech recognition in the presence of emotional speech, synthesis of emotional speech and emotion recognition. Concerning emotion recognition, it aims to the detection of the emotional state of a speaker from speech samples. For the task of robust emotion recognition, scientists usually perform either facial expression analysis or speech analysis. An extensive number of experiments have been conducted using signal processing techniques to explore which particular aspects of speech would manifest saliently the emotional condition of a speaker. The outcome of this research was that the most crucial aspects are those related to prosody [1], [2] (pitch contour, intensity and timing). Furthermore, voice quality [3] and certain co-articulatory phenomena [4] are high correlated with some emotional states.

In the present study we focus on the prediction of basic emotion categories based on knowledge extracted only from speech signals. Specifically, we present the exploitation of features carrying information regarding intonation and speaking style of a spoken sentence for the task of emotion recognition. For this purpose prosodic knowledge was extracted from the quantification of F0 contour derived from Fujisaki's model [5] of intonation. This model is based on the fundamental assumption that intonation curves, although continuous in time and frequency, originate in discrete events triggered by the speaker that appear as a continuum given physiological mechanisms related to fundamental frequency control. The model has been applied to several languages and good approximations of F0 contours have been presented. Fujisaki's representation of F0 is realized as the superposition of phrase and accent effects.

G. Antoniou et al. (Eds.): SETN 2006, LNAI 3955, pp. 443–453, 2006.

The outline of this paper is as follows. Initially we present a brief description of Fujisaki's model of intonation. In section 2 we present the methodology followed for the feature extraction from the utilized databases as well as the construction of the classification framework. Finally, we present and discuss the results of our evaluation.

2 Fujisaki's Model of Intonation

Fujisaki's model is the continuation of Ohman' s work [6] on the prosody of words. It is based on the fundamental assumption that intonation curves, although continuous in time and frequency, originate in discrete events triggered by the reader that appear as a continuum given physiological mechanisms related to F0 control, figure 1.

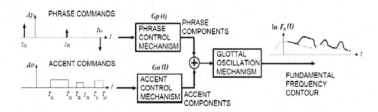

Fig. 1. Fujisaki's model for F0 contour generation

Unlike all other approaches for describing F0 contours, the Fujisaki model aims at modeling the generation process of F0 by giving an explanation on the physical and physiological properties behind it. The model generates F0 contours in the logF0 domain. The logarithm of the fundamental frequency contour is modeled superposing the output of two second order critically damped filters and a constant base frequency. One filter is excited with deltas (phrase commands), and the other with pulses (accent commands). With the technique of Analysis-by-Synthesis a given F0 contour is decomposed into its constituents (phrase and accent commands) and estimate the magnitude timing of their underlying commands by deconvolution. Equation 1 describes this relationship mathematically,

$$\ln F_0(t) = \ln F_b + \sum_{i=1}^{I} A_{pi} G_{pi}(t-T_{0i}) + \sum_{j=1}^{J} A_{aj}\{G_{aj}(t-T_{1j}) - G_{aj}(t-T_{2j})\} \tag{1}$$

F_b is the baseline value of fundamental frequency, I the number of phrase commands, J the number of accent commands, A_{pi} the magnitude of the i_{th} phrase command, A_{aj} the amplitude of the j_{th} accent command, T_{0i} the timing of the i_{th} phrase command, T_{1j} the onset of the j_{th} accent command and T_{2j} the end of the j_{th} accent command. The output of the second order filters, described in equations 2 and 3, will provide the accent and phrase components of the pitch contour representation.

$$Gp_i(t) = \begin{cases} a^2 t e^{-at}, & t \geq 0 \\ 0, & t < 0 \end{cases} \qquad (2)$$

$$Ga_j(t) = \begin{cases} \min[1-(1+\beta_j t)e^{-\beta t}, \gamma], & t \geq 0 \\ 0, & t < 0 \end{cases} \qquad (3)$$

$G_{pi}(t)$ represents the impulse response function of the phrase control mechanism and $G_{aj}(t)$ the step response function of the accent control mechanism as shown in figure 1, α the natural angular frequency of the phrase control mechanism, β the natural angular frequency of the accent control mechanism and γ the relative ceiling level of accent components. All the above parameters (timing of commands, their amplitudes as well as phrase and accent components) henceforth will be referred to as "Fujisaki-parameters". For the analysis of our data we have selected a value for *Fb* equal to the corpus-mean value yielded in the analysis. Concerning the time constants α and β they were chosen equal to 1.7 and 20 respectively. Furthermore, the parameter γ was set equal to 0.9.

3 Methodology

In this section the emotion classification framework of our endeavor will be described. It is consisted of the feature extraction and the classification stage. For the analysis of the proposed intonational features, experiments were conducted with the exploitation of two emotional speech databases. Both databases are composed of four emotions and a neutral session.

3.1 Speech Data

Initially, a Greek emotional speech (GrES) database [7] constructed in Wire Communication laboratory (WCL), was utilized. For the choice of the emotional states that were included in the database we have built upon the work of Oatley [8]. Therefore in our recordings we tried to capture the emotions of happiness, anger, sadness, fear plus a neutral session. A professional actress familiar with Radio Theater was employed for the enunciation of the text corpus. The thirty years old speaker had the standard Greek accent as spoken in Athens and has been a professional actress for almost ten years. To avoid the interference of a listener's decision on the emotional contents due to semantically meaning, we attempted to construct semantically neutral sentences. The use of identical utterances spoken with different expressive content was designed to normalize out the effects of non-expressive meaning in the utterances. The actress was asked to use her every day way of emotional expression and not an exaggerated theatrical approach. She was instructed to read all the utterances with one emotion then change it and start over again. In that way we assured that the speaker did not have to change emotion more than five times (expressing anger, joy, neutral, sadness, fear and neutral).

Secondly, a Danish emotional speech (DES) [9] corpus was employed; in this database the text corpus has been expressed with five basic emotional states, such as anger, happiness, neutral, sadness, and surprise by four speakers, two male and two female.

3.2 Features and Datasets

Appropriate acoustic feature selection is an important step in emotion recognition. In the proposed approach we have initially calculated eighteen basic acoustic features *(Basic set)* and secondly we have extracted features from Fujisaki's model of intonation *(Fujisaki set)*. The features that were extracted from both databases were such that they would not require prior segmentation of the speech data; thus, they could be obtained from raw speech data easily and would not need the inclusion of any phoneme recognizer in a real time application.

Previous research in the field of emotion recognition has shown that emotional reactions are strongly related to the pitch and energy of the spoken message. For example, the pitch of speech associated with anger or happiness is always higher than that associated with sadness or fear, and the energy associated with anger is greater than that associated with fear. As in similar research, in this study we adopt pitch and energy features for the construction of our datasets. Thus, our *basic set* of features consists of, F0 values in the logF domain *(logF0)*, the deltas of the pitch contour *(dlogF0)* extracted from speech, the first *(F1)* and second *(F2)* formant of the signal, the thirteen first Mel frequency cepstral coefficients *(MFCCs)* and the difference of energy *(dEnrg)* per frame. Pitch contour and formant frequency estimation was conducted with the utilization of Praat [10] software. A 256 sample window and 128 sample frame shift was employed; pitch frequencies were assumed to be limited to the range of 60-320 Hz for both male and female data. The calculation of the thirteen MFCC parameters was carried out from [11]; a total of 40 filters and a 512 samples FFT size were applied for the calculation.

On the other hand, *Fujisaki's set* consists of four novel features derived from Fujisaki's Analysis-by-Synthesis parameterization of pitch. The features extracted from Fujisaki's model are the phrase component *(PhrComp)*, the accent component *(AccComp)* per frame as well as the pitch resulted from Fujisaki's synthesis *(FujLogF0)* and the deltas of the resulted pitch contour *(dFujLogF0)*. We have used the *FujLogF0* as well as the *dFujLogF0* in order to take advantage of its smooth (no discontinuities) contour. With the application of Fujisaki's model we tried to benefit from the fact that phrase commands are related to the slow varying component of intonation while the accent commands are related to fast changes. In that way, changes in prosody due to different emotional state could be exposed more straightforward. For Fujisaki's parameters extraction we have utilized the freely available implementation of [12]. The datasets extracted from both databases contain only feature vectors corresponding to the voiced parts of the signal.

3.3 Emotion Recognition Classification Stage

The classification stage of our emotion recognition framework consists of two classifiers the C4.5 tree inducer and an implementation of instance base learning.

Both algorithms were acquired from the WEKA machine learning library [13] with a configuration resulted after a broad number of experiments with the resulted datasets. In the following subsections a brief description of the utilized machine learning algorithms is presented.

3.3.1 C4.5 Algorithm

In C4.5 [14], binary decision is carried out in the nodes of a decision tree producing a set of logical rules. Therefore, every path starting from the root of a decision tree and leading to a leaf represents a rule. The number of rules embodied to a given tree is equal to the number of its leaf nodes. The premise of each rule is the conjunction of the decisions leading from the root node, through the tree, to that leaf, and the conclusion of that rule is just the category that the leaf node belongs to.

For the growth of C4.5 trees the basic algorithm used was a greedy method constructing the tree in top-down recursive divide and conquer manner. In C4.5, the procedure of pruning is performed. Pruning is a process that is not included in some of its antecedent, such as the ID3 tree [14]. Unlike the stop splitting strategy, pruning is performed when a tree is grown fully and all the leaf nodes have minimum impurity. C4.5 selects a working set of examples at random from the training data and the tree growing/pruning process is repeated several times to ensure that the most promising tree has been selected. In our implementation of the algorithm only pre-prunning was applied and a confidence value of 25% was selected.

3.3.2 Instance Based Learning Algorithm

The Instance-Based (IBk) learning algorithm [15], represents the learned knowledge simply as a collection of training cases or instances. It is a form of supervised learning from instances; it keeps a full memory of training occurrences and classifies new cases using the most similar training instances. A new case is then classified by finding the instance with the highest similarity and using its class as prediction. Therefore, the IBk algorithm is characterized by a very low training effort. On the other hand, this leads to high storage demands caused by the need of keeping all training cases in memory. Furthermore, one has to compare new cases with all existing instances, which results in a high computation cost for classification.

This algorithm uses a distance measure to predict, as the class of a test instance, the class of the first closest training instance that is found. The similarity function used for IBk for k instances is,

$$Similarity(x, y) = -\sqrt{\sum_{i=1}^{n} f(x_i, y_i)} \tag{4}$$

where the instances are described by n attributes. As regards numeric valued attributes the f function equals to,

$$f(x_i, y_i) = (x_i - y_i)^2 \tag{5}$$

IBk is identical to the nearest neighbor algorithm except that it normalizes its attributes' ranges, processes instances incrementally, and has a simple policy for tolerating missing values. Furthermore, IBk saves only misclassified instances and employs a "wait and see" evidence-gathering method to determine which of the saved instances are expected to perform well during classification. The only limit to the complexity of this machine learning method is the limit on the ability to store instances. In our implementation of instance based learning, we adopted a number of 5 neighbors (IB5) as it provided the best classification results.

4 Evaluation

In this section we examine and discuss the contribution of Fujisaki's features to the task of emotion recognition. To increase the evaluation's validity we applied two well established machine learning approaches on two emotional databases. As a result, four frameworks were built. The configuration of the training datasets and the corresponding machine learning algorithms applied are summarized in table 1. To evaluate the derived recognition models we have utilized the 10-fold cross validation [16] method. Recognition performance was measured with the F-measure metric per each emotion category. F-Measure is defined as the harmonic mean of precision and recall and is calculated as shown in equation 6,

$$ F = 1 \Big/ \left(\alpha \frac{1}{P} + (1 - \alpha) \frac{1}{R} \right) \tag{6} $$

where α is a factor which determines the weighting of precision and recall. A value of $\alpha=0,5$ was adopted for our experiments.

Table 1. Emotion Recognition Frameworks

Database	Emotions #	Speakers #	Features Set	ML Method
GrES	5 Emotions (Anger, Fear, Joy, Neutral, Sadness)	1 female	Basic	C4.5
			Basic/Fujisaki	
			Basic	IB5
			Basic/Fujisaki	
DES	5 Emotions (Anger, Happiness, Neutral, Sadness, Surprise)	2 male, 2 female	Basic	C4.5
			Basic/Fujisaki	
			Basic	IB5
			Basic/Fujisaki	

4.1 Results

In order to evaluate the performance of the models recognition, total accuracy was calculated and the results are presented in table 2. From table 2 it can be noted that total accuracy increases significantly with the addition of Fujisaki's features for both databases with an average raise of 9.52%.

4.1.1 GrES Framework Evaluation

Due to the nature of the spoken data obtained from GrES database, the models trained with these datasets presented higher performance accuracy for all evaluation scenarios. This was expected since GrES database is considered as text and speaker dependent (it consists of the same text corpus across all emotions uttered by one speaker).

Table 2. Emotion Recognition Models Total Accuracy

Database	ML Method	Features Set	Total Accuracy (%)
GrES	C4.5	Basic	73,85
		Basic/Fujisaki	82,87
	IB5	Basic	86,16
		Basic/Fujisaki	90.47
DES	C4.5	Basic	50
		Basic/Fujisaki	66,01
	IB5	Basic	64,16
		Basic/Fujisaki	72,93

Figure 2 presents the F-Measure for GrES models of C4.5 and IB5 classification approaches; it shows that Fujisaki's set of features improved the recognition of all emotion categories, especially those with a lower prior F-Measure score, such as happiness, sadness and surprise. We can claim that this was a result of the fact that such emotions are manifested with pitch contours resulted from intonational phenomena that are less sharp, thus more accurately represented from Fujisaki's model.

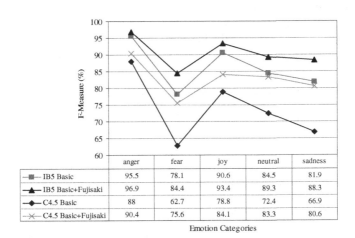

	anger	fear	joy	neutral	sadness
■— IB5 Basic	95.5	78.1	90.6	84.5	81.9
▲— IB5 Basic+Fujisaki	96.9	84.4	93.4	89.3	88.3
◆— C4.5 Basic	88	62.7	78.8	72.4	66.9
✕— C4.5 Basic+Fujisaki	90.4	75.6	84.1	83.3	80.6

Emotion Categories

Fig. 2. F-Measure for IB5 and C4.5 models trained with GrES datasets

In figure 3 the difference in F-Measure values between the models trained with *basic* and *basic+Fujisaki's* set of features is presented. High correlated emotion categories such as anger/joy and fear/sadness that share similar acoustical properties were more accurately predicted with the addition of Fujisaki's feature set. Table 3 contains information about the actual as well as predicted classifications performed by the GrES models. It reveals that employment of Fujisaki's features resulted higher recognition accuracy for the neutral category.

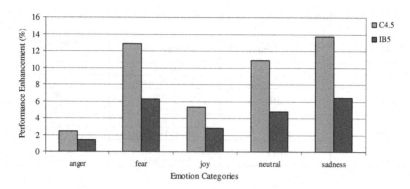

Fig. 3. Enhancement of F-measure for GrES datasets with the Fujisaki's set addition

Furthermore, classification models imbued with Fujisaki's features achieved better segregation of fear and sadness emotional states. In particular, recognition results of sadness category, that were achieved from models trained with the *basic set* of features, showed confusion with fear, joy and neutral category; on the contrary, inducing knowledge from Fujisaki's intonational model to our classification models presented segregation of the misclassified categories, as shown in the confusion matrix of table 3. We have to note here that in table 3 (as well as table 4), columns contain the instances that were classified as that class while rows represent the actual instances that belong to that class.

Table 3. GrES models confusion matrix for C4.5 and IB5 algorithms

C4.5						IB5				
Basic	**anger**	**fear**	**joy**	**neutral**	**Sadness**	**Basic**	**anger**	**fear**	**joy**	**neutral**	**sadness**
anger	**19496**	45	1799	13	821	anger	**21146**	13	632	9	374
Fear	40	**13494**	452	5298	2295	fear	12	**17040**	154	3332	1041
Joy	1753	440	**17984**	142	2473	Joy	596	452	**20483**	117	1144
neutral	10	5145	134	**17869**	1466	neutral	3	2757	34	**21420**	410
sadness	861	2343	2458	1444	**14280**	sadness	357	1809	1128	1195	**16897**
Basic + Fujisaki	**anger**	**fear**	**joy**	**neutral**	**sadness**	**Basic + Fujisaki**	**anger**	**fear**	**joy**	**neutral**	**sadness**
anger	**20057**	9	1724	0	384	anger	**21634**	3	420	1	116
fear	5	**16290**	87	3694	1503	fear	3	**18449**	48	2450	629
joy	1752	108	**19177**	5	1750	joy	634	104	**21130**	14	910
neutral	1	3573	13	**20570**	467	neutral	0	2169	5	**22293**	157
sadness	395	1521	1811	469	**17190**	sadness	230	1391	867	568	**17631**

4.1.2 DES Framework Evaluation

Following to GrES datasets evaluation, experiments with DES datasets were conducted. Figure 4 depicts the F-measure obtained from C4.5 and IB5 emotion

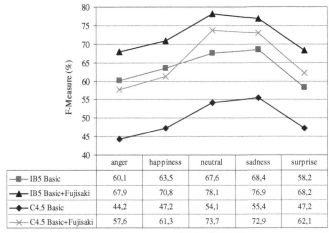

	anger	happiness	neutral	sadness	surprise
—■— IB5 Basic	60,1	63,5	67,6	68,4	58,2
—▲— IB5 Basic+Fujisaki	67,9	70,8	78,1	76,9	68,2
—◆— C4.5 Basic	44,2	47,2	54,1	55,4	47,2
—✕— C4.5 Basic+Fujisaki	57,6	61,3	73,7	72,9	62,1

Emotion Categories

Fig. 4. F-Measure for IB5 and C4.5 models trained with DES datasets

recognition models that were extracted from the DES datasets. And in this case the reported results clarify the contribution of Fujisaki's set of features to the task of emotion recognition since their inclusion outperformed the basic dataset models.

Consequently, figure 5 depicts the recognition improvement achieved for each emotion category for both classification algorithms. It is clearly shown that the classification of all emotion categories was enhanced with the addition of Fujisaki's features.

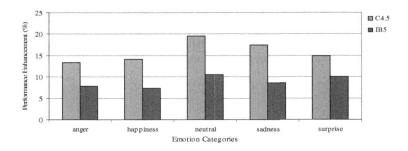

Fig. 5. Enhancement of F-measure for DES datasets with the Fujisaki's set addition

Finally, table 4 presents the confusion matrices resulted from the experiments carried out with the DES database. It is shown that the classification of certain emotion categories with acoustical similarities, such as neutral/sadness, surprise/happiness, was improved. It worth's mentioning that for DES models, neutral category had the highest F-Measure score for both classification algorithms.

Results achieved with our system through the DES datasets were comparable to previously conducted research [17].

Table 4. DES models confusion matrix for C4.5 and IB5 algorithms

C4.5						IB 5					
Basic	anger	happiness	neutral	sadness	surprise	Basic	anger	happiness	neutral	sadness	surprise
anger	**1947**	894	517	328	661	anger	**2481**	553	596	373	344
happiness	898	**3304**	814	599	1310	happiness	569	**4347**	789	520	700
neutral	524	829	**3687**	1166	576	neutral	250	373	**5152**	842	165
sadness	372	610	1162	**3294**	507	sadness	137	259	1102	**4302**	145
surprise	720	1434	657	561	**2872**	surprise	471	1240	813	598	**3122**
Basic + Fujisaki	anger	happiness	neutral	sadness	surprise	Basic + Fujisaki	anger	happiness	neutral	sadness	surprise
anger	**2508**	674	386	300	479	anger	**2887**	544	359	300	257
happiness	688	**4272**	480	390	1095	happiness	524	**4974**	451	413	563
neutral	344	474	**5044**	583	337	neutral	216	251	**5546**	673	96
sadness	284	393	641	**4335**	292	sadness	112	208	640	**4895**	90
surprise	538	1196	361	342	**3807**	surprise	416	1141	429	504	**3754**

5 Conclusion

The purpose of this study was to present the contribution of features calculated from Fujisaki's model of intonation for the task of emotion recognition from speech signals. All features were extracted from two emotional speech databases describing five basic emotional states each. Fujisaki's features contribution was measured and evaluated by comparing them to a basic set of attributes, which have been previously employed for this task. Extracted datasets were utilized for training the C4.5 and IB5 classification algorithms. The derived models evaluation revealed the effectiveness of Fujisaki's features for the task of emotion recognition. Further research will focus to the extraction of new features from statistical properties of the phrase and accent components of Fujisaki's model per utterance.

References

1. Murray I.R., Arnott J.L., "Towards a simulation of emotion in synthetic speech: a review of the literature on human vocal emotion", JASA 93(2), pp. 1097-1108, 1993
2. Cowie R. and Douglas-Cowie E., "Automatic statistical analysis of the signal and prosodic signs of emotion in speech", in Proc. of ICSLP, Philadelphia, pp. 1989–1992, 1998
3. Gobl C., Chasaide A.N. Testing Affective Correlates of Voice Quality through Analysis and Resynthesis, in Proc. of ISCA Workshop on Emotion and Speech, 2000.
4. Kienast M., Sendlmeier W. Acoustical Analysis of Spectral and Temporal Changes in Emotional Speech, ISCA Workshop on Emotion and Speech, 2000
5. Fujisaki, H. and Hirose, K. "Analysis of voice fundamental frequency contours for declarative sentences of Japanese". In Journal of the Acoustical Society of Japan (E), 5(4): pp. 233-241, 1984
6. Ohman, S., "Word and sentence intonation, a quantitative model," Tech. Rep., Department of Speech Communication, Royal Institute of Technology (KTH), 1967

7. Zervas, P., Geourga, I., Fakotakis, N., Kokkinakis, G., Greek Emotional Database: Construction and Linguistic Analysis, in Proc. of 6th International Conference of Greek Linguistics, Rethymno, 2003

8. Oatley, K., Gholamain, M., Emotions and identification: Connections between readers and fiction. In M. Hjort & S. Laver (Eds.) Emotion and the arts. (pp. 263-281). New York: Oxford University Press, 1997

9. Engberg, I., S., Hansen, A., V., Documentation of the Danish Emotional Speech Database (DES), AAU report, Person Kommunication Center, Denmark, 1996

10. Boersma, P., & Weenink, D., Praat: doing phonetics by computer (Version 4.3.01) [Computer program], 2005. Retrieved from http://www.praat.org/

11. Slaney M., Auditory Toolbox. Version 2. Technical Report n. 1998-010, Interval Research Corporation

12. Mixdorff, H., "A novel approach to the fully automatic extraction of Fujisaki model parameters," in Proc. of ICASSP, 2000, vol. 3, pp. 1281–1284, Istanbul, Turkey

13. Witten, I., H., Frank, E., Data Mining: Practical machine learning tools and techniques, 2nd Edition, Morgan Kaufmann, San Francisco, 2005

14. Quinlan, R., C4.5: programs for machine learning. Morgan Kaufmann Publishers Inc., 1993

15. Aha, D., Kibler, D., Albert, M., Instance based learning algorithms. Machine Learning, 6:37 - 66, 1991

16. Stone, M., Cross-validation choice and assessment of statistical predictions. Journal of the Royal Statistical Society, 36, 111-147, 1974.

17. Hammal Z., Bozkurt B., Couvreur L., Unay D., Caplier A., Dutoit T., "Passive versus Active: Vocal Classification System", in Proc. 13th European Signal Processing Conference, Turkey, 2005

Detection of Vocal Fold Paralysis and Edema Using Linear Discriminant Classifiers

Euthymius Ziogas and Constantine Kotropoulos

Department of Informatics,
Aristotle University of Thessaloniki,
Thessaloniki 54124, Greece
thimiouc@otenet.gr, costas@zeus.csd.auth.gr

Abstract. In this paper, a two-class pattern recognition problem is studied, namely the automatic detection of speech disorders such as vocal fold paralysis and edema by processing the speech signal recorded from patients affected by the aforementioned pathologies as well as speakers unaffected by these pathologies. The data used were extracted from the Massachusetts Eye and Ear Infirmary database of disordered speech. The linear prediction coefficients are used as input to the pattern recognition problem. Two techniques are developed. The first technique is an optimal linear classifier design, while the second one is based on the dual-space linear discriminant analysis. Two experiments were conducted in order to assess the performance of the techniques developed namely the detection of vocal fold paralysis for male speakers and the detection of vocal fold edema for female speakers. Receiver operating characteristic curves are presented. Long-term mean feature vectors are proven very efficient in detecting the voice disorders yielding a probability of detection that may approach 100% for a probability of false alarm equal to 9.52%.

1 Introduction

Speech processing has proved to be an excellent tool for voice disorder detection. Among the most interesting recent works are those concerned with Parkinson's Disease (PD), multiple sclerosis (MS) and other diseases which belong to a class of neuro-degenerative diseases that affect patients speech, motor, and cognitive capabilities [1, 2]. Such studies are based on the special characteristics of speech for persons who exhibit disorders on voice and/ or speech. They aim at either evaluating the performance of special treatments (i.e. LSVT [2, 3]) or developing accessibility in communication services for all persons [4]. Thus, it would possibly be a matter of great significance to develop systems able to classify the incoming voice samples into normal or pathological ones before other procedures are further applied.

In this paper, we are concerned with vocal fold paralysis and vocal fold edema, which are both associated with communication deficits that affect the perceptual characteristics of pitch, loudness, quality, intonation, voice-voiceless contrast etc, having similar symptoms with PD and other neuro-degenerative diseases [5]. In either case, a two-class pattern recognition problem is essentially studied.

G. Antoniou et al. (Eds.): SETN 2006, LNAI 3955, pp. 454–464, 2006.

Closely related previous works are the detection of vocal fold cancer [6], where a Hidden Markov Model (HMM)-based classifier was employed and the binary classification between normal subjects and subjects suffering from different pathologies in [7], where Mel frequency cepstral coefficients and pitch were used as features for classification that was performed by the linear discriminant classifier, the nearest mean classifier, and classifiers based on Gaussian mixture models or HMMs. Three parameters namely the number of discrimination, the level of clustering, and the average clustering were assessed for disease discrimination based on acoustic features in [8]. The performance of Fisher's linear classifier, the K-nearest neighbor classifier, and the nearest mean one for vocal fold paralysis and vocal fold edema was assessed in [9]. An attempt is presented to identify pathological disorders of the larynx such as vocal fold paralysis using wavelet analysis and multilayer neural networks in [10]. The detection of certain voice pathologies from the cepstral content of the mucosal wave that is reconstructed by inverse filtering based on findings from the behavior of a 2 m vocal cord model is discussed in [11].

In this paper, two techniques based on linear classifiers are developed. The first one is a sample-based optimal linear classifier design, while the second one is based on the dual-space linear discriminant analysis. The work presented in this paper extends previously reported results in [9]. We are not interested in the detection of pathological speech as in [7], but in the assessment of the discriminatory capability of the aforementioned classifiers for detecting vocal fold paralysis in male speakers and the detection of vocal fold edema in female speakers. The pattern recognition experiments were conducted by employing either frame-based 14th order linear prediction coefficients or their long-term mean vectors for each speaker. Leave-one-out estimates of the probability of false alarm and the probability of detection are derived and receiver operating characteristic (ROC) curves are demonstrated.

The outline of the paper is as follows. Section 2 describes the design of sample-based linear parametric classifiers. The design of dual space linear discriminant classifiers is discussed in Section 3. The data-set used is presented in Section 4 along with the feature extraction. Experimental results are reported in Section 5 and conclusions are drawn in Section 6.

2   Sample-Based Linear Parametric Classifiers

We focus on a two-class pattern recognition problem. Let X denote a sample (i.e. a feature vector). In this paper, linear parametric classifiers are studied regardless of the pattern distributions and hence the decision rule is of the form

$$
h(X) = V^T X + v_0 \underset{\underset{\Omega_2}{>}}{\overset{\overset{\Omega_1}{<}}{}} 0, \tag{1}
$$

where V is the classifier coefficient vector, v_0 is the threshold, and Ω_i, $i = 1, 2$ denote the two classes. The optimal linear classifier is of the form [12]:

$$V = [s\Sigma_1 + (1 - s)\Sigma_2]^{-1} (M_2 - M_1), \tag{2}$$

where Σ_i is the covariance matrix of the samples that belong to class Ω_i and M_i is the corresponding mean vector. The optimal linear parametric classifier can be designed using the iterative Algorithm 1.

Algorithm 1. Linear parametric classifier design

Step 1: Divide the available samples into two groups namely the *design sample set* and the *test sample set*.

Step 2: Using the design samples, compute the sample mean $\widehat{M}_i$ and the sample covariance matrix $\widehat{\Sigma}_i$, $i = 1, 2$.

Step 3: Change s from 0 to 1.

Step 4: Calculate V for a given s by $V = [s\widehat{\Sigma}_1 + (1 - s)\widehat{\Sigma}_2]^{-1}(\widehat{M}_2 - \widehat{M}_1)$.

Step 5: Using the coefficient vector V obtained in Step 4, compute $y_j^{(i)} = V^T X_j^{(i)}$, for $i = 1, 2$ and $j = 1, 2, \ldots, N$, where $X_j^{(i)}$ is the jth test sample in the class Ω_i.

Step 6: The scalar values $y_j^{(1)}$ and $y_j^{(2)}$ that do not satisfy $y_j^{(1)} < -v_0$ and $y_j^{(2)} > -v_0$ are counted as classification errors. Changing v_0 from $-\infty$ to $+\infty$ find v_0 that yields the smallest classification error.

Step 7: Record the classification error determined in Step 6 and go to Step 3.

Algorithm 1 makes no assumption concerning the distributions of the feature vectors X. It is known as *holdout method* and produces a *pessimistic bias* in estimating the classification error. If Step 1 is omitted and the classifier is designed using all the available samples and tested on the same samples in Step 5, then the so called *resubstitution method* results. The latter method produces an *optimistic bias* in estimating the classification errors. As the number of samples increases towards ∞, both the bias of the holdout method and that of the resubstitution method are reduced to zero. As far as the parameters are concerned, we can get better estimates by using a larger number of samples. However, in most cases, the number of the available samples is fixed.

3   Dual Space Linear Discriminant Analysis

A Dual Space Linear Discriminant Analysis algorithm was proposed for face recognition in [13]. In contrast to the linear parametric classifier described in Section 2, this algorithm is not restricted to a two-class problem.

Let the training set contain L classes and each class Ω_i, $i = 1, 2, \ldots, L$ have n_i samples. Then the within class scatter matrix S_w and the between class scatter matrix S_b are defined as

$$S_w = \sum_{i=1}^{L} \sum_{X_k \in \Omega_i} (X_k - M_i)(X_k - M_i)^T \tag{3}$$

$$S_b = \sum_{i=1}^{L} n_i (M_i - M)(M_i - M)^T \tag{4}$$

where M is the gross-mean of the whole training set and M_i, $i = 1, 2, \ldots, L$ are the class centers for Ω_i, $i = 1, 2, \ldots, L$. The Dual Space Linear Discriminant Analysis is summarized in Algorithm 2.

Algorithm 2. Dual space linear discriminant classifier design

At the *design (training) stage*:

Step 1: Compute S_w and S_b using the design set.

Step 2: Apply principal component analysis (PCA) to S_w and compute the principal subspace F defined by the K eigenvectors $V = [\Phi_1 | \Phi_2 | \ldots | \Phi_k]$ and its complementary subspace $\overline{F}$. Estimate the average eigenvalue ρ in $\overline{F}$.

Step 3: All class centers are projected onto F and are normalized by the K eigenvalues. Then S_b is transformed to

$$K_b^P = \Lambda^{-\frac{1}{2}} V^T S_b V \Lambda^{-\frac{1}{2}}, \tag{5}$$

where $\Lambda = \mathrm{diag}\{\lambda_1, \lambda_2, \ldots, \lambda_K\}$ is the diagonal matrix of the K largest eigenvalues that are associated with F. Apply PCA to K_b^P and compute the l_P eigenvectors Ψ_P of K_b^P with the largest eigenvalues. The l_P discriminative eigenvectors in F are defined as

$$W_P = V \Lambda^{-\frac{1}{2}} \Psi_P. \tag{6}$$

Step 4: Project all the class centers to $\overline{F}$ and compute the reconstruction difference as

$$A_r = (I - VV^T)A, \tag{7}$$

where $A = [M_1 | M_2 | \ldots | M_L]$ is a matrix whose columns are the class centers. A_r is the projection of A onto $\overline{F}$. In $\overline{F}$, S_b is transformed to

$$K_b^C = (I - VV^T)S_b(I - VV^T). \tag{8}$$

Compute the l_C eigenvectors of K_b^C with the largest eigenvalues Ψ_C. The l_C discriminative eigenvectors in $\overline{F}$ are defined as

$$W_C = (I - VV^T)\Psi_C. \tag{9}$$

At the *test stage*:

Step 1: All class centers M_j, $j = 1, 2, \ldots, L$ as well as the test samples X_t are projected to the discriminant vectors in F and $\overline{F}$ yielding

$$a_j^P = W_P^T M_j \tag{10}$$

$$a_j^C = W_C^T M_j \tag{11}$$

$$a_t^P = W_P^T X_t \tag{12}$$

$$a_t^C = W_C^T X_t. \tag{13}$$

Step 2: The test sample X_t is assigned to the class

$$j = \arg\min_{j=1}^{L} \left\{ \|a_j^P - a_t^P\|^2 + \frac{1}{\rho} \|a_j^C - a_t^C\|^2 \right\}. \tag{14}$$

4   Datasets and Feature Extraction

Due to the inherent differences of the speech production system for each gender, it makes sense to deal with disordered speech detection for male and female speakers separately. In the first experiment that concerns vocal fold paralysis detection, the dataset contains recordings from 21 males aged 26 to 60 years who were medically diagnosed as normals and 21 males aged 20 to 75 years who were medically diagnosed with vocal fold paralysis. In the second experiment that concerns vocal fold edema detection, 21 females aged 22 to 52 years who were medically diagnosed as normals and 21 females aged 18 to 57 years who were medically diagnosed with vocal fold edema served as subjects. The subjects might suffer from other diseases too, such as hyperfunction, ventricular compression, atrophy, teflon granuloma, etc. All subjects were assessed among other patients and normals at the MEEI [14] in different periods between 1992 and 1994. Two different kinds of recordings were made in each session: in the first recording the patients were called to articulate the sustained vowel "Ah" (/a/) and in the second one to read the "Rainbow Passage". The former recordings are those employed in the present work. The recordings made at a sampling rate of 25 KHz in the pathological case, while at a rate of 50 KHz in the normal case. In the latter case, the sampling rate was reduced to 25 KHz by down-sampling. The aforementioned datasets are the same used in [9]. However, in this work more frames are considered per speaker utterance.

As in [9], 14 linear prediction coefficients were extracted for each speech frame [15]. The speech frames have a duration of 20 ms. Neighboring frames do not possess any overlap. Both the rectangular and the Hamming window are used to extract the speech frames. In the first experiment, the sample set consists of 4236 14-dimensional feature vectors (3171 samples from normal speech and another 1065 samples from disordered speech) for male speakers. In the second experiment, the sample set consists of 4199 14-dimensional feature vectors (3096 samples from normal speech and another 1103 samples from disordered speech vectors) for female speakers.

Besides the frame-based feature vectors, the 14-dimensional mean feature vectors for each speaker utterance are also calculated. By doing so, a dataset of 21 long-term feature vectors from males diagnosed as normal and another 21 long-term feature vectors from males diagnosed with vocal fold paralysis is created in the first experiment. Similarly, a dataset of 21 long-term feature vectors from females diagnosed as normal and another 21 long-term feature vectors from females diagnosed with vocal fold edema is collected in the second experiment.

5   Experimental Results

The assessment of the classifiers studied in the paper was done by estimating the probability of false alarm and the probability of detection using the just described feature vectors and the leave-one-out (LOO) method. The probability of detection P_d is defined as

$$P_d = \frac{\text{\# correctly classified pathological samples}}{\text{\# pathological samples}} \qquad (15)$$

and the probability of false alarm P_f is given by

$$P_f = \frac{\text{\# normal samples misclassified as pathological ones}}{\text{\# normal samples}}. \qquad (16)$$

where # stands for number. There is no difficulty in the application of the LOO concept for long-term feature vectors. However, for frame-based feature vectors, the LOO method that excludes just one feature vector associated to speaker S leaves another $N - 1$ feature vectors of this speaker in the design set, where N is the number of feature vectors extracted from speaker S utterance. To guarantee that the test set is comprised of totally unseen feature vectors (i.e. samples), we apply the LOO method with respect to speakers and not the frame-based samples. Then the test set is comprised by feature vectors of the same speaker and a unique decision can be taken by assigning the test speaker to the class where the majority of the test feature vectors is classified to.

5.1   Sample-Based Linear Parametric Classifier

It is worth noting that for the linear parametric classifier the aforementioned probabilities of false alarm and detection are threshold-dependent. Accordingly, a ROC curve can be derived by plotting the probability of detection versus the probability of false alarm treating the threshold as an implicit parameter.

Vocal Fold Paralysis in Men

Frame-based feature vectors. Using the rectangular window and increments $\Delta s = 0.01$ Algorithm 1 yields the minimum total classification error 14.2857% for $s = 0.19$. The aforementioned classification error corresponds to a misclassification of 1 out of 21 normal utterances and 5 out of 21 disordered speaker utterances. The ROC curve is depicted in Figure 1a. Working in the same way with the Hamming window, Algorithm 1 yields the minimum total classification error for $s = 0.4$. However, in this case considerably more errors are committed in recognizing the normal patterns. Figure 1b depicts the corresponding ROC curve. By constraining the probability of false alarm at 10 %, the linear parametric classifier yields a probability of detection slightly higher than that achieved by the Fisher linear discriminant classifier [9].

Long-term feature vectors. If we design the classifier using the parameters derived by the LOO method on the frame-based feature vectors in order to classify the mean feature vectors per speaker, we obtain the ROC curve of Figure 1c, when the rectangular window is used. We see that the two classes are now considerably separable and we achieve a perfect classification for $P_f \approx 10\%$ that corresponds to 2 speakers. When the Hamming window is employed, the ROC curve plotted in Figure 1d results.

Vocal Fold Edema in Women

Frame-based feature vectors. Algorithm 1 yields the smallest total classification error of 9.5238% for $s = 0.92$ that corresponds to misclassification of 4 disordered speech utterances. Figure 2a depicts the ROC curve when the rectangular window is used. By comparing the ROC curves plotted in Figures 1a and 2a we notice that the classifier detects more efficiently vocal fold edema in women than vocal fold paralysis in men. A much better performance is obtained when the Hamming window replaces the rectangular one. The minimum classification error is only 7.1429% for $s = 0.84$, corresponding to misclassification of one normal and two disordered speech utterances. Indeed, the ROC curve of Figure 2b indicates a more accurate performance than that of Figure 2a. By constraining the probability of false alarm at 10 %, the linear parametric classifier yields a probability of detection 20% higher than that achieved by the Fisher linear discriminant classifier [9].

Long-term feature vectors. By using the rectangular window we can achieve a $P_d = 100\%$ for a misclassification of only one normal utterance, as can be seen in Figure 2c. The corresponding ROC is plotted in Figure 2d, when the Hamming window is used with the mean feature vectors.

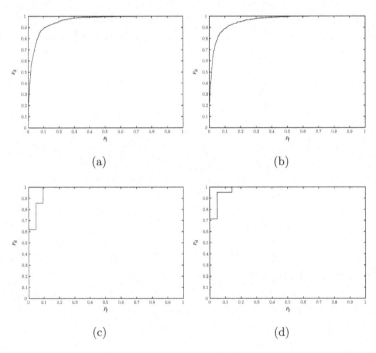

(a)

(b)

(c)

(d)

Fig. 1. Receiver operating characteristic curves of a linear parametric classifier designed to detect vocal fold paralysis in men using: (a) frame-based features and the rectangular window; (b) frame-based features and the Hamming window; (c) long-term feature vectors and the rectangular window; (d) long-term feature vectors and the Hamming window

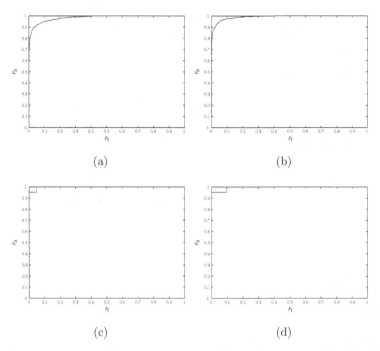

(a)   (b)

(c)   (d)

Fig. 2. Receiver operating characteristic curves of a linear parametric classifier designed to detect vocal fold edema in women using: (a) frame-based features and the rectangular window; (b) frame-based features and the Hamming window; (c) long-term feature vectors and the rectangular window; (d) long-term feature vectors and the Hamming window.

From the ROC curves of Figure 2c and 2d, we notice that no false alarm can by obtained at the expense of only one misclassified disordered speech utterance. By allowing for 2 misclassifications of the normal utterances, we can obtain a perfect detection of vocal fold edema.

Tables 1 and 2 summarize the performance of the parametric classifier when frame-based features and long-term features are used, respectively.

Table 1. Performance of the parametric classifier for frame-based features (E_N stands for normal speech errors - i.e. false alarms and E_D stands for disordered speech errors - i.e. miss-detections)

Pathology	Window	E_N	P_f	E_D	P_d
Paralysis	Rectangular	1	4.761905%	5	76.1905%
Paralysis	Hamming	1	4.761905%	5	76.1905%
Edema	Rectangular	0	0%	4	80.952381%
Edema	Hamming	1	4.761905%	2	90.47619%

Table 2. Performance of the parametric classifier for long-term features (E_N stands for normal speech errors - i.e. false alarms and E_D stands for disordered speech errors - i.e. miss-detections)

Pathology	Window	E_N	P_f	E_D	P_d
Paralysis	Rectangular	0	0%	8	61.90476%
Paralysis	Rectangular	2	9.52381%	0	100%
Paralysis	Hamming	0	0%	6	71.4286%
Paralysis	Hamming	3	14.2857%	0	100%
Edema	Rectangular	0	0%	1	95.2381%
Edema	Rectangular	1	4.761905%	0	100%
Edema	Hamming	0	0%	1	95.2381%
Edema	Hamming	2	9.52381%	0	100%

5.2   Dual Space Linear Discriminant Classifier

Before applying the dual space linear discriminant classifier (Algorithm 2) to either frame-based or long-term feature vectors, we must note the following:

- We are interested in a two class problem, hence $L = 2$.
- Considering the ratio of the largest to the smallest eigenvalue of S_w in either case, we found that it was of the order of 10^3 or larger. For this reason, we shall consider as null subspaces the ones defined by eigenvectors associated with eigenvalues that are ten times larger than the smallest eigenvalue at most. S_w is a full rank matrix in any case. Thus, we obtain $K = 12$ and hence the dimension of the null subspace of S_w is equal to 2.
- In our case, S_b is a rank 1 matrix. Therefore, $l_P, l_C > 1$ does not make any sense and we choose that $l_P = l_C = 1$.
- The probabilities of detection and false alarm are not threshold-dependent. Accordingly, the classifier operates at a single point and no ROC curve is obtained.

Having clarified the above, we applied the dual space linear discriminant classifier to the detection of vocal fold paralysis in men and vocal fold edema in women. The results are summarized in Tables 3 and 4.

Table 3. Dual space linear discriminant classifier applied to frame-based feature vectors (E_N stands for normal speech errors - i.e. false alarms and E_D stands for disordered speech errors - i.e. miss-detections)

Pathology	Window	E_N	P_f	E_D	P_d
Paralysis	Rectangular	1	4.761905%	7	66.6667%
Paralysis	Hamming	2	9.52381%	8	61.90476%
Edema	Rectangular	1	4.761905%	7	66.6667%
Edema	Hamming	5	23.80952%	4	80.952381%

Table 4. Dual space linear discriminant classifier applied to long-term feature vectors ((E_N stands for normal speech errors - i.e. false alarms and E_D stands for disordered speech errors - i.e. miss-detections)

Pathology	Window	E_N	P_f	E_D	P_d
Paralysis	Rectangular	2	9.52381%	7	66.6667%
Paralysis	Hamming	2	9.52381%	8	61.90476%
Edema	Rectangular	1	4.761905%	4	80.952381%
Edema	Hamming	4	19.04762%	4	80.952381%

From the cross-examination of either Tables 1 and 3 or Tables 2 and 4, we conclude that the parametric classifier is more accurate than the dual space linear discriminant classifier. For vocal fold paralysis, the use of the rectangular window yields better results than the use of the Hamming window. The opposite is true for vocal fold edema.

6 Conclusions

Two linear classifiers, namely the sample-based linear classifier and the dual space linear discriminant classifier have been designed for vocal fold paralysis detection in men and vocal fold edema detection in women. The experimental results indicate that the sample-based linear classifier achieves better results than the dual space linear discriminant classifier.

Acknowledgments

This work has been supported by the FP6 European Union Network of Excellence MUSCLE "Multimedia Understanding through Semantics, Computation and Learning" (FP6-507752).

References

1. F. Quek, M. Harper, Y. Haciahmetoglou, L. Chen, and L. O. Ramig, "Speech pauses and gestural holds in Parkinson 's Disease," in *Proc. 2002 Int. Conf. Spoken Language Processing*, 2002, pp. 2485–2488.
2. L. Will, L. O. Ramig, and J. L. Spielman, "Application of Lee Silverman Voice Treatment (LSVT) to individuals with multiple sclerosis, ataxic dysarthria, and stroke," in *Proc. 2002 Int. Conf. Spoken Language Processing*, 2002, pp. 2497–2500.
3. J. L. Spielman, L. O. Ramig, and J. C. Borod, "Oro-facial changes in Parkinson's Disease following intensive voice therapy (LSVT)," in *Proc. 2002 Int. Conf. Spoken Language Processing*, 2002, pp. 2489–2492.
4. V. Parsa and D. G. Jamieson, "Interactions between speech coders and disordered speech," *Speech Communication*, vol. 40, no. 7, pp. 365–385, 2003.
5. www.emedicine.com/ent/byname/vocal-fold-paralysis-unilateral.htm.

6. L. Gavidia-Ceballos and J. H. L. Hansen, "Direct speech feature estimation using an iterative EM algorithm for vocal fold pathology detection," *IEEE Trans. Biomedical Engineering*, vol. 43, pp. 373–383, 1996.

7. A. A. Dibazar, S. Narayanan, and T. W. Berger, "Feature analysis for automatic detection of pathological speech," in *Proc. Engineering Medicine and Biology Symposium 02*, 2002, vol. 1, pp. 182–183.

8. M. O. Rosa, J. C. Pereira, and M. Grellet, "Adaptive estimation of residue signal for voice pathology diagnosis," *IEEE Trans. Biomedical Engineering*, vol. 47, pp. 96–104, 2000.

9. M. Marinaki, C. Kotropoulos, I. Pitas, and N. Maglaveras, "Automatic detection of vocal fold paralysis and edema," in *Proc. 2004 Int. Conf. Spoken Language Processing*, 2004.

10. J. Nayak and P. S. Bhat, "Identification of voice disorders using speech samples," in *Proc. IEEE TenCon2003*, 2003, number 395.

11. P. Gómez, J. I. Godino, F. Rodríguez, F. Díaz, V. Nieto, A. Álvarez, and V. Rodellar, "Evidence of vocal cord pathology from the mucosal wave cepstral contents," in *Proc. 2004 IEEE Int. Conf. Acoustics, Speech, and Signal Processing*, 2004, vol. 5, pp. 437–440.

12. K. Fukunaga, *Introduction in Statistical Pattern Recognition*, Academic Press, San Diego CA, 2nd edition, 1990.

13. X. Tang and W. Wang, "Dual space linear discriminant analysis for face recognition," in *Proc. 2004 IEEE Computer Society Conf. Computer Vision and Pattern Recognition*, 2004, pp. 1064–1068.

14. Voice and Speech Laboratory, Massachusetts Eye and Ear Infirmary, Boston MA, *Voice Disorders Database*, 1.03 edition, 1994, Kay Elemetrics Corp.

15. J. R. Deller, J. G. Proakis, and J. H. L. Hansen, *Discrete Time Processing of Speech Signals*, MacMillan Publishing Company, N. Y., 1993.

An Artificial Neural Network for the Selection of Winding Material in Power Transformers

Eleftherios I. Amoiralis, Pavlos S. Georgilakis, and Alkiviadis T. Gioulekas

Technical University of Crete, University Campus, Kounoupidiana, Chania, Greece
{Eamoiralis, Pgeorg}@dpem.tuc.gr

Abstract. The selection of the winding material in power transformers is an important task, since it has significant impact on the transformer manufacturing cost. This winding material selection has to be checked in every transformer design, which means that for each design, there is a need to optimize the transformer twice and afterwards to select the most economical design. In this paper, an Artificial Neural Network (ANN) is proposed for the selection of the winding material in power transformers, which significantly contributes in the reduction of the effort needed in the transformer design. The proposed ANN architecture provides 94.7% classification success rate on the test set. Consequently, this method is very suitable for industrial use because of its accuracy and implementation speed.

1 Introduction

In today's competitive market environment there is an urgent need for the transformer manufacturing industry to improve transformer efficiency and to reduce costs, since high quality, low cost products, and processes have become the key to survival in a global economy [1]. In addition, the variation in the cost of the materials has direct impact in the optimum transformer design. This work investigates the selection of the material of the transformer windings, which can be copper (CU) or aluminum (AL). Since CU and AL are stock exchange commodities, their prices can significantly change through time. Consequently, in some transformer designs, it is more economical to use CU windings instead of AL windings and vice versa. However, this has to be checked in every transformer design, optimizing the transformer twice and afterwards selecting the most economical design. In this paper, an ANN technique is applied to power transformers for the selection of the winding material. The proposed method is very fast and effective, which makes it very efficient for industrial use.

2 Optimum Transformer

This section describes the method for the determination of the optimum transformer, namely the transformer that satisfies the technical specifications [2] and the customer needs with the minimum manufacturing cost. In the industrial environment considered, three-phase wound core power transformers are studied, whose magnetic circuit is of shell type. The optimum transformer is calculated with the help of a suitable

G. Antoniou et al. (Eds.): SETN 2006, LNAI 3955, pp. 465–468, 2006.
© Springer-Verlag Berlin Heidelberg 2006

computer program, which uses 134 input parameters in order to make the transformer design as parametric as possible [3]. Among the acceptable solutions, the transformer with the minimum manufacturing cost is selected, which is the optimum transformer. It is important to note that some of these 134 input parameters have very strong impact on the determination of the optimum transformer such as the unit cost (in €/kg) of the magnetic material and the type of the winding material (CU or AL).

3 Proposed Methodology

In this work, a fully connected three-layer feedforward ANN is trained in a supervised manner with the error back propagation algorithm [4]. This technique is applied to power transformers for the selection of the winding material, which is a classification problem [5] into two classes: CU or AL. In order to create the learning and test sets, 6 power ratings (250, 400, 630, 800, 1000 and 1600 kVA) are considered. For each transformer, 9 categories of losses are taken into account, namely AA', AB', AC', BA', BB', BC', CA', CB', CC', according to CENELEC [2]. For example, a 250 KVA transformer with AC' category of losses has 3250W of load losses and 425W of no load losses [2]. Five different unit costs (in €/kg) are considered for the CU and the AL winding. Based on the above, $6·9·5 = 270$ transformer design optimizations with CU winding and 270 transformer design optimizations with AL winding are realized. In total, $6·9·5^2 = 1350$ final optimum designs are collected and stored into databases. The databases are composed of sets of final optimum designs (FOD) and each FOD is composed of a collection of input/output pairs. The input pairs or *attributes* are the parameters affecting the selection of winding material. Thirteen attributes are selected based on extensive research and transformer designers' experience (Table 1). The output pairs comprise the type of winding (CU or AL) that corresponds to each FOD. The learning set is composed of 675 FODs and the test set has 675 FODs (different than the FODs of the learning set).

The number of neurons in the input layer is equal to the attributes, while the output layer comprises a single neuron, corresponding to the optimum winding material: CU or AL. We note that the input-output data are normalized by dividing the value of each attribute by its maximum value, contributing to the efficient ANN training [6].

Table 1. Thirteen attributes have been selected based on extensive research and experience

Symbol	Attribute Name	Symbol	Attribute Name
I_1	CU unit cost (€/kg)	I_8	Guaranteed winding losses (W)
I_2	AL unit cost (€/kg)	I_9	I_7/I_8
I_3	I_1/I_2	I_{10}	Rated power (kVA)
I_4	FE unit cost (€/kg)	I_{11}	Guaranteed short-circuit voltage (%)
I_5	I_4/I_1	I_{12}	I_7/I_{10}
I_6	I_4/I_2	I_{13}	I_8/I_{10}
I_7	Guaranteed FE losses (W)		

4 Results and Discussion

A wide range of different ANN architectures and training parameters were considered using the MATLAB ANN toolbox [7]. The number of hidden layers and the numbers of neurons in each hidden layer are parameters to be defined by trial and error. Nevertheless, it has been observed that in most applications, one hidden layer is sufficient [8]. In our method, one hidden layer is chosen. The number of the neurons in the hidden layer was varied from 7 to 39 (Fig. 1). After numerous experiments, the ANN with 13 hidden neurons was found to be sufficient for this work with favorable good results. In Fig. 1 we show the average accuracy (comes from ten different executions) of the learning and test set for each experiment. We note that the 13-13-1 topology (13 input neurons, 13 neurons in the hidden layer, and 1 neuron in the output layer) reaches the highest classification success rate on the test set, despite the fact that the learning set is not as good as the others.

In addition, a wide range of different transfer functions and training functions are used, taken from MATLAB ANN toolbox [7]. Thus, the log-sigmoid transfer function is used, which may have any value between plus and minus infinity, and squashes the output into the range 0 to 1 (modeled as logsig in MATLAB). In addition, a network training function is used that updates weight and bias values according to the conjugate gradient backpropagation with Polak-Ribiere updates (modeled as traincgp in MATLAB [6]) [9]. This function is capable of training any network as long as its weight, net input, and transfer functions have derivative functions. We note that all the experiments use maximum numbers of epochs equal to 100.

Based on the above, the optimal architecture for the proposed feedforward ANN [10] was reached after enough experimentation with various combinations structured as 13-13-1. In this case, the classification success rate on the learning set is 97.5% and 94.7% on the test set. It should be noted that the percentage of the learning and test set resulted in the average of ten different executions of the algorithm. This result is improved by 2.1% in comparison with the classification success rate obtained using decision trees [11].

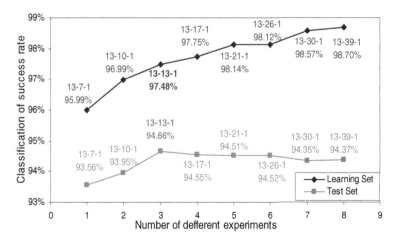

Fig. 1. Accuracy of each of the eight different topologies concerning the learning and test set

5 Conclusions

In this work, a fully connected three-layer feedforward ANN was proposed in order to select the winding material in power transformers. The knowledge base was composed of 1350 final optimum designs. Half of them composed the learning set and the rest the test set. Thirteen attributes were selected based on extensive research and transformer designers' experience, and afterwards, were used as inputs in the ANN. The output pairs comprised the type of winding (CU or AL) that corresponds to each FOD. The performance of the ANN was found to be exceptional, which emerged this method as an important tool for classification. Specifically, the classification success rate on the learning set was 97.5% and 94.7% on the test set. The proposed method is very suitable for industrial use, because of its accuracy and implementation speed, since the ANN method eliminates the need to optimize the transformer twice.

References

1. Georgilakis, P., Hatziargyriou, N., Paparigas, D.: AI Helps Reduce Transformer Iron Losses. IEEE Computer Applications in Power **12** (2005) 41-46
2. CENELEC harmonization document 428.1 S1, (1992)
3. Georgilakis, P.S., Tsili, M.A., Souflaris, A.T.: A heuristic solution to the transformer manufacturing cost optimization problem. Proceedings of the 4th Japanese-Mediterranean Workshop on Applied Electromagnetic Engineering for Magnetic, Superconducting and Nano Materials (JAPMED'4), Cairo, Egypt, (2005)
4. Haykin, S.: Neural Networks: A Comprehensive Foundation, 2nd edn, Prentice Hall, (1999)
5. Zhang, G.: Neural Networks for Classification: A Survey, IEEE Trans. on Systems, Man, and Cybernetics **30** (2000) 451-462
6. Moravej, Z., Vishwakarma, D.N., Singh, S.P.: ANN-Based Protection Scheme for Power Transformer. Elect. Mach. Power Syst. (2000) 875-884
7. Denuth, H., Beale, M.: Neural Network Toolbox. For Use with MATLAB, User's Guide, Version 4.0, March (2005)
8. Coury, D.V., Jorge, D.C.: Artificial Neural Network Approach to Distance Protection of Transmissions Lines. IEEE Trans. on Power Delivery, **13** (1998) 102-108
9. Scales, L. E.: Introduction to Non-Linear Optimization. Springer-Verlag, New York (1985)
10. Fine, T.: Feedforward Neural Network Methodology. 1st edn, Springer-Verlag, (1999)
11. Georgilakis, P., Gioulekas, A., Souflaris, A.: A Decision Tree Method for the Selection of Winding Material in Power Transformers. Proceedings of the 4th Japanese-Mediterranean Workshop on Applied Electromagnetic Engineering for Magnetic, Superconducting and Nano Materials (JAPMED'4), Cairo, Egypt, (2005)

Biomedical Literature Mining for Text Classification and Construction of Gene Networks

Despoina Antonakaki, Alexandros Kanterakis, and George Potamias

Institute of Computer Science, Foundation for Research and Technology (FORTH),
Vassilika Vouton, P.O. Box 1385,
71110 Heraklion, Crete, Greece
{antonak, kantale, potamias}@ics.forth.gr

Abstract. A multi-layered biomedical literature mining approach is presented aiming to the discovery of gene-gene correlations and the construction of respective *gene networks*. Utilization of the *Trie*-memory data structure enables efficient manipulation of different gene nomenclatures. The whole approach is coupled with a texts (biomedical abstracts) *classification* method. Experimental validation and evaluation results show the rationality, efficiency and reliability of the approach.

1 Introduction

Automatic extraction of information from biomedical texts appears as a necessity considering the growing of the massive amounts of scientific literature (11 million abstracts in PubMed; www.pubmed.com). In addition, a serious problem is the variety and multiplicity of utilized biomedical *terminologies* for naming genes. The need to organize and utilize the various biomedical terminological resources seems inevitable [4], [5]. Towards this target we introduce a method for the efficient storage and retrieval of gene terms based on the *Trie* memory data-structure. The method copes

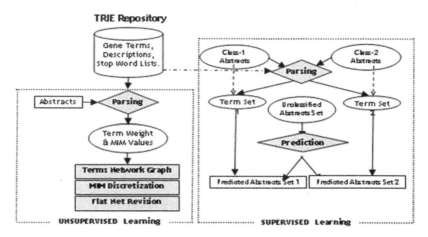

Fig. 1. General Architecture of the *MineBioText* system

G. Antoniou et al. (Eds.): SETN 2006, LNAI 3955, pp. 469–473, 2006.

with different sets of gene terms, their free-text descriptions, and a stop-words dictionary as well. Text-mining techniques are utilized in order to extract potential gene-gene, and gene-disease *correlations* from input biomedical abstracts [3], [5], [7]. The Mutual Information Measure (MIM – an entropic metric) is utilized in order to estimate the correlation strengths. The most *informative* correlations are inferred and respective *gene-networks* are formed and visualized. In addition, we introduce an approach for texts (abstracts) *classification* realized by a novel similarity matching scheme. The whole batch of techniques is implemented in the *MineBioText* system [1] – the system's general architecture is shown in figure 1.

2 Methodology

Input and Trie data-structure. Initially a corpus biomedical literature, including gene terminology and descriptions is collected from Entrez, BioMart and the Gene Ontology (www.geneontology.org). The respective terms are stored and retrieved by the *Trie* data structure [6] which, as shown in [2], is an efficient data structure used for frequent item-set mining. Concerning speed, memory requirements and sensitivity of parameters, *Tries* outperform hash-trees [4].

Mathematic Formulation. Assume $A = \{a_1, \ldots a_n\}$ the finite set of abstracts $a_i \subset \Lambda$, $a_i = \{\lambda_{i,1}, \ldots \lambda_{i,ki}\}$, Λ the potential set of words. If we denote the set of gene terms retrieved from HUGO, EMBL and GO as T_{HUGO}, T_{EMBL}, and T_{GO}, respectively then, we define $T_x = T_{HUGO} \cup T_{EMBL} \cup T_{GO}$. The set of all genes from Ensembl with the annotation of Ensembl IDs $S = \{s_1, \ldots s_m\}$, the set of descriptions T_D where, $t_D \in T_D$, t_D is the set of k words Λ_k $\forall t_D \in T_D$, $t_D \subset \Lambda$ where, $t_D = \{\lambda_{i,d1}, \ldots \lambda_{i,di}\}$, $d_i = /t_{di}$ and the stop-word list as $L = \{a \text{ dictionary set of English words}\}$ we may assert the following:

$$\forall t_x \in T_x, \exists s_{t_x} \in S \text{ such that } \exists T \rightarrow S \tag{1}$$

$$\forall t_D \in T_D, \text{ there is a corresponding } S_{t_D} \in S \tag{2}$$

Assume $k \in a_i$ where $a_i \in A$

if $(k \notin L)$

if $\exists t_{x_t} \in T_x$ such as $t_x = k$ $\left.\right\} \Rightarrow V_{t_x} = 1$

  Assuming Eq.1

else if $\exists 1\ t_{D_i} \in T_D$

assuming $T_{D_{\lambda_{ij}}} = \sqcup_{d_i} \in T_D : \lambda \in t_{D_i} \}$ such as $\lambda_{ij} = k \} \Rightarrow V_{t_D} = 1$

Eq.(2) $\Rightarrow$ for each $t_D \in T_D$ corresponds $S_{T_D} \in S$

else if $\exists t_{D_1}, t_{D2}, \ldots t_{D_N}$ where $t_{D_i} \in T_D \}\Rightarrow$

$\left(N : \text{number of descriptions}\right)$

  for the significant identifiers that

  correspond to $t_{D_1}, \ldots t_{D_N} : S_{t_{D_1}} \ldots S_{t_{D_N}} \}\Rightarrow$ we assign $V_{S_{T_D}} = \min\left(1, V_{S_{T_D}} + \frac{1}{n}\right)$

Fig. 2. Assigning weights to the gene terms

Term Identification. Identification of gene terms is divided in two parts according to the source that the terms belong. First, terms' localization is based on S_x and Tx and the combination of S_D and T_D. The corresponding relation indicates the occurence of a t_D in more that one descriptions. An algorithmic process is devised and used for the assessment of gene terms' *weights* (in figure 2; see also equation 3).

Mutual Information Measure (MIM), a well known entropic metric [8], is used to quantify gene-gene correlations, based on the co-occurrence of the respective terms.

Classification. We devised a novel texts (biomedical abstracts) classification approach based on supervised learning techniques. It is based on the computation of (gene) terms' *weights* (equation 3) and a special texts *classification scheme* based on the formula in equation 4[1].

$$\sum Vt_{Atrain_i} \tag{3}$$

$$\frac{rank_1 - rank_2}{count} \times weight \times \left| \frac{strength_1}{max_1} - \frac{strength_2}{max_2} \right| \tag{4}$$

3   Experimental Validation and Evaluation Results

Validation. We applied the whole approach (using the MineBioText system [1]) on different sets of abstracts targeting different biomedical tasks and inquiries, e.g., *"does gene-G_a correlates to gene-G_b?"* or, *"does gene-G correlates with disease-D?"* An indicative genes-genes / genes-diseases network is shown in figure 3.

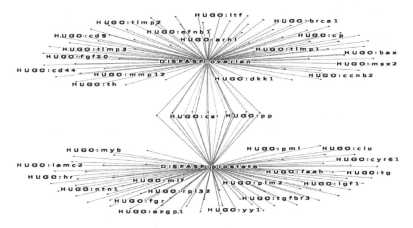

Fig. 3. A genes-genes/genes-diseases network; the network indicates an <u>indirect</u> relation between '*Prostate*' and '*Ovarian*' cancer via their correlations with gene '*cxcr4*' – a real discovery because in none of the input abstracts "*ovarian*" and "*prostate*" terms co-occur

---

[1] Rank$_1$, rank$_2$ are the ranks of the weight of s_x in the sorted lists of the strength values of train files of domain$_1$ and domain$_2$. Count is the total number the significant values. (term) Weight is assigned in the algorithm of Fig3. max$_1$, max$_2$ are the maximum strength values (train), strength$_1$ and strength$_2$ is the sum of the weight values of co-occurrence of the term in the train files 1 and 2 respectively.

Evaluation. Selecting the *most-informative* gene-terms (i.e., terms with high correlations) we applied the presented texts-classification approach on the same indicative sets of abstracts. The task was to classify abstracts to pre-defined categories (i.e., abstracts referring to *'breast cancer', 'colon cancer', leukemia* etc.; retrieved from PubMed). Prediction accuracy and AUC/ROC, on unseen (test) abstracts, results are summarized in tables 1 and 2 (abstracts' specifics are also included).

Table 1. The classified set of Abstracts

Dataset	Abstracts	Gene Terms	Train / Test	Classified
'Breast' cancer	9.278			4264
'Colon' cancer	4.594	168.019	50% / 50%	2036
'Leukemia' cancer	13.218			6358

Table 2. The Classification Results

Dataset	Total Accuracy	AUC*
Breast – Colon Cancer	93.0%	0.993
Colon –Leukemia Cancer	97.5%	0.996
Breast – Leukemia Cancer	90.0%	0.966
Breast-Ovarian Cancer	98.5%	0.998
Breast- Prostate Cancer	98.6%	1.000
Ovarian-Prostate cancer	97.6%	1.000

* AUC: Area Under Curve (ROC analysis assessment)

4 Conclusions

We presented an integrated biomedical literature mining methodology for the discovery of genes correlations accompanied and the construction of relative genes-networks. The methodology utilizes special data-structures for the efficient manipulation of biomedical terms, and the MIM entropic metric to assess correlation strengths. The methodology is coupled with a novel texts (abstracts) classification approach. It was validated on indicative biomedical tasks that reveal the rationality of the approach. Experimental texts-classification (prediction accuracy) results indicate the reliability of the methodology.

Acknowledgment. The reported work was partly supported by PrognoChip (EPAN, Greek Secretariat for Research & Technology), and INFOBIOMED (FP6/2002/IST-507585) projects.

References

1. Antonakaki, D. Mining the Biomedical Literature – The MineBioText system: Discovery of Gene, Protein and Disease Correlations. MSc thesis, dept. of Computer Science, Univ. Crete (2006).
2. Bodon, F.: Surprising results of trie-based FIM algorithms. Proc. Workshop on Frequent Itemset Mining Implementations (FIMI'04), v.90, Brighton, UK, (2004).
3. Chang, J.T., Raychaudhuri, S., Altman, R.B.: Improving Biological Literature Improves Homology Search. Pacific Symposium on Bio-computing, Mauna Lani, HI (2001), 374-383.

4. Collier, N., Nobata, C., and Tsujii, J.: Extracting the Names of Genes and Gene Products with a Hidden Markov Model. Proceedings of COLING, Saarbruecken, (2000), 201-207.
5. Frantzi, K. Ananiadou, S., and Mima, H.: Automatic Recognition of Multi-Word Terms: The C value/NC-value method. International Journal on Digital Libraries 3:2 (2000), 115-130.
6. Fredkin, E.: Trie Memory. CACM 3:9 (1960), 490-499.
7. Iliopoulos, I., Enright, A., Ouzounis, C., Textquest: Document clustering of Medline abstracts for concept discovery in molecular biology. Pac. Symp. Biocomput. (2001), 384-395.
8. Shannon, C.: 1948). A Mathematical Theory of Communication. Reprinted with corrections from The Bell System Technical Journal 27 (1948), 379–423, 623–656.

Towards Representational Autonomy of Agents in Artificial Environments

Argyris Arnellos, Spyros Vosinakis, Thomas Spyrou, and John Darzentas

Deptartment of Product and Systems Design Engineering,
University of the Aegean, Syros, Greece
{arar, spyrosv, tsp, idarz}@aegean.gr

Abstract. Autonomy is a crucial property of an artificial agent. The type of representational structures and the role they play in the preservation of an agent's autonomy are pointed out. A framework of self-organised Peircean semiotic processes is introduced and it is then used to demonstrate the emergence of grounded representational structures in agents interacting with their environment.

1 Introduction

There is an interesting interdependence between the three fundamental properties of *interactivity*, *intentionality* and *autonomy*, which are used to describe an agent. As it is suggested in [1], there is no function without autonomy, no intentionality without function and no meaning without intentionality. The circle closes by considering meaning (representational content) as a prerequisite for the maintenance of system's autonomy during its interaction. Moreover, the notion of representation is central to almost all theories of cognition, therefore being directly and indirectly connected with fundamental problems in the design of artificial cognitive agents [2], at the pure cognitivistic framework as much as at the embodied and dynamic approaches. Although an embodied agent seems to be able to handle very simple tasks with only primitive stimulus-response actions, its cognitive capabilities cannot scale to tackle more complex phenomena. These and other problems are evidences that the use of representations, even in reflexive behaviors, becomes essential [3]. However, representations should not be generic, context-free and predetermined, but they should be an emergent product of the interaction between an agent and its environment [2].

Self-organised and embodied systems admit no functional usefulness to representations. Based on the abovementioned, the incorporation of a process to support the vehicle of the representation which carries internal information about an external state seems imperative. This process should give the interactive dimension to the self-organising system and furthermore, it should correspond to the embedded structure of emergent representations. Peircean semiosis [4] can be seen as the process which drives the system into meaningful interaction. In the proposed framework, intelligence is not considered as an extra module, but as an asset emerging from the agent's functionality for interaction and the aim is the unification of the modality of

G. Antoniou et al. (Eds.): SETN 2006, LNAI 3955, pp. 474–477, 2006.

interaction, perception and action with the smallest possible number of representational primitives. In the present paper, there is an attempt to design a more generic architecture which will integrate aspects of self-organisation and embodiment with Peircean semiotics. There is in no way a demonstration of a totally autonomous system, but the introduced architecture overcomes the symbol-grounding problem, which is the fundamental obstacle for the frame problem, and by doing so, it introduces a type of representational structures that are integrated into the functional structure of the artificial agent. The proposed approach is in correspondence with contemporary works in AI, such as [5] and [6].

2 Emergent Representations Via Self-organised Semiotic Processes

The basic structural element of the proposed framework is the semiotic component. A possible representation is to use a frame-like structure, and to let individual slots express the respective qualities (*qualisigns*) of the object they represent. For indexing and interpretation purposes, two more slots should be reserved to describe the unique *id* of the component and the type of data it holds. In the case of artificial environments, possible objects that can be represented in the agent's knowledge base using semiotic components are *entities*: the individual visual elements that exist as geometries in the environment. The semiotic component should possibly contain their spatial properties (e.g. translation, rotation, bounding box size) and other custom qualities that better describe their nature. Semiotic components could also describe: *relations*, i.e. spatial (e.g. near), structural (e.g. part-of) or other relations between entities, *situations*, i.e. a collection of objects and relations between them that describes (part of) the environment and *actions*, i.e. preconditions (described as the initial situation), performance (series of motor commands) and effects (changes between initial and final situation). The slots can contain either crisp values or sets. In the latter case, the component describes not just one instance but a category (*legisign*).The abstract architecture rising from the interaction of a self-organised system with its environment based on Peircean semiotic processes is shown in Fig. 1. A detailed analysis of the architecture is given in [7].

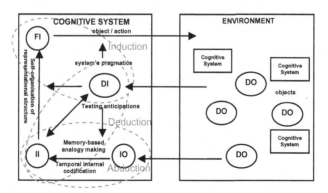

Fig. 1. An agent engaging in self-organised semiotic processes within the environment

As a first step towards a computational methodology for implementing the proposed framework, an example has been set up, where agents are wandering around an environment and try to learn simple actions. Each agent has its own abilities concerning perception and action and initially it has no representational structures regarding possible actions. A perception mechanism, which is constantly being informed by the environment, creates the Immediate Objects (IO) as components that will drive the semiotic process. These are stored in the *short term memory*, which agents are constantly examining and comparing to their representational structure to try and detect any *surprising phenomena*, i.e. objects that they cannot categorize. In the implemented example, the semiotic components describe *entities*, *spatial relations*, *situations* and *actions*. The process of semiosis is initiated by an agents's failure to categorize an observed situation. A completed semiosis consists of the three inferential procedures: *abduction*, *deduction* and *induction*, which drive the agent's logical argumentation.

The process of abduction begins with the observation and description of the nature of a surprising phenomenon on the basis of the anticipations of the agent. Hence, the interaction initiates from the dynamic object (DO), the environmental element of interaction. A representamen contains several IOs which in turn refer to several DOs. Which IO will eventually be actualized depends on the cognitive system's anticipations. The decision made is determined by the highest similarity score. If it reaches below a certain threshold, the IO is treated as belonging to a new category and is stored in the representational structure. A new semiotic component is created that contains all differences between the IO and the category with the most similarity. In the second part of the abduction, an analogy between the surprising phenomenon and the agent's anticipations is attempted, in order to indicate a possible direction of a hypothesis explaining the surprising phenomenon. The differences between an observed action a and a known category A can be found in both preconditions and effects of the action and may involve differences in quality values of the same entity, in the entities that take part in the action and in the relations between them. At the final part of the abduction a formulation of a possible explanation for the surprising phenomenon takes place. At this point the immediate interpretant (II) has been formed. In the end of the abductive phase, A' is created as a copy of A to describe the revised category if the hypothesis were true.

In the deductive phase the consequences of the formulated hypothesis are examined. In the first part, a possible direction of the consequences of the hypothesis is indicated based on the agent's anticipations. In the second part, the formulation of the consequences of the hypothesis takes place. Hence, there will be some tests needed in order this core meaning to be temporarily stabilized into a dynamic interpretant (DI). This process is the most complicated one as the self-organised system will try to incorporate the new representational structure (II) in its functional organisation. In the example, during the deductive phase the effects of the hypothesis are applied to A' based on a set of generalization and specialization rules. Both A and A' are kept in memory and linked to each other as A' is a descendant action of A. So, a surprising phenomenon will either create a new tree as a single node, or expand an existing tree by adding a descendant node to the most similar of its nodes.

The, in a way, objective meaning, which results from the semantic and pragmatic processes, should be open to revision. In case of acceptance, the hypothesis can be used to account for similar surprising phenomena in the future. Then, a new belief would be fixed and if such a hypothesis continues to persist through the agent's interaction with the environment, it will grow to a habit (FI), where a representational structure coincides with the intentionality of the respective object. In the example, if the perceived context meets the preconditions of an action, and that action involves at least one entity of type 'agent', the agent's behavior tries to imitate the action. If there is an anticipated change in the agent's position, the agent actually changes its position in order to meet the changes in the action effects. Each action in memory is assigned a score, and, whenever it is observed in the environment or it is the most similar to an action observed in the environment, its score is increased and the score of all other nodes in the same category tree is decreased. The nodes whose score is below a certain threshold are deleted from memory. With this process the agent manages to test its hypotheses by trying them, and to reinforce the correct ones, leading to the restructuring of its representational structure.

3 Conclusions and Future Work

An example has been presented as an application of the proposed framework, where agents evolve their own representational structures regarding new actions by observing the environment and trying to interact with it. The structure of the Peircean semiotic processes overcome the symbol grounding problem as they are already grounded by their nature. The fact that a representamen mediates between the DO and its interpretant provides a Peircean semiotic process with an embodied structure, since now agent's anticipations are grounded in agent-environment interaction. The authors plan to extend the analysis and implementation in more complex environments, where the representation of actions allow agents to anticipate long-term actions by embedding them seriously into time and enriching their degree of representational autonomy.

References

1. Collier, J.: Autonomy in Anticipatory Systems: Significance for Functionality, Intentionality and Meaning. In: Dubois, D. M. (eds.): The 2nd Int. Conf. on Computing Anticipatory Systems. Springer-Verlag, New York (1999).
2. Christensen, W. D., Hooker, C. A.: Representation and the Meaning of Life. In: Clapin, H., Staines, P., Slezak, P. (eds.): Representation in Mind: New Approaches to Mental Representation, Oxford: Elsevier (2004).
3. Pfeifer, R., Scheier, C.: Understanding Intelligence..MIT Press, Cambridge, M.A (1999).
4. Peirce, C. S.: The Essential Peirce. Selected Philosophical Writings. Vol. 1 1992 and 1998.
5. Vogt, P. (2005) The emergence of compositional structures in perceptually grounded language games.: Artificial Intelligence. 167(1-2) (2005): 206-242.
6. Roy, D.: Semiotic Schemas: A Framework for Grounding Language in the Action and Perception.: Artificial Intelligence. 167(1-2) (2005): 170-205.
7. Arnellos, A., Spyrou, T. and Darzentas, J.: Towards a Framework that Models the Emergence of Meaning Structures in Purposeful Communication Environments. The 47th Annual Conf. of the Int. Society for the Systems Sciences (ISSS) 3(103) (2003).

Combining Credibility in a Source Sensitive Argumentation System

Chee Fon Chang, Peter Harvey, and Aditya Ghose

Decision Systems Lab,
University of Wollongong, NSW 2522, Australia
{c03, pah06, aditya}@uow.edu.au

Abstract. There exist many approaches to agent-based conflict resolution which adopts argumentation as their underlying conflict resolution machinery. In most argumentation systems, the credibility of argument sources plays a minimal role. This paper focuses on combining credibility of sources in a source sensitive argumentation.

1 Introduction

Recent applications of argumentation in multi-agent systems have drawn great interest. Systems such as [1, 2, 3], provides formalisation to defeasible or non-monotonic reasoning focusing on representation and interaction that exist between arguments.

We view argumentation as being (simultaneously) a process for information exchange, a process for conflict resolution and an approach to knowledge representation/reason. We believed that multi-agent argumentation should not focus on logical "truth" but on convincing/persuading other agents of a particular view or position. As such, how an individual is perceived in their community will effect the acceptance of their arguments. In [4], we associated arguments with their sources providing a notion of credibility. We have demonstrated that the defeat of arguments varies depending on the perceived credibility of the participating agents. We will now demonstrate the need for credibility in accrual[5, 6] argumentation. Accrual argumentation simply prescribes that the combine attack of two or more arguments might defeat another argument (say α) where attack of each individual argument may not be sufficient to defeat that α.

For example, let's assume that Bill is a juvenile and has committed a crime. We pose a question: "Should Bill be punished?". Assuming that you are given the statements below:

Tom: *Bill has robbed someone, so he should be jailed.* (α)
Tom: *Bill has assaulted someone, so he should be jailed.* (β)
Dick: *Bill is a juvenile, therefore he should not go to jail.* (γ)

Let's assume that the individual arguments α and β are not strong enough to defeat argument γ and that the accrual of α and β provide sufficient strength to defeat argument γ. Now let's focus on Tom. If Tom was deemed credible then the previous defeat holds. However, should Tom be discredited (Tom was discovered to be a liar), then the combined strength of Tom's arguments will be influence and hence might not be sufficient to defeat Dick's argument. Now, assume the following:

G. Antoniou et al. (Eds.): SETN 2006, LNAI 3955, pp. 478–481, 2006.

Tom: *Bill has robbed someone, so he should be jailed.*
Harry: *Bill has assaulted someone, so he should be jailed.*
Dick: *Bill is a juvenile, therefore he should not go to jail.*

Given that the sources of arguments are different, we believe that the resulting combined strength of the *accrual* arguments should differ from the previous example. Furthermore, observe the following arguments

John: *Bill has robbed someone, so he should be jailed.*
Tom: *Bill has robbed someone, so he should be jailed.*
Dick: *Bill has robbed someone, so he should be jailed.*
Harry: *Bill is a juvenile, therefore he should not go to jail.*

In human argumentation, a set of logically identical arguments with different supporters are stronger then an argument with only one supporter[1]. However, in most logical and argumentation systems, a set of repeated arguments hold no additional weight and is sometime explicitly disallowed. We argue that repeating arguments, if provided from different sources, should be considered as distinct arguments and hence should strengthen the logical claim. In these situations, there should exist an approach in combining credibility, augmenting the strength of arguments hence influencing the defeat relation. In this paper, we will provide such an approach.

In the next section, a brief formalisation of source sensitive argumentation system for combining credibility and augmenting the strength of arguments is provided.

2 Formal Definition

In this section, we will provide a brief outline of source sensitive argumentation system. Interested parties are directed to [4] for a more detailed formalisation.

For simplicity, we will take any finitely generated propositional language $\mathcal{L}$ with the usual punctuation signs, and logical connectives. For any set of wffs $S \subseteq \mathcal{L}$, $Cn_L(S) = \{ \alpha \mid S \vdash \alpha \}$.

Definition 1. *(Well-founded Argument) An argument α is a triple $\langle F, A, C \rangle$ where F, A and C denote the sets of facts, assumptions and conclusion respectively. An argument α is a* well-founded *argument iff it satisfies the following conditions:*

- $F, A, C \subseteq \mathcal{L}$
- $F \cap A = \emptyset$
- $F \cup A \vdash C$
- $Cn (F \cup A \cup C) \nvdash \bot$

We will write F_α, A_α and C_α to respectively denote the facts, assumptions and conclusions associated with an argument α. A pair of well-founded arguments β and γ are said to be in *conflict* iff $Cn (C_\beta \cup C_\gamma) \vdash \bot$.

Definition 2. *(Tagged Arguments) Given a set of unique identifiers $\mathcal{I}$, we define $\mathcal{A}$ as a set of* tagged *arguments of the form $\langle S, A \rangle$ where*

---

[1] By supporter, we simply meant sources.

- $S \in \mathcal{I}$ represents the tagged *arguments'* source.
- A *is a set of* well-founded *arguments*.

We will write S_ϕ and A_ϕ to respectively denote the source and well-founded argument associated with a tagged argument ϕ.

Definition 3. *(Ordered additive group) An* ordered additive group *is a pair* $\mathcal{G} = \langle V, + \rangle$ *where*

- V *is a totally ordered set of elements with the identity element 0, and the inverse of the elements denoted with a prefix* $-$.
- $+$ *is a binary addition operator on* V *satisfying commutative, associative and closure (i.e., applying the* $+$ *operator to two elements of a* V *returns a value which is itself a member of* V.

For convenience, we will denote the inverse elements of V as *negative elements* and the non-inverse elements as *positive elements*.

Definition 4. *(Argument Strength) Given an argument is a well-founded argument* α *and an ordered additive group* $\mathcal{G}$, *we define the following functions:*

- S_F *is a* $f_{strength}$ *function if it maps all elements of* F_α *to positive elements in* V.
- S_A *is a* $a_{strength}$ *function if it maps all elements of* A_α *to negative elements in* V.

There exists many mapping for the functions S_F and S_A. We leave the details and what constitute a rational mapping to the designer.

Definition 5. *(Credibility Function) Given a set of unique identifiers* $\mathcal{I}$ *and an ordered additive group* $\mathcal{G}$, *we say* C *is a credibility function if it maps all values of* $\mathcal{I}$ *into* V.

For simplicity, we have define it as a function that maps a set of unique identifiers into a total ordered set V. However, one could define an arbitrary complex measure taking into account of the context in which the argument is situated.

Definition 6. *(Defeat) Given a set of* tagged *arguments* $\mathcal{A}$, *the strength functions* S_F, S_A *and the credibility function* C, *a relation* $D \subseteq \mathcal{A} \times \mathcal{A}$ *is said to be a* defeat *relation on* $\mathcal{A}$. *We will write* $\phi D \psi$ *iff* A_ϕ *and* A_ψ *are in conflict and* $S_F(F_{A_\phi}) + S_A(A_{A_\phi}) + C(S_\phi) > S_F(F_{A_\psi}) + S_A(A_{A_\psi}) + C(S_\psi)$.

Definition 7. *(Agent) Given a set of unique identifiers* $\mathcal{I}$ *and a set of tagged arguments* $\mathcal{A}$, *an agent is represented as* $\langle I, A, D, S_F, S_A, C \rangle$ *where*

- $I \in \mathcal{I}$.
- $A \subseteq \mathcal{A}$ *s.t.* $\forall \phi : \phi \in \mathcal{A}$, *if* $S_\phi = I$ *then* $\phi \in A$.
- D *is a defeat relation.*
- S_F *is a* $f_{strength}$ *function such that* $S_F(\emptyset) = 0$.
- S_A *is a* $a_{strength}$ *function such that* $S_A(\emptyset) = 0$.
- C *is a credibility function such that* $C(I) = 0$. *This represents the credibility (higher values are better) of other agents in the system as evaluated by the agent.*

Definition 8. *(Source Sensitive Argumentation System) A source sensitive argumenta-tion system is defined as:*

$$\mathcal{SAS} = \langle Agt, \mathcal{A}, \mathcal{G} \rangle$$

where

- *Agt is a set of agents.*
- *$\mathcal{A}$ is a set of tagged arguments.*
- *$\mathcal{G}$ is a totally ordered additive group.*

3 Conclusion

In most argumentation systems, the source and combining sources of the argument plays a minimal role. This paper illustrated that when dealing with accrual arguments, the defeat relation should be sensitive to the relationship between the argument and its source. We have provided an approach for combining credibility, augmenting the strength of arguments and within a source sensitive argumentation system.

3.1 Future Works

We acknowledge that there exists room for improvements. We point to improvements that can be made on mapping sources to credibility by augmenting the function to con-sider context. We also like to point out that the current mapping may not be satisfactory to some audience. Suggestion of generalising the mapping function via the use of semi-ring structure, combining two orthogonal metric (one measuring strength of the argu-ment, the other measuring the credibility) are currently under investigation. By using this approach, we are able to relax the constraints placed on the ordering. We are also in the position to provide a notion of graded defeat. This modification would provide a method to infer the global credibility and defeat relation from any given set of agents.

References

1. Prakken, H.: An argumentation framework in default logic. Annals of Mathematics and Artificial Intelligence **9**(1-2) (1993) 93–132 Bibsource = DBLP,http://dblp.uni-trier.de
2. Bondarenko, A., Dung, P.M., Kowalski, R.A., Toni, F.: An abstract, argumentation-theoretic approach to default reasoning. Artificial Intelligence **93** (1997) 63–101
3. Vreeswijk, G.: Abstract argumentation systems. Artificial Intelligence **90**(1-2) (1997) 225–279
4. Chang, C.F., Harvey, P., Ghose, A.: Source-sensitive argumentation system. In: Proceedings of the 8th International Conference on Enterprise Information Systems. (2006)
5. Verheij, B.: Accrual of arguments in defeasible argumentation. In: The proceedings of the 2nd Dutch/German Workshop on Nonmonotonic Reasoning. (1995) 217–224
6. Prakken, H.: A study of accrual of arguments, with applications to evidential reasoning. In: Proceedings of the 10th International Conference on Artificial Intelligence and Law. (2005) 85–94

An Environment for Constructing and Exploring Visual Models of Logic Propositions by Young Students

Christos Fidas[1], Panagiotis Politis[2], Vassilis Komis[1], and Nikolaos Avouris[1]

[1] University of Patras, 26500 Rio Patras, Greece
[2] University of Thessaly, Volos, Greece
fidas@ee.upatras.gr, ppol@uth.gr, {komis, avouris}@upatras.gr

Abstract. This paper presents the main characteristics of Logic Models Creator (LMC). LMC is a new educational environment for young students to build and explore logic models in graphical form. LMC allows visual representation of logic models using IF/THEN/ELSE constructs. In this paper we provide an overview of LMC architecture and discuss briefly an example of use of LMC. As discussed, LMC users in the reported case study managed to achieve effective communication and task evaluation during exploration of problems involving decision making.

1 Introduction

Logic Models Creator (LMC) is a new learning environment which supports logic modeling activities for students of 11 to 16 years old. LMC is a derivative of the decision support component of an earlier modeling environment, ModelsCreator version 2.0 (MCv2), originally built as a tool to be used for qualitative and semi-quantitative reasoning with real world concepts [1]. The original Decision Support component of ModelsCreator included a validation and model diagnosis module described in [2]. The limitations of that module have been tackled in LMC, as discussed more extensively in [3]. The logic propositions that can be built and explored with LMC meet the requirements of many curriculum subject matters, like mathematics, science etc., permitting interdisciplinary use of the logic modeling activity. LMC puts great emphasis on visualization of the modeling entities, their properties and their relations. In fig. 1 an example of a model built using LMC is shown. On the left the hypothesis is visualized and on the right hand side the conclusion of the logical proposition. In this example the conditions are tested for helping somebody that has received an electric shock.

An important aspect of LMC, as with the original MCv2, is its open character regarding the ability provided to the teachers to create new logical domains (i.e. new subject matters) as well as new primitive entities which are needed for the creation of the logic models.

In the rest of this paper we present first the architecture and basic functionality of the LMC environment. We describe then an example of use of LMC by groups of young students and discuss the implications.

G. Antoniou et al. (Eds.): SETN 2006, LNAI 3955, pp. 482–485, 2006.

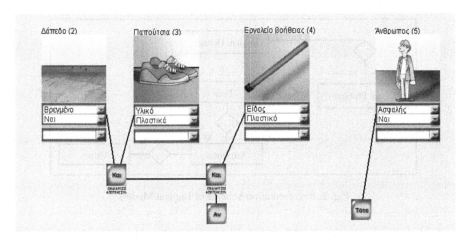

Fig. 1. A typical logic model: A solution to the "the electric shock" problem: IF FLOOR=WET AND SHOES=RUBBER AND STICK=PLASTIC, THEN MAN=SAFE

2   The Logic Models Creator (LMC) Environment

A typical LMC model to solve a given problem may be express according to the following syntax:

Proposition = *IF* Construct *THEN* Construct
          | *IF* Construct *THEN* Construct *ELSE* Construct
Construct = (Construct *AND* Construct)
          | (Construct *OR* Construct)
          | *NOT*(Construct)
          | Attribute=Value

The system considers two basic user categories: (a) the students and (b) the teachers, who interact with the visual environment in order to accomplish specific tasks. While the main task of the students is to build and check the correctness of their logical models the main task of the teachers is to create new logical domains and define the reference models, i.e. valid expressions for a given problem.

An important aspect of LMC is its open character regarding the ability provided to the teachers of creating new logical domains (i.e. new subject matters) as well as new primitive entities which are needed for the creation of the logical models. Each logical domain represents one or more logical problems which describes decision making concepts that the students must explore. For each logical problem the teacher can create entities which describe textually and visually the concepts included in the problem domain (e.g. the stick, the floor, etc.). Each entity may include a set of a attributes which describe specific characteristics of the entity. Furthermore to each attribute of an entity can be assigned one more possible values. These values belong to a set which is defined in the creation phase of an entity. Figure 2 depicts the main domain entities that define a logical problem.

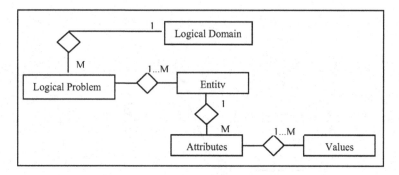

Fig. 2. Representation Scheme of Logical Models

In the frame of a specific domain a teacher can define more than one Reference Models against which the students models will be subsequently tested. We consider these as models which describe alternative correct solutions to a given logical problem. The Reference Model should not violate rules related with the syntax of logical propositions of LMC. The knowledge representation used for expressing the Reference Model has been a matter of discussion during development of LMC and the previous environment MC. As discussed in [3], a first attempt was to express the Reference Model through logical propositions, however this approach produced rigid logical models. An alternative proposed here is to use Truth Tables for representation of the Reference Model.

So for each Reference Model in LMC a teacher must complete a Truth Table which contains all the combinations of different events that exists in the Reference Model. If the hypothesis graph connects a set of $\{G_1,...,G_N\}$ events of different attributes and each attribute can take values from a set $\{G_{11},...,G_{1M})$ than the whole set of different states in which the hypothesis graph can be found is the Cartesian product $G_{if}=\{G_{1M} \times G_{2M} \times ...G_{NM}\}$.

In a similar way we can define the decision part of the statement. If it connects a set of $\{1,...,M\}$ events of different attributes then we add to the truth table M columns which will be associated with values by the teacher. These values of the attributes in the decision graph depend on the values of the attributes of the hypothesis graph.

We consider that a *logical problem* consists of a set of correct logical models L $L=\{l1,...,lN\}$. The purpose of the system is to support the student with appropriate feedback in order to build a model that is equal to a correct logical model in the knowledge base of the active logical domain. To attain this aim, the system creates and displays messages using a relevance factor.

In the case that the student model is equal to a model in set L a message is produced in order to inform the student about the correctness of his model. In any other case the system has diagnosed that the student model has no equal model in set L, it sttempts to find a model in set L which is similar to the students model. With the aim of achieving this goal, the validation module scores each model in set L in relation to the student model.

The logical model with the highest score is defined as the closest logical model to the developed student model. The validation module of LMC checks the level of similarity at (a) the Entities level (b) the Attributes level (c) the Attributes values level and (d) the Relations level and provides the student with appropriate feedback messages in order to support and scaffold the modelling process.

3 LMC in Use: Some First Findings and Conclusions

In a case study that had as the main objective to validate the use of this environment by typical users, a pair of two 11-year old students were asked to explore a logical model under the supervision of their teacher. The model is based on a scenario of a dog that is in conduct with a live wire and received an electric shock. The children were asked to investigate the conditions under which they could safely rescue the dog. The mode includes attributes like Material of the *stick* to touch the dog, Material of the *shoes* of the child, Material and condition of the *floor* (see figure 1). The teacher asked the students to investigate various alternatives and to check the validity of the model. The session that lasted one hour was recorded and subsequently analyzed using a dialogue annotation scheme. An extract of the dialogue follows:

Instructor: Well, let's try the iron stick.
Student A: OK, I select iron.
Student B: The iron is the worst choice!
Student A: Hmm, you are right; the iron is the worst...

An interesting finding of the study was that the two children were engaged in dialogue with the LMC environment and discussed their own experiences related to the subject domain. They investigated for instance the conducting capability of materials like plastic and rubber in relation to the shoes and inferred that plastic is insulating material, as in cables of household electric appliances. One of the children recalled that her grandmother received a strong shock when she touched a bare live cable. The messages received by LMC were considered relevant and supported the specific task.

The children seemed to trust the software environment when they engaged in dialogue with it and expressed their wish to further interact with models of this nature in other subject domains. Despite the fact that the children of this age group were lacking strong conceptual models of the domain, they managed to reason about it with the support of LMC.

References

1. Fidas, C., Komis, V., Avouris, N., Dimitracopoulou, A.: Collaborative Problem Solving using an Open Modelling Environment. In G. Stahl (ed.), Proc. CSCL 2002, Boulder, Colorado, USA, Lawrence Erlbaum Associates, Inc., (2002) 654-655.
2. Partsakoulakis I., Vouros G.. Helping Young Students Reach Valid Decisions Through Model Checking. Proc. 3td ETPE Conf., pp. 669-678, Rhodes, Greece, 2002.
3. Fidas C., Avouris N., Komis V., Politis P., On supporting young students in visual logic modeling, Proc. 3rd IFIP Conference on Artificial Intelligence Applications & Innovations (AIAI) 2006, Athens, June 2006.

Bridging Ontology Evolution and Belief Change

Giorgos Flouris and Dimitris Plexousakis

Institute of Computer Science, FO.R.T.H.,
P.O. Box 1385, GR 71110, Heraklion, Greece
{fgeo, dp}@ics.forth.gr

Abstract. One of the crucial tasks towards the realization of the Semantic Web vision is the efficient encoding of human knowledge in ontologies. The proper maintenance of these, usually large, structures and, in particular, their adaptation to new knowledge (ontology evolution) is one of the most challenging problems in current Semantic Web research. In this paper, we uncover a certain gap in current ontology evolution approaches and propose a novel research path based on belief change. We present some ideas in this direction and argue that our approach introduces an interesting new dimension to the problem that is likely to find important applications in the future.

1 Introduction

Originally introduced by Aristotle, *ontologies* are often viewed as the key means through which the vision of the Semantic Web can be realized [1]. One of the most important ontology-related problems is how to modify an ontology in response to a certain change in the domain or its conceptualization (*ontology evolution*) [6].

There are several cases where ontology evolution is applicable [6]. An ontology, just like any structure holding information, may need to change simply because of a change in the domain of interest. In other cases, we may need to change the perspective under which the domain is viewed, incorporate additional functionality to the ontology according to a change in users' needs, or otherwise improve our conceptualization of the domain.

In this paper, we argue that the currently used ontology evolution model has several weaknesses and present an abstract proposition for a future research direction that will hopefully resolve such weaknesses, based on the related field of *belief change* [4]. Due to space limitations, only part of our proposition will be presented; the interested reader is referred to the full version of this paper for further details [2].

2 Ontology Evolution: Discussion on Current Research Direction

Ontology evolution tools have reached a high level of sophistication; the current state of the art can be found in [6]. While some of these tools are simple ontology editors, others provide more specialized features to the user, like the support for evolution strategies, collaborative edits, change propagation, transactional properties, intuitive graphical interfaces, undo/redo capabilities etc.

G. Antoniou et al. (Eds.): SETN 2006, LNAI 3955, pp. 486–489, 2006.

Despite these nice features, the field of ontology evolution is characterized by the lack of adequate formalizations for the various processes involved. Most of the available tools attempt to emulate human behavior, using certain heuristics which are heavily based on the expertise of their developers. They are not theoretically founded and their formal properties remain unspecified; moreover, they require varying levels of human intervention to work. In short, current work on ontology evolution resorts to ontology editors or other, more specialized tools whose aim is to *help* users perform the change(s) manually rather than performing the change(s) automatically.

We believe that it is not practical to rely on humans in domains where changes occur often, or where it is difficult, impossible or undesirable for ontology engineers to handle the change themselves (autonomous robots or agents, time-critical applications etc). This is true because manual ontology evolution is a difficult task, even for specialized experts. Human supervision should be highly welcome and encouraged whenever possible, but the system should be able to work decently even without it.

In current approaches, a change request is an explicit statement of the modification(s) to be performed upon the ontology; these are determined by the knowledge engineer in response to a more abstract need (e.g., an observation). Thus, current systems do not determine the actual changes to be made upon the ontology, but rely on the user to determine them and feed them to the system for implementation. This way, whenever the ontology engineer is faced with a new fact (observation), he decides on his alternatives and selects the best one for implementation by the system. This decision is based on his expertise on the subject, not on a formal, step-by-step, exhaustive method of evaluation. However, an automatic ontology evolution algorithm should be able to track down all the alternative ways to address a given change, as well as to decide on the best of these alternatives; the resolution of such issues requires a more formal approach to the problem of ontology evolution.

3 Belief Change and Ontology Evolution

Our key idea towards resolving these deficiencies is to exploit the extensive research that has been performed in the field of *belief change*. Belief change deals with the *adaptation of a Knowledge Base (KB) to new information* [4]. Viewing ontology evolution as a special case of the problem of belief change motivates us to apply results and ideas developed by the belief change community to ontology evolution.

We believe that our approach allows us to kill several birds with one stone. The mature field of belief change will provide the necessary formalizations that can be used by the yet immature ontology evolution field. Belief change has always dealt with the automatic adaptation of a KB to new knowledge, without human participation; the ideas and algorithms developed towards this aim will prove helpful in our effort to loosen up the dependency of the ontology evolution process on the knowledge engineer. Finally, previous work on belief change can protect us from potential pitfalls, prevent "reinventing the wheel" for problems whose counterparts have already been addressed in the rich belief change literature and serve as an inspiration for developing solutions to similar problems faced by ontology evolution researchers.

Unfortunately, a direct application of belief change theories to ontologies is generally not possible, because such theories focus on classical logic, using assumptions that fail for most ontology representation formalisms. Despite that, the intuitions behind such theories are usually independent of the underlying logic. In the sequel, we briefly revisit some of the most important concepts that have been considered in the belief change literature, in order to demonstrate the main tradeoffs and issues involved in their migration to the ontological context. Unfortunately, space limitations only allow a brief outline of these issues; for more details refer to [2].

- **Foundational and Coherence Models:** Under the foundational model, there is a clear distinction between knowledge stored explicitly (which can be changed directly) and implicit knowledge (which cannot be changed, but is indirectly affected by changes in the explicit one). Under the coherence model, both explicit and implicit knowledge may be directly modified by the ontology evolution (or belief change) algorithm unambiguously. There are arguments in favor of both models in the belief change literature [5], which are also applicable in the ontological context.
- **Modifications and Facts:** The system could either be fed with the facts that initiated the change (observations, experiments, etc) or with the modifications that should be made in response to these facts. The former approach ("fact-centered") is commonly employed in belief change; the latter ("modification-centered") is more common in ontology evolution. We believe that the "fact-centered" approach is superior, because it adds an extra layer of abstraction, allowing the ontology engineer to deal with high-level facts only, leaving the low-level modifications that should be performed upon the ontology in response to these facts to be determined by the system. Moreover, this is the only approach that could lead to automatic determination of changes [2]. Finally, it allows the description of any type of change using 4 operations only (*revision, contraction, update, erasure* [2], [8]).
- **Primacy of New Information:** The common attitude towards the new information is that it should be accepted unconditionally. However, the distributed and chaotic nature of the Semantic Web implies that data in ontology evolution may originate from unreliable or untrustworthy sources. Thus, it might make sense to apply ideas from *non-prioritized belief change* [7], where the new information may be partially or totally rejected.
- **Consistency:** It is generally acknowledged that the result of an ontology evolution (and belief change) operation should be a consistent ontology (KB). Unfortunately though, in the ontological context, the term "consistent" has been used (others would say abused) to denote several different things. In the full version of this paper [2], we identify the different types of "consistency" that have appeared in the literature and determine those that are interesting in the ontology evolution context.
- **Principle of Minimal Change:** Whenever a change is required, the resulting knowledge should be as "close" as possible to the original knowledge, being subject to minimal "loss of information". The terms "closeness" and "loss of information" have no single interpretation in the belief change literature, each different interpretation resulting to a different belief change algorithm. However, the considerations that have appeared in the belief change context can generally be migrated to the ontology evolution context. For more details on this issue, refer to [2].

The above considerations form only a partial list of the issues that have been discussed in the belief change literature. This analysis did not intend at providing specific solutions for the ontology evolution problem, but at showing that the choice of the change(s) to be made in response to some new information is a complex and multifaceted issue and that several considerations need to be taken into account before determining the proper modifications to be made; this is true for any type of knowledge change, including ontology evolution. Unfortunately, in the ontology evolution literature, most of these issues are dealt with implicitly, if at all, with no formal or informal justification of the various choices and without considering the different alternatives.

4 Conclusion and Future Work

We introduced an alternative approach to ontology evolution, based on a view of the problem as a special case of the more general and extensively studied problem of belief change [4]. This way, most of the techniques, ideas, algorithms and intuitions expressed in the belief change field can be migrated to the ontology evolution context. Our approach is described in detail in the full version of this paper [2].

We argued that this approach will lead to several formal results related to ontology evolution and resolve several weaknesses of the currently used model. Our study did not provide any concrete solutions to the problem; our goal was to provide the foundations upon which deeper results (like [3]) can be based, thus paving the road for the development of effective solutions to the ontology evolution problem.

This paper only scratched the surface of the relation between ontology evolution and belief change. Much more work needs to be done on this issue, both in theoretical and in practical grounds, by attempting the application of specific belief change algorithms, results or theories in the context of ontology evolution.

References

1. Berners-Lee, T., Hendler, J., Lassila, O.: The Semantic Web. Scientific American 284(5) (2001) 34-43
2. Flouris, G., Plexousakis, D.: Handling Ontology Change: Survey and Proposal for a Future Research Direction. Technical Report FORTH-ICS/TR-362 (2005)
3. Flouris, G., Plexousakis, D., Antoniou, G.: On Applying the AGM theory to DLs and OWL. In Proceedings of the 4th International Semantic Web Conference (2005) 216-231
4. Gärdenfors, P.: Belief Revision: An Introduction. In: Gärdenfors, P. (ed): Belief Revision. Cambridge University Press (1992) 1-20
5. Gärdenfors, P.: The Dynamics of Belief Systems: Foundations Versus Coherence Theories. Revue Internationale de Philosophie 44 (1992) 24-46
6. Haase, P., Sure, Y.: D3.1.1.b State of the Art on Ontology Evolution (2004) web page: http://www.aifb.uni-karlsruhe.de/WBS/ysu/publications/SEKT-D3.1.1.b.pdf
7. Hansson, S.O.: A Survey of Non-prioritized Belief Revision. Erkenntnis 50 (1999)
8. Katsuno, H., Mendelzon, A.O.: On the Difference Between Updating a Knowledge Base and Revising It. Technical Report on Knowledge Representation and Reasoning, University of Toronto, Canada, KRR-TR-90-6 (1990)

A Holistic Methodology for Keyword Search in Historical Typewritten Documents

Basilis Gatos, Thomas Konidaris, Ioannis Pratikakis, and Stavros J. Perantonis

Computational Intelligence Laboratory,
Institute of Informatics and Telecommunications,
National Research Center "Demokritos",
153 10 Athens, Greece
{bgat, tkonid, ipratika, sper}@iit.demokritos.gr
http://www.iit.demokritos.gr/cil

Abstract. In this paper, we propose a novel holistic methodology for keyword search in historical typewritten documents combining synthetic data and user's feedback. The holistic approach treats the word as a single entity and entails the recognition of the whole word rather than of individual characters. Our aim is to search for keywords typed by the user in a large collection of digitized typewritten historical documents. The proposed method is based on: (i) creation of synthetic image words; (ii) word segmentation using dynamic parameters; (iii) efficient hybrid feature extraction for each image word and (iv) a retrieval procedure that is optimized by user's feedback. Experimental results prove the efficiency of the proposed approach.

1 Introduction

A robust indexing of historical typewritten documents is essential for quick and efficient content exploitation of the valuable historical collections. In this paper, we deal with historical typewritten Greek documents that date since the period of Renaissance and Enlightenment (1471-1821) and are considered among the first Greek typewritten historical documents. Nevertheless, the proposed methodology is generic having the potential to be applied to other than Greek historical typewritten documents.

Traditional approaches in document indexing usually involve an OCR step [3]. In the case of typewritten historical documents OCR, several factors affect the final performance like low paper quality, paper positioning variations (skew, translations, etc), low print contrast, typesetting imperfections. Usually, typewritten OCR systems involve a character segmentation step followed by a recognition step using pattern classification algorithms. Due to document degradations, OCR systems often fail to support a correct segmentation of the typewritten historical documents into individual characters [1]. In literature, two general approaches can be identified: the segmentation approach and the holistic or segmentation-free approach. The segmentation approach requires that each word has to be segmented into characters while the holistic approach entails the recognition of the whole word. In the segmentation approach, the crucial step is to split a scanned bitmap image of a document into individual

G. Antoniou et al. (Eds.): SETN 2006, LNAI 3955, pp. 490–493, 2006.

characters [4]. A holistic approach is followed in [2][5][6][8][11] where line and word segmentation is used for creating an index based on word matching.

In the case of historical documents, Manmatha and Croft [7] presented a holistic method for word spotting wherein matching was based on the comparison of entire words rather than individual characters. In this method, an off-line grouping of words in a historical document and the manual characterization of each group by the ASCII equivalence of the corresponding words are required. The volume of the processed material was limited to a few pages. This process can become very tedious for large collections of documents.

Typing all unique words as well as constructing an index is an almost impossible task for large document collections. To eliminate this tedious process, we propose a novel holistic method for keyword-guided word spotting which is based on: (i) creation of synthetic image words; (ii) word segmentation using dynamic parameters; (iii) efficient feature extraction for each image word and (iv) a retrieval procedure that is improved by user's feedback. The synthetic keyword image is used as the query image for the retrieval of all relevant words, initializing in this way, the word spotting procedure. The retrieval accuracy is further improved by the user's feedback. Combination of synthetic data creation and user's feedback leads to satisfactory results in terms of precision and recall.

2 Synthetic Data Creation

Synthetic data creation concerns the synthesis of the keyword images from their ASCII equivalences. Prior to the synthesis of the keyword image, the user selects one example image template for each character. This selection is performed "once-for-all" and can be used for entire books or collections. During manual character marking, adjustment of the baseline for each character image template is applied in order to minimize alignment problems.

3 Word Segmentation

The process involves the segmentation of the document images into words. This is accomplished with the use of the Run Length Smoothing Algorithm (RLSA) [10] by using dynamic parameters which depend on the average character height. In the proposed method, the horizontal length threshold is experimentally defined as 50% of the average character height while the vertical length threshold is experimentally defined as 10% of the average character height. The application of RLSA results in a binary image where characters of the same word become connected to a single connected component. In the sequel, a connected component analysis is applied using constraints which express the minimum expected word length. This will enable us to reject stopwords and therefore eliminating undesired word segmentation. More specifically, the minimum expected word length has been experimentally defined to be twice the average character height.

4 Feature Extraction

The feature extraction phase consists of two distinct steps; (i) normalization and (ii) hybrid feature extraction. For the normalization of the segmented words we use a bounding box with user-defined dimensions. For the word matching, feature extraction from the word images is required. Several features and methods have been proposed based on strokes, contour analysis, zones, projections etc. [2][3][9]. In our approach, we employ two types of features in a hybrid fashion. The first one, which is based on [3], divides the word image into a set of zones and calculates the density of the character pixels in each zone. The second type of features is based on the work in [9], where we calculate the area that is formed from the projections of the upper and lower profile of the word.

5 Word Image Retrieval

The process of word matching involves the comparison/matching between the query word (a synthetic keyword image) and all the indexed segmented words. Ranking of the comparison results is based on L_1 distance metric. Since the initial results are based on the comparison of the synthetic keyword with all the detected words, these results might not present high accuracy because a synthetic keyword cannot a priori perform a perfect match with a real word image. Motivated by this, we propose a user intervention where the user selects as query the correct results from the list produced after the initial word matching process. Then, a new matching process is initiated. The critical impact of the user's feedback in the word spotting process lies upon the transition from synthetic to real data. Furthermore, in our approach user interaction is supported by a simplified and user friendly graphical interface that makes the word selection procedure an easy task.

6 Experimental Results

For the evaluation of the performance of the proposed method for keyword guided word spotting in historical typewritten documents, we used the following methodology. We created a ground truth set by manually marking certain keywords on a subset of the available document collection. The performance evaluation method used is based on counting the number of matches between the words detected by the algorithm and the marked words in the ground truth. For the experiments we used a sample of 100 image document pages. The total number of words detected is 27,702. The overall system performance given in Fig. 1 shows the average recall vs. average precision curves in the case of single features as well as in the case of the proposed hybrid scheme. In Fig. 1 we demonstrate the improvement achieved due to user's feedback mechanism. It is also clearly illustrated that the hybrid scheme outperforms the single feature approaches.

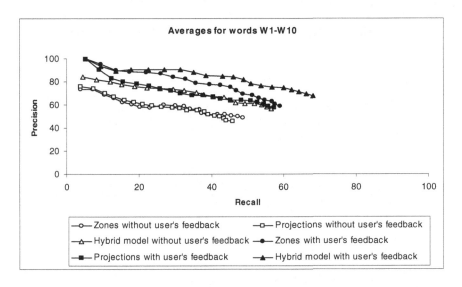

Fig. 1. Average Precision/Recall rates for all words

References

1. Baird H. S.: The state of the art of document image degradation modeling. IARP 2000 Workshop on Document Analysis Systems (2000) 10-13
2. Bhat D.: An evolutionary measure for image matching. In: Proceedings of the Fourteenth International Conference on Pattern Recognition, ICPR'98, volume I (1998) 850-852
3. Bokser M.: Omnidocument technologies. In: Proceedings of the IEEE, 80(7) (1992) 1066-1078
4. Gatos B., Papamarkos N. and Chamzas C.: A binary tree based OCR technique for machine printed characters. Engineering Applications of Artificial Intelligence, 10(4) (1997) 403-412
5. Lu Y., Tan C., Weihua H., Fan L.: An approach to word image matching based on weighted Hausdorff distance. In: Sixth International Conference on Document Analysis and Recognition (ICDAR'01) (2001) 10-13
6. Madhvanath S., Govindaraju V.: Local reference lines for handwritten word recognition. Pattern Recognition, 32 (1999) 2021-2028
7. Manmatha R.: A scale space approach for automatically segmenting words from historical handwritten documents. In: IEEE Transactions on Pattern Analysis and Machine Intelligence, vol. 27, No. 8 (2005) 1212-1225
8. Marcolino A., Ramos V., Ármalo M., Pinto J. C.: Line and Word matching in old documents. In: Proceedings of the Fifth IberoAmerican Sympsium on Pattern Recognition (SIARP'00) (2000) 123-125
9. Rath T. M., Manmatha R.: Features for word spotting in historical documents. In: Proceedings of the Seventh International Conference on Document Analysis and Recognition (ICDAR'03) (2003) 218-222
10. Waked B., Suen C. Y., Bergler S.: Segmenting document images using diagonal white runs and vertical edges. In: Proceedings of the Sixth International Conference on Document Analysis and Recognition (ICDAR'01) (2001) 194-199
11. Weihua H., Tan C. L., Sung S. Y., Xu Y.: Word shape recognition for image-based document retrieval. International Conference on Image Processing, ICIP'2001 (2001) 8-11

Color Features for Image Fingerprinting

Marios A. Gavrielides, Elena Sikudova, Dimitris Spachos, and Ioannis Pitas

AIIA Laboratory, Computer Vision and Image Processing Group,
Dept. of Informatics, Aristotle University of Thessaloniki,
Box 451 Thessaloniki, GR-54124, Greece

Abstract. Image fingerprinting systems aim to extract unique and robust image descriptors (in analogy to human fingerprints). They search for images that are not only perceptually similar but replicas of an image generated through mild image processing operations. In this paper, we examine the use of color descriptors based on a 24-color quantized palette for image fingerprinting. Comparisons are provided between different similarity measures methods as well as regarding the use of color-only and spatial chromatic histograms.

1 Introduction

Image fingerprinting (or perceptual hashing) refers to the extraction of a unique description of an image that would be resilient to transformations, in an analogous manner to human fingerprints. Detecting transformed versions of images could be used to fight piracy of such material.

Image fingerprinting differs from image *watermarking* in the sense that watermarking involves embedding information into the image, whereas fingerprinting, as defined here, involves descriptors extracted from the image content. Fingerprinting can be used to search for those copies of an image that have already been circulating in the internet with no watermarks embedded on them.

In order for such a system to be successful, it has to be robust against a number of frequent attacks, have good discriminating ability to avoid the retrieval of false alarms, provide efficient storage of extracted image descriptors that would be used for image matching and an efficient search mechanism that would compare the image description of the query image to those in a database of image descriptors. A number of approaches [1], [2], [3] have been presented in the literature.

In this paper, we examine the use of color-based descriptors for an image fingerprinting system and its robustness to most common attacks. We demonstrate the effect of various color descriptors including color-only and color-spatial information, reduced number of colors, and different types of histogram-similarity measures.

2 Color-Based Fingerprint Extraction

The fingerprint extraction procedure involves the quantization of the image colors and the calculation of color histograms based on the resulting colors. We used a quantization method based on a pre-defined color palette known as the Gretag Macbeth Color

G. Antoniou et al. (Eds.): SETN 2006, LNAI 3955, pp. 494–497, 2006.

Checker, which was designed to match human perception of colors. The Macbeth chart is a standard used to test color reproduction systems and it consists of 24 colors, scientifically prepared to represent a variety of different naturally occurring colors. The procedure for the generation of the color chart is reported in [4]. We created a color palette based on the Macbeth xyY values found in [5] in Table G.10.

Color histograms have been used extensively in CBIR systems due to the simplicity of their calculation and their robustness to common image transformations. Many types of histograms exist in the literature falling mainly into two categories: those based only on the quantized colors and those incorporating information on the spatial color distribution. We examined the use of both kinds of color histograms. The first one was the *normalized color-only histogram*, providing probability of the occurrence of a certain color in an image. The normalized color histogram depends only on the color properties of an image without providing any information on the spatial distribution of colors. In order to examine any advantages of using histograms incorporating color-spatial information for image fingerprinting, we also experimented with the *spatial chromatic histogram* proposed by Cinque et.al. [6]. The spatial chromatic histogram descriptor gives information on color presence, and color spatial distribution.

3   Color-Based Fingerprint Matching

Image matching between color histogram descriptors depends on the choice of similarity measures, so we investigated the use of three different measures given below to match the normalized color histograms. A fourth measure was used for the spatial chromatic histogram. The matching measures used were *Scaled L_1-norm* and *L_2-norm* distance, defined as $d_{L_1}(H_1, H_2) = 1 - 0.5 * \sum_{i=1}^{C_p} |H_{1_i} - H_{2_i}|$ and $d_{L_2}(H_1, H_2) = 1 - \frac{1}{2} * \sqrt{\sum_{i=1}^{C_p} (H_{1_i} - H_{2_i})^2}$.

The above two measures are scaled versions of the L_1-, and L_2-norms which have been previously used for matching color histograms.

Scaled Histogram Intersection defined as $d_{HI}(H_1, H_2) = \sum_{i=1}^{C_p} \min(H_{1_i}, H_{2_i}) * (1 - |H_{1_i} - H_{2_i}|)$ is a modified version of the Histogram Intersection measure. Only colors present in the image contribute to this metric.

Finally, in order to compare the spatial chromatic histograms between images I_1, I_2, we used the *spatial chromatic distance* defined in [6].

4   Results and Discussion

A database of 450 art images of variable sizes, provided by the Bridgeman Art Library, was used to evaluate the method. The following set of 20 transformations was applied to each image: Scaling (25,50,75,125,150 and 200%), Rotation (10 , 20 , 30 , 90), Cropping - (both sides by 10, 20 and 30%), Compression - (JPEG with 25, 50, 75 quality factor), Blurring (median with 3x3, 5x5,7x7 masks), and Combination of attacks (Rotation 10 , cropping 10%, resizing to 25%, median filtering 5x5 and compression with quality factor 50). The images were resized using nearest neighbor interpolation. For the image rotation, it has to be noted that a black frame was added around the image, thus producing an additional source of degradation, except for the case of 90 . The set of 450 original images defined the Original Image Set and the resulting set of 9000 transformation images defined the Transformed Image Set.

The use of color-based descriptors for the application of image fingerprinting was evaluated using Receiver-Operator Characteristic (ROC) analysis. Specifically, the evaluation consisted of taking the color descriptors from each of the 450 images in the Original Image Set and matching them against the descriptors from each of the 9000 images in the Transformed Image Set. Matches were determined by applying a threshold on the similarity measures and identifying those images with measures higher than the threshold. The well-known measures *True Positive Fraction* (TPF or sensitivity) and *False Positive Fraction* (FPF) were used. By sweeping the threshold and averaging the measures of TPF and FPF over all images in the Original Image Set, ROC curves were calculated.

The ROC curves for the four similarity measures described in section 4 are plotted in Figure 1. It can be seen from the graph, that the normalized color histogram with the similarity measures scaled L_1-norm and scaled histogram intersection show the best performance whereas the quadratic histogram measure shows the worst performance. The quadratic histogram measure incorporates information regarding the distance of colors in the color space, which might be more useful if the query was for images of *similar* color, as opposed to exact matches. It can also be seen that the spatial chromatic histogram shows slightly worse performance compared to the color-only histogram for this experiment. The spatial information could prove useful when two images have exactly the same colors but in different locations. However, we did not design a database having those requirements since the goal was to examine the robustness of color-based descriptors over transformation changes in a general database.

We also examined the robustness of color-based descriptors for specific transformations. The ROC curves, taken using the color-only histogram with the normalized histogram intersection measure, that have been evaluated (but will not be presented here due to space limitations), demonstrate the invariance of color-based descriptors to resizing, to JPEG compression, to median filtering, and to rotation of 90 , keeping in

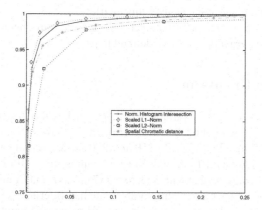

Fig. 1. ROC curves comparing the different similarity measures for matching of color histograms

mind that for that particular angle no black frame was added to the image. As expected, the performance dropped for higher degrees of cropping and for rotations where a black frame is added. However, even for cropping of 30% both sides, a sensitivity of 90% is achieved at only about 2.3% false positive rate.

The experimental results demonstrate the robustness of color-based descriptors for the application of image fingerprinting. The results were very good keeping in mind that the Transformed Image Set included images that were badly deteriorated.

In the future, we plan to examine the performance of the algorithm when the database includes similar images. For such a query, spatial descriptors might prove more useful. Moreover, we will address other attacks, such as illumination changes.

5   Conclusion

In this manuscript, we presented an image fingerprinting system that was designed to retrieve transformed versions of a query image from a large database. We examined the use of color-only and spatial chromatic histograms and the effect of different similarity measures. The results on a database of 450 original images and their 9000 transformation images, showed the robustness of color-based descriptors under high degrees of common attacks and are very encouraging for the use of this system for image finger-printing.

Acknowledgement

This work has been partly supported by EU and Greek national funds under Operational Programme in Education and Initial Vocational Training II through the Archimedes project Retrieval and Intellectual Property rights protection of Multidimensional Digital Signals (04-3- 001/4).

References

1. M. Schneider and S-F Chang, "A Robust content based digital signature for image authentication," in *Proc. 1996 International Conference on Image Processing (ICIP 1996)*, pp. 227-230, 1996.
2. R. Venkatesan and S.-M Koon and M. H. Jakubowski and P. Moulin, "Robust Image Hashing," in *Proc. of the 2000 International Conference on Image Processing (ICIP 2000)*, 2000.
3. M. Johnson and K. Ramchandran, "Dither-based secure image hashing using distributed coding," in *Proc. 2003 International Conference on Image Processing (ICIP 2003)*, pp. 495-498, 2003.
4. C.S. McCamy and H. Marcus and J.G. Davidson, "A color-rendition chart," *Journal of Applied Photographic Engineering*, vol. 2, no. 3, pp. 95-99, 1976.
5. A.S. Glassner, *Principles of Digital Image Synthesis*. Morgan-Kaufmann Publishers Inc., San Francisco, USA, 1995.
6. L. Cinque and G. Ciocca and S. Levialdi and A. Pellicano and R. Schettini, "Color-based image retrieval using spatial-chromatic histograms," *Image and Vision Computing*, vol. 19, pp. 979-986, 2001.

Neural Recognition and Genetic Features Selection for Robust Detection of E-Mail Spam

Dimitris Gavrilis[1], Ioannis G. Tsoulos[2], and Evangelos Dermatas[1]

[1] Electrical & Computer Engineering, University of Patras
gavrilis@upatras.gr, dermatas@george.wcl2.ee.upatras.gr
[2] Computer Science Department, University of Ioannina
sheridan@cs.uoi.gr

Abstract. In this paper a method for feature selection and classification of email spam messages is presented. The selection of features is performed in two steps: The selection is performed by measuring their entropy and a fine-tuning selection is implemented using a genetic algorithm. In the classification process, a Radial Basis Function Network is used to ensure robust classification rate even in case of complex cluster structure. The proposed method shows that, when using a two-level feature selection, a better accuracy is achieved than using one-stage selection. Also, the use of a lemmatizer or a stop-word list gives minimal classification improvement. The proposed method achieves 96-97% average accuracy when using only 20 features out of 15000.

1 Introduction and Related Work

The electronic mail is a crucial Internet service and millions of messages are sent every day. The flood of the user's mailboxes with unsolicited emails, a problem known as spam, consumes network bandwidth and can be seen as a Denial of Service attack. Many methods have been proposed to countermeasure spam but most of them do not employ machine learning but instead they use blacklists of known spammers, or dictionaries with phrase patterns usually found in spam messages. Other techniques require the users to manually identify and mark the spam messages in order to create personalized rules for each user.

Recent advances in text categorization (TC) have made possible the recognition of spam messages through machine learning techniques. The two key features that must be addressed in the TC problem are the feature selection and the classifier. The feature selection process is crucial and can improve performance because text contains a very large number of features (more than 20000 in an average in length corpus). In order to solve this problem, techniques like Singular Value Decomposition [7], term weighting based on text statistics [3] and latent semantic analysis (LSA) [8] have been used. The Vector Space Model (VSM) [3] and the nearest neighbor classifier [4] are primarily used as classifiers for document classification problems.

A simple k-NN classifier was used by Sakkis and Androutsopoulos [1], which is compared to a Naïve Bayes filter. The Information Gain (IG) is used to select the features. In the k-NN approach, the recall rate reaches 59.91% (using 600 features) while in the Bayesian approach is 63.67% (using 300 features).

G. Antoniou et al. (Eds.): SETN 2006, LNAI 3955, pp. 498–501, 2006.

The message preprocessing is another crucial factor in text categorization problems. Four different variations have been explored. A raw dataset (BARE), a dataset with its common words removed (STOP), a dataset with its words converted to their base form using a lemmatizer (LEMM) and a combination of the last two (LEMM-STOP).The authors in [2] explore the performance of a Naïve Bayes classifier on the four different datasets. Their results show that the LEMM-STOP gives better accuracy than the other approaches.

In this paper a genetic approach to the features selection problem for robust neural classification of e-mail spam is described and evaluated. In a two stages procedure, the initial set of a huge number of features are reduced using natural language tools, and selected the most stochastically important by measuring the features entropy. A fine-tuning selection is applied with the aid of a genetic algorithm.

In the following sections, the proposed method is described later and the corpus used for benchmark is presented. Finally, the experimental results are shown and the conclusions are given in the last section.

2 Feature Selection and Classification of E-Mail Spam

The method proposed in this paper consists of a feature selection process and a neural classifier. The feature selection process, in contrary with traditional methods, is performed in two levels. It has already been found that the proposed features selection outperforms other methods in text categorization, and especially in scientific abstract categorization [6].

The feature selection approach consists of two-level procedure. In the first level, the features are assigned a rank according to their entropy:

$$H(x) = -\sum_{y_i \in Y} p(y_i \mid x) \log p(y_i \mid x), \qquad i=1,2. \tag{1}$$

where y is the class (legitimate or spam) and x is each feature. From the original set of M features, a subset is defined by selecting N features based on their entropy rank.

In the second level, the subset of N is scaled down to K features by genetic selection. A genetic algorithm using tournament selection, detects the best K features that are to be used for classification. The genetic optimization function maximizes the correct classification rate using a RBF network. Therefore, the proposed fine-selection of features is optimal.

For the classification task, a neural classifier is used, and more specifically an RBF network. Although neural networks are very good classifiers, are uncommon in text categorization problems since they are problematic with high dimensionality. In this paper it is shown that if a proper set of features is obtained ($K \approx 20$), excellent accuracy can be achieved. The training process of the RBF network is generally fast and that is the main reason that it is used, since the combination of genetic selection with a neural classifier is a very time consuming training process.

3 Benchmark Corpus

The corpus used for training and testing in this paper is the PU1 corpus [5] which is available at (http://www.aueb.gr/users/ion/data/pu1_encoded.tar.gz). The PU1 corpus has been created from a normal user for a period of 36 months. It contains 1099 english messages, 618 of them are legitimate and 481 are spam, and consists of 4 subsets: a raw set, a raw set with a stop-word list used, a set with the words lemmatized, a set with the words lemmatized and with a stop-word list used. The 4 sets are split into 10 groups and used to perform 10-fold cross validation in all experiments presented below. The corpus is also pre-processed and three other variations are created: the STOP, LEMM and LEMM-STOP corpuses. These variations are described in [5].

4 Experimental Results

The genetic algorithm in all experiments runs for 100 generations and has a 0.05% mutation rate and a 0.95% crossover rate. The RBF network has 6 hidden neurons and 1 neuron in the output layer. The k-means algorithm is used to derive the synaptic weights in the hidden layer.

The experimental results shown in Table 1, give the average error of the 10-fold validation for each dataset when all features were used for genetic selection classification ($M=N$=approximately 16000). The results show that, when the LEMM-STOP dataset is used, better accuracy is achieved.

Table 1. Mean classification error for each corpus when only the fine-selection process is used (genetic selection)

Corpus	Number of Features (M)	Average Error (%)
BARE	16000	9.81
STOP	16000	9.63
LEMM	16000	8.71
LEMM-STOP	16000	6.79

Table 2. Mean classification error for the LEMM-STOP dataset when both feature selection steps are used

Corpus	Number of Features (N)	Average Error (%)
LEMM-STOP	3000	5.44
LEMM-STOP	6000	3.27
LEMM-STOP	8000	4.71

When the the complete features selection method is used, the genetic selection uses a subset of the original features. In Table 2, the mean classification error for the LEMM-STOP dataset is shown using the complete version of the features selection method. The experiments are completed only on the LEMM-STOP dataset, since this corpus gives lower classification error than the other three. It is obvious that the mean classification error drops significantly when only the genetic selection is used (Table 1). When a large number of features is selected, the classification error increases, because the search space of the genetic algorithm grows significantly. On the other hand, when keeping a small number of features, information helpful in the recognition process may be lost thus high classification error is measured. The use of a medium-size feature size (about 40-50% of the original) is found to give a low classification error. Although the results are promising, when the same method is applied to a classical text categorization problem, involving scientific paper abstracts ([6]), it performs significantly better. The smaller length in the email content can account for this divergence in performance.

5 Conclusions and Future Work

In this paper a two-step feature selection method is presented that uses term entropy to select a subset of the original features in the first step and genetic selection in the second step. An RBF network is used for the classification with 20 features as inputs producing a 3.27% classification error. Also, the use of a stop-word list and a lemmatizer is found to improve classification accuracy in the spam recognition problem. In future work, a larger corpus will be used and the performance of other classifiers will be explored.

References

1. G. Sakkis, I. Androutsopoulos, G. Paliouras, V. Karkaletsis, C.D. Spyropoulos, and P. Stamatopoulos: A memory-based approach to anti-spam filtering for mailing lists. In Information Retrieval, Vol. 6. Kluwer (2003) 49-73.
2. Androutsopoulos, J. Koutsias, K. V. Chandrinos, G. Paliouras, and C. D. Spyropoulos: An Evaluation of Naive Bayesian Anti-Spam Filtering. In Proc. of the workshop on Machine Learning in the New Information Age (2000).
3. Dik L. Lee, Huei Chuang, Kent Seamons: Document Ranking and the Vector-Space Model. IEEE Software, Vol. 14 (1997) 67-75.
4. Michael Steinbach, George Karypis, Vipin Kumar: A Comparison of Document Clustering Techniques. KDD Workshop on Text Mining (2000).
5. E. Michelakis, I. Androutsopoulos, G. Paliouras, G. Sakkis and P. Stamatopoulos: Filtron: A Learning-Based Anti-Spam Filter. Proc. of the 1st Conference on Email and Anti-Spam (2004).
6. Dimitris Gavrilis, Ioannis Tsoulos and Evangelos Dermatas: Stochastic Classification of Scientific Abstracts. Proceedings of the 6th Speech and Computer Conference, Patra (2005).
7. John M. Pierre: On the Automated Classification of Web Sites. Linkoping Electronic Articles in Computer and Information Science, Vol. 6 (2001).
8. S. Deerwester, S. Dumais, G. Furnas, T. Landauer and R. Harshman: Indexing by latent semantic analysis. Journal of the American Society for Information Science, Vol. 46 (1990) 391-407.

Violence Content Classification Using Audio Features

Theodoros Giannakopoulos [1], Dimitrios Kosmopoulos [2],
Andreas Aristidou [1], and Sergios Theodoridis [1]

[1] Department of Informatics and Telecommunications, National and Kapodistrian
University of Athens, Panepistimiopolis, Ilissia Athens 15784
{tyiannak, stud01144, stheodor}@di.uoa.gr
[2] Institute of Informatics and Telecommunications, National Center for Scientific Research
"Demokritos", Agia Paraskevi, Athens 15310, Greece
dkosmo@iit.demokritos.gr

Abstract. This work studies the problem of violence detection in audio data, which can be used for automated content rating. We employ some popular frame-level audio features both from the time and frequency domain. Afterwards, several statistics of the calculated feature sequences are fed as input to a Support Vector Machine classifier, which decides about the segment content with respect to violence. The presented experimental results verify the validity of the approach and exhibit a better performance than the other known approaches.

1 Introduction

In the following years a huge increase of the available multimedia content is expected. Almost everyone will be able to provide content, accessible by large portions of the population with limited central control. However, the increasing use of the related technology by sensitive social groups creates the need for protection from harmful content. The goal of the work presented here is part of a multimodal approach, which aims to contribute to the automated characterization of multimedia content with respect to *violence*. This approach will make possible for content providers to rate automatically their content and for the end user to filter the violent scenes in client terminal devices.

The violence characterization is quite subjective and this creates difficulties in defining violent content unambiguously. As violence we may define any situation or action that may cause physical or mental harm to one or more persons. Violent scenes in video documents regard the content that includes such actions. Such scenes are usually manifested through characteristic audio signals (e.g., screams, gunshots etc). For the specific problem the related literature is very limited and in most cases it examines only visual features such as in [1], and [2]. Audio data for violent detection is used as an additional feature to visual data in [3], where abrupt changes in energy level of the audio signal are detected using the *energy entropy* criterion.

We deduce from existing literature that although the audio is a very useful source of information, much simpler to process than video and in most cases self-sufficient for violent scene characterization, it has been rather overlooked. The use of additional

G. Antoniou et al. (Eds.): SETN 2006, LNAI 3955, pp. 502–507, 2006.

features as well as better classification methods is able to provide much better results and this is what we do in this work.

2 Audio Features

We extract six segment-level audio features, which will be used at a next stage by a Support Vector Machine classifier. For the feature calculation we assume that the signal x has already been segmented into semantically coherent *segments* (scenes). The segments are divided into W *time-windows* (*frames*) of predefined duration S, and for each one of them we calculate the frame-level features. Therefore, for each audio segment, six *feature sequences* of length W are calculated. In order to extract semantic content information it is necessary to follow how those sequences change from frame to frame. To quantify this variation, a number of statistics (e.g., mean value) have been calculated, for each feature sequence. In this paper, we use six popular frame-level features extracted both from the time and frequency domain ([4]). Afterwards, 8 statistics $f_1,\ldots,f_8$ have been calculated from the feature sequences, as described in the following. Those statistics are then used by the classifier as single-feature values of each audio segment.

2.1 Time-Domain Features

The *energy entropy* expresses abrupt changes in the energy level of the audio signal. In order to calculate this feature, the frames are further divided into K sub-windows of fixed duration. For each sub-window i, the normalized energy σ_i^2 is calculated, i.e., the sub-window's energy divided by the whole window's energy. Then, the energy entropy is computed for frame j using eq. (1). The value of the energy entropy is small for frames with large changes in energy level. Therefore, we can detect many violent actions like shots, which are characterized by sudden energy transitions in a short time period. This becomes obvious in figures 1 and 2, where the energy entropy sequences of two audio signals with violent content are presented. The features f_1 and f_2 that we use based on the energy entropy are the ratios of maximum to mean and maximum to median value of the energy entropy (eq. (2) and (3)).

Another feature stems from *the absolute value of the signal amplitude* (A_{0i} for each sample i). We use here as feature f_3 the ratio of the max to the mean absolute signal amplitude (4).

Short time energy N_j is another widely used feature in audio classification applications (*eq. (5)*). In the current project, we use the mean and variance of the short time energy (eq. (6) and (7)).

Zero crossing rate ([4]) is one of the most widely used time-domain audio features. It is calculated by the number of time-domain zero-crossings, divided by the number of samples in the frame, as presented in eq. (8) (*sgn* is the signum function). The statistic used for ZCR is the ratio of maximum to mean value (eq. (9)). In figure 3, the ZCR sequences for three different audio segments containing violence (gunshots), music and speech are presented. It is obvious that the plot justifies the selection of f_6.

Table 1. The features extracted from the employed criteria

Feature Name	Feature Equation	Statistics (Single Features)	
Energy Entropy	$I_j = -\sum_{i=1..K}\sigma_i^2 \log_2 \sigma_i^2$ (1)	$f_1 = \max_{j=1..W}(I_j) \Big/ \left(\frac{1}{W}\sum_{j=1..W} I_j\right)$ (2)	$f_2 = \dfrac{\max_{j=1..W}(I_j)}{median_{j=1..W}(I_j)}$ (3)
Signal Ampl.		$f_3 = \max_{i=1..L}(A_{0i}) \Big/ \left(\frac{1}{L}\sum_{i=1..L} A_{0i}\right)$ (4)	*(L: signal length)*
Short Time Energy	$N_j = \sum_{i=1..S} x_i^2$ (5)	$f_4 = \frac{1}{W}\sum_{j=1..W} N_j$ (6)	$f_5 = \frac{1}{W}\sum_{j=1..W}(N_j - f_4)^2$ (7)
Zero Crossing Rate	$Z_j = \frac{1}{2S}\sum_{i=1..S}|\operatorname{sgn}(x_i) - \operatorname{sgn}(x_{i-1})|$ (8)	$f_6 = \max_{j=1..W} Z_j \Big/ \left(\frac{1}{W}\sum_{j=1..W} Z_j\right)$ (9)	
Spectral Flux	$F_j = \sum_{k=0..S-1}(N_{j,k} - N_{j-1,k})^2$ (10)	$f_7 = \max_{j=1..W} F_j \Big/ \left(\frac{1}{W}\sum_{j=1..W} F_j\right)$ (11)	
Spectral Rolloff	$\sum_{k=0}^{m_c^R(j)}|X_{jk}| = \frac{c}{100}\sum_{k=0}^{S-1}|X_{jk}|$ (12)	$f_8 = \max_{j=1..W} m_c^R(j) \Big/ \left(\frac{1}{W}\sum_{j=1..W} m_c^R(j)\right)$ (13)	

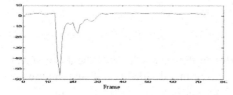

Fig. 1. Energy entropy of a shot   **Fig. 2.** Energy entropy of beatings

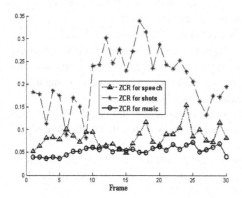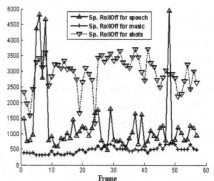

Fig. 3. ZCR for gunshots, music and speech   **Fig. 4.** Spectral rolloff for gunshots, music and speech

2.2 Frequency-Domain Features

Spectral flux is a frequency-domain measure of the local spectral change between successive frames, and it is defined as in equation (10). The related feature is the ratio of maximum to mean of the spectral flux, as presented in (11). $N_{j,k}$ is the spectral energy of the j-th frame for the k-th sample.

This frequency domain feature is called *spectral rolloff*, and it is defined as the frequency bin $m_c^R(j)$ below which the c percent (e.g., $c=90$) of the magnitude distribution of the Discrete Fourier Transform (DFT) X_k coefficients is concentrated for frame j (eq. (12)). It is a measure of skewness of the spectral shape, with brighter sounds resulting in higher values. The related statistic is the ratio of max to mean of the spectral rolloff (eq. 13). In fig. 4 an example of spectral rolloff sequences of three different audio segments (shots, music and speech) is presented. These differ in their mean values, but also in the way their peaks are distributed over time.

3   Classification

For the classification task we used the Support Vector Machine Classifier (SVM), which is known for its computational efficiency and effectiveness even for high dimensional spaces for classes that are not linearly separable ([5]). The classification task is twofold: (a) training, and (b) testing. During training we provided the normalized features extracted from audio segments to the classifier, along with labels Y indicating if the features correspond to violent (+1) or non-violent content (-1). The SVM gave as output a number of support vectors, which were used for the classification task. We have applied the linear, the Gaussian radial basis, the polynomial and the sigmoid hyperbolic tangent kernel functions for classification purpose with varying the C parameter, which expresses the trade-off between training error and margin.

4   Experimental Results

A database of audio segments, extracted from several movie genres, was created for training/testing purposes. The total duration of the samples was 20 minutes: 50% of that data was used for training, and the remaining 50% for testing. The sampling rate was 16 KHz and the sample resolution 16 bits (1 channel was used). The violent audio segments were extracted from scenes such as shots, explosions, fights and screams, while non-violent audio segments of music and speech were also extracted, along with non-violent sounds like fireworks, which have similar characteristics to violent sounds. The signal was divided into frames using Hamming windows of 400 msec, with a step of 200 msec (50% overlapping). All audio features described in section 2 were used. It has been experimentally found that the testing set was classified with minimum error rate when a polynomial kernel function had been used in the SVM classifier.

In table 2, we present the classification error rates of each individual classifier (feature), along with the error rates when all features are used (8-D space). Apart from the average error, the false negative and false positive errors are presented. It is obvious than no individual feature has overall performance better than 80%. Though, the error rate itself is not a criterion for deciding which of the features are better when

Table 2. Classification error rate for each feature

	f_1	f_2	f_3	f_4	f_5	f_6	f_7	f_8	8-D
% False Negative (FN)	9	12.5	13.5	12	9	11	10	12.5	**4.75**
% False Positive (FP)	13.5	13	15	17	12.5	12.5	10.5	12	**9.75**
Overall % Error	22.5	25.5	28.5	29	21.5	23.5	20.5	24.5	**14.5**

used in combination with the others. For this purpose, feature selection techniques may be used. On the other hand, the SVM has a classification error rate of 14.5% when all features are used.

For the 8-D case, the following measures were extracted (see Table 2): (a) *Recall (R):* The proportion of the violent segments, which have been correctly identified as violent, (b) *Precision (P):* The proportion of the data classified as violent, whose true class label was indeed violent and (c) *Accuracy (A):* The overall proportion of data classified correctly. The measures R, P, A are given by: $R=TP/(TP+FN)$, $P=TP/(TP+FP)$ $A=(TP+TN)/(TP+TN+FP+FN)$, where TP is the true positive rate and TN is the true negative rate. In our case, the two classes shared the same probability, i.e., the number of violent and non-violent test segments are the same. Therefore: $TP+FN=TN+FP=0.5$. Combining the results of Table 2, the definitions for R, P, A and the last equation, we found that recall was equal to 90.5%, precision 82.4% and accuracy 85.5%.

5   Conclusions and Future Work

In this work, we have used some popular audio features for detecting violence in audio segments with an SVM classifier. The whole system was tested using audio segments extracted from real movies and the results were promising. In average, 85.5% of the audio data was classified correctly, while the percentage of the violent segments that where correctly identified (recall) was 90.5%. This is a significantly better rate than that provided by any individual features, some of which have been used separately in the past for the same task.

In the future, other audio features (e.g., Mel-frequency cepstral coefficients - MFCCs) could be added to those presented in this paper. Furthermore, techniques for feature selection could be used, to find an optimal sub-set of features for the specific classification problem. Also, other classification algorithms can be employed like Hidden Markov Models (HMMs). Another direction of research could be the usage of multi-class recognition algorithms, for characterizing the audio segments as shots, screams, etc, instead of facing the problem as binary. On the other hand, it is needed to implement an audio *segmentation* algorithm, for dividing large audio streams into shorter homogenous segments. The computed segments will be fed as input to the feature calculation stage. Finally, is obvious, that the results of any audio violence detection system can be combined with synchronized visual cues.

References

1. Vasconcelos, N.; Lippman, A., *Towards semantically meaningful feature spaces for the characterization of video content*, Proc. International Conference on Image Processing, 1997., Volume 1, Oct 1997, Pages: 25 - 28 vol.1
2. A. Datta, M. Shah, N. V. Lobo, "Person-on-Person Violence Detection in Video Data", *IEEE International Conference on Pattern Recognition*, Canada, 2002.
3. J. Nam, A.H. Tewfik, "Event-driven video abstraction and visualisation", Multimedia Tools and Applications, 16(1-2), 55-77, 2002
4. Sergios Theodoridis, Konstantinos Koutroumbas, *Pattern Recognition*. Academic Press, 2005, 3rd Edtition.
5. N. Cristianini and J. Shawe-Taylor, "Support Vector Machines and other kernel-based learning methods", Cambridge University Press, ISBN 0-521-78019-5, 2000.

An Analysis of Linear Weight Updating Algorithms for Text Classification

Aggelos Gkiokas[1,2], Iason Demiros[1,2], and Stelios Piperidis[1]

[1] Institute for Language and Speech Processing,
Artemidos 6 & Epidavrou,
Athens 15125, Greece
Tel.: +30-210-6875300; Fax: +30-210-6852620
[2] National Technical University of Athens
{agkiokas, iason, spip}@ilsp.gr

Abstract. This paper addresses the problem of text classification in high dimensionality spaces by applying linear weight updating classifiers that have been highly studied in the domain of machine learning. Our experimental results are based on the Winnow family of algorithms that are simple to implement and efficient in terms of computation time and storage requirements. We applied an exponential multiplication function to weight updates and we experimentally calculated the optimal values of the learning rate and the separating surface parameters. Our results are at the level of the best results that were reported on the family of linear algorithms and perform nearly as well as the top performing methodologies in the literature.

1 Introduction

Text Classification can be defined as the assignment of free text documents to one or more predefined categories based on their content (Aas, 1999). The problem of text representation can be regarded at the level of meaningful units of text (lexical semantics). The most common choice is the representation of a text as a vector of words, often called the *bag of words* model (Sebastiani, 2002). Terms and phrases although they clearly possess superior semantic characteristics, however their application is not reported to improve the algorithm's performance except for a few cases.

In this paper we improve the performance of Balanced Winnow by introducing variable weight multiplicative rules into the updating mechanism of the algorithm.

2 Linear Text Classifiers

A linear Text Classifier classifies each new document according to the dot product of the weights and the strengths of the features in the document. Each document is represented as a set of features $d = \{f_1, f_2, ..., f_m\}$, where m is the number of active features in it (features that do exist). Features usually represent words, terms or phrases. The strength of the feature f in the document d is denoted by $s(f,d)$. The strength can range from a simple binary value indicating the presence or absence of the feature in the

G. Antoniou et al. (Eds.): SETN 2006, LNAI 3955, pp. 508–511, 2006.

document, to more sophisticated information-theoretic values like term frequency, tfidf and normalization factors according to the length of the document.

The classifier stores a weight vector for each category c of the collection. The weight vector is represented as $w_c = (w(f_1,c), w(f_2,c),..., w(f_n,c)) = (w_1, w_2,..., w_n)$ where n is the total number of features in the collection.. The scoring function of the document d for each category is represented by the dot product of the weights and the strengths of the document features:

$$F(d) = \sum_{f \in d} s(f,d) \cdot w(f,c) \tag{1}$$

2.1 Balanced Winnow

Balanced Winnow maintains a threshold value θ and two weight vectors w^+ and w^- for each category. In this case the prediction type is as follows:

$$\sum_{j=1}^{m} (w_j^+ - w_j^-) s_j > \theta \tag{2}$$

where the weights of the active features are simultaneously updated by two fixed parameters α (promotion) and β (demotion). Following a mistake on a positive example, updates are applied as follows: $w_j^+ := w_j^+ \cdot \alpha$ and $w_j^- := w_j^- \cdot \beta$ (positive part promoted, negative part demoted) while mistakes on a negative example result to a set of symmetric updates: $w_j^+ := w_j^+ \cdot \beta$ and $w_j^- := w_j^- \cdot \alpha$ (positive part demoted, negative part promoted). In our work, we have kept values α and $\beta = 1/\alpha$, allowing for a single update parameter to be used.

2.2 Threshold Range

When computing a multidimensional linear decision surface in the input space, as presented in the theory of Support Vector Machines (Cortes, 1995), the heuristic search for a thick separator (Dagan, 1997) that best separates the documents in a given category results to the introduction of two threshold values θ^+ and θ^-. The learning mechanism remains the same, except that a mistake is considered if a positive example has score below the threshold θ^+ or a negative example has score above θ^-.

2.3 Variable Multiplicative Weight Update

In our work, we parameterize the update rules by a learning rate $\eta > 0$ and by the strength s_j of feature j. While doing so, the learning procedure focuses on the stronger features of the category. This setting was described in (Kivinen, 1997) and results to the following weight update:

$w_j := w_j \cdot e^{\eta s_j}$ and $w_j := w_j / e^{\eta s_j}$ in the case of weight promotion and demotion respectively, where s_j is the strength of the active feature j. By replacing the above updates into (2) we obtain our final updating rules:

$$\text{If } d \in C \text{ and } \sum_{j=1}^{m}(w_j^+ - w_j^-)s_j < \theta^+ \text{ then } w_j^+ := w_j^+ \cdot e^{\eta s_j} \text{ and } w_j^- := w_j^- / e^{\eta s_j} \quad (3)$$

$$\text{If } d \notin C \text{ and } \sum_{j=1}^{m}(w_j^+ - w_j^-)s_j > \theta^- \text{ then } w_j^+ := w_j^+ / e^{\eta s_j} \text{ and } w_j^- := w_j^- \cdot e^{\eta s_j} \quad (4)$$

3   Experimental Work

Parameters and thresholds are derived experimentally through a series of incremental tests and by choosing the optimal value that maximizes the effectiveness of the algorithm in each particular case discussed. We have concluded experimentally that the choice of $\theta^+ = 1,4$ and $\theta^- = 0,6$ result to optimal F values. Analogously, a learning rate of $\eta = 0,01$ for the exponential version and $\alpha = 1,05$ for the fixed parameter α has given the best results.

A great number of experiments have been conducted on both versions of the Reuters corpus, experiments that involve the different versions of linear classifiers. Features are represented by words in the document. They were pre-processed by an English stemmer that we have developed and by standard stop-list filtering. We have experimented with a variety of different features. Words has so far given the best results.

The strength of each feature is determined as $\sqrt{tf}$ where tf is the term frequency, that is the number of occurrences of feature f in document d. In line with (Dagan, 1997) we found that $\sqrt{tf}$ produces better results than $tfidf$ or any other normalized version of term frequency in the document and no significant gain in success figures has been achieved by input space dimensionality reduction.

Out tests have been conducted on the standard benchmark collection Reuters-21578 Apte90 split. Applying the Winnow version with the fixed update parameter α we achieved a microaveraged break-even F point of 84.31%. The exponential version presented in this work achieved a microaveraged break-even F point of 85.61%

Table 1 summarizes a performance comparison of the most successful algorithms that are reported on the same corpus. For a detailed comparison see (Sebastiani, 2002).

Table 1. Comparative results on the Apte90 split of the Reuters corpus

Algorithm	Researcher	Score
Linear	(Lam, 1998)	82,2
Example-based	(Lam, 1998)	86,0
Neural Networks	(Yang and Liu, 1999)	83,8
Regression	(Yang and Liu, 1999)	84,9
Ada.Boost	(Weiss, 1999)	87,8
SVM	(Dumais, 1998)	87,0

4   Conclusion and Future Work

The Winnow family of algorithms exhibit several characteristics that make them attractive to apply in the domain of Text Classification. Among them we can stress their robustness to a great number of irrelevant features, their straightforward implementation, their low memory and processing power requirements, their ease of retraining and their high results that clearly fall within the state-of-the-art in this domain. In this paper we presented the results we obtained by applying an exponential multiplication function to weight. The basis of our work has been the BalancedWinnow algorithm. Our results are at the level of the best results that were reported on the family of linear algorithms and perform nearly as well as the top performing methodologies in the literature.

Acknowledgments

We gratefully acknowledge support from the grant eClassify (N.M/9), action 4.5.1 of the General Secretariat for Research and Technology of the Greek Ministry of Development.

References

1. Aas K. and Eikvil L. 1999. Text categorization: A survey. Technical report, Norwegian Computing Center.
2. Apte C, Damerau F. and Weiss S. 1994. Toward language independent automated learning of text categorization models. In Proceedings SIGIR-94.
3. Cortes C. and Vapnik V. 1995. Support vector networks. Machine Learning, 20:273-297.
4. Dagan I., Karov K., Roth D. 1997. Mistake-Driven Learning in Text Categorization. In: Proceedings of the Second Conference on Empirical Methods in NLP, pp. 55-63.
5. Kivinen J., Warmuth M. and Auer P. 1997. The Perceptron Algorithm vs. Winnow: linear vs. logarithmic mistake bounds when few input variables are relevant. Artificial Intelligence 97(1-2):325-343.
6. Littlestone N. 1988. Learning quickly when irrelevant attributes abound: A new linear-threshold algorithm. Machine Learning, 2:285#318.
7. Sebastiani, F. 2002. Machine learning in automated text categorization, ACM Computing Surveys 34(1), 1-47.

On Small Data Sets Revealing Big Differences

Thanasis Hadzilacos[1,2], Dimitris Kalles[1],
Christos Pierrakeas[1], and Michalis Xenos[1]

[1] Hellenic Open University, Patras, Greece
[2] Computer Technology Institute, Patras, Greece
{thh, kalles, pierrakeas, xenos}@eap.gr

Abstract. We use decision trees and genetic algorithms to analyze the academic performance of students throughout an academic year at a distance learning university. Based on the accuracy of the generated rules, and on cross-examinations of various groups of the same student population, we surprisingly observe that students' performance is clustered around tutors.

1 Introduction

Small data sets are usually suspect when used in a machine learning context. We present an application in a complex educational environment where a collection of small data sets can reveal surprisingly sensitive information about the processes that generate the data.

In the Hellenic Open University (HOU) we attempt to analyze whether tutoring practices have an effect on student performance. Using decision trees and genetic algorithms, we report significant differences in tutoring practices and we reflect on the implications and on the potential of these findings.

Key demographic characteristics of students (such as age, sex, residence etc), their marks in written assignments and their presence or absence in plenary meetings may constitute the training set for the task of explaining (and predicting) whether a student would eventually pass or fail a specific module.

Initial experimentation at HOU [1] consisted of using several machine learning techniques to predict student performance with reference to the final examination. The WEKA toolkit [2] was used and the key finding, also corroborated by tutoring experience, is that success in the initial written assignments is a strong indicator of success in the examination. A surprising finding was that demographics were not important.

We then followed-up with experimentation [3] using the GATREE system [4], which produced significantly more accurate and shorter decision trees. That stage confirmed the qualitative validity of the original findings (also serving as result replication) and set the context for experimenting with accuracy-size trade offs.

A decision tree like the one in Fig. 1 (similar to the ones actually produced by GATREE) tells us that a mediocre grade at an assignment, turned in at about the middle (in the time-line) of the module, is an indicator of possible failure at the exams, whereas a non-mediocre grade refers the alert to the last assignment. An excerpt of a training set that could have produced such a tree is shown in Table 1.

G. Antoniou et al. (Eds.): SETN 2006, LNAI 3955, pp. 512–515, 2006.
© Springer-Verlag Berlin Heidelberg 2006

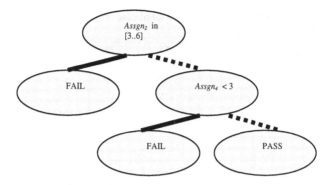

Fig. 1. A sample decision tree

Table 1. A sample decision tree training set

Assgn₁	Assgn₂	Assgn₃	Assgn₄	Exam
...	...	...	...	...
4.6	7.1	3.8	9.1	PASS
9.1	5.1	4.6	3.8	FAIL
7.6	7.1	5.8	6.1	PASS
...	...	...	...	...

2   The Experimental Environment

We use the student data sets to develop success/failure models represented as decision trees. We then calculate the differences between the models derived by data sets from different tutors to reflect on alternative educational policies.

The measurement is based on partitioned data sets. We have partitioned student populations into groups, according to how tutors are assigned to groups. This partitioning allows us to examine whether the grading practices of one tutor apply predictably well to a group supervised by another tutor at the same module. Table 2 shows how are these results are calculated.

A few words on notation are in order. D_i refers to the student group supervised by tutor i. D_0 refers to all students of a module. CV_i refers to the 10-fold cross-validation accuracy reported on data set D_i. $V_{i,j}$ refers to the validation accuracy reported on data set D_j, using the model of data set D_i.

We experimented with one senior (INF31) and two introductory (INF10, INF11) modules, chosen because one or more of the authors had a direct experience in tutoring a student group therein. INF31 data refer to the 2004-5 academic year. INF10 and INF11 data refer to the 2003-4 academic year (newer data has not been collected yet).

Table 2. A template for tabulating cross-testing results

Data Set	D_0	D_1	D_2	...	D_n
D_0	...	...	...	...	...
D_1	...	CV_1	...	...	...
D_2	...	$V_{2,1}$	CV_2	...	...
...	...	...	...	...	...
D_n	...	...	...	...	...

In INF31, six student groups were identified, with about 160 students in total. INF10 and INF11 have more student groups (over 30 and over 15 respectively) and stronger student populations (about 1000 and 500 respectively). The smallest groups had just over 10 students. The largest ones had just over 30 students.

We use GATREE for all experiments, with the default settings for the genetic algorithm operations (cross-over probability at 0.99 and mutation probability at 0.01) and set the bias to prefer short trees. Now, each table like Table 2 can be summarized by the average value of its cells; the initial results are shown in Table 3.

Table 3. INF31 accuracy results for decision trees

Data Set	INF31	INF10	INF11
Accuracy	92.05	83.60	82.31

Do we infer that senior course (INF31) tutors demonstrated a tighter homogeneity than their junior course (INF10, INF11) colleagues? Or, are the above findings the results of processes inherent (but, not yet identified) in the very different students populations (junior vs. senior)?

Herein lurks the danger of using statistics (even, sophisticated) without adequate domain knowledge. To further analyze the above data we went a step further. We noted that the overall exam success rate in INF31 is nearly 100%, whereas in the other two modules (before factoring in the students who drop out) the success rate is substantially below 50%. That sheds new light into the above findings. Indeed, it would be surprising if many differences could be spotted between groups who are overwhelmingly successful!

Now, note that the term "exam" actually aggregates two sessions; a student sits the second exam if the first one is unsuccessful. In this light, we observed that the near 100% rate of INF31 was due to the second exam, whereas the success rate for the second exam in INF10 and INF11 was very small (compared to the overall rate).

Now, the result for the first INF31 exam was $\boxed{62.31}$ (use Table 3 as a benchmark).

The findings are telling (and, incidentally, they suggest that any reference to standard deviations is superfluous). What initially appeared as homogeneity among tutors now turns out to be wide differences.

One can now reframe the question of homogeneity of tutoring practices, albeit in the opposite direction. However, we believe that the crux of the matter must be the identification of the gap. Bridging the gap is, as the cautious reader might suspect, more about human aspects than about technology.

3 Conclusions

The single most important contribution of this paper is the identification of a procedure for analyzing the level of homogeneity displayed by a group of tutors who are, theoretically, expected to smooth out differences that hinder their students' learning efforts. We have used an advanced combination of standard AI methods, in order to obtain information necessary for the reflection on educational policies.

There are some clear steps that can be taken to address differences. Some tutoring groups in HOU have invested in plenary virtual classes, whereas other groups are rotating the grading of exam papers. Either approach could be a legitimate candidate.

But, the purpose of this work is not to recommend a particular approach or to pit tutors' practices against each other; rather it is to develop a methodology whereby tutoring differences are raised and analyzed with respect to their importance. The role of the tutor in reflecting on one's own practices is as important as ever and, as this paper's experimental methodology has demonstrated, even small data sets can yield profound insight.

References

[1] Kotsiantis, S., Pierrakeas, C., & P. Pintelas (2004). Predicting students' performance in distance learning using Machine Learning techniques. *Applied Artificial Intelligence*, 18:5, 411-426.
[2] Witten, I., & E. Frank (2000). Data mining: practical machine learning tools and techniques with Java implementations. San Mateo, CA: Morgan Kaufmann.
[3] Kalles, D., & C. Pierrakeas (2006). Analyzing student performance in distance learning with genetic algorithms and decision trees (accepted for publication in: *Applied Artificial Intelligence*).
[4] Papagelis, A., & D. Kalles (2001). Breeding decision trees using evolutionary techniques. *Proceedings of the International Conference on Machine Learning*, Williamstown, Massachusetts.

A Significance-Based Graph Model
for Clustering Web Documents

Argyris Kalogeratos and Aristidis Likas

Department of Computer Science,
University of Ioannina,
GR 45110, Ioannina, Greece
{akaloger, arly}@cs.uoi.gr

Abstract. Traditional document clustering techniques rely on single-term analysis, such as the widely used Vector Space Model. However, recent approaches have emerged that are based on Graph Models and provide a more detailed description of document properties. In this work we present a novel Significance-based Graph Model for Web documents that introduces a sophisticated graph weighting method, based on significance evaluation of graph elements. We also define an associated similarity measure based on the maximum common subgraph between the graphs of the corresponding web documents. Experimental results on artificial and real document collections using well-known clustering algorithms indicate the effectiveness of the proposed approach.

1 Introduction

The problem of web document clustering belongs to Web Content Mining area [1] and its general objective is to automatically segregate documents into groups called clusters, in a way that each group ideally represents a different topic. In order to perform clustering of Web documents two main issues must be addressed. The first is the definition of a representation model for Web documents along with a measure quantifying the similarity between two Web document models. The second concerns the employment of a clustering algorithm that will take as input the similarity matrix for the pairs of documents and will provide the final partitioning. Although single-term analysis is a simplified approach, the Vector Space Model is still in wide use today. However, new approaches are emerging based on *graph representations* of documents which may be either *term-based* [1] or *path-based* [2]. The model we propose in this work utilizes term-based document representatives of adjustable size and achieves great modeling performance, while conforming to computational effort conditions (CPU, memory, time).

2 Significance-Based Graph Representation of Web Documents

At first an analysis task is performed to locate the 'useful' information in Web documents, which are primarily HTML documents using a set of tags to designate

G. Antoniou et al. (Eds.): SETN 2006, LNAI 3955, pp. 516–519, 2006.

different document parts, and thus assign layout or structural properties. An appropriate model should exploit this information to assign importance levels to different document parts, based on a predefined correspondence between HTML tags and significance levels. In our implementation four significance levels were used: {VERY HIGH, HIGH, MEDIUM, LOW}. Examples of document parts with very high significance are the title and metadata. High significance is assigned to section titles, medium to emphasized parts, and finally the lowest level is assigned to the remainder of normal text.

We represent a document as a directed acyclic graph, well known as *DIG* (*Directed Indexed Graph*), along with a weighting scheme. Formally, a document $d = \{W, E, S\}$ consists of three sets of elements: a set of graph nodes $W = \{w_1, ..., w_{|W|}\}$ each of them uniquely represents a word of the document (unique node label in graph), a set of graph edges $E = \{e_1, ..., e_{|E|}\}$, where $e_i = (w_k, w_l)$ is an ordered pair (directed edge) of graph nodes denoting the sequential occurrence of two terms in a document. Indeed, we call w_l *neighbor* of w_k and the *neighborhood* of w_k is the set of all the neighbors of w_k. These properties capture semantic correlations between terms. Finally, S is a function which assigns real numbers as significance weights to the *DIG* nodes and edges.

The simplest weighting scheme is actually a non-weighting scheme (*NWM*) [1]. The next step is the assignment of frequencies as graph weights for nodes (*FM*), whereas in this work we propose a more sophisticated significance-based weighting scheme (*SM*). We define the node (term) significance $g_w(w, d)$ as the sum of significance level of all occurrences of w in document d (possible values of significance level of i-th occurrence of w are {VERY HIGH, HIGH, MEDIUM, LOW}).

Regarding to the edges, we should keep in mind the key role they have for document's meaning content, since they represent term associations. Thus, we define the edge significance g_e as:

$$g_e(e(w_k, w_l), d) = \frac{g_w(w_k, d) \cdot g_w(w_l, d)}{g_w(w_k, d) + g_w(w_l, d)} \cdot freq(e(w_k, w_l), d) \cdot$$

where $e(w_k, w_l)$ is a document edge and $freq(e(w_k, w_l), d)$ is the edge's frequency in document d. We are now in a position to define the *document content*, which would be based on the weights of all elements of the document graph:

$$g_D^{(all)}(d) = \sum_{j=1}^{nodenum(d)} g_w(w_j, d) + \sum_{i=1}^{edgenum(d)} g_e(e_i(w_k, w_l), d) \cdot$$

where *nodenum(d)* and *edgenum(d)* are the number of different words and edges respectively in document d. Having estimated the significance values for all elements of the full document graph, we can simply apply a *filtering procedure* on the modeled dataset to keep the P more important nodes per graph. The evaluation criterion can be based either on the frequency weight of a term resulting in a Frequency Filtering (*FF*), or on the significance weight resulting in the proposed Significance Filtering approach (*SF*).

3 Similarity Measure

The next step is to define a measure $s(G_x, G_y)$ that quantifies the similarity between two given document graphs G_x, G_y. This can be enabled through a *graph matching process*, that is based on the maximum common sub-graph between the graphs of the corresponding web documents. The exact computation divides the size of $|mcs(G_x, G_y)|$ of filtered graphs by the $\max(|G_{dx}|, |G_{dy}|)$ of respective unfiltered graphs (note: the size of a graph $|G| = |W| + |E|$). Even though the *mcs* problem is *NP*-complete in general, in our case we have unique graph labels, therefore we deal a reasonable cost of $O(P)$, where P is the global filtering threshold for all documents. This similarity is called graph-theoretical and is used by *NWM*.

In fact, *mcs* ignores whatever information about element significances, even frequencies. We propose the *maximum common content* similarity measure that is based on the significance evaluation of common sub-graphs and is used in combination with the *SM*. In particular, we define two elementary similarity cases:

1. $E_w(w_i^{(x)}, w_j^{(y)}) = g_w(w_i, d_x) + g_w(w_j, d_y)$, which measures the similarity that derives from the mutual word $w_i = w_j$, where $w_i \in d_x$ and $w_i \in d_y$

2. $E_e(e_k^{(x)}(w_i, w_p), e_l^{(y)}(w_j, w_q)) = g_e(e_k(w_i, w_p), d_x) + g_e(e_l(w_j, w_q), d_y)$, which measures the similarity that derives from the mutual edge $e_k^{(x)} = e_l^{(y)}$, where $w_i = w_j$, $w_p = w_q$, $e_k \in d_x$ and $e_l \in d_y$.

If we could define the content union of two documents (at the full graph scale), we could also compute the percentage of common content. Supposing that the *mcs* has been calculated, we evaluate the overall normalized similarity matched sub-graphs:

$$s(G_x, G_y) = \frac{\sum_{i,j,k,l} \left(E_w(w_i^{(x)}, w_j^{(y)}) + E_e(e_k^{(x)}(w_i, w_p), e_l^{(y)}(w_j, w_q)) \right)}{g_D^{(all)}(d_x) + g_D^{(all)}(d_y)} .$$

4 Experiments and Conclusions

We conducted a series of experiments comparing the *NWM* model with the *SM* model proposed in this work. *NWM* uses frequency filtering (*FF*) and assigns no graph weights. The introduced novel *SM* model, on the other hand, uses term filtering based on significance (*SF*) and assigns significance-based weights to graph elements.

As clustering methods, we used an agglomerative algorithm (*HAC*) and two versions of *k-means* algorithm: the typical random center initialization (*RI-KM*) and the *global k-means* (*Global-KM*) [4], already been used to cluster web documents [3].

In our experiments, we evaluate clustering performance using three indices. The first index is the *Rand Index* (*RI*), which is a clustering accuracy measure focused on the pairwise correctness of the result. The second index is a *statistic index* (*SI*), which computes the percentage of *N* documents assigned to the "right" cluster, based on ground truth information. A third index we considered is the typical *Mean intra-Cluster Error* (*MCE*). Three web document collections were used: the *F-series*

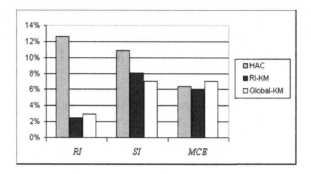

Fig. 1. *SM* vs *NWM* overall *improvement* on all collections using three indices

(95 web documents from 4 classes) and *J-series* (185 web documents from 10 classes) used in [7] and an artificially created dataset consisting of classes of high purity.

The experimental results (Fig. 1) indicate the overall improvement obtained using the proposed *SM* approach. We have found that *SM* is superior to *NWM* in all cases since a clear improvement for all indices was observed in almost all experiments. In what concerns the clustering algorithms, the agglomerative approach exhibits sensitivity on "difficult" data, while when used with the *SM* model, it can be competitive to k-means type of algorithms. From the k-means class of methods, *Global-KM* shows a clear qualitative superiority comparing to *RI-KM,* which nevertheless also remains a reliable and computationally "cheap" approach.

References

1. A. Schenker, M. Last, H. Bunke and A. Kandel: Clustering of Web Documents Using a Graph Model, Web Document Analysis: Chalenges and Opportunities, eds. A. Antona-copoulos and J. Hu, to appear
2. K. M. Hammuda: Efficient Phrase-Based Document Indexing for Web-Document Clustering, IEEE, 2003
3. A.Schenker, M.Last, H. Bunke, A.Kandel: A Comparison of Two Novel Algorithms for Clustering Web Documents, 2nd Int. Workshop of Web Document Analysis, WDA 2003, Edinburgh, UK, August 2003
4. A. Likas, N. Vlassis and J. J. Verbeek: The global k-means clustering algorithm, Pattern Recognition, Vol. 36, 2003, pp. 451 – 461

Supporting Clinico-Genomic Knowledge Discovery: A Multi-strategy Data Mining Process

Alexandros Kanterakis and George Potamias

Institute of Computer Science, Foundation for Research &
Technology – Hellas (FORTH) P.O. Box 1385, 711 10 Heraklion, Crete, Greece
{kantale, potamias}@ics.forth.gr
http://www.ics.forth.gr/~potamias/Potamias.htm

Abstract. We present a combined clinico-genomic knowledge discovery (CGKD) process suited for linking gene-expression (microarray) and clinical patient data. The process present a multi-strategy mining approach realized by the smooth integration of three distinct data-mining components: clustering (based on a discretized k-means approach), association rules mining, and feature-selection for selecting discrimant genes. The proposed CGKD process is applied on a real-world gene-expression profiling study (i.e., clinical outcome of breast cancer patients). Assessment of the results demonstrates the rationality and reliability of the approach.

1 Introduction

The completion of the human genome drives us to the *post-genomics* era. In this environment the newly raised scientific and technological challenges push for *trans-disciplinary* team science and *translational* research. In this paper we present a combined *Clinico-Genomic Knowledge Discovery* (CGKD) approach suited for linkage of patients' gene-expression (microarray) and clinical data. The whole approach composes a 'screening' scenario for the careful identification of those patient cases and genes, which are more suitable to feed a gene-selection process. The proposed process is inspired by respective multi-strategy machine learning [4]. The approach is based on the smooth integration of three distinct data-mining methodologies: (i) *Clustering* - based on a novel k-means clustering algorithm operating on categorical data, named *discr-kmeans;* (ii) *Association Rules Mining* - aimed for the discovery of 'causal' relations (rules with high confidence) between clusters of genes and patients' attributes; and (iii) *Feature Selection,* for the selection of the most discrimant genes to distinguish between different patient classes (e.g., prognosis and clinical outcome).

2 CGKD Methodology: The Data-Mining Components

Linking Genomic and Clinical Profiles: A Discretized k-means Approach. A lot of work has been done in identifying co-regulated groups or, *clusters* of genes, discriminant set of genes [1]. In this paper we introduce a *discretized two-dimensional k-means* clustering algorithm to identify co-regulated genes. Assume we have s

G. Antoniou et al. (Eds.): SETN 2006, LNAI 3955, pp. 520–524, 2006.

samples, g genes, and a 2-dimensional matrix $M(s \times g)$ that holds the gene-expression values of samples. Clustering of genes with the discretized k-means approach - called *discr-kmeans*, is inspired and resembles similar approaches reported in [2], [8]. It unfolds into the following two steps: *Step-1: Discretization.* We proceed with a method to overcome the error-prone variance of gene-expression levels by *discretizing* the respective continuous gene-expression values. A gene-expression value may be assigned to an (ordered) nominal value. Assume n such values - in the case of $n=2$, value '*1*' is interpreted as 'down'-, and value '2' as 'up'-regulated gene. The discretization of gene's g_i expression-values is based on a method reported in [3]. *Step-2: Clustering.* The main difference between normal k-means and discr-kmeans is that each cluster's center is not represented by the average value of the current cluster's genes but by a 2-dimensional matrix that contains the *percentage* of the discretised cluster's genes' values, $C_k(s,n)$. If s_i is a sample and $p \in [1, n]$ then, $C_k(s_i,p)$, the cluster's center, is the percentage of genes in cluster k the discretized expression-values of which is p for sample s_i. For example, in a domain with three samples and $n=2$, a (potential) cluster's center is presented by a matrix like:

Value → ↓Sample	'1' %	'2' %
1	80	20
2	55	45
3	10	90

In the above matrix, 80% from all genes that belong to the cluster, the discretized value of sample 1 is '*1*', which corresponds to a 'down'-regulated gene. Analogously in the same cluster, sample 3 exhibits an 'up'-regulated (value '2') gene. Now, the distance between a cluster $C_k(s,n)$ and a gene g_j may be computed by formula (1):

$$D(C_k, g_j) = \sum_{l=1}^{s} C_k \left(s_l, M_D \left(s_l, g_j \right) \right) \tag{1}$$

Initially we predefine the number of clusters, c, and we choose c random genes. We assume that each of the initialy chosen genes forms a unique cluster and we calculate its center. Then, we iterate through all genes and we assign each one to the closest cluster. As in regular k-means, this procedure is repeated until no change in cluster assignments appears or, until we reach a maximum number of iterations. We end-up, not only with clusters of genes but, with an indication of how '*strong*' a cluster is. A cluster is considered '*strong*' if it has a lot of 'extreme' discretized value percentages in the samples, i.e, close to 0%, or close to 100%.

From Genomic to Clinical Profiles: An Association Rules Mining Approach. We support discovery of associations across segments of combined clinico-genomic sample records, i.e., patient cases described with reference to clinico-genomic attributes, by using association rule mining [5], [7], or ARM for short. Using ARM we were able to establish significant and useful associations of the type: $G \Rightarrow C$, where G refers to a set of genes clusters, and C to a set of clinical attributes.

Selecting Discriminatory Genes via a Feature-Selection Approach. We applied a feature-selection method specially suited for the task of selecting discriminant genes – genes, the expression profiles of which is able to distinguish between particular pres-classified patient samples. A detailed description of the method may be found in [6].

The method is implemented in an integrated system for mining gene-expression (microarray) data – the MineGene system[1]. The method is composed by three components: discretization of gene-expression data, ranking of genes, and classification to predict patient class categories (e.g., clinical outcome and 'bad' or, 'good' prognosis). The overall multi-strategy process, named CGKD, is illustrated in figure 1, below.

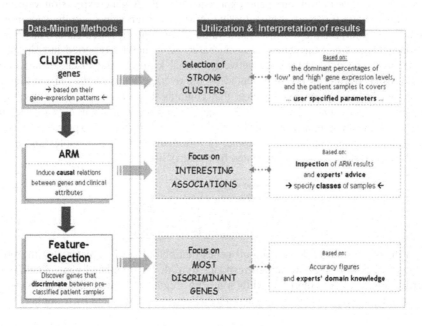

Fig. 1. A CGKD scenario enabled by the smooth integration of different data-mining methods

3 Utilizing CGKD in a Real-World Domain

We applied the CGKD process on a real world clinico-genomic study [9] (with which we compare our results). The data includes the gene-expression profiles of 24.481 genes over 78 patient samples; 44 of them with a status of over five years survival ('good' prognosis), and 34 with a status of less than five years survival ('bad' prognosis). The patients' clinical profiles are also provided – here we focus on the prognostic status trying to discover reliable associations between the prognostic profiles of patients and their gene-expression background.

Expriments and Findings. (a) *Clustering genes and selection of strong clusters.* For discr-kmeans clustering we set the number of clusters to 90. The next step was to select the clusters that show a strong relation with the respective clinical attributes. This process is performed by manual inspection on the clusters' samples coverage and

---

[1] Kanterakis, A.: Gene Selection & Clustering Microarray data: The MineGene System. MSc thesis, dept. of Computer Science, University of Crete, April 2005, Heraklion, Crete. http://www.csd.uoc.gr/~kantale/ Kanterakis_ THESIS.pdf

the number of included. The respective thresholds were, for #samples $\geq$10, and #genes $\geq$100, with the respective threshold for considering a sample as 'strong' to have at least 90% 'up'-regulated genes in the respective cluster. We end-up with a set of 13 gene-clusters. (b) *ARM and causal genomic-clinical relations.* We selected all the genomic attributes to participate in the 'IF' scope of the rule and the rest of the clinical attributes to participate in both sides. We set a minimum support and confidence threshold to 10 and 60 respectively and focused on "follow_up-time" in years (for clinical attributes), and on all 13 gene-clusters. In the resulted association rules only 3 out of the 13 gene clusters appeared. These rules cover: 37 out of the input 78 samples, and 5936 genes (5503, 284 and 149 for the three respective clusters). (c) *Gene-Selection.* Applying the feature-selection approach, presented in the previous section, on the set of 37 cases and the set of 5936 we end-up with the results presented in table 1, below.

Table 1. Comparative gene-selection accuracy results

	#SG*	37 samples**	78 total samples	19 test samples***
CGKD	100	100%	85.9%	89.5%
Ref. Study	70	NA⁺	80.8%	89.5%

*SG: number of selected genes; **The samples selected by the CGKD process; ***Independent set of samples (left-out during training); ⁺NA: Not Applicable

4   Conclusions and Future Research

Based on data-mining components we introduced an integrated clinico-genomic knowledge discovery process (CGKD). We applied CGKD on a real-world gene-expression case study ending-up into strong and causal relations between patients' genomic and clinical profiles. The results on applying the presented feature/gene-selection approach are encouraging, demonstrating the rationality of the approach and its reliability as well. Our future R&D plans focus on the design and implementation of a Web-based environment to support the presented CGKD process.

Acknowledgment. This work is already in progress and it is being partially supported by the INFOBIOMED NoE IST (IST-2002-507585), and PrognoChip (funded by the Greek General Secretariat for Research & Technology in the context of the EPAN program) projects.

References

1. Eisen, M., Spellman, P.T., Botstein, D. and Brown, P.O. (1998) Cluster analysis and display of genome-wide expression patterns. Proc. Natl. Acad. Sci. USA 96, 14863-14867.
2. Gupta, S.K., Rao, S., Bhatnagar, V. K-means Clustering Algorithm for Categorical Attributes. LNCS 1676 (1999) 203 - 208

3. Lopez, L.M., I.F. Ruiz, R.M. Bueno and G.T. Ruiz, Dynamic Discretisation of Continuous Values from Time Series, in Proc. 11th European Conference on Machine Learning (ECML 2000), eds. R.L. Mantaras E. and Plaza, LNAI 1810 (2000) 290-291.
4. Botta, M., and Giordana, A. (1993). SMART+: A Multi-Strategy Learning Tool, in Proc. IJCAI-93, pp. 937-943.
5. Potamias G., Koumakis L., and Moustakis V. (2004). Mining XML Clinical Data: The HealthObs System. Ingenierie des systems d'information, special session: Recherche, extraction et exploration d'information 10:1, 2005.
6. Potamias, G., Koumakis, L., Moustakis, V.: Gene Selection via Discretized Gene-Expression Profiles and Greedy Feature-Elimination", Lecture notes in Artificial Intelligence-LNAI, vol. 3025, pp. 256-266, (2004).
7. Agrawal,R., Imielinski, T., and Arun, Swami, N. (1993). Mining Association Rules between Sets of Items in Large Databases, in *Proc. of the 1993 ACM SIGMOD International Conference on Management of Data.*
8. San, O.M., Huynh, V-N., Nakamori, Y.: An alternative extension of the k-means algorithm for clustering categorical data. Int. J. Appl. Math. Comput. Sci., 14:2 (2004) 241–247.
9. van't Veer, L., Dai, H., Vijver, M.v.D., He, Y., Hart, A., Moa, M., Peterse, H., Kooy, K.v.D., Marton, M., Witteveen, A., Schreiber, G., Kerkhoven, R., Roberts, C., Linsley, P., Bernards, R., and Friend, S. (2002). Gene expression profiling predicts clinical outcome of breast cancer. Nature 415, 530–536.

SHARE-ODS: An Ontology Data Service for Search and Rescue Operations

Stasinos Konstantopoulos, Georgios Paliouras, and Symeon Chatzinotas

Institute of Informatics and Telecommunications,
NCSR 'Demokritos', Ag. Paraskevi 153 10, Athens, Greece
{konstant, paliourg, schatzin}@iit.demokritos.gr

Abstract. This paper describes an ontology data service (ODS) for supporting Search and Rescue (SaR) operations. The ontological model represents various aspects of the command, communication, and organisational structure of the SaR forces and the deployment and progress of a SaR operation. Furthermore, the ontology supports the semantic indexing of multimedia documents in the context of SaR processes and activities. This ODS supports a semantically-enhanced information and communication system for SaR forces. Modelling the spatio-temporal aspects of an operation in alignment with possibly-unreliable information automatically extracted from multimedia objects, introduces a number of challenges for the field of knowledge representation and reasoning.

1 Introduction

Search-and-rescue (SaR) operations are conducted by fire-brigade, rescue and medical units, operating under a complex unified command-and-communications structure. The communication channels of the emergency units are push-to-talk walkie-talkies and short hand-written message forms read over the radio. All status information necessary to decision making is processed manually.

The SHARE project[1] develops a Push-To-Share (PTS) advanced mobile service that provides communication support for emergency teams during SaR operations. We present here the SHARE Ontology Data Service (SHARE-ODS), which supports the PTS service with (quantitatively but also qualitatively) enhanced information, necessary for the decision-making process at all command levels of the operation. Furthermore, the information stored in the ODS serves as a complete log of the operation for the purposes of planning and evaluation.

Although several multimedia semantic modelling and spatio-temporal modelling ontologies have been proposed, there is no unifying approach of the two. Here we propose a model for the semantic indexing of multimedia objects in the context of processes and activities. This model not only unifies these two aspects of a SaR operation, but it also allows for the semantic cross-checking of possibly-unreliable information automatically extracted from multimedia objects.

---

[1] SHARE: Mobile Support for Rescue Forces, Integrating Multiple Modes of Interaction, IST-funded project, URL: http://www.ist-share.org/

G. Antoniou et al. (Eds.): SETN 2006, LNAI 3955, pp. 525–528, 2006.

Due to space limitations, the overview of the state-of-the-art and the description of SHARE-ODS is very concise. For a fuller overview and SHARE-ODS description, please see technical report DEMO-2006-1.[2]

2   Related Ontologies

Ontological resources that are relevant to our SaR ontology are both general purpose ontologies and related domain ontologies.

Various general-purpose space, time, and spatio-temporal ontologies have been proposed, generally speaking as part of a more complete concept and interface specification that aims to enhance interoperability between databases and applications that make geographic and temporal references. Most prominently:

- The Standard Upper Ontology Working Group of IEEE.
- ISO geo-reference standards 19107:2003, 19115:2003 and 14825:2004. ISO 19108:2002 standardises temporal characteristics of geographic information.
- The OpenGIS specification of the Open Geospatial Consortium[3].
- Temporal ontologies, e.g. OWL-Time[4] and OWL-S[5].

Domain ontologies and task ontologies describe the vocabulary for a generic domain, task, or activity by means of specialised terms. They can be used as a basis which can be expanded and specified into an application-specific ontology. Ontologies and projects that are related to the SHARE ontology include:

- The OntoWeb[6] and KnowledgeWeb[7] thematic networks, developing standards, infrastructure and ontologies for semantic annotation.
- The aceMedia project[8] on knowledge discovery from multimedia data and ontology-driven meta-data extraction.
- The Enterprise Ontology[9], capturing the structure and processes of large corporations with complex structures and business plans.
- The CoSAR-TS project, researching the semantic modelling of military SaR operations. CoSAR-TS is based on the <I-N-OVA> model.[10]

3   The Search-and-Rescue Ontology Data Service

Search-and-rescue operations (SaR) are conducted by fire-brigade, rescue and medical units, operating under a unified command-and-communications structure. Emergency forces use half-duplex channel walkie-talkie technology for simple push-to-talk voice communication. Furthermore they exchange hand-written

---

[2] http://www.iit.demokritos.gr/~konstant/dload/Pubs/demo-2006-1.pdf
[3] http://www.opengeospatial.org/
[4] http://www.isi.edu/~pan/OWL-Time.html
[5] http://www.daml.org/services/owl-s/
[6] http://www.ontoweb.org/
[7] http://knowledgeweb.semanticweb.org/
[8] http://www.acemedia.org/
[9] http://www.aiai.ed.ac.uk/project/enterprise/enterprise/ontology.html
[10] http://www.aiai.ed.ac.uk/project/{cosar-ts/index.html,oplan/inova.html}

message forms that are typically read over the radio. All status information, reporting and documentation for decision making is processed manually.

SHARE proposes replacing walkie-talkies and written message forms with a push-to-share (PTS) system that supports the transmission of audio, video and digital message forms. The new system integrates the PTS communications system with the ontologically-indexed data service, supporting the decision-making process by making all relevant information and documents easily retrievable by means of semantic indexing and searching.

3.1   SaR Operations

Emergency units participating in SaR operations, operate under a unified command and communications structure and are deployed in sections (B-Level deployments) and subsections (C-Level deployments). Deployments have three aspects: (a) operational, e.g. fire-fighting, first-aid, water supply, etc., (b) geographical, that is, the area they are responsible for, and (c) operation structural, defining command and communications channels. In addition to the B and C-Level units, the operation establishes (on site) an A-Level command and control centre, which is in charge of the whole operation.

3.2   The Ontology Data Service

The SHARE Ontology Data Service (ODS) is an intelligent storage, indexing and retrieval mechanism for (a) meta-data of documents created and transmitted during an operation, (b) spatio-temporal information pertaining to the operation, and (c) information regarding the structure of the operation. This information is accessed through the ODS interface, which offers functions for populating and querying an application-specific ontology through a Web Service (complying to the W3C SOAP[11] messaging recommendation). The web service uses Protégé[12] to manipulate the OWL representation of the ontology, and a reasoning engine (currently Jena[13]) to provide the back-end for the querying functionality, allowing for the retrieval of implicit (inferred) knowledge.

3.3   Ontological Model

The ontological model of the operation is organised into three sub-ontologies: *SaR, multimedia* and *event*. In addition, there are two auxiliary sub-ontologies (*time* and *space*) that represent spatio-temporal references and actual geographical features (buildings, streets, etc) present at the theatre of the operation.

The SaR ontology holds the concepts that are related to the Search and Rescue operation, the personnel involved, and the communications system. SaR concepts include deployment types (e.g. A-, B- or C-Level), operational rôles and actual personnel, units, vehicles, equipment, etc. Deployments comprise units

---

[11] http://www.w3.org/TR/2003/REC-soap12-part0-20030624/

[12] http://protege.stanford.edu/

[13] http://jena.sourceforge.net/

and are linked together in a partology, and also connected to operational rôles their require (e.g. deployment leader, dispatcher, etc) which, in their turn, are connected to the actual personnel members that fulfil each rôle.

The Multimedia conceptual model holds meta-data from all documents (text messages, audio, video, and infrared video) generated and transmitted during the operation. This meta-data includes 'logistical' information (creation time, session the document was transmitted in, sender and recipient, etc) and content meta-data extracted automatically by image, speech, and text processing systems.

Finally, events relate a temporal instance with some characteristic or instance of the operation. Action events, in particular, relate temporal instances with an agent (e.g. a PTS_USER instance), an object (e.g. a PTS_SESSION), and other action-specific properties (e.g., for session participation events, floor time).

4   Future Plans

We propose an ontological model that unifies SaR operation modelling with semantic annotation of documents, to offer an integrated model for an operation and all documents pertaining to it. Furthermore, we are putting together a set of tools for using the ontology at an actual SaR operation. These tools include the Ontology Data Server for updating and accessing the semantic data and the reasoning facilities that will augment the original data with inferred facts.

As a SaR operation unfolds, the ontology gets populated by various sources, some reliable (e.g. GPS) and some not (e.g. information extraction modules). Faulty data can be caught (and, possibly, corrected) when create inconsistencies, which can be resolved in favour of the more reliable source. In this manner, feedback can also be provided to the module responsible for the error, so that it can improve its performance over time. In cases where multiple sources corroborate towards accepting or rejecting multiple pieces of information, the problem of deciding which to accept as most reliable (and, inversely, distribution of responsibility in order to provide feedback) becomes a non-trivial problem. This problem has been approached in various domains, but not in the domain of responsibility distribution among multiple information extraction sources.

The other interesting direction we plan to pursue is spatio-temporal representation and reasoning for the purposes of operation planning and evaluation. At this point, the ontology models only the current situation, with a limited temporal EVENT ontology. In order to represent the operation through time, the EVENT ontology will be expanded. The temporal information will be used by a reasoning engine that supports spatio-temporal reasoning. Spatio-temporal reasoning applies to cases where we don't have precise, quantitative information about space and time, but only qualitative relationships between instances. Constraint-satisfaction spatio-temporal reasoning can be applied in these cases in order to effectively query the Knowledge Base.

Graphical Representation of Defeasible Logic Rules Using Digraphs

Efstratios Kontopoulos and Nick Bassiliades

Department of Informatics, Aristotle University of Thessaloniki,
GR-54124 Thessaloniki, Greece
{skontopo, nbassili}@csd.auth.gr

Abstract. Defeasible reasoning is a rule-based approach for efficient reasoning with incomplete and conflicting information. Nevertheless, it is based on solid mathematical formulations and is not fully comprehensible by end users, who often need graphical trace and explanation mechanisms for the derived conclusions. Directed graphs (or digraphs) can assist in this affair, but their applicability is balanced by the fact that it is difficult to associate data of a variety of types with the nodes and the connections in the graph. In this paper we try to utilize digraphs in the graphical representation of defeasible rules, by exploiting their expressiveness, but also trying to counter their major disadvantage, by defining multiple node and connection types.

1 Introduction

Defeasible reasoning [2] constitutes a simple rule-based approach to reasoning with incomplete and conflicting information. It can represent facts, rules, as well as priorities and conflicts among rules. Such conflicts arise, among others, from rules with exceptions (e.g. policies and business rules) and priority information is often available to resolve conflicts among rules. However, although defeasible reasoning features a significant degree of expressiveness and intuitiveness, it is still based on solid mathematical formulations, which, in many cases, may seem too complicated. So, end users might often consider the conclusion of a defeasible logic theory incomprehensible. A graphical trace and an explanation mechanism would certainly be very beneficial.

Directed graphs (or digraphs) are a special case of graphs that constitute a powerful and convenient way of representing relationships between entities [4]. In a digraph, entities are represented as nodes and relationships as directed lines or arrows that connect the nodes. The orientation of the arrows follows the flow of information in the digraph [5]. Digraphs offer a number of advantages to information visualization, with the most important of them being: (a) comprehensibility - the information that a digraph contains can be easily and accurately understood by humans [8] and (b) expressiveness - digraph topology bears non-trivial information [4]. Furthermore, in the case of graphical representation of logic rules, digraphs seem to be extremely appropriate. They can offer explanation of derived conclusions, since the series of inference steps in the graph can be easily detected and retraced [1]. Also, by going backwards from the conclusion to the triggering conditions, one can validate the truth of the inference result, gaining a means of proof visualization and validation. Finally,

G. Antoniou et al. (Eds.): SETN 2006, LNAI 3955, pp. 529–533, 2006.

especially in the case of defeasible logic rules, the notion of direction can also assist in graphical representations of rule attacks, superiorities etc.

There is, however, one major disadvantage, not only of digraphs but of graphs in general. More specifically, it is difficult to associate data of a variety of types with the nodes and with the connections between the nodes in the graph [4].

In this paper we attempt to exploit the expressiveness and comprehensibility of directed graphs, as well as their suitability for rule representation, but also try to leverage their disadvantages, by adopting an "enhanced" digraph approach.

There exist systems that implement rule representation/visualization with graphs, such as Graphviz [6], although we haven't come across a system that represents defeasible logic rules yet. Certain knowledge-based system development tools also feature rule and execution graph-drawing. Finally, there have been attempts of creating rule graphs for certain rule types, like association rules [3] or production rules [7], but they remained at an elementary stage of development.

2 Representing Rules with Digraphs

In an attempt to leverage the inability of directed graphs to use a variety of distinct entity types, the digraphs in our approach will contain two kinds of nodes, similarly to the methodology followed by [7]. The two node types will be:

- literals, represented by rectangles, which we call "*literal boxes*"
- rules, represented by circles

Thus, according to this principle, the following rule base:

$$p: \text{ if A then B} \qquad\qquad q: \text{ if B then } \neg C$$

can be represented by the directed graph:

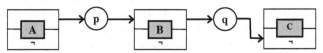

Each literal box consists of two adjacent "*atomic formula boxes*", with the upper one of them representing a positive atomic formula and the lower one representing a negated atomic formula. This way, the atomic formulas are depicted together clearly and separately, maintaining their independence.

r: if ¬A and B then C
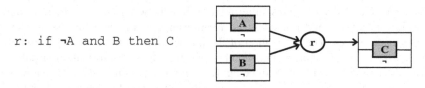

Fig. 1. Digraph featuring a conjunction

If the rule body consists of a conjunction of literals the representation is not profoundly affected, as illustrated in Fig. 1. As can be observed, digraphs, "enhanced" with the addition of distinct node types, offer a significant level of expressiveness in representing rules. The next step is to use directed graphs in the representation of defeasible logic rules, which are more demanding in representational capabilities.

3 Defeasible Logics and Digraphs

A *defeasible theory* D (i.e. a knowledge base or a program in defeasible logic) consists of three basic ingredients: a set of facts (F), a set of rules (R) and a superiority relationship (>). Therefore, D can be represented by the triple (F, R, >).

In defeasible logic, there are three distinct types of rules: strict rules, defeasible rules and defeaters. In our approach, each one of the three rule types will be mapped to one of three distinct connection types (i.e. arrows), so that rules of different types can be represented clearly and distinctively.

The first rule type in defeasible reasoning is *strict rules*, which are denoted by $A \rightarrow p$ and are interpreted in the typical sense: whenever the premises are indisputable, then so is the conclusion. An example is: *"Penguins are birds"*, which would become: r_1: penguin(X) $\rightarrow$ bird(X), and is represented by digraphs, as follows:

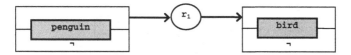

Notice that in the rule graph we only represent the predicate and not the literal (i.e. predicate plus all the arguments) because we are mainly interested in emphasizing the interrelationships between the concepts (through the rules) and not the complete details of the defeasible theory.

Contrary to strict rules, *defeasible rules* can be defeated by contrary evidence and are denoted by $A \Rightarrow p$. Examples of defeasible rules are r_2: bird(X) $\Rightarrow$ flies(X), which reads as: *"Birds typically fly"* and r_3: penguin(X) $\Rightarrow$ ¬flies(X), namely: *"Penguins typically do not fly"*. Rules r_2 and r_3 would be mapped to the following directed graphs, respectively:

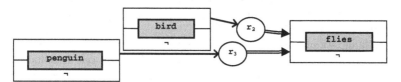

Defeaters, denoted by $A \sim> p$, are rules that do not actively support conclusions, but can only prevent them, namely they can defeat some defeasible conclusions by producing evidence to the contrary. An example is: r_4: heavy(X) $\sim>$ ¬flies(X), which reads as: *"Heavy things cannot fly"*. This defeater can defeat the (defeasible) rule r_2 mentioned above and it can be represented as:

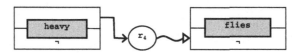

Finally, the *superiority relationship* is an acyclic relation > that is used to resolve conflicts among rules. For example, given the defeasible rules r_2 and r_3, no conclusive decision can be made about whether a penguin can fly or not, because rules r_2 and r_3 contradict each other. But if the superiority relationship $r_3 > r_2$ is introduced, then r_3 overrides r_2 and we can indeed conclude that the penguin cannot fly. Rule r_3 is called *superior* to r_2. Thus, a fourth connection type is introduced and the aforementioned superiority relationship is represented as follows:

The set of rules ($r_1 - r_4$) mentioned in this section form a bigger, compact directed rule graph that can indeed raise the level of comprehensibility on behalf of the user.

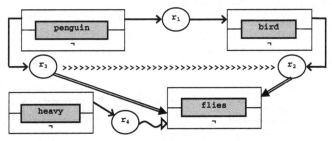

4 Conclusions and Future Work

In this paper we argued that graphs can be a powerful tool in the field of information visualization. Especially in the case of rules, directed graphs can be particularly useful, since by definition they embrace the idea of information flow, a notion that is also encountered in rules and inference. Directed graphs present, however, a major disadvantage, which is their inability to associate data of a variety of types with the nodes and with the connections between the nodes. In this paper we propose an approach that aims at leveraging this disadvantage, by allowing different node and connection types. Digraphs, "enhanced" with these extra features, can greatly assist in representing defeasible logic rules.

In the future we plan to delve deeper into the proof layer of the Semantic Web architecture, by enhancing further the rule representation with rule execution tracing, explanation, proof exchange in an XML/RDF format, proof visualization and validation, etc. These facilities would be useful for increasing the user trust for the Semantic Web and for automating proof exchange and trust among agents in the Semantic Web.

References

[1] Antoniou G., Harmelen F. van, *A Semantic Web Primer*, MIT Press, 2004.
[2] Antoniou G., *Nonmonotonic Reasoning*, MIT Press, 1997.
[3] Chakravarthy S., Zhang H., "Visualization of association rules over relational DBMSs", *Proc. 2003 ACM Symp. on Applied Computing*, ACM Press, pp. 922-926, 2003.

[4] Clarke D., "An Augmented Directed Graph Base for Application Development", *Proc. 20th annual Southeast regional Conf.*, ACM Press, pp. 155-159, 1982.

[5] Diestel R., *Graph Theory (Graduate Texts in Mathematics)*, 2nd ed., Springer, 2000.

[6] Graphviz - Graph Visualization Software, http://www.graphviz.org.

[7] Jantzen J., "Inference Planning Using Digraphs and Boolean Arrays", Proc. Int. Conf. on APL, ACM Press, pp. 200-204, New York, USA, 1989.

[8] Nascimento H.A.D. do, "A Framework for Human-Computer Interaction in Directed Graph Drawing", *Proc. Australian Symp. on Information Visualization*, pp. 63-69, 2001.

An Efficient Peer to Peer Image Retrieval Technique Using Content Addressable Networks

Spyros Kotoulas[1,*], Konstantinos Konstantinidis[2,**], Leonidas Kotoulas[2], and Ioannis Andreadis[2]

[1] Department of Computer Science, Vrije Universiteit Amsterdam, De Boelelaan 1081a, 1081HV Amsterdam, The Netherlands
kotoula@few.vu.nl
[2] Laboratory of Electronics, Department of Electrical and Computer Engineering, Democritus University of Thrace, Vas. Sofias 12, 67100 Xanthi, Greece
{konkonst, lkotoula, iandread}@ee.duth.gr

Abstract. We present a novel technique for efficient Content Based Peer to Peer Image Retrieval (CBP2PIR) that employs a Content Addressable Network (CAN). A two-stage color histogram based method is described. The first stage defines mapping into the CAN by use of a single fuzzy histogram; while the second stage completes the image retrieval process through a spatially-biased histogram. The proposed system is completely decentralized, non-flooding, and promises high image recall, while minimizing network traffic.

1 Introduction

In recent years, a wide range of Peer-to-Peer (P2P) systems have been developed to overcome the weaknesses of centralized approaches: single point of failure, lack of scalability, undisclosed or censored content and invasion of privacy just to name a few. Extensive research has been carried out on structured overlay networks to improve efficiency and scalability. Although these Overlays can be used to find specific peers or content, they are not directly usable for Information Retrieval, since they typically require some sort of fixed-size content or peer descriptor.

Meanwhile, image retrieval systems have mainly involved large static databases, with the disadvantages of centralized systems. However, such systems are computationally demanding and produce lengthy descriptors which cannot be used for P2P. Hence, methods that produce light though efficient image descriptors come in hand. Such a descriptor is the histogram which counts the color distribution of an image and disperses it into bins, producing a fixed-size vector. To prove efficient, most histogram extracting techniques, such as Swain's et al [1], produce large sized vectors (2048 bins) which are not optimal in this case. A more suitable one is fuzzy histograms [2] which only require 10 bins in order to be reasonably efficient. Once efficiently retrieving relevant images, a method of low computational complexity is

---

* Funded by the EU OpenKnowledge Project (IST-2005-027253).
** Funded by the EU-EPEAEK Archimedes-II Project (2.2.3.z,subprogram 10).

G. Antoniou et al. (Eds.): SETN 2006, LNAI 3955, pp. 534–537, 2006.

desirable to increase precision. Hence, we introduce the novel idea of spatially-biased histograms, ostensibly simple histograms of 128 bins, enriched with embedded information from the spatial distribution of the colors in an image.

Combining these image retrieval techniques with a Structured Overlay Network, we are aspiring to create a system with the benefits of both centralized systems, namely very high recall and small number of messages and P2P systems: scalability, fault tolerance, low setup cost and decentralization. Thus, we propose a 2-stage approach: Initially, we use the Overlay to route the query to the neighborhood where the majority of our results will lie. In the second stage, we perform a neighborhood search, via use of the proposed spatially-biased histograms, to increase the retrieval precision. To this effect, we map the histograms created by the classification process to a Cartesian space, maintained by a Content-Addressable-Network (CAN) [3].

The CAN is effective in storing and retrieving *(key, value)* pairs. Each key is a point in the coordinate space and its value is stored at the peer which is responsible for the zone that contains this point. To locate an object, it is sufficient to route to the peer with that zone. When a new peer joins the network, it splits an area owned by another peer and takes over half of it (including the corresponding keys). When a peer leaves the network, its area is taken up by its neighbors.

2 System Overview

In the proposed system, a large number of peers are organized in a CAN and collaborate to spread the computational load, data and network traffic. Organization of the peers is completely automatic and any peer in the system can be considered an entry point either for new peers joining or for retrieval of information.

Queries consist of 2 histograms and a range parameter. In the first stage, the query is routed to the peer whose zone contains the point defined by a 10-bin fuzzy histogram. Then, that peer takes control of the query and performs a second-stage query in its neighborhood using a 128 bin spatially-biased histogram.

Inserting images consists of extracting the histograms from the images, routing to the peer owning the zone that corresponds to the point defined by the fuzzy histogram and placing both descriptors there, along with a pointer to the original image, or the image itself. Peers may join/leave the network at any time without disrupting the system as CAN mechanisms provide fault tolerance through replication.

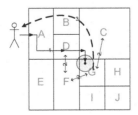

Fig. 1. System Overview

The first stage refers to creating a low-dimensional histogram to be used as coordinates to map images and queries into the CAN space. Histograms are extracted in the L*a*b* color space, a perceptually uniform color space which approximates the way that humans perceive color. For the preclassification stage to produce efficient results, the a* and b* components are subdivided into 5 regions, whereas L* is subdivided into only 3 regions. The fuzzification of the input is accomplished by using appropriate built-in membership functions (MF) for the three input components (L*, a*, b*) which represent the regions. A detailed description of this technique can be found in [2].

After the query has been routed to a single peer, the final stage of the scheme is the retrieval of the most similar images from that peer and its neighbors. To this end, a new method of histogram extraction from the HSV color space is proposed. The HSV color space was selected partially due to its approximation of the way humans perceive color, but mainly because most of the color information is stored in just one of its 3 dimensions; the component of Hue.

Global feature techniques lack in cases in which the images have similar colors, but are spatially distributed differently. This problem can be solved with the use of local histograms [4], which on the other hand suffer a severe lack of speed due to repetitiveness. This leads to the need of adopting global histograms with embedded local characteristics, such as the proposed spatially-biased histogram. In this method the three color components are interlinked (8Hx4Sx4V), thus creating a histogram of 128 bins. During the accessing of every pixel's value in the hue frame, the algorithm also searches around every pixel for pixels with similar colors in manners of a cross having 15 pixels height and width. When every pixel included in the vicinity of the full length of the cross possesses a color similar to the one of the central pixel, instead of increasing the value of the specified color bin by one as usual, it increases it by two more, considerably growing the number of pixels in the bins which contain colors with significant concentrations in the image. The cross was chosen due to its simplicity and therefore minimal computational burden in contrast to using other shapes. The rest of the histogram, including saturation and value, is created straightforwardly so that even the slightest of information is included.

Having concluded the histogram extraction process, the similarity metric of Bhattacharyya distance [4] was used, which measures the statistical separability of spectral classes; estimating the probability of correct classification.

3 Experimental Results

The Image Retrieval method was simulated and tested on a 10,000-image database extracted from "Label Me" [5], enriched with a collection of images representative for the general requirements of a web-based image retrieval system.

The retrieval outcome is presented through a query session which produces 100 images for the routing stage and 25 for the final retrieval ranked in similarity according to the value produced by the metric; the smaller the number which the metric produces, the higher the similarity to that specific image.

The measurement used in order to evaluate the system is the retrieval performance percentage, which is the percentage of similar images produced in the 25 first most similar images retrieved by the system. Precision is the proportion of relevant images retrieved R in respect to the total retrieved A, whereas recall is the proportion of similar images retrieved in respect to the similar images that exist.

Table 1. Filtering Performance achieved for seven representative image sets

Image Set	1	2	3	4	5	6	7
Precision (%)	84	72	84	100	60	28	100
Recall (%)	95	90	91	100	75	63	100

In Table 1 one can see a synopsis of th performance of the method for seven different image sets and notice the high recall percentage, which means that most of the existing similar images were retrieved in the first 25. These image sets were selected to be presented, as they are characteristic of the image database and also show the worst and best precision and recall performances of the proposed system.

4 Evaluation

The total cost of our retrieval process can be estimated by adding the cost of the 2 retrieval stages. For the first stage, the cost is one lookup in the CAN, which, as described in [3], is up to 5 hops with latency within a factor of 2 of the underlying network latency. The second stage consists of communicating with neighboring peers and should not be more that 15 short distance messages, but typically much fewer. Therefore, we expect the total number of messages to be less than 20, and most of them in a local network.

The size of each query is the size of the 2 histograms plus the size of the address of the sender, in total 10*4 Bytes for the fuzzy histogram, 128*4 Bytes for the spatially-biased histogram and up to 10 Bytes for the sender information.

Finally, image recall and precision will not be worse than what is presented in table 1. In fact, it will typically be higher because we are searching within the whole zone of the peers, instead of the first 100 results returned by the first stage.

References

1. M.J. Swain and D.H. Ballard. Color Indexing. Int. J. Comp. Vis 7 (1991) 11-32
2. K. Konstantinidis, A. Gasteratos, I. Andreadis. Image Retrieval Based on Fuzzy Color Histogram Processing. Opt. Comm. 248 4-6 (2005) 375-386
3. S. Ratnasamy, P. Francis, M. Handley, R. Karp, and S. Shenker. A scalable content-addressable network. Proc. ACM SIGCOMM '01 (2001) 161-172
4. K. Konstantinidis and I. Andreadis, Performance and Computational Burden of Histogram based Color Image Retrieval Techniques, J. Comp. Meth. Sci. Eng (JCMSE) 5 (2005) 1-7
5. B. C. Russell, A.Torralba, K. P.Murphy, W. T.Freeman (2005), LabelMe: a database and web-based tool for image annotation. *MIT AI Lab Memo AIM-2005-025*, September 2005

Predicting Fraudulent Financial Statements with Machine Learning Techniques[*]

Sotiris Kotsiantis[1], Euaggelos Koumanakos[2], Dimitris Tzelepis[1],
and Vasilis Tampakas[1]

[1] Department of Accounting, Technological Educational Institute of Patras, Greece
[2] National Bank of Greece, Credit Division
sotos@math.upatras.gr, koumanak@upatras.gr,
tzelepis@upatras.gr, tampakas@teipat.gr

Abstract. This paper explores the effectiveness of machine learning techniques in detecting firms that issue fraudulent financial statements (FFS) and deals with the identification of factors associated to FFS. To this end, a number of experiments have been conducted using representative learning algorithms, which were trained using a data set of 164 fraud and non-fraud Greek firms in the recent period 2001-2002. This study indicates that a decision tree can be successfully used in the identification of FFS and underline the importance of financial ratios.

1 Introduction

Researchers have used various techniques and models to detect accounting fraud in circumstances in which, a priori, is likely to exist. However few studies have tested the predictive ability of different types of models and methods used by means of a common data set. In this study, we carry out an in-depth examination of publicly available data from the financial statements of various firms in order to detect FFS by using alternative supervised machine learning methods. This study indicates that a decision tree can be successfully used in the identification of FFS and underline the importance of financial ratios.

The following section attempts a brief literature review. Section 3 describes the data set of our study and the feature selection process. Section 4 presents the experimental results for the representative compared algorithms. Finally, section 5 discusses the conclusions and some future research directions.

2 Literature Review

The financial statement audit is a monitoring mechanism that helps reduce information asymmetry and protect the interests of the principals, specifically, stockholders and potential stockholders, by providing reasonable assurance that management's financial statements are free from material misstatements. However, in real life,

---

[*] The Project is Co-Funded by the European Social Fund & National Resources - EPEAEK II.

G. Antoniou et al. (Eds.): SETN 2006, LNAI 3955, pp. 538–542, 2006.
© Springer-Verlag Berlin Heidelberg 2006

detecting management fraud is a difficult task when using normal audit procedures [6] since there is a shortage of knowledge concerning the characteristics of management fraud. Additionally, given its infrequency, most auditors lack the experience necessary to detect it. Moreover, managers deliberately try to deceive auditors [8].

Nieschwietz et al. [13] provide a comprehensive review of empirical studies related to external auditors' detection of fraudulent financial reporting while Albrecht et al. [2] review the fraud detection aspects of current auditing standards and the empirical research conducted on fraud detection. Bell and Carcello [4] developed and tested a logistic regression to estimate the likelihood of fraudulent financial reporting. Green and Choi [9] developed a Neural Network fraud classification model. Ansah et al. [3] investigate the relative influence of the size of audit firms, auditor's position tenure and auditor's year of experience in auditing on the likelihood of detecting fraud in the stock and warehouse cycle.

For Greek data, Spathis [17] constructed a model to detect falsified financial statements. He employed the statistical method of logistic regression. The reported accuracy rate exceeded 84%. Kirkos et al [11] investigate the usefulness of Decision Trees, Neural Networks and Bayesian Belief Networks in the identification of fraudulent financial statements. In terms of performance, the Bayesian Belief Network model achieved the best performance managing to correctly classify 90.3% of the validation sample in a 10-fold cross validation procedure. For both studies [17] and [11] 38 FFS firms were matched with 38 non-FFS firms.

The application of machine learning techniques for financial classification is a fertile research area [5], [11]. As a consequence, our main objective for this study is to evaluate the predictive ability of machine learning techniques by conducting a number of experiments using representative learning algorithms.

3 Data Description

Our sample contained data from 164 Greek listed on the Athens Stock Exchange manufacturing firms (no financial companies were included). Auditors checked all the firms in the sample. For 41 of these firms, there was published indication or proof of involvement in issuing FFS. The classification of a financial statement as false was based on the following parameters: inclusion in the auditors' report of serious doubts as to the accuracy of the accounts, observations by the tax authorities regarding serious taxation intransigencies which significantly altered the company's annual balance sheet and income statement, the application of Greek legislation regarding negative net worth, the inclusion of the company in the Athens Stock Exchange categories of "under observation and "negotiation suspended" for reasons associated with the falsification of the company's financial data and, the existence of court proceedings pending with respect to FFS or serious taxation contraventions.

The 41 FFS firms were matched with 123 non-FFS firms. All the variables used in the sample were extracted from formal financial statements, such as balance sheets and income statements. This implies that the usefulness of this study is not restricted by the fact that only Greek company data was used. The selection of variables to be used as candidates for participation in the input vector was based upon prior research work, linked to the topic of FFS [17], [18], [8]. Additional variables were also added in an attempt to catch as many as possible predictors not previously identified.

Table 1 provides a brief description of the financial variables used in the present study. Moreover, in an attempt to show how much each attribute influences the induction, we rank the influence of each one according to a statistical measure – ReliefF [16]. The average ReliefF score of each attribute according to our dataset are also presented in Table 1. The larger the value of the ReliefF scores is, the more influence of the attribute in the induction.

Table 1. Research Variables description and Average ReliefF score of each variable

Variables	Variable Description	ReliefF score
RLTC/RCR02	Return on Long -term capital / Return on Capital and Reserves 2002	0.02603371
AR/TA 01	Accounts Receivable/Total Assets 2001	0.02587121
TL/TA02	Total liabilities/Total assets 2002	0.02577709
AR/TA02	Accounts Receivable/Total Assets 2002	0.02257509
WC/TA 02	Working capital/total assets 2002	0.02118785
DC/CA02	Deposits and cash/current assets 2002	0.01364156
NFA/TA	Net Fixed Assets/Total Assets	0.0133596
NDAP02	Number of days accounts payable 2002	0.01085013
LTD/TCR02	Long term debt/total capital and reserves 2002	0.00798901
S/TA02	Sales/total assets 2002	0.00395956
RCF/TA02	Results carried forward/total assets 2002	0.00384807
NDAR02	Number of days accounts receivable 2002	0.00327257
CAR/TA	Change Accounts Receivable/Total Assets	0.00320415
WCL02	Working capital leveraged 2002	0.00254562
ITURN02	Inventory turnover 2002	0.00215535
TA/CR02	Total Assets/Capital and Reserves 2002	0.00208717
EBIT/TA02	Earnings before interest and tax/total assets 2002	0.00206301
CFO02	Cash flows from operations 2002	0.00169573
CFO01	Cash flows from operations 2001	0.0009421
CR02	Current assets to current liabilities 2002	0.00082761
GOCF	Growth of Operational Cash Flow	0.00073566
CAR/NS	Change Accounts Receivable/Net Sales	0.00071853
EBT02/EBIT02	Earnings before tax 2002/Earnings before interest and tax 2002	0.00049986
Z-SCORE02	Altman z-score 2002	0.00047192
CR/TL02	Capital and Reserves/total liabilities 2002	0.00041943

Thus, the attributes that mostly influence the induction are: RLTC/RCR02, AR/TA01, TL/TA02, AR/TA02, WC/TA02, DC/CA02, NFA/TA02, NDAP02, LTD/TCR02, S/TA02, RCF/TA02, NDAR02. With regard to the remaining variables, it seems that the other attributes do not influence the induction at all. For this reason, these attributes were removed from the training set.

4 Experimental Results

A representative algorithm for each learning technique was used. The most commonly used C4.5 algorithm [15] was the representative of the decision trees. RBF algorithm

[12] - was the representative of the Artificial Neural Networks. The K2 algorithm [10] was the representative of the Bayesian networks. The 3-NN algorithm was the representative of lazy learners [1] since we determined this best K=3 automatically through the minimization of the estimation error on a test set. Ripper [7] was the representative of the rule-learners. Finally, the SMO algorithm was the representative of the SVMs [14]. All accuracy estimates were obtained by averaging the results from stratified 10-fold cross-validation in our dataset. We also present the accuracy of simple logistic regression model (LR). It must be mentioned that we used the free available source code for our experiments by the book [19] in order to find the best parameters for each algorithm. The results are presented in Table 2.

Table 2. Accuracy of models in our dataset

	K2	C4.5	3NN	RBF	RIPPER	LR	SMO
Total Acc.	74.1	91.2	79.7	73.4	86.8	75.3	78.66
Fraud (F)	51.2	85.2	56.1	36.6	65.7	36.6	48.8
Non-Fraud (NF)	82.1	93.3	88.0	86.3	94.1	88.9	88.6

In a comparative assessment of the models' performance we can conclude that decision tree outperforms the other models and achieve outstanding classification accuracy. For this reason, we also visualize the produced classifier for better interpretation of the results (Fig 1). Decision tree performs well with this problem because the division of the instance space is orthogonal to the axis of one variable and parallel to all other axes. Therefore, the resulting regions are all hyperrectangles.

```
IF WC/TA 02 <0.180188
    THEN   IF TL/TA02 <0.6263
                THEN IF NDAR02 < 0.033637 THEN "non-fraud" ELSE "fraud"
                ELSE IF NFA/TA <0.800656 THEN "non-fraud" ELSE "fraud"
    ELSE    IF TL/TA02 >0.0939 THEN "non-fraud" ELSE "fraud"
```

Fig. 1. The produced classifier

5 Conclusion

The aim of this study has been to investigate the usefulness and compare the performance of machine learning techniques in detecting fraudulent financial statements by using published financial data. The results indicate that published financial statement data contains falsification indicators. In terms of performance, the decision tree learner achieved the best performance. It must be mentioned that our input vector solely consists of financial ratios. Enriching the input vector with qualitative information, such as previous auditors' qualifications or the composition of the administrative board, could increase the accuracy rate.

References

1. Aha, D., Lazy Learning, Dordrecht: Kluwer Academic Publishers (1997).
2. Albrecht, C.C., Albrecht, W.S. and Dunn, J.G., Can auditors detect fraud: a review of the research evidence, Journal of Forensic Accounting, Vol. 2 No. 1, (2001) 1-12.
3. Ansah, S.O., Moyes, G.D., Oyelere, P.B. and Hay, D., An empirical analysis of the likelihood of detecting fraud in New Zealand, Managerial Auditing Journal, Vol. 17 No. 4, (2002) 192-204.
4. Bell T. and Carcello J., A decision aid for assessing the likelihood of fraudulent financial reporting, Auditing: A Journal of Practice & Theory, Vol. 9 (1), (2000) 169- 178.
5. Calderon T.G., and Cheh J.J., A roadmap for future neural networks research in auditing and risk assessment, International Journal of Accounting Information Systems, Vol. 3, No. 4, (2002) 203-236.
6. Coderre G. D., Fraud Detection. Using Data Analysis Techniques to Detect Fraud. Global Audit Publications (1999).
7. Cohen, W., Fast Effective Rule Induction, Proceeding of International Conference on Machine Learning, (1995) 115-123.
8. Fanning K. and Cogger K., Neural Network Detection of Management Fraud Using Published Financial Data, International Journal of Intelligent Systems in Accounting, Finance & Management, Vol. 7, No. 1, (1998) 21-24.
9. Green B.P. and Choi J.H., Assessing the risk of management fraud through neuralnetwork technology, Auditing: A Journal of Practice and Theory, Vol. 16(1), (1997) 14-28.
10. Jensen, F., An Introduction to Bayesian Networks, Springer (1996).
11. Kirkos S., Spathis C., Manolopoulos Y., Detection of Fraudulent Financial Statements through the Use of Data Mining Techniques, Proceedings of the 2nd International Conference on Enterprise Systems and Accounting, Thessaloniki, Greece, (2005) 310-325.
12. Mitchell, T., Machine Learning, McGraw Hill (1997).
13. Nieschwietz, R.J., Schultz, J.J. Jr and Zimbelman, M.F., "Empirical research on external auditors' detection of financial statement fraud", Journal of Accounting Literature, Vol. 19, (2000) 190-246.
14. Platt, J. Using sparseness and analytic QP to speed training of support vector machines. In M. S. Kearns, S. A. Solla, & D. A. Cohn (Eds.), Advances in neural information processing systems 11. MA: MIT Press (1999).
15. Quinlan, J. R., C4.5: Programs for machine learning, Morgan Kaufmann (1993).
16. Sikonja M. and Kononenko I., An adaptation of Relief for attribute estimation in regression, Proc. of ICML'97, (1997) 296-304.
17. Spathis C., Detecting false financial statements using published data: some evidence from Greece, Managerial Auditing Journal, Vol. 17, No. 4, (2002) 179-191.
18. Spathis C., Doumpos M. and Zopounidis C., Detecting falsified financial statements: a comparative study using multicriteria analysis and multivariate statistical techniques, The European Accounting Review, Vol.11, No. 3, (2002) 509-535.
19. Witten I. & Frank E., Data Mining: Practical Machine Learning Tools and Techniques with Java Implementations, Morgan Kaufmann, San Mateo, (2000).

Discrimination of Benign from Malignant Breast Lesions Using Statistical Classifiers*

Konstantinos Koutroumbas[1], Abraham Pouliakis[2],
Tatiana Mona Megalopoulou[2], John Georgoulakis[3],
Anna-Eva Giachnaki[4], and Petros Karakitsos[3]

[1] Institute for Space Applications and Remote Sensing,
National Observatory of Athens, Greece
koutroum@space.noa.gr
[2] Department of Histology and Embryology, Medical School of Athens,
Athens University, Greece
[3] Department of Cytopathology, Attikon University Hospital, Athens, Greece
[4] Hellenic Cancer Society

Abstract. The objective of this study is to investigate the discrimination of benign from malignant breast lesions using: the linear, the feedforward neural network, the k-nearest neighbor and the boosting classifiers. Nuclear morphometric parameters from cytological smears taken by Fine Needle Aspiration (FNA) of the breast, have been measured from *193* patients. These parameters undergo an appropriate transformation and then, the classifiers are performed on the raw and on the transformed data. The results show that in terms of the raw data set all classifiers exhibit almost the same performance (overall accuracy $\equiv$ 87%), Thus the linear classifier suffices for the discrimination of the present problem. Also, based on the previous results, one can conjecture that the use of these classifiers combined with image morphometry and statistical techniques for feature transformation, may offer useful information towards the improvement of the diagnostic accuracy of breast FNA.

1 Introduction

Breast lesion is one of the most common applications of statistical classifiers in medicine. This may be due to the fact that several diagnostic dilemmas emerge in the interpretation of mammography and fine needle aspiration (FNA) cytology, concerning indications for biopsy of breast lesions.

The aim of this study was to investigate the capability of morphometry combined with the following statistical classifiers: the linear classifier, the feedforward neural network classifier, the k-nearest neighbor classifier and the boosting classifier using two-layer feedforward neural networks, in the discrimination of benign from malignant breast nuclei in routinely prepared smears, in order to undergo the diffculties mentioned above. These classifiers in combination with the selected features and transformations have never been reported in the literature.

---

* This study is supported in part by the Special Account for Research Grants of the University of Athens KAE:70/31703.

G. Antoniou et al. (Eds.): SETN 2006, LNAI 3955, pp. 543–546, 2006.

2 Materials and Methods

From the 3000 cases of solid breast lesions, collected at our laboratory during the last decade, 193 cases were selected as representatives for investigation. The study was performed on Giemsa stained smears taken by FNA. The cytologic diagnosis was made by two skilled cytopathologists and also confirmed by the histologic examination of surgical specimens. The data set is consisted of 128 malignant cases (6279 nuclei) and 65 benign cases (3165 nuclei). The classifiers were trained by the use of a training set consisted of 50% of the cases and tested by the remaining cases. Form each nucleus 25 parameters were extracted by a customised image analysis system [1](see Table 1).

Table 1. Nuclear features and the applied transformations

Symbol	Geometric features	Feature transformation
X_1	Area	$A^{1/28}$
X_2	Circularity	$cos(Circ^2)$
X_3	Major axis	$\ln(Mj)$
X_4	Minor axis	$Mn^{1/7}$
X_5	Perimeter	$sin(P)$
X_6	Form area (FormAR)	$FormAR^5$
X_7	Form perimeter (FormPE)	$(FormPE/(1 + FormPE))^{12}$
X_8	Contour index	$1/(CI^{13})$
X_9	Contour ratio	$1/(CR^6(1 + CR))$
X_{10}	Roundness factor	$1/RF^{13}$
X_{11}	Diameter	$(sin(D))^2$
	Textural features	
X_{12}	Mean value of histogram	$\mu_{h(k)}$ (no transformation)
X_{13}	Standard deviation of histogram	$(STD(h(k)))^{1/5}$
X_{14}	Variance of histogram	$(VAR(h(k)))^{1/9}$
X_{15}	Short run of run length matrix	$sin(RLM_{SR})$
X_{16}	Long run of run length matrix	$sin(1/(RLM_{LR}))$
X_{17}	Grey level of run length matrix	$sin(RLM_{GL})$
X_{18}	Distribution of run length matrix	$sin(RLM_D)$
X_{19}	Maximum of co-occurrence matrix	$ln(1/COM_{MAX})$
X_{20}	Entropy of co-occurrence matrix	$sin((COM_E)^{(1/21)})$
X_{21}	Inertia of co-occurrence matrix	$sin(COM_I + \frac{COM_I}{(1+COM_I)} + (\frac{COM_I}{(1+COM_I)})^2)$
X_{22}	Mean value of differences histogram	$ln(\mu_{h_d(k)} + 5)$
X_{23}	Variance of differences histogram	$(VAR(h_d(k)))^{(1/9)}$
X_{24}	Contrast of differences histogram	$(Contr(h_d(k)))^{(1/10)}$
X_{25}	Entropy of differences histogram	$sin((Entr(h_d(k)))^3)$

In this work three parametric and one non-parametric classifiers are considered[2], namely: (a) The *linear classifier*, a parametric classifier whose output y depends linearly on its input x via a parameter vector w and a scalar w_0, i.e. $y = w^T x + w_0$. If $y > 0(< 0)$ x is assigned to class 1 (-1). The parameters w and w_0 are estimated via the minimization of the sum of square error function,

J. (b) The *two-layer feedforward neural network (2LFNN)* parametric classifier, a classifiers whose output y depends nonlinearly on its input $\boldsymbol{x}$, via the equation $y = g(\sum_{j=1}^{m} v_j f(\boldsymbol{w}_j^T \boldsymbol{x}) + v_0)$, where $\boldsymbol{w}$'s, v's are parameters, f is a sigmoid function (e.g. hyperbolic tangent) and $g(x) = 1(-1)$ if $x > 0(< 0)$. The parameters are estimated via the minimization of J. (c) The *boosting classifier*, which consists of several small 2LFNNs created sequentially. Eacg 2LFNN tries to classify correctly the vectors that were classified incorrectly be the combination of the 2LFNNs generated so far. (d) The *k-nearest neighbor* non-parametric classifier, which assigns a vector $\boldsymbol{x}$ to a class taking into account the classes of its k nearest neighbors from a reference set Y. Here the classifiers have been applied to:

1. The raw data set, denoted by X^1.
2. The normalized data set (X^2), where the values of each feature are normalized in the interval $[-1, 1]$, via the transformation $x_i^{trans} = \frac{x_i^{raw} - \min_i}{\max_i - \min_i}$ where x_i^{raw} is the raw value of the i-th feature, x_i^{trans} is the transformed value of the i-th feature, and $\min_i$ and $\max_i$ are the minimum and the maximum values of the i-th feature.
3. The normalized data set (X^3), where each of the 25 features was transformed empirically, so as to follow the normal distribution (see Table 1) [3]. The normality of the data was tested through the skewness test[1] [3]. Note that transformations may not be unique.
4. The normalized data set, denoted by X^4, which follows from X^3 is further normalized in the interval $[-1, 1]$, via the previous transformation.

3   Results

The four classifiers under study are applied on the X^1, X^2, X^3 and X^4 sets, each X^i is partitioned into a training set, used to train each classifier, and a test set, used for the evaluation. The results are shown in Table 2 (variations of the parameters of the classifiers do not affect significantly their performance).

Table 2. Results of the four classifiers for the X^1, X^2, X^3 and X^4 sets

		Boosting clas.	2-layer FNN ($nodes = 10$)	k-nearest neigh. ($k = 13$)	linear clas.
X^1	Training set	90.21%	90.43%	88.33%	89.18%
X^1	Test set	87.44%	87.04%	87.13%	86.17%
X^2	Training set	88.21%	92.63%	88.74%	89.18%
X^2	Test set	81.63%	86.59%	85.91%	86.19%
X^3	Training set	91.73%	90.06%	79.36%	89.24%
X^3	Test set	80.80%	87.00%	78.17%	86.61%
X^4	Training set	92.76%	90.22%	74.03%	88.68%
X^4	Test set	82.48%	87.31%	73.87%	86.00%

---

[1] The Kolmogorov-Smirnov was not used because it is sensitive to large data sets.

4   Discussion

Fine Needle Aspiration (FNA) has reached a wide acceptance in the investigation of breast lesions because of the quite high overall accuracy. However in some cases the discrimination between benign and malignant lesions is difficult because of the lack of sufficient diagnostic criteria or of the paucity of cells in the smears [4]. To resolve the problem of safe and reproducible classification of breast lesions in cytologic as well as in histologic level, morphometric parameters have already been investigated using different methods with encouraging results [5].

In our study, the results of Table 2 show that all classifiers give more or less similar results on the raw data set. In addition, these are their best results compared to the results obtained for the transformed data sets. In addition, while the two-layer feedforward neural network classifier and the linear classifier give similar results for X^2, X^3 and X^4, the performance of the boosting classifier drops significantly on the transformed data sets. Also, the performance of the k-nearest neighbor classifier degrades significantly for X^3 and X^4.

It is worth noting that because in all X^1, X^2, X^3, and X^4 cases the performance of the linear classifier is almost identical to that of the two-layer feedforward neural network and the boosting classifier, the linear classifier seems to suffice for the discrimination of the two classes in the present problem.

The fact that despite the objectivity introduced by the measuring system, the classifiers can not obtain 100% classification performance for the breast nuclei. This indicates that there exists an overlap in the feature space and may explain the difficulties observed in the morphological diagnosis. A detailed analysis on the nuclei that have not been classified correctlly, indicated that the majority of the nuclei of the malignant cases that have been missclassified are from small cell carcinomas, which are easily diagnosed by cytopathologists. A combination of the methods considered above and a cytological examination may decrease dramatically the number of cases that require histologic confirmation before the therapeutic decision.

As future plans we intend to examine the discriminative capability of classifiers like the above to cells stemming from other organs as well as other classifiers (such as kernel-based methods).

References

1. Karakitsos, P., Megalopoulou, T.M., Pouliakis, A., Tzivras, M., Archimandritis, A., Kyroudes, A.: Application of discriminant analysis and quantitative cytologic examination to gastric lesions. Analytical and Quantitative Cytology and Histology **26**(6) (2004) 314–322
2. Theodoridis, S., Koutroumbas, K.: Pattern recognition. Second edn. Academic Press (2003)
3. Joseph, F., Hair, J., Anderson, R., Tatham, R., Black, W.: Multivariate Data Analysis. Fifth edn. Prentice-Hall International. London (1998)
4. Lindholm, K.: Breast (chapter 7). In Orell, S.R., Sterrett, G.F., Walters, M.N.I., Whitaker, D., eds.: Fine Needle Aspiration Cytology. 3 edn. Churchill Livingstone. ISBN 0 443 057141, Printed in China (1999)
5. Walberg, W.H., Mangassarian, O.L.: Computer-aided diagnosis of breast aspirates via expert systems. Anal. Quant. Cytol. Histol. **12** (1990) 314–320

Comparison of Data Fusion Techniques for Robot Navigation

Nikolaos Kyriakoulis[1], Antonios Gasteratos[1], and Angelos Amanatiadis[2]

[1] Department of Production and Management Engineering
[2] Department of Electrical and Computer Engineering,
School of Engineering, Democritus University of Thrace,
GR-671 00 Xanthi, Greece
agaster@pme.duth.gr

Abstract. This paper proposes and compares several data fusion techniques for robot navigation. The fusion techniques investigated here are several topologies of the Kalman filter. The problem that had been simulated is the navigation of a robot carrying two sensors, one Global Positioning System (GPS) and one Inertial Navigation System (INS). For each of the above topologies, the statistic error and its, mean value, variance and standard deviation were examined.

1 Introduction

Robot navigation is the process that a robot tries to follow a predetermined path, or an obstacle free path. In robotics we are able to use a wide range of different sensors to navigate. The most likely way to provide robustness and flexibility in robot navigation is to mount on the robot more than two sensors that they are integrated correctly and with a proper data fusion technique. However, any measurement is corrupted by noise and device inaccuracies and, thus, isolating this noise is straightforward [1]. Hence, there is a need of a filter in order to obtain measurements that are immune to noise and such one is the Kalman filter [3, 4]. In this paper three topologies were examined, involving the measurements of two sensors, a GPS and an INS. The three proposed topologies include a Kalman filter utilized along with one set of "if...then" rules or with the least mean square method. The data fusion occurs in these set of rules or in the least mean square system. The methods were examined comparatively in both quantitative and qualitative manner.

2 Sensors Selection

The scope of our navigation application is that the robot should be able to determine its real position fast and accurately, i.e. the estimated coordinates to be as close to the real ones as possible. Taking into account the above assumption the outputs of the sensors were obtained in absolute coordinates. The GPS selection was based on its technical characteristics, so that it also produces absolute coordinates, time etc. Besides using the time and the coordinates the robot velocity is obtained. The INS selection was based on its capability to produce output of the same format as the one of the

G. Antoniou et al. (Eds.): SETN 2006, LNAI 3955, pp. 547–550, 2006.

GPS. The GPS and INS are complimentary sensors and the disadvantages of each other are ideally cancelled. In case of an absence of the GPS signal (due to satellite signal loss), the INS is activated to navigate until the GPS signal is recovered [2].

3 Sensors Fusion for Robot Navigation

To establish accuracy, availability and robustness, the measurements from GPS and INS should be fused. The selection of Kalman filter was based on the nature of the problem itself, i.e. the requirement to compute the actual coordinates. This is to say that the navigation was not about path finding or object evasion. On the other hand, the Kalman filter is capable to manage the coordinates in such a way, that the noise is isolated and the final output is coordinates with lower noise corruption.

3.1 Topologies

Three different topologies were composed and studied. The different topologies involve, apart the Kalman filter, a least mean square function and an expert system, in different arrangements. They all were assessed towards our aim, i.e. the accurate estimation of the coordinates of the robotic platform. These three topologies are described below as thoroughly as possible.

3.1.1 If Then Rules Along with the Kalman Filter
This topology is depicted in Fig. 1. The Kalman filter function is cascaded to a simple "if...then" rules expert system. The system obtains the measurements from the sensors, which subsequently are fed into the "if...then" rules expert system, where the data fusion occurs. Only one measurement will be the input to the Kalman filter.

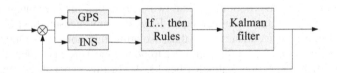

Fig. 1. A Kalman Filter utilized along with an "If...Then" rules expert system

The selection is based on a comparison of the distances between measurements and real coordinates which takes place. The shorter distance is preferred to the longer as it is corrupted lesser by noise. So the input to the filter exhibit as little noise as possible. In the case of both sensors sharing the same noise then the more reliable (comparing to) measurement is selected.

3.1.2 Least Mean Square with the Kalman Filter
The second of the proposed topologies utilizes a "least mean square method" followed by the Kalman filter, as illustrated in Fig. 2. The sensor data fusion occurs in the system that implements a least mean square method. The topology is competed with a cascaded Kalman filter, were the output of the least mean square method is fed, in order to produce the final output.

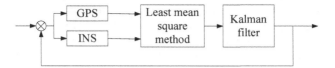

Fig. 2. A Kalman Filter in cascade with a least mean square method

3.1.3 Two Kalman Filters with Least Mean Square

This topology uses similar building blocks as the previous one. Here the sensor data is firstly filtered out by the Kalman filter module, whilst the fusion takes place afterwards. Two parallel Kalman filters are implied, each of which is applied on the sensor data. The outputs from the two filters are fused by the system with the least mean square, where the functions are exactly the same to the previous topology. A block diagram of the process is demonstrated in Fig. 3.

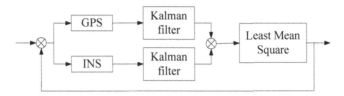

Fig. 3. Two Kalman Filters followed by a least mean square method

4 Comparative Study

All the above proposed topologies were statistically examined. The mean value, the standard deviation and the variance were used as benchmarks. The topology exhibiting the least mean value is the third one (Fig. 4c). The topology with the lowest variance and standard deviation is the second one (Fig.4b). As it is shown to the Fig. 4a, which refers to the first topology, the error's distribution range is quite long and the density is mostly about 6. In the Fig. 4b and 4c the distribution is bell shaped and the range of the error is from -0.2 to 0.15. Although Fig 4b and 4c are quite similar it is shown that the second one has bigger mean value as the density varies mostly about 5 to 6 above the zero, instead of the third one's where are distributed around zero.

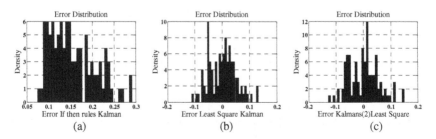

Fig. 4. The error density distribution of the proposed topologies presented in Figs 1, 2 and 3, respectively

Apart from the quantitative comparison, a qualitative one should be approached. Considering the Fig. 5a, 5b and 5c, it could be easily shown that the second topology provide better results. The second topology responses close enough to the ideal land-marks, the bold spots at the referring Figure. The third topology, though it responses closer to the ideal landmarks than the other two, is not as stable as the second one. As it is shown below to the Fig. 5a, 5b and 5c the robot has to follow the bold line which is the ideal one. There are some measurements that take place from the two sensors which are marked with the squares. The final output of the above topologies is the light gray line.

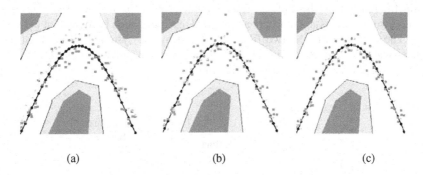

| (a) | (b) | (c) |

Fig. 5. A mobile robot trajectories corresponding to the topologies presented in Figs 1, 2 and 3, respectively. The rhombuses are the measurements, the bold squares are the real states and the gray cycles are the outputs of the fusion techniques.

5   Conclusion

A comparative study of three different topologies of sensor data fusion was carried out in this paper. The target application is that of determining the exact position of a robot, in order to perform autonomous navigation. The sensors utilized are a GPS and an INS. The choice among the three topologies relies strongly on the nature of the problem that the topology is to be implemented. There are cases in which we want to have a good mean value, but others that we want to have an overall low variance or standard deviation. Furthermore, it is obvious that the implementation of the topology with the If…Then rules requires a high cost, as there are more calculating resources, in contrary to the topology with the least mean square system.

References

1. Hall, D. L., Llinas, J.: Handbook of Multisensor Data Fusion. CRC Press, Boca Raton (2001)
2. Johnson, R. Sasiadek, J. Zalewski, J.: Kalman Filter Enhancement for UAV Navigation. Proc. SCS 2003 Collaborative Technologies Symposium Orlando, FL (2003)
3. Kalman, R.E, Bucy, R.: New Results in Linear Filtering and Prediction Theory. Journal of Basic Engineering 83 (1961) 95-108
4. Maybeck, P.S.: The Kalman Filter: An Introduction to Concepts. Springer-Verlag, New York (1990)

On Improving Mobile Robot Motion Control

Michail G. Lagoudakis

Intelligent Systems Laboratory*
Department of Electronic and Computer Engineering,
Technical University of Crete,
Kounoupidiana, 73100 Chania, Crete, Hellas (Greece)
lagoudakis@intelligence.tuc.gr

Abstract. This paper describes two simple techniques that can greatly improve navigation and motion control of nonholonomic robots based on range sensor data. The first technique enhances sensory information by re-using recent sensor data through coordinate transformation, whereas the second compensates for errors due to long control cycle times by forward projection through the kinematic model of the robot. Both techniques have been succesfully tested on a Nomad 200 mobile robot.

1 Introduction

The quest for artificial intelligence is best expressed in the field of robotics, where intelligent behavior and interaction are embodied and express themselves in the real world. The age of robot intelligence comparable to human intelligence may be still quite far away, however simpler, yet crucial, subproblems in this context are currently within the reach of the present technology. For example, a first step towards higher-level intelligence is the ability of a mobile robot to reason about its mobility and navigate safely in the environment.

Many mobile robots, from small laboratory robots to larger autonomous automobiles, rely on wheeled mobility and range data from sonar, laser, or infrared sensors to navigate. These robots are commonly nonholonomic [1], that is, their motion is constrained by steering. Despite significant differences at the higher level (path planning), most robot navigation algorithms at the lower level (motion control) rely on reactive controllers which take into account instantaneous range data in the robot's egocentric framework. This work indentifies two common problems in this context and proposes techniques to address them. The proposed techniques have been tested successfully on a Nomad 200 mobile robot in coordination with a neural map local path planner and a multi-objective motion controller in both simulated and real environments [2].

2 Sensor Data Transformation

Instantaneous sensor data are noisy and potentially inaccurate. To reduce instantaneous sensor uncertainty we maintain a short-term memory of the most

---

* Research conducted while the author was with the University of Louisiana, Lafayette.

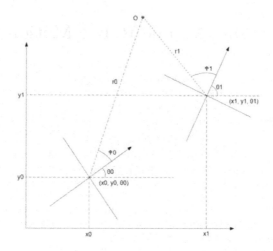

Fig. 1. Sensor range reading transformation

recent sensory information. Thus, the last few sensor readings are reused in the next few steps before they are discarded. This trick compensates for potential inaccuracies, providing at the same time a richer sense of the surrounding environment. A key parameter is the size of the memory window. A short window offers almost no advantage, whereas a large one leads to "inertia" in sensing changes. An interval of 2–3 seconds of real time is sufficient in most cases. Given an internal estimate of the cycle time through the robot's clock, the system automatically determines the required memory size.

The readings in the short term memory cannot be reused in a straightforward way; appropriate transformation is necessary. Due to robot motion, a previous reading may be reused at a configuration different than the one it was obtained from. Following Figure 1, consider a sensor range reading (r_0, ϕ_0) (with respect to the robot's local coordinate frame) corresponding to some obstacle O obtained from configuration (x_0, y_0, θ_0) (with respect to a global coordinate frame). Given a new configuration (x_1, y_1, θ_1) of the robot, what would the range reading (r_1, ϕ_1) corresponding to the same obstacle O from that configuration be? The transformation proceeds from the local coordinate frame at the first configuration to the global coordinate system and back to the local coordinate frame at the second configuration[1]:

$$r_1 = \sqrt{\big(x_0 + r_0 \times \cos(\phi_0 + \theta_0) - x_1\big)^2 + \big(y_0 + r_0 \times \sin(\phi_0 + \theta_0) - y_1\big)^2}$$

$$\phi_1 = \texttt{arctan2}\big(y_0 + r_0 \times \sin(\phi_0 + \theta_0) - y_1, x_0 + r_0 \times \cos(\phi_0 + \theta_0) - x_1\big) - \theta_1$$

To compute the transformation we use the odometry of the robot, which is quite accurate for short time frames. In summary, a cyclical buffer stores the last k range scans, obtained during the last k control cycles, along with the configuration

---

[1] `arctan2(y, x)` calculates `arctan(y/x)` and returns an angle in the correct quadrant.

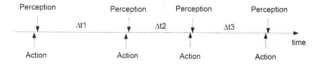

Fig. 2. The hybrid nature of discrete control on continuous robot motion

of the robot at each scan. Through the above transformation, the stored readings can be made to appear as if they were all obtained from the current (or any other) configuration. Through this technique it is possible for the robot to maintain sensory information even outside its current sensory scope.

3   Configuration Prediction

Mobile robots are typically controlled by computers either on-board or off-board. Thus, control commands are issued only at discrete points in time and not continuously because of the required computation time in each cycle. This is also true for sensing, since the world is perceived only at discrete points in time. Figure 2 shows the repeated control cycle: a control command is issued (action), the world is perceived (perception), and in time Δt_1 the next action is computed. In fact, the cycle time Δt_k between two consecutive control commands can vary due to contingent events (communication delays, running processes, etc.). In any case, there is a finite time interval Δt during which there is no control over the motion of the robot. Moreover, the control action issued at a particular time step corresponds to the world as it was perceived at the previous time step. The impact of this problem becomes apparent in high speed motion, where a fast moving robot might be in a completely different configuration by the time the control command is issued.

Our proposed solution is to estimate the time Δt between control steps and predict the configuration of the robot at the beginning of the next cycle. Then, the next action is computed with respect to the predicted configuration as if the robot was there. In particular, given the current configuration (x_0, y_0, θ_0) and the current rotational and translational velocities (u_0, v_0) of the robot, we seek the configuration (x_1, y_1, θ_1) after time Δt. A nonholonomic robot moving with constant speeds follows a trajectory given by the unicycle model equations [3]:

$$x(t) = \frac{u_0}{v_0}\sin(v_0 t) \qquad y(t) = \frac{u_0}{v_0}(1 - \cos(v_0 t)) \qquad \theta(t) = v_0 t$$

Given that speeds are held almost constant during the interval Δt, we can estimate the resulting configuration as follows:

$$x_1 \approx x_0 + x(\Delta t) \qquad y_1 \approx y_0 + y(\Delta t) \qquad \theta_1 \approx \theta_0 + \theta(\Delta t)$$

To obtain an estimate of the cycle time Δt, the controller measures the elapsed real time using the robot's clock. For averaging, we use a simple convex combination of the last two measured cycle times with a higher weight on the most

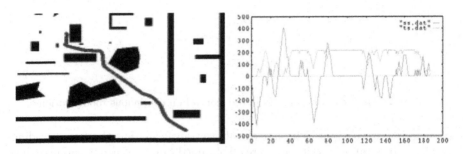

Fig. 3. A simple navigation task: robot path (left) and control commands (right)

recent one. Thus, the controller quickly adapts to the performance and load of the underlying platform, with some "inertia" to avoid contingent oscillations.

4   Improved Navigation and Consclusion

The proposed techniques have been integrated in a motion controller which issues incremental velocity commands guided by a holonomic path planner. The controller finds the best rotational and translational velocities by discrete optimization of a multi-criteria objective function defined over the *dynamic velocity window* [4] as determined by the current velocities and the maximum acceleration and deceleration ability of the robot. The objective function combines the proximity of the resulting configuration to the current goal with the potential of unforeseen, perhaps unavoidable, collisions and issues commands that eliminate or minimize collision impact. Such collisions may become possible due to dynamic obstacles, but also due to the holonomic nature of the path planner. The complete system achieves accurate, smooth, and safe navigation (an example is shown in Figure 3). The proposed techniques are quite general. Any robot navigation algorithm can project its knowledge (recent sensor data) in the near future (predicted configuration) and compute proactively and adaptively the next control command to improve navigation accuracy and performance.

References

1. Lafferriere, G., Sussmann, H.: Motion planning for controllable systems without drift. In Tarn, T., ed.: Proceedings of the 1991 IEEE International Conference on Robotics and Automation, Sacramento, California, IEEE Press (1991) 1148–1153
2. Lagoudakis, M.G., Maida, A.S.: Neural maps for mobile robot navigation. In: IEEE International Joint Conference on Neural Networks (IJCNN'99). Volume III., Washington, DC, IEEE Press (1999) 2011–2016
3. Luca, A.D., Oriolo, G.: Local incremental planning for nonholonomic mobile robots. In Straub, E., Sipple, R.S., eds.: Proceedings of the 1994 International Conference on Robotics and Automation, Los Alamitos, California, IEEE Press (1994) 104–110
4. Fox, D., Burgard, W., Thrun, S.: The dynamic window approach to collision avoidance. IEEE Robotics and Automation Magazine **RA–4** (1997) 23–33

Consistency of the Matching Predicate*

Dimitris Magos[1], Ioannis Mourtos[2], and Leonidas Pitsoulis[3]

[1] Technological Educational Institute of Athens, 12210 Athens, Greece
dmagos@teiath.gr
[2] University of Patras, 26500 Rion, Patras, Greece
imourtos@upatras.gr
[3] Aristotle University of Thessaloniki, 54124 Thessaloniki, Greece
pitsouli@gen.auth.gr

1 Introduction

Let $G(V, E)$ denote an undirected graph, V and E being the sets of its nodes and edges, respectively. A *matching* in $G(V, E)$ is a subset of edges with no common endpoints. Finding a matching of maximum cardinality constitutes the maximum cardinality matching (MCM) problem. For a thorough theoretical discussion we refer to [6]. The MCM problem is of specific interest from a Constraint Programming (CP) point of view because it can model several logical constraints (predicates) like the *all_different* and the *symmetric all_different* predicates [7]. Thus, the definition of a maximum cardinality matching constraint provides a framework encompassing other predicates. Along this line of research, we define a global constraint with respect to the MCM and address the issue of consistency. Establishing hyper-arc consistency implies the identification of edges that cannot participate in any maximum cardinality matching. Evidently, this issue (also called *filtering*) is related to the methods developed for solving the problem. Solving this problem for bipartite graphs was common knowledge long before Edmonds proposed an algorithm for the non-bipartite case [3]. Regarding hyper-arc consistency, the problem has been resolved only for the bipartite case [1].

In this paper, we adopt an approach alternative to the ones discussed above, since, through matroids and independence systems, we are able to deal with both the bipartite and the non-bipartite cases. More specifically, we present filtering algorithms for problems defined as independence systems and, since matching can be regarded as such, these algorithms become applicable to the MCM problem. Hence, our contribution is twofold. First, we provide filtering schemes for both bipartite and non-bipartite matching through a unifying theoretical approach and, secondly, the procedures described apply to *any* predicate that could be expressed as an independence system.

---

* This research has been partially funded by the Greek Ministry of Education under the program "Pythagoras II".

G. Antoniou et al. (Eds.): SETN 2006, LNAI 3955, pp. 555–558, 2006.

2   Preliminaries and Problem Formulation

We refer to [2] for formal definitions related to global constraints. We consider each element of E as a set consisting of two elements (nodes) belonging to V. Hence, for $e \in E$ and $v \in V$, one can write $0 \leq |e \cap \{v\}| \leq 1$. Similarly, edges $e_i, e_j \in E$ are incident to the same node if and only if $|e_i \cap e_j| = 1$. A set $M \subseteq E$ is called a *matching* if, for every pair of edges $e_i, e_j \in M$, it holds that $|e_i \cap e_j| = 0$. The MCM problem is defined as

$$\max_{M \ E:\ e_i\ e_j\ =0,\ e_i,e_j \in M} |M|$$

The *matching* constraint is imposed on a set of variables, each corresponding to a node of the graph $G(V, E)$. That is, for each $v \in V$ there exists a variable x_v. Let $d : E \to \mathbb{Z}_+$ be a bijection, i.e. d maps each edge to a unique positive integer. For $v \in V$, let E_v denote the set of edges incident to node v, i.e. $E_v = \{e \in E : |e \cap \{v\}| = 1\}$. The domain of x_v is defined as $D_v = \{d(e) : e \in E_v\} \cup \{0\}$, where value 0 is reserved and its meaning is explained next. The variables x_u, x_w are said to form a pair if they share the same value, which is also different than 0. Apparently, this value must belong to both D_u, D_w. This implies that nodes u, w are linked via the edge associated with the common value of the variables x_u, x_w. Hence, the global constraint

$$matching\{x_v : v \in V\},$$
$$x_v \in D_v, \forall v \in V,$$

asks for a maximum number of pairs with distinct pair values. The variables not selected to form a pair are assigned value 0.

Before proceeding, we should recall certain definitions related to matroids (see [5]). Denote the collection of subsets of a set A as 2^A.

Definition 1. *Given a finite set $\mathcal{E}$ and some family of subsets $\mathcal{F} \subset 2$, the set system $\mathcal{M} = (\mathcal{E}, \mathcal{F})$ is a matroid if the following conditions hold*

(I1) $\emptyset \in \mathcal{F}$,
(I2) *If $X \in \mathcal{F}$ and $Y \subset X$ then $Y \in \mathcal{F}$,*
(I3) *If $X, Y \in \mathcal{F}$ and $|Y| < |X|$, then there exists an element e of $X \backslash Y$ such that $Y \cup \{e\} \in \mathcal{F}$.*

If conditions (I1), (I2) hold, $\mathcal{M} = (\mathcal{E}, \mathcal{F})$ is called an *independent system* (IS). Hence, by Definition 1, a matroid is an IS for which (I3) also holds. The following definitions apply to any IS. $\mathcal{E}$ is called the *ground set*. A set $X \in \mathcal{F}$ is said to be an *independent set* of $\mathcal{M} = (\mathcal{E}, \mathcal{F})$. Any set which is not independent is *dependent*. A *maximal* independent set is called a *base*. An IS can be described by a set of matroids on the same ground set. Consider the matroids $\mathcal{M}_1 = (\mathcal{E}, \mathcal{F}_1), \ldots, \mathcal{M}_k = (\mathcal{E}, \mathcal{F}_k)$. Their intersection, also called *k-matroid inter-section*, is defined as $(\mathcal{E}, \bigcap_{i=1,\ldots,k} \mathcal{F}_i)$. Clearly this is an IS. Moreover,

Theorem 1 ([5]). *Any independence system is the intersection of a finite number of matroids .*

The connection between matchings in a graph and independence systems is direct: the set of matchings forms an IS, to be denoted by $M(G)$, on the ground set of edges E. An MCM is simply a maximum cardinality basis (MCB) in $M(G)$. Therefore, a filtering procedure identifying the elements of $\mathcal{E}$ that do not belong to any MCB is applicable to the MCM problem. Such a scheme, when applied to $M(G)$, produces the set of edges not participating in any maximum cardinality matching. The problem of finding a base of a matroid is quite different than that of finding an MCB of an IS, the latter being polynomially solvable only if the IS is the intersection of two matroids [5]. Further, it has been proved that the set of matchings in an arbitrary graph G is the intersection of at most $O(log|V|/loglog|V|)$ matroids [4].

3   Consistency of the Matching Constraint

Our aim is to establish a partitioning of E to sets $E_{ALL}, E_{SOME}, E_{NONE}$, which include the edges participating to all, some or none maximum cardinality matchings, respectively. Hereafter, $\mathcal{E}$ and E are interchangeably used to denote the ground set. The algorithm presented next computes this partitioning on any IS, under the conditions that we can compute the rank of any subset of the ground set $\mathcal{E}$ and we can find an MCB including a specific $e \in \mathcal{E}$ (denoted as $B(e)$). Note that, in the case of $M(G)$, this problem as well as the problem of computing the rank of any subset of edges are polynomially solvable.

Algorithm 1. Achieving hyper-arc consistency for the MCB problem on an IS

$X = \emptyset$;
$\mathcal{E}_{NONE} = \emptyset$;
$\mathcal{E}_{ALL} = \emptyset$;
$rank\mathcal{E} = r(\mathcal{E})$;
for all $e \in \mathcal{E} \setminus X$ **do**
    Compute a basis $B(e)$;
    if $r(B(e)) < rank\mathcal{E}$ **then**
        $\mathcal{E}_{NONE} = \mathcal{E}_{NONE} \cup \{e\}$;
    else
        $X = X \cup \{B(e)\}$;
    end if
end for
for all $e \in X$ **do**
    if $r(\mathcal{E} \setminus \{e\}) < rank\mathcal{E}$ **then**
        $\mathcal{E}_{ALL} = \mathcal{E}_{ALL} \cup \{e\}$;
    end if
end for
$\mathcal{E}_{SOME} = \mathcal{E} \setminus \{\mathcal{E}_{ALL} \cup \mathcal{E}_{NONE}\}$;

Theorem 2. *Algorithm 1 correctly determines in $O((\Omega_1 + \Omega_2) \cdot |\mathcal{E}|)$ steps the partitioning $\mathcal{E}_{ALL}$, $\mathcal{E}_{SOME}$, $\mathcal{E}_{NONE}$, where Ω_1, Ω_2 are, respectively, the computational complexities of computing the rank function and $B(e)$, for $e \in \mathcal{E}$.*

Proof. (Correctness) The algorithm consists of two loops. The first one separates the elements of $\mathcal{E}_{NONE}$ from those of $X = \mathcal{E}_{ALL} \cup \mathcal{E}_{SOME}$. The separation is achieved by identifying for each $e \in \mathcal{E}$ an MCB containing it. Apparently, if the rank of such a base is smaller than the rank of $\mathcal{E}$ then $e \in \mathcal{E}_{NONE}$; otherwise, all the elements of $B(e)$ belong to X. In the second loop, we identify those elements of X that belong to $\mathcal{E}_{ALL}$. Observe that $|\mathcal{E}_{ALL}| \leq r(\mathcal{E})$ and recall that for each $e \in X$ there is a basis containing it, whose rank is the same as $\mathcal{E}$. Thus, for each such element we check if its deletion from $\mathcal{E}$ decreases its rank. If this is true then the element belongs to $\mathcal{E}_{ALL}$; otherwise, it must belong to $\mathcal{E}_{SOME}$.

(Complexity) Let Ω_1, Ω_2 denote the computational complexity of computing the rank function and of finding $B(e)$, respectively. The first loop is performed at most $|\mathcal{E}|$ times. At each iteration, we need to compute $B(e)$, $r(B(e))$ and perform one comparison. Thus, the complexity of the first loop is $O((\Omega_1 + \Omega_2) \cdot |\mathcal{E}|)$. Similarly, the complexity of the second loop is $O(\Omega_1 \cdot |\mathcal{E}|)$.

Let us now examine in more detail how the critical steps of Algorithm 1 are implemented in the case of $M(G)$. The standard solution method for the maximum cardinality matching problem is the algorithm described in [3], which can be implemented in $O(|V|^3)$ steps. For $X \subseteq E$, by deleting all the edges in $E \setminus X$ and subsequently applying Edmonds' algorithm, we can determine the cardinality of a maximum matching consisting entirely of edges of X. In this way, we identify $r(X), \forall X \subseteq E$. Finally, the same algorithm can be used to determine $B(e)$, for $e \in E$. To achieve this for an edge $e \in E$, it is sufficient to delete all edges incident to nodes u, v, where $|e \cap \{u\}| = |e \cap \{v\}| = 1$. As a result, the graph decomposes into two components: one consisting of the edge e and its two incident nodes u, v and one consisting of the remaining nodes and all the edges not incident to either of u, v. Let B denote a maximum cardinality matching on the second component. It is easy to see that $B(e) = B \cup \{e\}$.

References

1. Costa M.C.: Persistency in maximum cardinality bipartite matchings. Operations Research Letters **15** (1994) 143–149.
2. Dechter R.: Constraint Processing. Morgan Kaufmann (2003).
3. Edmonds J.: Paths, trees and flowers. Canadian Journal of Mathematics **17** (1965) 449–467.
4. Fekete S.P., Firla R.T., Spille B.: Characterizing matchings as the intersection of matroids. Mathematical Methods of Operations Research **58** (2003) 319–329.
5. Korte B., Vygen J.: Combinatorial Optimization: Theory and Algorithms. Algorithms and Combinatorics **21**, Springer (1991).
6. Lovasz L., Plummer M.D.: Matching theory. Annals of Discrete Mathematics **29**, North-Holland (1986).
7. Régin J. C.: The symmetric alldifferent constraint. Proceedings of the IJCAI-99 (1999), 420–425.

Intrusion Detection Using Emergent Self-organizing Maps*

Aikaterini Mitrokotsa and Christos Douligeris

Department of Informatics University of Piraeus,
80 Karaoli and Dimitriou Str. Piraeus 18534, Greece
{mitrokat, cdoulig}@unipi.gr

Abstract. In this paper, we analyze the potential of using Emergent Self-Organizing Maps (ESOMs) based on Kohonen Self –Organizing maps in order to detect intrusive behaviours. The proposed approach combines machine learning and information visualization techniques to analyze network traffic and is based on classifying "normal" versus "abnormal" traffic. The results are promising as they show the ability of eSOMs to classify normal against abnormal behaviour regarding false alarms and detection probabilities.

1 Emergent Self Organizing Maps vs KSOM

In this paper, we propose an intrusion detection approach that is based on a class of neural networks known as Kohonen's Self-Organizing Maps (KSOMs) [1]. Our approach combines information visualization and machine learning techniques and enables us with the ability to have a visual view of network activity. The proposed approach produces promising results in its ability to classify normal against abnormal behavior. Emergent SOMs (ESOMs) are based on simple KSOMs but present some advantages over them that can be exploited in order to achieve better results in the detection of intrusions.

One of the basic disadvantages of SOM maps is that their abilities are limited to a few neurons. In a Kohonen's SOM to each neuron correspond the best matches of a great number of input data. So in a way each neuron represents a cluster. On the other hand, Emergent SOMs may expand from some thousands to tens of thousands of neurons. In some cases the number of neurons may be greater than the number of input data. The cooperation of such a big number of neurons leads to structures of a higher level.

We trained Emergent Self Organized Maps with logs ([2],[3]) of network traffic and exploited the main advantage of Emergent SOMs the large number of neurons. In order to visualize these structures the U-Matrix method is used. This method permits us to achieve a good visualization of the network traffic and observe the existence of possible intrusions.

Each log of network traffic is represented by a vector with some fixed attributes. Each vector has a unique spatial position in the U-Matrix [3] and the distance between

---

* This work was partially supported by the GSRT under a PENED grant.

G. Antoniou et al. (Eds.): SETN 2006, LNAI 3955, pp. 559–562, 2006.

two points is the dissimilarity of two network traffic logs. The U-Matrix of the trained dataset is divided into valleys that represent clusters of normal or attack data and hills that represent borders between clusters. Depending on the position of the best match of an input data point that characterizes a connection this point may belong to a valley (cluster (normal or attack behaviour)) or this data point may not be classified if its best match belongs to a hill (boundary). The map that is created after the training of the Emergent SOM, represents the network traffic. Thus, an input data point may be classified depending on the position of its best match. In order to achieve meaningful distance calculations the means and the variances of the features should be comparable. We have normalized the data with mean zero and variance one.

Mukkamala et al. [4] identified the most significant features from the KDD-99 dataset using two ranking methods for the SVMs (Support Vector Machines) and ANNs (Artificial Neural Networks). We have performed binary classification using the important features of each type of attacks and multi-class classification combining the most important features for the 4 types of attacks (DoS, probe, R2L, U2R) (13 features) and the most important features of each type of attack and normal data (18 features). We have to note here for features, whose values are alphanumeric, we map each instance of alphanumeric value to sequential integer values.

2 Experimental Results

According to the proposed approach ESOMs are trained to learn the normal behavior and attack patterns and then deviations from normal behavior are flagged as attacks. It is demonstrated that ESOMs are capable of making highly accurate attack/normal classifications. For the evaluation we have used the Databionics ESOM tools [5].

We performed various evaluation experiments. Table 1 presents the datasets that were used in order to train and test our approach. All the datasets are part of the available 10% KDD dataset [6] of various sizes that include normal data and DoS, Probe, R2L and U2R attacks. We performed binary classification (i.e. normal/attack) to classify each class of attacks (DoS, Probe, R2L, U2R) against normal traffic.

The ESOM of a trained dataset containing normal traffic and DoS attacks is depicted in figure 1. As it can be clearly seen the training data set has been divided into two classes that are very well distinguished, normal data class (dark color) and DoS data class (light color). In figure 2 the testing dataset for the corresponding training dataset is depicted. In order to evaluate the efficiency of the proposed approach we use two measures, i.e. the detection rate and the false alarm rate:

$$\text{Detection rate} = \frac{TP}{TP + FN}, \text{ False alarm rate} = \frac{FP}{TN + FP},$$

where TP is the number of true positives (attack logs classified as attacks), TN the number of true negatives (normal logs classified as normal), FP the number of false positives (normal logs classified as attacks) and FN the number of false negatives (attack logs classified as normal). The most effective approach should reduce as much as possible the *False alarm rate* and at the same time increase the *Detection rate*.

Table 1. Datasets used for evaluation

Dataset	Attacks		Normal
Dataset 1	3732 DoS		5065 normal
Dataset 2	3737 DoS		5064 normal
Dataset 3	2052 probe		3905 normal
Dataset 4	2055 probe		3503 normal
Dataset 5	562 R2L		1001 normal
Dataset 6	564 R2L		1001 normal
Dataset 7	3732 DoS	2052 probe	
	562 R2L		10072 normal
	6372 Total attacks		
Dataset 8	3737 DoS	2055 Probe	9669 normal
	564 R2L	27 U2R	
	6383 Total attacks		

Table 2. Evaluation Results

Experiment	Number of Features	Training Dataset	Testing Dataset	Detection Rate	False Alarm
Experiment 1	11	Dataset 1	Dataset 2	93,55%	0,21%
Experiment 2	7	Dataset 3	Dataset 4	91,33%	0,25%
Experiment 3	5	Dataset 5	Dataset 6	95,92%	2,6%
Experiment 4	13	Dataset 7	Dataset 8	93% DoS	6,39%
				96,29% U2R	
				98,97% probe	
				92,3% R2L	
				96,29% U2R	
				95,17% Total	
Experiment 5	18	Dataset 7	Dataset 8	99,49% DoS	3.4%
				99,75% probe	
				99,46% R2L	
				100% R2L	
				99,59% total	

Thus experiments have been performed with 50x82 neurons and 20 training epochs. The Gaussian function was used as a kernel neighborhood function and weight initialization method and the Euclidean as a distance function. The initial and final learning rate, were 0.5 and 0.1 respectively and the initial and final value for radius were 24 and 1 respectively. Moreover in order to avoid topology errors caused by border effects we have used boundless toroid grids.

As it can be seen from the table 2 where the evaluation results are presented the detection rate ranges from 91,33% to 95,92% for binary classification (experiments 1,2,3) and the corresponding false alarms from 0,21% to 2,6%. The highest detection

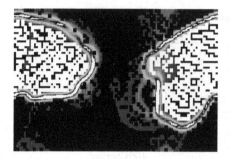
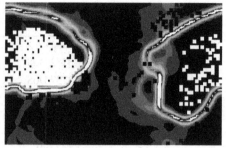

Fig. 1. U-Matrix of the training dataset   **Fig. 2.** U-Matrix of the testing dataset

rate and lower false alarm is achieved for DoS attacks while the R2L attacks present lower detection rate and false alarm equal to 2,6%. The ESOM approach presents good results with extremely low false alarms when only one attack is included in the training and testing dataset. When datasets include more than one attack the results are more promising, using 18 features that derive from the combination of important features of each type of attack and normal traffic.

By exploiting the visualization of network traffic our approach detects attacks by classifying malicious and normal actions. The proposed approach produces efficient results for randomly selected datasets. We should note that even though we employed small datasets of the 10% KDD dataset, the results are extremely promising.

References

1. S. Haykin, "Neural Networks: A comprehensive Foundation", Prentice- Hall, USA, 2nd edit.
2. A. Ultsch, "Data Mining and Knowledge Discovery with Emergent SOFMs for Multivariate Time Series", In Kohonen Maps, (1999), pp. 33-46.
3. A. Ultsch, "Maps for Visualization of High-Dimensional Data Spaces", Proc. WSOM, Kyushu, Japan, (2003), pp. 225-230.
4. S. Mukkamala, A.H. Sung, "Identifying Significant Features for Network Forensic Analysis Using Artificial Intelligent Techniques", International Journal of Digital Evidence,2003(1)4.
5. Databionic ESOM Tools, http://databionic- esom.sourceforge.net/devel.html.
6. The Third International Knowledge Discovery and Data Mining Tools Competition, May 2002. http://kdd.ics.uci.edu/databases/kddcup99.kddcup99.html

Mapping Fundamental Business Process Modelling Language to OWL-S

Gayathri Nadarajan[1] and Yun-Heh Chen-Burger[2]

[1] CISA, School of Informatics, University of Edinburgh, UK
[2] Artificial Intelligence Applications Institute, University of Edinburgh, UK

Abstract. This paper presents a conceptual mapping framework between a formal and visual process modelling language, Fundamental Business Process Modelling Language (FBPML), and the Web Services Ontology (OWL-S), aiming to bridge the gap between Enterprise Modelling methods and Semantic Web services. The framework is divided into a data model and a process model component. An implementation and an evaluation of the process model mapping are demonstrated.

1 Introduction

The need for more sophisticated Web based support tools has become apparent with the fast advancement of the Web and the Semantic Web vision. Business-to-Business (B2B) Electronic Commerce is fast becoming the most important application area of Semantic Web technology in terms of market volume [1]. Enterprise Modelling (EM) methods, on the other hand, are mature methods used as analysis tools for describing and redesigning businesses. They have been recognised for their value in providing a more organised way to describe complex, informal domain. For virtual organisations with business goals, the automation of business processes as Web services is increasingly important. Thus, traditional EM methods, such as Business Process Modelling (BPM) methods could be exploited by emerging technologies such as Semantic Web services to provide a more mature framework incorporating both business- and Web application-specific technologies. In a wider context this aims to bring business- and technical-oriented communities closer in order to achieve common organisational goals.

FBPML [2] is an inherited, specialised and combined version of several standard modelling languages that seeks to provide distributed knowledge- and semantic-based manipulation and collaboration. It provides graphical notation for describing business processes and has two sections to provide theories and formal representations for describing data and processes. OWL-S [3] is a Web service ontology that aims to describe Web services in machine-processable forms to facilitate the automation of Web service tasks, including automated Web service discovery, execution, composition and interoperation. Both languages have separate models to describe data and processes and are therefore structurally similar. Furthermore, OWL-S is also fast becoming the de facto standard for describing Web services, thus it is the most appropriate Semantic Web based language for FBPML to be mapped with.

G. Antoniou et al. (Eds.): SETN 2006, LNAI 3955, pp. 563–566, 2006.

2   The Conceptual Mapping Framework

A conceptual mapping framework was devised to map the two languages, motivated by the fact that both languages have a clear separation between their data and process schemas. FBPML's data model is described in the FBPML Data Language (FBPML DL) while OWL-S is described in the Web Ontology Language, OWL [4]. FBPML's process model is described by the FBPML Process Language (FBPML PL), while OWL-S contains its own classes to describe its process model. Thus the mapping framework was divided into a data model component and a process model component. Figure 1 illustrates this distinction and the general approach undertaken for this work.

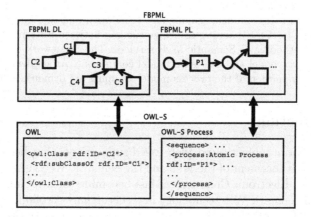

Fig. 1. The FBPML to OWL-S Conceptual Mapping Framework

The mapping of data models between FBPML and OWL-S involves the translation of representations of concepts (or classes), instances (of the concepts) and the relationships between the concepts and instances from FBPML DL to OWL. It also entails the translation of representations of properties and restrictions between the two data model languages. The process model mapping entails the mapping between FBPML PL and OWL-S. The primitives in FBPML were mapped to the primitives in OWL and OWL-S, resulting in Table 1.

3   Mapping, Implementation and Evaluation

Following the primitive mapping exercise, an exhaustive decomposition methodology was devised as an attempt to translate a FBPML process model into its OWL-S equivalent using worked examples on the data and process models. The worked examples are not shown here due to space limitation. Based on this methodology, a process model translator was developed using SICStus Prolog 3.10.1 on (Red Hat) Linux 9, that parses first-order logic (Horn) clauses into hierarchical OWL and RDF tree-like tags [5]. A data model translator was not developed due to time limitation. The main aim of the process model translator was to cater for any process model described in FBPML PL to be converted into OWL syntax. As pointed out in Table 1, the process model mapping does not encompass all the possible primitives and process constructs, and is thus limited. Hence the system was implemented to perform the translation as closely, accurately and directly as possible, taking into account some viable assumptions and interpretations. The mapping exercise using worked examples demonstrated

Table 1. Summary of mapping between FBPML and OWL-S primitives

Model Type	Primitive	FBPML	OWL/OWL-S
Data	Classes	Concrete Class	Class
		Abstract Class	Class
	Instances	Instance of Class	Instance of Class
Data	Relations	Class Relationship	Class Property
		Instance Relationship	Object Property
		Instance Attribute	Datatype Property
Process	Main Nodes	Activity	Composite Process
		Primitive Activity	Atomic Process
		Role	Participant
		Time Point	See *Note*
Process	Links	Precedence Link	(part of) Sequence
		Synchronisation Bar	See *Note*
Process	Junctions	Start	See *Note*
		Finish	See *Note*
		And-Joint	Split-Join
		Or-Joint	See *Note*
		And-Split	Split
		Or-Split	Repeat-While, Repeat-Until
		Xor-Junction	Choice
Process	Annotations	Idea Note	See *Note*
		Navigation Note	See *Note*
Process	Process Components	Precondition	Precondition
		Trigger	See *Note*
		Postcondition	Effect
		Precondition, Trigger and Postcondition	Input/Output
		Action	Atomic Process
		Conditional Action	If-Then-Else

Note: Limited (or no) equivalent convention provided by OWL-S.

that most of the data model components could be mapped directly, while not all the process model components, in particular the junctions, could be fully mapped. The implementation of the process model translator, although limited, decomposes the sequences and combination junctions in a methodical manner.

A constituent of a FBPML process model that could not be translated is recorded in the comment construct. The problem will arise if loops, which may cause partly overlapped processes, are added to the process model. When this happens, the process model may not be decomposed, thus causing mapping problems. Thus, we can conclude that the formal mapping between FBPML and OWL-S is very challenging and will require more insight and exploration before a reasonable mapping framework could be formulated. The essence of the analysis is that a much thorough understanding for both languages has been gained and this can work as the groundwork towards future directions.

4   Conclusion and Extensions

We have demonstrated a conceptual mapping framework between two formal languages, FBPML and OWL-S. The former is traditionally used in the context of business process modelling and the latter in the domain of Semantic Web services. We have also attempted to automate the translation of the process modelling aspect between the two languages. The conceptual mapping exercise and implementation have brought to light some vital differences between the constructions of the two languages which suggest that the mapping between them is partial. Furthermore, the specifications of some aspects of OWL-S are still in progress and, hence, the mapping is not complete. A complete formalism for rules and conditions within OWL would allow for some of the gaps between FBPML and OWL-S to be filled. The framework could also be further strengthened by incorporating ontologies to represent the data and process models together with sound mapping principles. As the future of OWL-S remains unclear, current effort towards converging OWL-S with Web Services Modelling Ontology (WSMO) could be a positive step towards the development of a stronger and more stable global standard for Semantic Web services.

References

1. Antoniou, G. and van Harmelen, F.: A Semantic Web Primer. MIT Press, Cambridge, MA, USA. (2004)
2. Chen-Burger, Y.-H., Tate, A., and Robertson, D.: Enterprise Modelling: A Declarative Approach for FBPML. In Proceedings European Conference of Artificial Intelligence, Knowledge Management and Organisational Memories Workshop. (2002)
3. Martin, D. et al.: OWL-S Semantic Markup for Web Services, Release 1.1.. World Wide Web Consortium (W3C), http://www.daml.org/services/owl-s/1.1/ (2003)
4. McGuinness, D. and van Harmelen, F.: OWL Web Ontology Language. World Wide Web Consortium (W3C), http://www.w3.org/TR/owl-features/ (2004)
5. Nadarajan, G.: Mapping Fundamental Business Process Modelling Language to a Semantic Web Based Language. MSc. Dissertation, School of Informatics, University of Edinburgh, UK. (2005) (unpublished)

Modeling Perceived Value of Color in Web Sites

Eleftherios Papachristos, Nikolaos Tselios, and Nikolaos Avouris

Human-Computer Interaction Group, Electrical and Computer Eng. Dept.,
University of Patras, GR-265 00 Rio Patras, Greece
{epap, nitse}@ee.upatras.gr, avouris@upatras.gr

Abstract. Color plays an important role in web site design. The selection of effective chromatic combinations and the relation of color to the perceived aesthetic and emotional value of a web site is the focus of this paper. The subject of the reported research has been to define a model through which to be able to associate color combinations with specific desirable emotional and aesthetic values. The presented approach involves application of machine learning techniques on a rich data set collected during a number of empirical studies.

1 Introduction

Recent work has shown that the design space of a web site is affected by both engineering and aesthetic issues and that the visual aesthetics of computer interfaces are a strong determinant of users' satisfaction and pleasure [1]. An effective web site design has to communicate not only its content and information architecture, but also wider values such as sense of professionalism, skillfulness and credibility. Additionally to this, recent studies, reinforce the theory that physically attractive sources have been perceived to be credible by showing that people rarely use rigorous criteria when evaluating credibility [2]. Furthermore, a web site's *perceived value* is influenced by cultural beliefs, traditions, as well as goals and usage expectations [3]. However, little is known about the influence of aesthetics and the role of the color. Most approaches modeling interaction with web sites have focused primarily on the cognitive aspects [3]. As a result, aesthetic design and color usage is primarily implemented via ad hoc, trial and error procedures. Therefore, the need to model color effect emerges in order to guide the design practices in this area.

In this paper, we use A.I. techniques to define a model, to select the most appropriate color combination for a web site of a given purpose. The goal is to identify methodologically the color combinations which communicate effectively desired emotional values. For example, a news web site should effectively communicate values such as consistency, reliability, objectivity, etc. Due to the fact that a direct evaluation of each color is heavily subjective, the methodology tackles this problem by indirectly evaluating the credibility influence of selected color combinations, and then breaking down the underlying influence of each factor using a Bayesian Belief Network. The developed *Emotional Color Model* has been encoded in a tool to suggest appropriate chromatic schemes according to the desired perceived web site values. An extensive discussion of the developed model is included, further elaborating earlier report on this study results [5].

G. Antoniou et al. (Eds.): SETN 2006, LNAI 3955, pp. 567–570, 2006.
© Springer-Verlag Berlin Heidelberg 2006

2   Emotional Color Model Definition

The goal of this study is to determine relations between color characteristics and descriptors of the web site perceived value. The benefit of such an approach is the application of a formal methodological process to select the appropriate color combination. Subsequently, the process can be applied reversely: For a web site of a given scope we can elicit the appropriate color characteristics. A *Color Model* has been defined first, combining physical, aesthetic and artistic dimensions to describe any web page color scheme. This includes aspects such as *dominant* and *secondary color, number of colors*, primary *color scheme* and secondary color scheme attributes such as *degree of saturation* and *brightness*. This Model is associated to descriptors of the perceived value of a web site using a methodology discussed more extensively in [5]. According to this methodology, typical users of the web site are requested to provide their subjective feeling about different color schemes applied on a web page layout.

The Perceived web site value dimensions are compatible with the thirteen emotional dimensions that have been used by Kim et al. [4] to describe the emotional value of web site design, deduced through a systematic process. The emotional descriptors are: *Pleasant, Formal, Fresh, Modern, Friendly, Aggressive, Professional, Attractive, Calming, Dynamic, Reliable and Sophisticated.* The process of deriving the Emotional Color Model is shown in Figure 1.

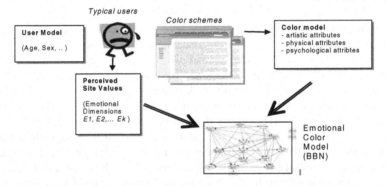

Fig. 1. Overview of the proposed methodology

The data collected have been used for training a Bayesian Belief Network (BBN). The BBN obtained has been proven a significant knowledge representation and reasoning tool, in this context. The proposed framework is supported by tools, to facilitate user data collection, and to permit user choosing which emotional descriptor has to be present on her web site and at what degree. Subsequently, the tool proposes a list of color schemes coupled with detailed explanations on the results.

3   Model Validation Study

An experiment took place to validate the proposed model, discussed in more detail in [5]. The goal was to involve users evaluating a series of mock web pages using the proposed descriptors to evaluate the affective impression to them. A common layout has been used, reproduced in a number of different color schemes. The data collected during the study were 4416 evaluations, used to train the BBN.

By analyzing the BBN we obtained *structural* and *statistical* conclusions. For example, according to the tree structure, dominant colour's *brightness* has a stronger emotional effect than its *hue*. And BBN's statistical analysis, led to the conclusion that *Green* should be used as a dominant color, if the priority of the designer is to communicate the emotional dimension *friendly*. On the other hand, *Blue* was found to have a variation between 35.68% and 35.77%. These values indicate that *Green* has higher sensitivity on "friendliness" than *Blue*. Consequently, we could assume that the existence of *Green* colour plays important role in whether a web page is perceived as friendly to its users, according to the subjects of this study.

Further processing of the BBN obtained, led to the ascertainment that the values perceived by the user were influenced in a layered way of variated impact by the encoded color charateristics. Those dinstictive four layers are (a)the *brightness* of the dominant color, (b) the *brightness* level of the secondary color, the *number of colors, contrast* between hues, and the *type of the secondary colo*r (warm or cold), (c) the *dominant color*, the *secondary color, color scheme, contrast levels of brightness* and finally (d) the *saturation and the type(warm or cold) of the dominant color.*

Table 1. A web site's color model with respect to the emotional dimension *friendliness*

Attribute	"Friendly" web page	Less "Friendly"
Dominant color	Green	Blue
Brightness of dominant color	Bright	dark
Saturation of dominant color	neutral	not saturated
Secondary color	Grey green	Blue
Brightness of secondary color	Bright	dark
Saturation of secondary color	not saturated	not saturated
Contrast of brightness between colors	high	neutral
Contrast between Hues	low	low
Number of colors	4	3
Color Scheme	monochromatic	monochromatic

Besides observations on the structure of the network, or performing sensitivity studies on various nodes, other interesting conclusions have been derived. For example, it seems to be preferable to use more than 4 colors and the best chromatic combinations are monochromatic and analogical. In addition, it seems to be preferable to use low contrast levels between colors. Cold colors are perceived as better than warm. If we adopt a monochromatic color scheme it is preferable to have high contrast in brightness. Finally, it was deduced that the best combination is a highly saturated dominant color with a low saturated secondary color. Table 1 presents the ideal color factors, proposed by the model, to communicate the emotional descriptor "friendly" to the greatest or lowest extent accordingly.

4   Conclusions

The objective of the study has been to derive conclusions related to specific color selections and their emotional impact, of general value and applicability. Many of the findings reported by this study confirm earlier empirical rules on color and current tendencies in web design, also discussed in our earlier study [5]. This confirms the validity of the proposed methodological approach. However, the reported results cannot be claimed to be of general value, mainly due to the small number of participants.

A subsequent research step is to conduct large scale studies with representative users. Towards this goal we are in the process of redesigning the data acquisition tool to gather the data online. The online tool has increased complexity due to the uncontrolled characteristics of users' workstations in terms of resolution and color depth. The tool will also normalize users' computer settings such as resolution color depth, gamma etc. and provide sufficient guidance to the user. Also, more primary and secondary color combinations are to be covered by adding more layouts to be presented randomly to the user. To further increase the reliability of the process, the emotional descriptors will be presented to the user in a random order. Finally, one may view the issue of appropriate chromatic combination to a broader context. We argue that various models of typical web user behavior engaged in typical tasks, like information foraging [6], may be extended to take into account color issues.

Acknowledgements

Research was funded by EPEAEK 2: 'Pithagoras 2: Models of information foraging on the web'. Valuable insight by Dr. Maragoudakis, M. should be also acknowledged.

References

1. Lavie, T. and Tractinsky, N. (2004). Assessing Dimensions of Perceived Visual Aesthetics of Web Sites, International Journal of Human-Computer Studies, 60(3):269-298.
2. Danielson, D.R. (2003). Transitional volatility in web navigation. Information Technology and Society, 1(3),Special Issue on Web Navigation, B. Shneiderman, J. Lazar, and M.Y. Ivory (Eds.), 131-158.
3. Wang, P., (2001). A survey of design guidelines for usability of web sites. Proceedings of the 2001 Human-Computer Interaction International Conference 1, 183-187.
4. Kim J., Lee J., Choi D., (2003). Designing emotionally evocative homepages: an empirical study of the quantitative relations between design factors and emotional dimensions, Int. J. Human-Computer Studies, 59, pp. 899–940.
5. Papachristos E., Tselios N., Avouris N., Inferring relations between color and emotional dimensions of a web site using Bayesian Networks, Proc. Interact 2005, Rome, Septembre 2005, Lecture Notes in Computer Science, Volume 3585, Sep 2005, Pages 1075 - 1078.
6. Pirolli, P. and Card, S. K. (1999). Information Foraging. Psychological Review 106(4): 643-675.

Introducing Interval Analysis in Fuzzy Cognitive Map Framework

Elpiniki Papageorgiou[1], Chrysostomos Stylios[2], and Peter Groumpos[1]

[1] Laboratory for Automation and Robotics,
Department of Electrical and Computer Engineering,
University of Patras, Rion 26500, Greece
Tel.: +30 2610 997293; Fax: +30 26120 997309
epapageo@ee.upatras.gr, groumpos@ee.upatras.gr
[2] Department of Communications, Informatics and Management,
TEI of Epirus, Artas Epirus, Greece
Tel.: +30 6974638830
stylios@teleinfom.teiep.gr

Abstract. Fuzzy Cognitive Maps (FCMs) is a graphical model for causal knowledge representation. FCMs consist of nodes-concepts and weighted edges that connect the concepts and represent the cause and effect relationships among them. FCMs are used in complex problems involving causal relationships, which often include feedback, and where qualitative rather than quantitative measures of influences are available. They have used for decision support to determine a final state given a qualitative initial knowledge for nodes and weighted edges. A first study on introducing Interval analysis in the FCM framework has been attempted and it is presented in this work. Here a new structure for FCM is proposed with interval weights and a new method for processing interval data input for FCMs is proposed.

Keywords: Fuzzy cognitive maps, Interval analysis.

1 Introduction

FCMs are qualitative models for a system, consisted of variables and the causal relationships between those variables [1]. They are useful for knowledge representation and processing for highly complicated domains [2], [3]. The usefulness of FCMs is highlighted for dynamic feedback systems for which conventional rule-based expert systems are inadequate [4]. Experts design and determine the nodes and weights of FCM, for each problem domain [5], [6]. Fuzzy variables are used for concepts and weights. Here it is introduced the treatment for nodes and the weights as interval numbers that lie within the range provided by the experts, rather than as fuzzy sets.

Interval analysis is a deterministic way of representing uncertainty by replacing a number with a range of values [7], [8]. It introduced to deal with numerical errors which occurred in mathematical computations performed on digital computers. Interval analysis has been used in many branches of mathematics, including numerical analysis, probability and logic [9], [10] and [11].

G. Antoniou et al. (Eds.): SETN 2006, LNAI 3955, pp. 571–575, 2006.
© Springer-Verlag Berlin Heidelberg 2006

In [12], Muata and Bryson used interval pairwise comparison techniques for generating consistent subjective estimates for the magnitudes of causal relationships in FCMs. Here it is introduced interval computations in all the FCM architecture.

2   A Brief Description of Fuzzy Cognitive Maps

A FCM is composed of nodes that represent the factors most relevant to the decision environment and weighted arrows that indicate the causal relationships among factors. One factor (variable) can have a positive or negative effect on another. Arrows have different numerical strengths. Experts describe their understanding of the relationships among the key factors. The directional influences are presented as all-or-none relationships, so the FCMs provide qualitative as well as quantitative information about these relationships [1].

Generally, the value of each node is calculated, computing the influence of the interconnected nodes to the specific node, by applying the following calculation rule:

$$A_i^{(k+1)} = f(A_i^{(k)} + \sum_{\substack{j \neq i \\ j=1}}^{N} w_{ji} \cdot A_j^{(k)}) \tag{1}$$

where $A_i^{(k+1)}$ is the value of node C_i at time $k+1$, $A_j^{(k)}$ is the value of node C_j at time k, w_{ji} is the weight of the interconnection from node C_j towards node C_i and f is the sigmoid threshold function. When a node(s) is stimulated, then the resulting activities can resonate through other nodes on the FCM until equilibrium is reached.

In the proposed methodology, both nodes and edges are fuzzy sets and are bounded in ranges provided by the inference method and the related membership functions. At follows, three different types for assessing FCM concepts and weights as interval values are introduced and a new mathematical form for FCM framework is proposed.

3   Introducing Interval Analysis in FCM Framework

Interval Fuzzy Cognitive Map (IFCM) is a FCM where its concepts (inputs, outputs) and weight take interval values. Interval FCMs are formed by processing units called Interval Concepts. An interval FCM is formed by three functions:

– Normalizer Function (T): This function analyzes the input nature and normalizes it in order to take only interval inputs.
– Sum Function (Σ): This function is the same as the sum function in the calculation for traditional FCMs.
– Activation Function: This function could be any interval derivable linear function, which restricts the output to interval values between [-1,1] or [0,1].

Interval FCMs can be classified in three different types depending on the concept's nature and nature of weights (fuzzy-interval). In the following subsection we describe the three different approaches for assessing FCMs using Interval Computations.

3.1 Type I of Interval FCM

In this approach, the initial concept values are interval numbers; the weights take crisp values and the output concepts take interval numbers. Fig. 1 represents the IFCM type I, with crisp weight values and interval values for input-output concepts.

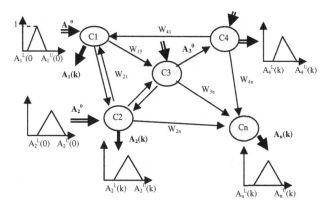

Fig. 1. Interval FCM model I with interval input-output concepts and crisp weigh++ts

The output concept value A_p, for a concept C_p is calculated by equations (2), (3):

$$A_{pi}^L(k) = A_{pi}^L(k-1) + \sum_{\substack{i=1, \\ wij \geq 0}}^{n} w_{ji} \cdot A_j^L(k-1) + \sum_{\substack{i=1, \\ wij \prec 0}}^{n} w_{ji} \cdot A_j^U(k-1) \tag{2}$$

$$A_{pi}^U(k) = A_{pi}^U(k-1) + \sum_{\substack{i=1, \\ wij \geq 0}}^{n} w_{ji} \cdot A_j^U(k-1) + \sum_{\substack{i=1, \\ wij \prec 0}}^{n} w_{ji} \cdot A_j^L(k-1) \tag{3}$$

Where the interval output concept is determined from the form:

$$A_p(k) = \left[A_p^L, A_p^U \right] = \left[f(A_{pi}^L), f(A_{pi}^U) \right] \tag{4}$$

3.2 Type II for Interval FCM

Type II of IFCM uses interval values for weights and crisp values for input concepts. The derived output concept values are calculated using equation (5):

$$A_{pi}(k) = \left[A_{pi}^L(k), A_{pi}^U(k) \right] = A_{pi}(k-1) + \sum_{i=1}^{n} \left[w_{ij}^L, w_{ij}^U \right] \cdot \left[A_j^L(k-1), A_j^U(k-1) \right] \tag{5}$$

The initial concept values $\mathbf{A}^0$ are crisp values derived from measurements and represent real numerical data.

3.3 Type III for Interval FCM

In this approach, all the FCM concepts and weights are determined as interval numbers producing an Interval FCM framework. The output concepts values are calculated through the equation (6), considering multiplication and addition of intervals.

$$A_{pi}(k) = \left[A_{pi}^L(k), A_{pi}^U(k) \right] = \left[A_{pi}^L(k-1), A_{pi}^U(k-1) \right] + \sum_{i=1}^{n} \left[w_{ji}^L, w_{ji}^U \right] \cdot \left[A_j^L(k-1), A_j^U(k-1) \right] \quad (6)$$

4   Conclusions and Future Directions

In this paper, interval analysis has been introduced to assess FCM's concepts and weights. This work proposes a new framework of Fuzzy Cognitive Map that updates the traditional Fuzzy Cognitive Map and has better characteristics. Only, Muata and Bryson [11] referred to interval pairwise comparison techniques for generating consistent magnitudes of FCM causal relationships. This paper proposes the inclusion of interval mathematics in the structure of the FCM, it is expected that the performance of the FCM with interval mathematics could be better to deal with interval types of input data eliminating numerical errors.

Our future work is directed towards the implementation of Interval Fuzzy Cognitive Maps in real problem from different scientific domains, proposing training algorithms for IFCM and comparing the results with other approaches. Furthermore, future research will be directed to fuzzy training algorithms for IFCMs in order to compare them with the recently proposed learning techniques for FCMs [5], [6].

Acknowledgements

This work was supported by the "PYTHAGORAS II" research grant co funded by the European Social Fund and National Resources.

References

1. Kosko, B.: Fuzzy Cognitive Maps, Int. J. Man-Machine Studies, 24 (1986), 65-75.
2. Stylios, C., Groumpos, P.P.: Modeling Complex Systems Using Fuzzy Cognitive Maps, IEEE Syst Man Cybern: Part A, 34, (2004), 155-162.
3. Park, K.S., Kim, S.H.: Fuzzy Cognitive Maps considering fuzzy relationships, Int. J. Hum.-Comp. Studies, 42 (1995), 157-168.
4. Taber, W.R.: Knowledge processing with Fuzzy Cognitive Maps, Expert Syst. Applic. 2, Number 1, (1991), 83-87.
5. Papageorgiou, E. I., Parsopoulos, K. E., Stylios, C. D., Groumpos, P. P., Vrahatis, M. N.: Fuzzy Cognitive Maps Learning Using Particle Swarm Optimization. Int. J. Intel. Inf. Syst., 25, 1 (2005), 95-121.
6. Papageorgiou, E.I., Stylios, C.D., Groumpos, P.P.: Active Hebbian Learning to Train Fuzzy Cognitive Maps, Int. J. Approx. Reasoning, 37 (2004), 219-249.
7. Moore, R.E.: Interval Analysis, Prentice Hall, New Jersey, (1966).
8. Aleferd, G., Herzeberger, J.: Introduction to interval computations. Academic Press, New York (1983).

9. Moore, R.E.: Methods and Applications of Interval Analysis. SIAM, Philadelpeia, (1979).
10. Kearfott, R.B., Kreinovich, V.: Applications of Interval Computations. Kluwer Academic Publisher (1996).
11. Ischibuchi, H., Nii, M.: Interval-Arithmetic-based Neural Networks. In: Brunke, H., Kande, A., (Eds): Hybrid methods in pattern recognition, Series in Machine Perception and Artificial Intelligence, 47 (2001).
12. Muata, K., Bryson, O.: Generating consistent subjective estimates of the magnitudes of causal relationships in fuzzy cognitive maps. Computers & Operations Research, 31, 8 (2004), 1165-1175.

Discovering Ontologies for e-Learning Platforms

Christos Papatheodorou[1] and Alexandra Vassiliou[2]

[1] Department of Archive and Library Sciences, Ionian University,
Palea Anaktora, Eleftherias Sq., Corfu, GR-49100, Greece
papatheodor@ionio.gr
[2] Division of Applied Technologies, NCSR "Demokritos",
PO Box 60228, Aghia Paraskevi, Athens, GR-15310, Greece
alex@lib.demokritos.gr

Abstract. E-Learning service providers produce or collect digital learning resources, derive metadata for their description, and reuse and organize them in repositories. This paper proposes a data mining approach to discover relationships between the learning resources metadata. In particular, it presents and evaluates methods for clustering learning resources and providing controlled vocabularies for each class description. The derived classes and vocabularies contribute to the semantic interoperability in learning resource interchanges.

1 Introduction

Ontology construction from a collection of documents in a domain requires the development of tools assisting their users to determine the existing concepts and their relations. OntoWeb Consortium has presented a survey on the ontology discovery tools, pointing out to two approaches [3]. The first one concerns RDF documents and exploits their structure [2]. The other approach exploits the content of the documents and is based on language engineering and machine learning techniques [5, 6]. A recent work [1] presents a method to form concept hierarchies (taxonomies) from text corpora based on the conceptual clustering technique named Formal Concept Analysis (FCA).

This paper is motivated by UNIVERSAL (http://www.ist-universal.org/), a European Union funded project (Information Society Technologies Programme), aiming to implement an open market place enabling the European Higher Education Institutes to exchange learning resources (LR). The platform hosts a variety of LR, covering many scientific domains and different educational needs. The LR descriptions are based on the known IEEE-LOM metadata standard and are encoded using the XML-RDF model. This paper presents a data mining approach that extracts the terms corresponding to the LR title, subject(s) and description from the RDF metadata files, using language engineering tools, and then tries to discover LR classes by clustering them as well as to define meaningful vocabularies for class descriptions. We combine the proposed clustering method along with a well-known feature selection method, the Singular Value Decomposition (SVD) for dimensionality reduction i.e. the selection

G. Antoniou et al. (Eds.): SETN 2006, LNAI 3955, pp. 576–579, 2006.

of appropriate terms comprising the vocabulary. Our aim is to compare the clustering outcomes, provide an evaluation framework, and decide if the application of SVD has improved the results produced by them.

2 Methodology and Evaluation

During the data preprocessing stage, LR metadata are gathered, and the title, subject and description fields of the metadata XML/RDF files are separated. Brill's tagger assigns to each word its most likely part of speech tag. The dataset is prepared as a $d \times t$ matrix $X = [x_{ij}]$, where d is the number of the LR and t the total number of the terms. Each cell in the data matrix X indicates the number of observed occurrences of a term in a LR.

For the pattern discovery stage we propose a variant of Cluster Mining algorithm [8], which discovers similar LR by looking for all cliques in a weighted graph $G(V,E)$. The set of nodes V corresponds to the set of the LR. If a term is common in the i-th and j-th LR, then the corresponding nodes v_i and v_j are connected by an edge e_{ij}. The weight on edge e_{ij} is equal either to frequency of the common terms in the two LR, or to a coefficient expressing the similarity (in the range [0,1]) between the two LR.

For the graph connectivity reduction we use a *connectivity threshold*, representing the minimum weight allowed for the edge existence. For each connectivity threshold a new clustering is generated. The algorithm allows the overlap among the LR of a clustering and Jaccard's coefficient measures the overlap between two clusters A and B (J= |A∩B| / |A∪B|). An acceptable clustering is that with the minimum LR overlap.

We applied the Cluster Mining algorithm on the original data matrix X (without rejecting of any terms) and then on reduced matrices X_k, produced by the application of the SVD, for different values of k, where $k \leq r$ and r the rank of the data matrix X ($r \leq d$). SVD is used for the reduction of noisy dimensions, rejecting the non-contributing to the analysis terms and projecting their vectors into a lower dimensional space spanned by the true "factors" of the term collection.

Finally we extract the terms that characterize the derived clusters. These representative terms form a prototypical model for each cluster. Their selection is achieved with the aid of a simple criterion called frequency increase criterion [8]. Given a term with frequency f in the entire dataset, and frequency f_i in a cluster i, the frequency increase criterion is defined as the difference of the squares of the two frequencies:

$$FI = f_i^2 - f^2,$$

A term is considered as representative of a cluster, if $FI > \alpha > 0$, where α is a threshold of the frequency increase.

The evaluation of the extracted ontologies aims to measure the adequacy of a specific set of concepts as a model of a given domain. There exist two approaches of ontology evaluation. The first one is based on formal methods [1, 4], while the second on the participation of domain specialists who compare the automatically learned concepts with their formal and intuitive knowledge of a domain [7].

For the evaluation of the effectiveness of our approach we considered a taxonomy acquired by a team of experts consisted of representatives from the brokerage platform administrators and the LR providers. The evaluation aims to measure the similarity of the produced clusters of LR, with the classes indicated by the experts. The evaluation is based on the following measures:

- *F-measure*: It is the harmonic mean of precision (*p*) and recall (*r*) (*F=2pr/(p+r)*), where (*p*) is the ratio of the number of the correctly recovered LR from a specific class in a cluster over of LR found in a cluster by a clustering algorithm. The precision in a clustering is the average precision over all classes with respect to the handcrafted taxonomy. Recall (*r*) is the ratio of the number of the correctly recovered LR from a specific class in a cluster over the number of LR in that class.
- *Discovered classes ratio(RCF):* the ratio of the discovered classes over the number of classes in the handcrafted taxonomy.
- *Classes recovered*: the clusters for which the *recall* equals to 1.
- *LR Coverage*: the ratio of the number of LR participating in a clustering over the number of LR in the data.
- *Efficiency*: The ratio of clusters found over the number of terms.

Concerning the selection of the best clustering, we consider the one with a relatively small overlap and a high value of LR coverage.

3 Experimental Results

The preprocessing of 134 LR descriptions stored in the UNIVERSAL repository returned 3,293 terms. The Cluster Mining algorithm has been applied on both the original data matrix X, and the approximated by SVD matrices (for 90, 100, and 125 eigenvalues), for connectivity thresholds $c=0.2,0.3,0.4,0.5,0.6$. After the selection of the best clustering, the application of the *FI* measure follows for the selection of the appropriate vocabulary. None of the clusterings has all the classes included in the experts' taxonomy.

Table 1. Evaluation resuts

	Original data threshold=0.2	90 eigenvalues threshold=0.5	100 eigenvalues threshold=0.4	125 eigenvalues threshold=0.4
F-measure	0.70	0.52	0.60	0.78
LR Coverage	0.45	0.51	0.72	0.70
classes found/total classes	6/10	7/10	8/10	6/10
Classes recovered (recall=1)	2	1	2	3
Efficiency	0.007	0.59	0.76	0.42

The evaluation of the clusterings' success process lays upon the evaluation measures, displayed in Table 1. For each one of the data sets the F-measure is calculated for $c=0.2,0.3,0.4,0.5,0.6$, with respect to the handcrafted taxonomy. The value of the connectivity threshold c for which the F-measure becomes maximum, is considered to be the most appropriate for the best clustering.

In general the combination of SVD with cluster mining provides better results. F-measure, acquires high values when SVD is used. Furthermore SVD using 100 eigenvalues exhibits the maximum LR coverage. The efficiency measure, representing the implementation costs for the derived vocabularies, is also optimized in the case of the SVD usage with 100 eigenvalues.

4 Conclusions

In this paper we examined a methodology for ontology engineering in learning resources repositories, based on the data mining approach. The development of ontology discovery tools is essential for the improvement of the e-learning systems and services. The experimentation with the presented methods proved that the combination of SVD with Cluster Mining is quite helpful and could be used for the organization of the LR to taxonomies, as well as the establishment of sufficiently rich vocabularies from the LR descriptions. The main advantages of this approach are the dimensionality reduction and scalability. Moreover the expressiveness, efficiency, and LR coverage are increased.

References

1. Cimiano, P., Hotho, A., Staab, S.: Learning Concept Hierarchies from Text Corpora using Formal Concept Analysis. Journal of Artificial Intelligence Research 24 (2005) 305-339
2. Delteil, A., Faron-Zucker, C., Dieng, R.: Extension of RDFS based on the CG formalism. In: Proceedings of the 9th International Conference on Conceptual Structures (ICCS 2001). Lecture Notes on Artificial Intelligence, Vol. 2120. Springer-Verlag, Berlin (2001) 275-289
3. Gómez-Pérez A., Manzano-Macho D., Alfonseca E., Núñez R., Blacoe I., Staab S., Corcho O., Ding Y., Paralic J., Raphael, T.: A survey of ontology learning methods and techniques. Deliverable 1.5, OntoWeb Consortium, IST Programme, project number IST-2000-29243, 30-05-2003 (2003)
4. Maedche, A., Staab, S.: Measuring similarity between ontologies. In: Proceedings of the 13th European Conference on Knowledge Engineering and Knowledge Management (EKAW 2002). Lecture Notes on Artificial Intelligence, Vol. 2473. Springer-Verlag, Berlin (2002) 251-263
5. Missikoff, M., Velardi, P., Fabriani, P.: Text Mining Techniques to Automatically Enrich a Domain Ontology. Applied Intelligence 18 (2003) 323-340
6. Navigli, R., Velardi, P.: Learning Domain Ontologies from Document Warehouses and Dedicated Web Sites. Computational Linguistics 50 (2004) 151 – 179
7. Navigli, R., Velardi, P., Cucchiarelli, A., Neri, F.: Automatic Ontology Learning: Supporting a Per-Concept Evaluation by Domain Experts. In: Workshop on Ontology Learning and Population, 16th European Conference on Artificial Intelligence (ECAI 2004), Valencia, Spain. Available at http://olp.dfki.de/ecai04/final-velardi.pdf (2004)
8. Paliouras, G., Papatheodorou, C., Karkaletsis,V., Spyropoulos, C.D.: Clustering the Users of Large Web Sites into Communities. In: P. Langley (ed): Proceedings of the 17th International Conference on Machine Learning (ICML 2000). Morgan Kaufmann, (2000) 719-726

Exploiting Group Thinking in Organization-Oriented Programming[*]

Ioannis Partsakoulakis and George Vouros

Department of Information and Communication Systems Eng.,
University of the Aegean, 83200 Karlovassi, Samos, Greece
{jpar, georgev}@aegean.gr

Abstract. This paper, based on the organizational model proposed in [2], investigates the organization oriented programming paradigm. The approach proposed, in contrast to other approaches, emphasizes on group thinking. To show how the organization oriented programming paradigm is applied the paper describes the implementation of the asynchronous backtracking algorithm used in distributed CSPs.

1 Introduction

An organization-oriented approach for developing MAS starts from the social dimension of the system, and is described in terms of organizational concepts such as roles (or functions, or positions), groups (or communities), tasks (or activities) and interaction protocols (or dialogue structure) [1]. Current organization-oriented approaches focus on self-interested agents with no group-thinking capabilities. As a consequence, the specification of interaction protocols has become an indispensable ingredient in almost every such approach, as well as on current develop-ment/engineering frameworks for building MAS. In contrast to these approaches, based on the organizational model proposed in [2] this paper investigates the *organization oriented programming* paradigm using agents that can act as group members in the core sense. According to this paradigm and the proposed organizationnal model, the developer may specify the expected behaviour of an organization in terms of roles, responsibilities and policies. The proposed approach does not focus on interaction protocols for the agents to accomplish their objectives; communication between agents is driven by the generic mechanisms agents exploit to achieve their group objectives. In our point of view, agents are not considered to be social because they do communicate, but because they are apt to *social deliberation*. To show how our paradigm is applied, we provide a specific example of organization oriented programming in distributed constraint satisfaction.

2 Organization Specification

The specification of an organization involves the specification of structural, deontic, and functional aspects of the organization.

---

[*] An extended version of this paper is in http://www.icsd.aegean.gr/incosys/Publications/

G. Antoniou et al. (Eds.): SETN 2006, LNAI 3955, pp. 580–583, 2006.

The specification of the *structure of organizations* is done in terms of roles. Roles are distinguished into *atomic roles,* that do not contain other roles and are played by individuals, and *composite roles* that contain at least one role and are played by groups of agents. The association between agents and roles is done through positions that are seen as instances of roles.

The specification of the *deontic aspects* of individual and group behaviour is done in terms of responsibilities. A responsibility comprises a goal state and a condition, and is denoted as a rule of the form $c => g$, where g represents the goal state and c the condition. Both, the conditions and the states of responsibilities are considered as first-order predicate logic formulae that may contain free variables. When an instance of c is recognized, then the corresponding instance of g must be achieved by the player (individual or group) of the corresponding role. Dealing with group responsibilities, the designer can distinguish between *individual*, *collaborative*, and *hybrid* responsibilities [3]. Positions inherit responsibilities from their corresponding roles as well as from the positions in which they are contained, and during the achievement of group goals they can be assigned additional ones. Recipes specify the *functional aspects* of groups in an organization, i.e. how collective goals are decomposed and achieved in the MAS. We distinguish between *state achievement recipes* (a-recipes) that specify how goal states can be achieved by assigning responsibilities to the subgroups and the individuals of the organization, and *state recognition recipes* (r-recipes) that specify how states can be recognized by means of acceptances of subgroups and beliefs of individuals. This paper focuses on recognition recipes. These are the building blocks of organizational policies for the formation of *acceptances* [3]. Each r-recipe belongs to a specific *relevant role*. Each group that plays the relevant role is a *relevant group* for this recipe. An r-recipe is associated to a *recipe state*. The body of an r-recipe comprises elements of the form $\rho_{ind}:s$, where ρ is a role contained in the recipe role, *ind* an indicator, and s is a subsidiary state of recipe's state. The indicator is a quantifier for the players of ρ and can take the value *all* or *one*, indicating *all* the players of ρ, or at least *one* of them, respectively. Examples of r-recipes are provided below. Individual agents recognize the occurrence of specific facts and events (and form the corresponding beliefs) by means of primitive recognition actions called *r-actions*.

3   Organization Oriented Programming Case Study

A distributed CSP is a CSP in which variables and constraints are distributed among multiple agents [4]. Each agent is responsible of assigning a value to a specific variable so as to satisfy the stated constraints. Agents send *"ok?"* messages to communicate their current value. There is a priority order of variables/agents, which is determined by the alphabetical order of the variable identifiers. Preceding variables in alphabetical order have higher priority. Each agent in its *agent_view* maintains a viewpoint that stores the current assignment of values to variables determined by other agents. If there exists no value that is consistent with the assignments of higher priority agents, the agent generates a new constraint (called *"nogood"*), and communicates it to the higher priority agents; Then, higher priority agents must re-evaluate their variables.

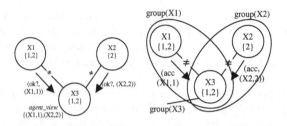

Fig. 1. Organization oriented programming in CSP

Fig. 1(a) shows the well-known example with three agents identified by their variables X_1, X_2 and X_3 [4].

Our aim in this section is to present a different conceptualization of the computations that have to be performed in asynchronous backtracking by converting a set of agents into an organization with common goals. Towards this aim, we must identify possible group settings, define one or more role hierarchies and specify roles' responsibilities and policies. Due to the dependency of the lower priority nodes from the higher priority ones, we specify groups with a *"master"* role and one or more *"peer"* roles. The role hierarchy is shown in Fig. 2, including the composite role *group* that contains the atomic roles. Each agent X_n assumes the existence of a group "group(n)" and assigns itself to the master position "master(n)" of this group. Moreover, it assigns each lower priority neighbour X_m to a peer position "peer(n,m)". Finally, it assigns itself to a "peer(m,n)" position of each group "group(m)" for each neighbour X_m with a higher priority. These assignments are done dynamically, through responsibilities of the role "myself" that all agents play, based on the constraints specified. So, for instance, in the setting shown in Fig. 1(a), as it is shown in Fig. 1(b), the agent X_1 defines a group with participants $\{X_1,X_2\}$. Each group is assigned the *hybrid* responsibility of selecting an appropriate value for the variable corresponding to the "master" agent. This value becomes known to all peers because of this responsibility. Fig. 2 shows two policies of the role "group". The first specifies that the value that a group accepts is the value that the master has selected for its variable. Since a master agent forms acceptances for the values selected by other groups in which is a peer, it selects values that are consistent with the values of its neighbor masters. According to the second policy in Fig. 2, each peer in a group must check for nogood lists, contributing towards the acceptance of nogood lists in the group in which it plays the role of peer. If a group cannot select a value, the master adds new constraints in the network. Since neighbour nodes are determined by the constraints, the addition of new constraints causes a kind of dynamic reorganization.

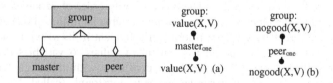

Fig. 2. The role hierarchy and policies

Therefore, these two recipes provide agents the means for (a) accepting values assigned to the variables, (b) notifying for inconsistencies, (c) re-structuring the organization by adding new constraints.

4 Concluding Remarks

This paper shows how MAS programming can be reduced to the specification of specific, explicitly specified group policies and responsibilities of socially delibe-rating agents. Most of the frameworks that are related to our proposal do not incor-porate the deontic, functional and structural dimensions, or they do not consider the collective recognition of states and the formation of group acceptances. Our first experiments to incorporate organizational aspects for implementing MAS that solve inherently distributed problems in dynamic settings are very encouraging. Further study and experimentation is needed for extending this "art" into a systematic way of programming MAS.

References

[1] V. Furtado, A. Melo, V. Dignum, F. Dignum, and L. Sonenberg. Exploring congruence between organizational structure and task performace: a simulation approach. In *Proc. of the AAMAS workshop: From Organizations to Organization Oriented Programming* (OOOP), 2005.

[2] I. Partsakoulakis and G. Vouros. Individual Beliefs and Group Acceptances within Agent Organizations. In *Proc. of AAMAS05*, 2005.

[3] I. Partsakoulakis and G. Vouros. Agent-Enhanced Collaborative Activity in Organized Settings. To appear in the *International Journal of Cooperative Information Systems*.

[4] M. Yokoo and K. Hirayama. Algorithms for Distributed Constraint Satisfaction: A Review. *Autonomous Agents and Multi-Agent Systems*, 3, pp. 185 – 207, 2000.

Multimodal Continuous Recognition System for Greek Sign Language Using Various Grammars

Paschaloudi N. Vassilia and Margaritis G. Konstantinos

Parallel and Distributed Processing Laboratory,
Department of Applied Informatics,
University of Macedonia,
156 Egnatia str., P.O. BOX 1591, 54006, Thessaloniki, Greece
{vpasx, kmarg}@uom.gr
http://macedonia.uom.gr/{~vpasx/, ~kmarg/}

Abstract. In this paper we present a multimodal Greek Sign Language (GSL) recognizer. The system can recognize either signs or finger-spelled words of GSL, forming sentences of GSL. A vocabulary of 54 finger-spelled words together with 17 signs, giving a total of 71 signs/words, is used. The system has been tested on various grammars and the recognition rates we achieved exceeded 89% in most cases.

1 Introduction

Sign Language (SL) is the usual method of communication between hearing-impaired people. SL words and sentences are combinations of hand movements and facial expressions. In the research works that have been developed, interest is concentrated mainly on hands forming *Signs*. Throughout this paper we use the term *Sign* to express a hand movement with a specific meaning. Each SL also provides its own hand-morph-alphabet. Words formed by the use of this alphabet are called *finger-spelled words* and usually describe uncommon concepts or proper names. We use the term *Word* to express a finger-spelled word. *Continuous recognition* is the case where the system is responsible to find the sing and word boundaries in a presented sequence of elements. Our system's main innovation is GSL handling; on the other hand its ability to recognize interchangeably both finger-spelled words and signs is also a novelty.

This paper is organized into 4 sections. In section 2, we present few research works. Our system together with the results obtained, are presented in section 3. Finally, in section 4 we give a few concluding remarks and refer to our future aims.

2 Related Work

SL recognition covers two areas of interest. The first one concerns the mean through which the computer senses the sign and could be either a *glove-based system* or a *visual-based one* [1]-[2]. The second area regards to the method used in building the

G. Antoniou et al. (Eds.): SETN 2006, LNAI 3955, pp. 584–587, 2006.

recognition system and could be based on Neural Networks [3], Adaptive Neuro-Fuzzy Inference Systems [4] or Hidden Markov Models [1]-[2], [6]-[7].

Hidden Markov Models (HMMs) are statistical models and have been used for recognition purposes by many researchers. Starner, *et al.* [1]-[2] presented a visual-based approach where a small feature vector was constructed from each image and an HMM-based system for the recognition of ASL sentences. An accuracy of 92%-99% per word on a 40-word lexicon was reached in various experiments. Vogler *et al.* [6] developed also an HMM-based system for recognition but used an electromagnetic tracking system for data obtaining. They achieved recognition rates between 83.6% and 89.9% over a 53 sign vocabulary. Hienz *et al.* [7] developed a video-based continuous SL recognition system for German Sign Language, using HMMs. In the feature extraction phase they calculated parameters regarding size, shape and position of the fingers and hands, while the signer was wearing cotton gloves with colour markers. Recognition rate exceeded 95%, working on a 52 sign vocabulary.

3 Our System

In our approach we use image-processing techniques in order to extract useful information from the signs performed. The idea is to extract feature vectors from images captured during sign forming. Each captured image corresponds to either a GSL alphabet letter or an unclassified hand morph (instance of a sign). The same feature vector is used for both kinds of elements and describes geometrical properties of the hand morph. The method is based on a work Al-Jarrah did [4] according to Jain [5]. The method involves finding the centre of mass and the orientation of the morph captured [5]. We calculate the lengths of vectors that originate from the center of mass and end up to the border. From the border points we use only those that lie in the fingertips area and their direction coincides to 0, ±5, ±10, ±15, ... ±90 degrees relatively to the morph direction. This led us to 37 border points or 37 elements for each feature vector.

In the system implementation part, that exploits the information obtained, we used HMMs. Each one of the elements under recognition, either word or sign, is represented by a single HMM, specifically trained for it.

Language modeling refers to syntax constraints that, are set, so as the number of candidate sentences to be reduced. We used various language models described below, to improve recognition, which support sentences formed according to the natural way of "speaking" with GSL.

Gr-1: [pronoun] noun {adjective} verb
Gr-2: pronoun noun {adjective} verb
Gr-3: pronoun noun adjective verb
Gr-4: pronoun noun verb
Gr-5: [pronoun] [noun] {adjective} verb [question word]

where square brackets [ ] denote optional selection of an item and braces { } denote zero or more repetitions of an item.

The grammar which permits maximum flexibility is Grammmar-5; in the opposite side lies Grammar-4, which accepts only small sentences with restricted form. The order of grammars in terms of increasing difficulty is: *Gr-4, Gr-3, Gr-2, Gr-1, Gr-5.*

3.1 Experiments and Results

The complete finger-spelled words' vocabulary consists of 6 pronouns, 22 nouns, 16 verbs, 6 adjectives and 4 question words. The complete sign vocabulary consists of 1 pronoun, 7 nouns, 7 verbs and 2 adjectives. Image-letters are formed by 4 users used to form the training and test examples of words and sentences.

An HMM is built for each one of the vocabulary words. Attentive experiments on HMMs' topology led us to tailoring 6 different topologies for "small" and "large" words.

HMMs are trained with a substantial number of examples and tested over examples that have never been used during the training phase.

In the tables below H represents the correct labels, D the deletions, S the substitutions, I the insertions and N the total number of labels that are used for testing; a *label* is the predefined word to which the output of the system is compared. The percentage number of labels correctly recognized is given by:

$$\% \, Correct \ = \frac{H}{N} x100 \tag{1}$$

The accuracy measure is calculated by subtracting the number of insertion errors from the number of correct labels and dividing by the total number of signs.

Various experiments have been performed using various grammar models and vocabulary sets. In Table 1 we present Continuous Recognition Results over the vocabulary of 54 finger-spelled words and 2 signs using various grammar models.

Table 1. Continuous Recognition Results over the vocabulary of 54 finger-spelled words and 2 signs using various grammar models

Type of Grammar		% Correct	%Accuracy	Numerical Results				
				H	D	S	I	N
Gr-1	SENT	90.44		265		28		293
	WORD	95.75	95.75	924	14	27	0	965
Gr-2	SENT	92.68		266		21		287
	WORD	97.36	97.36	922	0	21	0	947
Gr-3	SENT	94.17		97		6		103
	WORD	98.54	98.54	406	0	6	0	412
Gr-4	SENT	98.40		185		3		188
	WORD	99.47	99.47	561	0	3	0	564
Gr-5	SENT	89.10		286		35		321
	WORD	95.61	95.61	1003	10	36	0	1049

The higher recognition rates appear when we use Grammar-4, which supports the smallest sentences, fact that is quite expectable. Continuous recognition results over the whole vocabulary of 54 finger-spelled words and 17 signs using Grammar 5, appear in Table 2. Since Grammar 5 is the most flexible grammar, the results represent system's worst case.

Table 2. Continuous Recognition Results over the complete vocabulary of 54 finger-spelled words and 17 signs using Grammar-5

Type of Grammar		% Correct	%Accuracy	Numerical Results				
				H	D	S	I	N
Gr-5	SENT	89.31		309		37		346
	WORD	95.84	95.84	1061	12	34	0	1107

4 Conclusion and Discussion

In this paper we present a system that recognizes GSL sentences made of either signs or finger-spelled words. The recognizer is built over HMMs, each one representing a GSL word or sign. The data needed for HMM training is obtained through capturing video-frames in a time-sequential basis and applying image processing techniques to isolated hand morphs. A feature vector is extracted from each image. The system exploits the information obtained in sequences in order to train HMMs.

The vocabulary we used is easily extensible. Adding new words or signs requires a new collection of examples to train the new HMMs.

Such a system could be used for learning Greek Sign Language. Persons attempting to learn GSL could form signs and receive feedback from the system. Our future aim is to apply the recognition process in real-time. The process is quite the same and we expect equally high recognition rates.

References

1. Starner, T., Weaver, J. and Pentland, A.: Real-Time American Sign Language Recognition Using Desk and Wearable Computer Based Video, Pattern Analysis and Machine Intelligence, 1998.
2. Starner, T. and Pentland, A.: Real-time American Sign Language recognition from video using hidden Markov models. Perceptual Computing Section, Technical Report No. 375 MIT Media Lab Cambridge MA 1996.
3. Fels, S. and Hinton, G.: Glove-Talk: A Neural Network Interface Between a Data-Glove and a Speech Synthesizer, IEEE transactions on Neural Networks, Vol. 4, No. 1, 1993.
4. Al-Jarrah, O. and Halawani, A.: Recognition of gestures in Arabic Sign Language using neuro-fuzzy systems, Artificial Intelligence 133, pp.117-138, 2001.
5. Jain, A.K. Fundamendals of Digital Image Processing, Englewood Cliffs :Prentice Hall, NJ, 1989.
6. Vogler, C. and Metaxas, D.: ASL Recognition based on a Coupling Between HMMs and 3D Motion Analysis, Proceedings of the International Conference on Computer Vision, pp. 363-369, Mumbai, India,1998.
7. Hienz, H., Bauer, B. and Kraiss, K.-F.: HMM-Based Continuous Sign Language Recognition Using Stochastic Grammars, GesturE Workshop, Gif sur Yvette, France, 1999.

An Alternative Suggestion for Vision-Language Integration in Intelligent Agents

Katerina Pastra

Institute for Language and Speech Processing,
Artemidos 6 and Epidavrou, Maroussi, 151-25, Greece
kpastra@ilsp.gr

Abstract. State of the art artificial agents rely heavily on human intervention for performing vision-language integration; apart from being cost and effort effective, this intervention deprives artificial agents from the ability to react intelligently and to show intentionality when engaged in situated multimodal communication. In this paper, we suggest an alternative way of building vision-language integration prototypes with limited human intervention. The suggestions have emerged from the development of such a prototype for the verbalisation of visual scenes in a property-surveillance task.

1 Introduction

In Artificial Intelligence, vision-language association has been defined as an *integration* task that artificial agents perform for a number of applications, such as situated multimodal dialogue [1]. Vision-language integration has been theoretically explained as a *double-grounding* case [2], in which vision grounds language to its intended referents in the physical world (cf. the symbol grounding debate [3,4]), while at the same time language grounds vision to intentional aspects of the mental world (i.e., it renders e.g. object salience and token-type distinctions explicit). Double-grounding suggests that, ideally, a completely autonomous artificial agent with vision-language integration abilities can demonstrate human-like intentionality in certain multimodal situations. In a less ideal situation, the more "independent" from human intervention for performing integration an artificial agent is, the more intentional will appear to be. This autonomy requires that an agent is able to interpret its representations with computational mechanisms that go beyond mere instantiation of known association facts to *inferring* associations, so that the agent is able to generalise within and across domains and to recover from unexpected situations [5].

However, state of the art integration prototypes seem to be far from performing vision-language integration on their own. Through an extensive review of such systems, it has been shown that state of the art prototypes have major *scalability* problems; some of them deal with blocksworlds or miniworlds and therefore fail to generalise not only across but also within application domains [1], while others rely on *manually abstracted visual data*. Furthermore, their

G. Antoniou et al. (Eds.): SETN 2006, LNAI 3955, pp. 588–591, 2006.

association abilities are *restricted to instantiations* of *a priori* known image-language associations, failing therefore to deal with unexpected data even if common-sensical [1].

Is it feasible to shift all three drawbacks of state of the art integration prototypes, *i.e.*, build a prototype that will work with real world visual data (rather than blobs), that will analyse its visual input automatically and will have inference-making mechanisms that will allow for more scalable vision-language associations? How far can we currently go in achieving computational vision-language integration, minimising human intervention within core integration stages? VLEMA, a vision-language integration prototype developed for a property serveillance task has attempted to address these questions [5]. In what follows, we present suggestions on the direction research could take towards the goal of restricting human intervention in vision-language integration mechanisms as they emerged from the development of this prototype.

2   Suggestion One: Virtualised Reality Images as Visual Input

Object segmentation in 2D images of real world scenes is still quite restricted, with algorithms performing well only when the object(s) to be identified are very specific (e.g face recognition). Therefore, if one is to perform automatic analysis of real-world visual scenes with —more or less complex— configurations of a variety of objects, one is led to a dead-end; this is the most important reason why researchers usually resort to manual abstraction of visual data or to the use of blocksworlds when developing intelligent prototypes that require vision-language integration abilities.

There is, however, a recently emerged research field in which computer vision and computer graphics advances meet: that of *virtualised reality* [6]. Instead of relying on simplistic CAD models for building virtual worlds manually, image reconstruction algorithms construct virtual models of a real scene from multiple static or dynamic images of the scene. Simply put, the process involves the recording of a visual scene/event through (multiple) wide-range cameras, the recovery of the 3D geometry and/or photometric information of the scene from the images and the translation of this scene description into computer graphics models. The latter preserve the scene geometry through depth maps and they may also preserve the scene texture through mapping of the original 2D images of the scene onto the resulting 3D model. Novel views of the virtualised scenes are then easily synthesised on the fly in existing virtual reality hardware.

It is this type of visual data that VLEMA uses as input and suggests that should be used in similar prototypes, because it allows the system to work with real world, complex visual scenes in a format (*i.e.*, 3D) that is more promising for automatic image analysis due to the wealth of visual information it provides (e.g. there is no partial information on a specific object due to occlusion). While these images seem photo-realistic when rendered on screen by VRML browsers, the source code consists actually of very low-level visual information: indices of the coordinates of thousands of triangular faces that shape the scene in 3D. The faces are listed in no particular order,and their coordinates are expressed in relation to a common coordinate system (that of the whole scene) While not trivial, object segmentation in such data is feasible: in VLEMA, a face clustering algorithm decides which faces are boundary-forming ones in each dimension and produces three different clusterings of the faces into candidate-objects, according to the dimension that was taken to be the principle one each time. It then compares the different clustering results assuming that the first and last cluster in each clustering/dimension stand always for the *extrema* objects of the scene (i.e. the walls of an indoor scene). It also assumes that a cluster which is identified as such in more than one clusterings/dimensions stands for a single, non decomposable object. The remaining face clusters in each dimension may be clusters standing for the parts of an individual object (analysed differently in each clustering/dimension) or parts of more than one object; this distinction is left to an object naming module [5].

3   Suggestion Two: Naming Through a Feature-Augmented Ontology

VLEMA's suggestion for naming is the development and use of a domain ontology and knowledge-base with feature-based profiles of the entities of the domain. In particular, this resource should record information for each object regarding its:

- *structure*: the number of parts into which the object is expected to be decomposed in different dimensions
- *functionality*: visual characteristics an object may have which are related to its function e.g. whether an object has a surface on which things can be placed/fixed, and
- *interrelations*: these refer mainly to (allowable) spatial configurations of objects (e.g. whether an object could be *on* the floor or not), the dimension according to which size comparisons would be meaningful etc.

There are many arguments in favour of such feature selection for object naming in the literature [7, 8]. Still, one could argue, that relying on such features for drawing object name inferences would be risky when analysing e.g. a scene of a room with many different multi-part objects. Machine learning methods for associating words in an utterance with objects in view represent visual data through feature-value vectors, with features being usually shape, colour or/and texture [9, 10]; these approaches work for naming only very simple physical objects (e.g. a ball) or blobs, the image of which has been carefully stripped from any visual background during learning. However, approximate shape, colour or texture information alone cannot lead to any inferences in complex real world scenes. On the contrary, the suggested types of features allow a prototype's inference mechanisms: a) to go beyond differences in the appearance of similar objects (e.g.

different styles of sofas) and name these objects in the same way and b) to generalise over viewpoint differences; for example, VLEMA can identify a sofa as such even when seen from the side (rather than *en face*).

These are generalisations that machine learning-based object naming algorithms cannot do easily (or at all). In particular, identifying objects which differ in appearance as ones of the same type is something that cannot be achieved even with a very large amount of training data, if similar examples are not present in the training data. Similarly, learning approaches cannot deal with viewpoint differences in the appearance of an object; there is an almost infinite number of different images of the same object which may result from differences in the viewpoint from which the object is seen in a complex scene.

4   Conclusion

In this paper, we suggested that the development of vision-language integration agents could benefit from the combined use of *virtualised reality images* and a specific kind of a *feature-augmented ontology*. The automatic analysis of the former not only satisfies the requirement of working with real world scenes (rather than blocksworlds or one-object images), but it also allows for a wealth of information to be extracted. Combined with a feature-augmented ontology, this information can be used from an object naming module to perform structural, functional and relational (spatial or other) checks for determining the final number and identity of objects depicted in a scene.

References

1. Pastra, K., Wilks, Y.: Vision-language integration in AI: a reality check. In: Proceedings of the 16th European Conference in Artificial Intelligence. (2004) 937–941
2. Pastra, K.: Viewing vision-language integration as a double-grounding case. In: Proceedings of the AAAI Fall Symposium on "Achieving Human-Level Intelligence through Integrated Systems and Research". (2004) 62–69
3. Searle, J.: Minds, brains, and programs. Behavioral and Brain Sciences **3** (1980) 417–457
4. Harnad, S.: The symbol grounding problem. Physica D **42** (1990) 335–346
5. Pastra, K.: Vision-Language Integration: a Double-Grounding Case. PhD thesis, University of Sheffield (2005)
6. Kanade, T., Rander, P., Narayanan, R.: Virtualised reality: constructing virtual worlds from real scenes. IEEE Multimedia **4** (1997) 34–46
7. Minsky, M.: The Society of Mind. Simon and Schuster Inc. (1986)
8. Landau, B., Jackendoff, R.: "What" and "Where" in spatial language and cognition. Behavioural and Brain Sciences **16** (1993) 217–265
9. Kaplan, F.: Talking AIBO: First experimentation of verbal interactions with an autonomous four-legged robot. In: Proceedings of the TWENTE Workshop on Language Technology. (2000) 57–63
10. Roy, D.: Learning visually grounded words and syntax for a scene description task. Computer speech and language **16** (2002) 353–385

Specification of Reconfigurable MAS: A Hybrid Formal Approach

Ioanna Stamatopoulou[1], Petros Kefalas[2], and Marian Gheorghe[3]

[1] South-East European Research Centre, Thessaloniki, Greece
istamatopoulou@seerc.info
[2] Department of Computer Science, City College, Thessaloniki, Greece
kefalas@city.academic.gr
[3] Department of Computer Science, University of Sheffield, UK
M.Gheorghe@dcs.shef.ac.uk

Abstract. In this short paper we suggest that Population P Systems and Communication X-machines may be combined into one hybrid formal method which facilitates the correct specification of reconfigurable multi-agent systems.

1 Introduction: Formal Methods for MAS

Recently there has been an increasing interest towards biological and biologically-inspired systems such as insect colonies (ants, bees), flocks of birds, tumours growth etc. The motivation behind their development varies: (a) need of biologists to simulate and observe their behaviour, (b) understanding of how nature deals with various problematic situations has inspired problem solving techniques (Swarm Intelligence, Ant Colony Optimisation, robotics and DNA computing), (c) development of unconventional computational models [1].

These systems can be mapped to multi-agent systems (MAS). Each biological entity is an agent and the overall system's behaviour is the result of the agents' actions, the interactions among them and between them and the environment.

There is a number of agent engineering paradigms used in industry and academia but the more complex a MAS is, the less easy it is to ensure correctness at the modelling level. Correctness implies that all desired properties are verified for the model and that a testing technique is applied to prove that the implementation has been built in accordance to the verified model.

Another key aspect that has to be dealt with at the modelling level is the dynamic nature of the configuration of such MAS. Communication between two agents may need to be established or ceased at any point and also new agents may appear in the system while existing ones may be removed.

In order to formally model each agent as well as the dynamic behaviour of MAS, a formal method should be capable of rigorously describing knowledge, behaviour, communication and dynamics. A plethora of formal methods is available; some focus on the data structures of a system and the operations employed to modify their values, others on describing the control over a system's states and others on the concurrency and communication of processes. New computation

G. Antoniou et al. (Eds.): SETN 2006, LNAI 3955, pp. 592–595, 2006.
© Springer-Verlag Berlin Heidelberg 2006

approaches inspired by biological processes introduce concurrency and neatly tackle the dynamic structure of multi-component systems, e.g. P Systems [2].

In agent-oriented software engineering, there have been several attempts to use formal methods. An interesting comparison of formal methods for the verification of emergent behaviours in swarm-based systems is reported in [3].

Population P Systems provide a straightforward way for dealing with the change of a MAS structure, however, the rules specifying the evolution of the individual agents are not sufficient. On the contrary, *X-machines* are considered suitable as a specification language of a system's components [4], particularly well-suited for the modelling of reactive systems [5].

2 Population P Systems and Communicating X-Machines

A *Population P System* (PPS) [6] is a collection of different types of cells evolving according to specific rules and able of exchanging biological/chemical substances with their neighbouring cells.

Definition 1. A *Population P System with Active Cells* [6] is a construct $\mathcal{P} = (V, K, \gamma, \alpha, w_E, C_1^p, C_2^p, \ldots, C_n^p, R)$ where:

- V is a finite alphabet of symbols called objects;
- K is a finite alphabet of symbols, which define different types of cells;
- $\gamma = (\{1, 2, \ldots n\}, A)$, with $A \subseteq \{\{i, j\} \mid 1 \leq i \neq j \leq n\}$, is a finite graph;
- α is a finite set of bond-making rules of the form $(t, x_1; x_2, p)$, with $x_1, x_2 \in V$, and $t, p \in K$;
- $w_E \in V$ is a finite multi-set of objects initially assigned to the environment;
- $C_i^p = (w_i, t_i)$, for each $1 \leq i \leq n$, with $w_i \in V$ a finite multi-set of objects, and $t_i \in K$ the type of cell i;
- R is a finite set of rules dealing with object communication, object transformation, cell differentiation, cell division and cell death.

Communication rules allow an object inside a cell to be consumed and another object to be obtained by a neighbouring cell or by the environment or an object to be expelled to the environment. *Transformation rules* allow the replacement of an object. *Cell differentiation rules* allow the type of the cell to change. *Cell division rules* allow a cell to be divided into two cells of the same type. *Cell death rules* cause the removal of the cell from the system. *Bond-making rules* define the conditions under which a bond is created between two cells.

The transformation and communication rules take up the task of updating and communicating knowledge while other cell rules dictate when new agents appear in the system or existing ones are removed. The bond-making rules are responsible for establishing communication channels between two agents. However, a PPS is not as intuitive in specifying each of the participating agents in terms of their knowledge, actions and control over their internal states. An X-machine (XM) model consists of a number of states and also has a memory, which accommodates mathematically defined data structures. The transitions between states are labelled by functions.

Definition 2. The 8-tuple $XM = (\Sigma, \Gamma, Q, M, \Phi, F, q_0, m_0)$ defines a *stream X-machine* [7] where:

- Σ and Γ are the input and output alphabets respectively;
- Q is the finite set of states;
- M is the (possibly) infinite set called memory;
- Φ is a set of partial functions φ that map an input and a memory state to an output and a possibly different memory state, $\varphi : \Sigma \times M \to \Gamma \times M$;
- F is the next state partial function, $F : Q \times \Phi \to Q$, which given a state and a function from the type Φ determines the next state;
- q_0 and m_0 are the initial state and initial memory respectively.

XM models that are able to communicate are called Communicating XM components (CXM). The system structure is defined as the graph whose nodes are the CXM components and edges the communication channels among them.

In order to be able to dynamically redefine the structure of a CXM system model, we are in need of operators that will have an effect on the graph representation of the system structure by reconfiguring the communication channels.

The *Attachment operator* **ATT** is responsible for establishing communication between two CXM components. The *Detachment operator* **DET** removes communication channels between two CXM components. The *Generation operator* **GEN** creates a new CXM component. The *Destruction operator* **DES** is used for the removal of a CXM component from the communicating system. A detailed definition of these operators can be found in [1].

The rules that drive the evolution of the system structure are generally of the form *condition* → *action* whereby, if the condition allows, an appropriate action which includes one or more reconfiguration operations is being performed.

3   A Hybrid Approach

The idea behind combining PPS and CXM is that the first can be responsible for the reconfiguration of the system's structure while the other for the specification

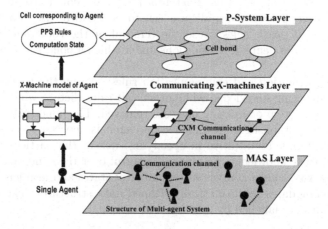

Fig. 1. The parallel computation of a CXM system and a PPS modeling a MAS

of the individual components. Both systems have the same physical structure, i.e. graph representation, at any time of the computation and the cells of the PPS correspond in a one-to-one manner to the CXM components. In order to achieve this the objects of each cell of the PPS need to capture information regarding the computation state of the corresponding CXM. Fig. 1 depicts the notion of a PPS working in parallel and in complete correspondence with a CXM system. An example illustrating the applicability of the approach can be found in [5].

4   Conclusions

This work has been motivated by the need for a formal framework for capturing the dynamics of the structure of biology or biology-inspired MAS during their modelling phase. XMs provide a solid mathematical framework and can therefore also support the formal verification of desired properties that should hold for each agent through the use of a model checking technique [8] as well as offer a testing strategy [7]. The result of our work suggests a hybrid approach whereby a PPS and CXM system compute in parallel, the first taking care of the dynamic aspects of a MAS and the second providing the means for the specification of the individual agents and the communication among them. Efforts will be directed towards implementing those features on top of existing XM and PPS animators. Finally, we are experimenting with the automatic transformation of XM models written using a particular notation into executable code for simulation and visualisation.

References

[1] Gheorghe, M., ed.: Molecular Computational Models: Unconventional Approaches. Idea Publishing Inc. (2005)
[2] Păun, G.: Computing with membranes. Journal of Computer and System Sciences **61** (2000) 108–143 Also circulated as a TUCS report since 1998.
[3] Rouf, C., Vanderbilt, A., Truszkowski, W., Rash, J., Hinchey, M.: Verification of NASA emergent systems. In: Proceedings of the 9th IEEE International Conference on Engineering Complex Computer Systems (ICECCS'04). (2004) 231–238
[4] Holcombe, M.: X-machines as a basis for dynamic system configuration. Software Engineering Journal **3** (1988) 69–76
[5] Kefalas, P., Stamatopoulou, I., Gheorghe, M.: A formal modelling framework for developing multi-agent systems with dynamic structure and behaviour. Number 3690 in Lecture Notes in Artificial Intelligence. Springer Verlag (2005) 122–131
[6] Bernandini, F., Gheorghe, M.: Population P Systems. Journal of Universal Computer Science **10** (2004) 509–539
[7] Holcombe, M., Ipate, F.: Correct Systems: Building a Business Process Solution. Springer-Verlag, London (1998)
[8] Eleftherakis, G.: Formal Verification of X-machine Models: Towards Formal Development of Computer-based Systems. PhD thesis, Dept. of Computer Science, Univ. of Sheffield (2003)

An Intelligent Statistical Arbitrage Trading System

Nikos S. Thomaidis[1,*], Nick Kondakis[1,2], and George D. Dounias[1]

[1] Decision and Management Engineering Laboratory,
Dept. of Financial Engineering & Management,
University of the Aegean, 31 Fostini Str., GR-821 00, Chios, Greece
Tel.: +30-2271-0-35454 (35483); Fax: +30-2271-0-35499
{nthomaid, kondakis, g.dounias}@fme.aegean.gr
http://decision.fme.aegean.gr
[2] Kepler Asset Management, 100 Wall Street, New York, NY 10005
nick@kondakis.com

Abstract. This paper proposes an intelligent combination of neural network theory and financial statistical models for the detection of arbitrage opportunities in a group of stocks. The proposed intelligent methodology is based on a class of neural network-GARCH autoregressive models for the effective handling of the dynamics related to the statistical mispricing between relative stock prices. The performance of the proposed intelligent trading system is properly measured with the aid of profit & loss diagrams.

1 Introduction

Statistical arbitrage is an attempt to profit from price discrepancies that appear in a group of assets. The detection of mispricings is based upon finding a linear combination of assets, or else a *"synthetic"* asset, whose time series is *mean-reverting* with finite variance. Given a set of assets $X_1,...,X_n$, a synthetic is a linear combination $\omega = (w_1, w_2, ..., w_n)$ such that

$$w_1 X_1 + w_2 X_2 + \cdots + w_n X_n \sim \text{mean reverting}\,(0, \sigma_t^2), \quad \sigma_t^2 < \infty$$

where in the above definition we allow for time-dependent volatility σ_t^2. The requirement of mean-reversion is to ensure that mispricings eventually "die out" and do not grow indefinitely. If they did, it would be impossible to control the risk exposure of the trading portfolio.

Several authors have suggested approaches that attempt to take advantage of price discrepancies by taking proper transformations of financial time-series; see e.g. [1, 2, 3] for stocks of FTSE 100 Stock Index, [4, 5] for equity index futures and [6] for exchange rates. Amongst them, [4, 1, 6] employ a neural network model to describe the dynamics of statistical mispricings. In this paper, we propose a new intelligent framework for the identification of statistical arbitrage

---

* This research is funded by the Public Benefit Foundation "Alexander S. Onassis" and by a grant from "Empeirikion" Foundation.

G. Antoniou et al. (Eds.): SETN 2006, LNAI 3955, pp. 596–599, 2006.

opportunities. Our approach deviates from the main trend in that it attempts to detect nonlinearities *both* in the mean and the volatility dynamics of the statistical mispricings. For this purpose, we use a recently proposed class of combined *neural network*-GARCH volatility models [7]. The methodology is applied to the detection of statistical arbitrage opportunities in a pair of two Indian stocks.

The remainder of the paper is organised as follows: Section 2 discusses the basic methodology used in detecting price discrepancies between stocks. Section 3 presents an empirical application and section 4 concludes the paper and discusses directions for further research.

2   Methodology

The methodology for detecting statistical arbitrage opportunities is outlined below.

2.1   Constructing a Synthetic

Let X_1, X_2 denote two assets (stocks in our case). In constructing the synthetic asset, we use an adaptive estimation scheme in which the coefficients of the linear combination of X_1 & X_2 are periodically re-calculated. In particular, we define the mispricing as Z_t $X_{2,t} - \alpha_{t-1} - \beta_{t-1} X_{1,t}$, where β_t mean $(X_{2j}/X_{1j}, j = t - W + 1, ..., t)$ and

$$\alpha_t \quad \text{mean}(X_{2j}, j = t - W + 1, ..., t) - \beta_t \, \text{mean}(X_{2j}, j = t - W + 1, ..., t)$$

Note that β is the mean price ratio between the two stocks in the window of W observations and α is chosen so as to minimize the total variation of Z_t within the window. This procedure has been experimentally found to give more reasonable estimates of the synthetic vector that also show more stability over time. The smaller is the value of W, the stronger is the mean-reversion of the synthetic and hence the more abrupt are the corrections of mispricings. In subsequent experiments, we report results obtained for a synthetic calculated on a window of 10 observations.

2.2   Modelling the Dynamics of the Statistical Mispricings

We describe the dynamics of statistical mispricings by means of autoregressive models that relate the current value of Z_t to its own lags. This gives us an idea of how mispricings of different size and sign (positive/negative) are corrected over time. We also take one step further in modelling *both* the mean and the volatility structure of statistical mispricings. In high sampling frequencies (i.e. intra-day data), the volatility of Z_t typically changes with time. In particular, large (positive or negative) shocks to Z_t are on average followed up by large shocks of either sign. We attempt to model both nonlinearities in the correction of mispricings as well as volatility spill-overs by means of a recently proposed class of joint neural network-GARCH models. Details on the specification of the model are given in [7].

2.3 Implementing a Trading System to Exploit the Predictable Component of the Mispricing Dynamics

The NN-GARCH model described above is used to obtain 1- and h-step-ahead confidence bounds on the future value of Z_t. Based upon these, we apply the trading strategy of buying the synthetic if $Z_t < \hat{Z}_{t+h}^{L,\alpha}$ and selling the synthetic if $Z_t > \hat{Z}_{t+h}^{H,\alpha}$, where $\hat{Z}_{t+h}^{L,\alpha}$, $\hat{Z}_{t+h}^{H,\alpha}$ denote the $(1-\alpha)\%$ low and high confidence bound on the value of the mispricing h steps ahead.

3   Empirical Application

For testing the arbitrage detecting methodology, we chose the stocks of Infosys Technologies Ltd and Wipro Ltd, both Application Software companies from the Indian stock market. We present the results from a "microscopic" arbitrage detector, in which the synthetic time series is calculated from 1-minute closing prices. The training set extends from August 2 to August 19, 2005 (4260 observations) and the test set from August 29 to September 12, 2005 (5060 observations). In this sampling frequency, we find both nonlinear corrections in mispricings and ARCH volatility effects. The specified NN-GARCH model includes lags 1-5 in the linear part, 1 hidden neuron with variables Z_{t-i}, $i = 3, 4, 5$ connected to it and a GARCH(1,1) equation. Table 1 shows the performance of a trading system, based on 5-minute-ahead forecasts, as a function of the confidence level (see 1st value of the pairs). For comparison purposes, we also report results from a linear model with the same set of input variables (2nd value of the pairs). Observe that the linear model places a much greater number of trades than the NN-GARCH, occasionally resulting in higher total profit at the end of the test period. However, trades tend to be less profitable on the average, especially for small confidence intervals, which renders the linear system inefficient from an economic point of view.

Table 1. The trading performance of arbitrage models as a function of the confidence level. The values in pairs correspond to the NN-GARCH and the linear model respectively. Second row shows the accumulated profit, third row shows the average profit per trade and fourth row shows the total number of trades in the specified period.

Confidence level $(1-\alpha)\%$	99	95	90	80	50	20
accumulated wealth	0,11.24	5.60, 26.09	8.37, 54.60	25.40, 67.64	60.32, 24.28	128.92, 17.91
average profit per trade	–, 0.66	0.80, 0.19	0.42, 0.14	0.33, 0.06	0.13, 0.01	0.10, 0.01
number of trades	17, 0	7, 137	20, 390	78, 1022	479, 1825	1294, 1981

4   Discussion-Further Research

This paper introduces a new computational intelligent framework for detecting and exploiting statistical arbitrage opportunities in a group of assets. Contrary to other intelligent approaches, we base the arbitrage trading strategies on *confidence bounds* on the future value of the mispricing rather than simple point forecasts. These confidence bounds are flexible in the sense that take into account short-term changes in the volatility of mispricing movements (ARCH effects). The results presented above show that our model is a good detector of arbitrage opportunities. At present, we are conducting further research on the optimal tuning of the parameters of our trading system (sampling frequency, forecasting horizon) as well as the possibility of combining forecasts from various sampling-frequency models so as to track both the long- and short-term behaviour of the mispricing time series. First results from the latter approach are rather encouraging.

References

1. Burgess, N.: Cointegration. In Shadbolt, J., Taylor, J.G., eds.: Neural Networks and the Financial Markets: predicting, combining and portfolio optimisation. Springer (2002) 181–191
2. Burgess, N.: Statistical arbitrage models of the FTSE 100. In Abu-Mostafa, Y., LeBaron, B., Lo, A.W., Weigend, A.S., eds.: Computational Finance 1999. The MIT Press (2000) 297–312
3. Towers, N.: Joint optimisation in statistical arbitrage trading. In Shadbolt, J., Taylor, J.G., eds.: Neural Networks and the Financial Markets: predicting, combining and portfolio optimisation. Springer (2002) 193–201
4. Burgess, N., Refenes, A.: Modelling nonlinear cointegration in international equity index futures. In Refenes, A., Abu-Mostafa, Y., Moody, J., Weigend, A., eds.: Neural Networks in Financial Engineering. World Scientific (1996) 50–63
5. Garrett, I., Taylor, N.: Intraday and interday basis dynamics: Evidence from the FTSE 100 index futures market. Studies in Nonlinear Dynamics nd Econometrics **5** (2001) 133–152(20)
6. Steurer, E., Hann, T.: Exchange rate forecasting comparison: neural networks, machine learning and linear models. In Refenes, A., Abu-Mostafa, Y., Moody, J., Weigend, A., eds.: Neural Networks in Financial Engineering. World Scientific (1996) 113–121
7. Thomaidis, N., Dounias, G., Kondakis, N.: Financial statistical modelling with a new nature-inspired technique. In: in Proc. of the 1st European Symposium on Nature-Inspired Smart-Information Systems (NISIS), Albufeira, Portugal. (2005)

Revising Faceted Taxonomies and CTCA Expressions

Yannis Tzitzikas[1,2]

[1] Computer Science Department,
University of Crete, Greece
[2] Institute of Computer Science,
FORTH-ICS, Greece
tzitzik@csi.forth.gr

Abstract. A faceted taxonomy is a set of taxonomies each describing the application domain from a different (preferably orthogonal) point of view. CTCA is an algebra that allows specifying the set of meaningful compound terms (meaningful conjunctions of terms) over a faceted taxonomy in a flexible and efficient manner. However, taxonomy updates may turn a CTCA expression e ill-formed and may turn the compound terms specified by e to no longer reflect the domain knowledge originally expressed in e. This paper shows how we can revise e after a taxonomy update and reach an expression e' that is both well-formed and whose semantics (compound terms defined) is as close as possible to the semantics of the original expression e before the update.

1 Introduction

Let F be a faceted taxonomy, i.e. a set of taxonomies $(\mathcal{T}_1, \leq_1), \ldots, (\mathcal{T}_k, \leq_k)$, and let $\mathcal{T} = \mathcal{T}_1 \cup \ldots \cup \mathcal{T}_k$. Each expression e of CTCA (Compound Term Composition Algebra) [3] specifies a set S_e^F of valid (i.e. meaningful) compound terms (conjunctions of terms) over $\mathcal{T}$. So an expression e actually defines the partition $(S_e^F, \mathcal{P}(\mathcal{T}) - S_e^F)$ where $\mathcal{P}(\mathcal{T})$ denotes the powerset of $\mathcal{T}$. An update operation u_F on F (resulting to a faceted taxonomy F') may turn the expression e obsolete (i.e. not well-formed), or it may make the derived compound terminology $S_e^{F'}$ to no longer reflect the desire of the designer, i.e. it may no longer reflect the domain knowledge that was expressed in e. For example, the deletion of a term t may make several compound terms (that do not even contain t) to no longer belong to $S_e^{F'}$. It would be very useful if we could update automatically e to an expression e' that is (a) well-formed (w.r.t. F'), and (b) $S_{e'}^{F'}$ is as close to S_e^F as possible. This would enhance the robustness and usability of systems that are based on CTCA, like FASTAXON [2]. We call this problem *expression revision* after taxonomy update. In the ideal case, we would like to find an expression e' such as: (α) e' is well-formed, and ($\beta^=$) $S_{e'}^{F'} = S_e^F$. Although condition (α) can be satisfied quite easily, condition ($\beta^=$) may be impossible to satisfy in some cases. We can relax condition ($\beta^=$) and consider that our objective is to find an expression e'

G. Antoniou et al. (Eds.): SETN 2006, LNAI 3955, pp. 600–604, 2006.

such that $S_e^{F'}$ is as *close* to S_e^F as possible. We can define the distance between two compound terminologies S, S' as the cardinality of their symmetric difference, i.e.: $dist(S, S') = |(S - S') \cup (S' - S)| = |S - S'| + |S' - S|$. Now let $\mathcal{S}^{F'}$ be the set of *all* compound terminologies over F' that can be defined by expressions of CTCA. We can express condition (β) formally as follows: $S_{e'}^{F'} = \text{arg}_S \min\{dist(S, S_e^F) \mid S \in \mathcal{S}^{F'}\}$. However, in some application scenarios, we may prefer $S_{e'}^{F'}$ to be a subset of S_e^F than being a superset, or the reverse. Consequently, we may state state two, different than (β), conditions: (γ) $S_{e'}^{F'} \subseteq S_e^F$ and $S_{e'}^{F'}$ is the biggest possible in $\mathcal{S}^{F'}$, and (δ) $S_{e'}^{F'} \supseteq S_e^F$ and $S_{e'}^{F'}$ is the smallest possible in $\mathcal{S}^{F'}$. Of course, to find the sought expression e' we would not like to investigate all expressions in $\mathcal{S}^{F'}$ (as this would be computationally inadmissible), but we rather want to find a method for *modifying* e to an e' that satisfies (α) and (β or γ or δ).

A complete treatment of this problem (with applications, examples, formal propositions and proofs) can be found at [1]. This paper is a short summary.

2 CTCA and Taxonomy Updates

The upper part of Table 1 recalls in brief the basic notions and notations about taxonomies and faceted taxonomies. Syntactically, a CTCA expression e over F is defined according to the following grammar ($i = 1, ..., k$): $e ::= \oplus_P(e, ..., e) \mid \ominus_N (e, ..., e) \mid \overset{*}{\oplus}_P T_i \mid \overset{*}{\ominus}_N T_i \mid T_i$. The initial operands, thus the building blocks of the algebra, are the *basic compound terminologies*, which are the facet terminologies with the only difference that each term is viewed as a singleton. In most practical settings, taxonomies have the form of trees and for reasons of space we confine ourselves to this case.

Plus-products and *minus-products*, denoted by $\oplus_P$ and $\ominus_N$ respectively, have a parameter that is denoted by P (resp. N) which is a set of compound terms over $\mathcal{T}$. In a P parameter the designer puts valid compound terms, while in a N parameter the designer puts invalid compound terms. The exact definition of each operation of CTCA (also including two auxiliary operations, called *product* and *self-product*) is summarized in the lower part of Table 1. An expression e is *well formed* iff every facet T_i appears at most once, and every parameter set P or N of e is always subset of the corresponding set of *genuine compound terms*. Specifically, the genuine compound terms in the context of an operation $\oplus_P(e_1, ..., e_k)$ (or $\ominus_N(e_1, ..., e_k)$) is denoted by $G_{e_1, ..., e_k}$ and it is defined as: $G_{e_1, ..., e_k} = S_{e_1} \oplus ... \oplus S_{e_k} - \cup_{i=1}^n S_{e_i}$.

We consider two update operations on subsumption relationships: $\texttt{delete}(t \leq t')$ (subsumption relationship deletion), and $\texttt{add}(t \leq t')$. Before $\texttt{delete}(t \leq t')$ we assume that the relationship $t \leq t'$ belongs to the transitive reduction (Hasse Diagram) of $\leq$, while before an operation $\texttt{add}(t \leq t')$ we assume that the relationship $t \leq t'$ does not already exist in $\leq$. We also consider three update operations on terms: $\texttt{rename}(t, t')$, $\texttt{delete}(t)$, and $\texttt{add}(t)$. Whenever a term t is deleted, all subsumption relationships in which t participates are deleted too,

Table 1. Notations and CTCA Operations

Name	Notation	Definition
terminology	$\mathcal{T}$	a finite set of names called terms
subsumption	$\leq$	a preorder relation (reflexive and transitive)
taxonomy	$(\mathcal{T}, \leq)$	$\mathcal{T}$ is a terminology, $\leq$ a subsumption relation over $\mathcal{T}$
faceted taxonomy	$F = \{F_1, ..., F_k\}$	$F_i = (\mathcal{T}_i, \leq_i)$, for $i = 1, ..., k$ and all $\mathcal{T}_i$ are disjoint
compound term over $\mathcal{T}$	s	any subset of $\mathcal{T}$ (i.e. any element of $\mathcal{P}(\mathcal{T})$)
compound terminology	S	a subset of $\mathcal{P}(\mathcal{T})$ that includes $\emptyset$
compound ordering over S	$\preceq$	Given $s, s' \in S$, $s \preceq s'$ iff $\forall t' \in s'$ $\exists t \in s$ such that $t \leq t'$.
immediate broaders of t	$Br_{(1)}(t)$	the smaller terms that are greater than t (w.r.t $\leq$), i.e. $minimal_<(\{t' \in \mathcal{T}\mid t \leq t', t \neq t'\})$
immediate narrowers of t	$Nr_{(1)}(t)$	the bigger terms that are smaller than t (w.r.t $\leq$), i.e. $maximal_<(\{t' \in \mathcal{T}\mid t' \leq t, t \neq t'\})$
broaders of t	$Br(t)$	$\{t' \in \mathcal{T} \mid t \leq t'\}$
narrowers of t	$Nr(t)$	$\{t' \in \mathcal{T} \mid t' \leq t\}$
broaders of s	$Br(s)$	$\{s' \in P(\mathcal{T}) \mid s \preceq s'\}$
narrowers of s	$Nr(s)$	$\{s' \in P(\mathcal{T}) \mid s' \preceq s\}$
broaders of S	$Br(S)$	$\cup\{Br(s) \mid s \in S\}$
narrowers of S	$Nr(S)$	$\cup\{Nr(s) \mid s \in S\}$
CTCA Operations		
Operation	e	S_e
	$\mathcal{T}_i$	$\{\ \{t\} \mid t \in \mathcal{T}_i\} \cup \{\emptyset\}$
product	$e_1 \oplus ... \oplus e_n$	$\{\ s_1 \cup ... \cup s_n \mid s_i \in S_{e_i}\}$
plus-product	$\oplus_P(e_1, ...e_n)$	$S_{e_1} \cup ... \cup S_{e_n} \cup Br(P)$
minus-product	$\ominus_N(e_1, ...e_n)$	$S_{e_1} \oplus ... \oplus S_{e_n} - Nr(N)$
self-product	$\overset{*}{\oplus}(\mathcal{T}_i)$	$P(\mathcal{T}_i)$
plus-self-product	$\overset{*}{\oplus}_P(\mathcal{T}_i)$	$S_{\mathcal{T}_i} \cup Br(P)$
minus-self-product	$\overset{*}{\ominus}_N(\mathcal{T}_i)$	$\overset{*}{\oplus}(\mathcal{T}_i) - Nr(N)$

however the other relationships are preserved, i.e. after deleting term t, for all $t' \in Nr_{(1)}(t)$ it holds $Br_{(1)}(t') \supseteq Br_{(1)}(t)$.

3 CTCA Expression Revision

Given a compound term s and a term t, we shall use $s\#t$ to denote the compound term $s - \{t\}$. Now given s and two terms t and t', we shall use $s\#t\#t'$ to denote the compound term s if $t \not\subseteq s$, otherwise the compound term derived from s by replacing t by t'. We can generalize and define:

$$s\#s1\#s2 = \begin{cases} (s - s1) \cup s2, & \text{if } s \cap s1 \neq \emptyset \\ s & \text{otherwise} \end{cases}$$

We have studied expression revision for each kind of update operation and below we summarize the results. The deletion of terms or subsumption relationships can be handled by extending the P/N parameters (so as to recover the missing compound terms from the semantics of the original expression). Table 2 shows the revised expression e' after each taxonomy update. In cases (1),(2) and (4) Table 2 shows how each P and N parameter of e should be revised to a P' and N' parameter of e'. In case (3), for every minus-product operation $\ominus_N(e_1, ..., e_k)$ and for every e_i $(1 \leq i \leq k)$ such that $f(a) \not\in f(e_i)$

Table 2. Expression Revision after Taxonomy Updates

	u_F	alg	Notes
(1)	rename(a, a')	$P' = \{s\#a\#a' \mid s \in P\}$, $N' = \{s\#a\#a' \mid s \in N\}$	
		$S_{e'}^{F'} = \{s\#a\#a' \mid s \in S_e^F\}$	$\sim (\beta^=)$
(2)	delete(a)	$P' = \bigcup_{s \in P}\{s\#a\#t \mid t \in Br_{(1)}^F(a)\}$	
		$N' = \bigcup_{s \in N}\{s\#a\#t \mid t \in Nr_{(1)}^F(a)\}$	(β)
		$S_{e'}^{F'} = S_e^F - \{s \mid a \in s\}$, thus $S_{e'}^{F'} \subseteq S_e^F$	
(3)	add(a)	$N' = N \cup \{\ \{a, u_i\} \mid e_i \in operands(cur_e),$	
		$f(a) \notin f(e_i), u_j \in maximal_{\preceq}(S_{e_i})\}$	
		$S_{e'}^{F'} = S_e^F \cup \{\{a\}\}$	$\sim (\beta^=)$
(4)	delete$(b \leq a)$	$P' = P \cup \{\ s\#Nr^F(b)\#\{a\} \mid s \in P\}$	
		$N' = N \cup \{\ s\#Br^F(a)\#\{b\} \mid s \in N\}$	
		$S_{e'}^{F'} = S_e^F$	$(\beta^=)$

(meaning the a belongs to a facet that does not appear in expression e_i), we have to add to N the parameter $\{a, u_i\}$ for each $u_i \in maximal_{\preceq}(S_{e_i})$. The most important result is that the addition of subsumption relationships cannot be handled so straightforwardly. The reason is that since the semantics of the operations $\oplus_P / \ominus_N$ are defined on the basis of the transitive relation $\preceq$ after the addition of a subsumption relationship we may no longer be able to separate (from the semantics) compound terms that were previously separable (i.e. compound terms which were not $\preceq$-related before the addition of the subsumption link). In such cases, the resulting compound terminology may neither be subset nor superset of the original compound terminology. This happens because the effects of adding a subsumption relationship is different in $\oplus_P$ and $\ominus_N$: the compound terminologies defined by $\oplus_P$ operations become larger, while those defined by $\ominus_N$ operations become smaller. Now the combination of $\oplus_P$ and $\ominus_N$ operations can lead to compound terminologies which are neither larger nor smaller than the original one. The following proposition gives sufficient and necessary conditions for satisfying condition $(\beta^=)$ after subsumption relationship addition.

Proposition 1. Let F' be the result of applying add$(b \leq a)$ on F. We can find an expression e' such that $S_{e'}^{F'} = S_e^F$ if and only if:

(i) for each $p \in P$ of every parameter P of e it holds:
   If $p \cap Nr^F(b) \neq \emptyset$ then $\exists p' \in P$ such that $p' \preceq_F (p - Nr^F(b)) \cup \{a\}$
(ii) for each $n \in N$ of every parameter N of e it holds:
   If $n \cap Br^F(a) \neq \emptyset$ then $\exists n' \in N$ such that $n' \succeq_F (n - Br^F(a)) \cup \{b\}$.

As a final remark we have to note that there is not any directly related work on the problem at hand because CTCA emerged relatively recently and its distinctive characteristics (range-restricted closed world assumptions) differentiate it from other logic-based languages (for more see [3]) and the corresponding literature on updates and revisions.

References

1. Y. Tzitzikas. "Updates and Revision in Faceted Taxonomies and CTCA Expressions". Technical Report 2005-11-18, TR 364, Institute of Computer Science-FORTH, Nov 2005.
2. Y. Tzitzikas, R. Launonen, M. Hakkarainen, P. Kohonen, T. Leppanen, E. Simpanen, H. Tornroos, P. Uusitalo, and P. Vanska. "FASTAXON: A system for FAST (and Faceted) TAXONomy design.". In *Procs of 23th Int. Conf. on Conceptual Modeling, ER'2004*, Shanghai, China, Nov. 2004.
3. Yannis Tzitzikas, Anastasia Analyti, and Nicolas Spyratos. "Compound Term Composition Algebra: The Semantics". *LNCS Journal on Data Semantics*, 2:58–84, 2005.

Neighboring Feature Clustering

Zhifeng Wang[1], Wei Zheng[1], Yuhang Wang[2], James Ford[1],
Fillia Makedon[1], and Justin D. Pearlman[1,3]

[1] Dept. of Computer Science, Dartmouth College, Hanover NH 03755, USA
[2] Dept. of Computer Science and Engineering, Southern Methodist University,
Dallas TX75205, USA
[3] Advanced Imaging Center, Dartmouth Hitchcock Medical Center,
Lebanon NH 03756, USA

Abstract. In spectral datasets, such as those consisting of MR spectral
data derived from MS lesions, neighboring features tend to be highly
correlated, suggesting the data lie on some low-dimensional space. Naturally, finding such low-dimensional space is of interest. Based on this
real-life problem, this paper extracts an abstract problem, neighboring
feature clustering (NFC). Noticeably different from traditional clustering schemes where the order of features doesn't matter, NFC requires
that a cluster consist of neighboring features, that is features that are
adjacent in the original feature ordering. NFC is then reduced to a piece-
wise linear approximation problem. We use minimum description length
(MDL) method to solve this reduced problem. The algorithm we proposed works well on synthetic datasets. NFC is an abstract problem.
With minor changes, it can be applied to other fields where the problem
of finding piece-wise neighboring groupings in a set of unlabeled data
arises.

1 Introduction

Clustering, or determining the intrinsic grouping in a set of unlabeled data in
an unsupervised manner, is a well studied subject. It is typically carried out
by using some measure of distance between individual elements to determine
which ones should be grouped into a cluster. Considerable work has been done
in devising effective but increasingly specific clustering algorithms. In this paper,
we propose a novel clustering scheme, *neighboring feature clustering (NFC)*.

Given an $m \times n$ matrix M, where m denotes m samples and n denotes n
(ordered) dimensional features (We assume that a natural ordering of features
exists that has relevance to the problem being solved). Our goal is to find a
intrinsic partition of the features based on their characteristics (as to spectral
datasets, such characteristics could be correlations) such that each cluster is a
continuous piece of features. For example, if we decide feature 1 and 10 belong
to a cluster, feature 2 to 9 should also belong to that cluster.

NFC is a generic abstraction. One possible application could be the analysis
of MR spectroscopy. MR spectroscopy are characterized by high dimensionality
and scarcity of available samples [1], presenting a challenge to classifiers due the

G. Antoniou et al. (Eds.): SETN 2006, LNAI 3955, pp. 605–608, 2006.

curse of dimensionality. However, MR spectral features are highly redundant (neighboring spectral features of MR spectra are highly correlated), suggesting that the data lie in some low-dimensional space. Using NFC, we can partition the features into clusters. A cluster can be represented by a single feature hence reducing the dimensionality. This idea can be applied to DNA copy number analysis too.

Unlike previous approaches [1], we propose a novel approach: reducing NFC into a one dimensional piece-wise linear approximation problem. Namely, given a sequence of n one dimensional points $< x_1,...,x_n >$, find the optimal step-function-like line segments that can be fitted to the points (as in Fig. 1. Piece-wise linear approximation [3] [4] is usually of 2D. Here we use its concept for a 1D situation) We use minimum description length (MDL) method [2] to solve this reduced problem.

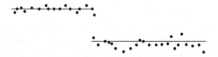

Fig. 1. 1D piece-wise linear approximation. With rather good accuracy, we can explain all the points by two line segments. The core issue with 1D piece-wise linear approximation is the balance of approximation accuracy and number of line segments. A compromise can be made using MDL.

2 Method

2.1 Reducing NFC to 1D Piece-Wise Linear Approximation Problem

1. Denote correlation coefficient matrix of M (defined in the previous section) as C. Let C^* be the strictly upper triangular matrix derived from $1-|C|$ (entries near 0 imply high correlation between the corresponding two features).
2. For features from i to j ($1 \leq i \leq j \leq n$), the submatrix $C^*_{i:j,i:j}$ depicts pairwise correlations. We use its entries (excluding lower and diagonal entries) as the points to be explained by a line in the 1D piece-wise linear approximation problem.
3. The objective is to find the optimal piece-wise line segments to fit those created points.

Points near 0 mean high correlation. We need to force high correlations among a set. Thus the points are always approximated by 0. For example, suppose we have a set with points all around 0.3. In piece-wise linear approximation, it is better to use 0.3 as the approximation. However in NFC, we should penalize the points stray away from 0. So we still use 0 as the approximation. Unlike usual 1D piece-wise linear approximation problem, the reduced problem has dynamic points (because they are created on the fly).

2.2 Encoding the Model and Data

There are two conflicting forces in the reduced problem: approximation accuracy and the number of line segments. A compromise can be achieved using MDL [2] [5] [6] . MDL provides a general framework for selecting a model for a set of data. It states that the best model is the one allowing the shortest encoding of the model and data given the model.

We consider the line segments as the model and the points explained by the line segments as the data. For the model, we need to encode the number of line segments and the boundaries. The number of line segments is an integer. Elias code [7] for integer k requires approximately $\log^* k$ ($\log^* k$ is defined as $\log k + \log\log k + ...$ over all positive terms) bits. If we have k line segments, we need to encode $k-1$ boundaries. A boundary is in $[1, n]$ where n is the number of points (features). Assuming a uniform distribution, the codelength for a boundary is $\log n$ bits. Thus the total codelength for the model is $\log^*(k) + (k-1) \times \log(n)$

For the data given the model, we encode them one line segment by one line segment. For a line segment explaining m_r points, we need to encode:

1. The number of points explained by the line. Using Elias code, the codelength is $\log^* m_r$ bits.
2. The distance d of each point from the line.
   (a) We assume d conforms to Gaussian distribution , i.e. $d \sim N(0, \sigma_d)$. We need to encode the parameter σ_d. Using Rissanen's precision optimization encoding method [8], the codelength is $\frac{1}{2}\log m_r$ bits.
   (b) Assuming d's are independent, the joint probability distribution is

$$p(d_{i+1}, d_{i+1}, ...d_{i+m_r}) = \prod_{r=i+1}^{i+m_r} \frac{1}{\sqrt{2\pi}\sigma_d} \exp(-\frac{d_r^2}{2(\sigma_d)^2}) = (\frac{1}{\sqrt{2\pi}\sigma_d})^{m_r} e^{-\frac{m_r}{2}}$$

By Shannon theory, the codelength is $-\log[(\frac{1}{2\pi\sigma_d})^m e^{-\frac{m}{2}}] = \frac{m}{2}\log 2\pi e\sigma_d^2$. With additional analysis beyond the page limit of this paper, we use codelength $\frac{m_r}{2}\log 2\pi e\sigma_d^2$ instead of $\frac{m}{2}\log 2\pi e\sigma_d^2$.

Since $\log^*(k) << (k-1) \times \log(n)$, we ignore $\log^*(k)$. Thus we compute the averaged codelength for a cluster from feature $i+1$ to $i+m$ as

$$L_{i+1,i+m} = \log(n) + \log^* m_r + \frac{1}{2}\log(m_r) + \frac{\sqrt{m_r}}{2}\log 2\pi e\sigma_d^2$$

2.3 Minimize the Total Codelength

We have the following codelength (upper triangular) matrix L

$$L = \begin{pmatrix} L_{1,1} & L_{1,2} & ... & L_{1,n} \\ & L_{2,2} & ... & L_{2,n} \\ & & & \\ & & & L_{n,n} \end{pmatrix} \quad R(n) = \begin{cases} 0 & \text{if } n = 0; \\ L_{1,1} & \text{if } n = 1; \\ \min_{0 \le i < n} (R(i) + L_{i+1,n}) & \text{otherwise.} \end{cases}$$

The aim of MDL is to minimize the total codelength. Thus we need to find a subsequence $1 = i_1 < i_1 < ... < i_k < i_{k+1} = n$ such that $L_{i_1,i_2} + \Sigma_{r=2}^{k} L_{i_r+1,i_{r+1}}$ is minimized. Denote the codelength of such a sequence as $R(n)$ for a sequence of length n. We have the above recursive function to compute $R(n)$.

We can compute the above recursive function efficiently by dynamic programming. By recording which branch we take in the recursive function to get the result for $R(n)$, we can get the clustering result. For example, if we compute $R(10)$ and find out (by recording which branch we take) $R(10) = L_{1,3} + L_{4,7} + L_{8,10}$, the corresponding clusters are {1,2,3},{4,5,6,7} and {8,9,10} for corresponding features.

With additional analysis beyond the page limit of this paper, we can find that the time complexity of our solution is $O(n^3)$

3   Experimental Results and Conclusion

We use synthetic data to test our algorithm. We assume that features within a cluster have correlation coefficients conforming to a normal-like distribution with zero mean and σ deviation (they should be in the range of $[0,1]$). Also we assume that features not within a cluster have correlation coefficients conforming to uniform distribution within the range of $[0,1]$. Synthetic datasets are thus derived.

We test synthetic datasets with different parameters (number of features, σ, cluster assignments). The results from our solution based on above synthetic datasets are very accurate and stable. Result analysis (both graphical and descriptional) is beyond the page limit of this paper.

References

1. Baumgartner, R., Somorjai, R., et al, "Unsupervised feature dimension reduction for classification of MR spectra", *Magnetic Resonance Image*, 22:251-256, 2004.
2. Banerjee, S., Niblack, W., Flicker, M. "A minimum description length polygonal approximation method", *IBM technical report*, 1996.
3. Teh, C.H., Chin, R.T.,"On the detection of dominant points on digital curves", *IEEE PAMI*, 11(8):859-872, 1989.
4. Pavlidis, T.,"Algorithms for shape analysis of contours and waveforms", *IEEE PAMI*, 2(4):301-312, 1980.
5. Barron, A., Rissanen, J., Bin, Y."The minimum description length principle in coding and modeling", *Information Theory, IEEE Transactions on*, 44(6):2743-2760, 1998.
6. Davies, R.H., Twining, C.J., et al, "A minimum description length approach to statistical shape modeling", *Medical Imaging, IEEE Transactions on*, 21(5):525-537, 2002.
7. Elias, P. , "Univeral codeword sets and representations of the integers", *Information Theory, IEEE Transactions on*, 2, 1975.
8. Rissanen, J., *Stochastic Complexity in Statistical Inquiry*, World Scientific, 1989.

Author Index

Lecture Notes in Artificial Intelligence (LNAI)